Tyndale New Testament Commentaries

Volume 2

TNTC

Mark

Tyndale New Testament Commentaries

Volume 2

Series Editor: Eckhard J. Schnabel
Consulting Editor: Nicholas Perrin

Mark

An Introduction and Commentary

Eckhard J. Schnabel

Inter-Varsity Press

IVP Academic
An imprint of InterVarsity Press
Downers Grove, Illinois

InterVarsity Press, USA
P.O. Box 1400
Downers Grove, IL 60515-1426, USA
ivpress.com
email@ivpress.com

Inter-Varsity Press, England
36 Causton Street
London SW1P 4ST, England
ivpbooks.com
ivp@ivpbooks.com

© 2017 by Eckhard J. Schnabel

Eckhard J. Schnabel has asserted his rights under the Copyright, Designs and Patents Act, 1988, to be identified as Author of this work.

All rights reserved. No part of this book may be reproduced in any form without written permission from InterVarsity Press.

InterVarsity Press®, USA, is the book-publishing division of InterVarsity Christian Fellowship/USA® and a member movement of the International Fellowship of Evangelical Students. Website: www.intervarsity.org.

Inter-Varsity Press, England, is closely linked with the Universities and Colleges Christian Fellowship, a student movement connecting Christian Unions throughout Great Britain, and a member movement of the International Fellowship of Evangelical Students. Website: www.uccf.org.uk.

Unless otherwise indicated Scripture quotations are taken from the Holy Bible, New International Version (Anglicized edition). Copyright © 1979, 1984, 2011 by Biblica (formerly International Bible Society). Used by permission of Hodder & Stoughton Publishers, an Hachette UK company. All rights reserved. 'NIV' is a registered trademark of Biblica (formerly International Bible Society). UK trademark number 1448790.

First published 2017

Image: © Scala/Art Resource, NY

USA ISBN 978-0-8308-4292-6 (print)
USA ISBN 978-0-8308-9497-0 (digital)
UK ISBN 978-1-78359-504-4 (print)
UK ISBN 978-1-78359-310-1 (digital)

Typeset in Great Britain by CRB Associates, Potterhanworth, Lincolnshire

Printed in the United States of America ∞

InterVarsity Press is committed to ecological stewardship and to the conservation of natural resources in all our operations. This book was printed using sustainably sourced paper.

Library of Congress Cataloging-in-Publication Data
Names: Schnabel, Eckhard J., author.
Title: Mark : an introduction and commentary / Eckhard J. Schnabel.
Description: Downers Grove : InterVarsity Press, 2017. | Series: Tyndale New
  Testament commentaries ; Volume 2 | Includes bibliographical references. |
Identifiers: LCCN 2017009560 (print) | LCCN 2017012805 (ebook) | ISBN
  9780830894970 (eBook) | ISBN 9780830842926 (pbk. : alk. paper)
Subjects: LCSH: Bible. Mark--Commentaries.
Classification: LCC BS2585.53 (ebook) | LCC BS2585.53 .S36 2017 (print) | DDC
  226.3/077--dc23
LC record available at https://lccn.loc.gov/2017009560

British Library Cataloguing in Publication Data
A catalogue record for this book is available from the British Library.

P	20	19	18	17	16	15	14	13	12	11	10	9	8	7
Y	37	36	35	34	33	32	31	30	29	28	27	26	25	

CONTENTS

General preface	vii
Author's preface	ix
Abbreviations	xi
Select bibliography	xvii

Introduction 1

1. Mark among the Gospels — 1
2. Characteristics of Mark's Gospel — 5
3. The origin of Mark's Gospel — 7
4. Theological emphases — 23
5. The structure of Mark's Gospel — 30

Analysis 31

Commentary 35

To Paul Schnabel,
my father in the truest sense of the word,
who has been preaching the gospel for seventy years

GENERAL PREFACE

The Tyndale Commentaries have been a flagship series for evangelical readers of the Bible for over sixty years. Both the original New Testament volumes (1956–1974) as well as the new commentaries (1983–2003) rightly established themselves as a point of first reference for those who wanted more than is usually offered in a one-volume Bible commentary, without requiring the technical skills in Greek and in Jewish and Greco-Roman studies of the more detailed series, with the advantage of being shorter than the volumes of intermediate commentary series. The appearance of new popular commentary series demonstrates that there is a continuing demand for commentaries that appeal to Bible study leaders in churches and at universities. The publisher, editors and authors of the Tyndale Commentaries believe that the series continues to meet an important need in the Christian community, not least in what we call today the Global South, with its immense growth of churches and the corresponding need for a thorough understanding of the Bible by Christian believers.

In the light of new knowledge, new critical questions, new revisions of Bible translations, and the need to provide specific guidance on the literary context and the theological emphases of the individual passage, it was time to publish new commentaries in the series. Four authors will revise their commentary that appeared in the second series. The original aim remains. The new commentaries are neither too short nor unduly long. They are exegetical and thus root the interpretation of the text in its historical context. They do not aim to solve all critical questions, but they are written with an awareness of major scholarly debates which may be treated in the Introduction, in Additional notes or in the commentary itself. While not specifically homiletic in aim, they want to help readers to understand the passage under consideration in such a way that they begin to see points of relevance and application, even though the commentary does not explicitly offer these. The authors base their exegesis on the Greek text, but they write for readers who do not know Greek; Hebrew and Greek terms that are discussed are transliterated. The English translation used for the first series was the Authorized (King James) Version, while the volumes of the second series mostly used the Revised Standard Version; the volumes of the third series use either the New International Version (2011) or the New Revised Standard Version as primary versions, unless otherwise indicated by the author.

An immense debt of gratitude for the first and second series of the Tyndale Commentaries was owed to R. V. G. Tasker and L. Morris, who each wrote four of the commentaries themselves. The recruitment of new authors for the third series proved to be effortless, as colleagues responded enthusiastically to be involved in this project, a testimony both to the larger number of New Testament scholars capable and willing to write commentaries, to the wider ethnic identity of contributors, and to the role that the Tyndale Commentaries have played in the church worldwide. It continues to be the hope of all those concerned with this series that God will graciously use the new commentaries to help readers understand as fully and clearly as possible the meaning of the New Testament.

Eckhard J. Schnabel, Series Editor
Nicholas Perrin, Consulting Editor

AUTHOR'S PREFACE

It is always a privilege to be invited to write a biblical commentary (let alone be the editor of a commentary series), and a particular privilege to write a commentary on one of the four Gospels which the early church placed at the beginning of the New Testament canon. Jesus' followers were called *Christianoi*, 'Messiah people' (Acts 11:26), probably by the Roman authorities in Antioch, the capital of the Roman province of Syria, who correctly recognized that the commitment and the message of this new movement was about Jesus, whom his followers regarded as the Messiah, the Jewish saviour. The preaching of Peter and Paul in the book of Acts is focused on Jesus' life, ministry, death and resurrection and their significance. Mark's Gospel reflects, supports, consolidates and provides material for the proclamation of the good news of Jesus' life and death in the early church. Mark knew that being a *Christianos*, a follower of Messiah Jesus, is connected with a particular set of convictions, but also, and even more importantly, with a personal and communal commitment to 'the good news about Jesus the Messiah, the Son of God' (Mark 1:1). This is why he wrote an account of Jesus' life and death. And this is why Christians, both individually and as groups, will and must read Mark's Gospel. It is my hope and prayer that this commentary will aid the reading and understanding of this important biblical text.

The Select bibliography lists forty-eight commentaries on Mark, thirty-two of which were written after 1989, the year of R. Alan Cole's revised edition of this Tyndale New Testament Commentary (the first edition came out in 1960). The commentaries most frequently consulted were those by Evans, France, Gundry, Marcus, Pesch, Strauss and Collins. References to the scholarly literature on Mark have been kept to a minimum. The explanation of Mark's Gospel is based on the Greek text; the translation used is the NIV (2011) unless indicated otherwise; NRSV, NASB, GNB and other versions are referred to when they reproduce the Greek text more directly or when they provide helpful interpretations of the Greek. When authors are cited without abbreviated titles, the reference is to commentaries on the Gospel of Mark.

I thank Rami Arav, Craig Keener, Heinrich von Siebenthal and Mark Strauss for readily answering queries. I thank Kelly R. Bailey, my assistant, and Allan Chapple, Senior Lecturer in New Testament at Trinity Theological College in Perth, Australia, for reading the manuscript and assisting in weeding out typographical errors and other infelicities. I thank Nicholas Perrin for reading the manuscript as co-editor of the new TNTC series. I thank the members of my weekly Sunday School class at the First Congregational Church in Hamilton, Mass., who listened to my exposition of the Gospel of Mark for one and a half years. And I thank Philip Duce and the staff at IVP UK for their dedication to the church worldwide in reissuing the TNTC series in a new edition, and for their competent work on this volume, in particular Suzanne Mitchell, Eldo Barkhuizen and Rima Devereaux.

I dedicate this commentary to my father, Paul Schnabel (born 10 November 1923), who has read, believed and preached the gospel for seventy years. For thirty-five years, my wife, Barbara, has supported my research and writing with her customary cheerfulness; as she consults commentaries in preparation for teaching in our local church, she is a model reader of both popular and advanced commentaries. I cannot thank her enough.

Eckhard J. Schnabel

ABBREVIATIONS

General

AB	Anchor Bible
ABD	*Anchor Bible Dictionary*, ed. D. N. Freedman (New York: Doubleday, 1972)
AThANT	Abhandlungen zur Theologie des Alten und Neuen Testaments
BAR	*Biblical Archaeology Review*
BDAG	*A Greek-English Lexicon of the New Testament and Other Early Christian Literature*, ed. W. Bauer, F. W. Danker, W. F. Arndt and F. W. Gingrich, 3rd edn (Chicago: University of Chicago Press, 2000)
BETL	Bibliotheca ephemeridum theologicarum lovaniensium
Bib	*Biblica*
BNP	*Brill's New Pauly*, ed. H. Cancik and H. Schneider (Leiden: Brill, 2002–2012)
CBQ	*Catholic Biblical Quarterly*
DJG	*Dictionary of Jesus and the Gospels*, ed. J. B. Green, J. K. Brown and N. Perrin, 2nd edn (Downers Grove: InterVarsity Press; Leicester: Inter-Varsity Press, 2013)
EDEJ	*Eerdmans Dictionary of Early Judaism*, ed. J. J. Collins and D. C. Harlow (Grand Rapids: Eerdmans, 2010)
EDNT	*Exegetical Dictionary of the New Testament*, ed. H. Balz and G. Schneider (Grand Rapids: Eerdmans, 1990–1993)

ET	English translation
FRLANT	Forschungen zur Religion und Literatur des Alten und Neuen Testaments
JBL	*Journal of Biblical Literature*
JRS	*Journal of Roman Studies*
JSHJ	*Journal for the Study of the Historical Jesus*
JSNT	*Journal for the Study of the New Testament*
JSNTSup	Journal for the Study of the New Testament Supplement series
JSS	*Journal of Semitic Studies*
LSJ	*A Greek-English Lexicon*, ed. H. G. Liddell, R. Scott and H. S. Jones, 9th edn, with rev. supplement by P. G. W. Glare (Oxford: Oxford University Press, 1996)
LXX	Septuagint (Greek translation of the Hebrew Scriptures)
MT	Masoretic Text
NEAEHL	*New Encyclopaedia of Archaeological Excavations in the Holy Land*, ed. E. Stern (Jerusalem: Israel Exploration Society, 2008)
NETS	*A New English Translation of the Septuagint*, ed. A. Pietersma and B. G. Wright (Oxford: Oxford University Press, 2007)
NewDocs	*New Documents Illustrating Early Christianity*, ed. G. H. R. Horsley and S. R. Llewelyn (Macquarie University, 1981–2012)
NIBC	New International Biblical Commentary
NICNT	New International Commentary on the New Testament
NIDB	*New Interpreter's Dictionary of the Bible*, ed. K. D. Sakenfeld (Nashville: Abingdon, 2006–2009)
NIGTC	New International Greek Testament Commentary
NIVAC	NIV Application Commentary
NovT	*Novum Testamentum*
NTS	*New Testament Studies*
NTTS	New Testament Tools and Studies
OEBA	*Oxford Encyclopedia of the Bible and Archaeology*, ed. D. M. Master (New York: Oxford University Press, 2013)

PNTC	Pillar New Testament Commentary
SBLDS	Society of Biblical Literature Dissertation Series
SNTSMS	Society of New Testament Studies Monograph Series
TANZ	Texte und Arbeiten zum neutestamentlichen Zeitalter
TDNT	*Theological Dictionary of the New Testament*, ed. G. Kittel and G. Friedrich (Grand Rapids: Eerdmans, 1964–1976)
TSAJ	Texts and Studies in Ancient Judaism
TynBul	*Tyndale Bulletin*
TZ	*Theologische Zeitschrift*
WUNT	Wissenschaftliche Untersuchungen zum Neuen Testament

Ancient texts

An.	Tacitus, *Annales*
Ant.	Josephus, *Antiquities of the Jews*
Ant. rom.	Dionysius of Halicarnassus, *Antiquitates romanae*
Ap.	Josephus, *Against Apion*
1 Apol.	Justin Martyr, *First Apology*
Barn.	*Epistle of Barnabas*
Cels.	Origen, *Contra Celsum*
CIIP	*Corpus Inscriptionum Iudaeae/Palaestinae*, ed. H. M. Cotton, L. Di Segni et al. (Berlin: de Gruyter, 2010–2014)
CIJ	*Corpus inscriptionum judaicarum*
Comm. Jo.	Origen, *Commentarii in evangelium Joannis*
De med.	Celsus, *De medecina*
De or.	Cicero, *De oratore*
Decal.	Philo, *De decalogo*
Dial.	Justin Martyr, *Dialogue with Trypho*
Did.	*Didache*
El.	Sophocles, *Elektra*
Ep. (Martial)	*Epigrams*
Ep. (Pliny the Younger)	*Epistulae*
Ep. (Seneca)	*Epistulae morales*

Ep. Arist.	*Epistle of Aristeas*
Exil.	Plutarch, *De exilio*
Flacc.	Philo, *In Flaccum*
Georg.	Virgil, *Georgica*
Haem.	Hippocrates, *De haemorrhoidibus*
Haer.	Irenaeus, *Adversus haereses*
Herc. fur.	Seneca, *Hercules furens*
Hist.	Tacitus, *Historiae*
Hist. eccl.	Eusebius, *Historica ecclesiastica*
IG	*Inscriptiones graecae*
Il.	Homer, *Iliad*
Inv.	Cicero, *De inventione rhetorica*
Legat.	Philo, *Legatio ad Gaium*
Life	Josephus, *The Life*
Lig.	Cicero, *Pro Ligario*
Lives	Eunapius, *Lives of the Philosophers and Sophists*
Mens.	Epiphanius, *De mensuris et ponderibus*
Mor.	Plutarch, *Moralia*
Morb.	Hippocrates, *De morbis*
Mos.	Philo, *De vita Mosis*
Nat.	Pliny the Elder, *Naturalis historia*
Nat. Fac.	Galen, *Natural Faculties*
Or.	Dio Chrysostom, *Orationes*
Pasch.	Melito of Sardis, *On the Pasch*
Philops.	Lucian, *Philopseudes*
Prov.	Philo, *De providentia*
Resp.	Plato, *Respublica*
Sacr.	Philo, *De sacrificiis Abelis et Caini*
Sib. Or.	*Sibylline Oracles*
Somn.	Philo, *De somniis*
Spec. leg.	Philo, *De specialis legibus*
Verr.	Cicero, *In Verrem*
Vesp.	Suetonius, *Vespasianus*
Vit. Apoll.	Philostratos, *Vita Apollonii*
War	Josephus, *The Jewish War*

ABBREVIATIONS   XV

Bible versions

ESV   The ESV Bible (The Holy Bible, English Standard
      Version), copyright © 2001 by Crossway, a publishing
      ministry of Good News Publishers. Used by
      permission. All rights reserved.
GNB   The Good News Bible published by The Bible
      Societies/HarperCollins Publishers Ltd UK,
      copyright © American Bible Society, 1966, 1971,
      1976, 1992, 1994.
JB   The Jerusalem Bible, published and copyright ©
      1966, 1967 and 1968 by Darton, Longman & Todd
      Ltd and Doubleday, a division of Random House,
      Inc., and used by permission.
KJV   The Authorized Version of the Bible (The King
      James Bible), the rights in which are vested in the
      Crown, reproduced by permission of the Crown's
      Patentee, Cambridge University Press.
NASB The NEW AMERICAN STANDARD BIBLE®,
      Copyright © 1960, 1962, 1963, 1968, 1971, 1972,
      1973, 1975, 1977, 1995 by The Lockman Foundation.
      Used by permission.
NET   The NET Bible, New English Translation, copyright
      © 1996 by Biblical Studies Press, LLC. NET Bible is
      a registered trademark.
NIV   The Holy Bible, New International Version
      (Anglicized edition). Copyright © 1979, 1984, 2011
      by Biblica (formerly International Bible Society).
      Used by permission of Hodder & Stoughton
      Publishers, an Hachette UK company. All rights
      reserved. 'NIV' is a registered trademark of Biblica
      (formerly International Bible Society). UK trademark
      number 1448790.
NJB   The New Jerusalem Bible, published and copyright
      © 1985 by Darton, Longman & Todd Ltd and
      Doubleday & Co., Inc., a division of Random House,
      Inc. and used by permission.

NLT	The *Holy Bible*, New Living Translation, copyright © 1996. Used by permission of Tyndale House Publishers, Inc., Wheaton, Illinois 60189, USA. All rights reserved.
NRSV	The New Revised Standard Version of the Bible, Anglicized edition, copyright © 1989, 1995 by the Division of Christian Education of the National Council of the Churches of Christ in the USA. Used by permission. All rights reserved.
REB	The Revised English Bible, copyright © Oxford University Press and Cambridge University Press 1989.
RSV	The Revised Standard Version of the Bible, copyright © 1946, 1952 and 1971 by the Division of Christian Education of the National Council of the Churches of Christ in the USA. Used by permission. All rights reserved.

SELECT BIBLIOGRAPHY

Commentaries on the Gospel of Mark

Achtemeier, Paul J. (1986), *Mark*, Proclamation Commentaries, 2nd edn (Philadelphia: Fortress).
Allen, Willoughby C. (1915), *The Gospel According to Saint Mark*, Oxford Church Biblical Commentary (London: Rivingtons).
Anderson, Hugh (1976), *The Gospel of Mark*, New Century Bible (Grand Rapids: Eerdmans).
Bayer, Hans F. (2008), *Das Evangelium des Markus*, Historisch-theologische Auslegung (Witten: R. Brockhaus).
Beavis, Mary Ann (2011), *Mark*, Paideia (Grand Rapids: Baker Academic).
Black, C. Clifton (2011), *Mark*, Abingdon New Testament Commentaries (Nashville: Abingdon).
Bock, Darrell L. (2015), *Mark*, New Cambridge Bible Commentary (Cambridge: Cambridge University Press).
Boring, M. Eugene (2006), *Mark*, New Testament Library (Louisville/London: Westminster John Knox).
Brooks, James A. (1991), *Mark*, New American Commentary (Nashville: Broadman).
Collins, Adela Yarbro (2007), *Mark*, Hermeneia (Minneapolis: Fortress).
Cranfield, C. E. B. (1959), *The Gospel According to Saint Mark*, Cambridge Greek Testament Commentary, repr. 1966 (Cambridge: Cambridge University Press).

Donahue, John R. and Daniel J. Harrington (2002), *The Gospel of Mark*, Sacra Pagina (Collegeville: Liturgical Press).
Dschulnigg, Peter (2007), *Das Markusevangelium*, Theologischer Kommentar zum Neuen Testament (Stuttgart: Kohlhammer).
Eckey, Wilfried (1998), *Das Markusevangelium* (Neukirchen-Vluyn: Neukirchener Verlag).
Edwards, James R. (2002), *The Gospel According to Mark*, PNTC (Grand Rapid: Eerdmans).
Ernst, Josef (1981), *Das Evangelium nach Markus*, Regensburger Neues Testament (Regensburg: Pustet).
Evans, Craig A. (2001), *Mark 8:27 – 16:20*, Word Biblical Commentary (Nashville: Nelson).
France, R. T. (2002), *The Gospel of Mark*, NIGTC (Carlisle: Paternoster; Grand Rapids: Eerdmans).
Garland, David E. (1996), *Mark*, NIVAC (Grand Rapids: Zondervan).
Gnilka, Joachim (1978–1979), *Das Evangelium nach Markus*, Evangelisch-katholischer Kommentar, 2 vols. (Neukirchen-Vluyn: Neukirchener Verlag).
Grundmann, Walter (1977), *Das Evangelium nach Markus*, 7th edn, Theologischer Handkommentar zum Neuen Testament (Berlin: Evangelische Verlagsantalt).
Guelich, Robert A. (1989), *Mark 1 – 8:27*, Word Biblical Commentary (Nashville: Nelson).
Gundry, Robert H. (1993), *Mark* (Grand Rapids: Eerdmans).
Hooker, Morna D. (1991), *The Gospel According to St Mark*, Black's New Testament Commentaries (London: Black).
Hurtado, Larry W. (1989), *Mark*, NIBC (Peabody: Hendrickson).
van Iersel, Bastiaan M. F. (2005), *Mark: A Reader-Response Commentary* (orig. 1998; London: Bloomsbury).
Juel, Donald H. (1990), *Mark*, Augsburg Commentary on the New Testament (Minneapolis: Augsburg).
Kertelge, Karl (1994), *Markusevangelium*, Neue Echter Bibel (Würzburg: Echter).
Lane, William L. (1974), *The Gospel of Mark*, NICNT (Grand Rapids: Eerdmans).
Légasse, Simon (1997), *L'Évangile de Marc*, Lectio divina (Paris: Cerf).

Lohmeyer, Ernst (1937/1967), *Das Evangelium des Markus*, Kritisch-exegetischer Kommentar (Göttingen: Vandenhoeck & Ruprecht).
Lührmann, Dieter (1987), *Das Markusevangelium*, Handbuch zum Neuen Testament (Tübingen: Mohr Siebeck).
Mann, Christopher S. (1986), *Mark*, AB 27 (New York: Doubleday).
Marcus, Joel (2000–2009), *Mark*, Anchor Yale Bible (New Haven: Yale University Press).
Mateos, Juan and Fernando Camacho (1994–2000), *Marcos*, 2 vols. (Córdoba: El Almendro).
Moloney, Francis J. (2012), *The Gospel of Mark*, 2nd edn (Grand Rapids: Baker Academic).
Oden, Thomas C. and C. A. Hall (1998), *Mark*, Ancient Christian Commentary on Scripture: New Testament (Downers Grove: InterVarsity Press).
Osborne, Grant R. (2012), *Mark*, Teach the Text Commentary (Grand Rapids: Baker).
Pesch, Rudolf (1976–1977), *Das Markusevangelium*, Herders theologischer Kommentar zum Neuen Testament, 2 vols. (Freiburg: Herder).
Robbins, Vernon K. (1984), *Jesus the Teacher: A Socio-Rhetorical Interpretation of Mark* (Philadelphia: Fortress).
Schmithals, Walter (1986), *Das Evangelium nach Markus*, Ökumenischer Taschenkommentar (Gütersloh: Mohn).
Schweizer, Eduard (1971), *The Good News According to Mark*, ET (London: SPCK).
Standaert, Benoît (2010), *Évangile selon Marc*, Études bibliques, 3 vols. (Paris: Gabalda).
Stein, Robert H. (2008), *Mark*, Baker Exegetical Commentary on the New Testament (Grand Rapids: Baker).
Strauss, Mark L. (2014), *Mark*, Zondervan Exegetical Commentary on the New Testament (Grand Rapids: Zondervan).
Taylor, Vincent (1981), *The Gospel According to St Mark* (orig. 1951; Grand Rapids: Baker).
Voelz, James W. (2013–2014), *Mark*, 2 vols. (Saint Louis: Concordia).
Witherington, Ben (2001), *The Gospel of Mark* (Grand Rapids: Eerdmans).

Other commentaries, books, monographs and articles

Adams, James N. (2003), *Bilingualism and the Latin Language* (Cambridge: Cambridge University Press).

Ådna, Jostein (2000), *Jesu Stellung zum Tempel: Die Tempelaktion und das Tempelwort als Ausdruck seiner messianischen Sendung*, WUNT 2/119 (Tübingen: Mohr Siebeck).

Aharoni, Yohanan (1979), *The Land of the Bible: A Historical Geography*, rev. edn (Philadelphia: Westminster).

Aland, Kurt (1979), 'Der Schluß des Markusevangeliums', in *Neutestamentliche Entwürfe* (München: Kaiser), pp. 246–283.

Allison, Dale C. (1993), *The New Moses: A Matthean Typology* (Minneapolis: Fortress).

Arav, Rami and Richard A. Freund (eds.) (1995–2009), *Bethsaida: A City by the North Shore or the Sea of Galilee*, 4 vols. (Kirksville: Truman State University Press).

Balabanski, Vicky (1997), *Eschatology in the Making: Mark, Matthew and the Didache*, SNTSMS 97 (Cambridge: Cambridge University Press).

Bammel, Ernst (ed.) (1970), *The Trial of Jesus* (London/Nashville: Nelson).

Bammel, Ernst and C. F. D. Moule (eds.) (1984), *Jesus and the Politics of His Day* (Cambridge: Cambridge University Press).

Bauckham, Richard J. (1994), 'The Brothers and Sisters of Jesus: An Epiphanian Response to John P. Meier', *CBQ* 56, pp. 686–700.

—— (ed.) (1995), *The Book of Acts in Its Palestinian Setting* (Exeter: Paternoster).

—— (ed.) (1998), *The Gospels for All Christians: Rethinking the Gospel Audiences* (Grand Rapids: Eerdmans).

—— (2002), *Gospel Women* (Grand Rapids: Eerdmans).

—— (2006), *Jesus and the Eyewitnesses: The Gospels As Eyewitness Testimony* (Grand Rapids: Eerdmans).

—— (2008), *The Jewish World Around the New Testament*, WUNT 233 (Tübingen: Mohr Siebeck).

Bauckham, Richard J. and Stefano De Luca (eds.) (2016), *Magdala, Jewish City of Fish* (Waco: Baylor University Press).

Baum, Armin D. (2008), 'The Anonymity of the New Testament History Books', *NovT* 50, pp. 1–23.

—— (2008), *Der mündliche Faktor und seine Bedeutung für die synoptische Frage*, TANZ 49 (Tübingen: Francke).
Beasley-Murray, George R. (1993), *Jesus and the Last Days: The Interpretation of the Olivet Discourse* (Peabody: Hendrickson).
Ben-David, Arye (1974), *Talmudische Ökonomie* (Hildesheim: Olms).
Best, Ernest (1981), *Following Jesus: Discipleship in the Gospel of Mark*, JSNTSup 4 (Sheffield: JSOT Press).
—— (1986), *Disciples and Discipleship: Studies in the Gospel According to Mark* (Edinburgh: T&T Clark).
—— (1988), *Mark: The Gospel As Story* (orig. 1983; Edinburgh: T&T Clark).
Bird, Michael F. (2012), *Jesus Is the Christ: The Messianic Testimony of the Gospels* (Downers Grove: IVP Academic).
Bird, Michael F. and Jason Maston (eds.) (2012), *Earliest Christian History: History, Literature and Theology*, WUNT 2/320 (Tübingen: Mohr Siebeck).
Black, David Alan (ed.) (2008), *Perspectives on the Ending of Mark: Four Views* (Nashville: B&H Academic).
Blinzler, Josef (1959), *The Trial of Jesus* (Cork: Mercier).
—— (1969), *Der Prozeß Jesu*, 4th edn (Regensburg: Pustet).
Blomberg, Craig L. (1990), *Interpreting the Parables* (Downers Grove: InterVarsity Press).
—— (1997), *Jesus and the Gospels: An Introduction and Survey* (Nashville: Broadman & Holman).
Bock, Darrell L. (2000), *Blasphemy and Exaltation in Judaism: The Charge Against Jesus in Mark 14:53–65* (Grand Rapids: Baker).
Bock, Darrell L. and Robert L. Webb (eds.) (2010), *Key Events in the Life of the Historical Jesus* (Grand Rapids: Eerdmans).
Bockmuehl, Marcus and Donald A. Hagner (eds.) (2005), *The Written Gospel* (Cambridge: Cambridge University Press).
Bond, Helen K. (2004), *Pontius Pilate in History and Interpretation*, SNTSMS 100 (orig. 1998; Cambridge: Cambridge University Press).
Booth, Roger P. (1986), *Jesus and the Laws of Purity: Tradition History and Legal History in Mark 7*, JSNTSup 13 (Sheffield: JSOT Press).
Breytenbach, Cilliers (1984), *Nachfolge und Zukunftserwartung nach Markus: Eine methodenkritische Studie*, AThANT 71 (Zürich: Theologischer Verlag).

Brooke, George J. (ed.) (2005), *The Dead Sea Scrolls and the New Testament* (Minneapolis: Fortress).

Brown, Raymond E. (1994), *The Death of the Messiah: From Gethsemane to the Grave. A Commentary on the Passion Narratives in the Four Gospels*, 2 vols. (London: Chapman).

Brown, Raymond E., Karl P. Donfried and John Reumann (1973), *Peter in the New Testament* (Minneapolis: Augsburg).

Burridge, Richard A. (2004), *What Are the Gospels? A Comparison with Graeco-Roman Biography*, 2nd edn (Grand Rapids: Eerdmans).

Cahill, Michael (1998), *Expositio Evangelii secundum Marcum* (Turnholt: Brepols).

Camery-Hoggatt, Jerry (1992), *Irony in Mark's Gospel: Text and Subtext*, SNTSMS 72 (Cambridge: Cambridge University Press).

Casey, Maurice (1999), *Aramaic Sources of Mark's Gospel*, SNTSMS 102 (Cambridge: Cambridge University Press).

Chapman, David W. and Eckhard J. Schnabel (2015), *The Trial and Crucifixion of Jesus: Texts and Commentary*, WUNT 344 (Tübingen: Mohr Siebeck).

Charlesworth, James H. (ed.) (1995), *Jesus and the Dead Sea Scrolls* (orig. 1992; New York: Doubleday).

—— (ed.) (2006), *Jesus and Archaeology* (Grand Rapids: Eerdmans).

Chilton, Bruce and Darrell L. Bock (2010), *A Comparative Handbook to the Gospel of Mark* (Leiden: Brill).

Cohen, Shaye J. D. (2010), *The Significance of Yavneh and Other Essays in Jewish Hellenism*, TSAJ 136 (Tübingen: Mohr Siebeck).

Collins, Adela Yarbro (2004), 'The Charge of Blasphemy in Mark 14.64', *JSNT* 26, pp. 379–401.

Collins, John J. (2010), *The Scepter and the Star: Messianism in Light of the Dead Sea Scrolls*, 2nd edn (Grand Rapids: Eerdmans).

Cook, John Granger (2011), 'Crucifixion and Burial', *NTS* 57, pp. 193–213.

—— (2014), *Crucifixion in the Mediterranean World*, WUNT 327 (Tübingen: Mohr Siebeck).

Corbo, Virgilio C. (1981–1982), *Il Santo Sepolcro di Gerusalemme*, 3 vols. (Jerusalem: Franciscan Printing Press).

Cotton, Hannah M. (1999), 'Some Aspects of the Roman Administration of Judaea/Syria-Palaestina', in W. Eck and E. Müller-Luckner (eds.), *Lokale Autonomie und römische Ordnungs-macht in den kaiserzeitlichen Provinzen vom 1. bis 3. Jahrhundert* (München: Oldenbourg), pp. 75–91.

Cox, Steven L. (1993), *A History and Critique of Scholarship Concerning the Markan Endings* (Lewiston: Mellen Biblical Press).

Crossley, James G. (2004), *The Date of Mark's Gospel*, JSNTSup 266 (London: T&T Clark).

Croy, N. Clayton (2003), *The Mutilation of Mark's Gospel* (Nashville: Abingdon).

Derrett, J. Duncan M. (1970), 'Herod's Oath and the Baptist's Head [1965]', in *Law in the New Testament* (London: Darton, Longman & Todd), pp. 339–362.

—— (1977–1995), *Studies in the New Testament* (Leiden: Brill).

Dorfbauer, Lukas J. (2013), 'Der Evangelienkommentar des Bischofs Fortunatian von Aquileia (Mitte 4. Jh.)', *Wiener Studien* 126, pp. 177–198.

Dunn, James D. G. (2003), *Jesus Remembered* (Grand Rapids: Eerdmans).

Dwyer, Timothy (1996), *The Motif of Wonder in the Gospel of Mark*, JSNTSup 128 (Sheffield: Sheffield Academic Press).

Eck, Werner (2007), *Rom und Judaea* (Tübingen: Mohr Siebeck).

Edwards, Douglas R. and C. Thomas McCollough (eds.) (1997), *Archaeology and the Galilee* (Atlanta: Scholars Press).

Ellis, Earle E. (1999), *The Making of the New Testament Documents* (Leiden: Brill).

—— (1999), 'The Synoptic Gospels and History', in B. Chilton and C. A. Evans (eds.), *Authenticating the Activities of Jesus*, NTTS 82/2 (Leiden: Brill), pp. 49–57.

Farmer, William R. (1974), *The Last Twelve Verses of Mark*, SNTSMS 25 (Cambridge: Cambridge University Press).

Fiensy, David A. (2014), *Christian Origins and the Ancient Economy* (Cambridge: Clarke/Cascade).

Fiensy, David A. and James R. Strange (eds.) (2014–2015), *Galilee in the Late Second Temple and Mishnaic Periods*, 2 vols. (Minneapolis: Fortress).

Finegan, Jack (1992), *The Archeology of the New Testament*, rev. edn (Princeton: Princeton University Press).
France, R. T. (1971), *Jesus and the Old Testament* (London: Tyndale).
Garland, David E. (2015), *A Theology of Mark's Gospel* (Grand Rapids: Zondervan).
Garnsey, Peter (1966), 'The *Lex Iulia* and Appeal Under the Empire', *JRS* 56, pp. 167–189.
Geddert, Timothy (2015), *Watchwords: Mark 13 in Markan Eschatology* (orig. 1989; London: Bloomsbury T&T Clark).
Geva, Hillel (ed.) (1994), *Ancient Jerusalem Revealed* (Jerusalem: Israel Exploration Society).
Gibson, Shimon (2009), *The Final Days of Jesus: The Archaeological Evidence* (New York: HarperOne).
Gibson, Shimon and Joan E. Taylor (1994), *Beneath the Church of the Holy Sepulchre, Jerusalem: The Archaeology and Early History of Traditional Golgotha* (London: Palestine Exploration Fund).
Gruen, Erich S. (1998), *Heritage and Hellenism: The Reinvention of Jewish Tradition* (Berkeley: University of California Press).
Hamilton, Gordon H. (1996), 'A New Hebrew–Aramaic Incantation Text from Galilee: "Rebuking the Sea"', *JSS* 41, pp. 215–249.
Hengel, Martin (1981), *The Atonement* (London: SCM).
—— (1985), *Studies in the Gospel of Mark* (Philadelphia: Fortress).
—— (1989), *The Zealots* (Edinburgh: T&T Clark).
—— (1995), *Studies in Early Christology* (Edinburgh: T&T Clark).
Hentschel, Anni (2007), *Diakonia im Neuen Testament*, WUNT 2/226 (Tübingen: Mohr Siebeck).
Heusler, Erika (2000), *Kapitalprozesse im lukanischen Doppelwerk*, Neutestamentliche Abhandlungen 38 (Münster: Aschendorff).
Hoehner, Harold W. (1972), *Herod Antipas*, SNTSMS 17 (Cambridge: Cambridge University Press).
Holmes, Michael W. (2007), *The Apostolic Fathers: Greek Texts and English Translations*, 3rd edn (Grand Rapids: Baker).
Hurtado, Larry W. (2006), *The Earliest Christian Artifacts: Manuscripts and Christian Origins* (Grand Rapids: Eerdmans).
Incigneri, Brian J. (2003), *The Gospel to the Romans: The Setting and Rhetoric of Mark's Gospel* (Leiden: Brill).

Instone-Brewer, David (1999), 'The Use of Rabbinic Sources in Gospel Studies', *TynBul* 50, pp. 281–298.
Iverson, Kelly R. (2006), 'A Further Word on Final Gar (Mark 16:8)', *CBQ* 68, pp. 79–94.
Jackson, Howard M. (1997), 'Why the Youth Shed His Cloak and Fled', *JBL* 116, pp. 273–289.
Jaubert, Annie (1965), *The Date of the Last Supper* (Staten Island: Alba House).
Jensen, Morten Hørning (2010), *Herod Antipas in Galilee*, 2nd edn, WUNT 2/215 (Tübingen: Mohr Siebeck).
Jeremias, Joachim (1971), *New Testament Theology* (London: SCM).
—— (1976), *The Eucharistic Words of Jesus* (London: SCM).
—— (1979), *Jerusalem in the Time of Jesus* (London: SCM).
Juel, Donald (1977), *Messiah and Temple: The Trial of Jesus in the Gospel of Mark*, SBLDS 31 (Missoula: Scholars Press).
Kee, Howard C. (1992), 'Early Christianity in the Galilee', in L. I. Levine (ed.), *The Galilee in Late Antiquity* (New York: Jewish Theological Seminary of America), pp. 3–22.
Kelhoffer, James A. (2000), *Miracle and Mission: The Authentication of Missionaries and Their Message in the Longer Ending of Mark*, WUNT 2/112 (Tübingen: Mohr Siebeck).
Kirner, Guido O. (2004), *Strafgewalt und Provinzialherrschaft* (Berlin: Duncker & Humblot).
Klassen, William (1996), *Judas: Betrayer or Friend of Jesus?* (Minneapolis: Fortress).
Kunkel, Wolfgang (1974), *Kleine Schriften zum römischen Strafverfahren und zur römischen Verfassungsgeschichte* (Weimar: Böhlau).
Lamb, Walter R. M. (2012), *The Catena in Marcum: A Byzantine Anthology of Early Commentary on Mark* (Leiden: Brill).
Leibner, Uzi (2006), 'Identifying Gennesar on the Sea of Galilee', *Journal of Roman Archaeology* 19, pp. 229–245.
—— (2009), *Settlement and History in Hellenistic, Roman, and Byzantine Galilee*, TSAJ 127 (Tübingen: Mohr Siebeck).
Lémonon, Jean-Pierre (2007), *Ponce Pilate* (Ivry-sur-Seine: Atelier).
Levine, Lee I. (2005), *The Ancient Synagogue: The First Thousand Years*, 2nd edn (New Haven: Yale University Press).
Lincoln, Andrew T. (1989), 'The Promise and the Failure: Mark 16.7,8', *JBL* 108, pp. 283–300.

Loffreda, Stanislao (1993), 'La tradizionale casa di Simon Pietro a Cafarnao a 25 anni dalla sua scoperta', in F. Manns and E. Alliata (eds.), *Early Christianity in Context: Monuments and Documents* (Jerusalem: Franciscan Printing Press), pp. 37–67.

Magness, J. Lee. (1986), *Sense and Absence: Structure and Suspension in the Ending of Mark's Gospel* (Atlanta: Scholars Press).

Marcus, Joel (1986), *The Mystery of the Kingdom*, SBLDS 90 (Atlanta: Scholars Press).

—— (1992), *The Way of the Lord: Christological Exegesis of the Old Testament in the Gospel of Mark* (Louisville: Westminster).

Marshall, Christopher D. (1989), *Faith As a Theme in Mark's Narrative*, SNTSMS 64 (Cambridge: Cambridge University Press).

Marshall, I. Howard (1980), *Last Supper and Lord's Supper* (Grand Rapids: Eerdmans).

Mason, Steve (2016), *A History of the Jewish War: AD 66–74* (Cambridge: Cambridge University Press).

Meier, John P. (1991–2016), *A Marginal Jew: Rethinking the Historical Jesus*, 5 vols. (New York: Doubleday).

Metzger, Bruce M. (1994), *A Textual Commentary on the Greek New Testament*, 2nd edn (Stuttgart: Deutsche Bibelgesellschaft).

Milgrom, Jacob (1991–2001), *Leviticus*, AB 3, 3 vols. (New York: Doubleday).

Millar, Fergus (1993), *The Roman Near East, 31 BC – AD 337* (Cambridge, Mass.: Harvard University Press).

Miller, Susan (2005), *Women in Mark's Gospel*, JSNTSup 259 (London: T&T Clark).

Moo, Douglas J. (1983), *The Old Testament in the Gospel Passion Narratives* (Sheffield: JSOT Press).

Moule, C. F. D. (1969), 'Mark 4:1–20 Yet Once More', in E. E. Ellis and M. Wilcox (eds.), *Neotestamentica et Semitica* (Edinburgh: T&T Clark), pp. 95–113.

Murphy-O'Connor, Jerome (2008), *The Holy Land: An Oxford Archaeological Guide from Earliest Times to 1700*, 5th edn (Oxford: Oxford University Press).

—— (2012), *Keys to Jerusalem: Collected Essays* (Oxford: Oxford University Press).

Myers, Ched (2008), *Binding the Strong Man: A Political Reading of Mark's Story of Jesus* (orig. 1988; Maryknoll: Orbis).
Myers, Eric M. and James F. Strange (1981), *Archaeology, the Rabbis, and Early Christianity* (London: SCM).
Neirynck, Frans (1992), *The Gospel of Mark: A Cumulative Bibliography, 1950–1990*, BETL 102 (Leuven: Leuven University Press).
Netzer, Ehud (2008), *The Architecture of Herod, the Great Builder* (orig. 2006; Grand Rapids: Baker).
Parker, Floyd O. (2003), 'The Terms "Angel" and "Spirit" in Acts 23:8', *Bib* 84, pp. 344–365.
Porter, Stanley (1994), 'Jesus and the Use of Greek in Galilee', in B. Chilton and C. A. Evans (eds.), *Studying the Historical Jesus*, NTTS 19 (Leiden: Brill), pp. 123–154.
Rapske, Brian M. (1994), *The Book of Acts and Paul in Roman Custody* (Exeter: Paternoster).
Reed, Jonathan L. (2000), *Archaeology and the Galilean Jesus* (Harrisburg: Trinity Press International).
Richardson, Peter (1999), *Herod: King of the Jews and Friend of the Romans* (orig. 1996; Minneapolis: Fortress).
Riesner, Rainer (1998), *Paul's Early Period: Chronology, Mission Strategy, Theology* (Grand Rapids: Eerdmans).
—— (2011), 'From the Messianic Teacher to the Gospels of Jesus Christ', in T. Holmén and S. E. Porter (eds.), *Handbook for the Study of the Historical Jesus*, Vol. 1 (Leiden: Brill), pp. 405–446.
Robertson, A. T. (2004), *Word Pictures of the New Testament*, Vol. 1: *The Gospel According to Matthew, The Gospel According to Mark*, rev. edn by W. J. Perschbacher (Grand Rapids: Kregel Academic).
Rocca, Samuel (2008), *Herod's Judaea: A Mediterranean State in the Classical World*, TSAJ 122 (Tübingen: Mohr Siebeck).
Sanders, E. P. (1985), *Jesus and Judaism* (Philadelphia: Fortress).
—— (1993), *The Historical Figure of Jesus* (London: Penguin).
Schiffman, Lawrence H. (2010), *Qumran and Jerusalem: Studies in the Dead Sea Scrolls and the History of Judaism* (Grand Rapids: Eerdmans).
Schnabel, Eckhard J. (1998), 'The Silence of Jesus', in B. Chilton and C. A. Evans (eds.), *Authenticating the Words of Jesus* (Leiden: Brill), pp. 203–257.

—— (2004), *Early Christian Mission*, 2 vols. (Downers Grove: InterVarsity Press).
—— (2011), 'The Meaning of βαπτίζειν in Greek, Jewish, and Patristric Literature', *Filologia Neotestamentaria* 24, pp. 3–40.
—— (2015), 'Persecution in the Early Christian Mission According to the Book of Acts', in S. E. Porter (ed.), *Rejection* (Eugene: Pickwick), pp. 141–180.
Schuol, Monika (2007), *Augustus und die Juden*, Studien zur Alten Geschichte 6 (Frankfurt: Antike).
Seaby, Herbert A. (1978/1968), *Roman Silver Coins*, 3rd/2nd edn (London: Seaby).
Sherwin-White, Adrian Nicolas (1992), *Roman Society and Roman Law in the New Testament* (orig. 1963; Grand Rapids: Baker).
Smallwood, E. Mary (2001), *The Jews Under Roman Rule* (orig. 1976; Leiden: Brill).
Sowers, Sidney (1970), 'The Circumstances and Recollection of the Pella Flight', *TZ* 26, pp. 305–320.
Standaert, Benoît (1984), *L'Évangile selon Marc: Composition et genre littéraire*, 2nd edn (Bruges: Saint-André).
Strobel, August (1980), *Die Stunde der Wahrheit: Untersuchungen zum Strafverfahren gegen Jesus*, WUNT 21 (Tübingen: Mohr Siebeck).
Taylor, Joan E. (1998), 'Golgotha: A Reconsideration of the Evidence for the Sites of Jesus' Crucifixion and Burial', *NTS* 44, pp. 180–203.
Telford, William R. (1999), *The Theology of the Gospel of Mark*, New Testament Theology (Cambridge: Cambridge University Press).
Theißen, Gerd (1983), *The Miracle Stories of the Early Christian Tradition* (Philadelphia: Fortress).
—— (1991), *The Gospels in Context: Social and Political History in the Synoptic Tradition* (Minneapolis: Fortress).
Twelftree, Graham H. (1999), *Jesus the Miracle Worker* (Downers Grove: InterVarsity Press).
—— (2011), *Jesus the Exorcist* (Eugene: Wipf & Stock).
VanderKam, James C. (2004), *From Joshua to Caiaphas: High Priests After the Exile* (Minneapolis: Fortress).
Wachsmann, Shelley (2013), *The Sea of Galilee Boat: An Extraordinary 2000 Year Old Discovery* (orig. 1995; Berlin: Springer).

Waldstein, Wolfgang (1964), *Untersuchungen zum römischen Begnadigungsrecht* (Innsbruck: Universitätsverlag Wagner).
Watts, Rikki E. (2000), *Isaiah's New Exodus and Mark* (orig. 1997; Grand Rapids: Baker).
Weder, Hans (1984), *Die Gleichnisse Jesu als Metaphern*, 3rd edn, FRLANT 120 (Göttingen: Vandenhoeck & Ruprecht).
Weeden, Theodore J. (1971), *Mark: Traditions in Conflict* (Philadelphia: Fortress).
Wenham, John (1991), *Redating Matthew, Mark and Luke: A Fresh Assault on the Synoptic Problem* (London: Hodder & Stoughton).
—— (1992), *Easter Enigma*, 2nd edn (Grand Rapids: Zondervan).
Wiarda, Timothy (2000), *Peter in the Gospels: Pattern, Personality and Relationship*, WUNT 2/127 (Tübingen: Mohr Siebeck).
Wieacker, Franz (2006), *Römische Rechtsgeschichte*, Handbuch der Altertumswissenschaft X/3.2 (München: Beck).
Williams, Joel F. (1995), *Other Followers of Jesus: Minor Characters As Major Figures in Mark's Gospel*, JSNTSup 102 (Sheffield: Sheffield Academic Press).
Wright, N. T. (1996), *Jesus and the Victory of God* (Minneapolis: Fortress).
Wuest, K. S. (1961), *The New Testament: An Expanded Translation* (Grand Rapids: Eerdmans).

INTRODUCTION

1. Mark among the Gospels

The New Testament book that we call 'the Gospel of Mark' is very possibly the oldest written account of the life of Jesus. Compared with Matthew and Luke, who report lengthy sections of Jesus' teaching, and compared with John, who provides more substantial and explicit theological interpretation, Mark wrote a vivid, action-packed narrative. Mark's accomplishments were not appreciated for long periods of time when Matthew's account was regarded as the most important Gospel. This changed when scholars came to accept the view that Mark's Gospel was the first of the four Gospels to be written.

a. History of interpretation

The oldest surviving fragments of the Gospel of Mark belong to Papyrus 45, dating from around AD 200–250. The fact that more papyrus fragments of Matthew, Luke and John survive may reflect the 'accident' of preservation, but it could also indicate that the other three Gospels circulated more widely than the Gospel of Mark at an early date. The latter possibility is reflected in the fact that Fortunatianus of Aquileia, who wrote a Latin commentary on the Gospels around AD 350, comments on texts mostly from the Gospel of Matthew as well as on some texts from the Gospels of Luke and John, but not on any text from the Gospel of Mark (Dorfbauer, 'Evangelienkommentar'). The earliest full text of Mark's Gospel is found in Codex Sinaiticus and Codex Vaticanus, both dating to the fourth century. The earliest commentary on Mark was written by Victor of Antioch in the late fifth century, a work that seems to have been a compilation of passages from earlier authors, primarily writers of homilies and commentaries on Matthew and Luke (Lamb, *Catena*). The first full-length commentary on Mark was written in the early seventh century; while initially attributed to Jerome, it is now recognized that the author, who might have been an Irish monk, 'appears to belong to a young church, the result of a Roman mission' (Cahill, *Expositio*, p. 117). Bede, a monk in the monastery of Saint Peter at Monkwearmouth in the Kingdom of Northumbria, between AD 724 and 731 wrote a commentary on Mark in four volumes which all survive. Other important commentaries were written by Theophylact (eleventh century) and Albertus Magnus (thirteenth century). Neither Martin Luther nor John Calvin wrote commentaries on the Synoptic Gospels. In the nineteenth century, important commentaries on Mark were written by A. Bisping, H. Ewald, H. J. Holtzmann, H. A. W. Meyer and B. Weiß. The major commentaries on Mark written in the twentieth and twenty-first centuries are listed in the Select bibliography.

A major reason why Mark's Gospel was neglected for a long time was the view put forward by Augustine (AD 354–430) that Matthew was written first and that Mark abbreviated Matthew, with Luke using both Matthew and Mark. The transition to a new paradigm is linked with Heinrich Julius Holtzmann, who argued in 1863 that Mark was the first written Gospel. This view became widely accepted, with the result that Mark's Gospel has become a foundational text in Jesus research.

The literature that has been produced on the Gospel of Mark is, literally, more than 'legion' (Mark 5:9): the cumulative bibliography of works written about Mark's Gospel between 1950 and 1990 lists 10,000 titles written by 3,000 scholars (Neirynck, *Bibliography*).

b. The priority of Mark's Gospel

Several arguments support the view that Mark was the first written Gospel. Mark's Gospel, with 11,025 words of Greek text, is much briefer than Matthew (18,293 words) and Luke (19,376 words); since over 97% of Mark's words have a parallel in Matthew and over 88% in Luke, and since Mark's accounts are often more detailed than the accounts of Matthew and Luke, it is more plausible to assume that Matthew and Luke 'used' Mark than that Mark condensed these two Gospels. If Mark summarizes Matthew and Luke, it is difficult to see why he omits Jesus' birth and important teaching such as the Sermon on the Mount. It is argued that it is easier to explain the rearrangement of material in Mark by Matthew and Luke than it is to explain a rearrangement by Mark of material in Matthew and Luke. Some passages have been explained in terms of 'editorial fatigue' or 'docile reproduction': they sometimes introduce incoherencies when they use material from Mark which they do not maintain throughout their narrative (cf. Matt. 9:14/Mark 2:18; Matt. 14:3–12/ Mark 6:17–29; and other passages where Matthew retained Mark's wording without assimilating it into his context). Another argument is related to Greek style. Mark sometimes uses rare or unusual words (Mark 1:10, 12, 16; 2:11, 21; 3:28; 9:3; 10:25; 11:8; 14:68, 72; 15:11) while Matthew uses more common words; it is easier to explain why Matthew would use a more common word than it is to explain why Mark would replace a common word with a more unusual word. The complexity of the matter can be seen in the fact that scholars who compared the use of Mark by Matthew and by Luke came to the conclusion that Matthew and Luke did not use the Gospel of Mark which has come down to us, but a lost earlier recension ('Proto-Mark') or a forgotten later revision of the present Gospel of Mark ('Deutero-Mark').

Many scholars acknowledge that the assumption of a straightforward literary dependence of some Gospels on one or two of the other Gospels is too simple. Some argue that the percentages of agreement between Mark, Matthew and Luke suggest not a literary relationship but independent, oral origins. Some point out that the

Synoptic tradition as a whole, comprising about 30,000 words (about 15,000 being words of Jesus), could be memorized – some Greeks memorized Homer's works, which are much larger, and some of the later rabbis seem to have memorized the entire Babylonian Talmud, which had almost two million words (Baum, *Faktor*). While the case for Markan priority continues to be plausible, these questions are more significant for commentaries on the Gospels of Matthew and Luke.

c. *The genre of Mark's Gospel*

The genre of a particular text signals expectations concerning the content, the purpose and the use of the text. Mark does not indicate what kind of book he wrote. The term *euangelion* ('good news', 'gospel') in 1:1 may or may not be meant as a literary self-definition; the term certainly refers to the good news *about* Jesus the Messiah or proclaimed *by* Jesus the Messiah. Justin Martyr (AD 100–165) calls 'Gospels' *apomnēmoneumata* or 'reminiscences', 'notes' (*1 Apol.* 66.3; 67.3; *Dial.* 107–117), historical sources for the life of Jesus; he uses the term *euangelia* (plural) as a reference to what we call the four canonical Gospels. Origen calls the Gospels *historiai* or 'histories', 'investigations', emphasizing historical reliability.

Form critics believed that the Gospels are *sui generis*, a unique genre created by Mark as the first author of a written Gospel. This assessment was linked with the Gospels' character as theological proclamation. In recent years, several studies have shown that the Gospels belong to the ancient category of *bios* ('Life' or biography). R. A. Burridge has compared the Gospels with Greco-Roman *bioi* ('Lives' or biographies) and concluded that the former fit quite comfortably into the genre category of the latter. He established that Jesus, about whom Mark writes (1:1), is the subject of about a quarter of the verbs (24.4%), with a further fifth of the verbs occurring in direct quotations from Jesus' teaching (20.2%) – that is, 44.6% of the verbs are 'controlled' by Jesus, a percentage similar to that found for those people whose lives are described in Greco-Roman *bioi* (Burridge, *Gospels*, pp. 190, 318).

Considering biographical material in the Old Testament, particularly in 1–2 Samuel and 1–2 Kings, and delineating a new classification of the genre biography in antiquity, A. Yarbro Collins (pp. 30–33) argues that Mark has an affinity with the *didactic* type of ancient biography (which aims at instructing the reader both about the life of a particular individual and about the way of life he founded). This is analogous to the *historical* type of ancient biography 'in that the life of Jesus is told, not for its own sake, not to illustrate his character or cultural achievement, but because his life was at the center of a crucial period of history from the point of view of Christian proclamation' (p. 33). Since the historical type of biography is very close to the historical monograph, which focuses on a single person, the Gospel of Mark could also be called a 'historical monograph' if Mark's focus is understood in terms of 'God's plan for the fulfillment of history' in which Jesus played a decisive role.[1]

2. Characteristics of Mark's Gospel

Mark's paratactical, anecdotal style leaves his hearers and readers with the impression of fast-paced action. The evangelist moves Jesus and the disciples quickly from event to event, first in Galilee, then in the Decapolis and finally in Jerusalem. Mark presents Jesus' ministry as a series of dramatic events with hardly a pause. When Jesus reaches Jerusalem, events are compressed within one week, with days and, during Jesus' crucifixion, hours marked by the evangelist. The use of the *historical present*, which was common in Hellenistic Greek, both in literary works and in popular texts, is used by Mark around 150 times (which is not reproduced in English translations). The historical present accounts for the vividness of the Greek text. Small details which are most plausibly understood as reflecting eyewitness memory – for example, in the feeding of the five thousand (6:32–44) the *five* loaves, the *two* fish, the *five* thousand, the *green* grass – also contribute to the vividness of the account (although such details could also be attributed to Mark's storytelling skills).

Mark uses the literary technique of *intercalation*, also called 'sandwich construction' – one narrative is bracketed by two halves

---

[1]. Collins, p. 33. Thus also Bock, France, Gundry (biographical and evangelistic/apologetic) and Stein in their commentaries.

of another narrative – at least on some occasions to help the reader understand the inner narrative and/or the flanking narratives. There are at least nine Markan intercalations: 3:20–35; 4:1–20; 5:21–43; 6:7–32; 11:12–25; 14:1–11; 14:17–31; 14:53–72; 15:40 – 16:8. It is not always clear whether Mark indeed intends his readers to see a connection between the inner narrative and the flanking narrative. For example, the narrative of Jesus' cursing of the fig-tree (11:12–14, 20–25), which 'surrounds' the narrative of Jesus' prophetic demonstration in the Outer Court of the temple (11:15–19) can be interpreted as emphasizing Jesus' authority over the temple. Many scholars go further and interpret the fig-tree incident as a symbolic action signalling divine judgment on Israel, based on Old Testament passages that use the fig-tree as a symbol for Israel. Others question whether Mark's readers would have understood an implicit reference to Old Testament symbols without Mark's help (as he writes for Gentile readers and often explains Jewish terms and customs); they point to Jesus' comments about the withered fig-tree in 11:22–25 which teach the disciples about the power of faith and prayer without hinting at judgment on Israel.

Richard Bauckham suggests that Mark's Gospel 'could depend closely on an already existing oral narrative, whether or not composed orally by the author of the Gospel, so that the written Gospel is a written "performance" of an oral narrative'; or Mark could have composed the Gospel 'in writing, making use of oral techniques because he was writing for oral performance of his text'.[2] Justin Martyr reports that at Sunday services 'the memoirs of the apostles [= Gospels] or the writings of the prophets are read for as long as time permits' (*1 Apol.* 67). To read the Gospel of Mark, without intermission, takes around two hours. In such a context, parataxis, repetition (redundancies) and the frequent use of the historical present (present tense of Greek verbs describing past events) are not indicative of a flawed style but signal its intended use in the life of the church.

---

2. Bauckham, *Eyewitnesses*, p. 233; cf. Hengel, *Studies in the Gospel of Mark*, p. 52: the Gospel of Mark probably 'was composed for solemn reading in worship'.

3. The origin of Mark's Gospel

a. Authorship

The author of the book that we call 'the Gospel of Mark' does not identify himself. Thus, technically, the book is anonymous. Some have suggested that the anonymity of the four Gospels and Acts is a specifically Christian phenomenon which reflects the authors' conviction that Jesus Christ is the exclusive authority besides whom any human authority should remain silent. While the anonymity may be without significance if the author simply assumed that the readers knew who wrote the book (cf. Marcus, p. 17), the correspondence between the anonymity of the four Gospels and Acts and the anonymity of the historical books of the Old Testament – the books from Genesis to Kings do not mention their authors' names, unlike the prophetic and sapiential books – seems significant. In contrast to the authors of Greek and Roman historical works, who are often explicitly motivated by the desire to earn praise and glory for their literary achievements,[3] the authors of the Gospels and the author of Acts adopted the literary device of anonymity, perhaps because 'they regarded themselves as comparatively insignificant mediators of a subject matter that deserved the full attention of the readers' (Baum, 'Anonymity', p. 23).

If we accept that Matthew and Luke accepted the 'guidance' of Mark's Gospel, whose material they incorporated into their own accounts of the life of Jesus, it follows that they were convinced of its reliability and authority. The initial success of the Gospel of Mark, demonstrated by its use by Matthew and Luke, indicates that the author cannot plausibly have been an unknown 'nobody'. The author's 'unusual work *cannot* have been circulated *anonymously* from the beginning, for that would have disqualified it from the start'.[4] It is in this context that the question of authorship is important – not so much for the *meaning* of the content of Mark's Gospel but for

---

3. Josephus, *Ant.* 1.1, says that historians write and publish because they are 'eager to display their literary skill and to win the fame therefrom expected'.
4. Hengel, in Bockmuehl and Hagner, *Written Gospel*, p. 80.

the *reliability* of the content. The question of the authorship of the Gospels is important because of its implications for the historical continuity between the tradition about Jesus and the Jesus of history.

The traditional view accepts the testimony of the early church that the author of the Gospel of Mark is *John Mark*, mentioned in Acts 12:12, 25, 15:37, and mentioned as *Mark* in Acts 15:39; Colossians 4:10; 2 Timothy 4:11; Philemon 24; 1 Peter 5:13 – and that he wrote the Gospel in *Rome*, largely on the basis of Peter's preaching, which Mark, as Peter's interpreter, knew well. The most incisive recent studies on the question have been written by Martin Hengel and, even more recently, Richard Bauckham, to whom frequent reference is made. The evidence is as follows.

i. The title of the book

Most extant manuscripts have the title 'According to Mark' or '(The) Gospel according to Mark' at the beginning of the text, at the end of the text or in a side margin. Martin Hengel has convincingly argued that the Gospels circulated with titles naming their authors when they were copied and sent out to other churches, particularly when more than one Gospel was in circulation (Hengel, *Studies in the Gospel of Mark*, pp. 64–84). Papyrus 66 (c. AD 200) has the title '(The) Gospel according to John', and Papyrus 75 (third century) has the title '(The) Gospel according to Luke' at the end of Luke's text and the title '(The) Gospel according to John' on the same page, after a small blank space, preceding John's text. The oldest manuscript for Mark, Papyrus 45 (third century), contains only portions of Mark, beginning with Mark 4:36–40 and ending with Mark 11:24–28, without the opening or the end of Mark. No other name appears in the manuscript tradition as a title for Mark's Gospel. It is unlikely that a fictional ascription of the Gospel to a non-apostle as author – one with a spotty record (Acts 13:13; 15:36–41) – would have gained early, wide and unanimous acceptance.

ii. Early tradition

Papias, bishop of Hierapolis in the province of Asia, who is identified by Irenaeus as writing as a 'hearer of John and companion of Polycarp' (*Haer.* 5.33.4), completed a five-volume work around AD 100–110 entitled 'Exposition of the Logia of the Lord' (which has not survived) in which he comments on Mark and on the book that Mark wrote. The passage is cited by Eusebius (c. AD 260–340):

> And the elder used to say: 'Mark, having become Peter's interpreter, wrote down accurately everything he remembered, though not in order (*ou mentoi taxei*), of the things either said or done by Christ. For he neither heard the Lord nor followed him, but afterward, as I said, followed Peter, who used to give his teachings in the form of *chreiai* but had no intention of giving an ordered account (*syntaxin*) of the Lord's sayings (*logia*). Consequently Mark did nothing wrong in writing down some things as he remembered them, for he made it his one concern not to omit anything that he heard or to make any false statement in them.' Such, then, is the account given by Papias with respect to Mark. (*Hist. eccl.* 3.39.14–16)[5]

Papias, who clearly speaks about the book we call the 'Gospel of Mark', constitutes the earliest explicit evidence that Mark wrote down the words and actions of Jesus.

Papias' testimony about Mark's connection with Peter is significant.[6] Papias is not an apologist for Mark – he treats Mark not as an eyewitness or original disciple but as an 'interpreter' of Peter, and he implicitly criticizes his book as lacking proper arrangement. As regards the content of the Gospel, the following observations are relevant for Mark's connection with Peter. (1) Mark makes Peter both the first disciple who is named and the last disciple named in the Gospel (1:16; 16:7). If this *inclusio* is intended by Mark to indicate that Peter is the main eyewitness source of his account of the life of Jesus, it is coherent with the fact that the names Simon and Peter occur with remarkable frequency in his Gospel, compared with the much longer Gospels of Matthew and Luke.[7] (2) The material about

---

5. The quotation is from Holmes, *Apostolic Fathers*, pp. 739, 741, with the exception of the sentence 'who used to give his teachings in the form of *chreiai*' (Holmes translates 'who adopted his teaching as needed').
6. For a defence of Papias' veracity cf. Gundry, pp. 1026–1045; Hengel, *Studies in the Gospel of Mark*, pp. 47–53; Bauckham, in Bird and Maston, *History*, pp. 151–157.
7. Bauckham, *Eyewitnesses*, pp. 125–126.

Peter in Matthew 16:17–29, Luke 5:1–11, 22:31–32, John 21:15–19, which is not paralleled in Mark concerns Peter's future and his authoritative role for the later followers of Jesus; the only such passage in Mark is Peter's call to 'fish for people' in 1:17, which is also addressed to Andrew. This 'reduction' of material on Peter in Mark's Gospel can plausibly be interpreted to be 'closer to the preaching of Peter, which would have been concerned with stories about Jesus, not with his own status in the church'.[8] (3) The assertion that Peter appears in Mark's Gospel not as a living individual but as a literary type[9] has been challenged by Timothy Wiarda, who has demonstrated that Mark characterizes Peter in various and distinctive ways, emphasizing his 'outspokenness or boldness of expression, quick initiative, overfunctioning, being an opinion leader, concern for Jesus, desire to honour and serve Jesus, determination to be loyal to Jesus, a distinctive sense of self-confidence in his discipleship, a measure of courage, and grief at awareness of disloyalty'.[10] (4) Some suggest that the connection between Peter and Mark was invented by Papias on the basis of 1 Peter 5:13 ('She who is in Babylon, chosen together with you, sends you her greetings, and so does my son Mark'). A better candidate for a fictitious author of the Gospel would have been Silas/Silvanus mentioned in 1 Peter 5:12, who is characterized as 'a faithful brother' and Peter's helper in writing the letter and who is mentioned in Acts and in the rest of the New Testament (Acts 15:22, 27, 32, 40; 16:19, 25, 29; 17:4, 10, 14–15; 18:5; 2 Cor. 1:19; 1 Thess. 1:1; 2 Thess. 1:1) much more frequently than John Mark. But Papias links Mark with Peter, not Silvanus.

Further early attestation of the view that Mark wrote the Gospel comes from the Anti-Marcionite Prologue (c. AD 150–180), Justin Martyr, *Dialogus cum Tryphone* 106.4 (c. AD 150), Irenaeus, *Adversus haereses* 3.1.1 (c. AD 170), Clement of Alexandria, in Eusebius, *Historica ecclesiastica* 6.14.6–7 (c. AD 180), Origen, in Eusebius, *Historica ecclesiastica* 6.25.5 (c. AD 200), Tertullian, *Adversus Marcionem* 4.5 (c. AD

---

8. Bauckham, in Bird and Maston, *History*, p. 153.
9. Marcus, p. 24; cf. Hengel, *Studies*, p. 51.
10. Wiarda, *Peter in the Gospels*, pp. 90–91.

200), Eusebius, *Historica ecclesiastica* 2.16–17 (c. AD 324) and Jerome, *Commentariorum in Matthaeum*, Prologue 6 (c. AD 400).

iii. The name of Mark
Some argue that since Mark was one of the most common names in the Roman Empire, and since Papias (and the other Early Church Fathers) refers only to 'Mark' rather than to 'John Mark', the patristic evidence has little value. It should be noted, however, that even though the Latin name *Marcus* was indeed used very commonly, this applies to its use as a *praenomen*, the first of three names of male Roman citizens which was not, however, used to refer to Roman citizens. The use of only *Marcus* (Gr. *Markos*) indicates that he must have been a slave or a non-Roman.[11] Given that the author of the Gospel was Jewish (see below), the evidence for the use of the name 'Mark' is extremely limited: only seven Jews with the name 'Mark' are attested. There would have been very few Jewish Christians in the first century with the name 'Mark', which suggests that the New Testament references to Mark refer not to three, or two, but only to one Mark.[12] And as far as Jewish Christian leaders or teachers are concerned, who could have written a Gospel or who could have a Gospel attributed to them, there may have been only one Mark – the John Mark of Acts.

iv. Ethnic identity
The author of the Gospel of Mark is most plausibly regarded as a Jewish Christian. He is aware of and explains Jewish customs and religious groups (7:1–5; 14:12; 15:42) and uses and translates Aramaic terms (3:17, 22; 5:41; 7:11, 34; 9:43; 10:46; 14:36; 15:22, 34), including Jewish technical terms (7:11), demonstrating that he knows Hebrew/Aramaic, which fits the John Mark of Acts whose home was in

---

11. Cf. Bauckham, in Bird and Maston, *History*, pp. 158–161.
12. The options are (1) John Mark, a Jewish Christian from Jerusalem, associated with Barnabas (Acts 12:12, 25; 13:5, 13; 15:37, 39); (2) Mark, a Jewish co-worker of Paul, a relative of Barnabas (Col. 4:10–11; cf. Phlm. 24; 2 Tim. 4:11); (3) Mark, a Christian in Rome with Silvanus (co-worker of Paul) and Peter, who calls him 'my son Mark' (1 Peter 5:12–13).

Jerusalem. Maurice Casey argues that substantial parts of Mark's Gospel were translated from Aramaic (Casey, *Sources*). The Gentile orientation of the Gospel – Jesus interacts positively with Gentiles and often disputes with Jewish leaders – does not prove that Mark was a Gentile (which would invalidate authorship by John Mark). Paul was a Jewish Christian, educated in Jerusalem (Acts 22:3), who interacted positively with Gentiles and often criticized Jews (cf. 1 Thess. 2:14–16; Rom. 9 – 10). And, of course, Jesus interacts for the most part positively with Jews, in particular with Jewish crowds (cf. 1:21–28, 32–39; 2:1–2, 12–13; 3:7–12; 10:17–22; 12:28–34; Marcus, p. 19).

v. Objections
The objection that a Palestinian Jewish Christian would not make the geographical errors that we find in Mark's Gospel is unconvincing. The question of the location of the exorcism in 5:1–17 is complex (see the commentary for an explanation of Gerasa as location). The journey described in 7:31 is not a geographical error but plausible in view of what we know about the Decapolis (Collins, p. 9). The fact that the topographical information gets clearer and denser in the Jerusalem area can be explained in terms of Mark's residence in Jerusalem (Gundry, p. 1039).

The claim that Mark is ignorant of Jewish laws and customs and that therefore the author of Mark's Gospel cannot have been John Mark of Jerusalem is also unconvincing. When Mark writes in 7:3–4 that 'all the Jews' wash their hands before they eat, seemingly in conflict with the fact that not all Jews followed Pharisaic tradition, it fits the statement in *Epistle of Aristeas* 305 that 'all the Jews' wash their hands before they pray: if Jews washed their hands before prayer, and if they prayed before eating, they washed their hands before eating. Since our knowledge of Jewish customs in Palestine around AD 30 is quite limited, and since the Gospels are our primary sources for this period, there are no more accurate sources which would warrant the verdict that Mark is inaccurate (Collins, p. 6).

b. Provenance and audience
Papias does not say where Mark wrote or when Mark wrote, although the association of Peter and Mark writing as Peter's interpreter could

explain the subsequent tradition that identified Rome, or more generally Italy, with the provenance of Mark's Gospel. Irenaeus seems to assume that Mark wrote in *Rome* after Peter's death (*Haer.* 3.1.1). The same view is held by an introductory note to the Gospel of Mark in some manuscripts of the Old Latin version ('Mark . . . was called stumpy-fingered, because for the size of the rest of his body he had fingers that were too short. He was Peter's interpreter. After the departure [or 'death'] of Peter himself, the same man wrote this Gospel in the regions of Italy'). According to Eusebius, Clement of Alexandria stated that the Gospel of Mark was written in Rome during Peter's lifetime (*Hist. eccl.* 6.14.5–7).

Frequent Latinisms in Mark's text can be taken as internal evidence for Rome as provenance of the Gospel (e.g. 2:4, 9, 11–12 *krabattos*, 'mat'; Lat. *grabatus*; 2:23 *hodon poiein*, 'make their way'; Lat. *iter facere*; 3:6, 15:1 *symboulion didonai*, 'form a plan, plot'; Lat. *consilium capere/dederunt*; 3:6, 6:27 *spekoulatōr*, 'courier, executioner'; Lat. *speculator*). Since many of these Latinisms are found in Koine Greek and also in the Gospels of Matthew and Luke, they do not prove that Mark wrote his Gospel in Rome, but their frequency in Mark favours a Roman origin.[13]

The older suggestion that Mark's Gospel was written in *Galilee* has been largely abandoned. Some scholars suggest *Syria* as the place of origin.[14] Arguments include the suggestion that Mark 13 reflects the events of the Jewish revolt against the Romans in AD 66–73, indicating that the Gospel was composed in geographical (and temporal) proximity to it (Marcus, pp. 33–35). A Syrian setting, it is argued, explains the instruction in Mark 13:14–15 to flee to the hills in the Transjordanian Decapolis region (cf. Eusebius, *Hist. eccl.* 3.5.3),

---

13. Hengel, *Studies*, p. 29; Standaert, *Marc*, pp. 470–473. A Roman origin is accepted by Bock, Cranfield, Edwards, France, Guelich, Gundry, Lane, Pesch, Strauss, Taylor, Witherington; Incigneri, *Gospel*, pp. 59–115.
14. Allen, pp. 4–6, combines Palestinian with Syrian origins: Mark wrote down Peter's teaching in Aramaic when the latter left Jerusalem in AD 44, and then, after going with Paul to Antioch, he translated it into Greek AD 44–47.

as well as the emphasis on persecution (Collins, pp. 12–13; Marcus, p. 36). On the connections between Mark 13 and the Jewish revolt, see below. As regards the context of persecution, the persecution during the Jewish revolt that Josephus describes is directed against Jews: he does not mention Christians in this context who, according to Mark 13:9, 13, would be persecuted 'on account of me [Jesus]'. There is no external evidence that supports Syria or the Decapolis as the provenance of Mark's Gospel. Not even Church Fathers from Syria located the composition of Mark's Gospel there. The theological perspectives of the Syrian (or Decapolis) churches that scholars assume are derived not from primary evidence but from the assumed provenance of New Testament texts. Alternatives to Rome are reduced to guesswork.

The city of *Rome* is the most plausible provenance. This does not mean that Mark wrote *for* the Roman churches, exclusively. The fact that Matthew and Luke valued and used Mark's Gospel when they wrote their own accounts of Jesus' life signals that the Gospel of Mark was regarded as useful in many different churches. The older paradigm that each of the four Gospels reflects the perspective of the community to which each evangelist belonged has been challenged by Richard Bauckham. He argues that this assumption turns each Gospel into an 'allegory by which the church tells its own story rather than the story of Jesus Christ'; since 'the early Christian movement was a network of communities in constant communication with each other, by messengers, letters, and movements of leaders and teachers', a network 'around which Christian literature circulated easily, quickly, and widely', the idea of writing a Gospel 'purely for the members of the writer's own church or even for a few neighboring churches is unlikely to have occurred to anyone' (Bauckham, *Gospels*, pp. 11, 44). The translation of Aramaic terms and the explanation of Jewish customs by Mark is particularly relevant for Gentile Christians who do not speak Aramaic. At the same time, the Gospel could have been read and would have been valued by Aramaic-speaking Christians in the East, even though they would not have needed the translations of Aramaic terms, and also by Jewish Christians who could be found in most if not all churches in the first century, even though they would not have needed an explanation of Jewish customs.

c. Date

Since the mid-twentieth century, most New Testament scholars have dated the Gospel of Mark to around AD 70.[15] This assessment is based on interpretations of Mark 13 which connect the references to wars between nations (13:7–8), persecution (13:9–13), the desolating sacrilege (the abomination that causes desolation) and the destruction of the temple and Jerusalem (13:14–20) with events in the recent past or in the not-too-distant future – that is, with the Jewish revolt against the Romans that began in AD 66 and the destruction of the temple by Titus in AD 70. Apart from the fact that the argument for a post-70 date presupposes that there can be no genuine prophecy, it is doubtful that Mark 13 represents plausible evidence concerning the date of composition of Mark's Gospel.

The references to wars between nations and rumours of wars in 13:7–8 represent traditional motifs which can be applied to any number of military conflicts, such as the war between Herod Antipas of Galilee and the Nabatean King Aretas IV in AD 36,[16] the invasion by Roman legions of Armenia in AD 58–60 or the civil wars in Rome after Nero's death in AD 69. The motifs of war, earthquakes and famines regularly occur in apocalyptic texts and, without information in the text explicitly specific to a unique location, cannot be used for establishing a date of composition. The reference to persecution in 13:9–13 does not fit the Jewish revolt of AD 66–70: there is no evidence that (Jewish) Christians were persecuted during this time. Josephus, *Jewish War* 2.457–480, reports massacres and imprisonments of Jews in nearly all the cities of Syria; the reference in 2:463 to 'Judaizers' who were affected refers to Gentiles who had become Jews; there is no indication that Josephus has Gentile Christians in mind.[17] Christians were persecuted in Rome by Nero after

---

15. Dschulnigg, pp. 55–56: AD 64–66; Edwards, p. 9: 64–70; Boring, p. 14: 65–70; Guelich, pp. xxxi–xxxii: 67–70; Collins, pp. 11–14: 68–69; Hengel, *Studies*, p. 22: 69; Marcus, pp. 38–39: 69–75; Pesch, I, p. 14: soon after 70; Incigneri, *Gospel*, pp. 202–207: 71.
16. Josephus, *Ant.* 18.109–105. Collins, p. 12; Theißen, *Gospels*, pp. 137–138.
17. Thus, however, Theißen, *Gospels*, p. 269, who suggests, without proof, that Christians 'could' also fall under the label *ioudaizontes*.

the fire of AD 64, and Peter was very probably executed during this time (Eusebius, *Hist. eccl.* 2.24), which would fit the view of some Church Fathers that Mark wrote his Gospel after Peter's death. However, since both Jewish and Gentile Christians were persecuted since the earliest days of the Jerusalem church, references to persecutions, if they are not explicitly specific to a particular time and place, cannot be used for dating a Christian text in the first century.

Details in Josephus' account of the siege of Jerusalem and the destruction of the city and of the temple are missing from Mark 13: the violent fighting and killing among the different Jewish factions, the thousands of Jews who were crucified by the Romans outside the city walls, and the incineration of the city and the temple by a catastrophic fire (Josephus, *War* 6.164–434). Mark does not actually describe the destruction of Jerusalem. The motifs that Mark uses are found in the language of prophecies of judgment in the Old Testament and Jewish apocalyptic literature. The description of events in Mark 13 'could very well have been spoken by Jesus himself and written down anytime between the mid-30s and the early 70s' (Stein, p. 15).

Some scholars argue for an early date of Mark's Gospel, around AD 35–45, 40, 45, 55 or 55–58.[18] James Crossley argues that since the early church debated the validity of biblical laws in the late forties and in the fifties, and since Mark portrays Jesus as directly involved in the Jewish debates of his day (e.g. Mark 2:23–28; 7:1–23; 10:2–12) but not in later Christian debates, he must have written his Gospel before the mid-forties. There is nothing in Mark 13 or in other Markan passages which make an early date inherently impossible. To argue that such an early date does not explain the silence of Paul about Mark's Gospel is unconvincing. Paul is largely silent about Jesus' ministry – why would he need to refer to a written Gospel? To argue that such an early date does not allow sufficient time for the development of the tradition that Mark uses is equally unconvincing. If Papias is correct that Mark wrote down Peter's teaching,

---

18. See, respectively, Crossley, *Date*; Casey, *Sources*, p. 259; Wenham, *Redating*, pp. 146–182; Mann, pp. 72–83; Ellis, *Making*, p. 375.

there was no need for a long development of oral traditions, as assumed by the older form criticism.

If one relies on external evidence, it is plausible to assume that Mark wrote in Rome before the death of Peter, whose teaching he wrote down, and that he wrote before the end of Paul's imprisonment (since Luke, who used Mark, ends the book of Acts without reporting the outcome of Paul's trial, which is plausibly explained by the suggestion that the trial had not yet taken place). This would mean that Mark wrote his Gospel between AD 60 and 62 (Gundry, pp. 1042–1043) or, if the relationship between Mark and Luke–Acts is made central to the argument, in the fifties. A very early date around AD 35–50 is possible given the internal evidence; a date around AD 50–64 is plausible given the external evidence.

d. Sources and historical reliability

Scholars who assume that Mark composed his Gospel using oral traditions that circulated in the Christian communities usually posit a pre-Markan passion narrative (Mark 14:1 – 15:47), eschatological discourse (13:1–37), parable collection (4:1–34), controversy stories (2:1 – 3:6; 11:27 – 12:37) and a miracle cycle containing Jesus' miracles in Capernaum, and in addition many 'free-floating' traditions (Marcus, pp. 57–59). While some argue that Mark was a conservative redactor of traditional material who faithfully reproduced extensive sources (Pesch), others think that Mark was a creative theologian who freely shaped his traditions (the standard critical view).

The early Christians were interested in the history of Jesus not primarily for the purpose of describing their self-identity but because Jesus was for them the source of salvation. That the early Christians sought to preserve the traditions about Jesus faithfully is seen in the fact that they transmitted them for their own sake and in their own right, not as attachments to evangelistic preaching or instruction in the community as is assumed in traditional form criticism and redaction criticism.[19]

Papias provides early evidence of the way in which the Gospel traditions were understood to be connected with eyewitnesses, some

---

19. Bauckham, *Eyewitnesses*, pp. 277–289.

of whom he knew personally, at a time that must be around AD 80 (Eusebius, *Hist. eccl.* 3.39.3–4). Papias was not interested in receiving material from collective memory: he did not record the Gospel traditions on the basis of their regular citation in his own church community. What mattered to Papias were eyewitnesses, some of whom were still alive, while others were the disciples of eyewitnesses and were reliable sources because they had direct personal links with the eyewitnesses. Since Papias knew that Mark wrote down the words and actions of Jesus as Peter's 'interpreter' (*Hist. eccl.* 3.39.14–16), Mark's Gospel is a written account of the teaching of Peter, Jesus' most important disciple. Peter's eyewitness accounts are the most significant – and perhaps the only – source for Mark's Gospel.

e. Mark's ending

The ending of Mark's Gospel has been in dispute since the fifth century. A few modern translations end the text at 16:8 and print 16:9–20 in smaller font (NIV), in brackets (NASB) or after headings which alert the reader to the fact that there is a 'shorter ending' and a 'longer ending' (NRSV), that 16:9–20 is 'an old ending to the Gospel' (GNB) or that 'some of the earliest manuscripts do not include 16:9–20' (ESV; cf. NLT). The standard editions of the Greek New Testament print 16:9–20 'out of deference to the evident antiquity of the longer ending and its importance in the textual tradition of the Gospel', but they place these verses in double square brackets 'in order to indicate that they are the work of an author other than the evangelist'.[20] The evidence for the four endings that appear in the manuscript tradition is as follows.[21]

1. The oldest manuscripts of the Greek New Testament (ℵ, Codex Sinaiticus; B, Codex Vaticanus) end Mark's Gospel at 16:8 and do

---

20. Metzger, *Textual Commentary*, pp. 105, 106.
21. The evidence has been set out most fully by Aland, 'Schluß', pp. 246–283. The letters and numbers refer to the labels for Greek manuscripts of the NT. The term 'minuscule' refers to manuscripts dating from the ninth to the sixteenth century which were written in a script of smaller letters in a running hand.

not contain verses 9–20. The ending at 16:8 is also attested in a minuscule manuscript (304; twelfth century) and in manuscripts of the Syriac (Sinaiticus, fourth/fifth century), Coptic (fourth/fifth century) and Armenian and Georgian translations, as well as by Eusebius (fourth century) and Jerome (fifth century).

2. One manuscript (the Latin manuscript k) ends the Gospel after 16:8 with the following sentence: 'And all that had been commanded them they told briefly to those around Peter. And afterward Jesus himself sent out through them, from east to west, the sacred and imperishable proclamation of eternal salvation' (printed as 'the shorter ending' in NRSV). This sentence is also included in some manuscripts between 16:8 and 16:9–20 (see point 5 below). The presence of many words that Mark otherwise does not use and the rhetorical tone which markedly differs from Mark's simple style indicate that this ending is not original.

3. Most Greek manuscripts have 16:9–20 following 16:8 in a continuous text. The longer ending is attested in three fifth-century manuscripts (A, Codex Alexandrinus; C, Codex Ephraemi Syri Rescriptus; D, Codex Bezae Cantabrigiensis) and found in virtually all Byzantine manuscripts, two of which Erasmus used when he produced the first edition of the Greek New Testament in 1516, which explains why the longer ending became the standard text until the nineteenth century. The earliest attestations of the longer ending are Tatian (Diatessaron, AD 172–175), Irenaeus (AD 170) and Eusebius (fourth century). Even in later manuscripts there is an acknowledgment of the fact that the originality of the longer ending is in doubt. Several manuscripts that have the longer ending indicate in scribal notes that older Greek manuscripts lack verses 9–20; for example, the manuscripts of Family 1 (minuscule manuscripts 137, 138, 1110, 1210, 1215, etc.) contain the following note: 'In some of the copies, the evangelist is set out fully up to this place; Eusebius also, the (pupil of) Pamphilus, only went this far in his canons; but in many (copies) this also is in circulation.' In the oldest commentary on Mark's Gospel, by Victor of Antioch, we find a note attached to the longer ending (in manuscripts of Victor's work dating from the tenth to the sixteenth century) that says, 'In most copies this additional material according to Mark is not found.'

4. Some manuscripts which contain 16:9–20 have an extended form of the longer ending. They interrupt the text between 16:14 and 16:15 and include what is called the 'Freer Logion':

> And they excused themselves, saying, 'This age of lawlessness and unbelief is under Satan, who does not allow the truth and power of God to prevail over the unclean things of the spirit [or, 'does not allow what lies under the unclean spirits to understand the truth and power of God']. Therefore reveal your righteousness now' – thus they spoke to Christ. And Christ replied to them, 'The term of years of Satan's power has been fulfilled, but other terrible things draw near. And for those who have sinned I was handed over to death, that they may return to the truth and sin no more, in order that they may inherit the spiritual and incorruptible glory of righteousness that is in heaven.'

This expanded longer ending is attested in a single manuscript (W, Codex Washingtonensis; fourth/fifth century) and hardly original.

5. Some manuscripts contain the shorter ending (see 2 above) followed by verses 9–20, attested in minuscule manuscripts from the sixth/seventh century (083, 099, 0112), Codex Regius (L; eighth century), Codex Athous Lavrensis (Ψ; ninth/tenth century), and in manuscripts of the Syriac, Sahidic, Bohairic and Ethiopic translations. This 'double ending', which combines the shorter and the longer ending, is certainly secondary.

There are essentially three options. First, the longer ending is original: Mark's Gospel ended with 16:1–20. However, the discussion since the publication in 1881 of *The New Testament in the Original Greek* by B. F. Westcott and F. J. A. Hort has established the virtually unanimous consensus[22] that the longer ending 16:9–20 was not part of the original Gospel of Mark but was composed by a scribe who believed that a Gospel could not end with a note of fear (16:8), without appearances of the risen Lord and without a missionary

---

22. Farmer, *Last Twelve Verses*, defended 16:9–20 as genuine in 1974; for a critique cf. Cox, *History*, pp. 84–90. For the latest defence by M. A. Robinson, in Black, *Perspectives*, pp. 40–79, see Bock, in ibid., pp. 132–133, 138–140.

commission. The external evidence (attestation in manuscripts) favours an ending at 16:8. The two earliest manuscripts end here; some Church Fathers (Clement, Origen) did not know the longer ending, while Church Fathers who did (Eusebius, Jerome) noted its absence in most of the Greek manuscripts they knew. Many later manuscripts include notes or scribal notations indicating awareness that manuscripts in circulation do not have the longer ending. The internal evidence (style and content of the text) indicates that the longer ending is not original: nine terms are found nowhere else in Mark, and two expressions (*tois met' autou*, 'those who had been with him', 16:10; *thanasimos*, 'deadly', 16:18) occur only here in the New Testament; the connection between verse 8 and verses 9–20 is awkward: there is no direct or clearly continuous link between verse 8 (the subject is the women at Jesus' tomb) and verse 9 (the subject is presumably Jesus, as assumed in NIV but not expressed in the Greek text); in verse 9 Mary is identified as being from Magdala, which is not necessary after the same identification in 15:47 and 16:1; verses 9–10 mention Mary of Magdala but forget the other women of verses 1–8; the expression *anastas de* ('when he arose') and the position of *prōton* ('first') between *prōi* ('early') and *sabbatou* ('of the week') is appropriate at the beginning of a narrative but awkward as a continuation of 16:1–8. If the longer ending were original, there would be no good explanation for its omission given the endings of Matthew and Luke. It is more likely that the Gospel ended at 16:8 and someone wished to supply a more appropriate conclusion. The text of the longer ending must have been written early in the second century.

The second option is that Mark's ending was lost before it was first copied.[23] It is argued that if the Gospel ended with 16:8, the announcement of Jesus meeting the disciples in Galilee would be unfulfilled, and that a Gospel with the bold start that 1:1 constitutes can hardly end with the negative responses of fear and fright. However, the announcement that the risen Jesus will meet the disciples in Galilee is not the only event that is not fulfilled in Mark's

---

23. Cf. Gundry, pp. 1009–12, 1021; Edwards, pp. 500–504; Evans, p. 539; France, pp. 671–674, 683–684; Stein, pp. 733–737.

Gospel: the prophecies about the destruction of the temple and the return of the Son of Man in Mark 13 are not fulfilled either. Mark's Gospel does *not* end with fear and fright but with an angel's announcement of Jesus' bodily resurrection and the promise of the disciples' restoration in Galilee in 16:7, an announcement and a promise that are a key component of Mark's ending. A variant of this second option, the hypothesis that the manuscript of Mark's Gospel was mutilated (Magness, *Ending*), reckons with two improbabilities: that the manuscript of Mark's Gospel deteriorated or was dismembered extremely rapidly within ten years or so (before being used by Matthew and Luke), and precisely at the end of a pericope.

The third solution is that the shorter ending is original: Mark's Gospel ended with 16:8. This view best explains the external and internal evidence of the manuscript tradition. Some suggest that it is likely that 16:9–20 'was excerpted from another document'.[24] More recently it has been argued that the author of the longer ending used copies of all four Gospels when he composed verses 9–20.[25] Since about 10% of the individual sections in Mark's Gospel end with *gar* ('for'; Gundry, p. 1011; cf. 1:38; 3:35; 6:52; 10:45; 11:18; 12:44), the final section could very well end with this preposition as well. Several studies have found evidence that chapters, lectures and books could indeed end with *gar*, which means that narrative texts also could end with *gar*, even though this is rare.[26] Open endings of literary works are attested in antiquity (Magness, *Ending*, pp. 25–85). In the Old Testament, the book of Jonah has an abrupt and puzzling end; in the New Testament, the book of Acts ends with Paul's legal case in the imperial court unresolved. Demetrius, who wrote an important work on ancient rhetoric and literary criticism, active perhaps in the first century AD (some suggest the third century BC), states with reference to Theophrastus that one 'should not elaborate on

---

24. Metzger, *Textual Commentary*, p. 105.
25. Kelhoffer, *Miracle and Mission*, pp. 48–156; he suggests that 16:9–20 was composed by a single author between AD 120 and 150 (pp. 157–244).
26. Examples are Plotinus, *Enneads* 5.5, treatise 32; Musonius Rufus, *Essay* 12.48; Lucian, *Dialogue of the Courtesans* 6.4. Cf. Croy, *Mutilation*, pp. 47–50, 180–185; Iverson, 'Word', pp. 79–94.

everything in punctilious detail but should omit some points for the listener to infer and work out for himself' (*De elocutione* 222). An ending at 16:8 makes sense 'because the decisive events in the history of salvation have occurred, and the prophesied appearances will only confirm what the angel has already proclaimed, that Jesus has been raised and yet remains the Crucified One' (Marcus, p. 1095). For interpretations of 16:8 as the ending of the Gospel, see the commentary on 16:8.

4. Theological emphases

a. Jesus, the Messiah and Son of God

Mark's Gospel is an account of Jesus' life, death and resurrection. This is made clear in the opening: 'The beginning of the good news about Jesus the Messiah, the Son of God.' The affirmation of Jesus' identity as the unique Son of God at the beginning, which is repeated by a declaration of God at Jesus' baptism (1:11), has a 'bookend' in the declaration of the Roman soldier at the cross who asserts, 'Surely this man was the Son of God!' (15:39). The question of Jesus' identity is like the proverbial red thread that runs through Mark's Gospel (cf. 1:27; 2:7; 4:41; 6:3, 14–16; 8:27–28, 29; 14:61–62).

The revelation of Jesus' identity happens gradually, which we may attribute not so much to Mark's literary artistry but to the historical progression during Jesus' ministry. After the declaration in 1:1 that Jesus is the Messiah and the Son of God, it is only God (1:11; 9:7) and demons (1:24, 34; 3:11–12; 5:7) who know this. It is not until Peter's declaration in 8:29 that the first human being acknowledges Jesus as Messiah, an identification that Jesus asks to be kept secret (8:30) before he qualifies it by speaking of the suffering, rejection, death and resurrection of the Son of Man (8:31). The first public identification of Jesus as the Messiah and Son of God happens in Jesus' Sanhedrin trial, affirmed by Jesus himself (14:61–62), which is again qualified by Jesus with reference to the Son of Man 'sitting at the right hand of the Mighty One and coming on the clouds of heaven' (14:62). The first public affirmation that Jesus is the Son of God comes as Jesus has just died on the cross (15:39). This gradual revelation of Jesus' identity as the messianic Son of God shows that both Jesus' disciples and his opponents found it impossible to connect the concept of Messiah with suffering and death; and it shows that Mark demonstrates that Jesus' suffering and death as a ransom for sins (10:45) was the underlying purpose of God in Jesus' life and ministry.

Mark's presentation of Jesus is enigmatic. He presents him as a human being with human emotions such as indignation (1:41; 10:14), exasperation (8:12; 9:19), anger (3:5), distress (3:5), amazement (6:6), love (10:21), with sometimes limited knowledge (13:32) and limited ability to do miracles (6:5). At the same time Mark describes Jesus as regularly driving out demons (1:21–28, 32–34; 5:1–20; 9:14–29), healing the sick (1:29–31, 32–34, 40–45; 2:1–12; 3:1–6, 7–12; 6:5, 53–56; 7:24–30; 8:22–26; 10:46–52), stilling a storm by verbal command (4:35–41), raising the dead (5:41–42), miraculously feeding large crowds of people (6:30–44; 8:1–10), walking on water (6:45–52), knowing the thoughts and hearts of people (2:8; 3:5), forgiving sins (2:9), and claiming authority over the Sabbath (2:28) and the purity stipulations of the law (7:14–18). In his parables, Jesus repeatedly explains his behaviour by pointing to God's action (4:1–20). Calming the storm is something only God can do (4:35–41; cf. Ps. 89:9), as is walking on water (6:45–51; cf. Job 9:8).

Jesus did not avoid the traditional titles of Messiah and Son of David, but he defined his role with reference to the Son of God who is Lord and with reference to the Son of Man who suffers before being vindicated by God.[27] Jesus is the Messiah, but in a paradoxical manner, both with regard to the transcendent dimension – he is the divine Son of God, the heavenly Son of Man – and with regard to the human dimension – he is the suffering Son of Man, the Servant of the Lord who brings redemption through vicarious death.

b. *The secrecy motif*

Jesus' commands that knowledge of his identity be kept concealed have been construed to constitute a 'messianic secret' (8:29–30; 9:9; in connection with exorcisms 1:25, 34; 3:11–12; in connection with healings 1:43–44; 5:43; 7:36; implied in 8:26). William Wrede, in a

---

27. For the title *Messiah* see 1:1; 8:29; 14:61–62; for the title *Son of God* see 1:1, 11; for the title *Son of Man* see 2:10; 8:31; 14:62.

study published in 1901 (*The Messianic Secret*, English translation from the German original in 1971), contended that the early Christians believed that Jesus was the Messiah only after Easter (Acts 2:36; Rom. 1:3–4; Phil. 2:6–11). As they proclaimed Jesus as Messiah, the fact that the traditions about Jesus contained little or no evidence for Jesus' messianic identity prompted early Christians to invent the motif of secrecy and introduce it into the story of Jesus; Jesus showed himself to be the Messiah, but he had forbidden the revealing of this to others. In other words, the secrecy motif was constructed to explain the unmessianic life of Jesus as well as the post-Easter belief that Jesus was the Messiah. Mark took over the notion of the 'messianic secret' from early tradition, amplified it and made it a predominant feature of this Gospel. Wrede regarded Peter's declaration that Jesus is the Messiah as unhistorical, and generally thought that Mark's Gospel was an unreliable historical source for the life of Jesus (a judgment that affects also Matthew and Luke, who are thought to have used Mark's Gospel for their own Gospels).

However, if Jesus was not regarded as Messiah by Peter and the other disciples (8:29), if there was nothing messianic about Jesus' ministry, and if Jesus did not himself declare that he was the Messiah (14:61–62), there is no explanation for why he was executed as 'the king of the Jews' (15:2, 9, 12, 18, 26; cf. Matt. 27:11, 29, 37; Luke 23:3, 37–38; John 18:33, 39; 19:3, 12, 14, 21). Furthermore, if Jesus' ministry was not messianic and if Jesus did not claim to be the Messiah, there is no explanation for why the early Christians would have been interested in transforming their unmessianic master into the Messiah after Easter.[28] Most scholars today do not believe that Wrede's hypothesis explains either the life of Jesus or Mark's Gospel.[29]

c. *The kingdom of God*
Mark summarizes Jesus' proclamation in the introduction to his Gospel with reference to the coming of the kingdom of God (*basileia*

---

28. Cf. Hengel, *Studies in Early Christianity*, pp. 1–72.
29. For detailed critique of the 'messianic secrecy' interpretation see Garland, *Theology*, pp. 371–385.

tou theou) which fulfils God's promises and which requires people to repent and believe in the good news (1:15). At the other 'end' of his Gospel, Mark reports that the crowds who witnessed Jesus' approach to Jerusalem on a donkey celebrated his coming as 'the coming kingdom of our father David' (11:9–10). When Mark uses the term 'kingdom' for other kingdoms (3:24; 6:23; 13:8), he refers to geographical–political entities, territories ruled by a king, an emperor, a tetrarch. When Mark refers to the 'kingdom of God', he synchronizes the coming of Jesus with the coming of the kingdom of God. Here, the expression 'kingdom of God' describes an activity of God – God's dynamic presence, God's powerful sovereignty becoming visible in history, God's transforming intervention in the lives of his people, a reality that is integrally connected with the person, proclamation, ministry of exorcism and healing, death and resurrection of Jesus. Jesus' transfiguration on the mountain provides three of the disciples with a preternatural experience of God's kingdom having come 'with power' (9:1, 2–9).

At the same time, the presence of the kingdom of God in Jesus' ministry is a mystery, a secret that only those with privileged information imparted by Jesus himself can understand (4:11; note the enigmatic parables in 4:1–34). The hidden presence of the kingdom of God in Jesus' ministry serves the purpose of revelation: as Israel's religious authorities have hardened hearts, they look but cannot see the reality of Jesus' mission (4:11–12); they reject Jesus and put him to death, a death that was a necessary and integral part of his mission according to God's purposes (8:31; 9:31; 10:32–34) – resulting in the open manifestation of Jesus' identity during Jesus' trial and in Jesus' resurrection, making possible the Christian gospel. This Jesus-focused (Christological) dimension of the kingdom of God is central in Mark's description of Jesus' ministry.

The kingdom of God has a temporal dimension: its arrival is evident in Jesus' proclamation of the presence of the kingdom, evidenced in his exorcisms and healings (1:15 as a summary of Jesus' entire ministry); at the same time, it awaits consummation in the future (14:25). The kingdom of God has a public, supernatural dimension: God's presence becomes visible in Jesus' exorcisms and healings (3:23–27) which transform the lives of many people in Galilee, in the Decapolis and in Syria. The kingdom of God has a private, supernatural dimension: it grows on account of God's initiative apart from human efforts (4:26–29); it is tied to understanding Jesus' message, an understanding that is impossible apart from divine initiative and apart from Jesus providing privileged information to his followers about the nature of God's kingdom (4:11; 10:23–27). The kingdom of God has a spatial dimension: people can and should enter it (9:47; 10:15, 23–25) and they can be near it (12:34); since it is connected with Jesus, the 'territory' of the kingdom of God is where Jesus is and where his followers are who proclaim what Jesus proclaims and who do what Jesus does (6:7–13, 30). The kingdom of God has a communal dimension: it consists of the company of those who are called by Jesus and who follow Jesus (1:16–20; 2:14–17). Jesus' followers constitute a family, created by and loyal to Jesus (3:31–35; 10:30). The kingdom of God has a cognitive dimension: it transforms the values and the way of life of those who belong to it on account of their commitment to Jesus (8:34 – 9:1; 9:33 – 10:31; 10:35–45). The kingdom of God has a spiritual dimension: Jesus' mission is fulfilled in his death and resurrection (8:31; 9:31; 10:32–34) as he gives his life as a ransom for many (10:45), forgiving the sins of those who repent (cf. 1:4 with 1:7–8; 1:15; 2:5, 6–11) and inaugurating the new covenant (14:22–25). The coming of the kingdom of God, inseparably synchronized with Jesus' mission, entails the destruction of the temple in Jerusalem (13:1–2, 14–19), the new covenant to which all belong who receive Jesus and the benefits of his sacrificial, atoning death (14:22–24; 10:45), and the later mission of the disciples, who will preach the good news to all nations (13:10).

d. The identity, requirements and mission of followers of Jesus

Jesus' first action is to extend a call to Peter, Andrew, Jacob (James) and John: he calls these four fishermen to come, to follow him and to be trained in order to be sent out to 'fish' for people (1:16–20). Jesus' disciples do not volunteer to follow Jesus, and Jesus does not call his disciples to study the law with him (as was the case with the disciples of the rabbis). It is Jesus who takes the initiative, and the primary loyalty of Jesus' followers is to Jesus himself. This 'structure' of discipleship established by Jesus is similar to the call that God extended to the prophets of the Old Testament. The readiness of the four fishermen in 1:16–20 to leave their nets and boats and follow Jesus demonstrates on the one hand Jesus' amazing authority and shows on the other hand that repentance and faith in the good news (1:15) entail the willingness to leave one's previous way of life and follow Jesus, who proclaims the kingdom of God.

The creation of the group of the Twelve (3:13–19) is significant. The figure twelve has symbolic value, recalling the twelve tribes of Israel. Jesus calls *all* Israel to repentance and to believe in the good news of the arrival of the kingdom of God, who fulfils his promises of end-time salvation. Although Mark does not develop this theme, the creation of the Twelve also means that those who hear and accept the proclamation of Jesus and of the Twelve (6:7–13, 30) belong to the *new people of God*, who are determined not by descent from Abraham and by loyalty to the law but by their commitment to Jesus and their faith in the good news of the coming of the kingdom of God in Jesus' ministry.

Mark portrays the disciples as responding positively to Jesus' call with immediate obedience (1:16–20). They leave everything when they follow Jesus (10:28). Jesus gives them privileged information about the nature of the presence of the kingdom of God and its connection with his ministry (4:11). Jesus allows some of the disciples to witness his raising of Jairus' daughter (5:37–43) and his preternatural transfiguration on the mountain (9:2–8). Jesus sends out the Twelve on a mission of proclamation, exorcism and healing in Galilee (6:7–13), which is successful (6:30). When Jesus sets out for Jerusalem and many of his followers are afraid of what might happen (10:32), the disciples stay with Jesus even though he tells them privately that he will be arrested by the Jewish religious authorities, condemned to death and executed by the Romans (10:33–34). Jesus' assurance to Jacob (James) and John that they will drink the 'cup' that he will have to drink (10:39), speaking of his suffering and death, is a prophecy that 'they will have become faithful proclaimers of the gospel' (Garland, *Theology*, p. 404). The same prophecy is implied in Jesus' assertion that his disciples will stand before governors and kings as witnesses (13:9): the disciples will be faithful, even when they are betrayed by family members and hated by all (13:12–13). When Jesus asserts that the gospel 'must first be preached to all nations' (13:10), he implies that this is what the disciples will actually do. When Jesus is arrested, Peter follows the arresting party into the courtyard of the high priest's house (14:54), demonstrating courage, even though his attempt to be close to Jesus ends miserably in denials that he knows Jesus. After his resurrection, Jesus conveys via the angel at the empty tomb the message that he will meet the disciples in Galilee (16:7), signalling their restoration after they had all deserted him in Gethsemane. A positive portrayal of disciples is also indicated in the reference to three women who are present at Jesus' crucifixion (15:40), at Jesus' burial (15:47, only the two Marys) and at the empty tomb (16:1).

Mark's portrayal of the disciples also reports their misunderstandings and failures. This aspect of Mark's description of the disciples has been (mis-)understood as a vendetta against the disciples, designed to discredit the view of false teachers in Mark's community by discrediting the disciples (Weeden, *Mark*; for a critique see Stein, pp. 26–31). This theory represents a mistaken model of 'mirror reading' Mark's Gospel and it ignores Mark's positive portrayal of the disciples. Mark's readers would have had a favourable pre-understanding of the disciples on the basis of the highly positive portrayal in the first chapters of his Gospel, even though they knew of Judas' betrayal and Peter's denial. The clearest negative description comes in 6:52; 8:17, 33. The fact that many of the passages in Mark's Gospel which give a severely negative portrayal of the disciples are also found in Matthew and Luke[30] indicates that misunderstandings and failures of the disciples were part of the Jesus tradition rather than a polemical construction of the evangelist.

---

30. For 7:18 cf. Matt. 15:17; for 8:4 cf. Matt. 15:33; for 9:5–7 cf. Matt. 17:4–5; Luke 9:33–34; for 9:18 cf. Matt. 17:16; Luke 9:40; for 9:32 cf. Luke 9:45; for 9:33–34 cf. Luke 9:46; for 14:32–42 cf. Matt. 26:36–46; Luke 22:39–46; for 14:50 cf. Matt. 26:56; for 14:66–72 cf. Matt. 26:69–75; Luke 22:56–62. Sometimes Matthew plays down the negative portrayals (see the parallels in Matthew to Mark 6:52; 8:17; 9:32, 34; 10:35), sometimes he intensifies them: for 4:38–40 cf. Matt. 8:25–27; for 8:32–33 cf. Matt. 16:23; for 9:28–29 cf. Matt. 17:19–20; for 14:4 cf. Matt. 26:8. Cf. Stein, p. 30.

Mark gives an unvarnished picture of the disciples. They fail to understand Jesus' parables (4:13), but then they receive Jesus' instruction (4:14–20, 33–34). They fail to understand Jesus' teaching about ritual purity (7:17); Jesus does not respond with a rebuke but provides them with an explanation (7:18–23). The disciples lose all hope when their boat is swamped by high waves on the Sea of Galilee (4:40); Jesus' statement that they 'still have no faith' does not censure them so much as point them to his presence as divine presence (4:41). The disciples' failure to understand Jesus' feeding of crowds of people (cf. 8:4) receives a harsh rebuke by Jesus, who says that they have hardened hearts (6:52; 8:17). The 'diagnosis' of having a hardened heart can be ominous since it is the condition of Jesus' enemies (3:5). The disciples' failure to understand and have faith, prompting Jesus' harsh rebukes in 4:40, 6:52, 8:17, takes place in view of Jesus' demonstration of his authority as divine authority. Similarly, the disciples' failure to understand Jesus' predictions of his suffering and death (8:32) earns them a stern admonition by Jesus. He links their opposition to his announcement that his death is an integral part of his mission with 'merely human concerns' which in this matter are opposed to 'the concerns of God' (8:33), an explanation that renders the disciples' lack of understanding of Jesus' prediction(s) of his suffering, death and resurrection plausible in the context of Jewish expectations which did not envision the Messiah's mission as entailing rejection by the Jewish religious leaders and death at the hands of the Roman authorities. Jesus' predictions of his suffering and death as central events of his saving mission required Jesus' resurrection as divine seal of approval (Stein, p. 31).

5. The structure of Mark's Gospel

The proposed outlines for Mark's Gospel fall into two main categories: outlines that focus on the geographical progression of Jesus' ministry from Galilee to Jerusalem (Cranfield, Lane, France, Marcus, Taylor, Garland) and outlines that focus on the revelation of Jesus as messianic Son of God and on his suffering and death (Boring, Guelich, Strauss). Some authors attempt to combine a geographical and a Christological outline (Bayer, Pesch). The outline that is assumed in this commentary largely follows Strauss and Garland.

ANALYSIS

1. **THE BEGINNING OF THE GOSPEL (1:1–13)**
   A. Heading (1:1)
   B. Jesus and John the Baptist (1:2–8)
   C. Jesus declared Son of God and conflict with Satan (1:9–13)

2. **JESUS' MESSIANIC AUTHORITY (1:14 – 8:21)**
   A. The kingdom of God and Jesus' authority (1:14 – 3:6)
      i. Jesus' proclamation of the kingdom of God (1:14–15)
      ii. Jesus' call of the disciples (1:16–20)
      iii. Jesus' teaching, healing and exorcism (1:21–45)
         a. Jesus teaches and exorcizes an evil spirit (1:21–28)
         b. Jesus heals Simon's mother-in-law (1:29–31)
         c. Jesus heals and exorcizes evil spirits (1:32–34)
         d. Prayer and mission in Galilee (1:35–39)
         e. Jesus heals a man with skin disease (1:40–45)
      iv. Controversies with religious leaders (2:1 – 3:6)
         a. Jesus forgives sin and heals a paralytic (2:1–12)
         b. Jesus calls Levi and eats with sinners (2:13–17)
         c. Jesus and fasting (2:18–22)
         d. Jesus and the Sabbath (2:23–28)
         e. Jesus and healing on the Sabbath (3:1–6)

B. The Twelve and the kingdom of God (3:7 – 6:6)
   i. Jesus' ministry: summary (3:7–12)
   ii. Jesus' call of the Twelve (3:13–19)
   iii. Jesus' family, opponents and authority (3:20–35)
      a. Jesus and his natural family (3:20–21)
      b. Jesus and the scribes from Jerusalem (3:22–30)
      c. Jesus' true family and the outsiders (3:31–35)
   iv. Parables about the kingdom of God (4:1–34)
      a. Parable of the four soils and true seeing (4:1–20)
      b. Analogy of the lamp and disclosure (4:21–23)
      c. Analogy of the measure and revelation (4:24–25)
      d. Parable of the growing seed (4:26–29)
      e. Parable of the mustard seed (4:30–34)
   v. Demonstrations of Jesus' authority (4:35 – 5:43)
      a. Authority over nature: the storm (4:35–41)
      b. Authority over demons: the Gerasenes (5:1–20)
      c. Authority over disease: the woman (5:21–34)
      d. Authority over death: Jairus' daughter (5:35–43)
   vi. Rejection in Nazareth (6:1–6)
C. The mission of Jesus Messiah and the Twelve (6:7 – 8:21)
   i. The mission of the Twelve (6:7–13)
   ii. The execution of John the Baptist (6:14–29)
   iii. The feeding of the five thousand (6:30–44)
   iv. Walking on water (6:45–52)
   v. Healing the sick in Gennesaret (6:53–56)
   vi. Controversy over tradition and purity (7:1–23)
   vii. The faith of the Syro-Phoenician woman (7:24–30)
   viii. Healing of a deaf mute (7:31–37)
   ix. The feeding of the four thousand (8:1–10)
   x. The Pharisees' demand for a sign (8:11–13)
   xi. Warning regarding the Pharisees and Herod (8:14–21)

3. **JESUS' MESSIANIC SUFFERING (8:22 – 15:47)**
  A. The revelation of the Messiah's suffering (8:22 – 10:52)
    i. Healing of a blind man at Bethsaida (8:22–26)
    ii. Peter's declaration that Jesus is the Messiah (8:27–30)
    iii. First passion and resurrection prediction (8:31–33)
    iv. The requirements of discipleship (8:34 – 9:1)

ANALYSIS   33

      v. The transfiguration of Jesus and Elijah (9:2–13)
     vi. Exorcism of a boy with an evil spirit (9:14–29)
    vii. Second passion and resurrection prediction (9:30–32)
   viii. Teaching on discipleship (9:33–50)
     ix. Teaching on divorce (10:1–12)
      x. Blessing the children (10:13–16)
     xi. The rich man and discipleship (10:17–31)
    xii. Third passion and resurrection prediction (10:32–34)
   xiii. The greatness of self-sacrificial service (10:35–45)
   xiv. Healing of Bartimaeus at Jericho (10:46–52)
B. The confrontation in Jerusalem (11:1 – 13:37)
      i. Jesus in the temple (11:1 – 12:44)
        a. Triumphal approach to Jerusalem (11:1–11)
        b. Prophetic action in the temple (11:12–25)
        c. Jesus' authority and the authorities (11:27–33)
        d. The parable of the tenants (12:1–12)
        e. Paying taxes to the emperor (12:13–17)
        f. The question about the resurrection (12:18–27)
        g. The question about the commandments (12:28–34)
        h. The question about David's Son (12:35–37)
        i. Warning against the teachers of the law (12:38–40)
        j. Commendation of the widow (12:41–44)
     ii. Jesus on the Mount of Olives (13:1–37)
        a. Prophecy of the destruction of the temple (13:1–2)
        b. The destruction of the temple (13:3–23)
        c. The coming of the Son of Man (13:24–27)
        d. The consequences for disciples (13:28–37)
C. The suffering and death of Jesus Messiah (14:1 – 15:47)
      i. The preparations for Jesus' arrest (14:1–11)
        a. The scheme to arrest Jesus (14:1–2)
        b. The anointing at Bethany (14:3–9)
        c. The betrayal by Judas Iscariot (14:10–11)
     ii. The Last Supper (14:12–31)
        a. Preparation for the Last Supper (14:12–16)
        b. Prediction of Judas Iscariot's betrayal (14:17–21)
        c. The bread and cup and Jesus' death (14:22–26)
        d. Prediction of Peter's denial (14:27–31)

      iii. On the Mount of Olives (14:32–52)
          a. Jesus' prayer in Gethsemane (14:32–42)
          b. Jesus' betrayal and arrest (14:43–52)
      iv. Jesus' trial before the Sanhedrin (14:53–72)
          a. Peter follows Jesus (14:53–54)
          b. Trial before the Sanhedrin and verdict (14:55–65)
          c. The denial of Peter (14:66–72)
      v. Jesus' trial before Pontius Pilate (15:1–20)
          a. Pilate's interrogation of Jesus (15:1–5)
          b. Unsuccessful attempts to release Jesus (15:6–15)
          c. The soldiers' mocking of Jesus (15:16–20)
      vi. Jesus' crucifixion (15:21–32)
          a. Conscription of Simon of Cyrene to carry the cross (15:21–22)
          b. Offer of wine mixed with myrrh (15:23)
          c. Crucifixion between two bandits (15:24–27)
          d. Mocking of Jesus at the cross (15:29–32)
      vii. Jesus' death and burial (15:33–47)
          a. Darkness and Jesus' last shout (15:33–34)
          b. Mocking of Jesus (15:35–36)
          c. Jesus' death (15:37)
          d. Splitting of the curtain in the temple (15:38)
          e. Declaration of the centurion (15:39)
          f. Presence of women supporters (15:40–41)
          g. Jesus' burial (15:42–47)

4. JESUS' RESURRECTION ANNOUNCED (16:1–8)
  A. The women at Jesus' tomb (16:1–5)
  B. The announcement of Jesus' resurrection (16:6–7)
  C. The reaction of the women (16:8)

COMMENTARY

1. THE BEGINNING OF THE GOSPEL (1:1–13)

Mark's account of Jesus' life, death and resurrection begins with a heading (1:1) which identifies Jesus Messiah and Son of God as the subject of the following narrative, followed by a scriptural comment (1:2–3) which links Jesus and John the Baptist, whose ministry is described in the next section (1:4–8), followed by an account of Jesus' baptism and of his testing in the wilderness (1:9–13). The prologue introduces the main *dramatis personae*: Jesus from Nazareth in Galilee, the crowds and the people of Jerusalem (John the Baptist is not a major actor after 1:13). And the prologue takes the readers behind the scenes of the following story: Jesus is identified from the outset as Messiah and Son of God (1:1), by God himself (1:11), an identity that is evident in the fact that his ministry is the fulfilment of Scripture (1:2–3) and that he is endowed with and directed by God's Spirit in the fulfilment of his messianic calling, himself dispensing the Spirit (1:8), which in the Old Testament only Yahweh himself does.

A. Heading (1:1)

Context

The first sentence of Mark's Gospel can be taken as the heading to the scriptural quotation in 1:2–3, to the account of John the Baptist in 1:2–8, to the prologue (1:1–13) or to the entire book. The connection of 1:2 to 1:1 renders the scriptural quotation in 1:2–3, formally, a comment on 1:1. At the same time, 1:2–3 introduces the account of John the Baptist in 1:4–8, which in turn introduces the account of Jesus' baptism in 1:9–11 in which the title 'Son of God' from 1:1 is taken up. However, 1:1 is not merely the introduction to the prologue: the term 'good news' (*euangelion*) in 1:1 is repeated in 1:14, 15, which begins the account of Jesus' public life, and occurs again in 8:35; 10:29; 13:10; 14:9. The prologue is only the 'beginning' of the 'good news' (1:1) which, in terms of its content, comprises Jesus' public life and ministry, whose account fills the rest of the book.

Comment

1. *The beginning of the good news about Jesus the Messiah, the Son of God.* The *beginning* (*archē*) of Mark's book is the ministry of John the Baptist (1:4–8) which initiates the fulfilment of messianic expectations (1:2–3) and leads to Jesus' baptism and testing (1:9–13). At the same time, these words announce the *beginning* of the book's central theme: the good news about the life, death and resurrection of Jesus, who is the promised Messiah. The suggestion that *beginning* echoes the opening phrase of Genesis 1:1 (LXX: *en archē*, 'in the beginning'; cf. John 1:1) is not convincing: while Genesis and John refer to the beginning of all things, Mark speaks of the beginning of the good news about Jesus.

The term *euangelion* ('good news')[1] is used in the New Testament as a quasi-technical term for the message of Jesus' followers. Traditionally *euangelion* was translated in English versions as 'gospel' (from

---

1. Cf. 1:14–15; 8:35; 10:29; 13:10; 14:9. Mark does not use the verb *euangelizomai* ('to bring good news, announce good news'), unlike Matt. (11:5) and Luke (1:19; 2:10; 3:18; 4:18, 43; 7:22; 8:1; 9:6; 16:16; 20:1).

Old English *godspel*, 'glad tidings'), while newer versions (NIV, NLT, NRSV) have 'good news'. Since both the noun and the verb *euangelizomai* are used in Greek texts for (the announcement of) good news in a variety of contexts, the assumption of an anti-imperial background – in the sense of a response to the emperor cult in which the terms were used for the announcement of the emperor's birthday or accession to the throne – is unnecessary. More important is the use of the verb in the LXX as the translation for Hebrew *biśśēr* ('to announce, tell, deliver a message'): key passages use the term to describe God's kingly reign, his victory over his enemies and the arrival of salvation.[2] In Isaiah, the 'herald of good news' announces and inaugurates the new era of God's kingly rule (Isa. 40:9–11; 52:7). Mark states that the content of his book is God's good news for God's people, conveyed in and through Jesus, who is the promised Messiah. It is the content of the book which is *euangelion*. It is possible, however, that Mark intended the term as a reference to the written narrative about the life of Jesus.[3]

Mark gives an account of the good news which is *about Jesus the Messiah*. In its Greek form (*Iēsous*), the name *Jesus* is the Hebrew name *Yĕhôšûʻa* (Joshua, meaning 'Yahweh saves', 'Yahweh is salvation'; the Aramaic form is *Yēšûʻa*). 'Jesus' was a popular name among Jews.[4] The Greek term *Christos* has traditionally been rendered with the transliteration 'Christ', which is easily misunderstood as a proper name. The Greek term is an adjective which renders the Hebrew term *māšîaḥ* ('anointed') which, by the first century, was used as a title for the promised king from the Davidic dynasty who would appear in the last days (Hebr. *ha-māšîaḥ*; Aramaic *mešîḥaʾ*; 'the Anointed One').[5] In 8:29, 9:41, 12:35, 13:21, 14:61, 15:32, *Christos* has

---

2. Cf. Pss 40:9[10]; 68:11[12]; 96:2 (LXX 95:2); Isa. 40:9; 41:27; 52:7; 60:6; 61:1; Nah. 1:15 (LXX 2:1).

3. Cf. Hengel, *Studies*, pp. 53–54; Collins, p. 131.

4. Bauckham, *Eyewitnesses*, p. 85: Among the ninety-nine most popular male names among Palestinian Jews before AD 200, 'Jesus' was the sixth most popular (after Simon, Joseph, Lazarus, Judas and John).

5. Cf. 2 Sam. 7:11–16; Pss 2; 89; 110; Isa. 9:1–7; 11:1–16; Jer. 23:1–6; Ezek. 34:23–24; 37:24–25. Cf. M. F. Bird, *DJG*, pp. 115–125.

clearly a titular meaning, emphasizing Jesus' perceived or claimed role as the Messiah.

The term *Son of God* here is not a synonym for *Messiah*, which is possible in the light of 2 Samuel 7:14, Psalm 2:7 and several Qumran passages,[6] but describes Jesus' identity in terms of divine dignity: Jesus is the unique, messianic Son of God, twice declared by the voice of God himself (1:11; 9:7), who shares God's power and glory (cf. 3:11; 5:7; 13:32; and note Jesus' miracles and exorcisms).

Theology

Mark's book relates the beginning of the good news about Jesus, who is the promised Messiah and indeed the unique Son of God. The appearance and the ministry of both John the Baptist and Jesus are not one more phase in the divinely guided history of salvation: John and Jesus mark a new beginning – the beginning of the promised, and long-awaited, salvation of Israel and of the world. The 'good news' that the prophets spoke and wrote about has become a reality, beginning with John and focused on Jesus. When the entire book is understood as a 'beginning', Mark asserts that the 'good news' continues in the churches in which his book is being read and heard by Jesus' followers who are in the process of taking the good news to all nations (13:10).

B. Jesus and John the Baptist (1:2–8)

Context

The beginning of the good news about Jesus the Messiah (1:1) is linked with the ministry of John which Mark introduces as constituting a fulfilment of Scripture (1:2–3). Mark's description of John's preaching focuses consistently on what he says about the One coming after him (1:7–8). Matthew and Luke elaborate John's preaching about repentance and the imminence of judgment (Matt. 3:7–10; Luke 3:7–9), and Luke includes John's reply to those who

---

6. 4Q174 I,11; 4Q246 II,1; perhaps 1QSa II,11–12; see on 14:61. In the OT the phrase 'son of God' refers to Israel (as God's firstborn son; 2 Sam. 7:14; Pss 2:7; 89:26) and to angels (Gen. 6:2, 4; Job 1:6; 38:7; Dan. 3:25).

question him about what he is doing (Luke 3:10–14). Assuming that Tiberius' fifteenth year mentioned in Luke 3:1 is reckoned from the beginning of his co-regency with Augustus in AD 11/12, and assuming that Jesus' crucifixion and resurrection took place in AD 30, John's ministry can be dated to AD 26/27.[7]

Comment

2–3. The 'beginning of the good news' of Jesus the Messiah fulfils Scripture. Mark prefaces the quotation with the traditional formula *it is written*; the perfect tense underlines that Israel's Scriptures are not texts that are relevant only for the past, but are God's living word in the present. The following quotation combines Exodus 23:20; Malachi 3:1; and Isaiah 40:3.[8] The ascription to Isaiah is not a mistake, but a deliberate device that places the story of John the Baptist and of Jesus in the context of Isaiah's vision of Israel's and the world's restoration and renewal in the last days (Watts, *New Exodus*, p. 89). The first sentence of the quotation comes from Exodus 23:20a (LXX), which speaks of the angel whom God promised to go before Israel in the wilderness at the time of the exodus: *I will send my messenger ahead of you* (lit. 'before your face'). The second sentence of the quotation comes from Malachi 3:1a: *who will prepare your way*. Mark's change from 'my way' (Mal.) to 'your way' allows for a messianic interpretation, and also implies that Jesus, who is thus directly addressed by Yahweh, is the embodiment of Israel's God. The third sentence is a quotation from Isaiah 40:3 (LXX): *a voice of one calling in the wilderness, 'Prepare the way for the Lord, make straight paths for him.'* Isaiah predicts a new exodus when the Lord (*kyrios*), Yahweh, the God of Israel, will return and lead his people out of the Babylonian exile into the Promised Land. The *voice* in the wilderness is the voice of John the Baptist, who calls God's people to repentance (1:4), thus preparing a path for the coming of the Messiah. Mark changes the phrase 'the paths of our God' in the LXX

---

7. Riesner, *Chronology*, pp. 39–41, 48–58. H. W. Hoehner and J. K. Brown, *DJG*, pp. 134–138, date John's ministry to AD 29 and Jesus' death to AD 33.
8. Conflation of several OT texts is also found in 1:11; 12:36; 14:24, 27, 62.

text to 'paths for him' (NIV) or 'his paths' (NRSV), referring to Jesus. The promised coming of God has taken place in the coming of Jesus. Where and when Jesus acts, God acts.

4. John is called *John the Baptist*. The title 'the Baptist' (*ho baptizōn*), which can be translated as 'the One who Baptizes' (NRSV 'the baptizer'), is the more functional equivalent of the title *ho baptistēs* in 6:25; 8:28. The Greek verb *baptizō* means 'to plunge, dip, immerse' – used, for example, of a knife that is plunged into a sacrificial animal, a ship that is submerged in water or fabric that is dipped into dye; in its metaphorical use it describes, for example, a person immersed in debt, overcome by an argument or overpowered by passions (Schnabel, 'Meaning'). Here, the meaning is 'immersion'. In Second Temple Judaism, self-administered and recurring ablutions such as hand-washing and immersion in water (in rivers or in *miqwāôt*, stepped immersion pools) were regularly practised by the pious, primarily to cleanse from impurity and to maintain purity. At Qumran immersion signified purification from defilement due to sin and initiation into the community as the true or pure Israel.

The location *in the wilderness* refers to an uncultivated and uninhabited country. The specific reference to the Jordan river in verse 5 identifies the valley between the lake of Galilee and the Dead Sea as the geographical region in which John was active. The crowds who came from Judea and Jerusalem suggest the southern part of the valley, not far from where the Jordan meets the Dead Sea near Jericho. The location of John's activity in the wilderness has theological significance. Yahweh had led Israel into the wilderness when he liberated them from bondage in Egypt and made them his people, meeting them at Sinai and giving them his holy law, and Israel experienced God's presence, provision and protection in the wilderness before they reached the Promised Land (Deut. 1 – 7, summed up in Deut. 8). John's ministry in the wilderness suggests hope and a new beginning, as his message confirms.

Mark describes John's activity with the verb *preaching*. The Greek term *kēryssō* denotes making an (official) announcement in the public sphere, often in the context of courts of law, with the implication of a demand to react to the content of the announcement. The prophets use the verb in connection with repentance (Jon. 1:2; 3:2, 4) and messianic forgiveness (Isa. 61:1). In the New Testament it is a standard term for the proclamation of God's redemptive action in Jesus the Messiah. People came to John because of his preaching.

Mark characterizes John's preaching with four nouns. (1) John preached *baptism* (Gr. *baptisma*); that is, the necessity for Jews to be immersed in the Jordan river in preparation for the coming of the One who would immerse them in the Holy Spirit (1:7–8). John's baptism purified those who repented from moral uncleanness (cf. Josephus, *Ant.* 18.117). To be born a Jew was not enough: in order to belong to the 'true Israel', prepared for the restoration of the last days connected with the Coming One who would grant the Holy Spirit, Jews had to accept John's preaching and respond by being immersed by John in the waters of the Jordan river. (2) John preached the necessity of *repentance*. The Greek term *metanoia* (lit. 'change of mind') describes regret or remorse for individual actions; the New Testament use of the term is deeply influenced by the prophets' call for the nation to return to Yahweh, implying a fundamental change in spiritual orientation and ethical behaviour. (3) John preached the necessity, and availability, of *forgiveness* (Gr. *aphesis*), a term that describes the act of freeing or liberating from something that confines or from an obligation, here the release from guilt and thus from punishment stipulated for the guilty. (4) John preached about *sins* (Gr. *hamartia*, 'sin'), a term that denotes the departure from human or divine standards of righteousness. Jews know that it is only God who can forgive sins.

The connection between the *baptism* that John preached, the *repentance* that he expected and the *forgiveness of sins* that he offered is debated. The term *repentance* that comes between *baptism* and *forgiveness* renders the assumption of a saving efficacy of baptism 'a less plausible deduction' (France, p. 67). John's baptism is not optional, but it is not the grounds for forgiveness, which only God can grant.

5. Mark now describes the effect of John's preaching: *The whole Judean countryside and all the people of Jerusalem went out to him*. The name of the region is used for its inhabitants: all people living in the Judean region came to John. *Judea*, which included Samaria and Idumea, had been under Roman administration since AD 6 when Augustus removed Archelaos, one of the sons of King Herod, who had ruled the southern part of the client kingdom of his father. The highest Roman official was a prefect (*praefectus*) from the equestrian order who was subordinate to the consular governor of the province of Syria.[9] *Jerusalem* was the capital of Judea when Herod I was king and it remained the *de facto* capital of Jewish Judea during direct Roman rule (with Caesarea as the political capital). In the first century AD, Jerusalem had a population of between 60,000 and 70,000 inhabitants.[10] Mark underlines the wide appeal of John's preaching. He notes specifically that the popular response to John's preaching included *all the people of Jerusalem*, who later responded positively to Jesus' preaching as well (3:8).

The people who came to John from all over Judea *were baptized by him in the river Jordan*. In contrast to Jewish self-administered immersions for the sake of purification from uncleanness, it is John who immerses people, perhaps indicating that the purification that prepares for the imminent coming of God and the Messiah is not dependent on what people do but on what is done to them. The phrase *confessing their sins* describes the people's response to John's preaching: they admit their wrongdoing, they express their remorse and they are then immersed in the Jordan river.

6. Mark pauses to describe John's clothing and diet: *John wore clothing made of camel's hair, with a leather belt round his waist, and he ate locusts and wild honey*. The description of his clothing comes from 2 Kings 1:8, where the prophet Elijah is described in nearly identical terms. This is significant since the 'messenger' of Malachi 3:1 (quoted in Mark 1:2) is identified in Malachi 4:5 as the Elijah of the last days, whom Jesus will identify with John in Mark 9:13. John's appearance portrays him at least as a prophet (cf. Zech. 13:4), and most likely more specifically as Elijah who was expected to appear in the last days. John's diet was simple, consistent with someone living off the land, but certainly nutritious. Locusts are the only type of insect permitted as food in the law (Lev. 11:20–23); they were also eaten, roasted or boiled, in the Qumran community (CD XII, 14–15).

7–8. Mark describes John's preaching, whose substance was described in verse 4, in two sentences in direct speech which explain

---

9. Cf. Cotton, 'Administration', pp. 75–81; Eck, *Rom*, pp. 1–51.
10. L. I. Levine, *EDEJ*, p. 796. Jeremias, *Jerusalem*, p. 84: 25,000–30,000; W. Reinhardt, in Bauckham, *Acts*, pp. 240–259, 263: 100,000–120,000.

more specifically why John's ministry is 'the beginning of the good news about Jesus the Messiah'. The first sentence announces the coming of One who is superior to John. The expression *the one more powerful than I* is not very specific. The superiority of the One whose coming John announces is explained with the image of the slave undoing the *sandal* thong of his master, his social superior. The second sentence provides a second clue for understanding the superiority of the One who will come. John's immersion of people in the water of the Jordan river is inferior to the immersion in the Holy Spirit effected by the One who is coming. Both the nature and the spiritual efficacy of the Coming One surpass what John accomplishes with his preaching and baptizing. The term *baptize* (*baptizō*; see 1:4) refers to physical immersion in *water* in the first part of the sentence, and to metaphorical immersion in the *Holy Spirit* in the second part of the sentence. Metaphorical 'immersion in the Holy Spirit' means being overcome or overwhelmed by the Holy Spirit. While John offers forgiveness of sins, symbolized in immersion in water, the One who is coming will grant the Holy Spirit. John's description leaves the Coming One incognito. In a Jewish context, and in the context of the passages quoted in verses 2–3 (Mal. 3:1; Isa. 40:3), the One more powerful than John who dispenses the Spirit would be Yahweh himself, who was expected to pour out his Spirit in the last days (Isa. 32:15; 44:3; Ezek. 36:26–27; 39:29; Joel 2:28–29). However, the reference to the removing of sandals, while a metaphor, does point to a human figure. Mark's readers know that John speaks of Jesus. The coming of God, who pours out his Spirit in the last days, takes place through the coming of Jesus, who pours out God's Spirit and thus effectively conveys the presence of God.

Theology
The contrast between John's water baptism and the immersion in the Spirit which the Coming One will bring means that 'water baptism is a preliminary rite, of lesser significance' which probably is intended to imply 'that even Christian water baptism on its own is inadequate' (France, p. 71). More significant than the rite of water baptism is the reality of God's very presence among his people and in the life of the individual who has confessed his or her sin and experienced God's forgiveness. Luke describes the fulfilment of

John's prophecy as having happened on the Day of Pentecost (Acts 2) and in the ongoing experience of Jesus' followers (cf. Acts 4:8, 31; 9:17; 13:9, 52; Eph. 5:18).

C. Jesus declared Son of God and conflict with Satan (1:9–13)

Context

In 1:9 Jesus is introduced for the first time. The focus in this passage is not so much on what Jesus did, nor on his baptism, but on his identity as the Son of God. The divine revelation is narrated as an experience of Jesus (1:10–11). While there is secrecy and paradox regarding Jesus' identity in the narrative that follows, Mark leaves no doubt for his readers as to who Jesus is: God's voice declares that Jesus is his messianic Son.

Comment

9. The 'date' that Mark provides for Jesus' appearance is general: *in those days* (NRSV) links Jesus' entry into the story with the ministry of John the Baptist described in the previous verses. Luke 3:1 provides an exact date for the beginning of John's ministry: the fifteenth year of Emperor Tiberius, probably dating from Tiberius' co-regency with Augustus in AD 11–12, was AD 27. Jesus' public ministry thus lasted three years from AD 27–30.[11] Jesus is identified, according to convention, with reference to the town in which he lived: Jesus comes *from Nazareth in Galilee*. Since Nazareth, which is not mentioned in the Old Testament (nor by Josephus nor in the Talmud), was a settlement with fewer than four hundred inhabitants, it could be contemptuously dismissed even by a Galilean like Nathanael (John 1:46).

Galilee, in Jesus' day a tetrarchy north of Roman Judea, was governed by Herod Antipas, the second son of King Herod. The two major Galilean cities Sepphoris and Tiberias are not explicitly

---

11. John 2:13, 6:4, 11:55 note three Passovers; according to John 2:20, the reconstruction of the temple had lasted for forty-six years, i.e. from 20 BC to AD 27.

mentioned in the New Testament. The population of Galilee is estimated for the first century at perhaps 25,000 to 30,000 people.[12] The One who is stronger than John comes, paradoxically, not from Bethlehem, the city of David which was linked with messianic expectations, nor from Jerusalem, the city of God's presence in the temple, but from Nazareth in Galilee.

A second paradox is the statement that Jesus *was baptized by John in the Jordan*. Mark has recounted John's message that the One who comes after him is stronger than he is and will 'baptize', not with water but, which is superior, with the Holy Spirit. Now the Coming One submits to John's water baptism. Mark does not comment on the paradox that the juxtaposition of verses 8 and 9 presents (unlike Matt. 3:14–15). Mark does not explain why Jesus, whom the voice of God declared to be his messianic Son (1:11), was immersed by John in the Jordan river in a baptism that is linked with repentance and the forgiveness of sins (1:4). Mark is content to point out that Jesus identified with John's message of Israel's need of repentance for the forgiveness of sins and the expectation of imminent restoration through the outpouring of God's Spirit.

10. The phrase *as Jesus was coming up out of the water* suggests full immersion in the Jordan river. Jesus *saw heaven being torn open*. The opening of heaven indicates a revelation of God (theophany).[13] Then Jesus saw *the Spirit descending on him like a dove*. The Spirit descends *on* (Gr. *eis*) Jesus, not as a temporary equipment for a specific task but as a permanent presence. As Jesus is the Messiah (1:1; cf. 1:11), the descent of the Spirit fulfils the prophets' expectation of a saviour figure who is endowed with God's Spirit (Isa. 11:2–4; 42:1; 61:1). The Spirit has no visible form, but Jesus *saw* something *like a dove*, which probably means something looking like a dove (not literally a dove). The dove has been interpreted as a symbol of Israel (*b. Ber.* 53b), as a reference to Noah's dove (Gen. 8:8–12) or to the hovering of the Spirit over the waters at creation

---

12. Rami Arav (private communication); Fiensy, in Fiensy and Strange, *Galilee*, I, p. 178, assumes 135,000 to 160,000 people, based on earlier estimations by E. M. Meyers, in Edwards and McCollough, *Archaeology*, p. 59.
13. Cf. Ezek. 1:1; John 1:51; Acts 7:56; 10:11; Rev. 4:1; 19:11.

(Gen. 1:2), none of which is convincing; the dove is probably mentioned simply because it was one of the most familiar birds. The connection between the gift of the Spirit and anointing in Isaiah 61:1 (cf. 1 Sam. 16:13) renders the descent of the Spirit on Jesus an affirmation of Jesus' identity as Messiah and his permanent empowerment for messianic service.

11. The *voice . . . from heaven* that Jesus heard is the voice of God, as the words that are spoken clearly indicate. God declares, in direct speech addressed to Jesus: *You are my Son, whom I love; with you I am well pleased.* The declaration of God's voice has three elements, all of which allude to Old Testament passages. First, *you are my Son* comes from Psalm 2:7, a psalm in which the kings of the earth conspire against Yahweh and against 'his anointed', with Yahweh declaring that he has established his king on Zion and that he has decreed that he is his, Yahweh's, son. The address 'you are my son' in Psalm 2 takes up Nathan's prophecy which designates David's son and successor as the son of God (2 Sam. 7:14). These two Old Testament passages were combined in the Qumran document 4Q174 as messianic texts, which fits with other Jewish documents that use 'Son of God' as a messianic title (e.g. 4Q246). The voice from heaven declares Jesus from Nazareth in Galilee to be God's Son, who is the promised royal Messiah. Second, the phrase *whom I love* (*agapētos*; NRSV 'the Beloved') may be an allusion to Genesis 22:2, where Abraham is commanded by God to offer as sacrifice Isaac, 'your only son, whom you love' (the LXX translates 'take your beloved son, whom you love'). If Mark intends his readers to see this connection, he would take Abraham's willingness to sacrifice his beloved son as prefiguring God's offering of his only, beloved Son; or, more generally, he alludes to the special relationship of Jesus to God as analogous to Isaac's special relationship with Abraham. The declaration that Jesus is God's 'beloved Son' is repeated by the voice from heaven at the transfiguration (9:7) and in Jesus' parable of the vineyard, where a 'beloved son' is the final messenger (12:6). Third, the phrase *with you I am well pleased* alludes to Isaiah 42:1, where the Servant of the Lord on whom Yahweh has put his Spirit is identified by Yahweh as 'my chosen one in whom I delight'. The Servant of Yahweh, directed by the Spirit, achieves justice for the nations by his patient faithfulness (Isa. 42:1–4). While the crowds later discuss who Jesus might be (8:27–28), Mark's readers are not left in doubt about Jesus' identity.

12–13. The Spirit who descended upon Jesus immediately sends him out *into the wilderness*, where Jesus is for forty days, *being tempted by Satan*. Unlike Matthew 4:1–11 and Luke 4:1–13, Mark does not explain the nature of the temptation. His focus is not on Jesus' temptation as such but on the description of the supernatural conflict behind Jesus' earthly ministry. On one side of this conflict is Jesus, directed by the Spirit, and God's angels; on the other side is Satan. This conflict is not resolved in these two verses in terms of a decisive victory, and the subsequent narrative which prominently recounts Jesus' encounters with demons indicates that the conflict is and remains a real conflict. The *forty days* may be an idiomatic expression for a long but limited period (cf. Gen. 7:4; Num. 13:25; 1 Sam. 17:16; Acts 1:3).

The Greek word *satana* is a transliteration of Aramaic *Sātānā'*, from the Hebrew noun *śāṭān* ('adversary, opponent', both in the military and political sphere and in the sense of a celestial figure opposing God and his people, Job 1:6–12; 2:1–7; Zech. 3:1–2), which had become the direct proper name of the anti-divine power (Sir. 21:27; *T. Dan.* 3:6; 5:6). The *wild animals* are often linked with Satan as highlighting the danger of the wilderness; perhaps more plausibly the reference signals that Jesus restores the coexistence of the human and non-human creation that existed in Eden (Gen. 1:28; 2:19–20) but was lost in the fall, to be restored in God's new world (Isa. 11:1–9; 65:25; Hos. 2:18; note that Isa. 11 speaks of the endowment of a Davidic figure with the Spirit, in the context of a future in which the enmity between wild animals and humanity will be overcome). The service of the *angels* who *attended him* is not explained. It can describe in general terms protection (cf. Pss 11–12); the analogy of Elijah (1 Kgs 19:4–8) and the account in Matthew 4:11 suggest the provision of food.

Theology

Jesus' baptism entails not repentance and forgiveness of sins but empowerment with God's Spirit and affirmation of his messianic and, indeed, divine status. Jesus is the Messiah and the unique Son of God who is God's servant. In combination with the allusion to

Psalm 2:7, Isaiah's prophecy in Isaiah 42:1–4 helps Mark's readers understand the paradox of the life and ministry of Jesus as a suffering Messiah: Jesus is indeed the Davidic Messiah and the unique Son of God, but he is also unrecognized as God's servant even though he is endowed with God's Spirit.

2. JESUS' MESSIANIC AUTHORITY (1:14 – 8:21)

The first of the two main parts of Mark's Gospel can be divided into three main sections. Mark first describes Jesus' proclamation of the kingdom of God and its presence in the reality of Jesus' authority (1:14 – 3:6). Most of these events take place in Galilee, where Jesus spends the bulk of his ministry of teaching, healing and exorcizing demons. Second, Mark describes Jesus' continued Galilean ministry as Jesus is now accompanied by the Twelve (3:7 – 6:6), in the context of the opposition of Jesus' family and of Jerusalem scribes, who argue that his authority comes from Satan. Third, Mark describes Jesus' further mission linked with the Twelve (6:7 – 8:21), which includes increased ministry in regions outside Galilee.

A. The kingdom of God and Jesus' authority (1:14 – 3:6)

Mark relates Jesus' proclamation of the kingdom of God in Galilee (1:14–15), Jesus' call of the disciples (1:16–20), Jesus' teaching, healing and exorcizing demons (1:21–45) and his controversies with the religious leaders on account of his claim to have the authority to forgive sin, his eating with sinners and his healing on the Sabbath (2:1 – 3:6).

i. Jesus' proclamation of the kingdom of God (1:14–15)
Context

Mark recounts Jesus' public ministry with a description of the content of his preaching, which will be known to Mark's readers from 1:14–15. The 'good news about Jesus the Messiah, the Son of God' (1:1) is the 'good news of God', whose content is specified in 1:14–15: the time has come when the prophetic hope of messianic deliverance is being fulfilled, as the kingdom of God is near. These two verses thus have foundational significance for Mark's entire narrative of Jesus' ministry: Jesus' teaching and the response that he expects can all be related to this passage, which presents the essential content of the good news.

Comment

14. Mark dates the beginning of Jesus' public ministry with John's arrest: *Jesus went into Galilee*; that is, he travelled to the towns and villages of Galilee (cf. 1:9), *after John was put in prison* (*paradothēnai*; lit. 'handed over', a technical term for being handed over into custody). The comment connects Jesus' ministry to John's ministry, with the emphasis that the ministry of the forerunner is over and Jesus now takes centre stage. Jesus proclaims in Galilee *the good news of God*[1] which is, according to verse 1, at the same time the 'good news about Jesus the Messiah, the Son of God', who has been described in 1:2–13 as affirmed by God himself as the promised Messiah, his unique Son and his Servant. The genitive *of God* can give the meaning 'good news about God' (whose kingdom is near) and 'good news coming from God' (conveyed through Jesus' proclamation).

15. Mark relates the content of Jesus' proclamation of the 'good news of God' in direct speech: *The time is fulfilled, and the kingdom of God has come near; repent, and believe in the good news* (NRSV). The summary of Jesus' proclamation consists of a twofold announcement and

---

1. The phrase is unique in the Gospels, but repeatedly used by Paul: cf. Rom. 1:1; 15:16; 2 Cor. 11:7; 1 Thess. 2:2, 8, 9; also 1 Peter 4:17.

two imperatives. The term *kairos* ('time') can mean 'decisive moment' (cf. 12:2) or 'span of time' (cf. 10:30; 11:13). Both meanings make sense here: the decisive moment of the fulfilment of God's promises of salvation has arrived with the coming of Jesus the Messiah; and the time of promise, hope and expectation has elapsed and the time of messianic deliverance has arrived. The hope of the prophets has become a reality; the time of fulfilment has come. The perfect tense of the verb (*peplērōtai*, 'is fulfilled') indicates that the fulfilment is a present reality. The phrase *kingdom of God* (Gr. *basileia tou theou*) describes God's kingship, his rule, his dominion.[2] The perfect tense of the verb translated as *has come near* (*ēngiken*) indicates that Jesus speaks not merely of the coming of God's kingdom as imminent (but still in the future), but – in the context of the preceding statement that the *kairos* has been fulfilled – as happening in the present. The *kingdom of God* is not to be reduced to a single referent, whether a time, place, event or situation: God's royal government is both fulfilled and awaited, present and future. Jesus proclaims that God is now fulfilling his purpose of messianic deliverance of Israel and, ultimately, the world. The coming of the kingdom of God requires that people *repent* (Gr. *metanoeite*; cf. 1:4). They need to acknowledge God's messianic intervention, which means they must listen to the proclamation of Jesus and be obedient to God's Messiah who is God's unique Son. The second response that the coming of God's kingdom entails is *believe the good news*. The verb 'believe' (*pisteuō*) denotes both acceptance that the *news* that Jesus proclaims is true and commitment to the reality of the present coming of God's kingdom. What this means for Jews, and also for Gentiles, is spelled out in the rest of Mark's Gospel.

Theology
The similarity and contrast between 'good news of God' in 1:14 and 'good news about Jesus the Messiah' in 1:1 are significant. Jesus proclaims the 'good news of God'; after Easter – when Mark writes his Gospel – the gospel is 'the good news about Jesus the Messiah'.

---

2. Relevant OT passages that speak of God's kingship are Exod. 15:18; Pss 47:7; 97:1; 99:1; 103:19; Isa. 24:23; 43:15.

This means that to speak of Jesus as the crucified and risen Messiah is to speak of God himself. The coming of the kingdom of God which is connected with Jesus' proclamation and with his identity and ministry requires a new orientation. Since the temple and the law were central for Israel's life with God, this new orientation implied in the term 'repent' entails a modification, here unspecified, with regard to these hitherto foundational realities: life lived in obedience to God's revelation now includes obedience to Jesus the Messiah. Repentance and faith are no longer exclusively bound up with Yahweh's presence in the temple and his revelation in the Mosaic law. They are now tied to God's present kingdom, which is bound up with Jesus' identity as the Messiah and as the unique Son of God, and thus with Jesus' proclamation and his ministry.

ii. Jesus' call of the disciples (1:16–20)
Context
The calling of the first disciples comes at the very beginning of Jesus' ministry, a large part of which consists in the training of disciples for future ministry. In Mark's narrative, the disciples are often a disappointment, but their role is critical in the proclamation of the good news and in the establishment of the kingdom of God.

Comment
16. The *Sea of Galilee* is the large lake in the Jordan Valley which separates Galilee from the Gaulan and Decapolis regions to the east. In the Old Testament the lake is called 'Sea of Kinneret'; in the New Testament, 'Sea of Galilee', 'Sea of Gennesar', 'Sea of Tiberias' or simply 'the lake'. Mark does not explain why Jesus, who is from Nazareth (1:9), about 18 miles (30 km) from the Sea of Galilee, walked beside the Sea of Galilee. Matthew explains that Jesus left Nazareth and made his home in Capernaum (Matt. 4:13). It has been suggested that Jesus moved to Capernaum because it was a larger town (but see on 1:21), was more strategically located for Jesus' itinerant ministry, was closer to the border with Perea allowing Jesus to escape Herod Antipas, and was economically more viable after Herod Antipas founded Tiberias as his new capital on the Sea of Galilee, allowing Jesus to take better care of his mother and brothers once Joseph had died and he was responsible for the family

(cf. John 2:12). The house in Capernaum in which Jesus stayed (Mark 2:1; 9:33) was the house of Simon Peter (cf. 1:29).

Jesus meets *Simon and his brother Andrew*. Simon (*Šímōn*) was the most popular male name among Palestinian Jews. The name is Greek, but was used as equivalent to the common Hebrew name *Šímōn*. Later in 3:16 Jesus gives Simon the 'by-name' Peter ('Rock'), after which Mark consistently uses this new name for the most famous disciple. Andrew (*Andreas*) is also a Greek name, which suggests that the family was open to Hellenistic influences, which was not unusual for the first century, particularly in view of the fact that the family, before moving to Capernaum (1:29), lived in Bethsaida (John 1:44) in the tetrarchy of Herod Philip at the northern end of the Sea of Galilee east of the Jordan river. The brothers were *casting a net* (Gr. *amphiballontas*) into the lake: they were fishing with a round 'cast net' (20–26 ft [6–8 m] in diameter) fastened to a rope and weighted with sinkers. The phrase *for they were fishermen* notes the profession of the two brothers. The term *fishermen* (*halieis*) prepares for the explanation of their future role in verse 17. The fact that Andrew is introduced as Simon's brother emphasizes the name of Simon, whose prominence is underlined by Mark's frequent references to Simon Peter,[3] singled out again at the end of the Gospel (16:7).

17–18. Jesus summons the two fishermen: *Come, follow me*. Jesus' call underlines his authority, which demands an immediate response, and it also provides a clue to his identity: it is only God who can command people to leave their profession with which they earn their livelihood in order to be devoted to his service (an OT parallel is the tribe of Levi who did not receive a share of the land since God chose them to serve in the tabernacle [Num. 1:47–54; 8:5–11; 18:6–7]). Jesus summons Simon and Andrew to be with him and learn what he teaches and do what he does (cf. 3:14).

Jesus' command is followed by a purpose statement which indicates that Jesus calls Simon and Andrew not only for their own sake but for the sake of others: *I will send you out to fish for people*. The

---

3. Simon: 1:16(2x), 29–30, 36; 3:16; 14:37; Peter: 8:29, 32–33; 9:2, 5; 10:28; 11:21; 13:3; 14:29, 33, 37, 54, 66–67, 70; 16:7.

phrase 'fishers of people' (*halieis anthrōpōn*; RSV/ESV translate 'fishers of men') has no obvious parallels in the Old Testament, Jewish or Greco-Roman sources.[1] Jesus seems to have coined the (positive) metaphor of 'fishing for people', which was natural enough given the scene of Simon and Andrew fishing in the Sea of Galilee. The two brothers and the other disciples whom Jesus will call are to assist Jesus in gathering people for the kingdom of God that has come near, challenging people to repent and to believe in the good news (1:14–15), and to learn from Jesus so that, eventually, they will be able to *fish for people* by themselves.

The description of Simon and Andrew's reaction suggests an immediate response: *At once they left their nets and followed him*. They recognize and acknowledge Jesus' unique authority and obey his summons: they drop their fishing nets (*diktya*); that is, they abandon their profession and their family (cf. 1:20; see, however, 1:29, 30–31), and follow Jesus. The term *akoloutheō* ('follow') is a standard term for discipleship; it means literally 'go behind someone' and has the metaphorical sense of 'follow as a disciple'. Simon and Andrew will no longer work as fishermen. They will follow Jesus and gather people for the kingdom of God. Jesus takes precedence over livelihood and family.

19–20. The same scene is repeated with two different brothers who are fishermen. Jacob (Gr. *Iakōbos*; Hebr. *Ya'ăqōb*; traditionally translated as *James*)[5] and his (probably younger) brother *John* (Gr. *Iōannēs*; Hebr. *Yōḥānān*) are identified with reference to their father Zebedee (Gr. *Zebedaios*),[6] to distinguish them from other well-known early Christians with the same names, Jacob (James), the brother of Jesus, and John the Baptist. Jacob (James) was killed by Herod Agrippa I in AD 41 (Acts 12:2), and John was one of the pillars of

---

1. In Jer. 16:16 LXX Yahweh sends 'many fishermen' to 'catch' his people in order to punish them. Threatening fishing metaphors are also used in Amos 4:2; Hab. 1:14–17 – when fish are caught, they die.
5. English *James* comes from Late Latin *Jacomus* (for *Jacobus*) and *Jamus*.
6. Zebedee is a relatively rare Jewish male name, no. 68 on the list of the most popular Jewish names; Jacob (James) is no. 11, John (*Yōḥānān*) no. 5.

the Jerusalem church, together with Simon Peter and Jacob (James), Jesus' brother (Gal. 2:9). Jacob and John are involved in the fishing operation of the family, which involves a *boat*, *nets* and *hired men*; the family was evidently well-to-do. They were fishing from a boat with a 'trammel net', which consisted of 'five nets combined in order to form a barrier with which to encircle schools of fish' (S. De Luca, *OEBA*, I, p. 172). The fishermen living in the towns on the Sea of Galilee produced not only for local needs but also for export (salted fish from Magdala; cf. 8:10). Jesus meets the brothers as they are *preparing*, that is, cleaning and mending the nets for the next day. As soon as he saw them, *he called them*, presumably with the same call with which he summoned Simon and Andrew (1:17). Jacob and John also respond without delay: they *left their father Zebedee*, who stays back in the boat with the hired workers, and *followed* Jesus – unprecedented in a society where honouring parents was one of the greatest values (cf. Exod. 20:12; Deut. 5:16; Prov. 23:22; also Sir. 3:1–16).

Theology

The proclamation of the kingdom of God is accompanied by the establishment of a community of followers who acknowledge and commit themselves to God's new initiative connected with Jesus. The members of this new community are defined by a threefold reality. First, they acknowledge Jesus' authority without reservation and without delay. Second, they are willing to leave their profession and their family. As regards the followers of Jesus more broadly, it is obvious that discipleship does not automatically, and not always, entail leaving everything behind to become an apostle (missionary) or evangelist. To be an 'apostle' is a special task (Acts 1:21–22; 1 Cor. 12:28; Eph. 4:11) among many other tasks that God and his Spirit gives to the church. Third, they are involved in the task of calling others to repent and believe in the good news of the kingdom of God, learning from Jesus how to 'fish for people'. As regards the metaphor of 'fishing for people', several elements are implied: fishermen have the unambiguous goal of catching fish; they need to be taught how to fish (by Jesus); they use different methods (a net in 1:18; a drag net in Matt. 13:47); they need patience (cf. Luke 5:5).

iii. Jesus' teaching, healing and exorcism (1:21–45)

Context

Mark began his account of Jesus' public ministry in Galilee with a summary of Jesus' message of the kingdom of God and the need for repentance and faith (1:14–15), and with a report on Jesus calling his first disciples at the Sea of Galilee, who will follow him and who will be trained by him to gather people for the kingdom of God (1:16–20). Now he narrates a series of healings and exorcisms that take place in and around Capernaum, apparently in a twenty-four-hour period (cf. 1:29, 32, 35; 2:1).

Comment

a. Jesus teaches and exorcizes an evil spirit (1:21–28)

21–22. Jesus and the two pairs of brothers already operate as a group: *they went to Capernaum*. Capernaum (*Kafarnaoum*; Hebr. *Kepar Naḥûm*, 'Village of Nahum'), further mentioned in 2:1, 9:33, was located about 3 miles (5 km) south-west of the Jordan river and the border to the neighbouring tetrarchy of Herod Philip. In the first century Capernaum had a population of perhaps 600; some estimates are as low as 100.[7] The *synagogue* of the first century, constructed of the local basalt stone (beneath a synagogue of the second/third century, which is beneath the prayer hall of a later synagogue of the fifth century whose ruins are still visible today), measured about 79 by 59 feet (24 by 18 m; Levine, *Synagogue*, pp. 51–52). Synagogues were centres of communal life: they functioned as courts and places for political discussions, storage of archives, education of children, public reading and teaching of Torah and prayer. Regular meetings in the synagogue took place on the *Sabbath* (Gr. *sabbaton*; Hebr. *šabbāt*), the day of rest at the end of the working week (cf. Gen. 2:3; Exod. 20:8–11; Deut. 5:12–15; see further on 2:23). Keeping the Sabbath, which involved not working on the seventh day, was,

---

[7]. Reed, *Archaeology*, p. 152: 600–1,500; S. De Luca, *OEBA*, I, p. 169: 1,000; Fiensy, in Fiensy and Strange, *Galilee*, I, p. 185: 2,000 or fewer. Rami Arav estimates 100 or even fewer (private communication). The estimates of France, p. 101 (10,000), Myers and Strange, *Archaeology*, p. 58 (12,000), and Kee, 'Galilee' (25,000) are unrealistic.

together with circumcision, the principal distinguishing mark of Jewish identity and a sign of one's commitment to God's covenant with his people (Exod. 31:16–17; Ezek. 20:12, 20). Violating the Sabbath, if done deliberately, was a capital offence (Exod. 31:14–15; 35:2; Num. 15:32–36; thus still in *Jub.* 50:8, 13; *m. Sanh.* 7:4). Pious Jews who resisted the demands of the Syrian king Antiochus IV Epiphanes were prepared to die rather than desecrate the Sabbath (1 Macc. 2:29–41).

Jesus attended synagogue services and was called upon by the synagogue officials to *teach* (*didaskō*; cf. 3:1; 6:2; cf. Luke 4:16–22). Teaching is Jesus' typical activity,[8] which is why he is called 'teacher' (*didaskalos*).[9] Here he teaches, presumably at the invitation of the 'ruler of the synagogue' (cf. Acts 13:14–16). The audience in the synagogue is *amazed* at Jesus' teaching since he taught *as one who had authority, not as the teachers of the law*. The people's amazement[10] implies the recognition that Jesus' teaching was out of the ordinary, indeed 'new teaching' (1:27). In view of 1:14–15, Jesus' teaching seems to have focused on the explanation of the fulfilment of God's promises that the prophets had spoken about and on the new period of history marked by the arrival of the kingdom of God. He taught that repentance, faith in God, membership of God's kingdom and thus identity as an authentic member of God's people depended on one's response to God's initiative connected with his own person and ministry (and no longer on the temple, on purity as defined by the law or on the keeping of the Sabbath; cf. 2:23 – 3:6; 7:1–23; cf. France, p. 102). The *authority* (*exousia*) that the audience recognizes probably consisted in the fact that Jesus did not explain Scripture with reference to other rabbis: he expounded the will of God with resolute immediacy. The *teachers of the law* (*grammateis*; often translated 'scribes') were professional experts in the Mosaic law who studied, explained and applied the law to specific situations. Mark mentions the 'teachers of the law' twenty-one times: they are mentioned beside the Pharisees (7:1, 5), the chief priests (10:33;

---

8. 1:21–22; 2:13; 4:1–2; 6:2, 6, 34; 8:31; 9:31; 10:1; 11:17; 12:14, 35; 14:49.

9. 4:38; 5:35; 9:17, 38; 10:17, 20, 35; 12:14, 19, 32; 13:1; 14:14.

10. Cf. 1:27; 2:12; 5:15, 20, 42; 6:51; 12:17.

11:18; 14:1; 15:31), and the elders and the chief priests (8:31; 11:27; 14:43, 53; 15:1).

23–24. As Jesus was teaching, a dramatic event happened: a man *who was possessed by an impure spirit* speaks. The term *impure spirit* is synonymous with 'demon' (cf. 6:7, 13; 7:25–26). The expression 'a man with an unclean spirit' indicates that the personality of the man 'has been so usurped by the demon that the demon has, as it were, swallowed him up' (Marcus, p. 192). Normally people stay away from impurity, uncleanness or dirt, whether literal, moral or ritual. The question *What do you want with us?* is an Old Testament idiom, a formula of disassociation, meaning 'go away and leave me alone' (cf. Judg. 11:12; 1 Kgs 17:18). Since this is the first of many confrontations between Jesus and demons, the plural form *us* may indicate that this particular demon speaks on behalf of the entire 'fraternity' of demons. The demon addresses him as *Jesus of Nazareth*, identifying Jesus by the town in which he grew up (cf. 1:9). As exorcists sought to gain power over a demon through knowledge of the demon's name, this particular demon may be attempting to counter Jesus' power by claiming to have himself the power of knowledge about Jesus. The demon knows, or senses, that Jesus' mission is *to destroy us*: Jesus is no ordinary exorcist who has mastered the techniques of manipulating spirits; rather, his arrival signifies the presence of God's powerfully effective reign which leaves no room for opposition to God by Satan and his demons. The day has come in which, according to the prophecy of Zechariah 13:2, the Lord of hosts will remove the unclean spirit.

25–26. Jesus *rebuked* (NRSV) the spirit (cf. 9:25): he forces the evil powers into submission, preparing the way for the establishment of the kingdom of God. The words of the rebuke are described in direct speech, underlining their importance. The first command, *Be quiet!*, orders the impure spirit to stop its defiant shouting. This command is the first example of Jesus giving the order not to reveal who he is (cf. 1:44; 5:43; 7:36; 8:26 in the context of healings; 8:30 in the context of Peter's confession of Jesus' messianic identity). Revelations about his identity spoken by demons could be a 'potential embarrassment' and could lead to 'premature and misdirected popular adulation' (France, p. 105). The second command, *Come out of him!*, orders the demon to exit the man whom he had controlled. The submission of the demon was a violent act: the impure spirit *shook the man violently and came out of him with a shriek*. The demon visibly shook the man with a loud shout as a final, desperate but unsuccessful protest. Jesus' power is superior to the destructive power of the evil spirit: his word of submission has to be obeyed.

27–28. Mark reports the reaction of the people in the synagogue, a reaction which quickly spreads to the entire region. People in the Capernaum synagogue are *amazed* at Jesus' teaching and his expulsion of the demon. The expression *they asked each other* means 'they discussed among themselves'. They wonder what the relationship is between the authority (1:22) of his *new teaching* about the coming of the kingdom of God, which requires repentance and faith, and his *authority* to give *orders to impure spirits* so that *they obey him*. The audience realizes that there is a connection between his authoritative teaching and his authority over demons.

b. Jesus heals Simon's mother-in-law (1:29–31)

29–31. After the synagogue service, Jesus and his four disciples go to the *home of Simon and Andrew*, which was evidently Jesus' base of operations during his Galilean ministry (cf. 2:1; 9:33). The octagonal Christian basilica (fifth/sixth century) whose ruins are visible today was built on top of a quadrilateral shrine (second to fourth century), with Christian graffiti from the second century, underneath which private domestic structures were discovered, which might very well be the 'House of Peter'.[11] This house is only about 30 m south of the synagogue. The mention of Simon's *mother-in-law* suggests that she was the lady of the house; perhaps the brothers' father and mother had died. Simon Peter's wife is mentioned in 1 Corinthians 9:5. His mother-in-law was *lying sick with a fever* (NASB; NIV, NRSV have 'was in bed'), indicating that the fever (*pyretos*) was severe (Luke 4:38 speaks, more dramatically, of a 'high fever'), which could have been due to malaria, but the Greek uses a general term. Mark reports three actions of Jesus: *he went to her, took*

---

11. Loffreda, 'Casa di Simon Pietro', pp. 37–67; cf. Charlesworth, *Jesus and Archaeology*, pp. 49–50.

her hand and helped her up: he touched her[12] and lifted her to a sitting or standing position. The cure was instant: *the fever left her*. The remark that *she began to serve them* (NRSV) demonstrates the completeness of the healing.

c. Jesus heals and exorcizes evil spirits (1:32–34)

32–33. In the dual time expression *that evening after sunset*, the second phrase indicates that the Sabbath day had come to an end so sick people could be carried about and Jesus could legitimately heal (see 3:2). The imperfect tense of the phrase *the people brought* (Gr. *epheron*) suggests a continuous procession of *ill and demon-possessed* people being brought to Jesus. Mark maintains the distinction between people who have a physical illness which Jesus heals (*therapeuō*), often with touch, and people who are possessed by demons which are cast out (*daimonia ekballō*), accomplished by a word of command (cf. 3:10–11; 6:13).

34. Jesus healed *many* who had *various diseases*, and he drove out *many demons*. The term *poikilai* ('various') indicates that there was no physical sickness that Jesus did not and could not heal. Mark relates healings of fever (1:29–31), skin disease (1:40–45), paralysis (2:1–12), atrophied muscles (3:1–6) and continual blood loss (5:25–34), and of people who were deaf and dumb (7:32–37), blind (8:22–26; 10:46–52), had epilepsy (9:14–29) or had died (5:21–43). In the exorcisms of evil spirits, Jesus *would not let the demons speak because they knew who he was*, a silencing that Mark already noted in verse 25. The problem was not primarily the inappropriate nature of the witness but the knowledge of the demons that he is 'the Holy One of God' (1:24), 'the Son of God' (3:11), the 'Son of the Most High God' (5:7), indeed 'the Messiah' (Luke 4:41, the parallel passage to Mark 1:34). The time and manner of the revelation of Jesus' identity as Messiah and unique Son of God is Jesus' own prerogative, revealed only to those close to him (8:29–30) and understood only in connection with Jesus' crucifixion. See Introduction 4b.

---

12. As often in physical healings; cf. 1:41; 5:41; 6:5; 7:23–33; 8:23–25; also 3:10, 5:27, 6:56, where Jesus is touched by the sick.

d. Prayer and mission in Galilee (1:35–39)

35–37. The time expression *very early in the morning, while it was still dark*, indicating the time from 3 to 6 am, suggests that even after a very busy day whose activities extended far into the night, Jesus did not rest. He left, without awakening his four disciples, and *went off to a solitary place*. It was in a deserted spot outside Capernaum that *he prayed*, spending time alone with God. Jesus' praying is mentioned three times in Mark: here at the beginning of his Galilean ministry, after the feeding of the five thousand (6:46) and in the garden of Gethsemane (14:32–39). He repeatedly exhorted his disciples to pray (9:29; 11:24; 13:18; 14:38).

The fact that Simon and his companions, presumably Andrew, Jacob and John, *found him* when they *went to look for him* may suggest that they had been meeting at that secluded spot before. The disciples inform Jesus, related by Mark in direct speech, that *everyone is looking for you*, a sentence that underlines the impact of Jesus' teaching in the synagogue and of the exorcisms and healings that had taken place in Capernaum the previous day. The people demand, and the disciples expect, Jesus to build on the previous day's triumph and continue his work in Capernaum.

38–39. Jesus' reply involves both a geographical statement and a statement of mission. The summons *let us go somewhere else – to the nearby villages* characterizes Jesus' mission as an itinerant ministry: Jesus does not want to remain in a town where he has had much success and which is strategically located, but he wants to reach all the towns and villages of Galilee. The purpose statement *so that I can preach there also* is explained with the sentence *that is why I have come*. Jesus' mission is to *preach* (*kēryssō*) the good news of the coming of God's kingdom and the necessity that people respond with repentance and faith (1:14–15) not only in one town. The purpose of Jesus' mission is to 'come out' (*exerchomai*); that is, to leave Capernaum and go to all villages and towns of Galilee to preach the good news of the coming of God's kingdom. Mark reports that Jesus did what he said his mission was, summarizing his ministry in Galilee: *he travelled throughout Galilee, preaching in their synagogues and driving out demons*. Jesus visited all towns and villages in Galilee; he preached (cf. 1:4, 14), taught (cf. 1:21) and drove out demons, demonstrating his messianic authority (cf. 1:21–28).

e. Jesus heals a man with skin disease (1:40–45)

40. Jesus encounters the *man with leprosy* at some unspecified place in Galilee, evidently outside the nearby village or town, as befitting a person with 'leprosy' (thus the traditional translation in the English versions). The Greek term is *lepra*, used for a variety of skin conditions wider than true leprosy (Hansen's disease; the Greek term *elephantiasis*, used for a skin disease similar to Hansen's disease, does not occur in the NT). According to Leviticus 13 – 14 LXX, *lepra* (Hebr. *ṣaraʿat*) refers to conditions of the surfaces of persons (Lev. 13:1–46), clothing (Lev. 13:47–59) and houses (Lev. 14:34–53). The Old Testament rules aim at distinguishing contagious from non-contagious conditions; people diagnosed with an infectious skin condition are to be excluded from society (Lev. 13:45–46). According to the Sadducean text 11QTemple XLVIII, 14–15, an area was to be set aside in every city for lepers and others who were not allowed to enter the city because they would defile it (Collins, p. 179). Infectious skin diseases were regarded as incurable apart from divine intervention (cf. Exod. 4:6–8; Num. 12:9–15; 2 Kgs 5:1–27; 2 Chr. 26:16–21); the cure is comparable to raising the dead (2 Kgs 5:7; also *b. Sanh.* 47a).

The man *came to him*: he takes the initiative to approach Jesus. He *begged him on his knees*: he requests healing with urgency and with deference to Jesus. His appeal is formulated in direct speech: *If you are willing, you can make me clean*. The conditional clause is not meant to express doubt about Jesus' interest in him or about his ability to heal; rather, the man expresses his appeal with humble politeness and diffidence.

41–42. Jesus was *moved with pity* (NRSV). The translation 'Jesus was indignant' (NIV) assumes that the Greek term *orgistheis* is original (as the more difficult reading; France, Guelich, Marcus, Pesch, Stein, Strauss). Jesus' indignation is seen in that his preaching was interrupted, or that the leper approached him in public disregarding the strictures of the law, or that evil such as leprosy and the suffering it caused are present in the world. More widely and earlier attested in the New Testament manuscript tradition is the word *splangchnistheis* ('moved with pity', NRSV; cf. GNB, NASB, NIV note), which should be preferred (so the standard editions of the Greek NT). The effect of Jesus' pity is described with three verbs: Jesus *reached out his hand*, he *touched the man* – disregarding the possibility of contracting leprosy himself, willing to become ritually unclean by touching the leper, and defying both the law and social taboo – and then he *said* to the man *I am willing; be clean*. The phrase *immediately the leprosy left him* suggests the instantaneous visibility of the cure. The touch that should have made Jesus unclean in fact cures the man with leprosy.

43–44. Jesus sends the cured man away, *with a strong warning* not to *tell this to anyone*. Jesus' prohibition of spreading the news about the dramatic healing corresponds to Jesus silencing the demons (cf. 1:25, 34). Publicity about spectacular, instantaneously effective and observable healings would lead to excessive and theologically uninformed enthusiasm that hindered Jesus' mission, as verse 45 indicates. Jesus sends the healed man *to the priest*, who would have to ascertain, in a process lasting eight days, that the leprosy had indeed disappeared (cf. Lev. 14). A priest with expertise to ascertain that the leprosy had disappeared might have been found in Galilee, but the *sacrifices that Moses commanded for your cleansing* had to be offered in Jerusalem, requiring at least a three-day journey. The phrase *as a testimony to them* most naturally means that by fulfilling the legal obligation of people with skin disease whose skin had cleared up, the man would give proof that he was truly healed and could be reintegrated into Jewish society.

45. The healed man *went out and began to talk freely, spreading the news*, either immediately before he travelled to Jerusalem, on his way to Jerusalem or upon his return. The verb *kēryssō* can be understood as a general term: the cured leper spreads publicly the *news* (*logos*) of his healing; or the verb, in the context of verses 4, 7, 14, 38, 39, could refer specifically to the man 'proclaiming' his healing as 'good news'. The man's dissemination of the account of his dramatic healing, in disobedience to Jesus' command but as a natural reaction, results in the fact that *Jesus could no longer enter a town openly*. Since the next episodes take place in town, the comment is best regarded as a hyperbolic assertion that underscores the excitement that news of Jesus' healing activity caused in the villages and towns of Galilee.

Theology
Jesus has the authority to expel evil spirits from people and to heal people from diseases, both in public and in private. The visible and

audible departure of the evil spirit from the afflicted man in the synagogue in Capernaum and the instantaneous disappearance of the skin condition of the man who approached Jesus outside the town demonstrate the reality of the present coming of the kingdom of God (1:14–15). These miracles confirm that Jesus is indeed the Messiah and unique Son of God (1:1) who is more powerful than John the Baptist since he is endowed with God's Holy Spirit (1:10–11). This is obvious for Mark's readers, but not for the people living in the villages and towns of Galilee: their excitement focuses on the exorcisms and healings (1:27–28, 32–33, 45), which is why Jesus commands the demons and the people he heals to remain silent.

iv. Controversies with religious leaders (2:1 – 3:6)
Context
This section, framed by statements about Jesus' popularity (1:45; 3:7), consists of five episodes that report controversies with Israel's religious leaders. The healing of a paralysed man in Capernaum leads to a discussion about whether Jesus has the authority to forgive sins, with scribes accusing Jesus of blasphemy (2:1–12). Jesus' call of Levi, a tax collector, and the banquet that ensues, provokes a discussion about eating with sinners (2:13–17). Then people wonder why Jesus and his disciples are not fasting (2:18–22). When the disciples pick some grain on the Sabbath, the Pharisees start a discussion about what is lawful on the Sabbath (2:23–28), a dispute that continues when Jesus heals a man with a shrivelled hand on the Sabbath (3:1–6). Jesus' behaviour prompts the Pharisees to contact the Herodians with the suggestion of a plot to kill Jesus (3:6). Mark again highlights Jesus' authority over physical diseases (first and fifth episode); and he now underscores Jesus' authority over questions pertaining to the law, such as fasting, eating with sinners and the Sabbath (second, third and fourth episodes), and, provocatively, his authority to forgive sins (first episode).

Comment
a. Jesus forgives sin and heals a paralytic (2:1–12)
1–2. After some time preaching and healing in Galilean villages and towns (1:38–39, 41–45), Jesus returns to Capernaum (cf. 1:21). He seems to have *entered Capernaum* before *people heard that he had come*

home. Again large numbers of people gathered *outside the door* (cf. 1:33), in the narrow lane outside, with *no room left* inside the house, as Jesus *was speaking the word to them* (NRSV). The expression 'speak the word' is also used in 4:33; 8:32. Both 'preaching' (1:14, 38–39) and 'teaching' (1:21–22) involve 'speaking'. The term *word* (*logos*) refers to the message of the kingdom of God (1:15), which, as verse 5 will indicate, entails repentance and forgiveness of sins conveyed by Jesus.

3–4. The throng of people in front of the house makes direct access to Jesus impossible, which presents a problem for the four friends who carry a *paralysed man* on a *mat* which must have had a wooden frame. The man is severely handicapped, perhaps a paraplegic: he is unable to walk. Mark does not comment on the cause of the paralysis, which might be congenital, damage caused by a disease such as multiple sclerosis, or the result of a stroke or fall resulting in a spinal cord injury. The term 'son' (*teknon*; v. 5) is a form of familiar address and does not provide information about age. The friends are not able to bring the paralysed man to Jesus *because of the crowd*. This is the first occurrence of the word *ochlos* ('crowd'),[13] a term that shows that Jesus' ministry did not take place in private but, nearly always in Mark's Gospel, in front of crowds of people. Crowds are never associated with the teachers of the law or with the Pharisees. The determination of the four to present their friend to Jesus causes them to carry the mat up to the roof of the house. The private houses in Capernaum were built of undressed basalt stones smoothed with plaster; the roofs seem to have been supported by wooden beams and covered with a bed of reeds, coated with layers of mud plaster. The friends *made an opening in the roof* (lit. 'they unroofed the roof'), *digging through it*, a graphic description of the improvised demolition of a substantial part of the roof. Once they opened the roof, they *lowered the mat the man was lying on*, expecting the people below to place it in front of Jesus.

---

13. Mark uses *ochlos* thirty-eight times; he refers in connection with Jesus' ministry to 'a very large crowd' (4:1), 'a great crowd' (5:21), 'a large crowd' (5:24; 6:34; 8:1; 9:14; 12:37), 'a considerable crowd' (10:46), 'crowds' (10:1); my own translations.

5. As the friends look through their hole into the room below, *Jesus saw their faith*. Faith (*pistis*) here, as elsewhere in Mark, is closely linked with Jesus' power to heal people miraculously from diseases.[1] Faith is the expectation that Jesus exercises the power of God to cure the illness. Jews would not expect to be healed by a demon, and they would know that only God has the power to heal a serious illness such as paralysis instantaneously. The phrase *their faith* most naturally refers to the faith of the four friends whose action Jesus had observed, but it probably includes the faith of the paralysed man who may have asked his friends to take him to Jesus.

Jesus' immediate response is not a word of healing but the statement *Son, your sins are forgiven*. Jesus deals with the man's paralysis by focusing first on his sins, with the implication that forgiveness of sins and physical healing are interrelated. Such a connection is often found in the Old Testament.[15] At the same time, the book of Job advances the argument that the suffering of an individual is not necessarily the result of specific sins. In the New Testament we find the same balance: sometimes suffering, illness and death are the result of specific sins of the people concerned,[16] while other passages deny that such a direct connection can always be made for the calamity that a person suffers.[17] Jesus may have been aware that the man's paralysis was the result of his sin. Or the man may have believed, rightly or wrongly, that his condition was the result of sin and was looking for more than physical relief. Alternatively, perhaps Mark intends the forgiveness of sins to be understood in the general context of repentance and faith that Jesus demands in view of the coming of the kingdom of God (1:14–15). It now becomes clear that the forgiveness of sins that John the Baptist put on Israel's agenda is conveyed in a new, previously unheard-of, sense by Jesus. The statement *your sins are forgiven* is understood by the scribes as not

---

1. Cf. 1:40–45; 2:1–12; 5:21–24, 35–43; 6:5–6; 7:31–34; 9:14–29; 10:46–52.
15. Num. 12:9–15; 2 Sam. 24:10–15; 2 Chr. 7:13–14; 26:16–21; Isa. 38:16–17.
16. John 5:14; Acts 5:1–11; 1 Cor. 11:30; 1 John 5:16.
17. Luke 13:1–5; John 9:2–3; 2 Cor. 12:7; Gal. 4:14–14.

merely stating a fact but as actually forgiving, an understanding that Jesus reinforces (vv. 8–12). The passive verb 'you are forgiven' is thus not a divine passive ('God forgives you'), which could be negatively interpreted by the scribes as implying that Jesus usurps the prerogatives of a priest (cf. Lev. 4:26, 31) or of an authorized prophet (cf. 2 Sam. 12:13). The context makes it clear that Jesus claims to have the authority to forgive sins.

6–7. The presence of *some teachers of the law* (cf. 1:22) who were *sitting* in Simon's house listening to Jesus' teaching may suggest genuine interest in Jesus, or, rather, their suspicion that his teaching is dubious at best or contradicting the law at worst. Jesus' declaration of forgiveness provokes unspoken misgivings, a *reasoning in their hearts* (NASB). The 'heart' (*kardia*) is the centre of human cognition and volition, the seat of the intellectual, spiritual and emotional life. The first question, *Why does this fellow talk like that?*, enquires about reasons why Jesus thinks he can pronounce a person to be forgiven. The second sentence, usually punctuated as a statement, could also be a question: *Is he blaspheming?* Blasphemy is not only the pronouncement of the divine name (Yahweh), as in the technical rabbinic sense (*m. Sanh.* 7:5), but covers a wider range of offences, including idolatry, arrogant disrespect towards God or insulting God's chosen leaders.[18] The third question, *Who can forgive sins but God alone?*, alludes with the phrase *God alone* (*heis ho theos*) to Israel's confession of faith, 'Hear, O Israel, the LORD our God is one' (*heis ho theos*; Deut. 6:4; part of the Shema), as well as to texts such as Exodus 34:6–7, Isaiah 43:25, 44:22 which declare that God is the one who has the power to forgive sins. The scribes think that if Jesus indeed claims that he can forgive sins, he infringes on God's prerogative, claiming to be able to do what only God can do, which would be tantamount to blasphemy. Blasphemy was a capital offence (Lev. 24:10–16). Jesus is eventually indicted on a charge of blasphemy (Mark 14:64).

8–9. Although the scribes do not voice their questions and their implicit and/or explicit accusations, *Jesus knew in his spirit* what they were thinking. Jesus had supernatural powers of discernment (also

---

18. Cf. Bock, *Blasphemy*, pp. 30–112.

5:30; 12:15), which here reinforces his unique authority. In the Old Testament it is God who knows the *hearts* of human beings.[19] It now becomes obvious that Jesus' commands to silence regarding the revelation of his identity are not connected with some 'secret': he deliberately and explicitly brings into the open the question whether he has the authority to forgive sins, which in Old Testament and Jewish thought only God can do. Jesus challenges the scribes with two questions. The question *Why are you thinking these things?* reveals that Jesus knows what they are thinking. The question *Which is easier: to say to this paralysed man, 'Your sins are forgiven,' or to say, 'Get up, take your mat and walk'?* forces the scribes to come to a decision regarding the nature of Jesus' authority. The either–or question implies an *a fortiori* argument (lit. 'from something stronger'). In terms of external proof, the 'easier' action is to declare sins forgiven: it is impossible for human beings to ascertain whether this has actually happened. The 'more difficult' action is to command a paralysed man to stand on his feet, take his mat and walk home: it will be immediately obvious whether this has actually happened. An instantaneous, observable healing is 'hard evidence'.

10. The expression *the Son of Man* (Gr. *ho huios tou anthropou*) occurs here for the first time.[20] The expression, translated into Greek from the Aramaic expression *bar 'enāš*, need not be a title, and in first-century Judaism was certainly not a messianic title with nationalistic overtones. In its most basic sense it refers to a human being in the sense of 'everyone' (humankind), or 'some' (a restricted group) or 'someone' (an individual). Jesus uses the expression as an indirect self-reference that sometimes, but not always, alludes to the heavenly 'son of man' in Daniel 7:13–14 (cf. Mark 13:26; 14:62). Jesus seems to have chosen the term because it was ambiguous, capable of representing humanity and the transcendent character of his mission. Both suffering and authority are attached to most of Jesus' uses of the term. In verse 10, the meaning is 'a unique man like me': only an extraordinary, unique man has the authority to forgive sins. Jesus

---

19. Cf. 1 Sam. 16:7; 1 Kgs 8:39; 1 Chr. 28:9; Ps. 7:10; Jer. 11:20; 17:10; in the NT cf. Luke 16:15; Acts 1:24; 15:8; Rom. 8:27.
20. Cf. 2:28; 8:31, 38; 9:9, 12, 31; 10:33, 45; 13:26; 14:21 (2x), 41, 62.

asserts that as the unique Son of Man, he has the *authority* (cf. 1:22, 27) to *forgive sins*. The phrase *on earth* does not limit the authority that Jesus claims to have, but underlines the boldness of his claim: forgiveness is now not exclusively a heavenly function, the prerogative of God in heaven, but is exercised *on earth* because of the presence of the Son of Man who, according to Daniel 7:13–14, was to receive from God authority over the earth (cf. France, p. 129).

11–12. Jesus' miracle-working word, introduced with the authoritative *I tell you*, consists of three imperatives: *get up, take your mat and go home*. The paralysed man had been lying on his pallet since the day of his paralysis, unable to get up – Jesus commands him to stand on his feet. The paralysed man had been unable to walk – Jesus commands him to walk to his house in which he lives. The command to carry his mat as he walks home implies that the man can now do what healthy people do: bend down, pick up loads and carry them. The effect of Jesus' words is both instantaneous and public: *he got up, took his mat and walked out in full view of them all*. His paralysis has disappeared and the atrophied muscles are restored: he can stand; he can bend; he can walk. Mark's comment on the public nature of the miracle underlines Jesus' claim that since he has the power to accomplish the 'harder' action and instantaneously and visibly heal the paralysed man, he also has the authority to forgive sins. *Everyone* who witnessed the miracle, evidently including the scribes, was *amazed* (cf. 1:27). The people *praise God* because they *have never seen anything like this*, acknowledging that the effectiveness of Jesus' miracle-working word is God's doing.

b. Jesus calls Levi and eats with sinners (2:13–17)

13. Mark once again notes Jesus' public teaching and his continuing popularity. Jesus leaves Simon's house and goes down to the Sea of Galilee. What Jesus did in the synagogue (1:21), he did in public by the lake: he was *teaching*, explaining his proclamation of the good news of the coming of the kingdom of God and the need for repentance and faith (1:15).

14. Jesus sees *Levi son of Alphaeus*. Most first-century Jews with the name Levi seem to have been Levites, people descending from Jacob's third son, whose hereditary task was service in the temple. The name Alphaeus (Hebr. Halpi, or Halfai) is attested as the name of Palestinian Jews.[21] Mark describes Levi *sitting at the tax collector's booth*: he was working in his day job at the tax office (*telōnion*). A tax collector (*telōnēs*) was a revenue officer. The principal tax was the direct tax on landed property (*tributum soli*), which under Herod and his son Antipas, who ruled Galilee, was paid, as far as we know, in produce; then there were sales taxes, probably levied in the marketplace (we do not know what kinds of sales were taxed, nor the rate that was assessed), as well as tolls and duties for trade within the cities and for goods transiting the cities.[22] The Jewish tax collectors seem to have collected tolls and duties. The New Testament knows of two specific tax collectors who became followers of Jesus: Levi/Matthew from Capernaum in Galilee and Zacchaeus, a 'chief tax collector' (*architelōnēs*) in Jericho in Roman Judea (Luke 19:1–10). It is unclear whether Levi collected duties for goods in transit between cities, which would have been taxed by Antipas, or taxes, tolls and duties for sales and trade within Capernaum, which would have been collected by the town.

Both Mark and Luke (5:27) identify the tax collector whom Jesus called in Capernaum as 'Levi'; Matthew identifies him as 'Matthew' in the same call narrative, and refers to 'Matthew the tax collector' in the list of the Twelve (Matt. 9:9; 10:3). Mark and Luke have a 'Matthew' in the list of the Twelve as well, but without identifying this Matthew as a tax collector (Mark 3:18; Luke 6:15; Acts 1:13). To complicate matters, Mark identifies Levi by the patronymic '(son of) Alphaeus' (v. 14), while he also has a 'Jacob/James son of Alphaeus' in his list of the Twelve (3:18), as do Matthew and Luke (Matt. 10:3; Luke 6:15; Acts 1:13). The easiest solution for this changing of names is to assume that Levi was also known under the name Matthew, and that Jacob son of Alphaeus was Levi's brother. Since Alphaeus was a rare name, it seems plausible to assume that Levi son of Alphaeus and Jacob son of Alphaeus (Mark 3:18) are brothers; in this case, Jesus calls three sets of

---

21. In the list of the ninety-nine most popular names of Palestinian Jews before AD 200, Alphaeus is no. 61; Levi is no. 17. Matthew (Mattathias) ranks no. 9.
22. Cf. F. Udoh, in Fiensy and Strange, *Galilee*, I, pp. 371–379.

brothers: Simon and Andrew, Jacob (James) and John, Levi/Matthew and Jacob.

Jesus' authoritative call, formulated with an imperative, is similar to that of Simon and Andrew, and Jacob and John (1:16–20). The command *follow me* uses the verb *akoloutheō*,[23] which increasingly becomes the standard term for the disciples' relationship with Jesus. The effect of Jesus' word is, as before, instantaneous: *Levi got up and followed him*. As a tax collector, Levi would have been able to read, write and take notes, which led later Christian tradition to assume that the other disciples made use of notes Levi made of Jesus' teaching (so Papias; cf. Eusebius, *Hist. eccl.* 3.39.16).

15. The verb translated *having dinner* (Gr. *katakeimai*) means here 'recline (on a couch) for the purpose of dining', suggesting a formal or festive meal. It appears that Levi gave a banquet in Jesus' honour and invited *many tax collectors* to eat with Jesus *and his disciples*. Mark mentions *sinners* together with tax collectors. The term 'sinners' (*hamartōloi*) has been understood as referring to the 'people of the land' (*'ammê ha'āreṣ*) who did not follow the scrupulous standards of ritual cleanness that the Pharisees demanded.[24] More plausible is the view that the term refers to flagrant violators of the Mosaic law.[25] Jesus' teaching about the kingdom of God resulted in sinners responding to his call for repentance.

This is the first reference to Jesus' *disciples*.[26] The term *mathētēs* describes a person 'who engages in learning through instruction from another' and someone 'who is rather constantly associated with someone who has a pedagogical reputation or a particular set of views' (BDAG, p. 609). The term is not restricted to the Twelve, as verse 16 indicates (cf. also 3:13). In most of Mark's Gospel, however, it designates those who are Jesus' constant companions.

---

23. BDAG, p. 36, lists three relevant meanings: (1) to move behind someone in the same direction; (2) to follow or accompany someone who takes the lead; (3) to follow someone as a disciple.
24. Jeremias, *New Testament Theology*, pp. 108–113.
25. Sanders, *Jesus and Judaism*, pp. 174–211; cf. Marcus, Strauss.
26. Mark uses the term *mathētēs* a total of forty-six times; in ch. 2 see 2:15, 16, 18, 23.

The concluding phrase *for there were many who followed him* probably explains not 'disciples' but 'tax collectors and sinners': many people responded positively to Jesus' ministry of healing and teaching.

16. Some *teachers of the law who were Pharisees* observed Jesus dining in Levi's house. The 'teachers of the law' or 'scribes' were mentioned in 1:22. The Pharisees are mentioned here for the first time.[27] The main source for understanding this religious Jewish group, apart from the New Testament, is Josephus. The designation 'Pharisees' (Aramaic *perišaya'*, 'separated, distinguished') was used early as a derogatory name, perhaps on account of the group's separation from the Maccabean resistance movement (cf. 1 Macc. 7:12–13). By the first century the term seems to have had a positive meaning. The Pharisees are repeatedly described as people who transmit, preserve and develop the tradition of the law in its written and oral form. Some Pharisees were formally trained scribes, which explains their presence in local synagogues. Their understanding of tradition was non-exclusive, which explains their interest in Jesus. Well-known Pharisees in the New Testament are Gamaliel (Acts 5:34) and Paul (Phil. 3:5; Acts 23:6). The conversations between Jesus and the Pharisees focus on questions of proper behaviour: fasting, working on the Sabbath, tithing and ritual purity.

When scribes who belonged to the Pharisaic movement saw Jesus *eating with the sinners and tax collectors* in Levi's house, they asked his disciples, *Why does he eat with tax collectors and sinners?* The twofold reference to eating in verse 16 suggests that the issue was one of purity: they knew, or assumed, that Jesus would be offered non-kosher food or food that had not been properly tithed, or that Jesus might be defiled by contact with unclean dishes or with the clothes of ritually unclean people in the close quarters of a meal (Marcus, p. 227). And since sharing a meal with someone might have been seen as a symbol of identification, Jesus' social contact with tax collectors and people who had the reputation of sinners was dubious, since righteous people heed the warning about 'becoming bedfellows with sinners' (*1 En.* 97:4).

---

27. Cf. 2:16, 18 (2x), 24; 3:6; 7:1, 3, 5; 8:11, 15; 10:2; 12:13. Cf. E. J. Schnabel, *NIDB* IV, pp. 485–496; R. Deines, *EDEJ*, pp. 1061–1063.

17. Jesus' response to the criticism of the Pharisaic scribes is given in two parts. First, Jesus cites a proverb: *It is not the healthy who need a doctor, but those who are ill.* The truth of this statement, which is found nearly verbatim in Plutarch,[28] is obvious. Jesus defends the company that he keeps: as a doctor attends to the sick, so Jesus meets with tax collectors and sinners. Then Jesus makes an explicit statement about his mission: *I have not come to call the righteous, but sinners.* If the statement is taken literally and if the *righteous* are identified with the scribes and Pharisees, Jesus would be excluding them from his mission, which is hardly plausible, even if 'righteous' is understood ironically in the sense of 'self-righteous' – the self-righteous need Jesus' attention as much as sinners. It is preferable to understand the antithetical statement as an expression not of exclusion but of priority. Jesus' main concern is *sinners*, whom he calls to repent and believe in the good news of the arrival of the kingdom of God (1:14–15) – not the Pharisees, who may be faultless as regards the righteousness based on the law, as Paul the Pharisee asserts that he was (Phil. 3:6), although they will also need to acknowledge that the coming of God's kingdom is connected with Jesus' ministry. One thinks of the parable of the father and the two sons in which the older, righteous son is confronted with the father's lavish mercy for the 'lost' son, which he must acknowledge – otherwise he will find himself outside the father's 'house' (Luke 15:11–32).

c. Jesus and fasting (2:18–22)

18. John's ministry had attracted *disciples*, people who were committed to his teaching and his baptism even after he was imprisoned and executed, and evidently not living in the wilderness as a community but integrated in everyday life, in Galilee and beyond (e.g. in Ephesus; Acts 19:1–4). They were *fasting*, as were the *Pharisees*. Fasting is not merely relinquishing food for a period of time, but an act of worship which expresses one's dependence on God. The

---

28. Plutarch, *Apophthegmata laconica* 230–231: 'It is not the custom of doctors to spend their time with the healthy, but where people are ill'; cf. Dio Chrysostom, *Or.* 8.5.

Old Testament mandated a day of fasting on the Day of Atonement (Lev. 16:29, 31). In the post-exilic period there were four additional annual fasts (Zech. 8:19), and Esther 9:31 adds another annual fast. Other references to fasting are a matter of individual choice: fasting accompanies mourning and grief (1 Sam. 31:13), petitions for aid (2 Sam. 12:16; Ezra 8:21), repentance and acts of piety (Neh. 9:1–3; Joel 1:14; Luke 2:37) and the pursuit of wisdom (2 Chr. 20:3). The prophets criticized fasting when done with an undevoted heart (Zech. 7:5), with pride (Isa. 58:4–6) or while acting with injustice towards the weak (Isa. 1:13–17). Some Jews thought that the fasting of the righteous atones for unknown sins (*Pss Sol.* 3:7–8). The Pharisees fasted twice a week, on Mondays and Thursdays (Luke 18:12; *Did.* 81; *b. Ta'an.* 12a), perhaps in connection with hopes for the coming of the last days (cf. *b. Sanh.* 97b–98a). Matthew reports Jesus' fasting for forty days and nights in the wilderness (Matt. 4:2; not mentioned by Mark). The subject of the sentence *they came* (NASB; NIV has 'some people came') is observers who noticed the difference in personal practice compared with John's disciples and the Pharisees. The 'why not' question implies an element of challenge, perhaps even reproach, but not necessarily hostility.

19. Jesus does not answer the question directly, but uses a series of analogies to assert that this is not an appropriate time for his disciples to fast, although they will fast in the future (v. 20; cf. Matt. 6:16–18; Acts 13:2–3; 14:23). The question *How can the guests of the bridegroom fast while he is with them?*, introduced in Greek with a negation which allows only a negative answer, states the obvious: weddings are festive affairs involving the entire village and lasting for a week or more. Guests at a wedding party do not fast, indeed *they cannot*, as they share the joy of the bridegroom. Jesus asks the questioners to recognize that his ministry of exorcism, healing and teaching constitutes an exceptional and joyful new reality, demonstrated by the excitement among the people in Galilee. His ministry marks a new beginning which calls for celebration, not fasting. At a deeper level, Jesus may be inviting his listeners to notice that as he compares himself to the bridegroom who is the source of joy, he connects the excitement among the people with his proclamation of the coming of the kingdom of God – which is a present reality connected with himself and his ministry, marking a new beginning and a new relationship between God and his people (as a wedding does), suggesting a messianic role for Jesus, and indeed connecting Jesus with the Old Testament portrayal of Yahweh as Israel's bridegroom and with the marriage imagery used for Yahweh's relationship with his redeemed people in the last days.[29]

20. Jesus asserts that *the days will come when the bridegroom is taken from them* (NRSV). The verb 'will be taken' (*apairō*) indicates removal by force rather than by natural causes. As Jesus sees himself as the bridegroom in verse 19, he predicts here his violent death, albeit in veiled terms in the context of an allegorical analogy. It is *on that day* that the disciples *will fast*. Fasting will become a spiritual discipline again in the future. Jesus does not say how they will fast; to take the phrase *on that day* as suggesting that the disciples will fast on Good Friday (so Marcus, Pesch), or more generally on Fridays, would be pedantic. The phrase is more plausibly synonymous with *the days will come*. Jesus refers to a time in the future 'when the immediate excitement of Jesus' ministry will give way to a more settled style of discipleship in which fasting will take its proper place' (France, p. 140).

21–22. Two further analogies illustrate the inappropriateness of fasting in the present time. When a *patch* (*epiblēma*) is used to repair a hole in a *garment* (*himation*), one has to use an old patch. If an *old garment* is repaired, one cannot use a piece of *cloth* (*rhakos*) that is *unshrunk* (*agnaphos*); that is, fresh from the weaver's loom, not fulled. If one uses a new piece of cloth to patch an old garment, the new *patch* (*plērōma*) will pull away from the old garment, since upon washing the patch will shrink, *making the tear worse*.

New wine (*oinos neos*) refers to freshly pressed grapes which had been allowed to ferment in a vat; after the lees had been strained out, the still fermenting new wine was put in skins made of leather, where the fermenting process continued. *Old wineskins* (*askoi palaioi*) which had been used for some time were potentially brittle. The still fermenting new wine *will burst the skins*, with the result that *both the wine and the wineskins will be ruined*. Combining the new with the old

---

29. Isa. 61:10; 62:4–5; Hos. 2:14–20; in the NT cf. Matt. 25:1–3; Eph. 5:23–33; Rev. 19:7–9; 21:2, 9.

will have disastrous consequences. The final clause *no, they pour new wine into new wineskins* is not an instruction for wine-makers, who do not need to be told the obvious, but a succinct statement challenging those who have understood the previous analogies to think through the implications of Jesus' presence and proclamation. The new patch and the new wine represent Jesus' preaching of the good news of the coming of the kingdom of God, which is thus characterized as a new era of salvation that cannot be contained in the structures and practices of the existing religious traditions (the old garment and the old skins), as represented by the Pharisees and the scribes, and even the movement of John the Baptist.

d. *Jesus and the Sabbath (2:23–28)*

23–24. Keeping the *Sabbath* was one of the principal marks of being Jewish (cf. 1:21). According to Exodus 31:14–15, the Sabbath was holy and was to be observed as a day of rest, that is, a day when no work should be done. Later discussion focused, inevitably, on what constituted 'work'; that is, on what was prohibited. (For lists of prohibitions cf. Exod. 16:22–30; 34:21; 35:2–3; Num. 15:32–36; Neh. 10:31; 13:15–22; Jer. 17:21–22; then *Jub.* 50:6–13; CD X, 14 – XI,18; *m. Shab.* 7:2 lists thirty-nine prohibitions.)

As Jesus and his disciples were walking through the *cornfields* (lit. 'standing grain') on a Sabbath, the disciples *began to pick some ears of corn*. The time must have been late spring or early summer, as harvest time was not far off (barley was ripe in April/May, wheat in May/June). The Pharisees (cf. v. 16) object to the disciples' behaviour, which evidently had Jesus' approval. They question not their action as such, which was permissible according to Deuteronomy 23:25 (cf. Lev. 19:9–10; 23:22); they are convinced that what they are doing *is unlawful* because it happened on the Sabbath. They evidently regard the action as 'reaping' or 'threshing', which, according to rabbinic definitions of 'harvesting' (which was explicitly forbidden on the Sabbath), fell within the classes of work prohibited on the Sabbath (Exod. 34:21; cf. *m. Shab.* 7:2).

25–26. Jesus responds with an appeal to Scripture, which he cites as precedent and which has primary authority compared with subsequent halakhic rulings. *In the days of Abiathar the high priest*, David entered the tabernacle and ate consecrated bread, and gave some of the bread to his companions as well (cf. 1 Sam. 21:1–6; according to the Hebrew text, it was Ahimelek, the father of Abiathar, who gave David the consecrated bread. There is some confusion in that 1 Sam. 22:20 calls Abiathar the son of Ahimelek, and 2 Sam. 8:17 and 1 Chr. 18:16; 24:6 make Ahimelek the son of Abiathar; when Mark 2:26 is translated 'when Abiathar was high priest' [NRSV], the problem persists, unless one assumes that Mark followed a different textual tradition that surfaces e.g. in 1 Sam. 22:20; a more general understanding of the Greek phrase such as 'in the time of Abiathar the high priest' [NASB; cf. NIV, ESV] avoids the problem; cf. Strauss).

Jesus introduces the scriptural reference with the explanation that David did what he did when he and his companions *were hungry and in need*. The same is seemingly not the case with regard to Jesus and the disciples: they were not eating because they were hungry; they were having a snack. Also, the illegality of David's action was not connected with breaking the Sabbath law (although this could be inferred from the fact that the removal and replacement of the bread in the tabernacle, mentioned in 1 Sam. 21:6, was a Sabbath duty according to Lev. 24:8), but the law that stipulated that only priests could eat the consecrated bread of the tabernacle. The logic of Jesus' scriptural argument implies the claim that he has personal authority at least as great as that of David. If David's authority was sufficient to obtain priestly approval for an action that was illegal, then Jesus can declare an action deemed illegal by the Pharisees to be permissible since his authority exceeds that of David (explicit in v. 28). The twofold reference to David's *companions* provides the precedent for the principle that the disciples' plucking heads of grain on the Sabbath is covered by Jesus' personal authority.

27–28. Jesus clarifies the purpose of the Sabbath and the nature of his authority in two pronouncements. The statement *the Sabbath was made for man, not man for the Sabbath* should be read not as a rejection of all obligations to keep Sabbath restrictions, but as a statement of priority. When considering specific questions concerning what God's people can and cannot do on the Sabbath, man (*anthrōpon*) whom God has created is more important than the Sabbath. The verb translated as *made* (*egeneto*) focuses here not on historical origins (the Sabbath is the seventh day, while Adam was created on the sixth day), but on purpose: the Sabbath rest is for the benefit of the workers and animals (Exod. 23:12; Deut. 5:14–15). Resting and being refreshed on the Sabbath is not a burden but a blessing (Isa. 58:13).

The second pronouncement emphasizes Jesus' authority: *So the Son of Man is Lord even of the Sabbath*. The expression *Son of Man* (cf. v. 10) is a self-reference of Jesus, who claims for himself authority over the Sabbath as the epitome of humankind. It is as the extraordinary, unique Son of Man that Jesus is the *Lord* (*kyrios*) of the Sabbath and thus has authority to override the Sabbath law and, certainly, interpretations of the Sabbath law advanced by the Pharisees. The claim to be *Lord of the Sabbath* affirms the unique authority that Jesus exercises in his ministry, affecting one of the most sacred institutions of the Jewish people, linking Jesus, again, most closely with Yahweh, who decreed the Sabbath, in whose honour the Sabbath was observed and to whom the Sabbath belongs (note the expression 'a Sabbath of/to Yahweh' in Exod. 16:25; 20:10; Deut. 5:14; or 'my Sabbaths', Exod. 31:13; Lev. 19:3; Ezek. 20:12–13).

e. Jesus and healing on the Sabbath (3:1–6)

1–2. Jesus again attends a synagogue service (cf. 1:21–28), presumably in Capernaum, and again a controversy on account of the Sabbath ensues (cf. 2:23–28), triggered by the presence of *a man with a shrivelled hand* or *arm* (BDAG, p. 1082), a hand paralysed as the result perhaps of nerve damage caused by an accident, or a paralysed arm and hand as the result of polio or a stroke. It appears that the Pharisees who had objected to the disciples plucking heads of grain in the cornfields outside town are now in the synagogue, *looking for a reason to accuse Jesus*. Their attitude has changed: they *watched him closely*, not out of curiosity and interest, but in order to collect evidence for Jesus' infringement of the Sabbath laws and *accuse* him; that is, bring legal charges against him. Local courts (cf. 13:9; Matt. 5:22) could inflict punishments such as the forty lashes minus one that the apostle Paul endured five times (2 Cor. 11:24). As the Pharisees watched whether Jesus would break the Sabbath law, which, if it were deliberate, was punishable by death (see on 1:21), they might have aimed at gathering evidence for an indictment on a capital crime; rabbinic law specifies that the transgressor must be warned by two witnesses, and executed only if he or she persists in violating the law (*m. Sanh.* 7:8).

The Pharisees wanted to see *if he would heal* the man with the paralysed hand/arm. Jesus had dramatically exorcized a demon on a Sabbath day in a previous synagogue service (1:21–28), and he had healed Simon's mother-in-law on the Sabbath (1:29–31). The Pharisees seem to expect that if Jesus notices the man, he will heal him even though it is the Sabbath. Since 'creative work' is prohibited on the Sabbath, when God rested from his work of creation, healing constitutes 'work' and is permitted only if there is the risk of death (cf. *m. Yom.* 8:6).

3–5. Jesus commands the man with the paralysed hand or arm, *Stand up in front of everyone.* Jesus accepts the challenge of the Pharisees, whose thoughts and intentions he seems to know, determined to force the issue of his authority as 'Lord of the Sabbath' (2:28). He does not delay the healing to a time after sunset when the next day begins, nor does he want to heal the man in a private setting. He is determined to heal him in public. Jesus formulates the principle that relief of suffering is permissible on the Sabbath with a rhetorical question: *Which is lawful on the Sabbath: to do good or to do evil, to save life or to kill?* To delay the healing of the man with the paralysed hand/arm by a few hours does not constitute evil, nor will it kill him. The negative terms (*do evil, kill*) highlight the positive principle: one should do good on the Sabbath, and one can indeed save life on the Sabbath. While healing the man now, during the synagogue service, is not a critical necessity, it is certainly a good act that gives the man and his family a great deal of joy. The Pharisees refuse to answer Jesus' question. Since Jesus is unwilling to engage in a discussion about halakhic details of the definition of 'work', they do not want to be drawn into a discussion of the fundamental difference between good and evil, life and death. If they answer in the positive, they will encourage Jesus to heal the man. If they answer in the negative, they will argue the impossible (nobody wants to do evil and kill, on any day of the week), and they will be exposed as people who do not seem to care for the well-being of the man with the paralysis.

Jesus looks at the Pharisees *in anger and deeply distressed*, an emotional reaction (cf. 1:41) triggered by *their stubborn hearts* (lit. 'the obstinacy of their hearts'). This expression describes people who cannot or will not acknowledge the truth (for the disciples in 6:52; 8:17; for Israel's failure to recognize Jesus as Messiah in Rom. 11:7, 25; 2 Cor. 3:14; John 12:40). If the heart (cf. 2:6 NRSV), the seat of discernment and volition, has become 'petrified', it cannot perceive new insight. The healing of the man with the paralysed hand is narrated with an extreme economy of words. Jesus says to the man, *Stretch out your hand [arm]* – an action that used to be impossible for the man, but is now suddenly possible: *he stretched it out*, which demonstrates, for all to see, that *his hand [arm] was completely restored*, its function re-established. Jesus did not touch the man: the only 'work' that he did was to utter a verbal command, formulated in Greek with three words.

6. The Pharisees left the synagogue and *began to plot with the Herodians how they might kill Jesus*. The Pharisees moved from a desire to condemn Jesus (v. 2), hostile silence (v. 4) and refusal to consider the significance of Jesus' ministry (v. 5), to a murder plot. The term 'Herodians' (*Hērōdianoi*; cf. 12:13/Matt. 22:16) is a Latinism (*Herodiani*) denoting supporters of Herod who owed their standing and their positions of influence to Herod and to the close relationship he had established with the imperial family. After King Herod's death, they seem to have formed a pressure group on the Roman government in Judea, believing in the necessity of a king in order to maintain independence. They would have regarded it as advantageous to have one of Herod's sons (Antipas, tetrarch of Galilee) or grandsons (Agrippa I) crowned king of Judea.[1] Their cooperation with the Pharisees is not really surprising, as 'the Pharisees were interested in both peace and independence of the sort that only a Herodian ruler could provide' (Rocca, *Herod's Judaea*, p. 261). The establishment of a Jewish king did not necessitate the overthrow of the Romans who ruled in Judea directly and in Galilee indirectly. As Herod had been appointed king of the Jews by the Senate of Rome, Herodians and Pharisees might very well cooperate in achieving the goal of establishing another Jewish king of Judea: in AD 41, Agrippa I, grandson of King Herod, was appointed king (he is called 'King

---

1. Cf. Richardson, *Herod*, pp. 259–260; Rocca, *Herod's Judaea*, pp. 259–261.

Herod' in Acts 12:1). The Pharisees and the Herodians agreed in principle that Jesus had to be silenced, and perhaps began discussing the tactical question of how this could be achieved, given Jesus' popularity. Jesus did not have the political credentials to be king of the Jews, and in the view of the Pharisees he was too unorthodox by far, eating with tax collectors and sinners, willing to violate the law in its traditional interpretation, and claiming to have a unique status that transcended that of King David.

Theology

Forgiveness and healing are connected with faith. Before Jesus' death and resurrection, faith is the expectation that Jesus can and will exercise the power of God to heal. Mark highlights the faith of the paralysed man's friends (2:5) who, presumably, would not have acted without the man's consent. Theories about vicarious faith should not be based on this passage. Mark will later explain that Jesus could do only a few miracles of healing in Nazareth because the people there did not believe in him (6:5–6). Since healing is a sign of the presence of the kingdom of God, and since the coming of the kingdom is connected with repentance and faith, faith is the prerequisite for healing and forgiveness.

Jesus' statement about the old garment and the old wineskins should not be interpreted as Mark signalling to his readers that Judaism is bad. Jesus asserts that his ministry constitutes a new reality which heralds a new beginning – for sinners, but also for the righteous. The old realities of responding to God's presence in Israel (in the law and in the temple) are incompatible with the new reality of the good news of the kingdom of God, present in Jesus' person, in his proclamation and in his ministry of exorcism and healing. The 'old' garment is not discarded, but needs to be mended properly, which means that God's revelation in his covenant with Israel is preserved as it is altered on account of the coming of his kingdom in Jesus' person and ministry.

B. The Twelve and the kingdom of God (3:7 – 6:6)

The first controversy with the teachers of the law and the Pharisees (2:1 – 3:6) ended with a reference to a plot to kill Jesus (3:6). This indicates that the next section (3:7 – 6:6) belongs to a new phase of Jesus' ministry, sometimes called the 'later Galilean ministry'. Mark relates further demonstrations of Jesus' authority and continues to report on the growing opposition to Jesus. Both Jesus' mighty acts and the opposition to Jesus intensify. After summarizing Jesus' ministry and popularity (3:7–12), Mark describes Jesus' call of the Twelve (3:13–19), then two groups of opponents: his natural family (3:20–21) and teachers of the law from Jerusalem who suggest that Jesus' authority is inspired by Beelzebul (3:22–30), followed by a section on Jesus' true family (3:31–35). Mark continues with the first major discourse, Jesus' parables about the kingdom of God (4:1–34). Then a series of miracles demonstrates Jesus' authority over nature (4:35–41), demons (5:1–20), disease (5:21–34) and death (5:35–43). Mark concludes with a report on Jesus' rejection by the people of Nazareth (6:1–6).

i. *Jesus' ministry: summary (3:7–12)*
Context
This summary of Jesus' Galilean ministry is a self-contained unit, unlike the previous summaries in 1:14–15, 32–34, 39 which are directly linked with their immediate contexts. Placed after the controversies between Jesus and the religious leaders (2:1 – 3:6), the summary provides a contrast to the growing opposition and conflict. Mark reminds his readers that Jesus was immensely popular, not only in Galilee but throughout the region that had belonged to the kingdom of King Herod I. And the summary provides the context for Jesus' selection of twelve disciples as his co-workers in distinction from the large crowds of enthusiastic followers.

Comment
7–8. The move *to the lake* may have been a tactical withdrawal from the Pharisees' and Herodians' opposition (3:6), or merely the attempt to get away from the crowds and find privacy on the shore of the Sea of Galilee. If the latter was the case, the attempt was unsuccessful, since *a great multitude from Galilee followed him* (NRSV). As Jesus travelled throughout Galilee, preaching and healing (1:38–39), people from Galilean towns and villages travelled to Capernaum and the Sea of Galilee to hear Jesus teach. Mark mentions five

regions to the south, east and north of Galilee, where people *heard all he was doing*. On *Judea* and *Jerusalem* see on 1:5. *Idumea* (derived from 'Edom'), which is mentioned only here in the New Testament, was the region between the southern Judean hill country and the northern part of the Negev Desert, with Hebron being one of its important cities. The Idumeans were forcibly converted to Judaism after 110 BC. King Herod's family was Idumean. After the death of Archelaos, son of King Herod, who ruled over the southern part of his father's kingdom, Idumea became part of Roman Judea (together with Samaria). The region *across the Jordan* is usually interpreted in terms of Perea (Gilead in the OT), the territory east of the lower Jordan opposite Judea and Samaria that belonged to Antipas' tetrarchy of Galilee. Since Mark mentions Galilee in verse 7, the geographical marker *across the Jordan* can plausibly also be interpreted in terms of the tetrarchy of Philip, another son of King Herod, which included the territories Paneas, Gaulanitis, Trachonitis, Batanea and Auranitis. The region *around Tyre and Sidon* refers to the southern part of the Roman province of Syria north of Galilee. On Tyre see on 7:24. Tyre is about 34 miles (55 km) north of Capernaum as the crow flies, and Sidon is about 25 miles (40 km) north of Tyre. The people who came to Jesus from this region could very well have included pagans, attracted by reports of Jesus' dramatic healings, just as Jews living in southern Syria would have been drawn to Jesus. Mark reports that *a great multitude* (same phrase as in v. 7; NIV translates here 'many people', NRSV 'great numbers') from these regions *came to him* because of reports that he had healed many (v. 10).

9–10. The presence of the *crowd* (cf. 2:4) causes people to *press against him* (NIV 'crowding him'; NRSV 'crush him'). This prompts Jesus to ask the disciples, four of whom are fishermen, to provide a *small boat* whose use, however, is not explained. In 4:1–2 Mark notes that Jesus used a boat as a mobile speaker's platform. The well-preserved first-century fishing boat discovered near Kibbutz Ginnosar in 1986 is 27 feet (8.27 m) long and 7.5 feet (2.3 m) wide; the planks and the forward part of the keel were made of Lebanese cedar and the frame of oak; it had a mast and it could carry about fifteen people (Wachsmann, *Sea of Galilee Boat*). People who were afflicted with various diseases *were pushing forward to touch him*, evidently believing that merely touching Jesus would heal them. Mark later relates that people were indeed healed by touching Jesus (5:25–34; 6:56; cf. Matt. 14:36; Luke 6:19; 8:44; see later Acts 5:15–16; 19:11–12; in the OT cf. 2 Kgs 13:21).

11–12. Apart from healings of physical diseases, Jesus also helps people possessed by demons. The focus is not on the exorcisms, but on the fact that *the impure spirits* recognized Jesus. When they *saw him*, they *fell down before him* and *cried out, 'You are the Son of God'* – the highest Christological confession in Mark's Gospel. This ultimate truth about Jesus had been declared by God himself at Jesus' baptism in the wilderness (1:11). It is declared here and in 5:7 by demons who are thus described as having insight into supernatural truth. It will be repeated by the heavenly voice to three disciples in 9:7. It is only at his trial that Jesus affirms that he is the Son of God (14:61–62), which is acknowledged at the cross by the centurion (15:39). Human beings, not even the disciples, do not have this insight. They are not yet ready for this revelation, which is given in 1:11 and 9:7 in private and in 3:11 and 5:7 by demons, whom Jesus silences: *he gave them strict orders not to tell others about him* (cf. 1:25, 34; on the 'messianic secret' cf. Introduction 4b). Demons are unsuitable witnesses to Jesus' true identity, which can be revealed only by God and by Jesus himself. And the time has not yet come when his true identity can be revealed to the public. It can be understood properly only in the context of his death and resurrection. And, perhaps most importantly, since the demons seem to think that they can control Jesus because they know his identity and shout his name as a pre-emptive defence measure, Jesus silences them and thus effectively drives them out.

Theology
Jesus' authority, the central theme of his Galilean ministry, is confirmed by further healings and exorcisms, and by the multitudes of people from Galilee and the adjacent provinces and territories who come to him because they have heard the reports of his healings and exorcisms. The fact that the basis of Jesus' popularity is not his proclamation of the kingdom of God, which from Mark's point of view is the most essential aspect of Jesus' ministry, sets up Jesus' parable of the four soils in 4:1–20 in which he distinguishes people who are merely excited, and who eventually turn to other matters,

from people who have a mature understanding of the word of God. Enthusiasm without faith in Jesus will not last.

The notion that touching a person who has power (*dynamis*) effects healing was widespread in antiquity. This has been called 'magical' thinking. Due to the ambiguous connotations of 'magic', some scholars speak in a more neutral fashion of the 'dynamistic' worldview of people. It is certainly not surprising that Mark includes such incidents in his description of Jesus' ministry. He does not depict Jesus inviting people to touch him, or as endorsing the 'dynamistic' notion that touching effects healing. The fact that people are healed of diseases by merely touching Jesus can be attributed to Jesus' compassion for the crowds (6:34; cf. 8:2).

ii. Jesus' call of the Twelve (3:13–19)
Context
Jesus' opponents mentioned so far include teachers of the law, Pharisees and the Herodians (2:6–7, 16, 24; 3:1–6), and they will soon include Jesus' family (3:20–21, 31–35) as well as teachers of the law from Jerusalem (3:22–30). In contrast to these groups, Mark introduces by name twelve constant companions of Jesus, five of whom he has described as having been called by Jesus to leave their profession and follow him (1:16–20; 2:14–15). They will be called 'the Twelve' (4:10; 6:7; 9:35; 10:32; 11:11; 14:10, 17, 20, 43). When Mark uses the term 'disciples' after 3:19, he refers to this group of twelve men whom Jesus trains as they are 'with him' (3:14).

Comment
13–15. The *mountain* on which Jesus perhaps sought refuge from the crowds remains unspecified. There is nothing that suggests that Mark alludes to Moses ascending Sinai, as some surmise (Allison, *New Moses*, pp. 174–175). Moses does not select disciples on Sinai, and Jesus does not receive divine revelation on the mountain. The closest mountain to Capernaum would have been Mount Meiron (3,963 ft [1,208 m] high, c. 25 miles [40 km] north-west); closer were the hills of Akchabaron (c. 9 miles [15 km] to the north); the Horns of Hittin overlooking Tiberias were around 16 miles (25 km) to the south. The verb translated as *[he] called to him* (*proskaleō*) is often used to introduce a significant pronouncement or action of Jesus (3:23;

6:7; 7:14; 8:1, 34; 10:42; 12:43). Jesus took the initiative in selecting from the larger crowd of followers the smaller group of the Twelve. Their response, described with the phrase *and they came to him*, indicates their willingness to be trained by Jesus, and it underlines again Jesus' authority.

The number *twelve* is symbolic, suggesting, against the background of the twelve tribes of Israel, the restoration of the people of God that was expected for the last days (a conviction which necessitated the replacement of Judas Iscariot in Acts 1:15–26). The Twelve are the nucleus of the new messianic people of God. Mark adds, *whom he also named apostles* (NRSV).[31] 'Apostle' (*apostolos*) occurs in 6:30, and more often in Luke's Gospel.[32] The term can be defined as 'messenger with extraordinary status' (BDAG, p. 122, *apostolos* meaning 2). Mark describes the goal of the creation of the Twelve with two purpose clauses. Jesus appointed the Twelve *that they might be with him*. The foundational reality of discipleship is to be in the presence of Jesus, to hear and learn from his teaching, and to be trained by him for the mission with which he entrusts his followers. And Jesus appointed the Twelve *that he might send them out to preach*. The verb *send out* (*apostellō*), which triggered the title *apostolos*, implies movement from Jesus' location by the Sea of Galilee to other places. Jesus did not stay in Capernaum waiting for crowds to come (which they did), but travelled throughout Galilee to preach in other towns and villages as an essential part of his mission (1:38). In the same manner, the Twelve are appointed as Jesus' envoys who would travel to other villages, towns and regions. For the verb *preach* (*kēryssō*) see on 1:4, 14. The Twelve are called to proclaim the good news of the fulfilment of God's promises, the

---

31. NIV omits the phrase, following some Greek manuscripts. Important early manuscripts include the phrase, which is printed in the latest editions of the Greek NT; it could well be original as the more difficult reading (Mark uses *apostolos* elsewhere only at 6:30). Most commentators regard the phrase as a secondary assimilation to Luke 6:13; cf. Collins, Cranfield, France, Marcus.

32. Luke 6:13; 9:10; 17:5; 22:14; 24:10; there are twenty-eight references in Acts.

coming of the kingdom of God and the need for repentance and faith (1:14–15). Connected with their task to preach is exercising the *authority to drive out demons*. The Twelve remain with Jesus for the time being, until they share with Jesus the task of preaching and driving out demons (6:7–13). The notice in 6:13 indicates that the Twelve were indeed able to drive out demons, while 9:14–29 cautions that this was not automatic: their authority is not on the same level as that of Jesus.

16–19. The list of the Twelve begins with *Simon* (see 1:16). He was called by Jesus, together with his brother Andrew, as the first disciple (1:16–18). Simon was the most common Jewish male name. Before Jesus gave him a nickname, Simon was distinguished by his patronymic 'son of John' (John 1:42) or 'Bar-Jona' (Matt. 16:17 RSV); Greek *Bariōna* probably represents Aramaic *Bar Yōḥānā'*, where *Yōḥānā'* would be not *Yōnāh* (Jonah) but an Aramaized form of *Yōḥānān* (John).[33] Mark states that Jesus gave him the name *Peter* (Gr. *Petros*); Matthew 16:18 and John 1:42 explain the significance of the name, which means 'stone' or 'rock'. *Petros* was not a name that Greeks used, nor was the Aramaic term *Kepha'* ('rock'; Gr. *Kēphas*, Cephas) a name current among Jews. According to John 1:42, *Kēphas* was the name given to Simon by Jesus, which John then translates into Greek as *Petros*.[34] Some have suggested that the nickname originally alluded to Simon's 'rough' character.[35] Jesus and the early church linked the name *Kēphas/Petros* with his foundational role (Matt. 16:18; Gal. 2:9). Mark uses 'Simon' only once more, when Jesus addresses him directly (14:37); otherwise he uses Simon's new name 'Peter'.[36] The change to Simon's name reminded biblically literate readers of God changing the name of Abram (to Abraham), Sarai (to Sarah) and Jacob (to Israel) (Gen. 17:5, 15; 32:28), all of whom have foundational significance in the history of Israel.

---

33. Cf. Bauckham, *Eyewitnesses*, pp. 103–104.
34. Paul uses Cephas; cf. 1 Cor. 1:12; 3:22; 9:5; 15:5; Gal. 1:18; 2:9, 11, 14.
35. Cf. Brown, Donfried and Reumann, *Peter*, p. 90 n. 210.
36. 5:37; 8:29, 32, 33; 9:2, 5; 10:28; 11:21; 13:3; 14:29, 33, 37, 54, 66, 67, 70, 72; 16:7.

Jacob (*Iakōbos*; Hebr. *Ya'ăqōb*; in English versions traditionally 'James') and his brother *John* (*Iōannēs*; Hebr. *Yokanan*), the sons of Zebedee, were introduced as followers called by Jesus in 1:19–20. The two brothers formed, together with Simon Peter, the inner circle of the Twelve (cf. 5:37; 9:2; 14:33). Jesus gave the nickname *Boanerges* to Jacob/James and John, which Mark explains as *sons of thunder*. It is assumed that the Hebrew phrase *bĕnê regeš* ('sons of commotion') or *bĕnê rōgez* ('sons of agitation or anger') was roughly rendered by Mark in Greek as *huioi brontēs*. The nickname is perhaps an allusion to their occasionally explosive characters (9:38; Luke 9:54), or positively to Jesus' later assertion that the two brothers will be, just like him, exposed to suffering (10:38–40).

Andrew (*Andreas*) is Simon Peter's brother; see on 1:16. In 13:3 Andrew joins Simon in Jesus' inner circle.

Philip (*Philippos*) was a common Greek name (e.g. Philip, the father of Alexander the Great), but relatively rarely used by Palestinian Jews.

Bartholomew (*Bartholomaios*) is a patronymic which evidently was used as a name. In Aramaic his name was probably Bar Tolmai ('son of Tolmai'); the biblical name is Talmai (2 Sam. 3:3; 13:37; 1 Chr. 3:2); the Greek name Ptolemaios (Ptolemy) was popular because it was the name of the Hellenistic kings of Egypt.[37]

Matthew (*Maththaios*) was a very common Jewish name, particularly since it was Mattathias from Modein who, together with his son Judas Maccabeus and his four brothers, started the rebellion against the Seleucid state.[38] The Gospel of Matthew identifies this Matthew as 'the tax collector' (Matt. 9:9; 10:3), which means he may be the tax collector Levi of Mark 2:14 (see there).

Thomas (*Thōmas*) is a nickname that was evidently used as the name of this disciple. 'Thomas' is the Aramaic word for 'twin' (*te'oma*),

---

37. In the list of common male names among Palestinian Jews, Philip is no. 61; Bartholomew/Ptolemy is no. 50.
38. Mattathias is no. 9 in the list of popular Palestinian Jewish names. The short form Mattai, which was the name of the disciple in the list of the Twelve (written in Greek as Maththaios), was not very common, with only six occurrences; neither was the name Philip, which is no. 61 in the list.

as John knows, who explains 'Thomas' with *Didymos*, the Greek word for 'twin' (John 11:16; 20:24; 21:2).[39]

Jacob (*Iakōbos*; traditionally 'James') is identified as the son of Alphaeus; since Levi is called 'son of Alphaeus', and since Alphaeus was rarely used as a personal name by Palestinian Jews, Jacob may be the brother of Levi/Matthew (2:14).

Thaddaeus (*Thaddaios*) is a Greek name (Theodosios, Theodotos or Theodoros) which was turned into a shorter Semitic name (Taddai) written in Greek as Thaddaios. The lists of the Twelve in Luke 6:14-16 and Acts 1:13 do not have Thaddaeus, but a Judas son of Jacob (James). It is possible that this is the same disciple, who had a Hebrew name (Yehudah, Judas) and a Greek name (Thaddaeus, Taddai), treated as sound equivalents.[40] To distinguish this disciple from the other member of the Twelve who bore the name Judas (Iscariot), Mark and Matthew use the Greek name of this disciple, while Luke uses the name Judas and adds the name of the father.

Simon is the second disciple with this name, and thus is distinguished from Simon Peter with the nickname *the Cananaean* (NRSV; *ho Kananaios*), from Aramaic *qan'ana'* ('the zealot'), which Luke reproduces in Greek (*ho zēlōtēs*, 'the zealot'; Luke 6:15; Acts 1:13). The nickname 'zealot' should probably not be linked with the political party of the Zealots who initiated the revolt against the Roman occupiers in AD 66, but with the fact that this disciple was evidently a 'zealot for the law' (cf. Acts 21:20; 22:3, 19). However, by the time Mark (and Luke) wrote his Gospel, the term 'zealot' had clear political connotations, which suggests that Mark expected his readers to view this disciple as a fervent patriot.[41]

Judas (*Ioudas*) is the Hebrew name Yehudah (Judah), the fourth most common name of Palestinian Jews. He is called *Iscariot*

---

39. Thomas is attested in an early second-century text (Papyrus Yadin 10, 15) as an Aramaic name of a Palestinian Jew. Cf. Bauckham, *Eyewitnesses*, p. 105.
40. Cf. Bauckham, *Eyewitnesses*, pp. 99-101. Thaddaeus is no. 39 on the list; seven individuals with the name Taddai are attested.
41. Hengel, *Zealots*, pp. 392-394, is not convinced that 'Zealot' could have been used by Mark, writing in the 60s, with an innocuous sense.

(*Iskariōth*), which is most plausibly understood as indicating his place of origin (Hebr. *'îš qĕriyyôt*, 'man of Kerioth'). John refers to him as 'Judas, the son of Simon Iscariot' (John 6:71; 13:2, 26), which renders it all but certain that 'Iscariot' is a place name used as a family name.[42] The family came from a town named Kerioth (Josh. 15:25; Jer. 48:24, 41; Amos 2:2), perhaps Kerioth-Hezron, about 12 miles (20 km) south of Hebron in Judea. If this is correct, Judas would have been the only non-Galilean disciple. Mark's readers would know that it was Judas Iscariot *who betrayed* Jesus. The verb *betray* (*paradidōmi*) means literally 'hand over' and is often used in connection with personal objects in a hostile sense, sometimes as a technical term for being handed over into custody; the same word is used in 1:14 with regard to John the Baptist. Even readers with no knowledge of Jesus' arrest would sense an ominous note, particularly as Jesus had spoken of the 'removal' of the bridegroom in 2:20.

Theology
Jesus' call of the Twelve is a model of the identity and work of full-time missionaries. They are followers of Jesus who have been specifically called to leave their professions, who are trained as Jesus' envoys and who are sent out to people, towns and villages to proclaim the kingdom of God and to cast out demons and heal those with diseases. The criteria for the replacement of Judas in Acts 1:21–22 define the significance of the Twelve for the church that is about to be constituted: the life and work of the church rests on the twelve apostles who have been with Jesus since the days of John the Baptist and thus on their testimony of Jesus' life, ministry, death and resurrection; and the life and work of the church rests on the twelve apostles being active witnesses of Jesus' resurrection, who can thus fulfil Jesus' summons to be his witnesses in Jerusalem, in all Judea and Samaria and to the ends of the earth (Acts 1:8). The witness of the Twelve was, and remains, foundational for the church. The fact that Jesus is not part of the Twelve underscores his unique

---

42. Cf. Meier, *Marginal Jew*, III, pp. 208–211; Bauckham, *Eyewitnesses*, p. 106. Some refer to the later targums and take Iscariot to mean 'the man from the city'; i.e. from Jerusalem.

status: he is not the expected earthly king who comes from one of the twelve tribes of Israel (in his case the tribe of Judah): he is the unique Son of God who has divine authority.

In a more general sense, Jesus' call of the Twelve is also a model of discipleship. Disciples are people who are 'with Jesus', who have repented and come to faith, who acknowledge Jesus' message of the kingdom, who observe and learn from Jesus, who do what Jesus did – preach the good news, help the needy – and who follow Jesus in the context of their ordinary professional lives, even amid present and growing opposition.

iii. *Jesus' family, opponents and authority (3:20–35)*
Context
The description of Jesus calling the Twelve, whom he trains to extend his ministry, is followed by a description of the opposition against Jesus. His family thinks that he is out of his mind (3:20–21). And teachers of the law from Jerusalem, who have come to Capernaum, evidently to challenge Jesus, have concluded that Jesus owes his authority to drive out demons to the chief demon, Beelzebul (3:22–30). The final scene contrasts Jesus' family and the Jerusalem scribes with Jesus' 'true family' consisting of those who do the will of God and who are around him as he teaches and heals (3:31–35). This section presents us with the first major intercalation (see Introduction, section 2): the story of Jesus' family (3:20–21, 31–35) is interrupted by the scene of the Jerusalem scribes (3:22–30). The opposition of Jesus' family is paralleled in the opposition of the Jerusalem scribes.

Comment
a. Jesus and his natural family (3:20–21)
20–21. As in 2:1–4, a *crowd* gathered, which was so persistent that Jesus and the disciples *were not even able to eat* (lit. 'eat bread', an expression used for eating any kind of food). The needs of the crowd render it impossible for Jesus and his disciples to meet their own need of a meal. In 6:3 Mark describes Jesus' *family* more fully as consisting of his mother, Mary, his brothers, Jacob, Joseph, Judas and Simon, and at least two sisters; as Joseph, the father, is not mentioned, he may be presumed to have died. Jesus' family want to

take charge of him; they want to 'seize' and thus 'take control' of him. The reason for their action is given in direct speech, which underlines the seriousness of what they are saying, and with a single Greek word, which highlights the unqualified certainty of their opinion: *he is out of his mind* (Gr. *exestē*). Jesus' mother and brothers think that Jesus is unable to 'reason normally' (BDAG), that he is no longer rational, that 'he's gone mad' (GNB). Having heard of his activities and, presumably, of the controversies with the teachers of the law, the Pharisees and the Herodians, and having seen the crowds, they think, perhaps, that Jesus brings shame on the family.

b. Jesus and the scribes from Jerusalem (3:22–30)

22. Teachers of the law (cf. 1:21–22) had accused Jesus of blasphemy (2:6–7) and of associating with notorious sinners (2:16), and they had observed Jesus overriding the Sabbath law (2:18, 24), perhaps agreeing with those Pharisees and Herodians who decided that Jesus needed to be eliminated (3:6). Mark now introduces a new group: *teachers of the law who came down from Jerusalem*. For Jerusalem see 1:5. This is a delegation from the Jewish capital who may have been tasked, perhaps by the Sadducees, the high priestly families or the Sanhedrin, to travel to Galilee on a fact-finding mission regarding Jesus and his activities. Another delegation of Jerusalem scribes, accompanied by Pharisees, is mentioned in 7:1. Here, their immediately hostile accusation suggests that they have come to a decision, indicated by the imperfect tense of the verb *[they] said*. They are convinced that Jesus is *possessed by Beelzebul! By the prince of demons he is driving out demons*. Their charge that Jesus is demon-possessed is parallel to the charge of Jesus' family that he is out of his mind (v. 21). The opposition to Jesus is escalating in its seriousness, both in terms of the nature of the accusations and in terms of the source of the opposition.

The Jerusalem scribes say, literally, 'he has Beelzebul'. The word 'have' expressing demon possession is also used in 7:25; 9:17. Beelzebul[43] is explained as *the prince of demons*, which suggests that the Jerusalem scribes understand Beelzebul as another name for

---

43. KJV has 'Beelzebub', from the Latin assimilation to 2 Kgs 1:2–6.

Satan. The name Beelzebul is not found in pre-Christian Jewish texts for demons or for Satan. In the Old Testament, 2 Kings 1:2–6 mentions as the name of a Philistine god 'Baal-Zebub', which can mean 'Baal the Prince' or 'Baal of the Exalted Dwelling'; in Ugaritic texts the Canaanite god Baal is known as *zbl baʻal* ('Exalted Baal'). The LXX translates the name as *Baal myian theon Akkarōn*, 'Baal the Fly God of Ekron' (2 Kgs 1:2–3, 6; cf. Josephus, *Ant.* 9.2.1), which is a contemptuous deformation of the Canaanite divine title. As *zebul* is used for both heaven and the temple, both understood as God's dwelling place, it is possible that the word 'Beelzebul' is a Greek version of *Beʻel Shemayin*, the Aramaic name for the chief god, Zeus Olympios, regarded by Jews as the chief demon. This interpretation fits verses 25, 27, where Jesus speaks of the earth as Satan's house. The Jerusalem scribes challenge Jesus' authority over demons, indisputably visible in the dramatic exorcisms, by attributing the source of Jesus' power to Satan. They accuse Jesus of sorcery, a charge which, if it could be proven before a court of law, would carry the death sentence. The suggestion that Jesus' ability to drive out demons derives from a satanic source has been falsified in 1:24: the demons themselves acknowledge that Jesus has nothing in common with them; they know more than the Jerusalem scribes do. In verses 23–30, Jesus refutes the charge himself, directly and in more detail.

23. Jesus *called them over to him*, initiating a direct conversation with the Jerusalem scribes. The Greek term *parabolē* ('parables') refers to 'a narrative or saying of varying length, designed to illustrate a truth especially through comparison or simile', and can be translated as 'comparison, illustration, parable, proverb, maxim' (BDAG, p. 759) and, also, as metaphor, simile, figure of speech, similitude, analogy or riddle, depending on the context and the literary theory that interpreters presuppose (see Context for 4:1–34). The meaning here is illustration, analogy, perhaps even riddle (Strauss). A parable uses figurative rather than explicit speech. Jesus' use of figurative speech in controversies with opponents reflects a prudential move: enigmatic language is less dangerous than straight speech. Jesus asserts in 4:11–12 that he uses explicit speech for 'insiders' and parables for 'outsiders', of which the Jerusalem scribes who accuse him of being empowered by Satan are extreme representatives.

Jesus first refutes the scribes' accusation in explicit, non-figurative speech, by pointing out its absurdity: *How can Satan drive out Satan?* Jesus identifies Beelzebul of verse 22 as Satan, not as a lesser demon, and he describes the act of exorcizing a demon as 'driving out Satan' since Satan, the chief demon, controls the lesser demons. Jesus implies that the fate of the demons whom he drives out determines the fate of Satan, the chief demon. In the context of Jesus' foundational confrontation with Satan in 1:12–13 (a victorious encounter, as the context of 1:9–11 indicates), Jesus' confrontations with demons are confrontations with Satan. Jesus asserts that it is absurd to assume that Satan drives himself out of the people he controls. The fact that Satan is driven out as demons are driven out 'is *prima facie* evidence of divine presence' (Marcus, p. 273).

24–26. The underlying argument of the analogies in these verses is the principle that power and survival depend on unity. A *kingdom* (Gr. *basileia*; cf. 1:15) that is *divided against itself*, fractured into warring parties, will not survive. When Jeroboam and Rehoboam fought in a civil war, Israel fractured into a northern and a southern kingdom (1 Kgs 12). The *kingdom* of Satan is doomed if Satan subdues other demons. A *house* (Gr. *oikia*) or dynasty in which rival claimants to the throne fight against each other will not survive. When the Hasmoneans Aristobulus II and Hyrcanus II vied for the throne, the kingdom of Judea was taken over by the Roman general Pompey with hardly a fight (Josephus, *Ant.* 14.34–77; Strauss). The same holds true if *oikia* is understood as referring to a household: a family will not prosper if there is infighting among the family members. The application of the two analogies to the question of the authority of Satan, and of Jesus, is self-evident. If *Satan has risen up against himself* (NRSV) and if his dominion has become *divided*, he *cannot stand* and his *end has come*. Satan himself will not work towards his own end. If his kingdom is under attack, it is not from the inside, but from the outside. Satan's dominion is not self-destructing: it is destroyed by a greater power, which can only be the power of God. This is what is in fact happening, as the following illustrates.

27. The parable of the strong man refers to two persons: a *strong man* and a thief ('thief' is not actually used in the story). The place of action is the *house* in which the strong man lives and the area outside his house where the thief is located. The action of the story is straightforward: the thief ties up the strong man, enters the house and steals the contents of the house. The latter two actions are only possible if the first action has been successfully completed. The explanation of the parable is obvious from the context. The *strong man* is Satan; the *house* is his dominion over people whom he controls through lesser demons; the man who has the power to bind the strong man is Jesus; the strong man's possessions are the people who are demon-possessed and whom Jesus rescues. Jesus' exorcisms prove that he has subdued Satan. The implication is that Satan's power has come to an end (v. 26) and that the kingdom of God (1:14–15) is established in the ministry of Jesus.

28–30. The solemn opening *truly I tell you* (*truly* translates the Greek term *amēn*)[44] reflects Jesus' claim to unique authority. In the Old Testament, the Hebrew term *'āmēn* is employed as an affirmative response[45] or the conclusion of a doxology.[46] The only non-responsorial *'āmēn* in the Old Testament is in Isaiah 65:16, where God is called 'God of the Amen' (Hebr. *'ĕlōhê 'āmēn*; NIV 'the one true God'; NRSV 'the God of faithfulness'; NASB 'the God of truth'). There is no parallel to Jesus' introductory, non-responsorial *amen* in pre-Christian Jewish literature. Jesus speaks in his own name; his words are truth, like Yahweh's words in Israel's history and in the Scriptures.

Jesus asserts that *people* (lit. 'sons of men'; i.e. humanity) can receive forgiveness for *all their sins*, including *blasphemies* (NRSV). For the term 'blasphemy' see on 2:7. The plural refers to various acts of speech that constitute blasphemy and that God forgives. But there is no forgiveness for a person who *blasphemes against the Holy Spirit*. The next two clauses formulate negatively and positively the ultimate fate of the people who commit this sin. They *will never be forgiven*: God will never forgive them their blasphemy against the Holy Spirit; *they are guilty of an eternal sin*: their liability to be punished for this particular sin will never come to an end. The guilt attached to this sin has eternal consequences; the liability is eternal punishment

---

44. Cf. 8:12; 9:1, 41; 10:15, 29; 11:23; 12:43; 13:30; 14:9, 18, 25, 30.
45. Cf. Num. 5:22; Deut. 27:15–26; 1 Kgs 1:36; Jer. 11:5; 28:6; Neh. 5:13; 8:6.
46. Cf. Pss 41:13; 72:19; 89:52; 106:48; 1 Chr. 16:36.

beyond the present life. In the context of the Jerusalem scribes' assertion concerning Jesus' authority (v. 22), the sin of blaspheming against the Holy Spirit is the allegation that Jesus drives out demons empowered by Satan. Jesus does not directly accuse the scribes of this unforgivable sin, but Mark clarifies in the editorial comment of verse 30 that Jesus' statement about the sin of blasphemy against the Holy Spirit that cannot be forgiven was directed against the Jerusalem scribes. Their claim that Jesus has an *impure spirit* implies the refusal to acknowledge that Jesus is empowered by God's Spirit (cf. 1:8, 10, 12–13). Rather than acknowledge the self-evident fact, as demonstrated in verses 23–27, that God's power is at work in Jesus' exorcisms, they deny that God's kingdom is coming in Jesus' ministry, preferring to believe that Satan visibly displays his power in the towns of Galilee. People who deny the reality of God's presence in Jesus' ministry have nowhere to go when they need forgiveness for their sins.

c. Jesus' true family and the outsiders (3:31–35)

31–32. The earlier scene of Jesus' family wanting to restrain Jesus because they believed that he was out of his mind (v. 21) is picked up as *Jesus' mother and brothers* arrive in front of the house in which Jesus is teaching (v. 20). Mary, Jesus' mother, is mentioned by name in 6:3, as are his brothers Jacob, Joseph, Judas and Simon. The term *brothers* implies that Mary had conceived again and that Jesus had siblings.[47] The absence of Joseph, who would be expected to lead the expedition to retrieve Jesus, suggests that he was no longer alive. Jesus' family stands *outside* while Jesus is inside the house, surrounded

---

47. Cf. Matt. 1:25: Joseph 'did not consummate their marriage until' she had given birth to Jesus. Based on the theory that Mary remained perpetually a virgin, (Roman Catholic) church tradition has interpreted Jesus' 'brothers' as 'stepbrothers', sons of an earlier marriage of Joseph, or as 'cousins' (Mary's sister, also called Mary, marries either Clopas [John 19:25] or Alphaeus [Mark 3:18]). The latter interpretation is exegetically improbable and dogmatically unnecessary, and has been abandoned by most scholars. For the possibility that 'brothers' refers to Joseph's sons from an earlier marriage, see 6:3.

by people who witnessed the debate with the scribes. Someone informs Jesus that his mother and brothers are outside *looking* for him.

33–35. The rhetorical question of verse 33 challenges the crowd to absorb the impact of Jesus' statement. Those *seated in a circle* around Jesus are not merely the Twelve but the crowd of verse 32, the wider group of Jesus' followers who listen to his teaching. Jesus gestures towards the people sitting around him and asserts that they are all *my mother and my brothers*; that is, his true family, a close-knit fellowship of people who share a common identity, which is clarified in the final sentence of the scene: *Whoever does God's will is my brother and sister and mother*. The foundational description of Jesus' preaching in 1:14–15, which includes the only general summons so far, explains what Jesus means. Doing the will of God is now intricately and consistently linked with the good news of the fulfilment of God's promises, with the coming of the kingdom of God, and with the summons to repentance and belief in the good news. The Pharisees, the Jerusalem scribes and Jesus' family have not accepted the good news of the coming of God's kingdom in Jesus' ministry and thus do not belong to the circle of Jesus' true family. The earlier reference to Jesus' mother and brothers does not prepare the reader for the explicit reference to 'sister', which reflects the fact that Jesus' followers included not only men but also women. In 15:40–41 Mark will mention Mary Magdalene, Mary the mother of Jacob/James and Joseph, and Salome. Luke mentions Mary Magdalene, from whom seven demons had been exorcized; Joanna the wife of Chuza, the manager of Herod's household; Susanna; 'and many others' who were 'with Jesus' and who supported Jesus and the Twelve (Luke 8:2–3).

Theology

Jesus' exorcism of demons is visible evidence of the presence of the power of God in his ministry, demonstrating the authority of Jesus and the collapse of the dominion of Satan on account of the arrival of God's kingdom. Jesus' exorcisms signal the terminal decline of Satan's power. The Jerusalem scribes do not share this conclusion: they choose to 'explain' Jesus as tapping into Satan's power. In later rabbinic polemic, Jesus continues to be accused as a sorcerer,[48] indicating that in dialogues between Jews and Christians, the identity of Jesus continued (and continues) to be the key stumbling block. The unforgivable sin against the Spirit is the sin of refusing to acknowledge the presence of God's power in Jesus' ministry and the perversion of the truth about the origin of Jesus' authority, ascribing the latter to Satan. People who link Jesus with Satan will not receive God's forgiveness. People who seek to determine what Jesus should and should not do, like Jesus' mother and brothers, do not belong to the new community that is created by the coming of the kingdom of God. Those who follow Jesus, who listen to his proclamation, and who accept his authority over demons as divine authority and his teaching as the will of God, like the crowd in the house and like the Twelve, constitute the true family of Jesus the Messiah.

iv. Parables about the kingdom of God (4:1–34)
Context
The first main block of Jesus' teaching consists of three parables and two analogies: the parable of the four soils (4:1–20), the analogy of the lamp (4:21–23), the analogy of the measure (4:24–25), the parable of the growing seed (4:26–29) and the parable of the mustard seed (4:30–34). Jesus' explanation of why he speaks in parables in 4:11–12 focuses on the 'secret of the kingdom of God', the first reference to the kingdom of God since 1:15. This first main block of Jesus' teaching is a discourse about the kingdom of God.

There is a second theme that the first parable of the section addresses: the varied response to Jesus' ministry. Jesus' teaching, exorcisms and healings had created widespread excitement in Galilee and in the entire territory of King Herod's former kingdom and beyond (1:22, 28, 32–33, 37, 45; 2:1–2, 12; 3:7–8, 10–11, 20). The excitement ranged from popular enthusiasm to the commitment of initially five, then twelve followers who accepted Jesus' call to stay with him and be trained for active involvement in his ministry. At the same time there was intense opposition (2:6–7, 18, 23–24; 3:1–4,

---

48. Cf. *b. Sanh.* 43a, 107b; *b. Shab.* 104b. Early Christian writers address this standard Jewish polemic; cf. Justin, *Dial.* 69; Origen, *Cels.* 1.6.

6, 21–22). The parable of the four soils explains why Jesus' proclamation of the good news of the coming of the kingdom of God is not universally and joyfully accepted but paradoxically met with puzzlement, lack of understanding, disregard, antagonism and fierce resistance.

Jesus teaches in parables (on the term *parabolē* see 3:23). The section includes three specific parables (4:3–8, 26–29, 30–32) and two analogies (4:21–23, 24–25) as well as teaching about the nature and the purpose of Jesus' parables (4:10–13, 33–34). The Sunday school definition of a parable as 'an earthly story with a heavenly meaning' is inadequate. Jesus' parables are not simple illustrations of theological truths or moral behaviour: they often confuse, shock and challenge the listener and reader. The parables transport meaning by means of a story. Their meaning is not immediately understood but requires insight as it lies 'in' or 'above' the story. The meaning is not exhausted by cognitive understanding: the parables push listeners and readers towards a personal response at the level of attitude, will and action. Jesus' parables have been compared to modern political cartoons which require prior knowledge of the persons depicted in the cartoons that want to elicit a response and, ideally, subsequent action (Moule, 'Mark 4:1–20', pp. 96–97).

Earlier generations of interpreters followed A. Jülicher, who had argued in a two-volume work on Jesus' parables (1886/1899) that a parable is a story taken from everyday life, that an allegory is an artificially constructed story, that Jesus' parables are not allegories and that Jesus' parables communicate one single truth. This theory has been critiqued and abandoned by many if not most scholars today, both in the light of modern literary study of metaphors and in the light of more than three hundred rabbinic parables which usually contain allegorical elements and application of more than one 'point' that the parable teaches (Weder, *Gleichnisse*, pp. 11–98; Blomberg, *Parables*, pp. 13–167). As regards the allegorical elements, the suggestion that they should be related to the main characters of the parables, as modelled in the rabbinic parables (Blomberg, *Parables*, p. 166), is plausible. Just as rabbinic parables usually contain two or three main characters, contrasting the wise with the foolish, often with God evaluating and judging their respective behaviour as a third 'character' in the story, Jesus' parables commonly, although not invariably, have a triadic structure which suggests that the message of his parables is tied to the main characters.

Two principles need to be kept in mind when interpreting Jesus' parables. First, since the coming of the kingdom of God is the foundational content of Jesus' preaching (1:14–15; cf. 9:1; 10:14), Jesus' parables must be related both to his message of the kingdom of God and to his ministry in which he proclaimed the kingdom of God and demonstrated its presence in exorcisms and healings. Second, the specific elements of Jesus' parables, including the allegorical elements, must be related to the context of Jesus' ministry and of the message of the kingdom of God, not to the context of the later church or the church today. We can apply Jesus' parables to the church today only *after* we have interpreted them in the context of Jesus' ministry.

Comment
a. *Parable of the four soils and true seeing (4:1–20)*

1–2. Jesus teaches *again* by the Sea of Galilee, as he had done before (cf. 1:16; 2:13; 3:7). Jesus' *teaching* (cf. 1:21–22; 2:13) is his proclamation of the coming of the kingdom of God (1:14–15), conveyed in this scene *by parables* (3:23; see Context above for details). The *boat* that was mentioned in 3:9 is now used as a mobile speaker's platform. Jesus was sitting in the boat some distance from the shore, the boat presumably being manned by the disciples (at least the four fishermen of 1:16–20), while *the biggest crowd yet* (translation of Marcus, p. 291) was sitting *along the shore at the water's edge* (lit. 'beside the sea on the land', NRSV). Mark again underlines Jesus' popularity, his teaching as a central part of his ministry, and specifically his teaching in parables.

3–8. The parable of the four soils is traditionally called 'the parable of the sower' since a sower is mentioned in the first sentence. However, the sower is not very important in the story, and not identified in the interpretation in verses 13–20. The focus in the story and in the interpretation is the four different soils and their different responses to the seed, which explains our title for the parable.

The introductory *Listen!* summons the listeners to pay attention, a theme that is repeatedly emphasized in this section (4:9, 15–16,

18, 20, 23–24). The one person mentioned in the parable is *a sower*.[49] In the process of sowing, some *seed* fell *along the path*, outside the prepared soil, where it would not be ploughed in but was exposed to the *birds* that promptly *came and ate it up*. Other seed fell on *rocky places*, areas with little topsoil. The initial success, described with the phrase *it sprang up quickly*, gave way to failure *when the sun came up*, at the time of intense heat, which *scorched* the plants that *withered because they had no root*. Other seed fell among *thorns*, which allowed the germinated seed to grow together with the thorns, which *choked* the plants that were not able to produce a crop due to the lack of light and nourishment. In Lower Galilee, different soil types are represented, often within the area of a single settlement, ideal for some but not for other crops.[50] There is a progression in the three failed seeds: the first never germinates, the second germinates but dies, while the third germinates and grows into a plant but does not produce any grain.

Other seed fell on *good soil* where normal growth was possible and successful, as described with three verbs: the seed *came up* – it germinated; it *grew* – it developed into a plant; it *produced a crop* – it generated grain. The crop yield is described as *some multiplying thirty, some sixty, some a hundred times*. The argument that the parable indicates miraculous growth since normal yields would be in the order of five- or tenfold at most works if it is assumed that the figures given refer to the number of bushels harvested per bushel sown. Since the story mentions seeds, not bushels, it is preferable to assume that Jesus speaks of the number of grains per plant; a hundred grains or more per plant is a good yield, but not abnormally high.

9. The exhortation *Whoever has ears to hear, let them hear* summons listeners to discern and apply the meaning of the parable. Jesus

---

49. NIV, NLT translate 'a farmer'; the Greek term *ho speirōn* specifically refers to someone who is sowing seed.

50. A. Choi, in Fiensy and Strange, *Galilee*, I, pp. 302–304: wheat and barley are grown on Pale Rendzina soils which are shallow to moderately deep, and frequently micronutrient-deficient; Terra Rossa is shallow to moderately deep as well but gravelly to a limited degree; Basalt-derived soils are shallow, with basalt rock protrusions.

challenges the crowds (v. 2) to discover the meaning of the story and to ascertain which of the soils describes their life. As verses 10–12 will show, not everyone has ears to hear; not everybody will benefit from the parable.

10–12. After the crowd had left and Jesus was back on shore, *the Twelve and the others around him* asked him about *the parables*, perhaps about the meaning of this particular parable, or about the reason for teaching by parables, or about the relationship between the parables and the kingdom of God. Jesus responds by explaining who understands and who does not understand his parables, which he supports with a scriptural quotation, before interpreting the parable of the four soils in verses 13–20. The *secret of the kingdom of God* is privileged information about the coming of God's kingdom (1:15) that not everyone possesses.[51] The Greek term *mystērion* is most plausibly understood in the context of its use in Daniel. The Aramaic term *rāz*, translated in the LXX as *mystērion*, refers to the interpretation of Nebuchadnezzar's dream which is a 'secret' in that it is hidden from Babylon's wise men but revealed by God to Daniel, who explains, 'not because I have greater wisdom than anyone else alive, but so that Your Majesty may know the interpretation' (Dan. 2:30; cf. 2:18–19, 27–30, 47; cf. Amos 3:7). The *secret of the kingdom of God* is privileged information about the nature of the kingdom of God proclaimed by Jesus and about the paradoxical effect of the present reality of the kingdom in Jesus' ministry – privileged information that can be known only as the result of divine revelation. Jesus asserts that the secret of the kingdom of God *has been given to you*: the disciples know the privileged information (perfect tense of the verb) about the coming of God's kingdom since God has revealed it to them (divine passive). *You* is the Twelve and other followers (v. 10). They are the 'insiders', the recipients who have been given insight into the nature of the coming of God's kingdom.

---

51. If the Greek *mystērion* is translated as 'mystery' (KJV, NASB), the connotation is one of incomprehensibility, which is not in view here. The translation 'secret' connotes hiddenness of information that has not been divulged, without the implication that the content is (esoteric) knowledge that is not to be publicly shared or a puzzle that is hard to grasp.

In contrast, *those on the outside* do not have access to the privileged information about God's kingdom. The 'outsiders' (*hoi exō*) are all who are 'outside' the circle of Jesus' true family (3:31–35). To 'outsiders', *everything is said in parables*, which indicates that the parables do not communicate the secret of the kingdom of God. The parables are not 'helpful illustrations' that reveal the secret of the kingdom of God to people who have difficulties understanding Jesus' teaching. They do not help outsiders become insiders.

Jesus cites an abbreviated form of Isaiah 6:9–10 which seems to suggest that the purpose of Jesus' teaching in parables is the concealment of the secret of the kingdom of God with regard to the outsiders. The conjunction *hina* ('so that') at the beginning of the quotation constitutes a conundrum that prompts some to regard the statement as one of the most difficult passages in the New Testament, seemingly suggesting that Jesus teaches in parables in order to blind the eyes of his listeners. Numerous interpretations have been suggested to come to terms with Jesus' statement. The most natural sense of *hina* is to express purpose which needs to be understood, however, in the narrative context of Isaiah 5 – 6 and Mark 3 – 4. Isaiah portrays God as the owner of the 'vineyard' (Israel) which has failed to produce fruit. Israel is unfaithful, so God will allow the Assyrians to bring divine judgment on Israel; Isaiah's words of warning fall on deaf ears because Israel is unfaithful to Yahweh and because Yahweh has pronounced judgment. Jesus asserts that God acts in the present as he has acted in the past. Some people are *seeing* what happens in his ministry of exorcisms and healings, but they are *never perceiving* what this means. They may be *hearing* Jesus' message of the kingdom of God and listening to his parables, but they are *never understanding* the presence of the kingdom in Jesus' ministry. If they did perceive and understand, they would *turn and be forgiven*. The fact that Israel broke God's covenant explains why God's message was met with indifference. When people attribute what Jesus says and does to demonic authority or to Jesus' (allegedly disturbed) state of mind, they do not perceive or understand God's presence in his preaching, exorcisms and healings, which results in divine judgment. Jesus' pronouncement that his teaching in parables before outsiders hides the truth about the kingdom of God presupposes the *result* of their rejection of his words and deeds. Its *purpose* now is 'to blind them to the truth so that they will inadvertently fulfil God's plan of redemption in the death of Jesus' (Strauss, p. 186). At the same time, the parable of the lamp and its explanation by Jesus in verses 21–22, emphasizing that what is now hidden must be brought to light, suggests that the verdict of verses 11–12 may be only temporary, leaving hope that the outsiders 'need not be permanently written off, that the division between insiders and outsiders is not a gulf without bridges' (France, p. 201).

13–20. Jesus' interpretation of the parable is not as unusual as some assume; in Mark's Gospel see also 3:27; 4:22, 25; 7:18–23; 12:10–11; 13:29, 32–33, 35–37. Private explanations of important pronouncements are found in 7:17–23; 8:16–21; 10:10–12; 13:3–37; for explanations of actions of Jesus see 9:28–29; 11:21–25. The question *Don't you understand this parable?* implies that the Twelve and other followers who had asked about Jesus' parables (v. 10) specifically enquired about the meaning of the parable of the four soils. They have been given the privileged information about the kingdom of God, but that does not mean that they have complete understanding of everything that Jesus says and does. The disciples' lack of understanding is a recurrent theme (cf. 4:40; 6:52; 7:18; 8:17–18, 32; 9:19, 32). The question *How then will you understand any parable?* suggests that the parable of the four soils is the key to all other parables and thus the key to understanding the paradox of the presence of the kingdom of God in Jesus' ministry, which is accompanied by resistance and hostility.

Jesus does not identify the *sower* who, in the context of growing opposition, is Jesus himself. Jesus identifies the seed as *the word (ho logos)* which, in the context of Jesus' ministry, is the 'good news' of the coming of the kingdom of God (1:14–15; cf. 2:2), including his teaching in parables (v. 2). God's kingdom comes through the word of Jesus' proclamation, not through military force as many Jews expected. While Jesus' exorcisms and healings display in dramatic fashion God's power, God's kingdom is most authentically connected with the word of Jesus' preaching the good news.

The *seed along the path* are people who *hear* the word, who hear Jesus' proclamation of the good news of the kingdom of God, but from whom *Satan* immediately *comes and takes away the word that was sown in them*. Just as the seed along the path fails to germinate and is lost, there are people who hear but do not understand, with the result that Satan, whom Jesus defeats in exorcisms (3:23–27), is active in their lives and prevents them perceiving the presence of God's authority in Jesus' ministry.

The second group of people are the *seed sown on rocky places*. These are people who *hear the word*, who *at once receive it with joy*, but who *last only a short time*. Their response is more promising, they are joyfully enthusiastic about Jesus, but their commitment is short-lived. The heat of the sun that scorches the plants growing in shallow soil is identified with *trouble or persecution because of the word*. The growing and increasingly official opposition to Jesus causes people to have second thoughts. They re-evaluate their enthusiasm triggered by Jesus' miracles in the light of pressure from the Jewish authorities and Jesus' challenges to traditional norms of behaviour (note the controversies about the Sabbath and purity), and so *they quickly fall away*: they stop listening to Jesus.

The third group of people are *like seed sown among thorns*. These are people who also *hear the word*, who listen to Jesus' preaching, but *the worries of this life*, the concerns and anxieties of the present evil age, *the deceitfulness of wealth*, the seduction that comes from affluence with its illusion of security, and *the desires for other things*, the constant pursuit of material possessions, *come in and choke the word*. These followers of Jesus allow secular values to undermine their loyalty to Jesus and to the kingdom of God, with the result that they are *unfruitful*. Fruitfulness is conformity to the values of the kingdom of God that Jesus proclaims.

The fourth group of people is *like seed sown on good soil*. These are the people who *hear the word* – who listen to Jesus' preaching – and who *accept it* – who acknowledge the presence of the kingdom of God in Jesus' ministry. True followers of Jesus *produce a crop*: they bear fruit, which is described with a repetition of the varying yields. The listener has to decide what the 'fruit' may be and whether the different yields have any significance (see Theology below). The lack of identification of the fruit and the yields proves that the interpretation of the parable is far removed from the 'allegorizing' that Mark is often accused of, and it confirms that the allegorical elements of the interpretation consistently focus on the three main characters of the parable: the sower sowing seed, the unfruitful seed (with three types of soil) and the fruitful seed (with three levels of yield). Jesus proclaims the good news of the coming of the kingdom of God. There are people who hear his preaching but do not accept it: they reject it, they do not allow it to penetrate, they refuse to allow its force to affect and change their lives. And there are people who hear his preaching and accept it and are committed to it, following Jesus.

b. Analogy of the lamp and disclosure (4:21–23)

21. The analogy of the lamp is formulated with a double question which expects a negative and a positive answer respectively. The audience indicated by *them* may be the disciples and other committed followers (v. 10) or, which is more plausible in the light of verses 2, 33–34, the crowds. The seemingly awkward Greek formulation *the lamp comes in*[52] alerts the reader to the symbolic nature of the statement. A *lamp* (*lychnos*) is a clay or metal lamp filled with olive oil, usually placed on a 'lampstand' (*lychnia*) to light rooms after sundown. Clay lamps were manufactured in Galilean workshops, but Galilean Jews, to a surprising degree, imported the new Herodian lamps from Jerusalem workshops; the lamps were characterized by a knife-pared nozzle, a simple style and no or minimal decoration.[53] The *bowl* (Gr. *modios*; Lat. *modius*; NRSV 'bushel basket') is a grain measure holding 16 *sextarii* or about 1.92 gallons (8.75 l). The term generally translated *bed* (Gr. *klinē*) is also used for dining couches. It is self-evident that no one would ever place a lamp under a container or under a bed or couch. Lamps are meant to give as much light as possible. No one hides a light. The unexpected use of the personal verb in the phrase *the lamp comes in* has been interpreted as a figure for Jesus himself, whose light shines despite his temporary hiddenness; this is a plausible, but not a necessary, interpretation. The context suggests that the light of the lamp represents the revelation of the secret of the kingdom of God, which is not meant to be kept hidden but made available as widely as possible (France).

22–23. The proverbial application is now formulated with a double statement. Things that are *hidden* (*krypton*) are meant to be

---

52. NIV has *you bring in a lamp*, NRSV 'a lamp brought in'.
53. M. A. Chancey, in Fiensy and Strange, *Galilee*, I, p. 120.

disclosed, and things that are *concealed* (*apokryphon*) are meant to be *brought out into the open*. Jesus asserts that the present hiddenness serves *the purpose of* revelation. This fits Jesus' statement in verses 11–12 about the nature of his parables: his disciples and other committed followers understand the parables as descriptions of the coming of the kingdom of God; those who do not follow Jesus do not perceive the truth of the kingdom and of Jesus. This blindness to the 'light' of Jesus' words and deeds, and the resulting rejection of Jesus, are part of God's salvation purposes (cf. 8:31; 9:31; 10:33–34). God will reveal the present secret of the kingdom of God (v. 11) one day – in the disciples' preaching following Jesus' resurrection, as 9:9 suggests (Marcus, *Mystery*, pp. 143–150). The summons to *hear* (cf. v. 9) challenges the disciples and other committed followers, who are being given special insight by God, carefully to discern the meaning of the analogy of the lamp.

c. Analogy of the measure and revelation (4:24–25)

24. The analogy of the measure is introduced with the summons to *see what you hear*.[54] The combination of the visual and aural senses underscores the importance of paying attention to what Jesus says. Hearing alone is not sufficient: one needs to pay careful attention to what is heard when Jesus speaks of the kingdom of God in parables. The proverbial saying *With the measure you use, it will be measured to you*, which reflects language used in commercial grain contracts, is used here not in terms of the appropriateness of God's judgment (thus Matt. 7:2 and in Jewish literature, where the 'two measures' are judgment and mercy) nor in terms of encouraging generosity in giving (cf. Luke 6:37–38). Mark uses the principle of 'measure for measure' with reference to carefully hearing what Jesus says about the kingdom of God when he speaks in parables. The willingness and the effort that are necessary for paying close attention to Jesus' parables will be proportionately rewarded. The next phrase *and still more will be given you* (NRSV) underscores the

---

54. The initial imperative is translated as 'consider carefully' (NIV), 'pay attention' (GNB, NRSV) or 'take care' (NASB), which loses the visual sense of the verb *blepō* ('to see').

positive, rich reward that comes from careful consideration of Jesus' parables.

25. Jesus formulates with another proverb the principle of reciprocity and of God's generosity that goes beyond strict equality. The expression *whoever has* refers to the disciples and the committed followers of Jesus who have heard and responded to Jesus' words and deeds, who have at least an initial understanding of his parables, the God-given capacity to receive the word (v. 11). The promise *will be given more* asserts that a positive response to Jesus will lead to even greater insight into the coming of the kingdom of God as the disciples hear and understand Jesus' parables. The phrase *whoever does not have* refers to those who do not have a true understanding of Jesus' words and deeds and who thus do not understand the parables either. The assertion *even what they have will be taken from them* formulates the effect of Jesus' teaching in parables: their lack of understanding increases their perplexity concerning Jesus' words and deeds. They see but do not perceive; they hear but do not understand (v. 12). Their blindness with regard to the truth of Jesus and the coming of the kingdom of God increases. Their encounter with God's presence in Jesus' ministry, which they do not understand, undermines any benefit which they should have gained.

d. Parable of the growing seed (4:26–29)

26. Jesus introduces the second parable with a formula that provides an explicit explanation of the reference of the parable: *This is what the kingdom of God is like*. The comparison is directed not to the man who scatters seed, but to the whole story that is being told. The story is simple. It begins with a *man* who *scatters seed on the ground*, presumably seeds of wheat or barley. Throughout the story the farmer is inactive, until the very end when the time for harvesting has come.

27–29. The farmer goes about his daily life without intervening in the germination of the seed and the growth of the plants. The remark that *the seed sprouts and grows* is explained with four expressions. The seed grows *night and day*; that is, continually, without interruption. It grows *whether he sleeps or gets up*; that is, independently of the farmer's actions. It grows *though he does not know how*: the farmer cannot explain how seeds germinate in the soil and grow plants producing grain. The growth of the seed in the soil happens *all by itself* (Gr. *automatē*), without visible cause, without the farmer handling and manipulating *the stalk*, the early grass-like stages of the grain, or *the ear*, the fruiting spike of the cereal grain, or *the full grain in the ear*, the fully ripened grain. When *the corn is ripe*, the man *puts the sickle to it*: he harvests that grain, *because the harvest has come*.

The context in Mark, and the reference to the kingdom of God in verse 26, alert Jesus' listeners and Mark's readers to the symbolism of the man who scatters seed: God has initiated the coming of his kingdom, and Jesus proclaims the kingdom of God. In view of Jesus' recruitment of disciples, who are being trained to extend his ministry (3:13–19), the man scattering seed also depicts the missionary activity of the Twelve and other followers of Jesus. The parable emphasizes the way the seed grows – not only during the day when the farmer is active but also by night when he sleeps; not as the result of the farmer's intervention but 'automatically'. The way the parable depicts the growth of the seed underscores the reality of the presence of God's kingdom despite its hidden nature, unrecognized by the Jewish leaders and Jesus' own family, as well as the certainty of future consummation when people will 'see that the kingdom of God has come with power' (9:1). The kingdom of God is a dynamic reality that has an inherent power which will ensure its consummation. The final clause echoes Joel 3:13 (LXX 4:13) and thus suggests that even if Jesus and his followers experience trials and suffering, the consummation of the kingdom will bring salvation and, for the enemies, judgment.

e. Parable of the mustard seed (4:30–34)

30–32. The two introductory questions alert the reader to expect another parable that describes what *the kingdom of God is like*. Jesus compares the kingdom of God to a *mustard seed*. The mustard (*sinapi*) in question is probably black mustard (*brassica nigra*), which could grow to a height of 10 feet (3 m) or more.[55] Pliny describes the use

---

55. *m. Kil.* 1:2, 5 distinguishes mustard (*khardal*; Lat. *brassica nigra*), Egyptian mustard (*khardal mitsry*; Lat. *sinapis alba*) and wild mustard (*laphsan*; Lat. *sinapis arvensis*).

of mustard to treat serpent and scorpion bites, toothache, indigestion, asthma, epilepsy, constipation, dropsy, lethargy, tetanus, leprous sores and other illnesses (*Nat.* 20.236–240). The seed of the mustard plant is described as *the smallest of all seeds on earth*. The smallness of the mustard seed was proverbial.[56] Mark describes the growth of the small seed which *becomes the largest of all garden plants* with reference to *big branches* on which *birds* (lit. 'birds of the sky'; i.e. wild birds) can nest. The large mustard shrub stands out among the garden plants.

The parable emphasizes the difference between insignificant beginnings and the impressively large end result. Jesus' followers know that the small beginnings of Jesus' proclamation of the kingdom of God must not be despised. And they are reminded that they should not be impatient as they wait for the revelation of the majesty of God's kingdom. The reference to the *big branches* seems a deliberate exaggeration, which suggests that the nesting birds in the branches may allude to the imagery of impressive empires and 'great nations' in Ezekiel 17:23, 31:6 and Daniel 4:12, 21 (LXX 4:9, 18), indicating the future inclusion of Gentile nations in the kingdom of God. The ministry of Jesus in Galilee, however unimpressive its impact on Jewish society and however insignificant its scope in political terms, considering that Jesus proclaims the kingdom of God Almighty, will prove to be of ultimate, far-reaching significance.

33–34. Mark comments that Jesus proclaimed *the word*, the message of the kingdom of God (vv. 26, 30), regularly[57] with *parables*, indicating that the parables in verses 1–32 are only a selection. The phrase *so far as they were able to hear it* (NASB) means that not all who heard Jesus' parables had the capacity to understand and respond by seeking further insight into the kingdom of God. Mark informs his readers that Jesus' public teaching always involved *using a parable*, whereas in his private teaching to his own disciples *he explained everything*. When Mark records Jesus' public teaching before his arrival in

---

56. C.-H. Hunzinger, *TDNT*, VII, p. 289, assumes 725–760 mustard seeds to a gram (0.3 oz). In the Islamic world, the 'grain of mustard' (*khabba min khardal*) was the smallest unit of weight (c. 0.00002 oz [0.0007 g]).

57. The imperfect tenses of the verbs in 4:33–34 indicate ongoing practice.

Jerusalem, the focus is indeed on epigrammatic sayings (*parabolai* in the wider sense; cf. 3:23), with subsequent explanation for the disciples (7:14–15, 17–18; 10:5–9, 10–12). The rest of Jesus' teaching is directed to the disciples (with the exception of the public dialogues in ch. 12, which Mark may not regard as 'speaking the word' as such). However, since Mark did not record everything that Jesus said, it seems pedantic to assume that Jesus offered only a series of un-interpreted parables, analogies and riddles when he taught in Nazareth (6:2) and in the villages (6:6).

Theology
The parables in 4:1–34 explain the paradoxical fact that Jesus' proclamation of the kingdom of God is both welcomed and ignored, accepted and opposed. The parable of the four soils helps Jesus' followers understand the varying reactions to Jesus, which range from explicit hostility to Jesus' claims to enthusiastic reactions to Jesus' miracles and robust decisions to follow Jesus as disciples being trained by him. Hearing Jesus' message is not sufficient: hearing must turn into true understanding, experiential acceptance and permanent commitment – precisely the repentance and the faith that were an essential part of Jesus' message (1:14–15). Because not all are willing to listen and accept what Jesus says, his ministry, and his teaching in parables, creates a distinction between 'outsiders' who hear but do not understand and 'insiders' who hear and understand and gain further insight through instruction by Jesus. Understanding Jesus' parables and thus the presence of God in Jesus' ministry in word and deed requires divine insight that Jesus can provide. Being able to repent and have faith in Jesus is the result of divine grace.

The growth of the kingdom of God, the success of Jesus' preaching and, later, the success of the missionary work of the disciples is the sovereign work of God, not the result of human planning, strategic thinking, superior tactical decisions, better technology or personal ambition. The manner of the growth of God's kingdom and the coming of final redemption are beyond human control. This does not mean that Jesus' followers are inactive: Jesus has called the Twelve to be trained by him so that they can fulfil the task of fishing for people after he sends them out to extend his own ministry (1:17; 3:14–15). The disciples' responsibility is to preach and teach the good news of the kingdom of God, to exorcize demons and to heal. The germination and growth of the seed, which is the word of God, is God's responsibility and God's promise.

v. Demonstrations of Jesus' authority (4:35 – 5:43)
Context
Having explained the paradox of people's reactions to Jesus varying from excited enthusiasm to fierce rejection and the hidden reality of the growth of the kingdom of God, Mark relates further examples of Jesus' authority displayed in miracles. He begins by recounting the first nature miracle,[58] the calming of the storm on the Sea of Galilee (4:35–41), which prompts the disciples to ask who this man is who is able to control wind and water (4:41). Controlling the forces of nature is even more dramatic and inexplicable than exorcisms and healings. Two miracles of physical healing follow: the exorcism of demons in Gerasa (5:1–20) and the healing of the woman with a chronic haemorrhage (5:21–34). Mark concludes the section with a miracle that trumps the nature miracle at the beginning of the section: Jesus raises a dead girl (5:35–43), which reinforces the significance of the earlier question concerning Jesus' true identity.

Comment
a. Authority over nature: the storm (4:35–41)

35–36. The double temporal notice *that day when evening came* suggests to Mark's readers that Jesus' teaching in parables recorded in verses 1–34 took place on a single day on the shore of the Sea of Galilee near Capernaum. At the same time, the changes in audience in verses 1, 10, 26, 33–34 allow the possibility that at least part of the material in the preceding teaching section was organized thematically, drawing in teaching presented on other occasions. In the Greek text, Jesus *says* to his disciples that they will go to the other side of the lake. The present tense of the verb, translated as past tense in the English versions ('he said'), is a historical present tense, frequently employed by Mark to give the narrative a sense of vivid

---

58. For the other nature miracles see 6:30–44, 45–52; 8:1–13; 11:12–14, 21–23.

realism; when he reaches the climax of the story, he uses the aorist tense 'to indicate Jesus' decisive action' (France, p. 222). The geographical notice *to the other side* indicates the east shore of the Sea of Galilee, Capernaum being the point of reference. As 5:1 suggests, Jesus' next miracle took place in one of the cities of the Decapolis (cf. 1:9, 16; see 5:20; on the problem of the geographical setting see 5:1), which means that they travelled to the south-eastern shore of the lake, a distance of about 7 to 11 miles (12–18 km). The phrase *just as he was* suggests that Jesus and the disciples embarked for the east shore of the lake immediately after Jesus had finished teaching the crowds from the boat, without first returning to Capernaum. The phrase *other boats with him* refers presumably to the wider group of followers mentioned in verse 10 who follow Jesus and the disciples. These boats are not mentioned again in the subsequent narrative, as Mark is evidently not concerned about their fate (they may have returned to Capernaum as the storm was approaching, or they may have made it to the east shore of the lake).

37–38. A *windstorm* (NRSV; NIV 'squall'; lit. 'storm wind') can arise on the Sea of Galilee on account of its location in the Jordan Rift, about 3,000 feet (900 m) below the plateau of the Golan east of the lake. The possibility of sudden and violent storms is real.[59] Interpreters who speculate, on the basis of similar terms and phrases, that Mark's description of the storm has been inspired by literary antecedents such as Homer's *Odyssey* or by the story of Jonah, have probably never experienced a violent storm at sea in which their ship could have sunk. Storms that sink ships always involve strong, violent winds and high waves. Similar descriptions suggest comparable experiences, not literary dependence. Mark describes the storm as *great* (NIV 'furious'; the Greek expression is *lailaps megalē*, 'great storm'), its effect with the phrase *the waves broke over the boat*, and its danger with the notice that the boat *was nearly swamped*. The comment that Jesus was *in the stern, sleeping on a cushion*, remarkable in the

---

59. Cf. Aharoni, *Land*, p. 33: the Sea of Galilee (Chinnereth) is 'famous for its sudden storms which blow down from the surrounding mountains and transform it into a boiling cauldron'. Cf. Murphy-O'Connor, *Holy Land*, p. 464.

circumstances, plausibly reflects personal memory of the event. The boat evidently had a platform at the stern of the boat where the helmsman was stationed, with an area underneath that provided some protection from the elements; the article of the Greek *hē prymna* ('the cushion') suggests a standard part of the boat's equipment, perhaps a sandbag used for ballast. The contrast with the disciples' panic is striking. Mark does not say whether Jesus' sleep was due to physical exhaustion after teaching for several hours, or whether it was caused by 'the untroubled serenity of divine omnipotence' (France, p. 223; Strauss, p. 207, thinks of restful sleep despite danger as indicating trust in God; cf. Pss 3:5; 4:8; Prov. 3:24). The panic-stricken disciples woke Jesus, addressing him as *teacher*, which reflects their relationship. The address is not banal: people had commented earlier on the relationship between Jesus' teaching and his authority, especially his authority to drive out demons (1:22, 27). The disciples' question *don't you care if we drown?* is formulated as an accusation, although it is probably a cry for help. They do not explicitly ask for a miracle but, since they have seen his power over demons and illness, they take it for granted that Jesus has a solution in this situation as well.

39. Mark describes Jesus' actions with three verbs: he *got up*, he *rebuked the wind* and he *said to the waves, 'Quiet! Be still!'* Jesus treats the forces of nature as if they are wild animals which he can control (cf. 1:13), or like demons which he can drive out and silence (cf. 1:25).[60] Jesus' words have an instantaneous, dramatic effect: *the wind died down* and *it was completely calm* (lit. 'there was a great calm'; ESV, RSV); that is, the high waves subsided. The Greek phrase *galēnē megalē* ('great calm') stands in deliberate, stark contrast to the *lailaps megalē* ('great storm') of verse 37. Jesus' explicit and effective rebuking of the wind and silencing of the waves is reminiscent of Old Testament

---

60. The fact that the verbs *epitimaō* ('to rebuke') and *phimoō* ('to silence') occur in 4:39 and in 1:25 does not signal that Mark portrays the raging sea as a demonic force (as in Near Eastern mythology) and the calming of the storm as an 'exorcism'. The language of rebuke appears in different contexts (8:30–33; 10:13, 48), and Jesus commands not only demons to be silent (cf. 1:44; 5:43; 7:36; 8:30; 9:9).

passages in which Yahweh, the Lord of creation, rebukes the waters and the waves obey (Pss 18:15; 106:9; Isa. 50:2; Nah. 1:4), commands the sea and silences the waves (Pss 89:9; 107:23–29).

40–41. The scene ends with the first of a series of rebukes of the disciples by Jesus (cf. 7:18; 8:17–18, 21, 32–33; 9:19), formulated as two questions, and the disciples' reaction to the miracle, also formulated as a question. Jesus' first question, *Why are you so afraid?*, challenges the disciples to evaluate their reaction to the storm and to the danger of drowning. Fear as a response to physical danger is natural, but fear in Jesus' physical presence is unnecessary. This is underscored by the second question, *Do you still have no faith? Faith* (*pistis*), as in 2:5 (and 5:34; 10:52; 11:22), is confidence in Jesus' supernatural power. If Jesus' ministry is indeed intimately connected with the coming kingdom of God, if Jesus is the Holy One of God identified as such publicly by demons in the presence of the first disciples (1:24), if he is Lord of the Sabbath (2:28) and if he is stronger than Satan (3:23–27), then he will not drown in a boat trip that he himself has suggested (v. 35). The disciples should have known that they would survive the storm on this occasion.

The disciples *were terrified* (lit. 'they feared a great fear'), not of Jesus' rebuke but of the stunning display of divine power evident in the effects of Jesus' command to the wind and the waves. Manifestation of divine power makes human beings afraid (cf. 5:15; 6:50; 9:6; 16:5–6). The cessation of the wind and the calming of the waves by a verbal command suggests the presence of God. After Jesus' first exorcism in which he controlled a demon that spoke to the congregation, the people in the Capernaum synagogue asked, 'What is this?' (1:27). Now the disciples have seen that *even the wind and the waves obey him*, which inevitably raises the question *Who is this?* The disciples' question is personal, the logical corollary of the manifestation of divine power in Jesus' command. Mark's readers know the answer to the disciples' question: Jesus is the Messiah, the unique Son of God (1:1, 11). When the disciples formally answer the question in 8:29, when Peter declares that Jesus is the Messiah, the continuation of Mark's narrative shows that the disciples have little real understanding of who Jesus truly is, failing to grasp the point that Jesus' identity and mission include a violent death and a subsequent resurrection after three days (8:31–33).

b. Authority over demons: the Gerasenes (5:1–20)

1. After the storm, Jesus and the disciples arrive on the shore *across the lake*, on the eastern side of the Sea of Galilee. The reference to *the region of the Gerasenes* and the later mention of pigs (vv. 11–14, 16) indicate that they were in Gentile territory. The geographical location is complicated by the fact that the Greek manuscripts have different names, both here in Mark and in the parallel accounts in Matthew 8:28–34 and Luke 8:26–39. The most plausible original reading in Mark 5:1 is *Gerasēnōn* ('Gerasenes'), referring to Gerasa (mod. Jerash), an important city of the Decapolis (cf. v. 20) which, however, is located 35 miles (55 km) south-east of the Sea of Galilee. It is unlikely that the city controlled the territory to the shores of the lake, which makes the drowning of the pigs running over a steep bank into the lake (v. 13) impossible. The original reading in Matthew 8:28 is most plausibly *Gadarēnōn* ('Gadarenes'), referring to the city of Gadara (mod. Um Qeis), about 5 miles (8 km) from the Sea of Galilee, whose territory bordered on the lake, as demonstrated by coins the city minted portraying a ship; the city itself is separated from the lake by the Yarmuk Valley. Some manuscripts of the Gospel of Mark read *Gadarēnōn* (including the later manuscripts of the Majority Text, which explains the translation in KJV); this reading seems to have been the result of the work of copyists who wanted to conform Mark to the reading in Matthew. Some manuscripts read *Gergesēnōn* ('Gergesenes'), probably resulting from a discussion by Origen who mentioned a town of Gergesa as being very close to the lake and having a steep bank abutting on the lake (Gergesa has never been identified; some have suggested it might be mod. El Kursi).[61] Gergesa fits the geographical location of the miracle best, but it has the least textual support (an important early manuscript reading in Luke 8:26, 37, but *Gerasēnōn* has better textual support, as in Mark 5:1). Most scholars regard 'Gerasenes' as the original reading. It is possible that Mark refers to Gerasa as a term designating the entire territory of the Decapolis.

---

61. Origen, *Comm. Jo.* 27; cf. Oden and Hall, p. 67. Gergesa 'historically may be right, if only because no other suitable site exists' (France, p. 227).

2–5. As Jesus disembarks, he is approached by a man *with an impure spirit*, possessed by a demon (cf. 1:23). Mark provides a detailed description of the man. First, he *lived in the tombs*, seeking shelter outside town in rock-cut tombs or burial caves (in the 'necropolis' of the town; lit. the 'city of the dead'), places which, for Jews, were unclean (cf. Num. 19:11, 15). Second, *no one could bind him anymore, not even with a chain*: he was exceptionally strong and his condition had worsened over time. Mark's readers would be reminded of the 'strong man' of 3:27, representing Satan. Third, *he had often been chained hand and foot*: his relatives had attempted to control him with leg irons and handcuffs. Fourth, *he tore the chains apart and broke the irons on his feet*: at one point he had become so powerful that he broke the restraints and left for the cemetery, unable to live near other human beings. Fifth, *no one was strong enough to subdue him*: his situation was utterly hopeless; his relatives must have given up any hope, since he had become a danger to them and to others. Sixth, *he would cry out* among the tombs and in the hills *night and day*: as he roamed around the necropolis and in the countryside, the demon made him scream and shriek (cf. 1:26). Seventh, he *cut himself with stones*: his self-destructive behaviour (cf. 9:22, 26) left him torn and bloodied.

6–7. The man's response to Jesus' presence is described with four verbs: he *saw* Jesus, and was irresistibly attracted to approach him, for reasons not mentioned; he *ran* towards him, which is unexpected and surprising in view of his antisocial behaviour described earlier; he *fell on his knees* in front of Jesus, acknowledging this stranger's superior power; he *shouted at the top of his voice* (lit. 'with a great voice', *phōnē megalē*, repeating the adjective used in the previous episode), evidently the voice of the demon trying to frighten Jesus with the roar of the man's voice.

The demon pursues a fourfold strategy. First, he seeks to disassociate himself from Jesus, using the formula *What do you want with me?* (cf. 1:24), challenging Jesus to mind his own business. Second, he claims that he has supernatural knowledge of who Jesus is, addressing him as *Jesus, Son of the Most High God*, which goes beyond the title used by the demon in 1:24 ('the Holy One God'; cf. 3:11 'Son of God' in a similar context), using the designation 'Son' that the voice of God had used for Jesus at his baptism (1:11). If the demon-possessed man was a Gentile, the title 'Most High' could be a reference to Zeus Hypsistos, but Gentiles also called the God of Israel 'Most High' (Num. 24:16; 1 Esd. 2:2; Dan. 3:26; 4:2; 2 Macc. 3:31), a designation that underscored the sovereignty of Israel's God over creation, including all supernatural beings. Third, the demon seeks to defend himself with the phrase *I adjure you by God* (NRSV; NIV 'in God's name'), using a verb that is usually employed by the exorcist directed at the demon (cf. Acts 19:13); the demon invokes God, probably as a defensive measure to ward off Jesus' anticipated assault, indicative of the mighty demon's desperate fear, begging Jesus for a favour (Stein, p. 254). Fourth, the demon petitions Jesus, *do not torment me* (NRSV), indicating his awareness that Jesus is not only superior in power and status but also hostile. The 'torment' is the threat of being evicted from the demon's home (v. 10) and perhaps the torment of God's judgment which is, as demons know, their ultimate fate; the latter would make the demon to be asking Jesus to delay immediate expulsion in view of God's decree of future judgment (Strauss, p. 217; this is made explicit in the parallel in Matt. 8:29; cf. Rev. 20:10).

8–9. Mark underscores Jesus' power over demons: he summons the demon to come out of the man without using the name of the demon – he has no need to employ traditional methods of exorcists. Mark envisions 'no bargaining session between Jesus and the demons' (Stein, p. 254). Jesus' question, *What is your name?*, is not an attempt to gain control over the demon by learning its secret name. Jesus is in total control, as the demon's response to Jesus' presence demonstrates (vv. 6–7). Jesus' question, together with the demon's answer, *My name is Legion, for we are many*, highlights the extent of the demonic oppression that had taken control of the man and helps with understanding the subsequent episode involving two thousand pigs. *Legion* (*legiōn*) is the term used for a unit of Roman military troops. At the time of Augustus a legion consisted of about 5,000 men together with 120 cavalry serving as bodyguards and messengers, commanded by a senator of praetorian rank.[62] The man is possessed by many demons. When the man is in the forefront of the narrative, Mark uses the singular 'he' (vv. 9–10); when the demons are in the forefront,

---

62. Cf. J. B. Campbell, 'Legio', *BNP*, VII, cols. 356–370.

he uses the plural 'we/they' (vv. 9–10, 12–13). Jesus encounters not just one demon, but the kingdom of Satan (cf. 3:23–27).

10–12. The account vacillates between the singular and the plural and between masculine and neuter gender. *He* (singular) begs Jesus that he will not *send them* (plural, neuter) *out of the area*. The reason for the demons' request for this concession is not clear. There is little clear evidence for the theory that demons operate in specific geographical areas and that their relocation to other areas renders them powerless in their initial area of operation.[63] Perhaps the demons do not want to be banished to a remote area from which they cannot control human beings. Equally unexplained is the demons' request *Send us among the pigs; allow us to go into them*. Perhaps they surmise that inhabiting the pigs will allow them to stay in the area. The presence of pigs underscores that the incident takes place in Gentile territory. Jews were forbidden to raise or eat pigs (Lev. 11:7; Deut. 14:8; cf. Isa. 65:4; 66:17; *m. B. Qam.* 7:7). From a Jewish point of view, the demons' request means that the unclean spirits who control a man living in unclean tombs transfer to unclean animals. The demons' plea that Jesus *send* them into the pigs underlines the demons' total submission to Jesus' superior authority.

13. Jesus *gave them permission*. Why he did so is not explained. Mark relates that *the impure spirits came out* of the man and *went into the pigs*, specifically into a *herd* of pigs numbering *about two thousand*. What the demons probably did not expect was that the pigs then *rushed down the steep bank into the lake and were drowned*. The stampede and the drowning of the pigs dramatically and visibly underscores the power of Jesus' authority — pigs are perfectly capable of swimming. The demons that controlled the man for many years are now not even able to control pigs, unless we assume that Jesus did not expect the pigs to run over the cliff, in which case the pigs' drowning would underline the demons' destructiveness (Marcus, p. 352). There is no hint that Jesus' elimination of unclean animals signifies that he delivers Gentile territory from uncleanness. Mark reports the instantaneous effectiveness of Jesus' command: the pigs drown and the demons are left homeless (or the demons are banished to the abyss,

---

63. See perhaps the apocryphal text Tob. 8:3.

before the day of judgment; cf. Matt. 8:29; Luke 8:31; 2 Peter 2:4; Strauss, p. 219).

14–17. Mark reports that *those tending the pigs* who had witnessed the destruction of the herd rushed home and informed the people in the city (*polis*) and in farms and estates (*agroi*) about what had happened (vv. 14, 16). The people from the region who *came to Jesus* saw a transformed man whom they knew as having been *possessed by the legion of demons*.

Mark notes a threefold change in the man. First, the violent behaviour (vv. 3–5) had disappeared, and instead of roaming around in tombs and the hills, he was *sitting* in Jesus' presence, presumably listening to him. Second, he was *dressed*: the torn clothes resulting from his living in the open and from his cutting (v. 5), described in Luke 8:27 as nakedness, have been replaced by proper apparel, ready for human society. The clothes were at least an undergarment (*chitōn*; Lat. *tunica*) consisting of two equal-sized pieces of cloth that were sewn at the top and sides, with openings for the head and the arms; perhaps he was also given an outer garment (*himation*; v. 15 uses the verb *himatizō*) which was draped around the body and which, for males, was made of white or yellow wool with notched bands woven into the fabric. In 6:9 Jesus tells the disciples whom he sends on a short-term preaching tour into the towns and villages of Galilee 'not to put on two tunics' (NRSV; NIV 'not an extra shirt'). At least some of the disciples travelled with an extra *chitōn* which would be worn when the other was washed. Third, he was *in his right mind*: he no longer had an urge to live in tombs and he no longer screamed (vv. 2–3, 5); he had regained self-control and he was able to think and speak in a sound manner.

The reaction of the people from the region was not one of amazement and excitement, as on the Jewish side of the lake. Mark reports a twofold response (vv. 15, 17). The people *were afraid*: they sensed the majesty of divine power which was far superior to the power of the legion of demons. This made them afraid of what Jesus might do next. The people *began to plead with Jesus to leave their region*: the loss of the pigs that they had been informed about (v. 16) suggests that their request was motivated by a sense that Jesus' presence might cause further harm; or they were convinced that they would not be able to handle the extraordinary power of Jesus demonstrated in the liberation of the man from the demons and in the destruction of the two thousand pigs.

18–19. Jesus does not force himself on people. He accepts the request of the local population that he leave. Since Mark had not mentioned the purpose of the trip across the lake (cf. 4:35–36; 5:1), it is impossible to say whether the people's request that he leave prevented Jesus from accomplishing a specific purpose. The man, whose name Mark does not mention, *begged* Jesus that he might be allowed to *be with him* (NRSV). Since Mark uses the same expression ('to be with Jesus') as in Jesus' appointment of the Twelve in 3:14,[64] he seems to suggest that the healed man has experienced the power of the kingdom of God and volunteers to be one of Jesus' disciples. The fact that *Jesus did not let him* is not explained. Jesus' words to the man clarify that there was no doubt about the man's sincerity or commitment. The reason for Jesus' refusal might be the fact that the circle of the Twelve had already been established, or that the man was a Gentile and this was not (yet) the time for the integration of Gentiles into the messianic community.

Over against these negative reasons stands the positive reason implicit in Jesus' summons to the man: *Go home to your own people and tell them*. Since he has been healed, he can return to his house and family and resume a productive life, and he can be given a task that involves communication. The content of what he shall tell his family and friends is indicated with a twofold sentence. *Tell them how much the Lord has done for you*: he shall explain his complete, permanent (perfect tense of the verb) liberation from the legion of demons that the intervention of God has accomplished. As used in Jesus' words, *Lord* (*kyrios*; cf. 1:3; 2:28) refers to the God of Israel. *How he has had mercy on you*: he shall explain that his extraordinary recovery is the result of God's compassion. The fact that the people of the region did not respond with enthusiastic excitement to the exorcism but requested that Jesus leave means that there is no need for Jesus to command the man to be silent: the amazement of the people (v. 20) will not hinder his ministry.

20. The man leaves Jesus and does as he has been told. He begins to *proclaim . . . how much Jesus had done for him* (NRSV). *Proclaim* (*kēryssō*)

---

64. The translation 'to go with him' (NIV; cf. GNB, NLT) obscures this parallel.

is the same term used for the proclamation of John the Baptist (1:4, 7), of Jesus (1:14, 38–39) and of the future proclamation of the Twelve (3:14). There is now a Gentile equivalent to the proclamation by Jesus (1:14, 38–39) and by his disciples (1:45; 3:14) among the Jews of Galilee (France, p. 233). The *Decapolis*, the region of the 'Ten Cities',[1] extended from Damascus (which belonged to the province of Syria) in the north to Philadelphia in the south. The reason for belonging to the Decapolis was, for many cities, liberation from Jewish rule in 63 BC by the Roman general Pompey who seems to have integrated these cities into a (loose) confederation which belonged through most (but not all) of the first century to the Roman province of Syria, as an enclave separated geographically from Syria, claiming special status as Greek cities of the Hellenistic period.

The healed man attributed his liberation from the legion of demons to Jesus himself since he knew that what *Jesus had done for him*, only God could have done. Mark's readers would be aware of the identification of the work of God with the work of Jesus. When Jesus appears in the Decapolis in 7:31–37, people expect Jesus to heal the sick, which leads to further proclamation and astonishment. The missionary activities of the unnamed man whom Jesus liberated from a legion of demons laid the groundwork for future missionary work in the area south of Damascus where Paul preached the gospel following his conversion.[66]

c. Authority over disease: the woman (5:21–34)

21. Following the Gerasenes' request that he leave, Jesus and the disciples crossed *by boat* (cf. vv. 2, 18) to *the other side* of the Sea of Galilee. The third and fourth miracles that Mark relates in 4:35 – 5:43 presumably take place in Capernaum, where again *a large crowd* listened to Jesus as he taught *by the lake* (cf. 2:13; 3:7; 4:1).

---

1. Cf. Millar, *Roman Near East*, pp. 408–414. The sources, which are not unanimous, list Abila, Dion, Gadara, Gerasa, Hippos, Kanatha, Pella, Philadelphia, Raphana, Scythopolis, later Damascus.
66. Cf. Schnabel, *Early Christian Mission*, II, pp. 1032–1045, for Paul's mission to Arabia/Nabatea. Nabatean cities of the Decapolis included Gerasa, Kanatha, Philadelphia, Dium and Adraa.

The healing of the woman and the raising of Jairus' daughter form a double episode, another example of Mark's intercalation technique (cf. 3:20–35). Mark inserts the episode of the woman with a chronic haemorrhage (vv. 25–34) into the episode of Jairus' daughter (vv. 22–24, 35–43). The intercalation has the effect of delaying the healing of Jairus' daughter, who is very sick and who dies before Jesus arrives. Several parallels between the two miracles stand out: both recipients of the miracles are females who are in a hopeless situation; both situations involve ritual impurity (blood flow and death); in both miracles a period of twelve years plays a role (the number of years that the woman has suffered and the age of the girl); in both episodes Jesus heals by touch and emphasizes the importance of faith (Strauss, p. 227). On the other hand, the intercalation of the two episodes may not be a literary device here but indicative of historical memory of events that happened in the sequence in which Mark narrates the two miracles (France, p. 234).

22–24. If this scene indeed takes place in Capernaum, *Jairus* is *one of the synagogue leaders* of the local synagogue in which Jesus had taught before (1:21). A 'synagogue leader' (*archisynagōgos*) was, often, a wealthy member of the community who had a role in the ritual, administrative and financial aspects of the synagogue (Levine, *Synagogue*, pp. 136–138). The plural 'synagogue leaders' seems to describe the 'elders' (*presbyteroi*, Luke 7:3–5; cf. John 12:42: *archontes*, 'leaders'). Jairus probably belonged to a group of several synagogue leaders; if so, the singular 'the synagogue leader' in verses 35–36, 38 has to be interpreted in the context of the plural in verse 22. Jesus is in contact with and ministers to not only the destitute and the marginalized but also more affluent people. Not all Jewish leaders oppose Jesus (cf. 12:34; 15:43). Most beneficiaries of Jesus' miracles are anonymous. It is thus significant that both Mark and Luke name Jairus (*Iairos*; from Hebr. *yā'îr*, 'he enlightens'; cf. Luke 8:41). Besides Jairus, Mark names Bartimaeus (10:46) and Simon (14:3) as people healed by Jesus.[67] Presumably Jairus was known in the early Christian movement.

---

67. Luke 8:2–3 also mentions Mary Magdalene, Joanna and Susanna as women who had been cured of evil spirits and diseases, but Luke records no miracle story. John mentions Lazarus in a miracle narrative (John 11:1–44).

Mark describes Jairus' actions with four verbs. He *came*; that is, he walked from his house to the shore. He *saw Jesus*, for whom he had been looking and whom he wanted to meet. He *fell at his feet*, either acknowledging his recognition of Jesus as a respected teacher with a celebrated reputation for miraculous power, or, which seems more likely, demonstrating his desperation. And he *pleaded earnestly with him*: he implores Jesus to heal his daughter. Jairus' plea is formulated in direct speech (v. 23). He first provides a succinct report: *My little daughter is dying*, using the diminutive *thygatrion* of the usual term for 'daughter' (*thygatēr*), which could be a term of endearment since *thygatrion* can denote a girl of marriageable age. In verse 39 she is called a 'child' (*paidion*), in verse 42 a 'little girl' (*korasion*, diminutive of *korē*) and in verse 42 we learn that she was twelve years old. The later rabbis recommended marriage at the age of puberty; that is, at twelve or thirteen (*b. Yebam.* 62b); in Rome, at the time of Augustus, the legal minimum age for girls to be married was twelve. The term translated *[she] is dying* (*eschatōs echei*) indicates that she is 'at the point of death' (Lat. *in extremis*). Then Jairus asks Jesus to *come* to his house; the request *put your hands on her* implies touch as a natural gesture of healing (cf. 1:31, 41; 6:5; 7:32; 8:23, 25). His daughter has not yet died: he hopes that Jesus' touch will result in her healing so that she will continue to *live*. The Greek verb *sōzō*, which later was a standard term for salvation, here means *be healed* in the sense of 'be cured of the illness'. Jesus consents, brings his teaching to a close and accompanies Jairus to his house, accompanied by the large crowd that listened to him by the lake (v. 21). The note that the people *pressed round him* (also v. 31) is unique. The term that can be translated 'crowd around so as to leave little room for movement' (BDAG, p. 972, *synthlibō*) occurs only here in the New Testament. The comment prepares the reader for the miracle of the woman with the flow of blood who is in the crowd.

25–28. The woman who approaches Jesus is portrayed with a series of seven participles. The woman *had had a hemorrhage for twelve years* (NASB; lit. 'a flow of blood'); she had been 'subject to bleeding' (NIV) for a long time. The ailment seems to have been a chronic haemorrhage rather than an abnormally heavy monthly flow (*menorrhagia*): the woman knows immediately that she has been cured. The woman would have been ritually unclean in both cases. Leviticus distinguishes uncleanness incurred by the menstruant (*nidda*) from uncleanness incurred by a vaginal discharge outside a woman's period (*zaba*, lit. 'oozer'; cf. Lev. 12:7; 15:19-33; 20:18). The Mishnah has a tractate devoted to each condition (*Niddah*, *Zabim*), treating the *zaba* together with the male counterpart. A ceremonially unclean woman was limited in her ability to participate in Israel's religious life since others had to avoid contact to prevent ritual defilement; the woman may even have been quarantined.[68]

She *had suffered a great deal under the care of many doctors*, which indicates that she had been able to consult and pay not only one physician (*iatros*) but many. Interpreters who regard Mark's description as perhaps deliberately humorous write from a male perspective which fails to appreciate the physical and social suffering of the woman. She *had spent all she had*, which suggests that her search for a cure had depleted her assets and she had become desperate. She was not *getting better*: the cures that the doctors had applied had not healed her. Rather, *she grew worse*, a statement that is critical of the competence of doctors, at least in this case. Physicians were sometimes praised, sometimes mocked (cf. Sir. 38:1-3, 15; cf. Martial, *Ep.* 1.47: 'Lately was Diaulus a doctor, now he is an undertaker. What the undertaker now does the doctor too did before'). Some of the later rabbis said that the best doctor was worthy of hell (*m. Qidd.* 4:14).

The woman had *heard about Jesus* on account of the numerous people he had healed in and near Capernaum (1:34; 2:1-12; 3:1-5, 7-10); even though Jesus had been teaching in public for some time, she apparently had not seen him or listened to him, due to her isolation. She *came up behind him in the crowd*, the surreptitious approach suggesting that she violated a taboo by being among the public. The finite verb at the end of the sequence of participles emphasizes the action of the woman as decisive: she *touched his cloak*, that is, his outer garment, expecting to be healed. The woman's expectation is given in direct speech: *If I just touch his clothes, I will be healed*. The same

---

68. Milgrom, *Leviticus*, I, p. 765. Cf. 11QTemple XLV, 7-17; XLVI, 16-18; XLVIII, 14-17; Josephus, *Ant.* 3.261; *m. Nid.* 7:4. Cohen, *Significance*, pp. 399-401: social isolation of a menstruant or a *zaba* was a later development.

popular expectation that touching Jesus' clothing would bring healing is mentioned also in 6:56 (cf. Matt. 14:36; Luke 6:19; cf. Acts 5:15; 19:12). Neither Jesus nor Mark seems to have concerns regarding this 'magical' view of healing which assumes that the body of a holy person contains power that can be stored, tapped or transmitted to other physical objects (in the OT cf. 2 Kgs 13:20–21; Gundry, p. 280; Marcus, p. 359). Jesus does not comment on the woman's beliefs, nor does he intentionally encourage such behaviour in 6:56. As the bleeding woman touched Jesus' clothing, Jesus became ceremonially unclean; this was an uncleanness that was less serious than impurity contracted through contact with Jesus' skin (cf. Lev. 15:7), but it was real impurity nevertheless.

29–31. The effect of the woman touching Jesus' robe was instantaneous: *her bleeding stopped* (lit. 'the flow of her blood dried up') and *she felt in her body* (lit. 'she perceived in her body') that *she was healed of her disease* (NRSV). The effect on Jesus was also instantaneous: he was *aware* that *power had gone forth from him* (NRSV). Mark clarifies that the transfer of power from Jesus to the woman was not a mechanical, physical transfer. Jesus, who is pressed by the jostling crowd, with many people touching him, as the disciples point out, asks, *Who touched my clothes?*, suggesting that more than mere physical contact had taken place; and in verse 34 Jesus asserts that it was the woman's faith that had healed her.

32–34. When Jesus *kept looking around*, he challenged the person whose touch had had a perceptible effect on him to come forward and identify him- or herself. Either his supernatural insight does not extend here to the ability to identify the woman in the crowd, or Jesus wants to give the woman the opportunity to speak in public, breaking through her isolation, and bear witness to what has happened. The woman's reaction is described with five verbs, in the following sequence (obscured in NIV, NRSV). She *came*, trembling *with fear*, filled with the awe of being in the presence of a powerful miracle worker, and embarrassed because Jesus wanted to speak to her in public, surrounded by a large crowd. She was *trembling*, exhibiting a physical reaction to her fear. The trembling resulted from the awareness of divine power that had healed her (Miller, *Women*, p. 59), or from the fear that Jesus was angry because she had touched him surreptitiously (Bauckham, *Gospel Women*, p. 292). She *came*: having started to disappear into the crowd, she returns. She *fell at his feet*, not in supplication as Jairus did (v. 22), but in awe and worship. And she *told him the whole truth*, a term that occurs in judicial proceedings, which underlines the fact that she is a witness to Jesus' miraculous power that has healed her instantaneously.

Just as Jesus addressed the paralysed man as 'son' (2:5), he addresses the woman as *daughter*, a term used as a friendly greeting that reassures the woman in the context of his earlier challenge (v. 30) and the woman's fear and trembling (v. 33). Jesus asserts, *your faith has healed you* (the same formulation is used in 10:52). It was not the touch that healed her, but her *faith*, which here is the personal conviction that Jesus has divine authority to heal her (cf. 2:5; 4:40; 5:36; 9:23–24). The traditional 'dismissal formula' *go in peace* (Judg. 18:6; 1 Sam. 1:17; 20:42; 29:7) is here more than a farewell greeting: the woman is restored to full integration into the community, after twelve difficult years, and is able to enjoy the *peace* (*eirēnē*; Hebr. *šālôm*), the well-being, of God's people. The imperative *be freed from your suffering* (lit. 'be healed of your scourge' or 'torment') implies that the healing is permanent.

d. *Authority over death: Jairus' daughter (5:35–43)*

35–36. Mark resumes the story of Jairus and his daughter (vv. 22–24) in the middle of Jesus' conversation with the woman. Jesus' delay in reaching Jairus' house has resulted in Jairus' daughter's death. The fact that the girl has died is relayed to Jairus by envoys from the synagogue leader's house, perhaps relatives or neighbours. They state the reality of the girl's death: *Your daughter is dead*, and they suggest that Jesus is no longer needed and should not be bothered any further. Their comment on Jesus reflects their respect of him as a *teacher* who is immensely popular and exceedingly busy, but it also underlines the hopelessness of the situation which even the miracle-working teacher would not be able remedy. Since Jairus came to Jesus out of fear for his daughter's life, a fear that has now become a reality, Jesus tells him, *Don't be afraid*. And since Jairus came to Jesus believing that Jesus could heal his very sick daughter, Jesus tells him, *just believe*, urging him to have faith even in the face of death.

37. Jesus limits the number of people he invites to accompany him to *Peter, James [Jacob] and John*, which is consistent with Jesus allowing the same three disciples to be present at events of special revelatory significance (cf. 9:2; 13:3; 14:22). The astounding miracle of raising the dead is 'for their eyes only' (France, p. 239). The fact that Jairus takes Jesus to his house seems to suggest that he believes Jesus has a solution.

38–40. The house of the synagogue official was filled with mourners. Jesus *saw a commotion*, the confusion of mourners milling about, and *people crying and wailing loudly*. These are family members, relatives and neighbours. According to Matthew 9:23, paid mourners playing flutes and singing dirges (cf. Matt. 11:17; Luke 7:32) had already arrived (see Jer. 9:17–18). According to *m. Ketub.* 4:4, 'even the poorest in Israel do not hire less than two flute players and one wailing woman'. The question *Why all this commotion and wailing?* interrupts the mourners. The declaration *the child is not dead but asleep* is met with derisive laughter. The mourners ridicule Jesus' suggestion that the girl may not be dead, misunderstanding his use of figurative language, thinking that he literally denies her death. In view of the report conveyed to Jairus, a report that Jesus overheard (v. 36), Mark's readers know that the girl was not in a coma, but dead. The mourners may have laughed at the suggestion that Jesus, who exorcized demons and healed the sick, thought that he could also raise the dead. How right they were, but how out of place was their laughter! 'Sleep' was a common metaphor for death,[1] although the verb used in the LXX and the New Testament is *kaimaomai*, not *katheudō* which is used here, allowing the phrase to be understood as more than a metaphor (which would yield the statement 'the child is not dead but dead'). The unusual formulation indicates that this girl's situation is unique: the finality of death 'does not apply to her, since Jesus is about to reverse the verdict of death and raise her as if from sleep' (France, p. 239). Without confronting their ridicule, Jesus forced everyone to leave, with the exception of *the child's father*, that is, Jairus, her *mother*, who remains unnamed, and *the disciples who were with him*. The six adults went into the room where the dead child was lying.

---

1. Cf. LXX Gen. 47:30; Deut. 31:16; Job 14:12; Isa. 14:8; Sir. 48:11; in the NT cf. 1 Cor. 15:20; in classical Greek cf. Homer, *Il.* 11.241; Sophocles, *El.* 509; also in funerary inscriptions, cf. *CIJ* I 281; *IG* XIV 1683.

41–42. Mark relates the spectacular, climactic miracle with minimal description.² Jesus, standing over or kneeling in front of the dead girl, *took her by the hand* (circumstantial participle), and uttered a word of command (imperative), which carries the emphasis and underlines Jesus' unique authority. Mark reproduces the Aramaic words spoken by Jesus, transliterating the command into Greek: *talitha koum* (קוּם טַלְיְתָא, *ṭalyĕtāʾ qûm*, or טְלִיתָא קוּם, *ṭĕlîtāʾ qûm*, 'girl, stand up').³ Mark translates this as *Little girl, I say to you, get up!* The verb *egeirō* ('get up') denotes 'movement from a fixed position'. The Aramaic words are ordinary, not magical, probably reproduced for dramatic effect and emphasis. The power of Jesus' command is not in the words, but in Jesus' divine authority.

The resuscitation of the dead girl happened *immediately*: it was instantaneous, as with previous examples of Jesus' miracle-working words (cf. 1:42; 2:12; 5:29; see also 1:25–26; 2:12; 3:5; 4:39). The most dramatic of all dramatic miracles is reported in a matter-of-fact manner: the girl (cf. v. 23) *stood up* and began to *walk around*. Since the nouns describing the girl have been diminutives, Mark clarifies that the girl was old enough to stand up (*anistēmi*) and walk (*peripatein*): *she was twelve years old*, 'ready to launch on a meaningful and fulfilled life' (Boring, p. 158), old enough to marry. The reaction of the five witnesses was also instantaneous: *immediately they were completely astounded* (NASB), as were the people who had witnessed other miracles of Jesus (1:27; 2:12; 4:41; 5:15–17).

43. Jesus, as earlier, issued a command of silence (1:44; 7:36; 8:26; cf. 1:25, 34; 3:11–12; 8:30; 9:9). Since the parents would present the dead girl as alive to relatives, friends and neighbours, the command was impossible to keep. The command to silence underscores 'the great mystery of the divine power at work in the raising of someone from the dead' (Collins, p. 286) and is intended to dampen messianic expectations (Strauss, p. 235). The command *to give her something to eat* confirms the healing and reveals Jesus as a compassionate healer who

---

2. Contrast the miracles of Elijah (1 Kgs 17:17–24) and Elisha (2 Kgs 4:29–37).

3. KJV, RSV/ESV follow mostly later manuscripts which reproduce the Palestinian rather than the Mesopotamian form טַלְיְתָא קוּמִי, 'talitha koumi'.

is concerned about the girl's restoration to full strength, perhaps after a debilitating illness that has weakened her. The parents' first meal with their girl was surely not an expression of 'the banality of ordinary life' (thus France, p. 240) but an occasion of overwhelming joy.

Theology
The four miracles of 4:35 – 5:43 demonstrate Jesus' authority over demons (5:1–20) and illness (5:21–34), and, even more dramatically, over nature (4:35–41) and death (5:35–43). A comparison of the endings of the first and the last miracle – the stilling of the storm and the raising of Jairus' daughter – underscores the ambiguity of Jesus' words and deeds. The nature miracle prompts the question 'Who then is this, that even the wind and the sea obey him?' (4:41, NRSV), with Jesus' disciples appropriately enquiring about the identity of their friend and leader who has power over wind and waves. The resuscitation miracle, which raises the stakes even more, prompts great amazement (5:42), but no question concerning Jesus' identity, nor an answer to the first question. Jesus' miracles raise important questions, but even the climactic miracle of restoring a dead girl to life does not provide answers at this point, not even to the disciples. Control of the elements of nature is an attribute of divinity, in distinction from human beings, who are helplessly exposed to the forces of nature – which explains why the disciples are not only amazed and afraid, but also unable to understand what the calming of the storm requires, which Jesus accomplished by simple verbal commands (France, p. 221). The 'seed' of the kingdom of God is indeed small and hidden, germinating unseen, maturing by the power of God, eventually growing into a large and theologically explicit 'harvest' of Jesus' followers truly knowing Jesus' divine identity. The disciples' question 'Who then is this, that even the wind and the sea obey him?' can be answered only if and when the people who observe Jesus, and the readers of Mark's Gospel, respond by faith, trusting Jesus to do what only God can do.

vi. *Rejection in Nazareth (6:1–6)*
Context
Jesus' ministry in Nazareth concludes the second phase of his Galilean ministry described in 3:7 – 6:6. Mark had introduced Jesus

as coming from Nazareth on the occasion of his baptism by John (1:9), and as 'Jesus of Nazareth' when he first taught in the synagogue in Capernaum (1:24). Just as the first phase of Jesus' Galilean ministry ended with opposition and rejection, indeed a plot to eliminate Jesus (3:1–6), so the second phase ends with the people of his home town taking offence as they have no faith in what he teaches.

Comment

1. Jesus travels from Capernaum to his *home town*, which we know from 1:9, 24 to be Nazareth (see on 1:9). Matthew and Luke identify Bethlehem as Jesus' birthplace and Nazareth as the town in which he was raised (Matt. 2:1, 23; Luke 2:4, 39). Jesus was *accompanied by his disciples*, who play no role in this episode but are mentioned to remind the reader that Jesus is in the process of training them to gather people for the kingdom of God (1:17; 3:14).

2. Jesus joined the people of Nazareth on the *Sabbath* in the *synagogue* (cf. 1:21) where the local synagogue officials (cf. 5:22) invited him to teach. Jesus' popularity throughout Galilee and beyond as a teacher and miracle worker guaranteed that there was initial goodwill towards the most famous person ever born in Nazareth. Mark does not record what Jesus taught (unlike Luke in 4:16–20). *Many*, evidently not all, *were amazed* as they listened to Jesus' teaching. If the healing of 'a few people who were ill' in town, mentioned in verse 5, happened before the Sabbath, their amazement is due not only to Jesus' teaching but also to his miracle-working power. The people attempt to understand the 'Jesus phenomenon' by asking six questions (NIV). The last two are rhetorical questions whose answers, which are obvious, underscore their puzzlement. The question *Where did this man get these things?* expresses amazement at Jesus' abilities which cannot be explained by his upbringing in Nazareth. The question *What is this wisdom that has been given him?* infers from Jesus' teaching that he could not have obtained his knowledge of Scripture, his understanding of God and his kingdom (the foundational theme of Jesus' teaching, cf. 1:14–15), and his intellectual capacity in Nazareth, which was not much more than a village. The question *What are these remarkable miracles he is performing?* refers to the miracles (*dynameis*; lit. 'deeds of power') in other Galilean towns, news of which had reached Nazareth (cf. Luke 4:23), or to healings in Nazareth (v. 5) that took place earlier.

3. The rhetorical questions of verse 3 point to the puzzling dichotomy between Jesus' origins in Nazareth and his awesome, entirely unprecedented public ministry. The first question identifies him as *the carpenter (ho tektōn)*, a term that describes a worker in wood and can be translated 'builder' or 'carpenter'. Jesus was a craftsman who manufactured doors, windows, roofs, cabinets, and agricultural implements such as ploughs. The term is not derogatory, although it raises the question how Jesus, who used to be busy working like 'the man who handles the plough' and like every 'carpenter and master-builder' (*tektōn kai architektōn*) who works 'day and night', had the leisure to 'become wise' (Sir. 38:25, 27). Jesus, who was about thirty years of age when he began his ministry (Luke 3:23), had lived these thirty years in Nazareth, working perhaps twenty years as a carpenter.

Jesus is further described as *Mary's son*, an expression that occurs nowhere else in the New Testament. The patronymic identification 'son of Joseph' occurs in Luke's parallel (4:22; cf. Matt. 13:55: 'the carpenter's son') and in John 1:45; 6:42. Some see this as 'a slur against his legitimacy' (Marcus, p. 375), suggesting that Joseph was not his real father. This is implausible since neither Matthew nor Luke describes Jesus' virginal conception as a matter of public knowledge. Since Jesus was conceived when Mary and Joseph were betrothed, and since Joseph did not accuse Mary of adultery, Joseph effectively accepted Jesus as his own son, which means that both legally and in public opinion Joseph was Jesus' father. The suggestion that Mark regarded Mary as the more important parent (there is evidence that a man could be named with reference to his mother if she had the more prominent lineage) since he did not know of Joseph's Davidic lineage is also not plausible: 10:48, 11:10 indicate that Mark believed in Jesus' Davidic descent, which was a widespread conviction in the early church.[72] Some suggest that Joseph had died and Mary was the only surviving parent. While Joseph may indeed have died, in a Jewish context Jesus would still have been known as

---

72. Acts 2:30; 13:23; 15:16; Rom. 1:3; 2 Tim. 2:8; Heb. 7:14; Rev. 5:5; 22:16.

'son of Joseph'. The identification by a matronymic could reflect the fact that in Nazareth Jesus was known as 'the son of Mary' because his brothers and sisters were the children of Joseph by a previous wife (Bauckham, 'Brothers and Sisters'). Alternatively, the phrase may not be a formal genealogical designation but an informal comment occasioned by Mary's presence in the synagogue, with Joseph having died earlier (Meier, *Marginal Jew*, I, pp. 226–227). Mary was portrayed in 3:21, 31 (without Mark mentioning her name) as thinking that Jesus was out of his mind. According to John 19:25 she was at the cross when Jesus died, and according to Acts 1:14 she was in Jerusalem with the disciples, together with her sons.

Jesus is also described with reference to the fact that he is *the brother of James [Jacob], Joseph [Joses], Judas and Simon*. The Greek term translated *brother* (*adelphos*) means 'full brother' in the sense of 'son of the same mother' (cf. 1:16, 19; 3:17), but it can also refer to other close kinship relationships (cf. Gen. 14:14: 'nephew'; Mark 6:17: 'half-brother'; see on 6:17). The suggestion that *adelphos* means, here, 'cousin' (Jerome) is implausible since Mark surely would have used the standard term for 'cousin' (*anepsios*) if the three named men were not children of Joseph or Mary. It is not impossible that the four 'brothers' were sons of Joseph from an earlier marriage who could be called Jesus' 'stepbrothers' (Epiphanius) or, better, 'adoptive brothers' (Bauckham). This is the earliest view unambiguously attested before Tertullian, and receives plausibility from the fact that Jesus is called 'son of Mary', which is significant since the Old Testament repeatedly distinguishes a man's sons by one wife from his sons by another wife,[73] and which may suggest that Mary was not the biological mother of the four brothers. However, since Mark does not indicate that Joseph was previously married, it seems best to understand the term *brother* in the most common sense of 'full brother' (Helvidius, in his book written before AD 383 against the belief in the perpetual virginity of Mary).[74]

---

73. Gen. 4:19–22; 22:20–24; Exod. 6:15; 1 Chr. 2:2–4, 18–19, 21, 24–26.
74. Cf. Collins, p. 291; France, p. 179; Marcus, pp. 275–276, 375; Pesch I, pp. 319, 322–324; Stein, p. 187; Strauss, p. 243; Meier, *Marginal Jew*, I, pp. 318–332.

Jacob (*Iakōbos*; 'James'), presumably the eldest of the four as he is mentioned first, met Jesus soon after the resurrection (1 Cor. 15:7) and was a prominent leader in the Jerusalem church after AD 41 (Acts 12:17; 15:13–21; 21:18; Gal. 1:19; 2:9, 12). He is traditionally regarded as the author of the letter of James. Josephus relates that he died as a martyr in AD 62 on the orders of the high priest Ananus (*Ant.* 20.200). *Joses* (*Iōsēs*)[75] stands for Hebrew Yosi, the abbreviated form of Joseph used to distinguish him from his father. *Judas* (*Ioudas*) is traditionally identified with the author of the letter of Jude, who identifies himself as the 'brother of Jacob/James'. *Simon* (*Simōn*) may have been the youngest of the four brothers, but since Matthew 13:55 reverses the sequence of Judas and Simon, this is not certain. Mark related in 3:21, 31 that Jesus' brothers, together with Mary, thought that Jesus was out of his mind. Later, Paul describes 'the Lord's brothers' as travelling missionaries who take their wives along on their journeys (1 Cor. 9:5). Their significance as well-known figures in the early church is supported by the fact that all four names of Jesus' brothers were preserved by Mark and Matthew. The *sisters* (*adelphai*) of Jesus are not named. There were at least two sisters since Matthew 13:56 refers to 'all his sisters' who are 'with us', suggesting that they lived in Nazareth (while his brothers may have moved to Capernaum; cf. comment on 1:16). Early church tradition gives the names Mary and Salome, which suggests that they played some part in the early Christian movement.

The statement *and they took offence at him* indicates that the people of Nazareth listened to Jesus' teaching in the synagogue but rejected it. Their questions suggest that they cannot believe that a carpenter from Nazareth whose family they know can be God's agent who inaugurates the kingdom of God.

4. Jesus responds to the rejection with a proverbial statement about a prophet's rejection by his own people. Similar maxims speak of the fate of philosophers, physicians and other notable men.[76] The

---

75. NIV prefers *Iōsēph* instead of the better-attested *Iōsēs* (NASB, NRSV, RSV).

76. Plutarch, *Exil.* 604D: 'You would find that the most sensible and wisest people are little cared for in their own hometowns'; cf. Dio Chrysostom, *Or.* 47.6.

Old Testament repeatedly speaks of prophets being spurned by their own people (2 Chr. 24:19; 36:15–16; Neh. 9:26). The reference to a *prophet* could be merely proverbial, but it more plausibly implies that Jesus regards himself as a prophet, a designation that other people will soon use for him as they did for John the Baptist before him (6:14–15; 8:28; 11:32). It is a designation that Jesus is willing to accept (8:27–30), even though it is not the whole truth. If we define prophecy as 'speaking for God, predicting the future, and the authority to speak thus, without resort to or the permission of tradition or any other human authority' (C. Rowland, *DJG*, p. 705), Jesus was a prophet: he proclaimed, in his own authority, the coming of the kingdom of God in the present; he asserted that he had the authority to forgive sins, demonstrated by a miracle that could be properly explained only by the presence of divine power; and he predicted the future (8:31; 9:31; 10:32–34; 13:1–37). Jesus was rejected in his *own town* (*patris*, 'home town'), in Nazareth, *among his relatives*, by his extended family; and *in his own home* (*oikia*, 'house, household'), by his mother and brothers, which Mark had described earlier (3:20–21, 31–35). Mark will pick up this theme in the parable of the wicked tenants (12:1–12).

5–6. Mark's description of the consequences of Jesus' rejection by the people of Nazareth is highly ironic. Jesus had *laid his hands on a few sick people and cured them* (NRSV); that is, several healing miracles had taken place in which the sick (*arrōstos*; lit. 'powerless') were healed. But *he could do no deed of power there* (NRSV) – further miracles requiring power (*dynamis*) had become impossible (*ou dynamai*). Mark speaks, more tersely, of a limitation of Jesus' miracle-working power. Mark reports Jesus' miracles in terms of a response to faith (2:5; 4:40; 5:34, 36; 9:23–24; 10:52; 11:22–24). Since there is a *lack of faith* (*apistia*, 'unbelief'), an unwillingness to respond to Jesus' words and deeds with an acknowledgment of his authority as representing the authority of God, Jesus' miracle-working activity in Nazareth is reduced to a minimum, presumably affecting the few people who do have faith in him. The statement that Jesus *was amazed* or 'dumbfounded' by their unbelief underlines Jesus' humanness, 'the very issue that had blinded those who knew him best' (Guelich, p. 312). Later examples of limitations of Jesus' knowledge occur in 13:32; 14:36 (the question in 15:34 is different).

Mark ends verse 6 with the comment that Jesus continued his ministry of *teaching* (*didaskō*; cf. 1:21–22) about the coming of the kingdom of God (1:14–15). The formulation suggests that Jesus planned his preaching tours in Galilee: he was 'travelling around' (*periagō*; NIV: *went*) from village to village (*kōmē*; cf. 1:38) 'in a circle' (*kyklō*; NIV *around*). Jesus did not stay very long in a place which did not welcome him (cf. v. 11).

Theology
Mark never explicitly describes Jesus' royal ancestry through David, and records no visit of magi from the East who look for 'the king of the Jews' (Matt. 2:1–2). He describes Jesus from the perspective of the people of Nazareth, who know him as a carpenter, and relates Jesus' surprise that the people he knows from living in Nazareth reject him. Familiarity with Jesus does not guarantee knowing who Jesus truly is. As the 'secret of the kingdom of God' is given to those who accept Jesus' words and deeds (4:11), faith which makes miracles possible is God's gift to those willing to listen to and learn from Jesus. Jesus does not force himself on people (5:17), not even the people living in Nazareth.

C. The mission of Jesus Messiah and the Twelve (6:7 – 8:21)

The third major phase of Jesus' mission includes the mission of the Twelve and relates the expansion of Jesus' ministry beyond Galilee (6:7 – 8:21). Mark describes in eleven sections the mission of the Twelve (6:7–13), the death of John the Baptist (6:14–29), the feeding of the five thousand (6:30–44), Jesus' walking on water (6:45–52), the healing of the sick in Gennesaret (6:53–56), the controversy over tradition and purity (7:1–23), the faith of the Syro-Phoenician woman (7:24–30), the healing of a deaf mute (7:31–37), the feeding of the four thousand (8:1–10), the Pharisees' demand for a sign (8:11–13) and Jesus' warning regarding the Pharisees and Herod (8:14–21). The central theme continues to be Jesus' authority in word and deed inaugurating the kingdom of God. At the same time, the opposition of the Jewish religious leaders grows, as does the spiritual incomprehension of the disciples.

i. The mission of the Twelve (6:7–13)

Context

Mark had reported earlier how Jesus called four fishermen to follow him and be trained for a mission that would involve 'fishing' for people (1:16–20). Then Jesus appointed twelve disciples from a larger group of followers to be with him so that he might send them out to preach (3:13–19). The first part of this description of the role of the Twelve – to be with Jesus – was fulfilled in the events of the second phase of Jesus' ministry, as the disciples witnessed the continued excitement about Jesus but also the growing opposition, as they learnt the teaching of Jesus and as they were present when Jesus demonstrated his power over wind and waves, demons, illness and death. Now Mark describes how Jesus sent them out to preach and heal, replicating his ministry in the towns and villages of Galilee (6:7–13). In 6:30 they report back to Jesus. As the three episodes involving Jesus' disciples come at the beginning of the three phases of Jesus' ministry in and around Galilee, they highlight the significance of the Twelve for Jesus' mission.

Comment

7. The *Twelve* constitute the inner circle of Jesus' committed followers whom he had called to be trained so that he might send them out to preach (1:16–20; 3:14–15). It is now that Jesus *began to send them out*. The term *began* may be intended to suggest that there were other occasions when he sent the disciples out on short-term preaching tours in Galilee (as related by Luke 10:1–12). The term for *send* (*apostellein*) is the Greek equivalent for Latin *mittere* ('to cause to go, send, send off') from which the term *missio* ('sending') is derived. On their return in verse 30, the Twelve are called *apostoloi* ('envoys, messengers, apostles'), a term that in Mark does not describe an office but the process of the Twelve being sent by Jesus to preach the coming of the kingdom of God and to exorcize demons and to heal, with the authority present in the one who sends them and to whom they report back. He sends them out *two by two* (Gr. *dyo dyo*), in pairs – in six groups of two disciples each. The pairing serves mutual encouragement and support, it attests the veracity of the testimony of two witnesses (Deut. 19:15; Num. 35:30) and it represents the new community that will be established. The early church followed this precedent (Acts 8:14; 9:38; 13:2). Jesus gives the Twelve *authority* (*exousia*) over impure spirits, and charges them to liberate people from the power of demons as they participate in Jesus' authority. We later discover that the mission of the Twelve involved not only exorcisms and healing the sick (v. 13) but also preaching (v. 12), which is what Mark's readers expect both from the appointment of the Twelve in 3:14 and from Jesus' ministry (1:14–15).

8–9. Jesus' instructions, which are given in direct speech, focus on material provisions for the short-term 'missions trip' through Galilee (vv. 8–11). Jesus forbids taking travel provisions: *Take nothing for the journey*, which is specified in terms of *no bread*; that is, no food; *no bag*, a term that refers to the leather pouch used by travellers; *no money in your belts*; that is, without financial independence; *not an extra shirt*, not wearing two undergarments (*chitōn*, 'tunic, shirt'; cf. 5:15) as additional protection from the cold. Jesus allows *a staff* (*rhabdos*), a traveller's staff consisting of a relatively slender piece of wood varying in length, used for protection against animals and human beings, and *sandals* (*sandalion*), footwear 'consisting of a sole made of leather or other fabric and held on the foot by means of thongs' (BDAG, p. 913). Jesus wants the disciples to travel light as they are sent out on a short-term mission during which they can take the hospitality of Galilean sympathizers of Jesus for granted, as Jesus had presumably visited most if not all towns and villages in Galilee in his ministry.

10–11. Jesus directs the disciples to look for accommodation after they arrive in a town or village. They can expect to be invited to stay in a *house* where they can sleep and share the meals of the family. The first response that Jesus describes is one of welcome and acceptance. As Jesus stayed in houses and received the hospitality of people (1:29, 31; 14:3; cf. 14:13–15), so the disciples may expect the welcome and the hospitality of people living in the villages which they visit. The instruction *stay there until you leave that town* tells the disciples not to shop around for the most comfortable lodgings.

The second type of response comes as no surprise to Mark's readers who know about the opposition to Jesus. There might be a *place* (*topos*) – a house or a town – that will not welcome the team of two disciples who come to teach, exorcize demons and heal. Jesus' experience in Nazareth might be repeated. To *shake the dust off your feet* was a gesture of disassociation (more fully described in Luke 10:10–11; cf. Acts

13:51). The phrase *as a testimony against them* describes the missionaries who have been rejected as witnesses for the (divine) prosecution: people who reject the words and deeds of the Twelve, and thus Jesus himself, are 'marked' as unrepentant and liable to God's judgment.

12–13. Mark emphasizes four features of the Twelve's evangelistic tour through Galilee. First, *they went out*: they left the town (perhaps Capernaum) in which Jesus had given them the instructions for their 'field education'. The task of proclaiming the good news as Jesus' envoys involves geographical movement, travelling to towns and villages and contacting people. Second, they *preached that people should repent*: they proclaimed the good news of the kingdom of God and the necessity of repentance. The focus on repentance does not mean that the Twelve preached what John the Baptist preached (cf. 1:4), 'merely' preparing the way for Jesus (Hooker, p. 157). Third, *they drove out many demons*. Fourth, they *healed* many sick people. The latter two statements clarify that the mission of the Twelve recapitulates and extends Jesus' threefold ministry of preaching/teaching, exorcism and healing. The core content of Jesus' proclamation was the good news of the coming of the kingdom of God, with repentance and faith as the proper response (1:14–15). Mark chooses to focus on the response of the people, referencing 'repentance' as the proper reaction to the inbreaking power of the kingdom of God evidenced in the exorcisms and healings.

The *anointing* with (olive) oil in association with healing those who were *ill* (cf. v. 5) is mentioned in the New Testament only here and in James 5:14 (where the anointing of sick believers is performed 'in the name of the Lord'). Jesus is never reported to have used oil, which suggests to some that Jesus' power to heal was direct and not in need of using the medicinally helpful oil. Olive oil was a staple of ancient medicine, typically used for the care of the skin, including surgical cuts, lesions and burns, and to soothe haemorrhoids and headaches. More likely the symbolic reference to oil is in view here: oil is a symbol of joy and honour, God's blessing or divine commissioning.[77]

---

77. Hippocrates, *Morb.* 2.10; 2.13; *Haem.* 3; Celsus, *De med.* 3.9. In the OT and NT Isa. 1:6; Jer. 8:22; 51:8; Luke 10:34; cf. Josephus, *War* 1.657. Symbolic uses of oil: Ps. 45:7; Isa. 61:3; Lev. 14:15–18; Exod. 40:15; Num. 3:3; 1 Kgs 19:16.

Theology

The mission of the Twelve recapitulates and extends the mission of Jesus. Followers of Jesus preach what Jesus preached and do what Jesus did. Sent by Jesus, they are his representatives, his envoys who do what he told them to do, their authority being Jesus' authority. They travel in order to meet people who need to hear Jesus' message. They exorcize demons and heal the sick, demonstrating the powerful presence of the kingdom of God. Given that Mark often depicts the Twelve as disciples who are proud, selfish and lacking in understanding (6:52; 7:18; 8:17–18, etc.), their mission demonstrates that Jesus uses even 'flawed instruments to accomplish his purposes' (Strauss, p. 254). The instructions for the short-term missionary tour in Galilee were not meant to be replicated in different historical contexts. In Luke's Gospel, Jesus tells the disciples at a later time to take a purse and also a bag (Luke 22:36), cancelling the earlier directive in 10:4. On the long journeys implied in the missionary work of Paul, a bag with a provision of bread, money in a belt and a second tunic for additional protection in the cold or for a change of clothes would have been mandatory.

ii. The execution of John the Baptist (6:14–29)
Context

Mark's description of the mission of the Twelve (6:7–13, 30) is interrupted by two scenes: Herod Antipas' concerns about Jesus (6:14–16) and an account of the execution of John the Baptist by Antipas (6:17–29). This intercalation (cf. 3:20–35; 5:21–43) underlines the fact that – like the mission of Jesus – the mission of the disciples takes place in the context of opposition and rejection that may result in death. In 3:6 Mark had reported that the Pharisees contacted the Herodians to plot Jesus' death. Both groups appear again in 12:13 as opponents who want to catch Jesus in his words, sent by the chief priests, the teachers of the law and aristocratic elders (12:12). Jesus' comments about the 'yeast' of the Pharisees and of Herod (8:15) refer to the same opposition. The Twelve are called to a mission of restoration and deliverance which includes the risk and reality of conflict in which they may have to pay the ultimate price, as the example of John demonstrates.

Comment

14-15. *King Herod* is Antipas, son of Herod I ('the Great') and Malthace, a Samaritan woman. Antipas was born around 25 BC and raised in Rome. When Herod I, who held the title 'King', died in 4 BC, Augustus divided his kingdom into three parts ruled by Herod's sons: Archelaos became ethnarch in Judea, Idumea and Samaria (deposed in AD 6, when Judea came under Roman control); Philip became tetrarch in Gaulanitis, Trachonitis, Batanea and Paneas (until AD 33); Antipas became tetrarch in Galilee and Perea, two non-contiguous areas (until AD 39). Antipas was a client of Emperor Tiberius, after whom he named his second capital, Tiberias. His title was 'tetrarch' (*tetraarchēs*). Mark calls him *king* (*basileus*; Hebr. *melek*; cf. Matt. 14:9), probably a reflection of popular custom: people would have used the Aramaic term *malka*, which has a wider range of meaning than the Greek term *basileus*. His forty-three-year reign suggests that he was a successful ruler. A new evaluation of the available evidence concludes that 'Antipas was a minor Roman client ruler, mediocre in both his successes and failures ... Antipas did not appear to Rome as a vigorous king, and was never promoted beyond the status of a tetrarch, allotted a larger realm or given the right to appoint high priests.'[78] In the New Testament he is simply called 'Herod' (*Hērōdēs*), as in Josephus and on the coins he minted.

The fact that *Jesus' name had become well known* in Galilee prompted popular speculation about his identity. Three answers are suggested (cf. 8:27-28, where these three opinions are repeated). First, some said that with Jesus, *John the Baptist has been raised from the dead*. For the title 'John the Baptist' see on 1:4. Since Jews do not believe in reincarnation, since Galilean Jews were unlikely to believe that an especially good or especially evil person could somehow come back from the dead, and since Jesus was already active when John the Baptist was alive, this first opinion seems not to reflect particular views about resurrection. The statement more likely expresses the notion that 'Jesus is John the Baptist all over again' (Cranfield, p. 207), or that the spirit of John the Baptist had come to rest upon Jesus, as Elijah's spirit came to rest on Elisha (2 Kgs 2:15),

---

78. Jensen, *Herod Antipas*, pp. 257, 268.

establishing continuity between John the Baptist and his ministry and Jesus (France, p. 253).

Second, some said that Jesus *is Elijah*. If some people thought that Jesus was John, it is not surprising that others thought he was Elijah, since John's appearance and ministry were described in language reminiscent of Elijah (1:6; cf. 9:11–13). Many Jews expected Elijah to return in the last days (Mal. 4:5–6), because of Elijah's unusual departure (2 Kgs 2:11–12). In Matthew 11:14 Jesus asserts that John *is* Elijah, which can hardly be a reference to reincarnation: Elijah had not died but ascended into heaven, and Jesus (and Matthew) are unlikely to have thought of John the Baptist descending from heaven, given the stories about John's infancy (Luke 1:5–25, 39–41, 57–66). The statement most likely means that John held Elijah's office, coming 'in the spirit and power of Elijah' (Luke 1:17) and preaching repentance in Israel. Similarly, some people evidently believed that Jesus operated in the spirit and power of Elijah, preaching about God's powerful intervention and challenging Israel to repent. The raising of Jairus' daughter (5:35–43) was similar to a miracle in Elijah's ministry (1 Kgs 17:17–24).

Third, some said that Jesus *is a prophet, like one of the prophets of long ago*: they disagree that Jesus is a prophet like John or Elijah, but think that he is comparable to another prophet. According to Matthew 16:14, some people believed that Jesus was Jeremiah. The consensus is that Jesus is a prophet (see on 6:4, where Jesus refers to himself as a prophet).

16. Mark relates, in direct speech, Antipas' own assessment of Jesus. He endorses the view that Jesus is *John*, who *has been raised from the dead*, a view made all the more noteworthy since it was Antipas himself who had *beheaded* John. It is unclear whether Antipas seriously believed that Jesus was a second John: he may have spoken ironically or in mockery since he would likely not have shared Pharisaic views of the afterlife and bodily resurrection. If he was superstitious and shared Hellenistic beliefs about the dead returning to haunt their killers, his conscience may have been troubled when he heard of the supernatural power evident in Jesus's ministry, and he may have regarded Jesus as a threat. If the latter was the case, Antipas did nothing about it. Mark does not portray Antipas as a threat in this episode; Jesus' warning against Antipas comes later

(8:15). On the other hand, Matthew, in his parallel account, asserts quite explicitly that Antipas wanted to kill Jesus, which prompted Jesus to leave his territory (Matt. 14:5, 13). Mark relates a similar retreat of Jesus by boat in 6:32, without, however, connecting it to Antipas, although it is probably significant that he relates little public ministry of Jesus in Antipas' tetrarchy after this point (France, p. 254). Antipas' comment about having beheaded John provides Mark with the opportunity to report John's imprisonment and execution, which foreshadows the fate of Jesus as the 'other' John.

17–18. It was Herod Antipas who ordered John to be *arrested*, *bound* and *put in prison*. Josephus reports on the execution of John the Baptist (*Ant.* 18.116–119) as a digression prompted by the destruction of Antipas' army in AD 36 in the war against the Nabatean King Aretas IV, whose daughter, who was his first wife, he divorced in order to marry Herodias. Josephus regards Antipas' defeat as God's punishment for this immoral behaviour. According to Josephus, John was held at Machaerus in Perea east of the Dead Sea (cf. 3:8), one of Antipas' fortified palaces, built by Alexander Jannaeus around 90 BC, destroyed by Pompey in 64 BC and rebuilt by King Herod I around 30 BC.

Mark explains that Antipas imprisoned John *because of Herodias, his brother Philip's wife, whom he had married*. Antipas had married the daughter of King Aretas IV who ruled over Nabatea (Arabia), which was to the east and south of the Decapolis, with Petra as the capital city, bordering on Perea which belonged to the tetrarch's territory. Antipas dismissed his royal Nabatean wife because he was infatuated with *Herodias*. Mark calls Herodias *his brother Philip's wife*. King Herod had ten wives and numerous sons, several of whom had the name 'Herod', and there were several incestuous marriage relationships between the king's descendants. Herod Antipas was King Herod's son by Malthace the Samaritan. His brother Herod Philip, the tetrarch, was King Herod's son by Cleopatra of Jerusalem. Herodias was the daughter of Aristobulos, King Herod's son by Mariamne I, and thus a granddaughter of King Herod. Herodias was first married to Herod, a son of King Herod by Mariamne II, who was thus her uncle; Mark calls him *Philip*, which could have been the personal name of the son whom Josephus simply calls 'Herod'. Herodias divorced her first husband, Herod (Philip), and married his half-brother Herod Antipas, who was also her uncle. Herodias' daughter (vv. 22–25, 28), whose name was Salome (mentioned by Josephus), was from her first marriage and thus Herod Antipas' stepdaughter; she was at the same time Herod Antipas' niece (on her father's side) and his great-niece (on her mother's side). She later married Philip the tetrarch, later Aristobulos, the son of Herod, the brother of Agrippa (*Ant.* 18.136).

John the Baptist voiced public objections when Herod Antipas married Herodias, arguing that the marriage was *not lawful* (Gr. *ouk exestin*). The scandal was not the dismissal of his first wife, which was not illegal under Jewish law, and which was not necessary since polygamy was permitted and practised in the Herodian family, notably by Antipas' father, King Herod. According to Josephus, Herodias had insisted that Herod Antipas dismiss his Nabatean wife. The scandal was that he had sexual relations with his brother's wife, which was prohibited according to Leviticus 18:16, 20:21, even after the brother's death (permitted only if the brother had died without leaving a son; cf. Deut. 25:5–10 on Levirate marriage). Later Jewish law specifically prohibited sexual relations between a man and the wife of a half-brother (*b. Yebam.* 55a). The Essene document CD V, 8–11, records the prohibition of marriage with a niece. Both prohibitions applied to the union between Herod Antipas and Herodias. Josephus asserts that Herod Antipas flouted ancestral tradition (*Ant.* 18.136). Mark's report that John told Herod Antipas that *it is not lawful for you to have your brother's wife* assumes a direct, personal confrontation. Josephus states that it was Herod Antipas' fear of sedition which led to John's death, which implies that John spoke for large segments of Jewish and Galilean society.

19–20. John's public denunciation of Herod Antipas' marriage infuriated Herodias: she *nursed a grudge* against John (lit. 'she had it in for him') and *wanted to kill him*. She was prevented from carrying out her plan because Antipas *feared John and protected him*. Some have suggested that he protected John by imprisoning him in Machaerus, far away from Tiberias, Galilee's capital, keeping him safe from Herodias' intrigues. According to Mark, Antipas knew John *to be a righteous and holy man*: he knew that John was innocent of charges that would warrant a legal death sentence, and he acknowledged that John was a prophet who spoke for God. He *liked to listen to him*, perhaps because John was the most popular preacher who drew large crowds of people, and certainly because he acknowledged him to be a prophet. It was surely John's stature as a prophet that explains why Antipas *feared* him and why he was *greatly puzzled*, 'at a loss', uncertain what to do, yet willing to continue to have conversations with him.

21. The *birthday* (*genesia*; 'birthday celebration') of Antipas, whose date is unknown, was an *opportune time* (lit. 'suitable day') for Herodias, a favourable occasion for negotiating her husband's indecision and making him order John's execution. Antipas organizes a *banquet* (*deipnon*; here 'feast, dinner, elaborate dinner celebration') to which he invites *his high officials* (*megistanes*), noblemen attached to his court; *military commanders* (*chiliarchoi*), high-ranking military officers who commanded his (small) army;[79] and the *leading men of Galilee* (*hoi prōtoi*; lit. 'the first'), the most prominent men of Galilean society. It is possible that Chuza, who was *epitropos* and thus a high-ranking official at Antipas' court, whose wife Joanna was a supporter of Jesus (Luke 8:3), was present as an eyewitness. The presence of the highest representatives of the Galilean 'state' suggests Tiberias as the location for Antipas' party, which seems to create a conflict with Josephus, who says that John was executed in Machaerus (*Ant.* 18.119). Some suggest that 'the nobilities of Galilee may have sent him a deputation on his birthday', which Antipas celebrated on this occasion in his palace at Machaerus (Hoehner, *Herod Antipas*, p. 148). It is also possible that Antipas had brought John to his palace in Tiberias.

22–28. Mark describes the events that transpired in seven steps. First, *the daughter of Herodias* came into the banquet hall and *danced*. She is described as a *korasion* ('girl'), a term used for girls up to marriageable age (used in 5:41 for Jairus' daughter, who was twelve years old). According to Josephus, the name of Herodias' daughter

---

79. Cf. Rocca, *Herod's Judaea*, p. 139, who estimates that in the final year of his reign, King Herod's army reached a total of 20,000 soldiers; only a small part of this army served Antipas. Since Antipas' annual income totalled 200 talents (Josephus, *Ant.* 17.318) compared with 1,000–2,000 talents for King Herod (Rocca, p. 208), Antipas' army might have had between 2,000 and 4,000 soldiers.

by her first marriage was Salome (who thus was Antipas' stepdaughter and, simultaneously, his niece and his great-niece; cf. v. 17). That a princess would appear before a male audience and perform a dance is not difficult to imagine for Antipas' court since the cultural preferences of the Herodian dynasty were informed more by Roman customs than by adherence to Jewish tradition. Josephus relates that Antipas' palace in Tiberias displayed images of animals, which was forbidden by the Mosaic law (*Life* 65). Mark leaves the nature of the dance to the reader's imagination, an opportunity that commentators and artists did not let pass. The notion that there was an 'atmosphere of wild abandon' (Marcus, p. 396) and that the girl performed a 'lascivious dance' (Osborne, p. 100) is nowhere indicated in the text. If the daughter was as young as twelve, Mark may be depicting 'a child's performance' (Donahue and Harrington, p. 199; cf. Stein, p. 306).

Second, the girl and her dance *pleased* Herod Antipas and his dinner guests. The verb *areskō* means 'to act in a fawning manner' with the focus on winning approval, and 'to give pleasure, satisfaction, to please, accommodate'; the term is used in honorary inscriptions 'to express interest in accommodating others by meeting their needs or carrying out important obligations' (BDAG, p. 129); the verb itself does not imply sexual arousal. Antipas enjoyed the performance and offered to give his (step-) daughter *anything you want*, promising with an oath that *whatever you ask I will give you, up to half my kingdom* (v. 23). Extravagant gifts to successful entertainers were not uncommon, but Antipas' oath (which recalls the words of King Ahasuerus [Xerxes] to Esther; cf. Esth. 5:3, 6; 7:2) is surely hyperbolic. Since Herod Antipas was a client of Emperor Tiberius, he did not have the authority to transfer part of his tetrarchy to another ruler. The *kingdom* (*basileia*) was in fact a tetrarchy, although Antipas would have loved to have had the status of 'king' ruling over a kingdom.

Third, the girl leaves the banquet hall and consults with her mother (v. 24), asking for her advice on what she should *ask for*, what demands she should make given her stepfather's extravagant 'blank cheque' offer. The fact that she consults Herodias indicates that the girl is young. And the consultation suggests that her dance was not planned in order to engineer the death of John the Baptist.

Fourth, Herodias asks the girl to demand *the head of John the Baptist*, a grisly request, made 'without batting an eyelash' (Marcus, p. 402), for John's execution by decapitation.

Fifth, the girl *at once . . . hurried* into the banquet hall (v. 25), underlining the eagerness of Herodias' determination to eliminate John. The girl's request, introduced with *I want*, emphasizes the impatience of Herodias finally to get rid of John: she wants John's head *right now* (*exautēs*, 'at once, immediately, soon thereafter'), and *on a platter* (*pinax*, NRSV), a flat large dish on which food is served.

Sixth, Antipas was *greatly distressed* (v. 26), knowing that John was a righteous and holy man (cf. v. 20) who did not deserve to be extrajudicially killed as a 'thank-you gift', and realizing that this was not the girl's idea but his wife trying to manipulate him. He was trapped, however, *because of his oaths* and because of *his dinner guests* who were present when he made his promise and whom he did not want to think that he held John the Baptist as more valuable than half of his territory. As a result, he *did not want to refuse her*. Antipas' distress is less the consequence of 'a terrible bind' (Stein, p. 306) than the result of the fact that he was a fearful, indecisive ruler susceptible to falling for his wife's cunning plans. An oath may have been irrevocable in biblical times (cf. Num. 30:2; Judg. 11:29–40), but as a member of the Herodian dynasty he could surely have found a way to release himself from the hasty oath. He should have known that David's oath (1 Sam. 25:22) to kill Nabal was thwarted due to Abigail's intervention (1 Sam. 25:23–35) and his oath regarding Shimei (2 Sam. 19:23) did not prevent him from having him killed (1 Kgs 2:9). Some interpret the phrase *he did not want* to imply that attempts to persuade Antipas to release himself from his oath 'were actually made' (Derrett, 'Herod's Oath', p. 349).

Seventh, John is executed by being beheaded with a sword. Antipas, weak as he was, tried to demonstrate his resolve and authority by *immediately* sending an *executioner*. The term *spekoulatōr* is a Latin loanword which originally denoted a scout in the Roman army, and then a member of the imperial bodyguard or one of the headquarters staff of a legionary commander or of a provincial governor whose duties included carrying out executions (*LSJ*, p. 1626). Here the term refers to a staff member of Herod Antipas' household. The staff member is commanded *to bring John's head*, which he promptly does after having *beheaded John in the prison*. It is not clear whether the executioner *brought* John's head into the banquet hall or straight to the girl, to whom he *presented* ('gave') the platter with the head; she then gave it to her mother, who had wanted John's head to be chopped off. There is no doubt that John is dead.

29. The *disciples* of John (cf. 2:18) travelled to Tiberias, if this is where the execution took place, retrieved John's body and buried it.

Theology

The execution of John the Baptist prefigures the execution of Jesus, who is 'the one more powerful' than John (1:7). Both Herod Antipas and Pontius Pilate are pressured by others to execute. Like John's, Jesus' execution is ordered by a ruler who acknowledges the victim's innocence of misdeeds that warrant a death sentence. Both choose to secure the favour of others in exchange for their souls (8:36). For both, the 'word' they had heard from John and Jesus, respectively, did not take root. Seen in this context, the episode of John's execution is an important example of the cost of discipleship. Jesus will say in 8:35 that 'whoever loses their life for me and for the gospel will save it'. As Mark interpolates John's execution between the beginning and the end of the mission of the Twelve, he underlines the fact that missionary work is dangerous and that discipleship is costly, both taking place in the context of admiration, opposition and rejection, and the real possibility of martyrdom.

iii. *The feeding of the five thousand (6:30–44)*
Context

Following the mission of the Twelve, the two nature miracles in 6:30–44, 45–52 reveal Jesus' unique authority which is on an altogether different level from the authority that the disciples have been given to exorcize and to heal. The miracle of the feeding reminds biblically literate readers of Elijah's multiplication of bread in Zarephath (1 Kgs 17:8–16) and Elisha's miracle in 2 Kings 4:42–44.

Comment

30. The Twelve had been sent as Jesus' envoys (*apostoloi*; cf. 3:14; the verb *apostellō* is used in 6:7) into the towns and villages of Galilee (vv. 6–13). Now they returned and *gathered round Jesus*; that is, they assembled as a group in Jesus' presence. They reported *all they had done*: they described the exorcisms of demons and the healings of the sick that had happened during their tour through Galilee (v. 13). And they reported *all they had . . . taught*: they described their preaching of the necessity of repentance (v. 12) and the positive and negative responses of people (vv. 10–11).

31–32. Jesus wants to take the disciples to a *deserted place* (NRSV) so that they can *get some rest* and recuperate from the rigours of travelling, teaching, exorcizing demons and healing the sick.[80] Mark explains the need for withdrawal with the comings and goings of *many people* who had been drawn to the lake on account of Jesus' immense popularity. As the disciples returned from all over Galilee, they may have been accompanied by people from the villages. The phrase *by yourselves* is emphatic: the disciples have ministered to others; now they need to be cared for. Jesus and the disciples left *by themselves*, without the crowds, taking the *boat* to a *deserted place* (NRSV). Luke 9:10 locates the scene in Bethsaida (cf. Mark 1:16; 6:45), only about 3 miles (5 km) north-east of Capernaum, presumably in the neighbourhood of the town as he also speaks of a 'deserted place' (9:12, NRSV).

33–34. Jesus' attempt to leave the crowd behind was not successful. People from *all the towns* in the region, including towns that the disciples had visited, *ran on foot* along the shore and *got there ahead of them*. Jesus reacts to the presence of the *large crowd* with *compassion*; the Greek term, which can be translated 'to have pity' or 'feel sympathy', expresses emotion. The reason for Jesus' compassion is expressed with the analogy of *sheep without a shepherd*. Sheep without shepherds cannot survive for very long: they need shepherds to find pastures and water. The people of Israel in the desert without the leadership of Moses were compared to 'sheep without a shepherd' (Num. 27:17). The phrase became a proverbial metaphor for the people suffering as the result of weak leadership (1 Kgs 22:17; 2 Chr. 18:16) or negligent leadership (Ezek. 34:1–8). Ezekiel prophesied 'against the shepherds' that Yahweh would remove them and look after the scattered flock himself, rescuing them from all the places

---

80. Cf. 2:4, 13; 3:9, 32; 4:1, 34, 36; 5:21, 24, 30–32; also 9:2, 28; 13:3.

where they were scattered, and promising that he would search for the lost, bring back the strays, bind up the injured and strengthen the weak (Ezek. 34:9–16). The verbal parallels are closest with Numbers 27:17; the thematic connection, in the context of Jesus' proclamation of the coming of the kingdom of God, is strongest with Ezekiel 34:1–16. In a similar passage, Jeremiah prophesies that when Yahweh raises up a new king from the line of David whose name will be 'The LORD Our Righteous Saviour', he will appoint new shepherds who will save Judah and make Israel live in safety (Jer. 23:1–6; cf. Mic. 5:2–4; Zech. 13:7; also *Pss Sol.* 17:40–41). Mark's comment presents Jesus as the promised saviour who is the Davidic Messiah (cf. 1:1) in the context of an indictment of Israel's leadership, including the teachers of the law, Pharisees from Jerusalem (3:22; 7:1) and Herod Antipas (6:14). Jesus' compassion was expressed in the fact that *he began teaching them many things*: his compassion is prompted by the people's need to hear and understand the good news of the coming of the kingdom of God and the need for repentance and faith (1:14–15).

35–36. *Late in the day* must mean mid-afternoon: nightfall was still some time off (v. 47), around 7.30 pm in the summer; the evening meal was usually eaten at the ninth hour, probably not long after three o'clock in the afternoon. The disciples remind Jesus of the time of day and that it is a *deserted place* (NRSV; NIV 'remote place') where they have come ashore and met the crowds. They are rightly concerned that the people have *something to eat*, which means that Jesus needs to bring his teaching to an end and 'dismiss' (NIV *send . . . away*) the crowds so that they can find 'farms' (*agroi*; BDAG, p. 16, *agros* meaning 2; NIV translates 'countryside') and *villages* (*kōmai*; cf. 1:38; 6:6, 56) where they can buy food. The disciples had reminded Jesus of his responsibilities earlier in 1:36–37 and 4:38 (cf. 10:13). How realistic the disciples' plan was is another matter. We learn in verse 44 that five thousand men were present; according to Matthew 14:21 women and children were present as well, which means that the crowd could have numbered ten thousand people. There were not many villages or towns in the area: nearby Bethsaida (cf. v. 45) was a rural settlement, as was Chorazin, about 3 miles (5 km) to the west; the 200 (or 600) people living in Capernaum, 3 miles (5 km) to the south-west, could not have met the needs of such a large crowd either. Most late Second Temple villages in Galilee did not have a makeshift market. And the reference to the 'green grass' (v. 39) indicates that the time was spring, before grass turned brown in the summer heat, and thus a time when the village people would have just about consumed the harvest of the previous year. The disciples have no plans to care for the crowds themselves. They have hardly enough for themselves, as verse 38 makes clear. Mark does not indicate that they should have expected a miracle. Their suggestion that the people take care of themselves does make sense: the people had run to the secluded location and listened to Jesus' teaching; now they can go back home.

37–38. Jesus' suggestion that the disciples themselves *give them something to eat* serves to reveal their inability to cope with the situation (France, p. 266). It does not seem plausible to assume that Jesus challenges the disciples to 'serve as extensions of his own miracle-working power and authority' (Stein, p. 314). There is no indication that the disciples should have thought that they could miraculously feed these people. In the Gospels, nature miracles, which are few in number, are connected with Jesus, never with the disciples. The disciples' answer seems to be ironic, unless they had *half a year's wages* (lit. 'two hundred denarii') readily available, which is not completely out of the question considering the financial support of Mary, Joanna (the wife of Chuza, one of Herod Antipas' courtiers), Susanna and others (Luke 8:2–3).[81] The NIV (*Are we to go and spend that much on bread?*) implies that the disciples were not prepared to spend such an amount on food 'for a crowd of strangers' (France, p. 266). The Greek text does not suggest such an implication. The inventory of food that the Twelve had available, stored, perhaps, in the boat (*Go and see*), was not much: they had *five* loaves and *two fish* (according to John 6:9, the five loaves and two fish came from a boy who gave them to Andrew). Bread, in the form of round flat loaves

---

81. Ben-David, *Ökonomie*, pp. 300–301: an income of 200 denarii for a family of six sufficed to buy 400 loaves of bread yearly for each family member, a total of 2,400 loaves of bread (1 lb [500 g] each; *m. Pe'ah* 8:7); this would be a half-day's ration for the five thousand men present; cf. Gundry, p. 330.

(0.39 in. [1 cm] thick and 19.6 in. [50 cm] in diameter), and fish was the staple food of most Galileans. Salted and dried fish was a common provision for a journey and probably in view here (Marcus, p. 411). The numbers, which have no symbolic significance, highlight the magnitude of the miracle.

39–40. Jesus instructs the disciples to have the people sit 'dinner party by dinner party' (*symposia symposia*), and so they sit 'row by row' (*prasiai prasiai*) in hundreds and fifties. English versions generally translate the doubled nouns in the distributive sense of 'in groups'. The Greek term *symposion* denotes literally a 'drinking-party' or 'banquet' and refers here to 'a party of people eating together' (BDAG, p. 959). The term *prasia* means 'garden plot, garden bed' (cf. Sir. 24:31; the meaning 'group' is attested only here in Mark) and refers to the regularity of how the people were arranged. Five thousand men can be arranged in fifty groups of a *hundred* and in one hundred groups of *fifty* (if we assume ten thousand people to be present, the figures double). In a different context the arrangement and the numbers could have a military connotation, but there is no hint that this is meant here. The people are arranged in groups and rows to facilitate the distribution of the food. The vivid description of the scene, including the reference to the *green grass* (*chlōros chortos*), which indicates spring time, suggests eyewitness memory. The Greek verbs *anaklinō* ('to cause to recline at a meal, place as a guest'; NIV 'sit down') and *anapiptō* ('to recline on a couch to eat'; NIV 'sit down') suggest a festive atmosphere. Even though Jesus does not explain his instructions, the Twelve now must expect a miracle, as they organize the crowd into groups who get ready for the evening meal to be served. The same holds true for the thousands of people who must have known that the fishing boat did not hold provisions of bread and fish sufficient for such a large crowd. The anticipation must have been immense.

41. The miracle that takes place is not performed by a verbal command. Jesus did what the head of a Jewish family would do. He took the loaves and the two fish, placing the food that was about to be eaten in front of him. He looked up to heaven, addressing the prayer at the beginning of the meal to God (cf. 7:34; Job 22:26–27; Luke 18:13; John 11:41; 17:1). He *gave thanks*: he pronounced the blessing, which, for bread, was: 'Blessed are you, Lord our God,

King of the world, who brings forth bread from the earth' (*m. Ber.* 6:1). He *broke the loaves* – this might have been the moment when the miracle happened. He then *gave* the loaves to the disciples, who distributed them to the people. The same miracle happened when he *divided* the two fish among all the people. Since the sequence of the verbs 'take', 'give thanks', 'broke', 'gave' corresponds to 14:22 (minus the reference to 'looked up'), this suggests to many interpreters that Mark intends an allusion to the Last Supper (Eucharist). While Christian believers who read or hear the episode for the second or third time might be aware of such a connection, neither the wording nor the context requires such an interpretation (nor the reference to fish). The verbs correspond to what regularly happened at Jewish meals when food was blessed and distributed.

42–44. The result of Jesus taking the loaves and the fish, giving thanks to God, breaking the loaves, dividing the fish and giving them to the disciples for distribution was that *they all ate and were satisfied*. Both verbs underline the fact that a dramatic miracle had happened. Everybody in the crowd was eating bread and fish, and they all ate not only a little, but so much that they were 'filled with food' (*chortazō*), an experience that the poorer people in the crowd may not have had since the last wedding feast.

The description of the disciples who *picked up twelve basketfuls* of pieces of bread and fish also underscores that a spectacular miracle had just occurred: there were vastly more leftovers than the five loaves and two fish they started with. A *basket* (*kophinos*) was used for carrying things. The term does not describe the size: it could be 'a large, heavy basket' (BDAG, p. 563); it could refer to a wicker basket holding 'such things as a light lunch and general odds and ends' (Lane, p. 231). In the papyri the term is used for baskets holding 40 or 20 litras (1 litra is 2.09 pt. [0.99 l.]). Some interpret the figure *twelve* as an allusion to the restoration of the twelve tribes of Israel, but Mark does not hint at a symbolic significance to the figure.

The number *five thousand* men underlines the scale of the miracle as well; this was perhaps ten times the total population of Capernaum. According to Matthew 14:21, where this figure is also mentioned, there was an additional unspecified number of women and children. In contrast to many other miracles where Mark notes the amazement of the people who were the recipients or the witnesses of them

(1:22, 27; 2:12; 5:15, 20; 5:42; 6:51; 12:17), there is no comment here on their response. The explanation that most of the crowd were unaware of the miraculous origin of the food is hardly satisfactory: the disciples learnt what had happened, and their reaction is not mentioned either, unlike in the very next episode (v. 51). Readers of Mark's Gospel do not need a comment recording the amazement of the people or of the disciples since the twelve baskets and the number *five thousand* provide more than enough information to indicate their amazement.

Theology
It is surely not a coincidence that this is the only miracle recorded by all four evangelists (Matt. 14:13–21; Mark 6:30–44; Luke 9:10–17; John 6:1–15). The disciples had exercised authority over demons and illnesses during their tour through Galilee, but Jesus exercises power on an altogether different level. The reference to Jesus teaching the large crowd of people (6:34) because of the compassion he had for them should not be missed: Jesus' authoritative teaching and Jesus' powerful acts are two aspects of one single truth – the kingdom of God has come; its presence is seen, felt and tasted.

iv. Walking on water (6:45–52)
Context
The miracle of Jesus walking on water is the second storm scene, after 4:35–41, and follows immediately after the nature miracle of the multiplication of the loaves of bread and the fish in 6:30–44. The episode has been read as a rescue story (as 4:35–41); however, the disciples are not portrayed as being in any danger. The episode is best understood as a theophany: Jesus reveals his divine presence – he walks on water amid strong winds, something that only the creator of water and wind can do. At the same time Mark reminds his readers that the Twelve still do not truly understand who Jesus is, despite the fact that they have witnessed Jesus' demonstrations of divine authority.

Comment
45–46. The reference *to the other side* (NRSV; NIV leaves the phrase untranslated) raises geographical questions: where did the feeding

miracle take place, and what was the destination of the disciples when they got into the boat? According to Mark, Jesus sent the disciples towards *Bethsaida*, which suggests that the feeding miracle had taken place west of the Jordan river. Bethsaida has been identified with the archaeological remains at et-Tell, east of the Jordan river close to the northern shore of the Sea of Galilee. During the First Temple period, Bethsaida was the capital of the Aramean kingdom of Geshur (El Amarna Letters; 2 Sam. 3:3: Absalom was the son of King David by Maakah, daughter of King Talmai of Geshur). The substantial city was apparently destroyed during the Assyrian conquest in the late eighth century. During the Second Temple period, Bethsaida was a notably less remarkable town. Even when it was elevated to *polis* status in AD 30 by Herod Philip, who dedicated the town to Livia/Julia, the wife of Augustus and mother of Tiberius, it lacked the scale of wealth of Sepphoris and Tiberias in the Galilee tetrarchy of his brother. The archaeological remains suggest that Bethsaida 'was filled with unrealized delusions of grandeur not actualized in the humble basalt structures'.[82] The total population is estimated at two hundred residents. Bethsaida was the home town of three of the Twelve (Andrew, Peter, Philip; John 1:44; 12:21). If the miracle took place west of the Jordan river, the directive of verse 45 to go to the 'other side' would refer to the east side of the lake, a location east of the Jordan river, which fits Bethsaida. In verse 53 they return to the west side of the lake after a period of time, which means 'there is no need to accuse Mark of ignorance concerning the geography of Galilee' (Stein, p. 322).

After Jesus *dismissed the crowd*, having taken leave of the disciples, he retreats to a *mountain* (NRSV; *oros* also means 'hill') in order to pray in solitude (cf. 1:35; 14:35). Jesus causes spectacular miracles to happen, which imply divine control of nature, but he remains dependent on the Father, expressed in personal communion with God.

47–48. It was now after sundown, *later that night* (NIV; BDAG, p. 746, *opsios* meaning 1). The translation 'when evening came' (ESV,

---

82. Arav and Savage, in Fiensy and Strange, *Galilee*, II, p. 260. For the population figure cf. M. Appold, in Arav and Freund, *Bethsaida*, II, p. 32.

NRSV, RSV; cf. NASB) does not take into account the time needed for the events mentioned. The comment that *the boat was in the middle of the lake* and that Jesus *was alone on land* does not describe a problem that needed to be solved: the disciples were not in danger, and Jesus could have walked to Bethsaida by himself. The contrast sets up the miracle that will take place shortly. The fact that Jesus *saw the disciples straining at the oars* (lit. 'they were subject to severe distress in propelling [the boat] along', or 'they had a rough going in the waves') signals that the time was the pre-dawn period which allowed faint visibility. This is confirmed by the comment that this happened *at about the fourth watch of the night* (NASB; NIV 'shortly before dawn'; NRSV 'early in the morning'). The reference reflects the Roman custom of dividing the time between sundown and sunrise, about 6 pm and 6 am, into four equal periods of watches during each of which assigned persons were responsible for security. The 'fourth watch' (Lat. *quarta vigilia*) corresponds roughly to 3 am to 6 am. The time reference indicates that the disciples had been rowing for hours, failing to make much progress due to the fact that *the wind was against them*, blowing from a westerly direction.

Mark records the miracle with two simple verbs, describing what happened as a matter of course: *he went out to them, walking on the lake*. The drama is in what happens, not in the language. Biblically literate readers might notice an echo of Job 9:8 where God is referred to as the one who 'alone stretches out the heavens and treads on the waves of the sea'.[1] Jesus is doing what only God the Creator can do. Since Jesus' departure on his 'lake walk' is prompted by his seeing the disciples' distress, the comment that *he intended to pass them by* (NRSV) is confusing. Interpretations of the statement include the following: the verb 'intended' means 'about to' (NIV); the

---

1. References to the exodus, when God 'made a way through the sea, a path through the mighty waters' (Isa. 43:16; cf. Ps. 77:19; Sir. 24:5–6), are less relevant since they do not speak of walking on water. There are a few examples of stories of a hero walking on water: Xerxes, enabled by Zeus (Herodotus 7.56), Heracles (Seneca, *Herc. fur.* 319–324); other references to a person striding over the sea seem to be figures of speech; cf. Bock, p. 215.

formulation reflects the disciples' point of view; the verb 'pass by' should be understood as 'save' (in line with Amos 7:8; 8:2); Jesus intended to test the disciples' faith; Jesus intended to walk alongside the disciples; Jesus intended to walk ahead so that the disciples could 'follow' him. While some of these explanations are possible, a more plausible interpretation sees an intentional echo of theophany language of the Old Testament where God reveals himself to his people by 'passing by' them (Exod. 33:22; 33:19; 34:6; 1 Kgs 19:11; Job 9:11). The sentence could thus be translated: 'He intended to manifest himself to him.'

49–50. Since nobody had ever seen a person walking on water in the middle of a lake before, the reaction of the disciples, who *all saw him*, is understandable: they *cried out* and *were terrified* and *thought he was a ghost*. The term *phantasma* denotes an apparition, a phantom or a ghost, the disembodied spirit of a dead person. The disciples could not have thought that they were seeing Jesus' ghost, since they had no reason to believe that Jesus was dead. When they cried out in terror, they had not yet recognized him. Jesus, approaching the boat, still walking on the water, assures them that their fear is unnecessary. He summons them to *take courage*: they have no reason to be afraid. Then he identifies himself: *It is I*. He tells the disciples that they know him and they should recognize him. The phrase *egō eimi* ('It is I') is used when God reveals his name to Israel (Exod. 3:14; Deut. 32:39 LXX); in Isaiah God identifies himself as the one true God with the designation 'I am he' (Isa. 41:4; 43:10, 13, 25; 46:4; 48:12; 51:12; the Hebrew phrase *'ănî-hû* is translated in the LXX as *egō eimi*). However, since the context calls for a self-identification of Jesus for the benefit of the disciples who do not recognize him, it is not plausible to assume that the statement is a declaration of divinity ('I am Yahweh').

51–52. As Jesus climbs over the railing into the boat, *the wind died down*. The sudden cessation of the winds that had made the disciples' progress on the lake agonizingly slow is a second miracle, recalling the calming of the storm in 4:35–41. Jesus has absolute power over nature. The disciples were *completely amazed*, which is a recurrent feature of people's reactions to Jesus' miracles (cf. 1:22, 27; 2:12; 5:15, 20, 42; 12:17). Mark explains the disciples' amazement with the surprising statement *for they had not understood about the loaves*. He censures them for being 'only' amazed: they should have moved 'beyond the stage of instinctive astonishment to one of understanding who Jesus is' (France, p. 273). After the calming of the storm, they asked the question 'Who is this?' After the miracle of the loaves, they should have been able to answer this question more fully and seen Jesus' ministry in a new light, a fact that Jesus points out to them in 8:14–21. Mark traces their failure truly to understand Jesus to the fact that *their hearts were hardened*, a serious condition that afflicted Pharaoh (Exod. 7:3, 13, 22; 8:15, 32; 9:12; 10:1) and the people of Israel at the time of Isaiah (Isa. 6:10), the latter example having been alluded to by Jesus in the description of the 'outsiders' who fail to understand his message of the kingdom of God (4:12). The charge of having a 'hardened heart' is levelled against the disciples again in 8:17 in the context of Jesus' warning about the Pharisees and Herod Antipas. This is the beginning of a less flattering portrayal of the disciples.

Theology
The main emphasis of the text is the divine power of Jesus. He walks and talks with his disciples, as any master would do with his students, but he is more than an ordinary human being. As God, the creator of the world, walks on the mighty seas (Job 9:8), so Jesus walks on the water of the Sea of Galilee. As Yahweh 'passed before' Moses and Elijah (Exod. 33:18–23; 1 Kgs 19:10–12) to reveal his glory, so Jesus reveals his divine authority on the lake as he walks towards the boat in which the disciples, struggling with the wind, are terrified. Rationalistic explanations that attempt to remove the element of the miraculous face the irony of Job 9:10: God performs 'wonders that cannot be fathomed, miracles that cannot be counted'.

v. Healing the sick in Gennesaret (6:53–56)
Context
The report of Jesus healing at Gennesaret on the west side of the Sea of Galilee concludes Mark's report of the movements of Jesus and the disciples after the disciples' return from their preaching tour through Galilee (cf. 6:7–13, 30–32, 45). Mark provides another summary of Jesus' ministry, highlighting his healing ministry. Earlier

summaries which also emphasize Jesus' popularity are given in 1:32–34; 3:7–12.

Comment

53. On the geographical movement of Jesus and the disciples see on verse 45. *Gennesaret* was a plain on the west side of the Sea of Galilee between Capernaum in the north and Magdala in the south (mod. el-Ghuweir). Josephus describes the temperate climate and the beauty of the plain, with fruitful soil that allowed the people to plant all sorts of trees, in particular walnut trees, palm trees, fig trees, olive trees and grapes (*War* 3.516). The valley has been linked with the inhabitants of Taricheae (Magdala). It is disputed whether a town named Gennesaret (Ginnosar) existed. Archaeological remains at Tel Kinrot (Tell el-'Oreme), 3 miles (5 km) south-west of Capernaum, probably the Old Testament town of Kinnereth (Josh. 19:35), attest to a farmstead and perhaps a harbour. Some identify Gennesaret as a village (mod. Khirbet Abu Shushe) in the western part of the valley, at one point probably the most important town on the western shore of the Sea of Galilee, giving its name to the lake (Leibner, 'Gennesar'). The term *they . . . anchored* means literally 'to bring a ship into harbour'.

54–55. Jesus' arrival in an area close to Capernaum prompts general excitement. People immediately recognize Jesus and inform *that whole region*, that is, the villagers in the Gennesar Valley, that Jesus is in the area. The reference to running highlights the excitement, and perhaps also the concern that he might leave soon. Jesus did not stay on the shore. He travelled in the valley, followed by people who *carried those who were ill on mats* – seriously ill people who were unable to walk – to wherever they heard Jesus was.

56. The result of Jesus' ministry is formulated in terms of people from every village (*kōmē*; cf. 1:38), town (*polis*) and farm (*agros*; cf. 5:14; 6:36) carrying their sick family members and putting them in the *marketplaces*. The *agora* was the public space where the locals sold food and other products (7:4), where scribes expected to be greeted (12:38), where people looked for work (Matt. 20:3) and where children played (Matt. 11:16). The sick lying on their mats plead with Jesus to be allowed to touch *the edge of his cloak*; that is, the fringe of his robe (*himation*; cf. 5:15). For the idea that merely touching Jesus would bring healing see on 3:10; 5:28. The term *kraspedon* refers to the 'edge, border, hem' of a garment. If Jesus followed Numbers 15:38–39, Deuteronomy 22:12, the term may refer to the 'tassel' (Hebr. *ṣîṣit*) that an Israelite had to wear on the four corners of his outer garment. In 3:7–12 people touch *Jesus*; in 5:21–34 the woman touches Jesus' *garment*; and the people of the Gennesar Valley touch only the *fringe of his garment*. It is unclear whether this 'progression' is deliberate, whether Mark points to the humility of the people, or whether he implies that the fringe of Jesus' outer garment was the most easily accessible part of Jesus that they could touch. Even the very sick know that Jesus can heal them with unprecedented power. They do not simply touch the hem of Jesus' robe: they ask for permission. The request for him to authorize their touch suggests an implied reference to faith: the sick take the initiative, but they know that healing is totally dependent upon Jesus' will.

Theology
Jesus is the focus of the excitement of the people. Jesus is not the subject of the verbs in this short text: 'Jesus does not go out looking for patients; it is the people who take the initiative' (France, p. 275). Mark underscores again the dramatic power of Jesus. The comment that the sick lying on mats in the marketplace pleaded with Jesus to let them touch the fringe of his robe indicates that faith reaches out to Jesus and acknowledges the sovereign, divine power of Jesus in the act of healing.

vi. Controversy over tradition and purity (7:1–23)
Context
After a series of miracles around and on the Sea of Galilee, Mark returns to the controversy that accompanied Jesus' ministry. Pharisees and law experts from Jerusalem had assessed Jesus' authority as being inspired by Satan (cf. 3:22). Now they continue to observe Jesus whose new pronouncements (7:15, 19) are potentially more radical than his behaviour on the Sabbath and his statements about the Sabbath (2:23–27; 3:1–6). When we connect Jesus' pronouncements about purity with his subsequent ministry outside Jewish territory (7:24 – 8:10), the growing polarization between Jesus and the Jewish leaders becomes obvious. The controversy over ritual purity is the hinge between the Jewish and the Gentile phases of Jesus' ministry

in the north, and it foreshadows the conflict that awaits him when he makes his way to Jerusalem (10:1, 32).

Comment

1–2. After *teachers of the law* from Jerusalem had accused Jesus of being possessed by Beelzebul (3:22) in an earlier episode, a new delegation from Jerusalem arrived in Galilee, collaborating with the local Pharisees in their continued investigation of Jesus and his teaching.[2] The subject they raise suggests that these scribes were Pharisees. Local Pharisees had been described as opposing Jesus concerning his practice of eating with sinners and on questions of ritual purity (2:16, 24; 3:6). Now Jerusalem is mentioned as the source of opposition to Jesus.

The point of contention is connected with the behaviour of Jesus' disciples: the Pharisees and scribes had observed some of the disciples *eating food with hands that were defiled*. The term *defiled* (*koinos*) is translated by Mark for his Gentile readers as *unwashed* (*aniptos*). In Leviticus, the term for things or people that were ceremonially impure is *akathartos* (Hebr. *tāmē'*). In the struggle against Antiochus IV who ordered the Jews to slaughter for sacrifice pigs and other animals whose edibility was 'common' (*koinos*) to the surrounding peoples, but which the Mosaic law had defined as ritually unclean and forbidden for consumption, the term *koinos* became a term for ritually impure food.[3] The only handwashing for the purpose of ritual purity stipulated by the Mosaic law concerns the priests before offering sacrifice (Exod. 30:18–21; 40:30–32). Scribes discussed whether washing of hands should be extended to the eating of ordinary food and be required of Jews other than priests. The later Mishnah devotes the tractate *Yadayim* ('Hands') to these matters, developing the principle that since the hands are 'ever busy' (*m. Toh.* 7:8), liable to be in contact with unclean things, they are a source of ritual impurity.

---

2. On the teachers of the law cf. 1:22; on Jerusalem, 3:8; on the Pharisees, 2:16.

3. Booth, *Purity*, p. 120. For *koinos* denoting ritual impurity cf. Acts 10:14–15, 28; 11:8–9; 21:28; Rom. 14:14; Heb. 9:13; 10:29.

3–4. Mark clarifies Jewish rituals of purity in a parenthetical comment aimed at Gentile readers. Pharisees *give their hands a ceremonial washing* (lit. 'wash their hands with the fist', meaning 'up to the fist or wrist', 'with a fistful of water' or 'with a cupped hand') before they eat. The statement that *all the Jews* wash their hands before they eat is not strictly correct: the Pharisees had great influence on the people in Judea and Galilee, but their 'expansionist' view of the impurity of hands was not a general norm among the ordinary people at the time. On the other hand, Diaspora Jews practised handwashing before prayers, as a text from Alexandria attests: 'Following the customs of all the Jews, they washed their hands in the sea in the course of their prayers to God' (*Ep. Arist.* 305). If Jews washed their hands before prayer, and if they prayed before eating, they would have washed their hands before they ate (Marcus, p. 441). Mark explains that ceremonial washing of hands was a practice regulated by *the tradition of the elders*, a formulation that refers to the legal instruction that had been developed from the written Mosaic law by earlier teachers of the law (scribes, rabbis, legal scholars), here called *elders* (*presbyteroi*), in the course of history, codified in the Mishnah around AD 200.

Another Jewish practice Mark describes concerns Pharisees who return from the *marketplace* (*agora*; cf. 6:56) where they might have inadvertently come into physical contact with unclean persons or unclean food: they do not eat *unless they wash* (lit. 'immerse'). The term *baptizō* ('immerse'; cf. 1:4) denotes here not normal 'washing' but immersion in water (in a *miqveh*, a stepped immersion pool) for the purpose of ritual purification. There is no rabbinic regulation that requires pious Jews to immerse themselves after a trip to the local market. Mark adds that the Pharisees also follow the tradition of *washing* (lit. 'immersion') *of cups, pitchers and kettles*. Certain kinds of containers and utensils that could contract ritual impurity needed to be ritually cleansed (Lev. 11:32; 15:12). Stone vessels contracted ritual uncleanness less easily and were therefore preferred, for example, for storing water used for ritual purification (John 2:6). Some manuscripts add *and of beds*, which, if original, describes the desire to provide 'an even more comprehensive account of Jewish purification rites' by including the theme of Leviticus 15 (France, p. 283), or a passing phase of Pharisaic zeal, or 'the sharp edge of Markan sarcasm' (Marcus, p. 443).

5. The Pharisees and the Jerusalem scribes accuse the disciples of *eating their food with defiled hands* and thus refusing to *live according to the tradition of the elders*. The verb translated *live* (*peripateō*) means literally 'to walk' and is used here, as in many passages, figuratively in the sense of 'to conduct one's life, to comport oneself, behave, live as a habit of conduct' (BDAG, p. 803). The Hebrew term *halakhah* ('walking') was used to describe the content of the tradition resulting from the development of the Mosaic law in terms of regulations that were meant to help Jews keep the law.

6–7. Jesus responds to the accusation in two parts (vv. 6–8, 9–13). The word *hypocrite* (Gr. *hypokritēs*) originally meant 'one who expounds, interprets' and described an 'interpreter of the poet' or 'the speaker who through his interpretative words made intelligible the myth of which the songs of the chorus sang' (U. Wilckens, *TDNT*, VIII, p. 559); in Attic Greek, the term describes 'one who plays a part on the stage' (*LSJ*, p. 1886), a role-player or actor in the theatre. Later the term was used in a negative sense for the stage as a sham world and for the actor as a deceiver. Here, the term is used, as throughout the New Testament, in the sense of a 'pretender' whose words and actions contradict actual reality. The Pharisees and the rabbis from Jerusalem claim to declare the will of God but in truth they are only asserting human traditions. Jesus makes this accusation in verse 8.

Jesus' use of the word *hypocrite* and the reference to the prophet Isaiah, with the following scriptural quotation, is rhetorically effective. Jesus begins to unmask the Pharisees and scribes with an appeal to the authority of God speaking through Isaiah before offering his own comments. The statement *Isaiah . . . prophesied about you* applies the words Isaiah spoke to his eighth-century contemporaries to *you*, the Pharisees, a 'contemporarizing' use of the Old Testament that assumes a typological understanding of continuity in the relationship between God and his people, 'such that earlier events and situations appropriately serve as models for a later era of fulfilment, even though in themselves they had no predictive force' (France, p. 284). Isaiah charged his contemporaries with engaging in worship focused on external matters rather than on a close relationship with Yahweh. In describing the *worship* of Israel in which people *honour* God, the prophet sets up a contrast between *lips* which speak words addressed to God and *hearts* (cf. Mark 2:6 NRSV) which are far from God. They do not truly mean what they say; they speak the traditional prayers but they do not allow Yahweh to control their thinking, their decisions and hence their behaviour. They worship Yahweh with words, but since they do not worship him with their entire person involved, their worship is *in vain*: it serves no purpose; it is for nothing. This dichotomy between external worship and internal commitment has consequences in that *their teachings are merely human rules*: what they command as officially binding (*entalmata*, 'rules, commandments') has a purely human origin. Jesus counters the critique of his disciples who eat without having ritually cleansed their hands by pointing out that the Pharisees and scribes are more concerned with external regulations devised by human interpreters than with their fundamental relationship with God and the internal response of their thinking, their will and their commitment.

8. Jesus' basic charge is formulated with three contrasting pairs of words: the Pharisees and scribes *abandon* God's words and instead *hold to* human words; they exchange God's *commandment* for the elders' *tradition*, and thus their worship is not focused on *God* but on *human* activity (NRSV). God's revelation is 'commandment', which requires obedience, while 'tradition' developed by human beings may or may not be valuable, but cannot have the same authority as that which comes from God.

9. The second part of Jesus' response escalates the argument. The word 'abandon' in verse 8 is replaced by the more deliberate word *rejecting*; the phrase 'human tradition' becomes the more pointed *your tradition*; and the sense of intention is heightened by the purpose clause *in order to keep your tradition*, which suggests that they deliberately removed the *commandment of God* so that they could establish their tradition (NRSV). The Pharisees' wrong sense of priorities, focused as they are on external matters, has led to a deliberate evasion of God's demands. The phrase *a fine way* expresses not approval, but sarcasm.

10–12. Jesus illustrates the 'commands of God' (v. 9) with two quotations from the law. He specifically mentions *Moses* as the author who wrote down God's commands, in distinction from later interpretations and elaborations of the law that the Pharisees emphasize.

Jesus first quotes the fifth commandment from Exodus 20:12 (Deut. 5:16). The subsequent quotation of Exodus 21:17 illustrates the seriousness of the commandment to honour one's *father and mother*: breaking the fifth commandment carries the death sentence (Lev. 20:9). The fifth commandment is in a completely different league from the issue of washing hands for ritual purification before eating. In Jewish tradition, honouring one's parents included especially caring for their physical needs in old age (cf. Sir. 3:3, 8, 12–16; Philo, *Decal.* 116–118). Withholding support from parents is tantamount to *speaking evil* of them (NRSV; NIV 'curse') or 'insulting' them.

The 'tradition of the elders' had found a way to say *but* to the fifth commandment, allowing a son to shirk his responsibility to support his parents. Jesus refers to the scribal regulation that allows a son to tell his parents, *Whatever support you might have had from me is Corban* (NRSV). The verb 'support' (*ōpheleō*) means 'to provide assistance, help, aid, benefit, be of use'. The word *Corban* (*korban*), which is a transliterated Hebrew term (*qorbān*) meaning 'sacrificial offering' (cf. Lev. 2:1, 4, 12, 14), is explained by Mark for his Gentile readers with the Greek word 'gift' (*dōron*); English translations add *to God*, which is not in the Greek text but technically correct: *qorbān* is an offering consecrated to the temple; that is, to God. If a son declares that the material support he might have given his parents is *qorbān*, he pledges these particular possessions to God and removes them from ordinary human use. Uttering the word *qorbān* renders the vow binding, and vows must not be broken (Num. 30:2; Deut. 23:21–23; the Mishnaic tractate *Nedarim* is devoted to vows). It is not clear how the son in verse 11 who declares some of his possessions *qorbān* can retain the benefit of these possessions which he denies to his parents. An example of how this worked comes from an Aramaic ossuary inscription that says, 'Whatever benefit a man may derive from this ossuary (is a) qorban (sacrificial offering) to God from him who is in it' (*CIIP* I/1, No. 287). The person whose bones are in the ossuary uses a *qorbān*-vow to prevent violations of the bone casket by addition or removal of bones. The rabbis discussed conflicts between the obligations of the fifth commandment and the obligation of keeping a *qorbān* vow. According to *Mishnah Nedarim* 9:1 the commandment to honour parents overrules any vow. Jesus addresses the position and practice of more rigorous rabbis who refused to allow the release from an ill-considered or wrongly motivated *qorbān*-vow. It seems that the earlier Pharisaic strictness regarding vows was relaxed by the rabbis after AD 70, as Pharisaic sectarianism and stringency was replaced by rabbinic inclusiveness and leniency. If the Jerusalem scribes were priests, they would have a motive for insisting that *qorbān*-vows be honoured (Marcus, pp. 445–446). The phrase *you no longer permit doing anything* (NRSV) suggests that such cases were brought before a rabbinical court in which the scribes refused to release a son from his vow, even when he wished to be released (France, p. 287).

13. Jesus repeats what he has said in verses 8, 9, now using the formally legal term *nullify* (*akyroō*, 'make void, invalidate'). These scribes dared to rule *the word of God* to be unlawful, giving priority to their own *tradition* that they had *handed down*, passed on from rabbi to rabbi. The phrase *word of God* refers here not to the 'Bible' nor to the Christian message but to the specific divine pronouncement of the fifth commandment. The statement *and you do many things like that* accuses the Pharisees and Jerusalem scribes of the fact that the way they circumvent the obligations of the fifth commandment is only one example of their tendency to give priority to external matters rather than to a person's personal response to God.

14–16. The account shifts from a private discussion to a public conversation that involves *the crowd*, the people who are present to listen to Jesus' teaching. Jesus' initial response to the Pharisees and Jerusalem scribes in verses 6–13 did not specifically address the matter of eating with 'defiled hands' but examined their priorities in terms of external versus internal piety and in terms of the location of authority. Now Jesus addresses the principle of defilement by means of external contacts. The summons *Listen to me, everyone, and understand this* reminds Mark's readers of the language of chapter 4 and underlines the fact that 'hearing' (4:3, 9, 15–16, 18, 20, 23–24) needs to progress to 'understanding', otherwise one falls under the verdict of Isaiah 6:9–10 quoted in 4:12.

Jesus' answer to the Pharisees' position on defilement and purity is conveyed with a 'parable' or analogy (v. 17), 'an epigrammatic saying whose potentially wide application is balanced by its enigmatic form, so that it is for the hearers to work out its significance for themselves' (France, p. 288). Jesus' pronouncement is formulated as an antithetical parallelism ('not... but'; cf. 2:17, 22; 10:43; 12:25). The negative pronouncement comes first: *nothing outside a person can defile them by going into them*; then the contrasting, positive pronouncement: *it is what comes out of a person that defiles them*. The first part of the pronouncement assumes that the Pharisees believe that hands that have not been immersed and ritually purified transmit their impurity to the food they touch, which in turn, when eaten, transmits its impurity to the person who eats the food. The second part of the pronouncement is not to be taken literally in the sense that bodily discharges (*what comes out of a person*) are in view and that Jesus argued for the regulations of Leviticus 15 (bodily discharges) over against those of Leviticus 11 (clean and unclean food). Jesus argues basic principles, not the priority of one set of regulations over another set of regulations.

Several matters should be noted. (1) Ritual uncleanness is not always tantamount to sin. The uncleanness of the 'impure spirits' that Jesus drives out of demon-possessed people is not the basic paradigm for describing Jewish notions of purity and impurity. (2) Ritual defilement (impurity) that excluded from public worship and close social intercommunication until a purification ritual was completed (cf. Lev. 7:19–21) could be contracted not only by food but also by touching unclean things (e.g. corpses), by skin disease and by various bodily emissions. Jesus' pronouncement concerns, specifically, food laws (*kashrut*), not necessarily all purity regulations (*toharot*). (3) Jesus' double pronouncement could be understood, in a Semitic context, as a comparison rather than an absolute contrast: what comes out of a person defiles more than what goes into a person (cf. Isa. 1:11–17; Jer. 7:22–23; Hos. 6:6; Amos 5:21–27). Some interpreters claim therefore that Jesus did not actually abrogate the principle of unclean food; they regard the explicit statement in verse 19 as Mark's later interpretation (Booth, *Purity*, pp. 69–71). However, Jesus' pronouncement clearly formulates an outright antithesis: it is *not* possible for *anything* from outside a person to defile that person (cf. v. 18). There is no ambiguity: food that is eaten does not defile; what defiles is the evil that is inherent in human beings. Jesus' response to the disciples' question (vv. 17–18) suggests that the point of his pronouncement was too obvious to need an explanation. (4) Jesus' (assumed) participation in the temple cult and the approval of priestly purification of healed lepers (1:44) suggests to some that he did not abolish the purity laws. (5) When Jesus touched lepers (1:41), the dead (5:41) and a haemorrhaging woman (5:27), he deliberately disregarded purity laws. In these cases purity is transferred by touch from Jesus (the pure) to the impure, healing the disease and raising the dead. This does not necessarily imply that Jesus' presence abrogates the purity laws, although it differs from later rabbinic literature, which is much more interested in the reverse contact in which impurity is transferred by touch to the pure. At the same time, Jesus never defends ritual purity as a symbol of moral purity. The fact that the early church struggled with the question of food suggests that Jesus' pronouncement could be heard in different ways.[86]

17–19. The disciples ask Jesus about the meaning of the *parable* or 'analogy' (*parabolē*; cf. 3:23). Jesus' initial response with two questions – *Are you so dull?* ('void of understanding') and *Don't you see?* – suggests that they should have understood the meaning of the analogy of food entering a person and of things that do defile a person. This is not the first time, nor the last time, that Jesus censures the disciples for a lack of understanding (6:52; 8:17, 21). What differentiates the disciples from the 'outsiders' of 4:11–12, who do not understand is not an inherent ability to grasp Jesus' pronouncements but the fact that they receive privileged instruction from Jesus.

Jesus explains the first part of the pronouncement in verse 15 in verses 18b–19, and the second part in verses 20–23. Jesus first repeats the first line of the pronouncement, replacing 'nothing (outside) ... can defile' with *whatever ... (from outside) cannot defile* (v. 18b, NRSV). It is *not* possible for *anything* from outside to defile a person. Verse 19a states what happens to food that enters a person: it enters the *stomach* (*koilia*, 'the digestive tract in its fullest extent', the belly, stomach; BDAG, p. 550) and what remains of the food after digestion goes out into the *sewer* (NRSV *aphedrōn*; 'toilet, latrine, privy'). The food that enters a person does not go *into their heart*: the progress of the food through the body makes no contact with the part of a person that really matters, namely the heart. The term

---

86. V. 16 ('If anyone has ears to hear, let them hear') is absent from the earliest manuscripts; it is a scribal gloss, introduced from 4:9, 23.

heart should not be confused with 'emotion' but be linked with the intellectual, cognitive and spiritual faculties of a person (cf. 2:6, 8; 3:5; 6:52; 7:6). A person's thinking and will are not affected by food. Mark adds the editorial comment *In saying this, Jesus declared all foods clean* (lit. 'he cleansed all food'). The food laws (*kashrut*) of the law no longer apply. This is not a contradiction to the pronouncement in verse 15, as some interpreters suggest, but an inevitable deduction from the principle stated in verse 15 and its further elaboration in verses 18b–19a. Since Jesus accepts Moses' authority as conveying the word of God (1:44; 7:10; 10:3; 12:26; cf. Matt. 5:17–20), the pronouncement of Jesus points to his authority as the Messiah and Son of God (1:1) who proclaims the new reality of the kingdom of God in which food no longer defiles a person, taking his followers back to the time before Moses when all food was clean.[87]

20–23. Now Jesus interprets the second part of the pronouncement verse 15, explaining why true defilement comes from *within, out of a person's heart*. Defiling things are not external but things that originate in the *heart* (*kardia*) of a person. What follows is a 'vice list'. Such lists were used by Jewish and early Christian authors to illustrate severe and representative offences that people commit.[88] *Evil thoughts* is the overarching category that explains the defiling evil that resides in a person's heart: what controls the heart, the seat of thought and will (cf. 2:6), controls the reasoning and the actions of a human being. The following list mentions twelve items. The first six nouns are plural and take up commandments of the Decalogue (Exod. 20:13–15; Deut. 5:17–19, 21); the other six are singular, an arrangement that is probably rhetorical. Most of the first six nouns describe repeatable actions, while the items in the second half denote vices in the abstract (but not *greed*, unconvincingly translated in NASB as 'deeds of coveting').

---

87. Bock, p. 225; Stein, p. 345; for the last point cf. Witherington, p. 231.
88. Wis. 14:25–26; *1 En.* 91:6–7; 4 Macc. 1:2–8; 1QS IV, 9–11; Philo, *Sacr.* 32 (listing 150 items); in the NT cf. Rom. 1:29–31; 1 Cor. 5:10–11; 6:9–10; 2 Cor. 12:20–21; Gal. 5:19–21; Col. 3:5–8; 1 Tim. 1:9–10; 3:2–5; Titus 3:3; 1 Peter 4:3. With the exception of 'evil thoughts' and 'lewdness', all the items in Mark 7:21–22 are mentioned in the NT lists.

Sexual immorality (*porneiai*) or 'fornication', an extension of the seventh commandment, denotes unlawful sexual intercourse, including, in a Jewish context, adultery, prostitution and homosexual acts. *Theft* ('stealing'), taking the property that belongs to another person, contravenes the eighth commandment. *Murder*, the extrajudicial killing of a person, breaks the sixth commandment. *Adultery* (*moicheia*), marital sexual unfaithfulness of a husband or wife, breaks the seventh commandment, which carried the death sentence (Lev. 20:10; Deut. 22:22), a fact that shows the seriousness of the offence. *Greed* ('avarice, covetousness') is the desire to have more than one's due, addressed in the tenth commandment. *Malice* ('wickedness, baseness, maliciousness, sinfulness') describes a disposition without moral or social values. *Deceit* ('cunning, treachery') is taking advantage of another person through underhand methods. *Lewdness* ('self-abandonment, licentiousness, debauchery') is a lack of self-constraint which involves a person in behaviour that violates the bounds of what is socially acceptable. *Envy* (lit. 'evil eye') is a lack of generosity. *Slander* (*blasphēmia*, 'reviling, denigration, disrespect'; cf. 3:28) is speech that denigrates or defames. *Arrogance* ('haughtiness, pride') is the state of having an undue sense of one's importance, bordering on insolence. *Folly* ('foolishness, lack of sense') describes a person who lacks prudence or good judgment; in the Old Testament wisdom texts the 'fool' is the 'wicked' person whose foolishness consists in 'the wrong attitude to God which prevents him from knowing how to behave properly' (France, p. 293). Jesus concludes by restating the assertion of verse 20 which explains the second part of the pronouncement in verse 15: *all these evils* which reside in a person's heart and control his or her thinking, will and behaviour, *defile a person*. Sin, not food, makes impure.

Theology

Peter's vision in Joppa, his visit to Gentiles in Caesarea, the necessity to explain his actions in Jerusalem (Acts 10:1 – 11:18), the clash between Paul and Peter in Antioch (Gal. 2:11–14), and the deliberations and decisions of the so-called Apostles' Council in Jerusalem (Acts 15) all demonstrate that the leaders of the early church needed time, and privileged revelation, to settle the matter of ritual purity. Paul's declaration in Romans 14:14, 'I am convinced, being fully persuaded in the Lord Jesus, that nothing is unclean in itself', suggests that not all (Jewish) believers agreed with this pronouncement.

Jesus did not make ritual purity a test case of loyalty to God. As Jesus associated with 'sinners', he demonstrated that his mission had no place for keeping separate from the impure. As Jesus is the Son of Man who is 'Lord even of the Sabbath' (2:28), he is also Lord of the Mosaic law which, according to the prophet Jeremiah, would one day no longer be written on tablets of stone but on the hearts of God's people (Jer. 31:33), who would be empowered by God's Spirit (Isa. 44:3; Ezek. 11:19; 36:26; 39:29; Joel 2:28). The good news of the kingdom of God is like new wine that breaks open old structures (Mark 2:22). It is in this larger context that Jesus' pronouncement about food, ritual purity and true impurity needs to be understood.

vii. *The faith of the Syro-Phoenician woman (7:24–30)*
Context
After his pronouncement that all foods are clean (7:19), Jesus' second move outside Jewish territory into 'unclean' Gentile territory (cf. 5:1–20) assumes a deeper significance. The tour into Phoenicia in Syria (7:24–25) and the travel to the Decapolis (7:31) marks a new phase in Jesus' ministry in the course of which Gentiles are the beneficiaries of a second feeding miracle (8:1–10); it is interrupted by two episodes in Jewish territory (8:11–13, 14–21), after which Jesus travels again to regions east of the Jordan river, first to Bethsaida (8:22–26), then to Caesarea Philippi (8:27–30). The story of the Syro-Phoenician woman needs to be read in this context. Far from pointing to Jesus' reservation about helping Gentiles, his initial reluctance to liberate the woman's daughter from an impure spirit dramatically underlines the new possibilities of contact with Gentiles.

Comment
24. Jesus left Galilee and travelled *to the region of Tyre* (NRSV; cf. 3:8); the term *horion* means 'boundary', and used in the plural it denotes a region or district, here the administrative district in southern Syria controlled by Tyre. The population of Tyre had repeatedly participated in anti-Jewish actions (1 Macc. 5:15). After the Roman annexation of Syria in 63 BC, Tyre retained administrative

autonomy. King Herod I expelled the Tyrians from three fortresses in Galilee at the beginning of his reign, but then released the captured Tyrians and gave them gifts; he financed several buildings in Tyre, including colonnaded halls and an *agora*, visited the city on numerous occasions and employed Tyrian soldiers in his army.[89] The city of Tyre, about 35 miles (55 km) north-west of Capernaum, was the main urban centre near Galilee. The coins that the city minted in mass quantities were the most stable currency, used throughout Galilee and beyond. The bad blood between Tyrians and Galileans – Josephus describes Tyrians as 'notoriously our most bitter enemies' (*Ap*. 1.70) – was in part due to the fact that Jewish trade in the region was dependent on the wealthy merchants of Tyre; the agricultural production of Jewish Galilee supported the higher standard of living of the Tyrians.[90]

Mark does not provide a reason for Jesus' move to Gentile territory. Jesus may have wanted to escape the attention of Herod Antipas (cf. 6:16), create some distance between himself and the Pharisees and Jerusalem scribes (7:1, 5) or deliberately spend time among Gentiles. The comment that Jesus entered a *house* suggests that some of the people around Tyre who had travelled to Capernaum to hear Jesus teach and to see him drive out demons and heal the sick (3:8) remained sympathizers, or had become followers who were able and willing to provide accommodation for Jesus and the Twelve. Jesus wanted to be alone with his disciples (cf. 1:35; 3:13; 4:10; 6:31–32), but he was not able to escape people in need.

25–26. The *woman* who approached Jesus presumably had heard about Jesus before (cf. 3:8); now she hears that he is in the area. The reason for her arrival at the house in which Jesus is staying is the condition of her *little daughter* (cf. 5:23, Jairus' daughter), who has *an unclean spirit* (NRSV; 1:23, 26–27; 3:11; 5:2, 8, 13; 6:7), a *demon* (1:34, 39; 3:15; 5:13; 6:13) that she wants expelled. The daughter is evidently tormented by the demon to the extent that she cannot travel with

---

89. Josephus, *Ant.* 14.297–299; *War* 1.231–238, 422.
90. Cf. Theißen, *Gospels*, pp. 72–80. In the OT, Tyre is often condemned for its wealth and materialism; see Isa. 23:8–9; Ezek. 27 – 28; Joel 3:4–6; Zech. 9:2–4. For the later Christian community in Tyre see Acts 21:3–6.

her mother. Mark describes the woman as *a Greek* (*Hellēnis*), a term that describes not merely ethnic Greeks but often more broadly a person who is 'Greek' in language and culture, a description that may suggest that the woman was a member of the upper classes, a possibility that may also be indicated by the fact that she acts independently (Theißen, *Gospels*, pp. 70–71). This interpretation of the term is more plausible than the alternative that understands *Hellēnis* in terms of 'Gentile' or 'polytheist'. The latter is indicated by the description of the woman as *Syro-Phoenician* (*Syrophoinikissa*): she is a Gentile living in the Phoenician territory of Syria. If the woman had indeed upper-class status, the statement that *she begged Jesus* to free her daughter of the demon implies a reversal of roles: a wealthy woman from Tyre seeks help from Jesus, a Galilean.

27. Jesus' response to the woman's request for help seems offensive. Using an analogy, he calls the Jewish people *children*, meaning 'God's children' (cf. Deut. 14:1; Isa. 1:2), and the Gentiles *dogs*. The diminutive *kynarion* refers to a pet dog, a form of the term either to soften the saying by avoiding *kyōn*, which is sometimes used for a large, fierce and savage dog, or because the context requires dogs present at a meal in the house.[91] In the biblical tradition, dogs are often mentioned in parallel with pigs and prostitutes and associated with the wicked.[92] To call someone a 'dog' was an insult (1 Sam. 17:43; Isa. 56:10–11). As wild dogs scavenged for carrion, including that of unclean animals (Exod. 22:31; 1 Kgs 14:11), they were regarded as unclean. In some Jewish texts, dogs are symbols for Gentiles (*1 En.* 89:42, 46–49). It should be noted that some Jewish texts write about friendly dogs (Tob. 6:1; 11:4; *b. 'Abod. Zar.* 54b); in a later text, domestic dogs symbolize righteous Gentiles (*Midr. Ps.* 4:11). The label *dogs* formulates 'a challenge to the woman to justify her request' (Hooker, p. 183).

A surface reading of the text has Jesus refuse the woman's request with ethnocentric language. This interpretation is called into question not only by the fact that in Mark, Jesus is never caught off guard,

---

91. A. L. Connolly, in *NewDocs*, IV, pp. 157–159. In several epitaphs, pet dogs are depicted near the tables of their reclining owners.
92. 1 Kgs 22:38; Ps. 22:16; Matt. 7:6; Phil. 3:2; 2 Peter 2:22; Rev. 22:15.

but also, and more importantly, by the ending of the passage. Verse 29 does not support an interpretation in terms of 'because you have changed my mind'; it means, rather, 'because you have passed the test'. Jesus' words in verse 27 are, in Mark's plot, a test of faith.[93] A positive agenda is also suggested by the term *first* (*prōton*) at the beginning of Jesus' initial response: *first* the children eat, then the dogs. Jesus describes his mission as initially directed at the Jewish people, but now also extending to Gentiles, challenging the Greek woman with a provocative statement 'to claim what is rightfully hers' (Strauss, p. 313).

28. The woman evidently regards Jesus' response as an invitation to press the analogy further: since Jesus had been active among the 'children' of Israel for months and since he has now taken the initiative to come to the region of Tyre, he surely would be willing to do for her daughter what he had done 'first' for many Jews. The address *Lord* is deferential and perhaps indicates that the woman acknowledges Jesus' authority and her dependence upon his help. She expresses her confidence that Jesus will help by utilizing the potential of Jesus' analogy: the *dogs under the table* do indeed eat, even if it is *the children's crumbs*. The term *psichion* (diminutive of *psix*, 'bit, crumb', especially of bread) describes the crumbs of bread that fall from the table (*trapeza*) when children eat. Since children let breadcrumbs fall under the table while they eat, the woman seems to be saying that the dogs under the table do not have to wait until the children have finished eating but can now eat the crumbs that fall from the table (Strauss, p. 314). Note that *psichion* does not mean 'leftover' (GNB): the response of the woman does not describe the dogs eating after the children have finished their meal but suggests simultaneous eating.

29–30. On account of her *reply* (*logos*) Jesus grants the woman's request that he drive a demon out from her daughter. In the context of Mark's narrative, where the incident is placed at the beginning of Jesus' ministry in Gentile territory, Jesus' words are a test of the

---

93. Marcus, p. 468. Camery-Hoggatt, *Irony*, pp. 150–151, sees witty, 'peirastic' irony, 'a form of verbal challenge intended to test the other's response. It may in fact declare the opposite of the speaker's actual intention.'

woman's faith. In the parallel text in Matthew 15:28 Jesus explicitly comments on the woman's 'great faith'. Jesus dismisses the woman with the announcement that *the demon has left your daughter*, who had remained 'in her house' (NIV 'home') lying on her *bed* (*klinē*). When the woman returned, she found *the demon gone*. Mark records no command of Jesus, who heals from a distance, highlighting again his unique authority.

Theology
Since the Jewish people have been entrusted with the words of God (Rom. 3:1–2), they have priority in salvation history (cf. Rom. 1:16; 3:1–2). Jesus emphasizes this point, all the more remarkable in view of the opposition of the Jewish leaders. At the same time, Gentiles have been promised God's blessing in the Abrahamic promise of Genesis 12:3, which is now being fulfilled in the mission of the believers in Jesus Messiah. The move beyond Judea (Matt. 28:19; Acts 1:8) is foreshadowed in Jesus' ministry, both here and in 5:1–20.

The Syro-Phoenician woman is an example of persistent faith (mentioned by Matthew, implied by Mark). She responds to news about Jesus and his authority. She approaches Jesus, convinced that he has the power to free her daughter from demons. She perseveres with both boldness and humility in the face of an initial lack of positive response to her request. She has spiritual discernment in terms of what Jesus can and might do. She is 'willing to be last instead of first' (Strauss, p. 317). She trusts that Jesus has healed her daughter when he sends her home. She believes in Jesus as having unique, unprecedented authority.

viii. Healing of a deaf mute (7:31–37)
Context
The second of three miracles in Gentile territory (7:24 – 8:10) that follow Jesus' teaching about clean and unclean things takes place in the Decapolis. The episode reinforces the impact of the previous episode: the effects of the kingdom of God are experienced not only by Jews but also by Gentiles. The miracle, recorded only by Mark, is notable for the use of saliva for healing and for the use of an Aramaic word in the healing (cf. 5:41). The healing of a man who was both deaf and mute represents the fulfilment of Isaiah

35:5–6 and thus signals that the days of God's promised salvation have arrived.

Comment

31. Mark describes a circuitous journey from the region of Tyre, where the previous episode had taken place, north to Sidon (24 miles [40 km] north of Tyre), and south again to the Sea of Galilee, apparently reaching the lake on its eastern shore, and then into the region of the Decapolis. Jesus seems intent on avoiding Capernaum, the centre of his earlier ministry. On Tyre see on 3:8; 7:24; on Sidon see on 3:8. Jesus had visited the Decapolis earlier when he exorcized a legion of demons from a man who, after Jesus' departure, proclaimed the news of his healing in the Decapolis (5:1–20; on the Decapolis cf. 5:1, 20). Hippos, about a mile (2 km) east of the Sea of Galilee, was one of the cities of the Decapolis, built on a Roman grid system with urban architectural infrastructure, including a minting authority, controlling the villages in the area (Josephus, *Life* 42). It is not impossible, but is not indicated in the text, that this is the location where this episode took place.

32. Relatives or friends brought a man who was *deaf*. The term *kōphos* (orig. 'blunted, dulled') could refer to the organs of either speech or hearing and can thus describe either the lack of speech capability ('mute') or a lack of hearing capability ('deaf'). In the New Testament, the term generally refers to being mute[94] but here is used of being deaf (also in 9:25; Matt. 11:5; Luke 7:22) since Mark adds the explanation that he *could hardly talk*; the term *mogilalos* can mean 'speaking with difficulty, having an impediment in one's speech' or 'mute, unable to articulate'. Since the cure involved both hearing and speech, the man was both deaf and mute. The muteness was a serious speech impediment rather than a lack of all power of speech (in v. 35 he speaks 'normally', suggesting that before he was healed he was unable to speak properly). The man probably had had a stroke which affected his abilities to articulate what he was hearing and what he wanted to say. The people who brought the man to Jesus were convinced that he could heal him: they *begged* him to *place his*

---

94. Matt. 9:32–33; 12:22; 15:30, 31; Luke 1:22; 11:14.

hand on him, which has been a standard feature in Jesus' healings of illnesses (cf. 1:31, 41; 5:23; 6:5; 8:25), although in this case the healing will turn out to be more complex.

33–35. Jesus was surrounded by a *crowd* (cf. 2:4), mentioned here in passing, but indicative of Jesus' popularity that now extends into the Gentile territory of the Decapolis. Jesus *took him aside*, wanting to heal the man in private, which agrees with the later command to remain silent about what had happened (v. 36; the verb '[he] commanded them' suggests that the man's relatives or friends witnessed the miracle). Mark reports six actions of Jesus related to the healing. First, he *put his fingers into the man's ears*: the request that Jesus place his hands on the man (v. 32) is taken up, specifically with respect to the organs that were malfunctioning; Jesus first touches the ears, perhaps indicating that the more serious affliction was the inability to hear. Second, *he spat*, perhaps into his fingers before he touched the man's tongue (although in 8:23 he spits into the man's eyes). Saliva is mentioned both in ancient miracle stories and in normal medical practice.[95] Third, he *touched the man's tongue*: he applied the saliva with his fingers to the second organ that was afflicted by disability. Since the man could not hear Jesus speak, touching him in the ears and then on the tongue signalled to the man that Jesus was present and in the process of healing him. Fourth, *he looked up to heaven*: he prayed. Fifth, he uttered *a deep sigh*, perhaps exhaling breath carrying the force of life and thus conveying healing power; perhaps a sign of deep compassion for the man; perhaps an indication of emotional involvement in the healing; or perhaps an expression of heartfelt prayer (in support of the latter cf. Rom. 8:26). Sixth, he *said to him, 'Ephphatha!'*, an Aramaic word (*'ethpetakh*) that Mark translates into Greek, and which translates into English as *Be opened!* The healing happened instantaneously: *the man's ears were opened and his tongue was loosed* so that he was able to speak *normally*. The term *orthōs* means 'acting in conformity with a norm or standard' and can be translated as 'rightly, correctly, normally, properly'

---

95. Tacitus, *Hist.* 4.81; Suetonius, *Vesp.* 7: the saliva of the emperor Vespasian heals a blind man in Alexandria. Cf. Galen, *Nat. Fac.* 3.7; Pliny, *Nat.* 28.5.25; 28.7.37; cf. Collins, pp. 370–371.

(BDAG, p. 723; most English versions translate as 'plainly'). The man was now able to hear, and his speech was intelligible. Two of the promised events that Isaiah prophesied for the time when God came (Isa. 35:5–6) had taken place.

36–37. Jesus commanded the man and his relatives and friends *not to tell anyone*. He had given the same command in 1:44; 5:43 (cf. 8:26). In the context of Galilean crowds, the command to silence was intended to avoid publicity leading to excessive, theologically uninformed enthusiasm which would hinder the mission of Jesus. Here in the Gentile Decapolis, the command is surprising, given that earlier Jesus had commanded the man whom he had liberated from demons to announce what the Lord had done for him (5:19). Perhaps the activities of this man had triggered enthusiasm for Jesus comparable to that in Galilee. The people do not maintain silence, which is hardly surprising. People spoke about the miracle that had happened because *they were utterly astonished* (NASB), a natural and repeated reaction to Jesus' miracles (cf. 1:27–28; 2:12). The rare term *hyperperissōs* ('beyond all measure, utterly'), used only here in the New Testament, underscores the dramatic nature of the miracle. The sentence *he has done all things well* (NASB) reports a somewhat general assessment of the Gentile crowd. It is unclear whether Mark wants his readers to note an echo of Genesis 1:31 LXX ('And God saw all the things that he had made, and see, they were exceedingly good', *NETS*), reinforcing the notion of the restoration of creation at the time of God's present coming.

Theology
The miracle of the healing of the deaf and mute man in the Decapolis again demonstrates Jesus' unique power and his compassion for Gentiles. The episode is closely paralleled in 8:22–26 (healing of a blind man at Bethsaida): in both miracles saliva is mentioned and Jesus touches the organs affected. When we read the passage for modern audiences we should beware of allegorical interpretations that emphasize spiritual deafness and blindness (the subject of 4:12) while losing sight of the dramatic reality of the miracle in the Decapolis. Here was a man who was severely disabled, unable to hear and unable to articulate in an intelligible manner, who now, having encountered Jesus, could hear and could speak, able to

function fully in a society that did not make allowances for disabled persons, most of whom 'worked' as beggars.

ix. The feeding of the four thousand (8:1–10)
Context
The third in a series of miracles outside Jewish territory (7:24–30, 31–37) repeats the feeding miracle of 6:30–44 for a Gentile crowd. The second feeding miracle has a smaller scale: there are fewer people, more loaves and more fish, and less food is left over. There is no plausible reason to assume that the two narratives of feeding miracles go back to one single event or that the second narrative is a creation of Mark's to make a theological point concerning Gentiles: in 8:19–21 the two feeding miracles are mentioned as two separate events, with a specific distinction in the details. It is 'more economical to accept that there were two such incidents, separately remembered and passed down in tradition' (France, pp. 306–307).

Comment
1–3. The time reference *during those days* links the miracle of the feeding of the four thousand with the previous episode in which a deaf–mute man was healed in the region of the Decapolis, perhaps near Hippos (cf. 7:31). The description *another large crowd* alerts Mark's readers that a similar event has taken place before, inviting them to compare the two miracles. Mark does not explain what Jesus means when he says that the people – in verse 9 we are told that the crowd numbered four thousand – have been with him for a period of *three days*, and he provides no details when he records Jesus as saying that some had *come a long distance*. The diminishing food supplies did not diminish the crowd but, after three days, were becoming a problem. We are left to assume that the large number of people came from all over the Decapolis, the region in which the man from Gerasa from whom Jesus had exorcized the legion of demons had been spreading the news about Jesus and his miraculous powers (5:20), prompting people to bring the deaf–mute man to Jesus in the earlier episode (7:32), a healing which was widely reported in the area (7:36–37). The miracle is traced back to Jesus' *compassion* (cf. 1:41; 6:34), expressed in direct speech, which underlines the significance

of the statement in verses 2–3. Jesus is concerned about the physical well-being of the people who are listening to him.

4. The disciples' question has been interpreted as highlighting their dullness or as corresponding to Israel's murmuring in the desert (Exod. 16:3). It seems preferable to interpret it as a perplexed reaction to the dilemma posed by the geographical location of the crowd. The fact that they do not draw on their experience of the previous feeding miracle 'is not entirely surprising' (Bock, p. 233). Jesus does not comment negatively on their question (vv. 17–18 belong to a different context). The disciples may have regarded it as presumptuous to assume that 'Jesus would meet the situation with a miracle' (Cranfield, p. 205); Jesus is not a 'vendor of miracles' and demanding miracles is a sign of Jesus' opponents (cf. vv. 11–13); and the disciples know Jesus' servant posture 'sufficiently well not to prod him for miraculous intervention' (Edwards, p. 230).

5–7. The narrative proceeds along the lines of 6:38–41 (see there for comment on details). The description is less vivid, and the numbers are different: there are seven loaves rather than five, and 'a few small fish' rather than two fish. The fish, which are mentioned as though they formed a second course of the meal, are connected with a separate blessing. Seven loaves and a few small fish are inadequate for feeding a large crowd of people, and thus underline the scope of the miracle.

8–9. The effects of the miracle are described with an extreme economy of words: the people *ate* and they *were satisfied* (or 'filled'). The disciples gathered the *broken pieces that were left over*: they collected what was not eaten 'out of the total number of pieces that were broken off in the course of distribution, not scraps left by the diners' (BDAG, p. 805, *perisseuma*). They filled seven *baskets*; in Acts 9:25 a *spyris* is a 'basket' or 'hamper' large enough to carry a person. The baskets (*kophinoi*) in the first feeding miracle were smaller wicker baskets. The number of people who were fed is given as *four thousand*, without the qualifier 'men'.

10. Since Jesus and the disciples had been in Gentile territory on the east side of the lake, the trip with the boat takes them to the west side. Their destination is *Dalmanutha*, which is otherwise not attested; Matthew 15:39 refers to Magadan, which goes back to the same Hebrew word (*migdāl*, 'tower') as Magdala. Dalmanutha seems to be the Greek version of Aramaic Migdal Nunyyaa ('Tower of the fish'), to be identified with Magadan/Magdala/Taricheae/Migdal Nunayya/Migdal Saba'ayya (mod. el-Mejdel), about 3 miles (5 km) north of Tiberias. The term 'tower' refers to the promontory of Arbel which towers over the site, or to some monumental tower that gave the name Migdal to two distinct areas of the same settlement, called Taricheae ('factories for salting fish') in Greek and Latin sources.[96]

Theology
The second feeding miracle highlights the same themes as the first (cf. 6:30–44). Here Mark underscores in particular Jesus' compassion for Gentiles. The messianic banquet that Isaiah prophesies is not for Israel alone but for 'all peoples' everywhere (Isa. 25:6). The east side of the Sea of Galilee is not 'the ends of the earth' that God's salvation will reach in Isaiah's vision in 49:6 (cf. Acts 1:8) but, as Gentiles, these are people 'far off' (Acts 2:39) who are beginning to be reached by the good news of the kingdom of God.

x. The Pharisees' demand for a sign (8:11–13)
Context
The final two episodes in the first main part of Mark's Gospel in which he presents Jesus' messianic authority (1:14 – 8:21) reveal how little Jesus' enemies – the Pharisees (8:11–13) – and his disciples (8:14–21) have been able to understand of the true significance of Jesus' teaching about the coming of the kingdom of God, exorcizing demons and healing the sick. The Pharisees' demand for a sign has its counterpart in 7:1–20, and Mark's readers will not have forgotten the coalition of Pharisees and Herodians who were plotting to eliminate Jesus (3:6). The episode is the last scene of conflict with the religious leaders during Jesus' Galilean ministry (cf. 2:16, 18, 24; 3:6; 7:1, 5) before the final conflict in Jerusalem.

---

96. Cf. Leibner, *Settlement*, p. 229; S. De Luca and A. Lena, in Fiensy and Strange, *Galilee*, II, pp. 286–298; cf. Bauckham and De Luca, *Magdala*.

Comment

11. Jesus is on the west side of the lake in the region of Dalmanutha (v. 10). The *Pharisees* have been mentioned before alone (2:24), with teachers of the law (2:16; 7:1) and with the Herodians (3:6) as discussion partners of Jesus who, in stark contrast to the enthusiasm of the crowds, voice objections against Jesus, culminating in the plan to destroy him. The Pharisees here are local members of the movement. Mark describes their actions with four verbs. They *came* to where Jesus was staying, or from the town to the shore if this is where Jesus was teaching (cf. 2:13; 3:7; 4:1; 5:21; 6:32–34, 53–54). They *began* their conversation with a challenge. They *question* Jesus – they have not come for an open dialogue (thus the meaning of *syzēteō* in 1:27; 9:10) but for a dispute. They *asked him* ('requested', 'demanded') for a *sign from heaven*. The word *sign* (*sēmeion*) is not just another miracle (for which Mark uses the term *dynamis*, 'power', 'deed of power') but an event that confirms the intervention of divine power, authenticating Jesus as a *bona fide* prophet. The expression *from heaven* indicates that they demand a sign that has a supernatural character. They seem to be thinking of a cosmic 'portent' in the sky connected with the sun, the moon or the stars[1] that only God could cause to take place ('heaven' is a circumlocution for Yahweh). As biblically literate Jews, the Pharisees knew that not all miraculous signs could be trusted (Exod. 7:11–12, 22; 8:7; Deut. 13:1–3), but they would also have remembered the unambiguous fire from heaven that Elijah called down on the priests of Baal (1 Kgs 18:38) and the shadow cast by the sun that moved back ten steps at the time of Ahaz (Isa. 38:7–8). The Pharisees demand a sign with the intention to *test* Jesus, a term that has connotations of examination, temptation and provocation (as in 10:2; 12:15). Perhaps they intend to provoke Jesus to 'test' God as Israel did in the desert at Massah and Meribah (Exod. 17:1–7; Deut. 6:16; Ps. 95:8–9), unwittingly assuming the role of Satan the 'tempter' (1:13; cf. Matt. 4:3; 1 Thess. 3:5). Perhaps they intend to tempt Jesus to try to cause to happen a sign greater than any of the spectacular miracles he has done, expecting that

---

1. Cf. Matt. 24:30; Luke 11:16; 21:11, 25; Acts 2:19; Rev. 12:3; 13:13; 15:1.

he will fail miserably in the attempt, proving that his power is not authenticated by God.

12. Jesus comments on the Pharisees' demand for a sign with a question that challenges their motivation. The expression *this generation* goes beyond the Pharisees who want to test Jesus: it refers to his contemporaries who are still not sure who he is. There is no need for anyone to ask for a *sign* to authenticate the source of his power since the numerous exorcisms, the healings and the nature miracles have attested to the presence of the kingdom of God in his words and deeds. If these events have not persuaded them that Jesus' authority is divine authority, nothing else will convince them. The phrase *this generation* recalls the sinful generation of the flood (Gen. 7:1) and, more importantly in the present context of 'testing' God's agent, the grumbling generation of Israelites in the desert (Deut. 1:35; 32:5, 20; Ps. 95:10–11). The rabbis commented that these generations were unworthy of having a share in the world to come (*m. Sanh.* 10:3). In 8:38 Jesus will speak of 'this adulterous and sinful generation', in 9:19 of this 'unbelieving generation'. It seems that the enthusiastic excitement triggered by Jesus' exorcisms and miracles abated towards the end of Jesus' ministry and that many shared the Pharisees' scepticism. The phrase *truly I tell you* (cf. 3:28) solemnly introduces a word of judgment: *no sign will be given to it* – to 'this generation', including the Pharisees. The passive *will be given* implies divine action: God will not remove people's scepticism and authenticate Jesus' authority. They have sufficient evidence to be moved to repentance and faith and perceive the presence of the kingdom of God (1:15). Later, Jesus will say that false prophets will perform signs that will deceive many (13:22, 30).

13. The statement that Jesus *left them* may be a literary device to indicate geographical movement. In the context of the word of judgment in verse 12, the expression signals deliberate disengagement from the Pharisees and the people ('generation') they represent. They left Galilee by boat and *crossed to the other side* of the lake, rowing towards Bethsaida on the north-east shore (v. 22).

Theology
The episode recalls the continued and climactic opposition of the Pharisees, pious Jews committed to keeping the Mosaic law. They

have observed Jesus' exorcisms and miracles but they do not acknowledge that their source is the power of God. Miracles, not even spectacular deeds of power, cannot lead sceptics to faith, since miracles can have a Satanic source or can be left unexplained, if one so chooses. The Pharisees and the people they represent demand a sign as an excuse for refusing to draw conclusions from the evidence available in Jesus' teaching and ministry. Since they want to test Jesus without a willingness honestly to consider the consequences if Jesus indeed were to give a 'sign from heaven', Jesus rebukes them and refuses to perform such a sign. God does not send a supernatural sign that will 'power through' their unbelief and unresponsiveness. Paul asserts in 1 Corinthians 1:22 that Greeks demand wisdom and 'Jews demand signs', and argues that conversion to faith in Jesus is always, for Gentiles *and* for Jews, the result of the power of the Holy Spirit and the power of God (1 Cor. 2:4–5). Spiritual blindness can be lifted, and is lifted, when people are willing to listen to the good news and when they allow God to convince them of the truth of the gospel.

xi. Warning regarding the Pharisees and Herod (8:14–21)
Context
The last episode in the first main part of the Gospel (1:14 – 8:21) reveals how little the disciples have understood the true significance of Jesus' ministry. Like the Pharisees in the previous episode, they do not truly understand the significance of Jesus' miracles, in particular the two feedings miracles. Unlike the Pharisees, however, they do not test Jesus by demanding a sign, and nor does Jesus leave them.

Comment
14–15. The disciples had forgotten to stock up on supplies before leaving by boat from Dalmanutha. They had only *one loaf* of bread with them (cf. 6:38), sufficient for one dinner but not for thirteen – which was hardly a problem since they would be able to buy provisions in Bethsaida, only 7 miles (12 km) away. There is no reference to a need for food, and no miracle happens to make the one loaf suffice for all thirteen men on board the boat. Jesus' warning in verse 15 is not a comment on the disciples' oversight (he speaks of yeast, not of loaves of bread) but sets up Jesus' comment on their lack of

understanding. Jesus' warning is emphatic, formulated with two verbs of seeing: *Be careful* ('pay attention, be alert, be on guard, look out'), and *Watch out* ('look to, beware of'). *Leaven* (*zymē*; Hebr. *ḥāmēṣ*; ESV, NASB, RSV) is not synonymous with 'yeast' (Hebr. *śĕ'ōr*, 'sourdough'; so NIV, NRSV, GNB), which was rare in antiquity. Dough was leavened by mixing it with a batch of the previous week's dough, which had been preserved for that purpose. 'Leaven' is more or less synonymous with 'leavened bread' (Lev. 7:13). In Israel, all leaven in a house was removed at the beginning of the yearly festival of Unleavened Bread, which was later merged with Passover (Exod. 12:14–20), in commemoration of Israel's exodus from Egypt when the people did not have time to prepare food (and no time for the bread to rise). Leaven can be a positive symbol (growth of the kingdom of God, Matt. 13:33), but mostly it is a negative symbol, presumably because of the requirement to remove all leaven from the house before Passover.

The meaning of the analogy implied in the phrase *the leaven of the Pharisees and the leaven of Herod* (NASB) is not immediately clear. Matthew identifies the leaven with 'the teaching of the Pharisees and Sadducees' (Matt. 16:12), and Luke speaks of the 'hypocrisy' of the Pharisees (Luke 12:1). Suggestions regarding the meaning in the present passage include the demand for a sign by the Pharisees (8:11–12) and by Herod Antipas (Luke 23:8); a politically infectious and dangerous nationalism; the evil impulse that has hardened the heart of the Pharisees and Herod, who refuse to acknowledge the truth; and the unbelief of the Pharisees and Herod reflected in their lack of openness to what God is doing in Jesus' ministry and in their opposition to Jesus. The last suggestion is the most plausible in the context of verses 11–12 and 3:6. Jesus does not explain the analogy of 'leaven', but he clearly warns of the Pharisees and Herod. On the Pharisees see on 2:16; on Herod Antipas see 6:14; on the Herodians and their connection with Antipas see 3:6.

16. It is not clear whether the disciples' argument is triggered by the reference to leaven. As the imperfect tense of the verb *they discussed* signals duration, Mark states that the disciples had been arguing about the minimal supply of bread on board the boat for some time, ignoring Jesus' discourse about the Pharisees and Herod. Since Mark does not explain whether the disciples had understood, or misunderstood, Jesus' discourse on the Pharisees, their 'dullness' is not the main emphasis of the passage: Mark emphasizes the miracle-working power of Jesus against the foil of the disciples' discussion about the lack of sufficient bread (cf. Gundry, p. 408; Stein, p. 382).

17–20. Jesus' response is caused by their concern for bread *and* by their failure to be concerned about the more important issue of the Pharisees and of Herod (v. 15). What follows is a series of eight questions which all underline the failure of the disciples fully to understand what is happening in Jesus' ministry. The first five questions are rhetorical: by forcing the disciples to provide the obvious answers to these questions, he wants to draw them in towards a more mature faith.

The first question, *Why are you talking about having no bread?*, points to the negligible importance of the insufficient supply of bread. They will not die of hunger on the short trip to Bethsaida, and whoever was responsible for replenishing the supplies might have had good reasons for neglecting to buy more bread.

The second question, *Do you still not see or understand?*, could refer to the miracles which they had seen and which should have prompted them to understand Jesus' truly unique authority, and/or it could refer to the opposition of the Pharisees and Herod Antipas and the Herodians which had been a real threat since 3:6 and which, as Jesus will explain shortly, will lead to his execution (8:31). Jesus challenges the disciples to realize that they are 'insiders' who have been given understanding of the mystery of the kingdom of God (4:11).

The third question, *Are your hearts hardened?*, challenges the disciples to realize that they are not 'outsiders' like the Pharisees who have petrified, hardened hearts (3:5) and asks them to make sure that they do not have hardened hearts (6:52).

The fourth question, *Do you have eyes but fail to see, and ears but fail to hear?*, uses the metaphor of sense organs which do not function properly and draws on the Old Testament theme of God's people lacking spiritual awareness (Isa. 6:9; cf. Jer. 5:21; Ezek. 12:2). Jesus warns the disciples of the danger of becoming 'outsiders' to whom the words of Isaiah 6:9–10 apply (as in the explanation of the parable of the four soils in 4:12). He challenges them to hold fast to their privileged insight into the mystery of the kingdom of God.

The fifth question, *And don't you remember?*, challenges the disciples to remember what they have seen (Jesus' exorcisms and miracles) and what they have heard (Jesus' teaching of the coming of the kingdom of God).

The sixth question, *When I broke the five loaves for the five thousand, how many basketfuls of pieces did you pick up?*, reminds the disciples of the first feeding miracle (6:30–44) and solicits facts and figures that force them to confront the immature nature of their understanding and the pettiness of their argument about the insufficient supply of bread in the boat. The disciples have not forgotten what happened, of course: they collected *twelve* baskets full of bread, having distributed five loaves and two fish.

The seventh question, *And when I broke the seven loaves for the four thousand, how many basketfuls of pieces did you pick up?*, reminds them of the second feeding miracle (8:1–10) and challenges them to realize that they do not have to worry about going hungry or perishing on the lake, as long as they are with Jesus, who has twice met the needs of thousands of hungry people and who has twice demonstrated his power right on the lake (4:35–41; 6:45–52).

21. The eighth and last question, *Do you still not understand?*, repeats the second question and challenges the disciples to acknowledge the magnitude of Jesus' miracles and their connection to his proclamation of the coming of the kingdom of God. In the miracles Jesus has revealed – for eyes that can see – his unique authority as Messiah and Son of God (1:1), and in his proclamation he has revealed – for ears that can hear – that the coming of God takes place in his own person and ministry.

Theology
Even 'insiders' like the twelve disciples are prone to spiritual blindness and deafness. True spiritual insight is bound up with acknowledging and accepting Jesus' identity as the unique Messiah and Son of God who causes astounding exorcisms and miracles to happen since in his words and deeds the coming of God's kingdom has become a present reality. Peter will soon confess Jesus to be the Messiah (8:29), but he has not yet understood (8:32) that this entails Jesus' suffering, death and resurrection (8:31). A lack of understanding and a hardened heart can infect others, just as a small batch

of leaven affects an entire lump of dough. Judas Iscariot was one disciple who did not heed Jesus' warning: he joined the opposition and betrayed Jesus. Paul uses the same metaphor in 1 Corinthians 5:6 when he warns the church in Corinth that 'a little yeast leavens the whole batch of dough': if they do not remove the believer who is committing a very serious sexual sin, they may soon regard sinning as acceptable.

3. JESUS' MESSIANIC SUFFERING (8:22 – 15:47)

In Part One (1:14 – 8:21), Mark described Jesus' ministry in and around Galilee, emphasizing Jesus' authority in word and deed. In Part Two, Mark describes Jesus as the suffering Messiah. The first of three main sections describes Jesus' revelation of his suffering (8:22 – 10:52). Jesus predicts his suffering, death and resurrection in the context of Peter's declaration that he is the Messiah, repeating it twice in the context of instruction for his disciples in which he teaches them the values of the kingdom of God which are very different from the conventional values of society. In the second section, Mark describes the confrontation in Jerusalem (11:1 – 13:37), beginning with Jesus' entry into Jerusalem and ending with Jesus' discourse on the destruction of the temple and the signs before his climactic return. In the third section Mark describes Jesus' suffering and death (14:1 – 15:47), beginning with the plot to arrest Jesus and Jesus' betrayal, and ending with Jesus' crucifixion, death and burial.

A. The revelation of the Messiah's suffering (8:22 – 10:52)

The first section of Part Two is framed by two miracles: the healing of a blind man at Bethsaida (8:22–26) and the healing of blind Bartimaeus in Jericho (10:46–52). The only other miracle story – the exorcism involving a boy with an evil spirit (9:14–29) – comes in the middle of the section. These are the last miracles that Mark relates (apart from the fig-tree incident in 11:12–14, 20–21). After the 'introductory' miracle, Mark relates Peter's confession that Jesus is the Messiah (8:27–30), followed by Jesus' first passion prediction (8:31–33) and, since the disciples do not understand the connection between Jesus' ministry and his prediction of suffering, death and resurrection, his teaching on the requirements of discipleship (8:34 – 9:1). In the transfiguration scene (9:2–13), three disciples witness God affirming his purposes in the coming of Jesus, who is his unique Son. After the second passion prediction (9:30–32), Mark presents five sections of teaching: on discipleship (9:33–50), on divorce (10:1–12), on receiving the kingdom of God like children (10:13–16), on riches and discipleship (10:17–31) and on self-sacrificial service (10:35–45). Before the concluding healing of Bartimaeus in Jericho (10:46–52), Jesus predicts his passion and resurrection for a third time (10:32–34). The 'high' of Peter's confession (8:29) and the 'low' that immediately follows (8:31–33) establish a pattern that shows the inadequacy of a simplistic understanding of the mission of the Messiah. Jesus' teaching serves to instruct the disciples concerning the need of a thorough rethinking of traditional values.

References to being 'on the way' and related language (1:2–3; 8:27; 9:33–34; 10:17, 32, 52) describe the geographical movement of Jesus and his disciples; at the same time they hint at the nature of discipleship as a journey. The 'journey' of Jesus, a journey that ends in Jerusalem, is thus a study in discipleship. Mark reminds his readers throughout this section of the necessity of participating in this suffering as disciples pick up their cross and follow Jesus (8:34).

i. Healing of a blind man at Bethsaida (8:22–26)
Context
The episode of the healing of a blind man at Bethsaida is transitional. It is connected with the preceding context as a parallel to the

healing of the deaf–mute man in the Decapolis (7:31–37), and it picks up the theme of blindness which afflicts the Pharisees and which is a danger for the disciples (8:18), whose blindness Jesus addresses through his teaching, culminating in another healing of a blind man at the end of the section (10:46–52).

Comment

22. After the journey from Dalmanutha (v. 10) on the west side of the Sea of Galilee across the lake in a north-easterly direction, they arrive at *Bethsaida*, east of the Jordan river in the tetrarchy of Philip (see on 6:45). People brought *a blind man* to Jesus and implored him to *touch* the blind man, that is, to heal him by touching him (cf. 1:31, 41). Mark had not reported the healing of a blind man as yet, but in view of the previous summary statements concerning Jesus' healings – he healed 'many who had various diseases' (1:34) and many 'with diseases' (3:10) – Mark's readers would not have been surprised about the request of the Bethsaida residents who brought the blind man to Jesus. Visual impairment in general and blindness in particular were common afflictions, as demonstrated by their extensive treatment by ancient medical writers, descriptions in literature and letters, and ex-voto dedications in temples of Asclepius, the Greek deity of healing. Causes of visual impairment and blindness include congenital anomalies (the entire eyeball is absent or smaller than normal from birth), diseases, accidental or intentional injuries, and old age. Physicians performed cataract operations which, not surprisingly, did not always turn out well: Martial, *Epigrams* 8.74 jokes that an eye doctor (*opthalmicus*) is like a gladiator (*oplomachus*) who harms the eyes of his victims. In rare cases spontaneous cures seem to have taken place, even after twenty years of blindness (Pliny, *Nat.* 11.149).

23–24. Jesus took the blind man *by the hand* and led him outside the village to heal him in private. Jesus' action involved two elements: he *spat on the man's eyes* and he *put his hands on him*. On the use of saliva see on 7:33. The perhaps more poetic term *ommata* for 'eyes' (the normal term, *ophthalmoi*, is used in v. 25), together with the use of saliva, might suggest a more formal process of healing. The physical touch of the eyes is particularly meaningful for a blind man. The use of a question – *Do you see anything?* – is unique in a healing miracle.

Jesus enquires about the progress of the healing process. The man responds by 'looking upwards', not for prayer (as in 6:41; 7:34) but as an indication that he is regaining his eyesight. His reply, *I see people; they look like trees walking around*, indicates that the healing has begun but is incomplete: he can see, but not perfectly. He sees moving shapes that are walking and thus should be people, but he cannot see them clearly enough to identify them: they might easily be trees.

25. The second laying on of *hands on the man's eyes* – one hand on each eye – is not a 'second attempt' at healing the blindness of the man but a continuation of the process that has been set in motion and that is now being completed. Mark describes the complete healing with three expressions: *his eyes were opened* (*dieblepsen*; lit. 'he saw through', here 'he opened his eyes wide' or 'he saw clearly'); *his sight was restored* (*apekatestē*, 'he was restored'), which may suggest that he used to be able to see; and *he saw everything clearly* (*eneblepen*, 'he looked at, gazed on, could see, had a clear view of'). The distinction between *dieblepsen* and *eneblepen* 'is probably that the beam of light within the man's eye breaks through the internal barrier that has been blocking it and is therefore free to travel out into the external world (*dieblepsen*) and begin striking objects there (*eneblepen*), thereby restoring his sight' (Marcus, p. 595). The word *clearly* (*tēlaugōs*) means 'far-shining, far-beaming' (of the sun or the moon) or 'far-seeing', often used in descriptions of the radiance of the sun or things that are like it in brightness or splendour; the term reflects 'the most common ancient theory of vision, according to which sighted creatures see by means of light beams that come *out* of their eyes' (Marcus, p. 596). The words *everything* and *clearly* emphasize the complete nature of the healing, which is also highlighted by the threefold description. The two-stage process of the man's healing does not point to an embarrassing inadequacy on the part of Jesus, who is always in control throughout the episode. The complete healing of the man is never in doubt; 'it simply involves two stages' (Stein, p. 392).

26. Jesus sends the man *home* and commands him not to *go into the village*. If Jesus' command is understood in the context of the secrecy motif (cf. Introduction 4b), Jesus may simply be 'buying time' to allow himself and his disciples to leave Bethsaida before the news of the man's miraculous healing gets around (France, p. 325). Since Mark does not explicitly record a command by Jesus that the healed man keep silent about what has happened, such a command should not be read into the text. It is preferable to interpret the instruction not to go into the village as tantamount to Jesus telling the man to abandon his old occupation of begging in the village and to go home, without needing people to help him get there, as a public demonstration of the miracle (Gundry, pp. 419–420).

Theology
The healing of the blind man in Bethsaida reveals who Jesus is. Jesus brings the fulfilment of Isaiah 35:5–6 (cf. 29:18), which prophesied the opening of the eyes of the blind in the coming age of salvation. Jesus is indeed the Messiah, the unique Son of God (1:1). Like God himself (Ps. 146:8), Jesus, in a demonstration of divine power, gives sight to the blind. Many offer a symbolic interpretation: the miracle depicts the disciples' blindness concerning Jesus (as described in 8:14–21) and their gradual 'seeing' or understanding, resulting from Jesus' teaching concerning his passion (8:31 – 10:52).[1] The first stage of their healing is Peter's declaration that Jesus is the Messiah (8:27–30), and after Easter they receive the 'second touch', when they come to a true understanding of who Jesus is. Such a symbolic interpretation is not as evident as interpreters think. The disciples are still 'blind' in 8:27 – 10:52: they fail to understand the import of each of the three passion predictions, despite Jesus' teaching, and despite Jesus' rebuke to Peter 'Get behind me, Satan!' (8:32–33). They remain 'blind' concerning the necessity of Jesus' death and the reality of the prophesied resurrection of Jesus throughout 11:1 – 16:8 as well. It is preferable to interpret the healing of the deaf–mute and of the blind man 'not as analogies but in contrast to the deafness and blindness of the disciples' (Stein, p. 389).

ii. Peter's declaration that Jesus is the Messiah (8:27–30)
Context
Jesus has twice used the enigmatic expression 'the Son of Man' in comments about his authority (2:10, 28), without providing further

---

[1]. Best, *Following Jesus*, pp. 134–139; Guelich, pp. 430–431; Hooker, p. 197; France, p. 322; Marcus, p. 597; Strauss, pp. 352, 355; Bock, p. 238.

explanation. The people in Galilee think that Jesus is a prophet, while Herod Antipas thinks that he is John the Baptist raised from the dead (6:14–16). Now, as Jesus has reached the most northerly point of his travels, he forces the disciples to commit to an answer regarding the question of his identity. This is the watershed moment in the Gospel: Peter, speaking for the Twelve, declares that Jesus is the Messiah. The continuation of the Gospel indicates that his understanding of the role of the Messiah is flawed; he is unable to understand Jesus' clarification that he is the Son of Man who will suffer, who will be rejected by Israel's leaders, who will be killed and who will rise again after three days (8:31–33).

Comment

27. Jesus and the Twelve travel from Bethsaida about 25 miles (40 km) north, along the Jordan river, to *Caesarea Philippi* (Paneas, mod. Banyas) in the north-west corner of Philip's tetrarchy. Located on a plateau on both sides of the boundary between the Golan and Mount Hermon at the site of an old grotto shrine of Pan where King Herod had built a temple in honour of Augustus and Roma (Josephus, *Ant.* 15.363–364; *War* 1.400), Paneas was where Herod Philip founded his capital around 2–1 BC, naming it 'Caesarea' in honour of Augustus Caesar. The mixed population of Philip's tetrarchy included Syrians, Arabs, Itureans and Jews; there were no Jewish settlements in the district of Paneas, but the city itself had a Jewish community (Josephus, *Life* 11). Jesus and the Twelve did not stay in the city but in the *villages* (*kōmai*; cf. 6:6) located in its territory. As they are *on the way*, walking between villages in this remote part of the former territory of King Herod, Jesus first asks the disciples what people are saying about him. The question of Jesus' identity has repeatedly been a theme, beginning in the very first line of the Gospel in which Jesus was identified as Messiah and Son of God (1:1), and confirmed in God's acclamation at Jesus' baptism (1:11). Demons had recognized Jesus (1:34) as the Holy One of God (1:24), the Son of God (3:11) and the Son of the Most High (5:7). The disciples recognized the presence of divine power in the miraculous stilling of the storm, but they had not answered their terrified question 'Who is this? Even the wind and the waves obey him!' (4:41).

28. Popular opinion about Jesus' identity has not made any advances since the earlier report in 6:14–16. Some people, including Herod Antipas, the tetrarch of Galilee, believe that Jesus is John the Baptist come back from the dead. Other people believe that Jesus is Elijah or another great prophetic figure of the past who has reappeared. To describe Jesus as one of Israel's great prophets is indeed highly laudatory and certainly correct: only a few verses later Jesus prophesies his rejection, execution and resurrection (v. 31). To believe that Jesus is one of Israel's great prophets who has come back from the dead may be a wild idea implying notions of reincarnation, resulting from a failure to integrate Jesus into traditional Jewish categories. Alternatively, it is a more general recognition of an uncanny resemblance between Jesus' ministry and the ministries of the great prophets of the past who taught, performed miracles and were persecuted. To identify Jesus as a prophet is correct, but it is not the whole truth.

29. The question *But what about you?* indicates that the disciples can give a better answer. And the question *Who do you say I am?* signals that it is the responsibility of the disciples to give an answer that explains more fully who Jesus is. Since they have been entrusted with privileged information about the mystery of the kingdom of God (4:11), and since they have witnessed Jesus' miracles in 5:1 – 8:26, they should be able to 'connect the dots' and describe Jesus' identity in view of his powerful ministry in word and deed. Peter, whose given name was Simon and whom Jesus had called *Petros* ('rock'; 3:16), answers as the spokesman of the Twelve, indicated by the fact that both Jesus' response to Peter's declaration in verses 30–31 and Jesus' response to Peter's rebuke in verses 33–34 are directed to the disciples as a group.

Peter declares: *You are the Messiah*. This is the first time since the first line of the Gospel that the term *ho Christos* is used, a Greek expression that translates the Hebrew term *ha-mašiaḥ* ('the Anointed One') which was used by Jews as a title for the promised king from the Davidic dynasty who would appear in the last days (see 1:1). The explanation of Jesus which follows in verse 31 and Peter's reaction in verse 32 demonstrate that Peter's declaration that Jesus is the Messiah is not accompanied by an understanding of what the title 'Messiah' means as applied to Jesus. In the Second Temple period, the hope that a Davidic descendant would take the throne according to the prophecy of 2 Samuel 7:12–16 remained alive and was interpreted in terms of an idealized Davidic kingship in the context of end-time hopes for the restoration of Israel.[2] But there was no agreement on what kind of messiah would appear. In Qumran texts we find at least two if not three messianic figures: a royal messiah ('messiah of Israel'), a priestly messiah ('messiah of Aaron') and perhaps a prophetic messiah. The *Psalms of Solomon*, written during the rule of King Herod, possibly by Pharisees, anticipate a messiah who establishes David's throne, destroys sinners, purges Jerusalem of Gentiles, gathers the twelve tribes of Israel and inaugurates a period of holiness and covenant righteousness (*Pss Sol.* 17–18). In the context of the Old Testament images of a coming deliverer, the messiah could be viewed as a human figure who assumed royal office and who had superlative qualities of leadership and military prowess which he would use to liberate the nation of Israel; or he could be viewed as a superhuman and transcendent figure whom God would send from heaven to defeat God's enemies on earth and to lead Israel into paradise (Bird, *DJG*, p. 116).

30. Jesus' warning *not to tell anyone about him* indicates that the truth of his messianic identity is not to be publicly proclaimed. This is the one place in Mark's Gospel where a specifically *messianic* secret is mentioned (cf. Introduction 4b). The time for a public declaration of Jesus' true identity will come later (14:61–62), and then it will be Jesus himself who breaks the secrecy (France, p. 330). In view of the popular enthusiasm about Jesus, triggered by his exorcisms and healings, a public proclamation of Jesus as the Messiah would most likely be seriously misunderstood. While there was a widespread recognition of the need for a spiritual restoration of Israel, the strong strand of nationalistic hopes for political liberation and royal restoration would hinder a true understanding of Jesus' mission which is, as Jesus will shortly explain (v. 31), bound up with rejection by Israel's leaders, execution and resurrection.

---

2. Pss 2; 72; 89; 110; 132; Isa. 9:1–7; 11:1–16; Jer. 23:1–6; Ezek. 34:23–24; 37:24–25; Dan. 2:44–45; 9:24–27; Zech. 4:12–14; 6:11–12; 12:7 – 13:1.

Theology
The fact that the title *Christos* ('Messiah') had become standard terminology of the early church[3] shows that Mark recognizes the ambivalence of the term when he reports Jesus prohibiting the disciples from divulging in public Peter's declaration that he is the Messiah. Since the first line of the Gospel in 1:1, Jesus' identity has been the subtext of Mark's description of Jesus' ministry in word and deed. Jesus' teaching, his exorcisms and his miracles all invite, indeed demand, an answer to the question 'Who is this?' Peter's declaration that Jesus is the Messiah is correct in that Jesus fulfils the Old Testament promises of a new, powerful, redemptive initiative by God to restore God's people and a fallen world. At the same time Jesus is *not* the Messiah of the standard Jewish expectations: while he demonstrates the presence of the power of the kingdom of God in his exorcisms and miracles, he is not about to establish a powerful earthly kingdom with the capital in Jerusalem, defeating Israel's enemies and purging the land from Gentiles. Jesus will start to explain this in verse 31: the power of his status of Messiah is the spiritual power that is inextricably connected with his suffering, death and resurrection.

iii. *First passion and resurrection prediction (8:31–33)*
Context
This passage is intricately connected with Peter's declaration of Jesus as Messiah in verses 27–30 but is treated separately in order to emphasize Jesus' first explicit prediction of his suffering, rejection by the Jewish leaders, execution and resurrection. Despite the sombre theme, the tone is neither gloomy nor fatalistic since Jesus' path to suffering, rejection, death and resurrection is the fulfilment of a divine imperative that controls his messianic mission. Coming right after Peter's messianic declaration, Jesus' teaching about his suffering, death and resurrection clarifies the sense in which Jesus is Israel's Messiah. This is the first of three explicit passion

---

3. Cf. Acts 2:36; 3:18, 20; 4:26; 5:42; 9:22; 17:3; 18:5, 28; 26:23; in Paul's letters, the title *Christos* is used 383 times; cf. the expressions *Iēsous Christos* (127 times) and *Christos Iēsous* (91 times).

predictions (8:31; 9:31; 10:33–34) that vary in wording but that all agree on the concluding phrase 'he must be killed and after three days rise again'.

Comment

31. The phrase *he . . . began to teach them* signals that Jesus' death and resurrection is a new and central theme in his teaching to his disciples. The expression *Son of Man* (cf. 2:10) replaces 'Messiah' as a lesser-known and more ambiguous title. Since 'Son of Man' was not used in Jewish tradition as an obvious title for the Messiah, there was no blueprint for the mission of such a figure. The word *must* (Gr. *dei*) indicates that the following description of Jesus' mission is a necessary part of God's mission: his suffering, rejection, death and resurrection are not the unfortunate result of Judean and Roman politics but the purpose of God. Since the passion prediction in 9:12 is linked with the expression 'it is written' (cf. 14:21, 49), the *must* specifically refers to God's purposes revealed in Scripture. The scriptural references implied in *must* are not found in Daniel 7, which is the source of the 'Son of Man' title: the saints who are suffering (Dan. 7:25) are represented by the 'Son of Man' not in their suffering but in their victory; and in later Jewish texts that use the expression, the 'one like a son of man' appears as a victorious figure (as in Dan. 7:13–14). Relevant texts which explain the *must* of Jesus' suffering, rejection, death and resurrection include passages about the persecution of God's prophets by Israel's leaders, the righteous sufferer (Pss 22; 69; 118), the Suffering Servant whose death is connected with the restoration of God's people (Isa. 53), and the redeemer figure who is rejected by his people, pierced and smitten (Zech. 11:4–14; 12:10–14; 13:7–9). Jesus describes the mission of the 'Son of Man' that follows Peter's messianic declaration with four verbs (infinitives) which are all dependent on the word 'must'.

First, he must *suffer*: he will experience ill treatment and bodily harm; he will be on the receiving end of violence. The phrase *many things* could mean 'greatly' but refers, in the light of 10:33–34, specifically to being mocked, spat on and flogged.

Second, he must be *rejected* (*apodokimazō*): he will be 'declared useless', 'regarded as unworthy and therefore to be rejected' (BDAG,

p. 110).⁴ The people who render this verdict on Jesus involve the three main power groups in Judean society. The *elders* (*presbyteroi*) are the prominent lay members of the Sanhedrin (cf. 14:55), the non-priestly aristocrats sitting in the highest Jewish court in Jerusalem. The *chief priests* (*archiereis*) are the high priest, any former high priests, and the adult male members of the elite priestly families. The *teachers of the law* (cf. 1:22) are the experts of the Mosaic law, the scribes, probably mostly priests and Levites, but also Pharisees. The elders are mentioned again as Jesus' opponents in 11:27, 14:43, 53, 15:1, always in connection with the chief priests and scribes. The chief priests are mentioned here for the first time as Jesus' opponents; after 10:33 they are mentioned more than any other group, appearing either alone (14:10, 55; 15:3, 10–11) or at the head of the list of opponents (10:33; 11:18, 27; 14:1, 43, 53; 15:1, 31; the only exception is 8:31; Marcus, p. 1101). Teachers of the law from Jerusalem had been mentioned in 3:22, 7:1 as hostile to Jesus during his Galilean ministry. While there were 'elders' and 'teachers of the law' in Galilee, the reference to the chief priests indicates that the suffering that Jesus prophesies will take place in Jerusalem. The reference to these three groups, who represent the religious, political and theological power brokers in Judea, indicates a comprehensive rejection of Jesus by the Jewish leadership and marks 'the paradox of an unrecognised Messiah' (France, p. 335). Peter and John will face the same officials (Acts 4:5–7).

Third, he must *be killed*: the rejection by the Jewish leaders will lead to the most extreme punishment a human being can suffer, namely execution. Jesus does not specify the manner of execution that he will have to endure.

Fourth, he must *after three days rise again*: each of Jesus' passion predictions ends with a prophecy of his rising from the dead (9:31; 10:34). This resurrection takes place not at the end of history but as a bodily resurrection in history, in space and time, three days after his execution. The active verb *anistēmi* ('rise up'; Matthew uses the

---

4. The term occurs in Ps. 118:22 (LXX 117:22) for the 'rejected stone', a passage that Christians came to regard as a prophecy of Jesus' fate; cf. Mark 12:10; Matt. 21:42; Luke 20:17; 1 Peter 2:4, 7.

passive of the verb *egeirō*, 'to be raised') is probably used by Mark to suggest that 'despite whatever people can do to him the Son of Man will have the last word' (France, p. 336). The expression *after three days* means, in Jewish usage, 'the day after tomorrow', but could also generally refer to a short period of unspecified duration. Matthew and Mark use the expression 'on the third day', which agrees with the later report that Jesus was crucified on Friday and rose from the dead on Sunday, about thirty-six hours after his burial (and thus on the third day, Jesus being in the tomb on Friday late afternoon, Saturday, and Sunday early morning).

32. Jesus *said all this quite openly* (NRSV). The expression translated *all this* (*ton logon*) refers to Jesus' announcement that he will suffer, be rejected and be executed, and that he will rise from the dead after three days. The phrase *quite openly* (*parrēsia*; NIV 'plainly') describes 'a use of speech that conceals nothing and passes over nothing' (BDAG). Jesus spoke clearly to his disciples about his coming suffering, death and resurrection, not with an ambiguous allusion as in 2:20 ('But the time will come when the bridegroom will be taken from them').

Peter did not understand that Jesus *must* experience suffering, rejection, execution and resurrection after three days. Thus he *took him aside* to speak to him privately, and began *to rebuke him*, expressing his strong disapproval. He understood Jesus' ministry of teaching, exorcism and healing by acknowledging Jesus as Israel's Messiah. But he did not understand that Jesus' death and resurrection were connected to Jesus' ministry. Peter seems to have understood Jesus' mission as the promised Messiah in nationalistic terms, a mission in which the anticipated victory would involve 'a military assault on flesh-and-blood enemies' (Marcus, p. 614) and thus a mission in which there was no place for the rejection of the Messiah by Israel's leaders. Peter presumably protests in an attempt to clarify for Jesus the mission that God's Messiah will accomplish for Israel.

33. Jesus *turned and looked at his disciples* because Peter's protest reflects their viewpoint as a group. His reply, while directed to Peter specifically, involves all twelve disciples. The fierceness of Jesus' rebuke, *Get behind me, Satan!*, is shocking. The command *Get behind me* can be understood as an order for Peter to get out of Jesus' sight, in terms of a temporary dismissal; as an injunction for Peter to get out of Jesus' way and cease being an obstruction to his mission; or as 'a command to Peter to resume the path of discipleship rather than trying to *lead* Jesus' (Marcus, p. 607, who prefers this interpretation). The name *Satan* occurred in 1:13, 3:23, 26, 4:15 as the Jewish term for the devil (called Beelzebul in 3:22). The use of the name for a human being has no parallel, not even as a term of ultimate abuse. Jesus' point is that since Peter's rebuke reflects *merely human concerns*, in particular concerns that are opposed to God, his thoughts are 'so much at odds with the thoughts of God as to be attributed to a more supernatural source' (France, p. 338). Peter has temporarily become a 'Satan' because he sides with God's ancient opponent who wants to thwart God's redemptive purposes.

Theology
Peter and the disciples had listened to Jesus' teaching and received privileged information (4:11); they had seen the exorcisms and the miracles; and now they acknowledge and declare that Jesus is the Messiah. Jesus will confirm this before the Sanhedrin (14:61–62), before Pilate (15:2) and by his crucifixion (15:26). Jesus immediately defines his messianic status in terms of suffering, rejection, death and resurrection, events that are a divine necessity – something that Mark's Christian readers would know as they celebrated the atoning purpose of Jesus' death and the empowering reality of Jesus' resurrection in the Lord's Supper (cf. 1 Cor. 11:23–26). The fact that Peter cannot understand this, combined with Jesus' rebuke that Peter is thinking human thoughts, indicates that God's purposes cannot be grasped from a human perspective. If even the disciples, with the privileged teaching about the kingdom of God (4:11) they have received, and the privileged information about Jesus' coming suffering, rejection, death and resurrection (8:31–32), cannot understand what all this means, nobody can – unless God's Spirit and God's power lead to faith, as the apostle Paul later emphasizes (1 Cor. 2:4–5).

iv. The requirements of discipleship (8:34 – 9:1)
Context
Jesus has rebuffed Peter's attempt to define his mission as Israel's Messiah (8:32–33). The disciples need to see Jesus' life and mission

in the new light of his passion prediction. This episode teaches the disciples, and indeed the crowd, that they need to see their lives in a new light as well. They must learn to replace human values, which promote self and ambition, with the divine logic of triumph through death. This is the first of several passages on the nature, cost and consequences of discipleship.

Comment

34. The presence of a *crowd* of people who are at least potentially followers of Jesus suggests that Jesus and the disciples have started to move south into Jewish territory. In 9:14 we find the disciples surrounded by a large crowd and teachers of the law, and in 9:33 Jesus and the disciples arrive in Capernaum. If the 'high mountain' on which the transfiguration took place (9:2) was Mount Meiron in northern Galilee, the present scene could have taken place in a settlement such as Meroth (mod. Horbat Marus) on the northern boundary of Upper Galilee (Josephus, *War* 3.40). If so, there is no need to assume that Mark has taken the sayings of this passage from elsewhere in the Jesus tradition and placed them here as a complement to Jesus' passion prediction. The introductory conditional statement *If any want to become my followers* (NRSV) indicates that the subsequent teaching applies not only to the Twelve but to anyone who *wants* to join Jesus and his movement (*thelō* means 'have a desire for something' and 'to have something in mind for oneself, of purpose, resolve'; BDAG, p. 448). Jesus describes the conditions of discipleship with three pronouncements.

First, Jesus' followers *must deny themselves*: not things that the self wants, but the self itself. Jesus calls for a deliberate refusal to be guided by self-interest, for a conscious surrender of control over one's life, for an intentional renunciation of self-determination. When Simon and Andrew accepted Jesus' call and left their nets to follow him (1:18), they accepted Jesus' complete authority over their lives; they abandoned their identity as fishermen on the Sea of Galilee and joined Jesus, confident in their conviction that to be with Jesus was more important than anything else. The pronouncement is formulated as an imperative. The surrender of self-determination is not an option relevant perhaps for specially dedicated disciples or the inner circle, but a command for all who want to follow Jesus.

Second, Jesus' followers *must . . . take up their cross*. This is the first reference to the word *cross* (*stauros*; cf. 15:21, 30, 32). Jesus' predictions of his death (8:31; 9:31; 10:33–34) do not specify the manner of execution. In a Jewish context, crucifixion would not automatically come to mind: Jewish authorities usually executed by stoning (cf. Acts 7:58), although on some occasions Jewish rulers did execute by crucifixion (cf. Josephus, *War* 1.96–98; *Ant.* 13.380–381); Roman authorities carried out death penalties by decapitation, burning alive, throwing victims to the beasts in the arena and poisoning; crucifixion was reserved for the execution of slaves, brigands and rebels and, in the case of Roman citizens, for high treason;[5] sometimes they allowed a free choice of death (by cutting one's veins, taking poison, starving oneself, falling on one's sword, strangling oneself). The expression 'take up the cross' refers to the practice of criminals condemned to crucifixion carrying to the place of execution the *patibulum*, the heavy horizontal beam or crossbar to which their outstretched arms were eventually attached with nails or ropes; this was then hoisted up on a post so that the criminal could be exposed to the public until he died (cf. 15:21; Matt. 27:32; Luke 23:26; John 19:17). The preservation of the shocking image of walking as a convicted criminal with the crossbar to the place of the most shameful of executions suggests that it originates from Jesus' own prophetic awareness of the manner of his own execution (France, p. 339). Jesus speaks metaphorically, which is confirmed by the fact that in verse 38 the community of his followers is described as existing until the return of the Son of Man (note that Luke 9:23, in the parallel passage, speaks of carrying the cross 'daily'). The metaphor is a radical one: his followers have to be willing to risk their lives, literally, if indeed they resolve to follow him in a context where the political leaders are determined to put to death Jesus and his followers. Since crucifixion was regarded as the most shameful death, evident in vulgar taunts, curses and jests in which the word 'cross' was used, the metaphor challenges Jesus' followers to accept the shame that is involved in following him. In the context of the

---

5. Cf. Chapman and Schnabel, *Trial and Crucifixion*, pp. 532–638; on the *patibulum*, pp. 282–292; on the shamefulness of crucifixion, pp. 697–754.

first pronouncement on discipleship, the focus of the imperative is not on the possibility of martyrdom but on the experience of denying one's own self-interest, even to the point of death.

Third, disciples must *follow* Jesus. The repetition of the verb *follow* (*akoloutheō*; cf. 1:18; 2:14–15) is somewhat clumsy (and avoided in the NIV, which translates the first occurrence in v. 34 as 'be my disciple'). Following Jesus requires 'continuing determination to stick to the chosen path' (Marcus, p. 617).

35–37. The following statements explain the three pronouncements on discipleship in verse 34, describing the first reason for accepting Jesus' invitation to follow him. The words *save*, *lose* and *life* possess double meanings. People who *want to save their life* (NRSV) are people who refuse to deny themselves (negative sense of 'save'), whereas people who lose their life for Jesus' sake *will save it* (positive sense of 'save'): they will achieve eternal salvation on the final day (cf. v. 38). People who *lose* their life, because they want to save it, by refusing to follow Jesus, will not acquire eternal salvation (negative sense of 'lose'), whereas people who *lose their life* for Jesus' sake, because they deny themselves as they commit themselves to Jesus, will acquire eternal salvation (positive sense of 'lose'). The *life* (*psychē*) of those who want to save it but who lose it is human existence ('being alive') that refuses to follow Jesus and insists on self-determination (negative use of 'life'). The *life* of those who lose it for Jesus' sake and who will save it is the true human self ('real life') that exists beyond earthly life in eternity (positive use of 'life'). The phrase *for my sake, and for the sake of the gospel* (NRSV) underlines the radical centrality of Jesus and the good news of the kingdom of God, whose present reality is bound up in Jesus' person and ministry in word and deed. Followers of Jesus are willing to risk their lives as they follow him. They know and accept that as Jesus himself is killed by his opponents, they may suffer the same fate in future persecution. And they are willing to risk their lives for the gospel, a point that indicates that the disciples will have a role in the missionary proclamation of the good news.

To *gain the whole world* describes with a hyperbolic expression the height of human self-determination and ambition. People who set their sights on the *world* are people who are not committed to Jesus and the good news of the kingdom of the one true God who has created the world: they will *forfeit their life* (NRSV). They will lose the 'true life' of the kingdom of God, being deprived of eternal salvation. Earthly success, prestige and riches cannot compare with eternal life in the presence of God, the creator of the cosmos. The rhetorical question of verse 37 has an obvious negative answer: nobody can give anything *in return for their life* (NRSV). Eternal life cannot be bought, not even by the richest man who owned the world: it can be acquired only in following Jesus, in abandoning self-determination, in accepting the shame of the cross, and in being committed to the gospel and its proclamation.

38. There is a second reason for becoming and remaining a follower of Jesus. The contrast between 'earthly life' and 'true life', between purely human values and the values of Jesus and the kingdom of God, is stark, now expressed in terms of the Greco-Roman values of shame and honour. The phrase *If anyone is ashamed of me and my words* parallels 'saving one's earthly life' and involves repudiating Jesus and the gospel (v. 35). People who are *ashamed* of Jesus conceal their allegiance to Jesus and to his teaching since they are afraid of suffering a loss of status. They think that they will lose the honour they have in human society if others know about their commitment to Jesus and his shameful death. The expression *this adulterous and sinful generation* picks up Old Testament language of Israel as an unfaithful wife to God, her true husband (Isa. 1:4, 21; Ezek. 16:32; Hos. 2:3). The word *generation* refers, beyond Jesus' contemporaries, to any group of people whose common characteristics involve the repudiation of Jesus and the way of the cross, and thus rebelling against God and his Messiah (cf. 8:12 'this generation').

People who repudiate Jesus will suffer the consequences of their decision when the Son of Man (cf. 2:10, 28; 8:31) *comes in his Father's glory with the holy angels* – on that day, the Son of Man *will be ashamed of them*. The event that is in view here is most plausibly understood as a reference to Jesus' return at the end of days to judge and to save (cf. 13:26; 14:62), the event called *parousia* ('coming, advent') in Matthew 24:3, 27, 37, 39; 1 Corinthians 15:23; 1 Thessalonians 2:19; 3:13; 4:15; 2 Thessalonians 2:1, 8 (neither Mark nor Luke uses the term). Jesus identifies himself as the Son of Man who comes 'in the glory of his Father': he shares the divine glory that God has as the Creator. This is the first time in Mark's Gospel that Jesus identifies himself as the 'Son' of God the Father (in 1:1 the identification was made by Mark; in 1:11 by the heavenly voice; cf. later 13:32; 14:36). Since the Messiah was regarded as having a unique father–son relationship with God (4QFlor I,11; 2 Sam. 7:14; Pss 2:7; 89:26), and since Jesus accepted Peter's declaration that he was the Messiah (8:29), this is not surprising. What is surprising, however, is the assertion of sharing the *Father's* divine attribute of glory. The description of his return in terms of the Son of Man coming in the glory of God with the angels is an allusion to Daniel 7:9–10, 13–14, where the Son of Man is presented before the throne of God in the presence of angels and is given sovereignty over all nations. Here, instead of the Son of Man entering the presence of God's glory, he comes from God's presence sharing the Father's glory, judging all who repudiated him when he lived on earth. Would-be followers who are ashamed of Jesus will have to face Jesus on judgment day, when Jesus will be *ashamed* of them and deny them a place in the eternal kingdom of God.

9:1. Jesus' last pronouncement in this section is regarded as one of the most difficult statements of Jesus in the Gospels since it appears to predict that Jesus will return before the death of some of the twelve disciples and people in the crowd mentioned in 8:34. The saying seems not to have been difficult for Mark, since he could easily have omitted it if he found it embarrassing. The introduction *Truly I tell you* (cf. 3:28) identifies the following statement as an authoritative pronouncement. Jesus asserts that some of those present *will not taste death*. The subject of death arises from 8:34–38, where Jesus has mentioned death as a possible fate for disciples. Some of the disciples will experience an event before they die that those who have died earlier will not experience: they will *see that the kingdom of God has come with power*. The following explanations have been suggested. (1) It describes the coming of the Son of Man to judge the world, mentioned in 8:38. In this case, Jesus uttered a false prophecy, which some have interpreted as demonstrating Jesus' human nature. This view is implausible: since Jesus asserts in 13:32 that he does not know the time of the end, why would he predict it here? (2) It refers to the destruction of Jerusalem in AD 70 as a preview of the final judgment and as the event at which the authority of the Son of Man supplanted the authority of the earthly city. It is not clear, however, why the fall of Jerusalem would demonstrate the powerful presence of the kingdom of God. (3) It refers to the crucifixion of Jesus, or his resurrection from the dead, as the inauguration of the kingdom of God. This interpretation makes theological sense. However, since Jesus had referred to his death and resurrection explicitly in 8:31, it is difficult to explain the enigmatic nature of 9:1. (4) It describes the present manifestation of the kingdom of God in Jesus' words and deeds that disciples need to see with eyes of faith. This interpretation has difficulties in explaining the reference to the death of some disciples, and the fact that Mark relates only one more exorcism (9:14–29) and one more healing miracle (10:46–52). (5) It describes the experience of the realized dimension of the coming of the kingdom of God after Jesus' death and resurrection, set in motion at Pentecost. If Jesus' statement in 9:1 is treated as an isolated saying, this interpretation is plausible, and it provides a natural understanding of the phrase 'some of you who are standing here': some of the people who are present will be in Jerusalem when Jesus pours out the Spirit of God on his followers who will then begin to live and proclaim the reality of the kingdom of God; Judas Iscariot will have died, and many in the crowd will not be in Jerusalem to witness these events. (6) The close link between 9:1 and 9:2 ('after six days') suggests that in the present context, the most natural explanation of 9:1 is a reference to the transfiguration as a preview of the glory of the kingdom of God that will be revealed on the day of Jesus' return. Some of those present – Peter, Jacob (James) and John (9:2) – experience 'already now' a foretaste of the 'not yet' of the future consummation of the kingdom of God at the parousia of the Son of Man. The objection that the phrase *some who are standing here will not taste death* is ludicrous if it refers to an event that takes place a week later misses the significance of the word *some*: only three of the disciples were with Jesus on the mountain, while the rest would indeed *taste death* without seeing anything comparable (Cranfield, p. 288; France, p. 345).

Theology
Following Jesus has personal consequences regarding the human tendency to self-determination, self-aggrandization and self-promotion. Jesus speaks of a reorientation of values that he will

explicate later. The supreme significance of Jesus and the ultimate value of the kingdom of God calls Jesus' followers to accept the shame of Jesus' crucifixion as an integral part of God's purposes and to accept the possibility that walking on the path of the cross can literally cost them their lives.

v. *The transfiguration of Jesus and Elijah (9:2–13)*
Context

The transfiguration follows Peter's declaration that Jesus is the Messiah (8:29), Jesus' first explicit prediction of his death and resurrection (8:31) and Jesus' teaching on the sacrificial cost of true discipleship (8:34 – 9:1). Jesus' consultation of Elijah and Moses on the mountain sets the stage for the final journey to Jerusalem, where Jesus will accomplish his messianic task. The experience on the mountain reassures the disciples that Jesus is indeed the Messiah and Son of God (8:38), God's agent of salvation who will be glorified after he completes his mission. The visual experience is unique in the Gospels; the voice from heaven echoes the voice of God after Jesus' baptism (1:11): the two pronouncements offer direct testimony to Jesus' identity as the Son of God (1:1).

Comment

2–3. Peter, Jacob (James) and John, who formed the inner circle of the twelve disciples (cf. 5:37), are invited to a special revelation of Jesus' identity. Mark does not identify the *high mountain*. If Jesus and the disciples were still in the area of Caesarea Philippi (8:27), they could have ascended Mount Hermon (9,232 ft [2,814 m]), about 15 miles (25 km) to the north-east as the crow flies. However, the presence of a crowd in 8:34 and in 9:14, the latter including teachers of the law, suggests that Jesus had returned to Jewish territory. Tradition localizes the transfiguration on Mount Tabor, about 30 miles (50 km) south-east of Capernaum and about 11 miles (18 km) west of the Sea of Galilee, rising 1,640 feet (500 m) above the Jezreel Valley.[6]

---

6. Eusebius (d. 340) hesitated between Tabor and Mount Hermon; in AD 348 Cyril of Jerusalem decided on Tabor, supported by Epiphanius and Jerome.

Since Jesus and the disciples are in Capernaum in 9:33, they would have had to travel from Tabor north again, contrary to the impression that after leaving Caesarea Philippi they are moving south towards Jerusalem (10:32–33). A more plausible possibility is therefore Mount Meiron, about 50 miles (80 km) from Caesarea Philippi and 10 miles (16 km) east of Meroth (see comment on 8:34) as the crow flies, on the northern boundary of Upper Galilee.

The expression *there he was transfigured before them* uses a verb (*metamorphoō*) which means here 'to change in a manner visible to others' (BDAG, p. 639). Mark asserts that Jesus was 'changed' or 'transformed'. Luke 9:29 elaborates that 'the appearance of his face changed'; Matthew 17:2 says that 'his face shone like the sun'. Mark uses the passive voice (*he was transfigured*): he describes not a self-revelation of Jesus but a revelation of Jesus' glory by God (cf. v. 7). Jesus' clothes *became radiant and exceedingly white* (NASB). The word translated *radiant* means 'to cast rays of light' and can be translated as 'to shine, glitter, gleam'; the verb is used of glittering metal and the shining of the stars. The colour of the clothes became white (*leukos*) 'to a high degree' (Gr. *lian*): they were exceedingly white (NIV, NRSV 'his clothes became dazzling white'). The comment that Jesus' clothes were *whiter than anyone in the world could bleach them* (lit. 'no cloth refiner can whiten them') points to the otherworldly nature of the incident. Shining white clothing is mentioned in the narratives of Jesus' resurrection (16:5; cf. Matt. 28:3; Luke 24:4; John 20:12; Acts 1:10). Heavenly beings wear shining white clothing (Dan. 7:9; *1 En.* 14:20; *2 En.* 22:8–9). According to Psalm 104:1–2, God wears light like a garment. Mark's language describes God revealing the divine glory of Jesus.

4. Two long-deceased men of God appeared: *Elijah with Moses* (NRSV); Moses lived in the thirteenth century BC, Elijah in the ninth century. The sequence is unusual since Moses lived before Elijah and was the more prominent man in Jewish tradition. Elijah is mentioned first presumably because the dialogue in verses 11–13 will focus on Elijah (the order is reversed in v. 5). Elijah and Moses are not mentioned because they represent the law and the prophets; Moses was also a prophet, and Elijah hardly represents the prophets who wrote the prophetic books of the Old Testament canon. There are two explanations, which are not mutually exclusive, for the

appearance of these two figures. (1) Both Elijah and Moses featured in end-time hopes: Elijah was expected to return (Mal. 4:5), which prompted Jesus' being identified with him (6:15; 8:28; cf. vv. 11–13), and there were traditions that a 'prophet like Moses' would come (Deut. 18:15–19; cf. Acts 3:22; 7:37). The mysterious circumstances of the deaths of both figures (for Moses see Deut. 34:5–6, but later Jewish traditions said that Moses was translated directly to heaven; cf. Josephus, *Ant.* 4.326; for Elijah see 2 Kgs 2:11) may also play a role in their appearance on the mountain, prefiguring not only Jesus' resurrection but also his suffering (cf. vv. 12–13). The appearance of these two figures signals the presence of the messianic age that the Jewish people had long hoped for. (2) Both Elijah and Moses encountered God on Mount Sinai (Horeb) and heard his voice (Exod. 19 – 24; 34; 1 Kgs 19). Now Jesus, on another high mountain, meets with them before God speaks, again, from the cloud, confirming him in their presence as the messianic Son who brings to fulfilment the promises of God.

5–6. Peter reacts to the perplexing situation by assuring Jesus, whom he addresses as *Rabbi* ('master', 'sir'), which is rather inadequate in the circumstances, that he is enjoying the pleasant encounter, and then comes up with the fantastic suggestion of erecting three shelters for each of the great men. Sensing the extraordinary nature of the event, he tries his best to rise to the occasion and make himself useful, thinking that the meeting may last some time, during which they may need shelter from the sun. Mark, writing later, knows that Peter *did not know what to say*, and recalls hearing that Peter as well as Jacob (James) and John were *terrified* (NRSV) of what might happen next.

7. The *cloud* – which probably covered the entire mountain top: it *overshadowed* (NRSV) Jesus, the disciples and the two visitors – symbolizes God's presence[7] on the mountain, as in the Sinai narrative (Exod. 19:9, 16; 24:15–16; 34:5) when God's voice spoke from the cloud (Exod. 19:9; 24:16; 24:18 – 25:1; 34:5). The disciples hear God say, *This is my Son, whom I love. Listen to him!* God repeats the declaration that Jesus is his unique Son, spoken at Jesus' baptism (1:11),

---

7. Cf. Exod. 13:21–22; 16:10; 33:9; 40:34–38; Num. 11:25; 1 Kgs 8:10–13.

for the benefit of the disciples. If *my Son* alludes to Nathan's prophecy in 2 Samuel 7:14 and to Psalm 2:7, the heavenly voice affirms Jesus as the messianic Son of David. The command *Listen to him!* echoes Deuteronomy 18:15 where the promised 'prophet like Moses' is to be acknowledged as having the same authority as Moses himself at Sinai. As pious Jews, the disciples had listened to Moses (and the law) and anticipated the coming of Elijah in the last days. Now they are to listen to Jesus, whose supernatural splendour is identified by God's voice as the glory of his unique Son, the Messiah who conveys God's new revelation which involves Jesus' suffering, death and resurrection (8:31–32).

8–10. The sudden disappearance of the cloud, the voice and Elijah and Moses confirms both the miraculous nature of the incident and the pre-eminent status of Jesus. Jesus commands the three disciples *not to tell anyone what they had seen*, presumably not even the other nine disciples. Jesus sets a time limit on their silence: they could speak about the incident after *the Son of Man had risen from the dead*. It is only after his death and resurrection, which Jesus predicts here, that their report will not spark triumphalistic hopes and activism that a premature disclosure of the encounter on the mountain might trigger (cf. 8:30). Jesus' divine splendour can be properly understood only in the context of his suffering, death and resurrection. The disciples obey Jesus' command: they keep *the matter* (*logos*) to themselves. The terms of Jesus' time limit confuse them: they discuss what *rising from the dead* means, bewildered since there was no precedent of an individual rising from the dead before the general resurrection at the end of history.

11. The presence of Elijah on the mountain in visible form, the earlier discussion about the return of the Son of Man (8:38) and the popular speculation that Jesus is Elijah (8:28) prompt the disciples to ask Jesus why the *teachers of the law* (cf. 1:22) *say that Elijah must come first*. They seem to wonder how the prophecies about the coming of Elijah connect with the mission of Jesus, whom they now know to be the unique Son of God, the Messiah whose identity includes divine glory. Elijah's coming was to happen 'before that great and dreadful day of the LORD' (Mal. 4:5).

12–13. Jesus answers the disciples' question by asserting that the teaching of the scribes is correct: *Elijah does come first*, before the day of judgment. The statement that he *restores all things* summarizes the purpose of Elijah's coming (Mal. 4:6: 'He will turn the hearts of the parents to their children, and the hearts of the children to their parents'; cf. Sir. 48:10). Then Jesus asks a rhetorical question that challenges the disciples to understand Elijah's coming in the new light of the mission of the *Son of Man* who *is to go through many sufferings and be treated with contempt* (NRSV). The statement in verse 13, emphasized with the introductory *But I tell you*, clarifies the logic of the connection between the statement about the prophecy of the coming of Elijah to restore all things and the statement about the suffering of the Son of Man. The assertion *Elijah has come* (NRSV) clarifies that the prophecy of Elijah's return has been fulfilled: the experiences of Jesus as Son of Man correspond to the sequence of events as the prophesied return of Elijah. Also, the experience of Elijah was one of rejection and ill treatment (contrary to the expectations raised by Mal. 4:5–6), which foreshadowed the suffering and ill treatment of Jesus as Son of Man.

Mark does not say so explicitly, but his readers would probably see an allusion to John the Baptist (cf. Matt. 11:14; see on 6:14–15) and his frivolous execution by Herod Antipas in the statement *they did to him whatever they pleased* (NRSV). The experience of Elijah, who was rejected and ill treated, foreshadowed what happened to John the Baptist. At the same time, the experiences of both Elijah and John the Baptist foreshadow what will happen to Jesus as the Son of Man who will suffer much and be treated with contempt. Jesus had been linked with John the Baptist and Elijah (6:14–15; 8:28), John's imprisonment marked the beginning of Jesus' public ministry (1:14) and John's martyrdom had been extensively reported (6:16–29). Despite the fact that Malachi's prophecy about Elijah's return has been fulfilled in John the Baptist, the appearance of Elijah on the mountain is significant: the Greek perfect tense of the phrase *Elijah has come* (NRSV) speaks of an ongoing state of affairs, a fulfilment of Malachi's prophecy that is not exhausted by the ministry of John the Baptist. The brief appearance of Elijah, which happened after John's ministry had ended, signals that it is not John but Jesus the Son of Man who is the focus of the hopes of the prophets.

Theology
God's declaration on the mountain is succinct yet far reaching: Jesus is the Messiah and Son of Man as he is the beloved, unique Son of God, and his mission involves all that he said it would involve. The disciples are to take seriously the divine command to listen to him, and believe that Jesus' suffering, death and resurrection are part of his divinely ordained mission. The three disciples still do not fully understand, particularly Jesus' prediction of his resurrection soon after death. They will truly understand Jesus' death and resurrection only after both have happened (which is a story Mark will leave to others to tell). Peter will later remember, and describe, his experience on the mountain where he and the others were 'eye-witnesses of his majesty' (2 Peter 1:16–18).

vi. Exorcism of a boy with an evil spirit (9:14–29)
Context
The exorcism related in this episode is one of three miracles in Part Two of Mark's Gospel, the other two being the healing of the blind man at Bethsaida (8:22–26) and the healing of the blind man at Jericho (10:46–52) which frame the first main section of Part Two. The episode corresponds in broad terms to similar narratives of exorcisms; it is unique in that it relates the failure of the disciples to drive out the demon, a task for which they had been given authority in 3:15 and 6:7 and which they had carried out successfully (6:13). Unique is also the subsequent question why they had failed (9:14–18, 28–29). As is typical for Part Two, the focus is on the disciples, not on the crowd. The disciples receive an object lesson on the essential significance of faith (9:23) and prayer (9:29).

Comment
14–15. Jesus, Peter, Jacob (James) and John join the remaining nine disciples who are surrounded by a *large crowd* (cf. 2:4; 5:21, 24) which included *teachers of the law* (cf. 1:22) with whom they were *arguing*. The reason for the (presumably hostile) argument (cf. 8:11; 12:28) would have been the disciples' attachment to Jesus and their attempt to drive the demon out of the demon-possessed boy (cf. v. 28) with the authority that Jesus had given them (3:15; 6:7, 13), and perhaps also the fact that they had not been able to drive out the

demon. The scribes play no further role in the episode. Unlike in 7:1, Mark does not suggest that these were scribes on a fact-finding mission concerning Jesus' ministry. The comment that the people, when they saw Jesus, *were overwhelmed with wonder and ran to greet him* is surprising: such a reaction is usually the response of the crowd after a miracle or after Jesus' teaching (1:22, 27; 2:12; 5:15, 20, 42; 6:33). A comparable reaction is that of people running throughout Galilee to carry the sick to the villages that Jesus was visiting (6:55), although here the amazement is motivated simply by 'seeing' Jesus. Some see here an echo of the people's awe at Moses' radiance when he descended from Mount Sinai (Exod. 34:29–35). However, since Mark did not make the allusions to the Sinai narrative explicit, since in Exodus 34 the Israelites are afraid to approach Moses while here they come running, and since the demand of secrecy in verse 9 would not make much sense if the experience on the mountain lingered on Jesus' face, visible for all to see, this is not a necessary interpretation. It seems more plausible to interpret the comment in terms of 'the powerful impression which Jesus' personal presence by now created' (France, p. 364).

16–18. Jesus' question about the subject of the argument seems to be addressed to the crowd who have come running to him, since *a man in the crowd answered*. As the people approach Jesus, he may initially not be aware of who has been arguing with whom. The man addresses Jesus as *teacher* (cf. 5:35) and tells him about his demon-possessed son whom the disciples could not heal. He says that he brought his boy 'to you'; that is, to Jesus; in Jesus' absence he had asked his disciples *to drive out the spirit* (cf. 1:34, 39; 3:15, 22–23).

The man reports the effect that the spirit has on his boy by describing six elements. He obviously has seen these manifestations numerous times. The demon *has robbed him of speech* (lit. 'he has a mute spirit'; Gr. *alalos* means 'mute, unable to speak'). The boy is unable to speak, perhaps only when the demon attacks him, although this is not clear. There are occasions when the demon *seizes* or 'comes upon him' with hostile intent; on such occasions, the demon *throws him to the ground*: he casts him down in convulsions; then the boy *foams at the mouth*; he *gnashes his teeth*: he grinds his teeth, which makes a shrill, creaking sound; then he *becomes rigid*: he is immobilized and becomes stiff. The symptoms that the man describes are similar to those known today as manifestations of epilepsy, a term that derives from the Greek word *epilēpsia* or *epilēpsis* ('seizure' in the sense of 'epileptic fit'; *LSJ*, p. 643). Many Greeks saw the disease as a divine visitation and called it 'the sacred disease' (*hiera nosos*). A 'diagnosis' in terms of epilepsy is sometimes related to the term *selēniazetai* used in Matthew 17:15 (lit. 'to be moonstruck'; thus KJV 'lunatick', from Latin *luna*, 'moon'), but the term can be connected with epilepsy 'only by the prior assumption' that Matthew describes an epileptic (France, p. 362). Mark clearly speaks of possession by an evil spirit which in this case caused violent symptoms similar to those produced by the electric disturbance in the brain that causes an epileptic seizure. Epilepsy, which has physical causes, should not be equated with demon possession. At the same time, one should not reduce the biblical accounts of demon possession to descriptions of a malfunction of the brain. Demon possession can manifest symptoms comparable to those of epilepsy, and vice versa. The description here and in verses 20, 26 indicates a temporary physical seizure that the demon controlling the boy caused sporadically. The father asserts that the disciples *could not* drive out the spirit. The verb *ischyō* translated *could* (*not*) denotes 'to have requisite personal resources to accomplish something' and can be translated as 'to have power, be competent, be able' (BDAG, p. 484).

19. Jesus' response, *You unbelieving generation . . . how long shall I stay with you? How long shall I put up with you?*, echoes passages such as Deuteronomy 1:35, 32:5, 20, Psalm 78:8, Jeremiah 7:29, where God expresses his exasperation with this 'unbelieving' or 'faithless' generation of the people of Israel. The referent of *you* is ambiguous. It can refer to the last speaker (the father of the son), to the disciples (whose inability to drive out the demon from the boy has just been mentioned), to the scribes (who had been arguing with the disciples) or to the crowd. The nine disciples who could not drive out the demon surely do not constitute a 'generation', nor do the scribes or the father by themselves. It is best to link the *unbelieving generation* with all who are present: the disciples, the scribes, the father who will ask Jesus for help to overcome his unbelief (v. 24) and, in view of the term *generation* (*genea*; cf. 8:12), particularly the crowd. The statement is perhaps an allusion to the 'warped and crooked generation', which is the people of Israel in the Song of Moses (Deut.

32:5). The rhetorical questions introduced by *how long* express not only Jesus' exasperation with the faithlessness of the people which makes demon possession possible and dealing with demons difficult, but also the fact that the time for Jesus' departure is drawing near. Jesus' exasperation with this *unbelieving generation* does not preclude him from having compassion on people in need. He asks the father to *bring the boy* to him.

20–22. Mark describes the demon's control over the boy. When the evil spirit *saw Jesus*, it demonstrated its control by triggering a seizure. It *threw the boy into a convulsion* (lit. 'he pulled him about') which caused the boy to fall *to the ground* where he *rolled around*, turning over and over while *foaming at the mouth*. The enquiry regarding the duration of the condition underlines the dramatic nature of the deliverance, but it may also be part of Jesus' diagnosis of the very serious condition. The father reports the duration of his boy's affliction: the demon started to control the boy with violent seizures *from childhood*. He describes the dangerous nature of these seizures: the demon has *often*, many times, *thrown him into fire or water*. Through the convulsions the demon had attempted to drag the boy into the open cooking fire in the courtyard and into cisterns or immersion pools (cf. 1:4) in which an immobilized and convulsing boy could easily drown. The evil spirit wanted *to kill him*; it was only on account of the repeated interventions of the boy's father (and mother and other relatives) that he was still alive.

The father prefaces his request with the conditional clause *if you can do anything*: the inability of the nine disciples to drive out the demon has evidently generated doubt whether Jesus has the ability to heal the boy, whose condition is not only serious but seemingly an extremely difficult case. The word *anything* (Gr. *ti*) indicates the father's belief that even a little bit of help will be beneficial.

23–24. Jesus answers the father's tentative request with the critical question *'If you can?',*[8] challenging his assumption that he, Jesus, may have the power to do 'something', mitigating the condition of the

---

8. The Greek construction has been taken as a quotation: *the 'if you can'* (Marcus, p. 654), and as an idiomatic exclamation: *'if you can' indeed!* (France, p. 367).

boy to some degree, but not the power to do 'everything' and drive out the evil spirit once and for all. The following pronouncement removes any doubt: *everything is possible for one who believes*. The referent of the phrase 'the one who believes' (*tō pisteuonti*) can be the father: the man takes it as a reference to himself (v. 24), and elsewhere miraculous healings are linked with the faith of the petitioner (2:5; 5:34, 36; 10:52; cf. 6:5–6). On the other hand, the phrase *everything is possible* (*panta dynata*, 'all things are possible') refers in 10:27, 14:36 to the omnipotence of God, who has created 'all things' and who has the power to do 'all things'. Jesus asserts that since he acts in God's authority, he can do *everything*: he is not limited by the severity of the boy's condition. Mark probably wants his readers to see both aspects: Jesus asserts that he believes in the One who holds all power and that the all-sufficiency of his faith as the Son gives him the ability to do all things; and Jesus asks the father to surrender his scepticism prompted by the seemingly hopeless situation and to believe that he, Jesus, has the ability to do all things.

The father's reply formulates a paradox: *I do believe; help me overcome my unbelief!* The father is deeply honest: he does believe (*pisteuō*; cf. 1:15) in God who can do all things, he believes that Jesus can heal his boy – this is why he brought him – and yet, as 'the father of the boy' who is afflicted with the evil spirit, he is afflicted with *unbelief* (*apistia*) as to whether his wishes for a complete recovery will actually be realized. He acknowledges his lack of faith, which is not an unwillingness to commit to Jesus' power but an inability to believe in the face of immense odds, given that the nine disciples were unable to heal the boy. As he acknowledges his unbelief, he asks Jesus to help him to overcome it, addressing the One who can do all things as the source of faith that believes so that 'all things' can happen. His faith that Jesus can help his unbelief was all that was needed for the healing to take place.

25. The demon which had been referred to as a 'spirit' is now described as an *impure spirit* (cf. 1:23, 26–27; 3:11, 30; 5:2, 8, 13; 6:7; 7:25) and, in Jesus' direct address to the demon, as a *spirit that keeps this boy from speaking and hearing* (NRSV): the demon rendered the boy unable to speak (*alalos*; v. 17) and to hear (*kōphos* can denote lack of speech capability or lack of hearing capability). During the demonic attacks, the boy's sensory organs were shut down. Jesus utters a word of *command*, demanding that the spirit *come out* of the boy and *never enter him again*. In the phrase *I command you*, the Greek emphasizes the personal pronoun *I*: the impure spirit was able to resist the disciples' authority but it will not be able to resist Jesus' authority (which demons regularly do recognize: 1:24; 3:11; 5:7, 10). The command to *come out* is standard in exorcisms (1:25; 5:8; cf. 1:34, 39; 3:15, 23; 5:13; 7:29; cf. Lucian, *Philops.* 11, 16; Philostratos, *Vit. Apoll.* 4.20); the command *never enter him again* is unique in the Gospels (cf. Matt. 12:43–45 for the possibility that a demon returns). Jesus commands complete and permanent healing.

26–27. The demon *shrieked* (cf. 1:26), *convulsed* the boy repeatedly (or 'violently'; cf. 1:26) and then *came out*, leaving the boy *like a corpse*, completely but temporarily comatose. The spectators thought that the demon had killed the boy. Jesus took the boy *by the hand* and *lifted him to his feet*, restoring him to normality after the violent exorcism. The use of similar language in 5:41–42 is prompted not by an allusion to resurrection but by the fact that both the girl and the boy were lying on the ground and by Jesus' compassion in fully restoring them to normal life.

28–29. Mark does not specify the geographical location of the *house* (NRSV) in which Jesus and the disciples stayed. If the transfiguration which immediately precedes the episode of the exorcism took place on Mount Meiron (see on 8:34; 9:2), the miracle could have taken place in Meiron, a town south-east of the mountain, which is where Jesus and the disciples would have found accommodation. The disciples' question, *Why couldn't we drive it out?*, is legitimate, since Jesus had given them authority to drive out demons, and since they had effectively driven out demons during their tour through Galilee (3:15; 6:7, 13, 30). Jesus answers that *this kind* of impure spirit *can come out only by prayer*.[9] The phrase *this kind* could suggest that Jesus differentiates between different categories (Gr. *genos*) of demons, which then would indicate that a 'spirit that keeps from speaking and hearing' (v. 25) is more difficult to cast out than

---

9. The majority of manuscripts add the phrase 'and fasting' (KJV; accepted by France, p. 361, with a 'perhaps'); the shorter reading is well supported in the manuscript tradition and is preferred by most scholars; Collins, p. 434.

other demons. On the other hand, no other passage in the New Testament distinguishes between types of demons or assesses various levels of difficulty in exorcizing them. When Jesus drove out demons, he did so with a simple word of command, even in the severe case of the man with the legion of demons (5:3–5). Jesus' answer to the disciples' question suggests that they did not pray before the exorcism, which they presumably attempted to accomplish with a simple command. The phrase *by prayer* does not prescribe an extended time of intensive prayer but merely states that prayer is necessary. Jesus' point is this: while his personal authority allows him to drive out a demon, even a legion of demons, with a simple word of command, the disciples' authority is delegated authority, which means that in their encounters with demons they always need to acknowledge their dependence upon God by praying that God will help them drive out the demons.

Theology
Jesus' pronouncement about faith – 'everything is possible for one who believes' (v. 23) – is not a 'blank cheque' that can be cashed by his followers for whatever 'sum' they desire. The context of severe demon possession helps us understand that the phrase 'everything is possible' refers to the power of God, who alone is almighty, not to the power of the one who believes. It is not the father who should exorcize the demon, but Jesus who acts with the divine power that can do all things. Faith that leads to divine intervention is faith in God, not my faith in myself, nor my belief that my faith is strong. Jesus corrects the limited faith of the father and clarifies the nature of authentic faith, which is unreserved confidence in the sovereign power of God the Creator for whom nothing is impossible and who acts through his Son. Authentic faith involves overcoming doubt; it entails asking God to intervene, expecting, with unconditional trust, that he will act as he sees fit. Faith that overcomes unbelief is a gift from Jesus.

vii. Second passion and resurrection prediction (9:30–32)
Context
The second passion prediction (after 8:31) continues the instruction of the disciples, who need to learn that Jesus' suffering, rejection,

death and resurrection are an integral part of his mission, and who need to understand the connection between his proclamation of the kingdom of God and his coming death and resurrection.

Comment

30–31. *That place* refers to the house in which Jesus and his disciples stayed immediately after the experience on the mountain and the exorcism of the demon from the boy (cf. 9:28). They *passed through Galilee*, arriving in Capernaum in verse 33. If they started out from Meiron, they would have travelled south-east via Sepph and Chorazin to Capernaum, a distance of perhaps 12 miles (20 km). Jesus wanted to avoid recognition, not in order to rest (as in 6:31 and perhaps 7:24) but *because he was teaching his disciples*. As Jesus approaches his last journey, south to Jerusalem, instruction of his disciples concerning the purpose and climax of his mission takes precedence over public ministry. The second explicit prediction of his suffering and death (cf. 8:31; for implicit references to his death see 2:20; 9:19) reminds Mark's readers of what Jesus has been teaching the disciples over a period of time, indicated by the imperfect tense of the verb *he was teaching*.

The summary is brief. The Son of Man (cf. 2:10, 28; 8:31, 38; 9:9, 12) will be *delivered into the hands of men*: Judas will turn Jesus over to the Jerusalem authorities (14:10, 43–53), and the Jewish authorities will turn Jesus over to the Roman governor Pontius Pilate (15:1, 10) who has the political authority to indict Jesus on a death-penalty charge and to carry out the execution. The passive voice of the verb ('he will be delivered') can also be understood as a divine passive, with God as the subject of the actions of those who are responsible for Jesus' arrest, trial, conviction and execution (as in Rom. 4:25; 8:32; 1 Cor. 11:23; cf. Gal. 2:20; Acts 2:23). The phrase *they will kill him* predicts Jesus' execution; the unspecified plural leaves open whether Jesus (and Mark) holds the Jewish leaders (Acts 2:23; 4:10; 5:30; 7:52) or Pontius Pilate (Acts 10:39; 13:28), or both, responsible for Jesus' execution. The prediction *after three days he will rise* repeats 8:31.

32. Peter's reaction in 8:32 to Jesus' first passion prediction implied that he did not comprehend the necessity of Jesus' suffering, death and resurrection. This lack of understanding is now stated explicitly. Even after repeated instruction about the divine purpose of his death and resurrection, the disciples still *did not understand* what Jesus *meant* (lit. 'his word'). Their reluctance to ask Jesus what his statement means is atypical: they are normally very eager to clarify the meaning of Jesus' teaching, which they find difficult to understand (cf. 4:10; 7:17; 9:11, 28; 10:10; 13:3). Mark's comment that they *were afraid to ask him about it* suggests that they knew what the answer would be yet did not want to hear it, and they certainly would not want to be linked with 'Satan' as when Peter thought he could help Jesus understand what his mission was (8:33). It would take Jesus' bodily resurrection and his appearance to the disciples for them to understand that the kingdom of God would be established by the death and resurrection in history of the Messiah, before the day of judgment.

viii. Teaching on discipleship (9:33–50)

Just as the first passion prediction, which the Twelve did not understand, was followed by teaching on discipleship (8:34 – 9:1), so the second passion prediction (9:30–32) is also followed by teaching on discipleship which challenges the natural human assumptions and values that the disciples have. Jesus speaks of true greatness, personal ambition, the opposition to him, welcoming the least of God's people, and the cost of discipleship in view of the coming judgment.

33–34. Jesus and the disciples arrive at Capernaum (1:21; 2:1), his base of operations during his Galilean ministry which is now coming to an end. Mark relates no public ministry of Jesus (cf. vv. 30–31). The *house* is presumably the house of Peter and Andrew (cf. 1:29). When Jesus asks the disciples, *What were you arguing about on the road?*, he does not want to elicit new information since he clearly knows what they have been discussing, either having overheard their conversation or through supernatural insight. He wants them to admit to having had a debate they are ashamed of acknowledging. They had argued about *who was the greatest*, the most important disciple. The discussion may have been sparked by the fact that Jesus had selected Peter, Jacob (James) and John to go with him up the mountain, leaving behind the other nine disciples, who promptly failed to drive out a demon. Mark does not hint at the reasons that one of the other nine disciples may have advanced for not being included in the inner circle; perhaps Andrew wanted to be included in the inner circle next to his brother, as both Jacob (James) and his brother John were included. Alternatively, they sense that Jesus will indeed die soon and they start to raise the question who should be the leader of the group. The bid for leadership will soon surface again when Jacob (James) and John ask for prominent roles at Jesus' side (10:35–45). While self-promotion is a vice not a virtue, it was quite acceptable in Greco-Roman society to emphasize and promote one's honour.

35. Jesus' response again reveals their lack of understanding. The reference to Jesus *sitting down* characterizes what follows as deliberate, formal instruction. Jesus teaches that pre-eminent status in the kingdom of God has two characteristics. A 'great' disciple acknowledges that he is *last* (Gr. *eschatos*): the least, the most insignificant, the lowest in rank. And a 'great' disciple is active as *the servant of all*, as befits the most insignificant member of a group. *Servant* (*diakonos*) does not describe a 'server' who waits on tables, or somebody who engages in hands-on, practical ministry. The word *servant* (and 'serve') speaks of a person who has been commissioned for a task by a superior who gives to the *diakonos* any necessary rights and authority that he needs in order to fulfil the assignment given to him, and who is obligated to carry out the assignment according to the rules, quickly and reliably (Hentschel, *Diakonia*, p. 86). Here, the one who commissions is Jesus, who has called the Twelve and given them specific tasks (1:17; 3:13–14). In this context, the word *all* in the phrase *servant of all* is not primarily the other disciples but all people without exception, the people whom they 'fish' for the kingdom of God (1:17), and all who follow Jesus. Jesus speaks of conscious and constant self-assessment and of calculated and ceaseless action that benefits others. The ultimate model of such servant leadership is Jesus who came not to be served but to serve and 'to give his life as a ransom for many' (10:45).

36–37. The *little child* (Gr. *paidion*) denotes a boy or girl normally below the age of puberty, presumably a member of the family living in the house (v. 33). Jesus places the child *among them* (lit. 'in the middle'), a prominent position that was not typical for a child in Near Eastern society. The image of Jesus *taking the child in his arms* is a picture of personal, familial intimacy (not a symbolic act of adoption, as Marcus, p. 675, suggests). The phrase *one of these little children* broadens the object lesson beyond children to those who are regarded as insignificant and without social status like children (in first-century society). The illustration of a little child highlights status, not a particular character trait supposedly typical of children (such as humility, which is not even typical of children). To *welcome* (or 'receive') a child means treating the child as significant rather than ignoring the child or chasing him or her away. The child represents Jesus' followers, since receiving a child is the same as receiving Jesus, who is represented by his followers (cf. vv. 41–42). Jesus challenges the disciples, each of whom he has commissioned to be 'the servant of all' (v. 35), to treat all of his followers as significant, especially those who are regarded as lowly and insignificant. This is why arguments about who is the greatest are absurd. As Jesus has commissioned the disciples to 'fish for people' (1:17), he also challenges the disciples to treat all people as significant, including and particularly those who are at the bottom of the social hierarchy, who have no power and no influence, who are despised, who live in poverty. Authentic followers of Jesus do not despise the 'little people' because Jesus pronounced little children to have significance 'in the middle'.

The phrase *in my name* may refer to acting on the authority of Jesus (thus the use of the phrase in vv. 38–41), but probably has here the broader sense of 'doing as I would do' (France, p. 374). Jesus asserts that welcoming one of the *little children* means welcoming him. The *little children* represent Jesus: as the disciples treat people who are deemed insignificant with respect and honour, they are treating Jesus with respect and honour. Not only that: as they *welcome* Jesus, they welcome *the one who sent me*. The notion that Jesus was 'sent' occurs only here in Mark.[10] For Jesus' conviction that he has to fulfil a mission see 8:31; 9:12; cf. 10:33–34, 38, 45. His assertion that to receive him means to receive God does not necessarily imply divinity, since an envoy can represent the one who commissions him without equal status. But at the time when Mark wrote, the assertion

---

10. But see 12:6, the parable of the tenants. Cf. Matt. 10:40; 15:24; 21:37; Luke 4:18, 43; 9:48; 10:16; John 3:34; 4:34; 5:23–24, 30, 36–38, etc.

that receiving Jesus means receiving God would indeed have indicated Jesus' divine dignity. Given this meaning, the notion of being sent by God presupposes that Jesus was with God before he was sent, which implies Jesus' pre-existence.

38. The phrase *in your name*, which here clearly means 'by your authority' (repeated in vv. 39, 41; cf. v. 37), connects verses 38–41 with the previous scene (vv. 33–37) in which Jesus taught the disciples to receive people they might naturally reject. *John*, son of Zebedee (1:19–20), appears here on his own. Together with his brother Jacob (James), John will play an even more unfortunate role in 10:35–45. They are both members of the inner circle (5:37; 9:2; 13:3; 14:33). John takes the lead in demonstrating the disciples' lack of understanding regarding the values of the kingdom of God. He reports that he and other disciples saw *someone*, who remains unidentified, *driving out demons* by appealing to Jesus' name and authority. Jesus and the twelve disciples were not the only Jewish exorcists in Galilee and Judea and beyond (cf. Matt. 12:27, 43–45; Acts 19:13). Some, in their attempt to exorcize demons, invoked the name of Jesus as a magical formula (Acts 19:13–16), the only 'success' being adverse effects for the exorcists themselves, who were beaten up by the man who had the evil spirit. Since in the present case the exorcisms were successful (v. 39), the exorcist whom John saw was not invoking the name of Jesus in a magical formula while disbelieving in Jesus; he seems to have been a true follower of Jesus. When Jesus sent out seventy-two followers, they preached, healed and cast out demons (Luke 10:9, 17).

John and other disciples tried *to stop* the man from invoking Jesus' name. The reason given is the fact that the successful exorcist *was not following us* (NRSV). The term 'to follow' (*akoloutheō*) is frequently used as a term for discipleship (1:18; 2:14; 8:34); the object of the verb is always Jesus, not the disciples. John and other disciples were looking not for personal allegiance to Jesus but for institutional exclusivity, evidently believing that the authority to exorcize demons with reference to Jesus' authority should be limited to the circle of the Twelve. John himself had been with Jesus on the mountain when the nine remaining disciples were unable to drive out the demon from the boy (9:14–18) and thus cannot be accused of hypocrisy. However, he is concerned about the status of the Twelve in a manner that suggests that he has not understood Jesus' teaching about welcoming people deemed insignificant.

39. Jesus instructs his disciples *not* to stop the man who exorcizes demons in his name. He gives three reasons, expressed in three sentences beginning with *for* (cf. ESV, NASB, RSV; only partially retained in NIV, NRSV). First, since people who perform a miracle in the name of Jesus cannot go on to *say anything bad* about Jesus, they should not be opposed. The word for *miracle* (*dynamis*, 'deed of power') is the same word used for Jesus' miracles in 6:2, 5: the miracles caused by the man who exorcizes in the name of Jesus are in the same class as Jesus' exorcisms. For the phrase 'in the name of Jesus' see 9:37–38. The verb 'to say something bad about' means 'to speak evil of, insult, malign'. The expression *in the next moment* indicates that this is a general truth, not an absolute certainty that will always be valid (Matt. 7:21–23 mentions exceptions to the rule). In general, people who associate themselves with Jesus by invoking his name and who are instrumental in healing or exorcizing demons are followers of Jesus who should not be opposed.

40. Second, since the man who exorcizes demons in the name of Jesus *is not against us*; he is *for us*. Since there is no middle ground, an unaffiliated sympathizer who associates himself with Jesus is not to be put into the category of a declared enemy. He should be welcomed because he is on the side of Jesus and his closest followers. The maxim 'whoever is not against us is for us' is found in similar form in the first century BC (Cicero, *Lig.* 11: 'For we have often heard you [Cicero] assert that, while we held all men to be our opponents save those on our side, you counted all men your adherents who were not against you').

41. Third, since even basic acts of kindness done as a response to Jesus in the person of his disciples will be rewarded, unaffiliated followers should be welcomed. To give *a cup of water to drink* (NRSV) was a self-understood courtesy which required no reward. It may indicate, beyond the act of providing something to drink, the provision of hospitality more generally. Jesus reminds the disciples that there are people who give them a cup of water because they *belong to the Messiah*. The word *Christos* is used only here by Jesus as a title referring to himself (in 12:35; 13:21 Jesus' use of *Christos* is not explicitly self-referential but 'objective'). It is the title 'Messiah', not the enigmatic 'Son of Man', which will be 'the basis of people's treatment of Jesus' disciples after his death' (France, p. 378). Since Jesus accepted Peter's declaration that he is the Messiah (8:29), there is no plausible reason to doubt the authenticity of a pronouncement in which Jesus uses the title 'Messiah' for himself, in the context of private instruction.

Jesus does not say that benevolence and charity will be rewarded. He asserts that people who provide even basic support for Jesus' disciples, knowing that they belong to and work for Jesus the Messiah, support the kingdom of God and will be rewarded (cf. Matt. 10:42; 25:31–46). The affirmation formula *Truly I tell you*, which is inserted right before the reference to the reward at the end of the sentence (NASB; most English versions place it at the beginning of the sentence), underlines the certainty of God rewarding them on the day of judgment with eschatological blessing (Marcus, p. 688; cf. Matt. 5:12; Luke 6:35; 1 Cor. 3:14; Rev. 11:18; 22:12).

42. The pronouncement of verse 42 is linked by some with what follows (on account of the catchword 'cause to stumble'; cf. NIV, NRSV), but by others with the preceding assertions (on account of the construction 'anyone who' and the conceptual antithesis to verse 41; cf. Stein, p. 447; Strauss, p. 412). The expression *little ones* denotes disciples, probably an allusion to their weakness which invites others to cause them to stumble. In 9:35–37 Jesus had used a child as an illustration of discipleship; in Zechariah 13:7 'little ones' is a term for God's people in their weakness, subject to suffering; in Luke 12:32 Jesus alludes to this Old Testament passage and calls his followers the 'little flock'. The verb 'cause to stumble' (*skandalizō*; cf. 4:17; 6:3) describes here a person who causes followers of Jesus to *stumble*; the metaphor of 'tripping' indicates the 'downfall' or failure of their commitment to Jesus, as in 14:27, 29 where the verb is used to describe the failure of the disciples when Jesus is arrested. A *large millstone* (*mylos onikos*, lit. 'a millstone worked by donkey-power') refers to the large, industrial biconical (hourglass-shaped) Pompeian mill worked by donkeys, much heavier than the domestic rotary hand mills worked by women (the so-called Olynthus mill).[11] The

---

11. For such basalt tools found in Capernaum see S. De Luca, *OEBA*, I, p. 171.

notion of a millstone around the neck was a proverbial metaphor for suffering or difficulty. The reference to a *large* biconical millstone (Lat. *catillus*), whose height ranged from 17 to 40 inches (45 to 100 cm), underlines the certainty of immediate drowning of those thrown into the sea with a millstone around their neck.

The pronouncement can be understood as an encouragement: Jesus assures the disciples that those who persecute them will eventually be judged by God while his followers will be vindicated. In view of the context, it seems more plausible to take the pronouncement as a warning: those who cause followers of Jesus to stumble will face a horrible fate. The warning is stark: nobody survives being thrown into the sea with a gigantic millstone around his or her neck. As great as the reward is for even so small an act of kindness as giving a believer a cup of water (v. 41), equally great is the punishment for an act causing a believer to stumble (Stein, p. 447). Jesus does not explain how one might cause another believer to stumble. One could think of John's suggestion of stopping a believer who does not belong to the circle of the Twelve but who exorcizes demons in Jesus' name (v. 38): if the man is forced to stop using Jesus' name in exorcisms, he might stop believing in Jesus altogether.

43–48.[12] In three parallel sayings, Jesus links sins to different parts of the body, connected to verse 42 with the catchword 'cause to stumble' (*skandalizō*). Here the 'stumbling' is not caused by pressure from others but by internal temptations of the believer who faces the danger of stumbling. Each of the three pronouncements begins with a conditional clause (*if*), followed by a clause stating the recommended course of action, followed by a comparative statement asserting that it would be better to enter eternal life maimed than to be thrown into hell with a complete body.

The word *the life* (*hē zōē*; English versions do not translate the Greek article) refers here to eternal life in the presence of God, without fear of judgment; the third pronouncement (v. 47) replaces

---

12. Later manuscripts include the words of v. 48 after vv. 43 and 45, translated in KJV as vv. 44, 46. These two verses are generally regarded as secondary additions and not printed in newer English translations.

'life' with the phrase *the kingdom of God*, which indicates that here the 'kingdom of God' does not relate to the nature and effect of Jesus' earthly ministry (cf. 1:15; 3:24; 4:11, 26, 30; 9:1) but has a new and more otherworldly reference (as in 10:15, 23–25 in the context of 10:17, 30; cf. 14:25; note the contrast with *hell*). Here *life* and *kingdom of God* refer to eternal life in God's presence as the ultimate state of the faithful disciple.

The term translated *hell* (*geenna*, 'Gehenna') is the Grecized form of Hebrew *gē' hinnōm* ('Valley of Hinnom'), a reference to the valley on the south side of Jerusalem called 'Valley of the Sons of Hinnom' where human sacrifices had been offered to the Canaanite gods Molech and Baal (2 Chr. 28:3; 33:6; Jer. 7:31; 19:5–6; 32:35). King Josiah stopped such sacrifices (2 Kgs 23:10); subsequently the valley became a place for dumping and burning garbage. In the Second Temple period, the name was used as a symbol for the place of divine punishment (cf. *1 En.* 27:2; 2 Esd. 7:36; *2 Bar.* 59:5), the fires of hell prepared for the devil and the demons (Matt. 25:41; cf. Rev. 20:10). The phrase *where the fire never goes out* (v. 43) perhaps alludes to the continuously burning garbage dumps outside Jerusalem. The word *fire* is a metaphor for judgment. In verse 48 the metaphor of *fire* that *is not quenched* is taken from Isaiah 66:24, together with the metaphor of *the worms that eat them do not die*, referring to the dead bodies of God's enemies that are decomposing and burning on the battlefield. The ghastly combination of fire and worms as the fate of the wicked also occurs in Judith 16:17 and Sirach 7:17. Both fire and worms destroy, and are used here as symbols for the horrors of divine judgment.

The three body parts signify what people do, where they go and what they see and desire. The *hand* (*cheir*; cf. 3:1) is the basic human instrument for accomplishing one's purposes (Exod. 19:13; Deut. 28:12; Eccl. 2:11; 9:10; Pss 28:4; 90:17; cf. *1 En.* 100:9 regarding sinners and the 'works' of their 'hands', with reference to judgment 'in a blazing fire'; Marcus, p. 689). The *foot* (*pous*) is the basic human means of transport which includes walking to the place where sins are committed. The *eye* (*ophthalmos*) is the organ of sense perception by which the temptation to commit sin enters. The eye is often linked with lust and sexual sins (Gen. 39:7; Matt. 5:28; cf. Sir. 9:5; 1QS I, 6) but also with pride, envy, avarice and other sins that have to do with attitude and proclivity (Isa. 5:15; Eccl. 4:8; Matt. 20:15; Marcus, p. 692).

The reference to cutting off a hand or a foot and plucking out an eye is metaphorical. Self-mutilation is prohibited in biblical tradition, the special case of Deuteronomy 25:11–12 notwithstanding; see Deuteronomy 14:1. Most rabbis interpret the formula 'eye for eye, tooth for tooth, hand for hand, foot for foot' as allegorical, specifically as a reference to financial compensation (*b. B. Qam.* 83b–84a). The demands for self-amputation are clearly not meant literally, seen in the fact that only one of each paired member is to be amputated or plucked out, even though both were probably involved in the sin (in particular both feet and both eyes). The metaphor of self-amputation is shocking and underlines the utter seriousness of the consequences of sin, the reality of divine judgment, the horror of hell and the supreme value of eternal life in God's presence. Jesus challenges his disciples to renounce any and all sin with utter seriousness.

49–50. Jesus concludes his instruction for the disciples with three sayings about salt (*halas*), the first two concluding the theme of judgment, the third concluding the teaching on discord among his followers. The saying *everyone will be salted with fire* is perhaps the most enigmatic pronouncement of Jesus. If the saying is linked with the preceding verses where 'fire' is a symbol of judgment, the 'salting with fire' can be understood as stating that everyone, not only the wicked, will have to pass through judgment. Such an interpretation might be alluding to the judgment of Sodom in which fire rained down from heaven and Lot's wife was turned into a pillar of salt (Gen. 19:24–26; cf. Deut. 29:23: a cursed land becomes like Sodom and Gomorrah, 'a burning waste of salt and sulphur'). If the saying is linked with the next two sayings in which salt is explicitly said to be a good thing (v. 50), the 'salting with fire' can be understood as stating that the disciples will be purified as they continue to follow Jesus. In this interpretation the saying alludes to Leviticus 2:13, which requires that grain offerings, which were burned with fire, be accompanied by salt, called 'salt of the covenant of your God', with the added general injunction 'add salt to all your offerings'. In Ezra 6:9, 7:22 salt is included among the provisions that are necessary for restoring the temple ritual (cf. Ezek. 43:24). In Exodus 30:35 salt, an ingredient of the incense used in the tabernacle, is linked with the qualities 'pure and sacred'. To be 'salted with fire' evokes the holy sacrifices in the temple. Here it is Jesus' followers themselves who are *salted with fire*, an image which indicates that the disciples' dedication to Jesus, who has predicted his suffering, death and resurrection, 'is like that of a burnt offering, total and irrevocable' (France, p. 384). Fire is an image for both persecution and purification (1 Cor. 3:13–15; 1 Peter 1:7; 4:12; Rev. 3:18). The enigmatic nature of the metaphorical saying suggests that one probably need not decide between these interpretations: the fire of judgment punishes the wicked but purifies the righteous (cf. Isa. 43:2); the fire connected with taking up one's cross and following Jesus (8:34) involves self-sacrifice that requires total dedication to Jesus.

The second saying speaks of salt as *good*, a quality that must be preserved. Since salt cannot *lose its saltiness*, interpreters often refer to the salt of the Dead Sea which is not pure sodium chloride but contains substances such as carnallite which leaves a stale taste once the pure salt has been dissolved. Interpreted against this background, Jesus challenges his disciples 'not to lose the characteristics that bring preservation and life to the world' (Strauss, p. 415). Alternatively, the saying simply uses a metaphor, sometimes used as a symbol for wisdom (cf. Col. 4:6; Plutarch, *Mor.* 514EF; Cicero, *De or.* 1.34.159), asserting that since unsalty salt is worthless, the disciples must recognize the critical importance of their commitment to Jesus which they cannot afford to trade for anything (Marcus, p. 698).

The third saying challenges the disciples to *have salt among yourselves*, an expression that is explained with the following demand, *be at peace with each other*. In the Old Testament salt symbolizes the covenant (Lev. 2:13), and salt was associated with meals in general and with covenantal fellowship and conviviality in particular (Num. 18:19; 2 Chr. 13:5). Jesus calls on the disciples to have peaceful, harmonious relationships among themselves.

Theology
The disciples' discussion about their relative greatness reflects their confusion about what it means to follow Jesus and how following Jesus is connected to the kingdom of God. Glory comes through self-sacrificial service demonstrated in Jesus' suffering and death that

he has just predicted for the second time (8:30–32; cf. Phil. 2:1–11). Followers of Jesus need to understand, acknowledge and apply the reversal of values: their thinking and their behaviour must be shaped by the self-sacrifice of Jesus, who gives his life for the benefit of others (cf. 10:45), not by the domination that characterizes the world, not by attempting to promote their own status. The application of the metaphor of the hand, foot and eye is left to the reader. Every follower of Jesus needs to determine which specific aspects of his or her behaviour or interests may cause a spiritual catastrophe, and take action accordingly. The demand for (symbolic) self-mutilation underlines how serious dealing with temptation and sin in one's life is and remains. Followers of Jesus need to ensure that they maintain their integrity as people on the path of the cross who are willing to bear the cost of counter-cultural values while living as a community of peace.

ix. *Teaching on divorce (10:1–12)*
Context
Jesus' pronouncement on divorce is both similar to and different from his pronouncement on purity in 7:1–15. Responding to a challenge from Pharisees, Jesus argues with scriptural material that his interlocutors did not deem directly relevant for the matter being discussed, and he calls for a more basic obedience to the will of God than Jewish traditions required. The difference is the direction of Jesus' pronouncement: his emphasis on the priority of inward purity seems to justify a less rigorous attitude regarding the legal stipulations on purity matters, while his prohibition of divorce rules out the more 'liberal' attitude and practice of scribal teaching.

Comment
1. The phrase *that place* (lit. 'from there') seems to refer back to the last specific location mentioned, Capernaum (9:33). The next specific locations will be Jericho (10:46) and Jerusalem (11:1). The travel route presupposed by the statement that Jesus *went into the region of Judea and across the Jordan* has been regarded as geographically confused. However, there is no compelling reason to assume that Jesus followed what seems to have been the conventional route for Galilean pilgrims to Jerusalem who, wanting to avoid Samaria, used

the road *east* of the Jordan river through Perea ruled by Herod Antipas (6:14), crossing the Jordan river into Judea in the vicinity of Jericho. Mark's notice presumes that after Jesus left Capernaum, he travelled south through Samaria and, after reaching Judea at Akrabeta (60 miles or 95 km south of Capernaum, using the road *west* of the Jordan river), he travelled east into Perea, crossing the Jordan perhaps between Koreai/Zaretan and Adam near the Jabbok river. Mark does not say why Jesus crossed into Perea after travelling through Samaria and northern Judea. The reference to *crowds* indicates that Jesus and his ministry in word and deed were still immensely popular despite the opposition from scribes and Pharisees. The following debate about divorce takes place in the context of Jesus' public teaching.

2. The mainstream Jewish teachers agreed that it was *lawful for a man to divorce his wife*. The controversy between the Pharisaic schools of Hillel and Shammai concerned the legitimate grounds allowing a husband to *divorce* (lit. 'let go, send away, dismiss') his wife. The school of Shammai, probably the minority view, allowed divorce only in the case of immorality, while the school of Hillel allowed divorce over a spoiled meal or the greater beauty of another woman (*m. Git.* 9:10). The Jewish teacher Ben Sira said that a husband should not allow 'boldness of speech' of his wife and suggested that 'if she does not go as you direct, separate her from yourself' (Sir. 25:26). Mark's phrasing of the Pharisees' question suggests that they do not ask Jesus which grounds of divorce he allows but whether divorce itself is permissible. The question is relevant because the Essenes may have prohibited divorce and remarriage (CD IV, 20 – V, 1; Evans, p. 81; others point to 11Q Temple LIV, 4–5, also CD XIII, 15–17, suggesting that divorce was recognized). In the Saducean text 11Q Temple LVII, 16–19, the king of Israel is prohibited from divorcing; the Qumran community seems to have accepted this ruling and 'regarded divorce as a concession to human sinfulness' (Marcus, p. 700).

The Pharisees (cf. 2:16) *tested* Jesus; their enquiry was hostile (cf. 8:11). It is possible that news of Jesus' opposition to divorce preceded him and that the Pharisees wanted to establish that he contradicted Moses, who allowed divorce in Deuteronomy 24:1–4 (although Mal. 2:13–16 asserted that God hates divorce); but see on verse 10. Alternatively, if the Essenes indeed prohibited divorce and if John, who challenged Antipas over the divorce of his wife and subsequent (re-) marriage to Herodias (6:18), shared this view, the Pharisees may have wanted to establish that Jesus agreed with John's view and that his view was 'just as politically dangerous as John's had been' (Evans, p. 81).

3–4. Jesus' question, *What did Moses command you?*, invokes Moses as an authority that Jews accept, although the pronoun *you* may suggest a limiting nuance when compared with the more general question one might expect ('What did Moses command *us*'; Gundry, p. 529). In Deuteronomy 24:1–4 Moses does not *command* divorce, or even 'permit' it: he assumes that a divorce has taken place and that it has been duly certified, and then provides the legal ruling that the husband who has divorced his wife may not remarry her after her second husband has divorced her. Jesus seems to invite the Pharisees to 'correct' him by acknowledging that Moses never actually commanded divorce but merely presupposed its existence.

The Pharisees' answer, *Moses permitted a man to write a certificate of divorce and send her away*, is not a quotation from Deuteronomy 24 but a summary of what the scribes assumed was its 'permission'. The 'permission' is inferred from the fact that a divorce that becomes a fact after a certificate of divorce (or 'bill of relinquishment') has been issued is not met with disapproval in Deuteronomy 24. Since this statement is not the end of Jesus' comment on the question of divorce, his question in verse 3 does not intend to draw a contrast between the ultimate will of God, who does not 'command' divorce, and a concession of God, who 'permits' divorce in some specific circumstances (an interpretation which the Pharisees would accept and which would require a discussion about these special circumstances).

5. The *commandment* (NRSV) that Moses wrote refers to the long sentence in Deuteronomy 24:1–4 which concludes with a legal stipulation (that the divorced, remarried and 'redivorced' wife may not return to her original husband). Jesus explains that Moses' recognition of the reality of divorce and the provisions for divorce were a concession to human sinfulness. The expression *hardness of heart* (NRSV) describes people's stubborn resistance to God (Deut. 10:16; Prov. 17:20; Jer. 4:4; Ezek. 3:7). Divorce occurs when people rebel against the will of God in their behaviour, and it was for such situations that Moses legislated when he mentioned certificates of divorce.

6–8. Jesus emphasizes God's original intention for people who are married over against later legal provisions for divorce. He asserts that the situation that prevailed *at the beginning of creation*, before the fall, is the standard to which human behaviour should conform as regards marriage and divorce. Jesus first quotes Genesis 1:27: *God 'made them male and female'*. The fact that the sexual differentiation of male and female existed from the beginning (rather than being a result of the fall) is the basis for the sexual union between man and woman spelled out in the second quotation. Genesis 2:24 describes the basic pattern of heterosexual, lifelong monogamy as the order for marital relationships that God has created. A man will *leave his father and mother* and thus the home in which he grew up: he starts his own family. He is *united to his wife*: God himself attaches the man to his wife (divine passive), a joining that results in *the two* (Gr. *hoi dyo*) becoming *one flesh* (Gr. *sarx mia*). The last point is repeated for emphasis: the union that God creates between a husband and his wife results in the fact that *they are no longer two, but one flesh*. They are a single, indivisible unit exemplified in the sexual union of a husband and his wife that consummates the covenant God establishes between husband and wife.

9. Since it is *God* who has *joined together* the husband and his wife, *man* (RSV, NASB) must not separate them: a husband must not dismiss his wife. Divine actions shall not be cancelled by human actions. The expression *joined together* (lit. 'yoked together') is a metaphor for the union of husband and wife in marriage which is described as a *fait accompli*, 'not a matter of provisionality or choice' (France, p. 392). The present tense of the imperative *let no one separate* (NIV) emphasizes the durative aspect of the prohibition: the prohibition is always valid; husband and wife should never divorce. The fact that Mark does not record a response by the Pharisees may suggest that he wishes to leave the impression 'that they are thunderstruck and silenced by his retort' (Marcus, p. 711).

10–12. Jesus' explanation, which is even more shocking for the disciples (cf. Matt. 19:10), consists of two balanced statements referring both to a husband divorcing his wife and to a wife divorcing her husband. The implication of verse 12 that a woman might contemplate divorcing her husband and marrying another man is not exclusively a Roman practice but attested among Jews as well: a woman could show a court grounds for divorce and have the court persuade her husband to divorce her (*t. Ketub.* 12:3). Generally, however, only men could initiate divorce proceedings (Josephus, *Ant.* 15.259).

Jesus explains that it is not only divorce which is contrary to the will of God: remarriage (which is the issue in Deut. 24:1–4) is contrary to the will of God as well. A husband who divorces his wife and marries another woman *commits adultery against her*. The pronouncement extends the logic of the pronouncement on marriage and divorce in verses 6–9. Since the original one-flesh union between a husband and his wife is permanent in the eyes of God, a divorce does not cancel this union. Entering a second union and having marital relations within that relationship is as much adultery (*moicheia*; here the verb *moichaō* is used) as if the husband of a wife had intercourse with a woman married to another man. The divorce and the subsequent remarriage, which in first-century society would have been a common expectation, is just as much an offence against God and his purpose for marriage as it is an offence against the (first) wife who is wronged. The idea of adultery 'against the wife' implies the equality of man and woman in marriage (cf. 1 Cor. 7:4).

Theology

Marriage is much more than a contract between two people for mutual benefit: it is a heterosexual, monogamous, lifelong union that fuses two individuals, husband and wife, into one single, permanent reality established by God, a union of 'one flesh' that shall not be destroyed. The pronouncement in verses 11–12 does not mean that Jesus prohibits remarriage but allows divorce: Jesus does not change the topic in verses 11–12, but clarifies the implications of the pronouncement of verses 5–9. Jesus' argument 'is simple and complete, and Jesus sees no need to qualify the uncompromising conclusion: marriage is for life' (France, p. 329).

Jesus' pronouncement on divorce and remarriage has been, and continues to be, interpreted in different ways. Some argue that for

Christians, divorce is always prohibited and that divorce that has taken place is regarded as illegitimate in God's eyes. Situations in which, for example, one spouse abuses the other are to be resolved by counselling and by (temporary) separation, but not by divorce. Others say that while divorce is not God's ideal, it happens and is thus permitted on grounds that are strictly defined (adultery, often with reference to Matt. 5:32; 19:9) or broadly defined (breaking any of the marriage vows). Remarriage is not allowed by some who hold this position; others do allow remarriage. Good pastoral considerations which are cited for allowing divorce and remarriage are based on values drawn from Jesus' teaching on other subjects. However, 'no approach can claim his support which does not take as its guiding principle the understanding of marriage set forth in vv. 9 and 11–12' (France, p. 394). Jesus' pronouncement that marriage is permanent and divorce (and subsequent remarriage) is contrary to the will of God is clear and unequivocal. Paul refers approvingly to a word of the Lord which affirms that a wife should not divorce her husband and a husband should not divorce his wife (1 Cor. 7:10–11). If we find Jesus' teaching uncompromising, so did his disciples, whose conventional thinking on these and other matters Jesus challenges.

x. *Blessing the children (10:13–16)*
Context
Jesus' teaching on the values of true disciples again uses a child as illustration. While 9:36–37 spoke about receiving a child in Jesus' name, illustrating the reversal of values regarding status, greatness and service, this episode speaks of receiving the kingdom of God as a child receives it, highlighting the necessity of being entirely dependent upon God as well as emphasizing the importance of children. The transition from a consideration of marriage and its permanence (10:1–12) to the related theme of children is entirely natural.

Comment
13. The *little children* are boys and girls below the age of puberty (cf. 5:39; 9:24). The people who brought them were presumably their parents who want Jesus *to place his hands on them* (lit. 'touch them'): they seek a blessing from the renowned teacher. The background

of the requested touch is probably the parental blessing of children (Gen. 9:26–27; 27:21–29; 28:1–4; 48:14). Mark does not explain why *the disciples rebuked them*. Suggestions range from a conviction that Jesus' touch should be reserved for healing or fear that the children would exhaust Jesus, to concern that they might distract Jesus from teaching the crowds. The disciples have forgotten the lesson of 9:37.

14–15. Jesus is *indignant* at the disciples' refusal to let the parents and their children come to him, angry at their pride in thinking that they have an 'exclusive right to Jesus' authority' (9:38; Strauss, p. 432) and irritated at their failure to learn the lesson about receiving children in 9:37. The command *Let the little children come to me* instructs the disciples to let the parents and their children approach him, reinforced by the phrase *do not hinder them*. The fact that the verb 'hinder' (*kōlyō*) occurs in the context of water baptism in Acts 8:36, 10:47, 11:16–17 does not prove that the latter is in view here: the Acts passages explicitly refer to water, which is not the case here; verse 16 speaks of arms, hands and a blessing, not of immersion in water. The verb *kōlyō* means 'to keep something from happening; to hinder, prevent, forbid' and 'to keep something back; to refuse, deny, withhold', and is used in many different contexts. Jesus commands the disciples to stop obstructing the children.

The statement *the kingdom of God belongs to such as these* is not a pronouncement about children but about people who are *like* children, who share a child's status. In antiquity, the dominant features linked with children were their vulnerability, their dependence on their parents and their social marginality before they reached adulthood. Jesus commands the disciples to allow the children to come to him because they represent the kind of people to whom the kingdom of God belongs – those who come in utter dependence upon God, including especially those who are vulnerable and socially marginalized.

The emphatic 'Amen' saying states that to *receive the kingdom of God* requires accepting it *like a little child*. Just as children are completely dependent upon their parents, so receiving the kingdom of God requires utter dependence on God. The word *receive* reflects the passive stance of little children: they need their parents to take care of them; they receive their parents' care and provision as a matter of course. People who refuse to be 'like children' *will never enter* the kingdom of God. Jesus underlines the active stance that is required of people who desire to belong to God's dominion.

16. When Jesus *took the children in his arms*, and *placed his hands on them*, presumably one by one, and *blessed them*, he demonstrated the reality of the kingdom of God who accepts those who readily come to him in passive acceptance of his mercy and in active dependence on his care. The laying on of hands is 'a natural sign of association' (France, p. 398) often used in healings (1:41; 5:23; 6:5; 7:32; 8:23, 25) and a traditional symbol of blessing (cf. Gen. 48:14–18).

Theology
Jesus does not favour children because they have virtues that qualify them for the kingdom of God (suggestions range from their innocence, gentleness, purity, humility – stances that are not characteristic of the normal behaviour of children). He points to children as exemplifying the disposition of people who receive, enter into and belong to the kingdom of God – people who are not defined by social status and self-perceived significance but by the receptivity of those who don't have anything unless others give it to them, by the dependence of those who need the care and provision of others. Only those belong to the kingdom of God who are willing to receive God's mercy passively, as they are 'carried', and actively, as they 'enter' into the realm of his dominion. The paradox of simultaneous passivity and activity corresponds to the paradox of salvation by grace on account of faith in Jesus emphasized by Paul in Romans 1:16; 3:24–26; 5:2. While the emphasis is on the values of the kingdom of God that the disciples are still in the process of learning, the text also serves to guide Christians' attitude towards children and their spiritual welfare.

xi. The rich man and discipleship (10:17–31)
Context
Jesus' teaching on discipleship which characterizes the material after the first passion prediction (8:31–33) continues the reorientation of his disciples concerning the values of the kingdom of God. The episode picks up the themes of status and entrance into the kingdom of God of the previous episode (10:13–16). Jesus' pronouncements on wealth and on the criteria that determine whether one belongs

to the kingdom of God are as radical and uncompromising as his pronouncements on divorce (10:1–12). The threefold repetition of the phrase 'enter the kingdom of God' (10:23, 24, 25) points to the central focus of the episode. The references to 'eternal life' at the beginning and end of the text (10:17, 30), to 'heaven' (10:21), to being 'saved' (10:26) and to the gains enjoyed by committed disciples who have left everything (10:29–30) describe the results of following Jesus and deepen the disciples' understanding of the kingdom of God.

Comment

17. Jesus is *on his way* from Perea (v. 1), where he had taught in an undisclosed locality (v. 10), to Jericho (v. 46) and eventually Jerusalem (11:1). Mark does not describe the *man* who ran up to Jesus. We learn in verse 22 that he had 'great wealth'. Luke 18:18 calls him a 'ruler' (*archōn*), a governing official or an individual in a distinguished position. According to Matthew 19:20, he was a young man. He evidently belonged to the aristocratic, land-owning elite of Perea which was ruled by Antipas, the tetrarch of Galilee. The fact that he *ran up* to Jesus and *fell on his knees before him* points to the effect Jesus had on people, and indicates the deference of the man towards Jesus. He addresses Jesus as *good teacher*, which indicates the sincerity of his question and his respect for Jesus as an authority on one of the most important subjects in Jewish theology.

The expression *eternal life* describes ultimate salvation beyond the present life (for 'eternal' see on 3:29; for 'life', 9:43). In the context of verses 23, 25 and 26, *eternal life* is synonymous with entering the kingdom of God and being saved. The concept of eternal life as an 'inheritance' fits the idea of Israel as God's children (cf. Exod. 4:22; Deut. 14:1; Isa. 43:6; Jer. 3:4, 19; Hos. 11:1). The man believes in a future resurrection of the body and in life after death, but he knows that participation in the eternal life cannot be taken for granted. The question *what must I do?* should not be burdened with questions about the relationship between faith and works: Jesus' response involves things to 'do' (vv. 19, 21). The man asks how he can qualify for eternal life.

18–19. In his response, Jesus defines *good* to mean 'perfect' by asserting that *God alone* is good. The context shows that Jesus is not intent on making a statement about himself, somehow implying that he himself is not good in the sense in which only God is good.[13] As the man will shortly assert that he has been keeping God's commandments, Jesus challenges him to examine his idea of 'goodness' and his qualifications for obtaining eternal life.

Jesus assumes that the man knows the Decalogue (Exod. 20:1–17; Deut. 5:6–21), confirming its importance in Second Temple Judaism. The *commandments* that Jesus quotes represent the second part of the Decalogue which govern behaviour towards other people and which can be more objectively assessed than the commandments of the first part. The commandments are cited in the order 6, 7, 8, 9, 10, 5. *Murder* is the extrajudicial taking of another person's life. *Adultery* refers to sexual relations of a married man or woman with the wife or husband of another married person. To *steal* refers to the theft of property that belongs to someone else. To *give false testimony* is to provide false evidence as a witness before a court of law. The stipulation *you shall not defraud* seems to be a substitution of the tenth commandment ('you shall not covet'), drawing out in behavioural terms the practical result of coveting; the verb, which means 'cause another to suffer loss by taking away through illicit means' (BDAG, p. 121), is sometimes used in contexts of social oppression – for example, keeping back workers' wages or cheating the poor out of their living (cf. Mal. 3:5; Sir. 4:5; cf. Jas 5:4) – and may relate the man to the exploitative behaviour of the landed aristocracy (Marcus, p. 722). To *honour your father and mother* means to recognize their importance, to respect, love and obey them, and to take care of them in their old age. Jesus' quotation from the Decalogue is not meant to set up the man for failure (Strauss, p. 441). The law that God gave to Israel at Sinai was to be obeyed, and could be obeyed, so that Israel could enjoy fellowship with God, who would dwell among his people. God promised Israel life and blessing if they loved him and obeyed his commandments (Lev. 18:5; 25:18; Deut. 30:15–16).

---

13. On Jesus' sinlessness cf. 2 Cor. 5:21; Heb. 4:15; 7:26; 1 Peter 1:19; 2:22. Jesus' pronouncement in Mark 10:18 is an assertion about his humanity, which is 'relative' to the perfection of God; it does not imply that Jesus sees himself as a sinner.

20. The man asserts that he has kept *all these* commandments quoted by Jesus. Taken as rules of conduct, without presuming Jesus' interpretation of some of these commandments (Matt. 5:21–28), the six commandments that Jesus quoted could be kept to the letter (although honouring one's parents was not easy to quantify). If *all* refers not only to these six commandments but to all other commandments of the law, the man's answer does not imply a claim that he had never broken any of the commandments of the law. Rather it implies that if infringements of the law had taken place, he followed the procedures prescribed in the law to put things in order with God and with his fellow human beings (by offering sacrifices, ritual immersion, monetary restitution). Jesus' response in verse 21 implies that he acknowledged not only that one could observe the commandments of the law but also that this man was a pious, law-abiding Jew who had in fact observed the commandments. Paul says of his time before his conversion to faith in Jesus Messiah, 'As far as a person can be righteous by obeying the commands of the Law, I was without fault' (Phil. 3:6, GNB).

21. The statement that *Jesus looked at him and loved him* confirms that the man's question concerning eternal life was sincere and his assertion that he had kept the commandments was truthful. Jesus invites the man to *come* and *follow* him, joining the Twelve and other close disciples. This invitation is Jesus' answer to the man's question what he must do to inherit eternal life (v. 17). Following Jesus is the *one thing* that qualifies for entering the kingdom of God and obtaining salvation and eternal life. The man acknowledges the teaching authority of Jesus. Now Jesus challenges him to acknowledge the connection between himself and the kingdom of God, salvation and eternal life.

If the man accepts that obtaining eternal life is inseparably connected with following Jesus, he will do what Jesus commands him: *Go, sell everything you have and give to the poor*. Peter, Andrew, Jacob (James) and John left their nets and boats and followed Jesus because they acknowledged Jesus' authority to demand that they give up their professions and their way of life. If the rich man acknowledges Jesus' authority, he will divest himself of his possessions, donate the proceeds to the poor and follow Jesus, joining Jesus' closest disciples, who depend on the material support of others. Having *treasure in heaven* means, in the context of the man's question, eternal life. The expression implies a contrast with the treasures of earth which cannot compare with the treasures of heaven. The emphasis is not on self-sacrificial almsgiving but on following Jesus, which is confirmed by the aorist tense of the imperatives *sell* and *give* and the present tense imperative *follow* which underscores the permanence of the attachment to Jesus.

22. The reaction of the rich man to Jesus' invitation was immediately visible: his *face fell*, that is, he was shocked at Jesus' demand, with the result that dismay registered on his face (BDAG, p. 949, *stygnazō*), and he *went away*, terminating the encounter. His reaction had an internal component as well: he went away *grieving* (NRSV), feeling sad and distressed, which again confirms his sincerity and suggests that he wanted to accept Jesus' invitation to follow him but was unable to do so because he was not willing to part with his *great wealth*. The sincere, law-abiding man had expected an answer that would allow him to continue his life essentially unchanged. He had immense respect for Jesus as a teacher, but he was not willing to commit his life to him at the expense of his wealth. His wealth and the status quo had more power than Jesus' words and the power of the kingdom of God.

23–25. When Jesus *looked round*, he apparently registered the disciples' shock about what had just transpired. He comments on the rich man's departure with a pronouncement which makes them even more amazed: *How hard it is for the rich to enter the kingdom of God!* The Old Testament repeatedly warns against the danger of riches and critiques the rich who oppress and exploit the poor.[14] On the other hand, wealth was regarded as a sign of divine blessing.[15] The wealthy had both the means and the leisure to give alms to the poor and do good deeds and thus express their commitment to God. In this context, the statement that it is hard (or 'difficult') for the rich to enter the kingdom of God, that is, to gain eternal life (v. 17),

---

14. Pss 10:2–11; 12:5; 37:12–22; Prov. 11:28; 16:8; 19:1, 10; Isa. 10:1–4; 53:9; Amos 2:6–8; Mic. 2:1–5.
15. Prov. 10:22: 'The blessing of the LORD brings wealth'; cf. Deut. 28:1–14; Job 1:10; 42:10; Ps. 128:1–2; Isa. 3:10; cf. Sir. 11:17.

seems counter-intuitive. Jesus responds to the disciples' amazement by repeating the statement (v. 24). The omission of 'for the rich' renders the saying more universal. The difficulty for wealthy people to enter the kingdom of God is a symptom of the basic difficulty for all people, irrespective of their economic circumstances, to enter the kingdom of God and obtain salvation (Pesch, I, p. 141).

The formula *It is easier for . . . than . . .* designates an impossible event to which another impossible event is compared. Jesus asserts that just as it is impossible *for a camel to go through the eye of a needle*, so it is impossible *for someone who is rich to enter the kingdom of God*. The camel (*kamēlon*) was a proverbially large animal, the largest animal native to Palestine, a beast of burden that could carry heavy loads; and there was no other hole (*trymalia*) that was as small as the hole in a needle (*rhaphis*) used for sewing. It is impossible for a camel to walk through the eye of a needle. Attempts have been made to ameliorate the metaphor by 'miniaturizing' the camel or 'growing' the eye of the needle: some Greek manuscripts and a few early translations replaced the word *kamēlon* with the word *kamilon* ('rope'). As early as Theophylact (eleventh century), interpreters suggested that Jesus spoke of a small gate within the large double gate in the city wall of Jerusalem through which pedestrians could enter (suggesting that once the camel strips off its load and bends its knees and neck it can get through); but there is no evidence whatsoever that any gate in Jerusalem was ever called 'The Needle's Eye'. Such interpretations ignore the grammar of the statement and undermine the point that Jesus makes, a point that the disciples grasp: it is impossible for a rich person to enter the kingdom of God.

26. The progression from 'hard' to 'impossible' moves the disciples' reaction from being 'amazed' (v. 24) to being 'even more astounded' (lit. 'exceedingly struck out of their senses'). If the rich cannot enter the kingdom of God, *Who then can be saved?* In the context of the question of the rich man, 'to be saved' (*sōzō*) is here synonymous with 'eternal life' (v. 17), 'treasure in heaven' (v. 21) and 'entering the kingdom of God' (vv. 23, 24, 25). The law-abiding man who has kept God's commandments, who has been blessed with riches and who, because he is pious, would have given alms to the poor and thus stored up 'treasure in heaven' can be expected to be commended. An early Jewish text links keeping God's commandments with giving alms to the poor, promising that if you 'do not turn your face away from anyone who is poor, ... the face of God will not be turned away from you' (Tob. 4:5). If such a man cannot obtain eternal life, then nobody can be saved.

27. Jesus *looked at them*, knowing their thoughts, and replies by accepting the logic of their deduction: *With man this is impossible*. The rich, law-abiding man cannot obtain eternal life on account of his behaviour, and, indeed, nobody can be saved by his or her way of life, however law-abiding and pious a person may be. Then Jesus shifts the focus from the types of people who can be saved to the agent of salvation: it is impossible for rich and poor alike to be saved, *but not for God; for God all things are possible* (NRSV). From the perspective of human behaviour, no human being can achieve entry into the kingdom of God and obtain the salvation of eternal life by personal effort. From the perspective of the kingdom of *God*, who is the Creator and who can do everything (9:23), the salvation of the rich and indeed of any human being becomes a possibility. The salvation of the rich is a miracle, as is the salvation of everybody else.

28. Peter speaks for the Twelve when he reminds Jesus that *we have left everything to follow you*. Peter and the other fishermen left their nets and boats when Jesus called them (1:18, 20); Levi left his tax collector's booth (2:14); and the Twelve all 'came' when Jesus called them in order to prepare them for a ministry of preaching (3:13–14). At the same time, Peter and Andrew still possessed a house in Capernaum (1:29), and some disciples still owned a fishing boat (3:9; 4:1, 36; John 21:3). Since Jesus does not challenge Peter's assertion in his response, the phrase *we have left everything* is a relative statement describing the fact that they have left their professions and their way of life to follow Jesus in his itinerant ministry, to be trained by him and to participate in his mission.

29–30. Jesus accepts Peter's observation and describes, in another 'Amen' saying (3:28; 8:12; 9:1, 41; 10:15), the rewards of discipleship. The Twelve who travel with Jesus and who in teams of two visit the villages and towns of Galilee (6:7–13) have left houses, brothers, sisters, mothers, fathers, children or fields. The reference to children implies married disciples such as Peter (1:30) who have children and who later, after Pentecost, travel with their wives (1 Cor. 9:5). The omission of 'wives' in the list perhaps reflects the permanence of marriage emphasized in 10:2–12. The reference to *fields* implies well-to-do disciples who may have owned more than one field, among the Twelve perhaps Levi the tax collector. Since Peter and Andrew still had their house in Capernaum and since some disciples continued to own a boat, the word 'leave' does not describe the disposal of all property and the total renunciation of all family ties, but the leaving behind of home and family for the period of their itinerant ministry of preaching and healing. The Twelve have been willing to leave home, family and possessions *for my sake and for the sake of the good news* (NRSV). They obeyed Jesus' call not for the sake of treasures in heaven or as a means to enter the kingdom of God and obtain salvation and eternal life. They obeyed Jesus because it was *Jesus* who called them with an authority which they acknowledged as the legitimate authority over their lives. The parallel expression confirms the close connection, indeed identification, of Jesus with the good news of the kingdom of God (1:15). To follow Jesus means to participate in the kingdom of God, as the reality of God's kingdom is present in Jesus.

The symmetry of the clauses in verses 29 and 30 highlights the fact that 'nothing of consequence will be lost through discipleship' (Marcus, p. 737). Disciples who have left everything will *receive a hundred times as much* in houses, brothers, sisters, mothers, children, fields. From the previous list the word 'fathers' is omitted, perhaps because believers have one Father in heaven (cf. Matt. 23:9). The phrase *in this present age* refers to an earthly reward. The hundredfold increase is not meant to be understood literally (one hundred mothers and one hundred children are of 'dubious desirability', France, p. 408). Jesus speaks of the extended family of his followers (cf. 3:34–35) with new familial relationships and the sharing of possessions (cf. Acts 2:44–45; 4:32–37) – a new reality whose value is far greater than the security that personal possessions can ever give.

The item *along with persecutions* is a prediction that committed followers of Jesus, especially those engaged in full-time itinerant ministry, will experience the same kind of opposition that Jesus is experiencing (2:6–7; 3:2, 6, 21–22; 6:2–4) and will experience shortly in Jerusalem, as predicted (8:31; 9:31; 10:32–34). Similar warnings of future persecution are given in 10:39 and 13:9–13. If the 'gain' of discipleship is a 'mixed' blessing, this is nothing compared with the ultimate reward: *in the age to come eternal life*. This is the 'treasure in heaven' (v. 21) that the rich man missed out on when he left Jesus. The conclusion of Jesus' pronouncement confirms that 'eternal life', 'entering the kingdom of God' and 'following Jesus' are inseparably connected.

31. The epigram *But many who are first will be last, and the last first* expresses the difference between human values and the values of God's kingdom, between life in this age and life in the age to come. In the context of his encounter with the rich man and the ensuing dialogue about the entrance requirements of the kingdom, Jesus asserts that the rich and powerful who are regarded as 'first' in the present age will be 'last' in God's judgment in the age to come if they do not follow Jesus, and those who are regarded as 'last' by the rich and powerful in the present age will be 'first' in the eyes of God, who does the humanly impossible and brings them into his kingdom, granting them the salvation of eternal life.

Theology

The main emphasis of this text is the answer to the question how one can enter the kingdom of God and obtain eternal life and salvation. While the text indeed teaches about wealth and affluence, it does *not* teach that Jesus requires renunciation of wealth as a prerequisite for salvation. Jesus emphasizes that it is impossible for *both* rich people *and* everybody else to enter the kingdom of God on the basis of personal behaviour. Entrance into the kingdom of God is possible only if and when God himself 'transports' people into the realm of his dominion. Only God can grant eternal life in his presence; only God can give salvation to human beings. The key demand for the rich man is that he follow Jesus, which requires him to acknowledge Jesus' authority over his life – which, if he accepts it, will render him capable of doing what Jesus asks: he will be able to sell his possessions. The primary problem of the man is not that he is wealthy but that he does not understand who Jesus is. People who understand who Jesus is do what he says.

xii. Third passion and resurrection prediction (10:32–34)

Context

The third passion and resurrection prediction (after 8:31–32 and 9:30–31), the most detailed of the three, describes what will happen once they reach Jerusalem, which they are approaching. The request in the next episode by Jacob (James) and John for the best seats in Jesus' kingdom reveals that the disciples still fail to understand that Jesus' death is the goal and purpose of his mission, a fact that Jesus reiterates in a pronouncement on his life which he will give as a ransom for many.

Comment

32. Mark identifies, for the first time, Jerusalem as the goal of Jesus' travels, Jesus having left Capernaum (cf. 9:33; 10:1). The expression *going up to Jerusalem* (NRSV) is the standard phrase for describing travels to Jerusalem, due to its location in the Judean hill country at an elevation of 2,600 feet (800 m) above sea level, a steep climb from Jericho just north of the Dead Sea (1,407 ft or 429 m below sea level) and because it was the Holy City of the Jewish people. Jerusalem had been mentioned earlier as the source of opposition focused on the teachers of the law (3:22; 7:1). The arrival in Jerusalem will be a few days before the Passover festival. Jesus and the disciples would have been part of a large crowd of pilgrims travelling to Jerusalem. Since they have yet to arrive in Jericho (v. 46), the passion prediction and the ensuing discussion about greatness take place in Perea, east of the Jordan river. If the group were in a town opposite Jericho, they might have been staying in Bethennabris or Betharamphtha (Livias, renamed Julias), both towns around 5 miles (9 km) from the Jordan river. The Twelve were *astonished*, evidently on account of Jesus purposefully walking *ahead of them* (NRSV) on the road to Jerusalem, intent on reaching the city, despite the fact that he had foretold his rejection, suffering and death by the elders and chief priests. Those who were among the larger group of followers *were afraid*, affected by the approaching climax of Jesus' ministry and the impending confrontation between Jesus and the political and religious leadership in Jerusalem. Jesus instructs the Twelve privately about what will happen as the result of God's purposes for his ministry.

33–34. Jesus' prediction of his passion and resurrection retains elements of the two earlier predictions but adds more detail. The phrase *we are going up to Jerusalem* notes specifically that Jesus' violent death will take place in the religious capital of Judea, with the temple and the Sanhedrin, this highest Jewish court, being the most important Jewish institutions at the time. As in 8:31 and 9:31, Jesus speaks of himself in terms of the *Son of Man* (cf. 2:10) who will be handed over *to the chief priests and the teachers of the law*. The elders mentioned in 8:31 are omitted, which is not significant since it was the chief priests who controlled the Sanhedrin. Scribes from Jerusalem had travelled to Galilee, examined Jesus and concluded that he performed exorcisms with the power of Satan (3:22; 7:1). The passive verb *will be handed over* (NRSV) refers to Judas' betrayal of Jesus by which he hands Jesus over to the Jewish authorities (14:10, 43–53), but simultaneously points to God's action in the process (cf. 1:14; 9:31).

The imminent events are then described in two phases: there will be a Jewish trial and a Roman trial. The Jewish trial before the chief priests and scribes is described with two verbs: *They will condemn him to death*; that is, they will pronounce a sentence after a determination of guilt (*katakrinō*), a sentence that will impose the penalty of death (*thanatos*). Then *they . . . will hand him over to the Gentiles*, since it was the Roman governor who had the authority in a Roman province to indict suspects in death-penalty cases and carry out a death sentence. The word *Gentiles* (*ethnē*; cf. 10:42; 11:17; 13:8, 10) refers here specifically to the administration of Roman Judea, headed up by the prefect Pontius Pilate. The Roman trial is described with four verbs: they will *mock him* – they will subject him to derision, make fun of him as a pathetic would-be king (cf. 15:16–20); they will *spit on him*, treating him with utter contempt (cf. 15:19; in 14:65 it is members of the Sanhedrin who spit on Jesus); they will *flog him* – beat him with a whip (cf. 15:15); and they will *kill him* – Pilate will condemn Jesus to be executed by crucifixion (cf. 15:15, 24). Each of these four elements (although not the verbs) is mentioned in the suffering of Isaiah's Servant of the Lord (mockery and spitting, Isa. 53:3; flogging, 53:5; death, 53:8–9, 12), a figure who is important for Jesus' explanation of the purpose and the consequences of his death in verse 45. The resurrection prediction is formulated with the same words as in 8:31; 9:31: *three days later he will rise*. The ultimate outcome of Jesus' mission as the Messiah and Son of God (1:1) is formulated with climactic succinctness. But the emphasis is on Jesus' suffering and death.[16]

xiii. The greatness of self-sacrificial service (10:35–45)

The request of Jacob (James) and John to sit at Jesus' right and left in the glory of his kingdom presumes either that they have not heard what Jesus has just said when he predicted his trial in Jerusalem which would end in his execution (10:32–34), or that they understood Jesus' reference to the Son of Man in terms of possible royal connotations in the light of Daniel 7:13–14. As the disciples had responded to the first two passion predictions with a complete lack of understanding (8:32; 9:32), so they do here: while Jesus spoke of being mocked, spat upon, flogged and killed, Jacob and John pursue personal ambitions.

35–37. For *Jacob [James]* and *John* see 1:19; 3:17. Their request seems to have been made privately, although eventually the other ten disciples hear about it (v. 41). Together with Peter they belong to the inner circle of the Twelve (5:37; 9:2; 13:3; 14:33). They might have thought that the leading role of Peter, who had acted as their spokesman in 9:5, was not unassailable in view of Jesus' pronouncement about the first being last (v. 31; France, p. 415). Their plea that Jesus grant them *whatever we ask* is either a roundabout approach that reflects their awareness of the delicacy of their self-centred request or an attempt to manipulate Jesus into giving them *carte blanche*. Jesus responds cautiously, asking *what* exactly they want him to do for them.

Jacob and John request positions of honour in an implied hierarchy within the kingdom of God. The word *sit*, associated with *glory*, suggests a royal throne with the places of pre-eminent honour on either side. In Daniel 7:9, 13–14, 27 the glory of the Son of Man is connected with the holy people of the Most High sharing in his

---

16. The 'Secret Gospel of Mark', which consists of eleven verses that allegedly belong after 10:34, and two further verses allegedly coming after 10:46, is a modern forgery or a hoax; cf. Collins, pp. 486–493.

enthronement and his judicial authority (cf. Matt. 19:28; Luke 22:30; Rev. 3:21; 4:4). The seat on the *right* is the more prestigious (the notion is rooted in the dominating role of the right hand as the more active and more powerful). The *left* was regarded as the side from which bad omens came, which may explain why the word *aristeros* ('left') is replaced in verse 40 by the word *euōnymos* ('honoured', used euphemistically for 'left, on the left'; cf. *LSJ*, p. 740); however, sitting immediately on the left of the king was obviously a place of honour. Jacob and John evidently deduce from Jesus' teaching about the kingdom of God and his use of the title Son of Man, understood against the background of Daniel 7:14, that Jesus is King. Jesus' reply in verse 40 does not reject that notion. Jacob and John ignore Jesus' talk of rejection, suffering and death which has been prominent since 8:31, evidently hoping that it is a mistake (as Peter did in 8:32) and assuming that Jesus will establish his messianic kingdom once he arrives in Jerusalem. This would not automatically involve a messianic war with the Roman authorities (in which case they would have asked to be made Jesus' leading generals): Herod I and Agrippa I were kings of Judea with the approval of the Senate in Rome and the emperor.

38. Jesus' answer consists, first, of the assertion that their request is misguided. They do not understand the necessity of his death and the nature of his kingship. Second, Jesus asks a rhetorical question that highlights the uniqueness of this imminent death. The *cup* is sometimes an image of blessing, but more often a symbol of judgment, and occasionally a symbol of the suffering of God's people.[17] The expression *the cup I drink* refers to Jesus' suffering and death predicted in verses 33–34. If the notion of symbolized judgment is paramount, Jesus speaks of his suffering and death as vicariously accepting God's judgment for the sins of humankind: he drinks the *cup* which the wicked deserve. Since the image of the cup is also used for the suffering of God's people, it is not certain

---

17. Blessing: Pss 16:5; 23:5; 116:13; judgment: Ps. 75:8; Jer. 25:15–29; Ezek. 23:31–34; Hab. 2:16; cf. 1QpHab XI, 14; Rev. 14:10; 16:19; suffering of God's people: Isa. 51:17–23; Lam. 4:21. Note Jer. 49:12, where the innocent may have to drink a cup of suffering that they do not deserve.

that Jacob and John would have understood the connotation of vicarious suffering and death; the use of the metaphor in verse 39 is a non-vicarious application. Jesus will use the metaphor of the cup again in Gethsemane (14:36; cf. John 18:11).

The second metaphor is generally translated as *baptism*, which is misleading since the English term 'baptism' connotes Christian water baptism which the Greek terms *baptisma/baptizō* do not automatically denote. The Greek word *baptizō* means, in a physical sense, 'to plunge, dip, immerse' and, in a metaphorical sense, 'to be overpowered, overwhelmed, immersed' (see on 1:4). Since Jesus speaks of his death, not of immersion in water, the words *baptisma* and *baptizō* have a metaphorical meaning. In 1:8b the verb refers metaphorically to immersion into the Holy Spirit who 'overwhelms' those who belong to the Coming One. The background of the metaphor of 'immersion' is texts which describe suffering as an overwhelming deluge (Pss 42:7; 69:1–2; Isa. 43:2; 1QH XI [III], 28–36). Jesus asks Jacob/James and John whether they are willing to be 'overwhelmed' with the 'immersion' into suffering with which he is about to be 'overwhelmed' (cf. Wuest, *New Testament*: 'with the immersion with which I am to be overwhelmed, are you able to be immersed?').

39–40. Jacob/James and John respond that they can indeed be overwhelmed by suffering and death. They lack understanding, but they are courageously loyal. Jesus affirms that they will indeed *drink the cup* he is about to drink and be 'overwhelmed with the immersion' he is about to be overpowered with, suggesting that they will experience suffering and martyrdom. Luke relates the martyrdom of Jacob/James in AD 41 when Agrippa I was king of Judea (Acts 12:2). His brother John seems to have outlived all the other apostles, ministering into the last decade of the first century (Irenaeus, *Haer.* 3.1.1–2; 3.3.4); if he is the John who wrote the book of Revelation, he also suffered at the hands of Roman authorities who sentenced him to live in exile on the island of Patmos (Rev. 1:9–11).

Jesus does not deny that there are places of honour at his right and left, but he asserts that it *is not for me to grant* these places. He will not reserve them for Jacob and John. Their future suffering does not guarantee them places of honour. God will grant these *to those for whom they have been prepared*. While several passages speak of God 'preparing a place' for his people (Exod. 23:20 LXX; Matt. 25:34; 1 Cor. 2:9;

Heb. 11:16), it remains an open question who the favoured people are to whom Jesus refers. The context suggests that this will *not* be Jacob and John but those who are last (9:35), the lowliest (10:15), the 'servants' and 'slaves' (10:43–44). Mark's readers who knew about Jesus' crucifixion would probably have seen the irony that the two people who would soon be at Jesus' right and left were two bandits, not sitting on gilded thrones but hanging on wooden crosses (15:27).

41. When the other ten disciples heard of the scheme of Jacob and James, *they became indignant*. This is not righteous indignation (as Jesus' response to the disciples in 10:14), but, as the implicit rebuke in verses 42–44 shows, annoyance that the sons of Zebedee were trying to get ahead of them in the competition for the more prominent positions in the kingdom of God.

42. The following instruction is private. The expression *Jesus called them together* is used several times as an introduction to important and usually surprising pronouncements (3:23; 7:14; 8:34; 12:43). Jesus takes up the notion of royal privilege from the brothers' request and discusses the more general and universal subject of political rule. The phrase *you know* characterizes the following statement as a matter of common knowledge, which makes the 'not so with you' in verse 43 all the more conspicuous. The expression *those who are supposed to rule* (RSV) is probably an idiomatic way of saying 'those recognized as rulers' (NASB, NRSV; BDAG, p. 255); if the verb has the meaning 'appear' ('those who appear to rule'), Jesus would be saying that the power of political rulers is delegated power that comes from God, the only sovereign Lord (cf. John 19:11; Rom. 13:1–2). The word *ethnē* ('Gentiles') could refer to 'nations', including the Jewish nation: what Jesus says applies also in Galilee and Perea, where Antipas ruled, and in Judea where the chief priests and the members of the Sanhedrin had real power in religious matters. Since the word more often denotes non-Jewish people, Jesus probably refers to Gentile leaders, in particular Roman governors and the emperor, where absolute power could be observed. Neither the word *rule* nor the term *high officials* (lit. 'the great ones') describes a particular political office. Jesus describes people who are in a position to impose authority on others. The two verbs translated in NRSV as *lord it over* (*katakyrieuō*, 'to bring into subjection, subdue; to have mastery, lord it [over], rule') and *[be] tyrants over* (*katexousiazō*, 'exercise authority', perhaps 'tyrannize over someone'; BDAG, p. 531) have a pejorative meaning. Jesus speaks of oppressive domination, the unfair and cruel exercise of power, often for personal gain.

43–44. The phrase *it is not so among you* (NRSV) sums up the fact that the kingdom of God (1:15; 9:47; 10:14) is a recognizably alternative society, and that Jesus' family of his followers (3:34) operates with completely different values. Here the conventional expectations and structures are reversed. Jesus repeats earlier teaching: the word *great* recalls the question 'who is the greatest' in 9:34; the word *first* recalls Jesus' assertion that 'anyone who wants to be first must be the very last' (9:35) and that 'many who are first will be last, and the last first' (10:31). *Slave* (Gr. *doulos*) is a new term, denoting people who are owned by a master, indicating more strongly than the word *servant* (Gr. *diakonos*) the idea of subordination and service subject to directives by others. The synonymous parallelism of Jesus' statement which moves from *servant* to *slave* is a climactic declaration of the values of the kingdom of God, where greatness means service and prominence means working for the benefit of fellow believers. The phase *slave of all* indicates that this reversal of values does away with conventional hierarchies in which people of lower rank recognize those of higher rank. In the kingdom of God, leaders give precedence to everyone.

45. Jesus explains the reversal of values in the kingdom of God in which leaders, paradoxically, do not rule but serve, by pointing to his own mission: for *even the Son of Man did not come to be served, but to serve*. The expression Son of Man describes in Daniel 7:13–14 a human being who comes with the clouds of heaven before God, who gives him authority, glory and sovereign power, and who is worshipped by all nations and receives an eternal kingdom. No one would expect the exalted Son of Man to come as a lowly servant.

And certainly no one would expect that he would *give his life as a ransom for many*. The word 'ransom' (*lytron*) is used for sums of money paid to secure the freedom of prisoners of war, slaves and debtors; in the LXX also for the expiation of a life that was forfeited (Exod. 21:30; 30:12), specifically the price paid to redeem the firstborn son whose life was legally forfeited (Num. 8:17). The verb *lytroō* ('redeem') is used in the LXX for God's 'redemption' of his people, from slavery in Egypt (Exod. 6:6; Deut. 7:8) or from spiritual oppression (Ps. 59:2

LXX). Texts such as Exodus 21:30, 30:12, Numbers 35:31 which indicate the connection between 'ransom' and 'atonement' – a ransom is paid for a life that is forfeited – are important for Jesus' statement in verse 45. The preposition *for* in the phrase *for many* connotes substitution ('in place of, instead of') and benefit ('on behalf of, for'). The ransom payment is *his life* (Gr. *psychē*), referring to the life of the Son of Man. Jesus gives his own life as 'payment' so that *many* who are unable to pay themselves can be released and thus saved. The term *many* has been interpreted as a Semitic expression meaning 'all' (J. Jeremias, *TDNT*, VI, pp. 536–545: the sum total of humanity), but the context in verses 43–44 suggests those who follow Jesus (Marcus, p. 750). The implied contrast, however, is not between 'many' and 'all' but between the one life of the Son of Man and the many who are saved.

The background to Jesus' ransom saying is Isaiah 52:13 – 53:12.[18] Even though Isaiah uses *pais* for 'servant', not *diakonos* or *doulos*, the terms are conceptually similar and the verb *diakonoō* occurs in Isaiah 53:11 LXX. The language of service in verses 43–45 corresponds to the role of the Suffering Servant, who gives his life as a sacrifice for others. The phrase *to give his life* is close to Isaiah 53:12 where the Servant 'poured out his life unto death'. The word *ransom* corresponds conceptually to the Lord making the life of the Servant 'an offering for sin' for others (Isa. 53:10; cf. 53:4–6, 12). And the notion of the 'one' suffering for 'the many' occurs in Isaiah 53:11–12. The Son of Man of Daniel 7 will some day 'be served', but he must himself first serve, even suffer and die, as the Servant of the Lord. As the Servant of Isaiah 53 suffers and dies for the redemption of the people, God offering the life of the Servant as a substitute for their guilt, so the purpose of Jesus' mission is to die vicariously for the sins of the people.[19] Jesus' exorcisms and healings, his teaching, his confrontation with Israel's leaders, his challenging the norms of society – all these are subordinate to, and need to be

---

18. Evans, pp. 120–124; France, p. 420; Pesch, II, pp. 163–164; Strauss, p. 460; Hengel, *Atonement*, pp. 49–65; Watts, *New Exodus*, pp. 349–365.
19. For a defence of the authenticity of the ransom saying cf. Evans, pp. 124–125; Gundry, pp. 587–593; Stein, pp. 288–289; Strauss, pp. 461–462.

seen in the light of, Jesus' death by which people far and wide are redeemed from their sins.

Theology
God's sovereign purpose requires that Jesus suffers, dies and is raised after three days, and, specifically, that Jesus dies as a ransom for the people, who cannot pay the price for their redemption. Paul will later emphasize that Jesus on the cross was the place of God's atoning presence (*hilastērion*) accomplishing the redemption of sinners, the forgiveness of sins that God in his grace grants to Gentiles and Jews who believe that the crucified and risen Jesus is Israel's Messiah and Saviour of the world (Rom. 3:24–25). The writer to the Hebrew Christians emphasizes that Jesus' death represents his entry into the Holy of Holies to achieve eternal redemption once and for all (Heb. 7:27; 9:11–12). John and Peter also emphasize the atonement of Jesus' death of redemption (1 John 2:2; 1 Peter 1:18–19; Rev. 5:9–11; 7:14). The disciples must recognize that even though they cannot replicate Jesus' death, which redeems people from their sins, the spirit of service and self-sacrifice that characterizes Jesus must also characterize the life in Jesus' family in which they will be servant-leaders. The authority that drives Christian leaders is the needs of others, just as Jesus gave his life so that people in need would benefit.

xiv. *Healing of Bartimaeus at Jericho (10:46–52)*
Context
The last healing miracle is the final episode before Jesus' entrance into Jerusalem. It forms an *inclusio* with the healing of a blind man at Bethsaida (8:22–26) at the beginning of the section in which Mark describes Jesus' revelation of his suffering (8:22 – 10:52). Bartimaeus' cry 'Jesus, Son of David' prepares the reader for the pilgrims who welcome Jesus in Jerusalem with the shout 'Blessed is the coming kingdom of our father David!' Jesus is the Davidic Messiah who is about to enter Jerusalem and fulfil the mission of the Messiah, culminating in his death that redeems sinners.

Comment
46. Jesus, with his disciples and other followers and pilgrims, coming from Perea, crossed the Jordan river and arrived in *Jericho*

(mod. Tell es-Sultan), about 5.5 miles (9 km) north of the Dead Sea, at the foot of the ascent to Jerusalem. Conquered by Joshua (Josh. 6), Jericho was one of the main centres of the tribe of Benjamin where the prophet Elisha later healed the bitter waters of a spring (2 Kgs 2:19–22). In the Hellenistic period, the Hasmonean rulers built a palace complex, rebuilt by King Herod after the destructive earthquake of 31 BC. Besides the palace site, several settlements spread around the oasis, a fact that may explain the discrepancy between Mark's account in which the healing took place when Jesus was leaving Jericho (v. 46) and Luke's account according to which the miracle happened as Jesus approached Jericho (Luke 18:35: the verb 'approached' may mean 'in the vicinity of'; Luke relates in 19:1–10 how Zacchaeus became a follower of Jesus).

Besides Jesus and his disciples, *a large crowd* witnessed the healing of a *blind man*, whose name is given as *Bartimaeus (Bartimaios)*, translated by Mark as *son of Timaeus*. Evidently people called the man not by his personal name but by his patronymic. Timaeus is a Greek name that is attested only here as a name used by Jews, either in Palestine or in the Diaspora. Bartimaeus is the only healed person whose name Mark provides, which suggests that he was a member of the early Christian movement, as indicated by verse 52. Blind and lame people often gained their living through *begging*, and the main road through Jericho was a strategic location, particularly when pilgrims travelled through town.

47–48. Bartimaeus seems to have enquired about who was causing a commotion on the road, and people told him that *it was Jesus of Nazareth*. Since Jesus (Gr. *Iēsous*; Hebr. *Yĕhôšûʻa*; see on 1:1) was a very popular Jewish name, he was identified by his place of origin (cf. 1:24; on Nazareth see on 1:9). Evidently Bartimaeus has heard of Jesus' power to heal, because he begins to shout into the crowd, *Jesus, Son of David, have mercy on me!* The title *Son of David*, which was a functional equivalent among Jews for 'Messiah' (Gr. *Christos*) and highlighted royal and nationalistic connotations,[20] is surprising:

---

20. Cf. 2 Sam. 7:11–16; Ps. 89; Isa. 9:1–7; 16:5; Jer. 23:5–6; Ezek. 34:23–24; 37:24–25; Mic. 5:1–5; then *Pss Sol.* 17:21–22. Neither David nor the Son of David was linked with healing. Solomon, David's son, was linked with

nothing in Mark's account has prepared his readers for this designation. The disciples seem to have observed Jesus' ban regarding the Messiah's designation after Peter's declaration in 8:29. Mark does not relate that others suggested that Jesus was pursuing a messianic mission. It is possible that Bartimaeus had unusual spiritual insight such that he concluded from his knowledge of Israel's prophets that the coming Davidic king would help the needy and the poor and open the eyes of the blind (Isa. 11:4; 35:5–6) and that therefore Jesus was the Messiah. Alternatively, he might have used the most dramatic address he could think of in order to get Jesus' attention. In the next episode, when Jesus enters Jerusalem, messianic language is used quite openly (11:10), without Jesus objecting. Here, too, Jesus does not comment, still less rebuke the blind man. The secrecy Jesus imposed on the disciples (8:30) is slowly being lifted, preparing the way for his entry into Jerusalem and his open declaration in the trial that he is the Messiah (14:62).

People of Jericho and presumably pilgrims who were on the road *rebuked* the blind man and *told him to be quiet*, perhaps so that they could continue to listen to Jesus' teaching, or because they regarded him as too insignificant to bother the famous teacher, or because they were embarrassed on account of the messianic title. But the man continues to shout, addressing Jesus as *Son of David* and pleading for mercy. The persistence of the man, reflected in the fact that Mark reports his shouts twice in direct speech, is a sign of his faith in Jesus (2:5; 5:23, 34; 7:27–29, 32; 8:22; 9:24).

49–50. When Jesus *stopped*, so did the disciples as well as the larger group of followers and the pilgrims, all turning their attention towards the blind beggar. The verb *call*, which occurs three times in verse 49, means 'to summon' or call over (it does not render the episode a call narrative; in 1:16–20, 3:13–14 the verbs *kaleō* and *proskaleō* are used, not *phōneō*). The people's change of behaviour reflects Jesus' authority: having been dismissive, they now call out

---

exorcism (cf. the apocryphal text *Testament of Solomon*, written by a Christian author), which, however, is not the same as healing a blind man. There is no example in Judaism before or during the first century that speaks of the Son of David as a healer.

to the blind man and speak to him. They tell him, *Cheer up!* ('take heart; it's all right'; the verb is often a rallying cry to people in distress; cf. 6:50), *On your feet!* ('get up, stand up'), *He's calling you.* The man responds immediately and with vigour, so as not to lose any time. His *cloak* (*himation*; cf. 5:15) was the outer garment that he was wearing or that was lying in front of him to collect the alms. The rare verb *he jumped to his feet* is another graphic term describing the man's desire to *come to Jesus* without any delay.

51–52. Jesus does not immediately heal the man. His question *What do you want me to do for you?* is not a cautious enquiry into the wishes of the man, as in verse 36. Jesus engages him in a dialogue which allows Bartimaeus to express his faith, which he does by addressing Jesus as *rabbouni* and by asking him to heal him. The word *rabbouni* ('my master' or 'my teacher'; the latter is offered as a translation in John 20:16) represents the early Palestinian Aramaic term *rabbān*, which is a heightened form of *rab*, 'great one', a frequent designation for teachers of the law. Bartimaeus states his request to be healed with bold simplicity: *I want to regain my sight* (NASB; *anablepsō*). Bartimaeus expects an instantaneous and complete recovery of his eyesight, acknowledging Jesus' power to heal.

Jesus replies by granting Bartimaeus' request. The command *Go* dismisses the man and confirms that the healing has happened (cf. 1:44; 2:11; 5:19, 34; 7:29). Jesus heals in this case without touch (1:31, 41; 5:27, 41; 7:33–34; 8:22–26) and without a word of authority (2:11; 3:5). It is Bartimaeus' *faith* that has healed him: his conviction that Jesus has divine authority to restore his eyesight (cf. 5:34), which indeed is *immediately* restored. The verb *sōzō* (cf. 5:23) means here *healed* in the sense of 'cured of the illness'. In the context of verse 26 and the reaction of the man who begins to follow Jesus, it also means *saved* in the spiritual sense of eternal life, treasure in heaven and entering the kingdom of God (vv. 17, 23, 24, 25). Bartimaeus responds to the healing with the same immediacy with which his eyesight was restored: he *followed Jesus along the road*. The word 'follow' (*akoloutheō*; 1:18; 2:14) speaks of discipleship, as does the word 'road' or 'way' (*hodos*) later in the early church (Acts 9:2; 18:25, 26; 19:9, 23; 22:4; 24:14, 22). Bartimaeus follows Jesus on the way to Jerusalem, which is the 'way' of the cross (cf. 8:34).

Theology
Jesus' power to heal blind Bartimaeus demonstrates his unique, divine authority, underlined by the fact that the healing happens as the result of Jesus' word alone and that it takes place immediately. While the people of Jericho refer to Jesus as 'Jesus of Nazareth', the shouts of the man, twice given in direct speech, call Jesus the 'Son of David', identifying him as the royal Messiah promised in the Scriptures and longed for in Jewish tradition. Mark's readers know that Jesus is the Son of God (1:1; 3:11; 9:7) and Son of Man who will suffer, die and be raised (8:31; 9:9, 12, 31; 10:33). He is the royal Messiah – not as a king who is about to establish an earthly, political kingdom but as the Servant who has come to serve and give his life as a ransom for many (10:45). The encounter in Jericho also teaches what discipleship involves: calling out to Jesus for mercy, understanding that Jesus is the messianic Son of David, acknowledging Jesus' authority, coming to Jesus in faith, experiencing healing and transformation of one's life, and following Jesus on the way of the cross.

B. The confrontation in Jerusalem (11:1 – 13:37)

The second of three sections of the description of Jesus' messianic suffering (8:22 – 15:47) follows Jesus' repeated prediction of his suffering, death and resurrection during the last phase of his ministry which took place mostly outside Galilee (8:22 – 10:52), during which Peter declared that Jesus is the Messiah and Bartimaeus shouted that Jesus is the Son of David (8:29; 10:47–48). The second section describes the confrontation between Jesus and the Jewish authorities in Jerusalem (11:1 – 13:37), beginning with Jesus' approach to Jerusalem and his prophetic action in the temple, continuing with debates about political and theological questions, and culminating in private teaching for the disciples about the coming destruction of the temple and the signs of the end times. The third section (14:1 – 15:47) will report Jesus' arrest, his Jewish trial and his Roman trial, culminating in his execution by crucifixion.

i. Jesus in the temple (11:1 – 12:44)
Jesus' confrontation with the religious leaders in Jerusalem takes place explicitly in the temple (11:1 – 12:44) and implicitly on the

Mount of Olives (13:1–37). The confrontation in the temple can be divided into ten sections: Jesus' approach to Jerusalem which takes him directly into the temple (11:1–11), his prophetic action in the temple (11:12–25), the dispute with the Jewish leaders about his authority (11:27–33), the parable of the tenants (12:1–12), the discussions about paying taxes to the emperor (12:13–17), about the resurrection (12:18–27), about the commandments (12:28–34) and about David's Son (12:35–37), ending with a warning about the law experts (12:38–40) and a commendation of the widow (12:41–44).

In Mark's Gospel, this is Jesus' first visit to Jerusalem. John dates Jesus' arrival in Bethany six days before Passover and the triumphal entry into Jerusalem takes place the next day (John 12:1, 12–15). As Jesus was crucified on a Friday (14 Nisan, 8 April, AD 30), the anointing in Bethany took place on *Saturday evening* (9 Nisan, 2 April); the triumphal approach to Jerusalem and the return to Bethany on *Monday* (10 Nisan, 3 April) (Mark 11:1–11); the cursing of the fig-tree, the prophetic action in the temple and the return to Bethany on *Tuesday* (11:12–19); the discovery of the withered fig-free, the controversies with the religious leaders and the discourse on the destruction of the temple on *Wednesday* (11:20 – 12:34) and *Thursday* (12:35 – 13:37); the Last Supper, the arrest in Gethsemane, the Jewish trial, the Roman trial, the crucifixion and the burial on *Thursday evening/night* and *Friday*, 14 Nisan (14:1 – 15:47).

a. Triumphal approach to Jerusalem (11:1–11)
Context
Jesus travelled from Jericho (10:46–52) to Bethany on the Mount of Olives and from there into Jerusalem, entering the temple courts (11:11). Mark spends considerable time describing the acquisition of a colt (11:1–6) before he reports on Jesus' approach to Jerusalem, accompanied by outbursts of praise from Galilean pilgrims. Their nationalistic acclamation alludes to Zechariah's prophecy of the king who comes into Jerusalem riding on a donkey. Jesus' action is deliberate, and he does not check the acclamation of the pilgrims with its messianic connotations, just as he had not checked Bartimaeus' shouts addressing him as the Son of David (10:47–48).

Comment

1. Approaching *Jerusalem* (see 1:5), Jesus and the disciples, and presumably other followers such as Bartimaeus (10:52), arrive on the slopes of the *Mount of Olives*, about 2.2 miles (3.5 km) from the Temple Mount. The distance from Jericho is around 17 miles (28 km), the road ascending 4,000 feet (1,250 m). The Mount of Olives is part of a ridge of hills east of Jerusalem across the Kidron Valley, rising some 330 feet (100 m) above the city. In Zechariah 14:4 the Mount of Olives is mentioned as the place where God will stand on the day of judgment (cf. Ezek. 11:23; 43:2). Mark mentions *Bethphage* (*Bēthphagē*), whose location is uncertain, and *Bethany* (*Bēthania*; mod. Al-Eizariya, which preserves the name of Lazarus), located on the eastern slopes of the Mount of Olives. Bethany was the village in which Lazarus and his sisters Mary and Martha lived (John 11:1; cf. Luke 10:38). Jesus and the disciples seem to have stayed in their house when he visited Jerusalem, leaving Bethany for Jerusalem each morning (11:1, 11–12; 14:3). Since the Roman road from Jericho to the Mount of Olives passed north of Bethany, it appears that Bethphage was located on the ridge between the Roman road and Bethany, which means that Jesus and the disciples passed by Bethphage before reaching Bethany. Since Jesus stayed in Bethany (11:1, 12; 14:3), the village (v. 2) to which he *sent two of his disciples* would most likely be Bethphage.

2–3. Jesus dispatched two disciples to the nearby village to requisition a colt. It has been claimed that the word translated *colt* (Gr. *pōlos*; cf. vv. 4–5, 7; Luke 19:30, 33, 35) refers to a horse if the word stands alone and if the context does not indicate that it is a foal (BDAG, p. 900); however, this has been shown to be incorrect: *pōlos* can denote a donkey in such circumstances (Collins, p. 517; Marcus, p. 772). Horses, which were rare and expensive and mostly used by the military and the elite, were too valuable to be kept in the street. Matthew 21:2, 7 refers to a donkey (*onos*) and a colt (*pōlos*), John 12:14 to a young donkey (*onarion*), and both quote Zechariah 9:9 with a Greek text that has *onos* and *pōlos*; the LXX text has *pōlos neos* ('new' or unused donkey), which translates the Hebrew word *'ayir* (male donkey). The comment that *no one has ever ridden* the *pōlos* reflects Zechariah 9:9 and echoes the value of unused animals for religious purposes (sacrifices: Num. 19:2; Deut. 21:3; pulling the ark of the covenant: 1 Sam. 6:7). A rabbinic tradition says that the horse of the king cannot be used by anyone except the king (*m. Sanh.* 2:5).

Jesus' instructions seem to reflect the system of official transport called *angaria* ('pressed transportation') in which a government official could temporarily requisition an item or person (Evans, p. 142). The precise directions given to the two unnamed disciples suggest either Jesus' supernatural knowledge or a plan that had been arranged in advance. The instructions in verse 3 suggest the latter. The owner of the colt is not named, perhaps because loaning a colt for an event that turned out to be a declaration of Jesus' messianic role could be regarded as being complicit in a politically subversive act and thus in Jesus' arrangements the owner need not be directly implicated.[21] The one who *will send it back here immediately* (NRSV) is the owner of the colt who will agree to loan it to Jesus.

4–7. The scenario plays out exactly as Jesus has outlined. Mark reports that the colt was *outside in the street*, that it was *tied at a doorway* and that *people standing there* asked what the disciples were doing. Since the donkey had never been ridden, it was not prepared for use and had no saddle cloths. The two disciples who bring the donkey to Jesus *threw their cloaks over it*, presumably their outer garments (*ta himatia*; cf. 5:15). Up to this point, the Gospels never report Jesus riding on an animal. The special attention given to Jesus procuring a donkey and riding on the donkey into Jerusalem is significant since this was a deliberate departure not only from his usual practice of travelling by foot but also from the tradition that Passover pilgrims who were physically able to walk should enter Jerusalem on foot (cf. *m. Hag.* 1:1, which exempts 'one who cannot go up [to Jerusalem] on his feet' from the requirement to travel to Jerusalem for the main festivals). Jesus deliberately enacts the prophecy of Zechariah 9:9–10 which speaks of a king who comes into Jerusalem riding on a donkey.

8. Jesus' approach to Jerusalem has been compared to the coronation of Solomon, who entered the city on David's mule, accompanied by music and great rejoicing (1 Kgs 1:32–48); the

---

21. Cf. Bauckham, *Eyewitnesses*, p. 188; Mark signals that 'from this point on Jesus enters a danger zone in which he must employ caution and subterfuge'.

anointing of Jehu as king on the orders of Elisha, with people spreading their garments under his feet (2 Kgs 9:1–13); the entrance of the Davidic redeemer in Zechariah 9:9–10, explicitly quoted in the parallels Matthew 21:5; John 12:15; the entrance of Simon Maccabaeus into Jerusalem, accompanied by music, praise and the waving of palm branches (1 Macc. 13:50–51). People spread their *cloaks* as well as *branches* (*stibada*, reeds, leaves, rushes; John 12:13 mentions *baia tōn phoinikōn*, palm branches), cut in the nearby fields, providing a festive covering of the road in honour of Jesus.

9–10. Jesus, riding on the donkey, and the disciples are surrounded by people *who went ahead* and by people *who followed* – a description of the festival pilgrims walking into Jerusalem five days before Passover. It seems that it was customary for pilgrims to arrive several days in advance of Passover, if only to secure a place to stay in view of the 300,000 pilgrims who travelled (Sanders, *Figure*, pp. 249–251). It is presumably the people who have accompanied Jesus from Jericho who now celebrate his approach to Jerusalem. The first two lines of their shouts come from Psalm 118:25–26, the last of the Hallel psalms (Pss 113 – 118) that were recited at the major festivals in Jerusalem. The balanced structure of the shouts may suggest antiphonal chanting of the psalm.

Hosanna (Hebr. *hôšî'â nā'*, 'Save, now!' or 'Save, please!'; the LXX does not transliterate the Hebrew expression but translates *sōson dē*, 'Save, now!'), in Psalm 118, is a plea to God to save his people. Since Jesus' Hebrew/Aramaic name (*Yĕhôšû'a*, *Yešû'a*) is derived from the verb *yāša'* ('save'), some have suggested that the shout 'Hosanna' was directed to Jesus (Gundry, p. 630). Since the shout is directed to God in Psalm 118, it is more likely that the people who accompany Jesus on the road into Jerusalem cry out to God to fulfil his promises and deliver Israel – through Jesus (Evans, p. 145). Alternatively, 'Hosanna' may have been used as a shout of praise, 'with the element of entreaty largely forgotten' (France, p. 434).

Blessed is he who comes in the name of the Lord! is a benediction with which the people in the temple courts welcomed newly arriving pilgrims. The formulation in the singular made the blessing appropriate for greeting Jesus, the individual rider on the donkey at the centre of the procession. It is possible, on the basis of Zechariah 9:9–10, which the entire scene echoes, that those shouting these words perceived Jesus' approach to Jerusalem as the arrival of the expected royal saviour through whom God would bring deliverance.

Blessed is the coming kingdom of our father David!, which is not drawn from Psalm 118, continues the celebratory blessing of Jesus, who is coming into Jerusalem, but now it is the kingdom of David whose arrival is greeted. The expression 'kingdom of David' has political and nationalistic connotations which, if they express hopes for a new political reality, assume a messianic meaning. The crowd recalled Bartimaeus calling Jesus 'Son of David', and now it greets Jesus as the saviour riding into the city of David, expecting him to restore 'the kingdom of David', Israel's national sovereignty. David is not mentioned in Zechariah 9:9–10, but the king riding on a donkey into Jerusalem as 'your king' is modelled on David. The Palestinian version of the fourteenth of the Eighteen Benedictions which were used in the synagogues addresses God as 'Lord, God of David, who builds Jerusalem', and prays for 'the kingship of the house of David, your righteous Messiah'. In his trial before the Jewish court, Jesus will affirm that he is indeed the Messiah, the Son of Man sitting at the right hand of God (14:62), and in the Roman trial, when Pilate asks him whether he is the king of the Jews, Jesus answers in the affirmative, although with some reluctance (15:2), and Pilate orders his execution as 'king of the Jews' (15:26; cf. 15:9, 12, 18). The final *Hosanna in the highest heaven!* could be a plea that God will save him, the Messiah, as he is about to enter Jerusalem. However, the deliverance that the crowd celebrates and anticipates is the salvation of Israel as a whole.

11. Jesus *entered Jerusalem*, either through one of the gates in the Kidron Valley south of the Temple Mount or through a gate in the eastern wall of the Temple Mount. The word *temple* (*hieron*; NIV 'temple courts') refers to the entire complex of buildings, courts and colonnaded stoas on the Temple Mount, including the Outer Court accessible to all people, also Gentiles, as well as the courts of the Inner Enclosure accessible only to Jews (see on v. 15 for details). Mark reports what happened: Jesus *looked around at everything*, noticing the crowds of worshippers, the people who were buying and selling sacrificial animals and the money-changers. Jesus is not portrayed as a 'wide-eyed provincial'; he looks around 'as the Son of God to see what needs doing' (Gundry, p. 679, with reference to 3:5, 34;

5:32; 10:23). Because *it was already late*, Jesus and the Twelve returned to Bethany, where they stayed overnight. Mark's account is not as anticlimactic as many commentators think: the fact that the celebration of the pilgrims who accompany Jesus is not replicated by at least a greeting from the chief priests once Jesus arrives in the temple sets up the following controversies and their determination to eliminate Jesus.

Theology
Mark presents Jesus' entry into Jerusalem as a messianic action: the pilgrims acclaim Jesus as the messianic deliverer as he enters Jerusalem, the city of David. The silence imposed earlier on those whom Jesus healed (1:44; 5:43; 7:36; 8:26), on demons (1:25, 34; 3:11–12) and on his disciples (8:30; 9:9) is ending. As Jesus deliberately enters Jerusalem riding on a donkey, fulfilling Zechariah 9:9 with its promise of the coming of Israel's King, he signals that his mission is indeed a messianic mission that fulfils God's promises given to Israel. Mark's readers know that the blessings of the kingdom of God proclaimed by Jesus are different from the messianic blessings that most Jews expected – blessings dependent upon Jesus' followers denying themselves and 'taking up the cross' (8:34), and being eager to be last and servant of all (9:35) and willing to endure persecutions (10:30). Since the messianic kingdom that Jesus brings is not the sovereign, prospering kingdom that the Jewish people expected, it is not surprising that Jesus is not welcomed when he enters Jerusalem and visits the temple.

b. Prophetic action in the temple (11:12–25)
Context
The first event that happens once Jesus returns to Jerusalem takes place in the temple (11:15–19), the heart of Israel's religious life and a central symbol of its national identity. Jesus' action of clearing the temple's Outer Court of merchants is not an attempt to 'cleanse' the temple from a corrupt management and re-establish its original purity. Rather, it is a prophetic action that symbolizes the abrogation of the temple cult, the destruction of the temple and the inauguration of the messianic era in which the Gentiles come to faith in Israel's God and worship him on Zion. The symbolic nature of the

event is suggested, first, by the event itself, which must have been a small-scale action of limited duration since it did not provoke a reaction either from the captain of the temple who was the official in charge of all temple affairs or from the Roman cohort stationed in the Antonia Fortress overlooking the temple courts; and, second, from Jesus' teaching on this occasion, related by Mark in direct speech. The action in the temple is sandwiched between the cursing of a fig-tree in Bethany and the discovery that the fig-tree is dead (11:12–14, 20–25), an event that underlines Jesus' authority. John places a similar event in the temple at the beginning of Jesus' ministry (John 2:14–22). Many interpreters suggest that John moved the episode forward for theological reasons. It is by no means impossible that Jesus acted in a similar manner twice: Jesus did not attempt to reform the temple cult by use of force but engaged in a prophetic symbolic action that did not provoke any reaction from the Jewish temple police or the Roman authorities.[22]

Comment

12–13. At the beginning of Jesus' second day in Jerusalem, when he and the Twelve were setting out from Bethany (cf. vv. 1, 11), Jesus *was hungry*. Mark does not explain this curious notice. Probably Jesus was up before sunrise in order to pray (1:35) and did not eat before setting out on the hour-long walk into Jerusalem.

The common cultivated *fig-tree* (Gr. *sykē*, *Ficus carica*) is the first fruit tree mentioned in the Bible (Gen. 3:7). The deciduous tree which grows to a height of 19 feet (6 m) sheds its leaves in November and sprouts new leaves in late March. It grows two types of figs: first, the early figs (Hebr. *paggîm*) develop from green knobs on the old branches in March before the tree sprouts new leaves, ripening in late spring after the leaves have appeared and (marginally) edible in late March or early April; second, the later mature summer figs (Hebr. *tĕ'ēnîm*) which grow on the new branches and which are harvested in August through October. Since it was near Passover (the first week of April in AD 30), the fact that Jesus saw *a fig-tree in leaf* suggested that he could expect to find early figs; note that the

---

22. Strauss, pp. 489–490; Blomberg, *Jesus and the Gospels*, pp. 263, 368–369.

leaves are mentioned twice. This is implied in the formulation *he went to see whether perhaps he would find anything on it* (NRSV; NIV's 'if it had any fruit' supplies 'fruit' for the Greek word *ti* which, however, means 'anything, something'). If we take the expression 'anything' (*ti*) in the preceding clause seriously, it becomes obvious that Mark's comment *because it was not the season for figs* 'takes two steps backward to explain why Jesus went to find "something" instead of "figs" or "fruit"' (Gundry, p. 636). Jesus expected to find edible fig buds, not ripe figs.

14. As the tree 'spoke' to Jesus by providing only inedible leaves, Jesus 'answered' (*apokritheis*, generally translated *he said*) with the pronouncement: *May no one* 'any longer' (generally omitted in English versions) *ever eat fruit from you again*. The double negation 'no one . . . any longer' and the phrase 'ever again' (or 'to eternity') strengthens the 'curse', as Peter characterizes Jesus' pronouncement (v. 21). Mark's comment that *his disciples heard him say it* suggests that the cursing of the fig-tree entails private teaching for the Twelve.

Most interpreters see a symbolical meaning in the cursing of the fig-tree, pointing to Old Testament passages in which a fig-tree represents Israel (Jer. 8:13; Isa. 28:3–4; Hos. 9:10, 16–17; Mic. 7:1), 'judged by its Messiah because, despite its appearance and religious activity (symbolized by the leaves), Israel has failed to produce the appropriate fruit' (Stein, p. 514). While some see Jesus' curse as a verdict on the failure of Israel as a whole (France, p. 441), others argue that only the Jewish leaders are in view since at this point in the story the people in general are still responsive to Jesus while the ruling priests and scribes oppose him (Evans, p. 154; Marcus, p. 790). Not all interpreters are convinced. Some question the capability of Mark's readers to understand the assumed Old Testament background (see 7:2–4 for an explicit explanation of ceremonial washing of hands for non-Jewish readers), and the relevance of the Old Testament passages (in which the fig-tree does not represent the temple but Israel and which do not provide close parallels; e.g. in Jer. 8:13 the lack of figs on the tree is the result of judgment, in Mark supposedly the reason for judgment; in Isa. 28:3–4 eating a first-ripe fig symbolizes destruction, while in Mark there are no first figs or buds to be eaten). Mark does not say that Jesus went to the tree specifically to find fruit: he writes that Jesus approached the tree to find 'something'. Thus, some scholars conclude that a symbolic interpretation in terms of judgment on Israel is not intended.[23] A symbolic interpretation is further rendered unlikely on account of the fact that Jesus' comments on the withered fig-tree in verses 22–25 teach the disciples regarding the power of faith and prayer: judgment on Israel is neither mentioned nor implied. If indeed the fig-tree without figs symbolizes Israel without spiritual fruit, the disciples would have perceived such a symbolic meaning only later – not after Jesus' explanation in verses 22–25 and not necessarily after 13:1–2 where Jesus' prophecy of the temple's destruction is not linked with a failure on the part of Israel.

15–16. Jesus enters Jerusalem on the day after the triumphal procession and the brief visit to the temple (11:1–11). The phrase *he entered the temple* (RSV, NRSV, NASB) means, in view of the following description, that he entered the Outer Court. The Greek term *hieron* refers to a temple including temple courts and surrounding colonnaded halls. The modern label 'Court of the Gentiles' is misleading: this court was not specifically constructed as a place for Gentiles to worship, nor was it reserved for Gentiles – most of the people one would encounter in the Outer Court were Jews, but the area was accessible to Gentiles as well since it was not sacred, in contrast to the area inside the Inner Enclosure which Gentiles could not access.

Herod I had rebuilt the Second Temple, built at the site of Solomon's First Temple under the leadership of Zerubbabel after the return from the exile. Herod extended the temple area in the north and in the south beyond the sacred area of the Second Temple, building immense retaining walls and bridges that gave access from the city to the Temple Mount.[24] The eastern and the western walls of the Temple Mount were 1,542 and 1,591 feet (470 and 485 m) long, and the northern and southern walls were 1,033 and 918 feet (315 and 280 m) long. The platform, enclosed on all four sides by colonnaded halls, including the triple-colonnaded Royal Portico (see on 13:1), was exceptionally large, capable of accommodating over 70,000 people. The Court within the Outer Court, an area of 820 by

---

23. Dschulnigg, pp. 300–301; Gundry, pp. 672–673; Pesch, II, p. 197.
24. Cf. Netzer, *Architecture*, pp. 137–178.

820 feet (250 by 250 m), was surrounded by a stone balustrade 5 feet (1.5 m) high; this seems to have been the area of the original temple precinct before Herod's extension; it was regarded as sacred and thus forbidden for Gentiles. Signs warned Gentiles of being punished by death if they violated the restriction: 'No foreigner is to enter within the balustrade and forecourt around the sacred precinct. Whoever is caught will himself be responsible for (his) consequent death' (*CIIP* I/1 2). Inside the Court within the Outer Court was the Inner Enclosure, between 10 and 13 feet (3–4 m) higher than the Outer Court and surrounded by a wall about 65 feet (20 m) high. The Inner Enclosure contained the temple proper (*naos*), its entrance facing east, with the vestibule, the Inner Sanctuary and the Holy of Holies; the Court of Priests with the altar and the slaughtering place in front of the temple; and the Court of Israel accessible to Jewish males. The Court of Women, which served as the main access to the temple for the men, was attached to the eastern side of the Inner Enclosure.

The actions described in verses 15–17 most probably took place in the Outer Court south of the Inner Enclosure between the openings of the staircase emerging from the Huldah gates near the Royal Portico, which is where commercial activities took place. Some suggest that animals were sold at the northern end of the Outer Court near the only gate of the temple complex in the north wall that communicated directly with the open countryside (Sheep Gate or Tadi Gate; John 5:2; *m. Mid.* 1:3).[25] Since Jesus' actions took place in the Outer Court which was not sacred, they were not designed to restore the holiness of the temple. The location of the incident is important for understanding Jesus' teaching implied in the quotation of Isaiah 56:7. Mark describes what Jesus did in the Outer Court in terms of four specific actions.

First, Jesus *began driving out*[26] merchants who were *selling* and customers who were *buying* presumably blemish-free animals for

---

25. Cf. Murphy-O'Connor, *Keys to Jerusalem*, p. 61.
26. The fact that the same verb is used for expelling demons (1:34, 39; 3:15, 22–23) is irrelevant: the same verb was used for the 'throwing out' of all kinds of objects or persons. Mark does not portray the sellers and buyers as 'Satan's tools' who profane the temple (thus Marcus, p. 782).

sacrifices (John 2:14 mentions cattle and sheep), which would have been convenient for pilgrims from outside Jerusalem, as well as other items needed for worship (wine, flour, oil). Some assume that items unrelated to worship were sold and bought as well, items that pilgrims would have found significant, perhaps food or crafts. While this may be correct, the primary purpose of the commercial activities would have been the temple cult with its atoning sacrifices which required the provision of blemish-free animals.

Second, Jesus *overturned the tables of the money-changers* and *the benches of those selling doves*. Money-changing seems to have been the main source of income for the temple, generated with a 4–8% surcharge, from which not only were priests paid but also public works initiated. The system of the money-changers ensured the validity of the temple tax which had to be paid by every Jewish male twenty years or older in the Tyrian half-shekel (the silver drachma of Tyre) rather than with coins of varying quality minted in a multitude of cities, regions and provinces of the Roman world. Also, the money-changers provided pilgrims with the opportunity to acquire the currency needed to buy sacrificial animals and thus enabled them to participate in the temple cult. Pigeons or doves were the sacrifices of the poor (Lev. 12:6–8; 14:22).

Third, Jesus *would not allow anyone to carry merchandise* through the Outer Court. The word *skeuos* ('merchandise') denotes any 'thing' or 'object' used for any purpose, and also a container of any kind. Perhaps Jesus prevented people from carrying an ordinary, profane container or implement from outside the Temple Mount through the Outer Court.

Jesus did *not* attempt a *takeover* of the temple, which would have required the removal of the high priest, who was appointed by the Roman governor, an action that would in turn have required either collaboration with the Roman authorities in an attempt at temple reform or a hostile confrontation with the latter, which would have been quickly crushed. Jesus' action did not trigger an intervention of the Roman troops stationed in the Antonia Fortress on the north-west corner of the Temple Mount, as was the case on the occasion of Paul's arrest when the crowd was about to lynch him in the Outer Court (Acts 21:27–33). Jesus did *not* attempt a *reform* of the temple, which could be effectively achieved only by winning over the aristocratic priestly families for a reform programme. He did not want to 'reclaim' the Outer Court as a place where Gentiles should have been worshipping – the Outer Court, which was not sacred (and was thus accessible for pagans) in contrast to the Inner Enclosure, had not been built as a 'place of prayer', and the four colonnaded halls surrounding it provided sufficient space for Gentiles who came to Jerusalem to pray to Israel's God (note that the early church in Jerusalem, numbering in the hundreds and thousands, was able to congregate in Solomon's Colonnade on the eastern side of the Outer Court; Acts 3:11; 5:12). The fact that Jesus drives out not only sellers but also buyers makes it unlikely that his action was primarily directed against the exploitation and corruption of the chief priests, who controlled the activities on the Temple Mount, and their agents. Some Jews complained about corruption connected with the temple (Evans, pp. 167–168),[27] but it is difficult to know what the situation was in AD 30. Mark does not report a negative reaction of the chief priests. It is difficult to explain why Jesus is accused by the Jewish authorities of having plotted the destruction of the temple (14:58; cf. 15:29) if the purpose of his action was a symbolic protest against corruption. Jesus' actions against the money-changers and the sellers of sacrificial animals were symbolic, evident in the location in the Outer Court and in the small scale of the event. The sabotage of the services of the money-changers and the sellers of doves symbolizes the interruption of the sacrificial cult (Ådna, *Stellung*, p. 385). In combination with Jesus' teaching regarding the destruction of the temple (v. 17), this symbolic disruption is tantamount to an announcement of the abrogation of the temple cult and of the atoning function of the sacrifices, replaced by Jesus' atoning death (10:45).

17. The fourth action in the Outer Court was teaching. What Jesus *taught them* is summarized with quotations from Isaiah 56:7 and Jeremiah 7:11. The marked quotation (*Is it not written?*) from Isaiah

---

27. 1QpHab VIII, 7–13; IX, 2–16; 4QpNah Frag. 3–4 1:10; CD A VI, 14–17; 4QMMT 82–83; and *Test. Levi* 14:1 – 15:1; *Test. Judah* 23:1–3; *Test. Moses* 7:1–10; *Pss Sol.* 1:8; 8:9–13; Josephus, *Ant.* 20.179–181, 205–207.

56:7 summarizes Jesus' teaching on this occasion about the Old Testament promises concerning the conversion of Gentile nations: *My house will be called a house of prayer for all nations*. The author of 1 Maccabees 7:37 relates that when the Syrian general Nicanor came to Jerusalem and threatened the temple, the priests wept and quoted Isaiah 56:7, emphasizing that God had chosen the temple as 'a house of prayer' – not 'for all nations' but, eliminating the universalistic phrase and restricting the statement to Israel, 'for your people'. Jesus retains and, standing in the one court accessible to Gentiles, emphasizes the phrase *for all nations*. Isaiah's prophecy is part of a series of promises that in the coming ('messianic') age foreigners and other outsiders such as eunuchs will have full rights in the worship in the temple. Jesus retains the future tense of the verb (*will be called*) as he teaches in the Outer Court accessible to Gentiles. The passive tense of the verb describes an action of God. The point of Jesus' symbolic demonstration in the non-sacred Outer Court is not so much a critique of commercial activities that may have prevented Gentiles from worshipping as an announcement that the time has come for the fulfilment of the Old Testament prophecies about the last days in which the nations will stream to the Lord's temple on Mount Zion (Isa. 2:2–5; 49:1–6; 66:18–24; Mic. 4:1–5; Zech. 8:20–23). In other words, Jesus symbolically declares the entire Outer Court to be the place of worship for the nations and thus announces the beginning of the Gentile mission. When Jesus directs the Twelve to reach the nations with the good news of the kingdom of God and with his teaching (implied in Mark 13:10; see explicitly Matt. 28:19–20; Luke 24:47; Acts 1:8), he reverses the Jewish expectations of Gentiles coming from the periphery to Jerusalem and initiates a centrifugal mission which corresponds to his own travels through the villages and towns of Galilee. Since King Solomon, on the occasion of the dedication of the temple, had spoken of worshipping in the temple (1 Kgs 8:41–43), and since it was kings such as Joash and Josiah who had restored the temple (2 Kgs 12:2–17; 23:1–37), and as some Jewish texts expected the Davidic Messiah to 'purge Jerusalem' so that all nations would 'come from the ends of the earth' to see God's glory (*Pss Sol.* 17:30–31), Jesus' action was not only prophetic – it had royal–messianic overtones (Evans, pp. 178–179).

The introductory *Is it not written?* would have allowed Jesus' listeners to understand the next statement as an Old Testament quotation (from Jer. 7:11) as well: *you have made it 'a den of robbers'*. The word *lēstēs* ('robber') refers to someone who robs others by violence, a robber, highwayman, bandit; the word is later used by Josephus for the Jewish revolutionaries in the revolt against Rome. The word *spēlaion* ('den') means 'hideout' or 'grotto, cavern'. Jesus does not seem to use this expression to describe contemporary problems regarding the sellers or the temple management (who may be charging exorbitant prices but do not use force). Jesus uses the memorable phrase of Jeremiah 7:11, which occurs only here in the Old Testament, in Jeremiah's great 'Temple Sermon' delivered 'at the gate of the LORD's house' (Jer. 7:2), because it recalls the prophet's denunciation of the false confidence of the people of Judah who think that they can commit the most serious sins since the temple guarantees their safety (Jer. 7:2–10). Jeremiah's oracle was directed at the acceptance of sinful behaviour that cannot be compensated for by verbally acknowledging that the temple is 'the temple of the LORD' that keeps them safe. Since a 'hideout of bandits' is not reformed but destroyed, and since Yahweh, who speaks through Jeremiah, does not anticipate that the people will repent, the prophet's Temple Sermon is not an offer of repentance and restoration but a prophecy of judgment and destruction (Jer. 7:12–15). Jesus taught publicly, albeit in an allusive manner, that the confidence of the priests and the people that the temple would guarantee national and salvific security was misplaced and that the temple would be destroyed, an inference that corresponds to the fact that he predicted, privately and explicitly, the destruction of the temple (13:1–2).

This interpretation corresponds to the fact that Jesus will be accused within a few days of having threatened to destroy the temple, both in the trial (14:58) and during the crucifixion (15:29; cf. Acts 6:14). This means that when Jesus, by quoting Isaiah 56:7, announces the beginning of the time when the Gentiles will worship the God of Israel, he does not anticipate a reformation of the Second Temple. Rather, he anticipates the worship in a temple 'not made with hands', as witnesses state in the Jewish trial (14:58) – a spiritual temple in which Gentile believers worship as well. Since worshipping Israel's God without atonement for sins is impossible,

Jesus' twin prophetic announcements of the Jerusalem temple's destruction and of Gentile worship of Yahweh point to the crucial significance of Jesus' atoning death as predicted and described in 10:45.

18. The *chief priests* had been mentioned by Mark in the context of Jesus' predictions of his suffering, rejection and death (8:31; 10:33). Now they are introduced as Jesus' opponents who want to kill him. The *teachers of the law* (cf. 1:22) who have listened to Jesus' teaching are probably the same scribes who had travelled from Jerusalem to Galilee (3:22; 7:1) and who had become convinced that Jesus' activities could be explained only by the presence of the power of Satan, and that he and his followers rejected the tradition of the elders in matters related to ritual purity. Members of the priestly aristocracy and their law experts have been listening to Jesus' teaching about the temple in the Outer Court. Their reaction required an interpretation of Jesus' actions (vv. 15–16) and teaching (v. 17) in terms of a threat to the temple and to their authority. They realized that Jesus was threatening the status quo, with regard to the status both of the temple and of the Torah, and therefore they *began looking for a way to kill him*, as had been the case earlier in Galilee when some Pharisees and the Herodians plotted Jesus' death (3:6).

In contrast to the ruling priests and the law experts, *the whole crowd was amazed at his teaching*. The crowd would have included inhabitants of Jerusalem and Jewish pilgrims who were in town for the imminent festival of Passover, and perhaps some Gentiles who might have been visiting the city. Jesus' announcement of judgment was directed not at the Jewish people as a nation but at the temple and its leaders. Mark's comment reminds his readers of the amazement of the people in the synagogue in Capernaum at the beginning of Jesus' ministry, who were astounded because of Jesus' authority in word and action (1:22), as was the case here. The ruling priests and their law experts *feared* Jesus on account of his influence with the people which made an arrest impossible for the time being.

19–21. The Greek phrase usually translated *when evening came* might better be rendered 'late in the day': sunset in Jerusalem in early April is around 7 pm, and since the walk to Bethany (cf. vv. 1, 11–12) takes about an hour, Jesus and the Twelve would probably have left the Temple Mount around 5 pm.

When they left Bethany to return to Jerusalem (presumably) on Wednesday morning, they passed the fig-tree that Jesus had cursed the previous morning (vv. 12–14). The disciples noticed that the fig-tree had *withered from the roots*: it was completely dead; there was no life in any of its branches. Healthy and even sick fig-trees do not completely wither within twenty-four hours: a miracle had happened. This is the only miracle of judgment reported for Jesus in the Gospels.[28] For Mark, the term *cursed* is not an embarrassment: it was Jesus' powerful utterance that brought harm to the tree.

22–23. Jesus responds to Peter's comment on the withered fig-tree by drawing an explicit lesson for the disciples, focused on the theme *have faith in God*. In the context of the destruction of the tree on account of Jesus' command, *have faith in God* means to have faith in God's power. For the Jewish disciples, having faith in God was a matter of course. Jesus reiterates for the disciples the truth that they have already accepted, namely that the power which is manifest in his miracles is the power of God. Since verses 12–14 do not refer to Jesus' judgment of the temple there is no reason to regard Jesus' lesson on faith as a 'secondary' application of the fig-tree episode.

Much more startling is the next statement, introduced as an authoritative Amen-saying (cf. 3:28; 8:12; 9:1, 41; 10:15, 29): that trusting in the power of God makes it possible for seemingly impossible things to happen. Moving a *mountain* is proverbial for what is impossible for human beings (cf. 1 Cor. 13:2). Throwing a mountain into the sea is 'as useless and destructive an act as causing the death of a fig tree' (France, p. 448). Since the fig-tree is on the Mount of Olives, this would be the mountain in Jesus' saying. According to Zechariah 14:4, the Mount of Olives will split in two on the day of the coming of the Lord, 'with half of the mountain moving north and half moving south' – it is not removed into the sea, which means there is no reason to think that Jesus speaks here of the last days or the end of the world. Since the Temple Mount was visible from the Mount of Olives, it could be in view here as well; however, since Jesus and the Twelve were walking away from Jerusalem towards

---

28. Cf. Exod. 7:14 – 12:30; 1 Kgs 13:1–5; 2 Kgs 1:4, 10–14; 2:23–24; 5:27; cf. 2 Chr. 26:16–21; in the NT cf. Acts 5:1–11; 13:6–12.

Bethany, they would be facing the Mount of Olives, not the Temple Mount (Isa. 2:2/Mic. 4:1, Zech. 4:7 do not speak of the removal of Mount Zion into the sea, which means that if indeed the Temple Mount were in view, these eschatological passages are not relevant here either). Jesus does not comment on the fate of a particular mountain in the future. He asserts that what is humanly impossible becomes possible for those who believe in the power of God. Jesus states the condition for achieving the impossible both negatively: *if anyone . . . does not doubt in their heart*; and positively: *if anyone . . . believes that what they say will happen*. Mark has already made it abundantly clear that faith is the prerequisite for miracles.[1]

24–25. In a new saying, highlighted with the introductory *I tell you*, Jesus applies the statement about the power of faith that believes in the power of God specifically to prayer (*therefore*). The phrase *whatever you ask for in prayer* describes all requests in prayer, not only the spectacular commands of 'moving mountains'. Since prayer is addressed to God, it goes without saying that *whatever you ask* will be granted by God if and when it is in agreement with the will of God. Jesus' statement is not a blank cheque with believers invited to 'write' anything they wish on the empty line, as Jesus' prayer in Gethsemane (14:36) shows. The sequence of the verbs in the phrase 'all things for which you *pray* and *ask*' (NASB; the translation 'ask for in prayer' in ESV, NIV, NRSV obscures this) is probably significant: 'the requests that are answered are not just the first thing that pops into the supplicant's head but petitions that emerge from a state of meditation' (Marcus, p. 795).

Conditions for effective prayer are faith (v. 23) and forgiveness. To *stand praying* was a traditional posture for prayer (1 Sam. 1:26; 1 Kgs 8:22; Matt. 6:5; Luke 18:11, 13). To *forgive* others is a condition for receiving forgiveness from God, and both are conditions for answered prayer (cf. Matt. 6:14–15; 18:15–35; Luke 17:3–6). The word *anyone* suggests that the sins of the petitioner need to be forgiven, as the petitioner needs to forgive those who have sinned against him or her. Faith in God (v. 22) and God doing the seemingly impossible (v. 23) through the believers' prayers (v. 24) is possible if

---

1. 1:40; 2:5; 5:34, 36; 6:5–6; 7:29, 32; 9:23–24; 10:52.

and when the believers perceive that they are children of the *Father in heaven* – and that is possible only if and when their sins have been forgiven, which in turn means that they will forgive as they have been forgiven.[2]

Theology
The fig-tree incident emphasizes the power of Jesus and his word: his word can heal but it can also destroy, which also means, as the fig-tree miracle frames Jesus' action in the temple, that Jesus has the authority to announce judgment over the temple. The fig-tree incident also highlights the responsibility to bear fruit. Jesus' explanation of the withered fig-tree links the lesson that he wanted to teach not with Israel and her leaders but with the necessity of having faith in God. The proverbial saying about believing that impossible things can happen (v. 23) is tied to faith in God (v. 22), which means that Jesus does not describe the power of a faith that can move mountains but, rather, the power of God who alone can do the impossible. The phrase 'whatever you ask for in prayer' is qualified in John 14:13 in the phrase 'whatever you ask in my name' and in John 15:7 in the sentence 'If you remain in me and my words remain in you, ask whatever you wish, and it will be done for you'.

Interpreters who object to understanding Jesus' actions and teaching in the temple as symbolically announcing the destruction of the temple point to the fact that 'for many Jews any thought of the future kingdom involved reform and, in many cases, rebuilding of the temple' and that the kingdom 'could not be present if it did not involve the temple'.[3] This and similar arguments fail to convince. Jesus' view of the kingdom of God and his understanding of his messiahship challenge conventional Jewish notions of God's kingdom and of the role of the Messiah. The kingdom of God that Jesus proclaims is crucially connected with his mission as Messiah which is climactically focused on his death 'as a ransom for many'

---

2. V. 26 'But if you do not forgive, neither will your Father who is in heaven forgive your sins' (KJV, NASB in brackets) is a secondary accommodation to Matt. 6:15 in (mostly later) manuscripts.
3. Snodgrass, in Bock and Webb, *Key Events*, p. 473.

(10:45) and on his resurrection (8:31; 9:31; 10:33–34), events that have foundational significance for the life and ministry of Jesus' followers, who must deny themselves, take up their cross and refuse to be ashamed of Jesus, the rejected Messiah, in the time until his return in glory (8:34–38). Jesus' proclamation of the kingdom of God and his description of his messianic mission as the Servant whose death is a ransom for many leave no room for conventional Jewish expectations of a reform of the temple. When Jesus asserts that he is the stone the 'builders' rejected, the 'cornerstone' of a new building (12:10), he speaks of a new temple of God. As Jesus regarded his death as atoning for sins (10:45), and as he instituted a new 'Passover' focused on his (imminent) death rather than on sacrifices of lambs, 'he likely envisioned the ultimate replacement of the temple and its sacrificial system'.[4] His symbolic actions in the Outer Court of the temple, combined with this prophetic teaching which explained his actions, imply his claim to messianic authority.

c. Jesus' authority and the authorities (11:27–33)
Context
This is the first of six controversies between Jesus and the temple authorities (11:27 – 12:37). After Jesus has demonstrated his authority in the Outer Court of the temple and prophesied both the era of messianic fulfilment when the nations would worship Israel's God and God's judgment of the temple, the Jerusalem authorities question Jesus about the source of his authority, evidently in an effort to further their plans to have him executed (11:18). Queries by other groups that oppose Jesus are reported in 12:13, 18, 28. In these controversies Jesus holds his own, not only in the discussion about the source of his authority but also in the subsequent dialogues in which he develops the messianic claims implied in the manner of his approach to Jerusalem and in his actions in the temple.

Comment
27–28. The third entry into Jerusalem (cf. vv. 11, 15), on the Wednesday before Passover, took place on the same morning the

---

4. Strauss, p. 497; cf. Ådna, *Stellung*, p. 429.

disciples had discovered the withered fig-tree (v. 20). The fact that Jesus was *walking in the temple courts (hieron)* confirms that his actions on the previous day were symbolic, prophetic actions on a small, temporary scale. Jesus returns to the Temple Mount to teach, which he did daily (14:49) until his arrest on Thursday evening. As Jesus was teaching, perhaps in Solomon's Colonnade (1,542 ft [470 m] long, 49 ft [15 m] wide) on the east side of the Outer Court, the commercial activities on the south side would have resumed. The *chief priests* represent the ruling priestly families of Jerusalem. They included at the time the families of Phiabi, Camith, Boethus, Cantheras and, most prominently at the time, Ananus (Annas): Annas, high priest in AD 6–15, was involved in the interrogation of Jesus (John 18:12–13); he was followed in the high priesthood by his son-in-law Caiaphas (AD 18–36/37), who presided at Jesus' trial before the Sanhedrin, followed by Annas' sons Jonathan, Theophilus and later Matthias.[5] The chief priests were mentioned in Jesus' predictions of his death in 8:31, 10:33, and described in 11:18 as plotting his death, together with the *teachers of the law* (cf. 1:22), the law experts, probably the same scribes who had travelled from Jerusalem to Galilee (3:22; 7:1) and who had concluded that Jesus' authority had a satanic origin. The *elders* are the non-priestly aristocrats sitting in Jerusalem's highest court; they were also mentioned in Jesus' prediction of his death (8:31). The approach of the official Jewish leaders is hostile. They ask two questions.

They want to know *by what authority* Jesus is doing *these things*, quite obviously a reference to Jesus' disruptive actions in the Outer Court the day before (vv. 15–16), and possibly also a reference to the manner of his approach to Jerusalem on a donkey and accepting the pilgrims' shouts of blessing for 'he who comes in the name of the Lord' (vv. 7–10). If *poios* ('by what') is read as an equivalent of the interrogative *tis*, they ask 'by whose power or by whose name' (BDAG, p. 844) he is claiming authority over what happens in the temple. In the context of the latter meaning, the second question – *And who gave you authority to do this?* – draws out the implication of the first question: since *we* did not give you the authority to disrupt

---

5. Cf. VanderKam, *High Priests*, pp. 420–453.

the commercial activities in the Outer Court, who did? Jesus has no official authorization that gives him a voice in the affairs of the temple. Jesus' actions in the temple the day before, following his triumphant approach to Jerusalem, implied a claim to authority that the official leaders cannot afford to ignore.

29–30. Jesus' answer seems evasive. He asks a counterquestion, promising an answer if they will first answer whether *John's baptism* was *from heaven*, done by God's authority, or *of human origin*, an activity devised by John without divine sanction. Asking a counterquestion was a recognized debate move (cf. 10:3). That the Jewish officials do not challenge it suggests that they did not regard Jesus' question as an evasive change of subject, tacitly acknowledging that an answer to the question regarding John's authority would suggest an answer to their question about Jesus' authority, 'and their refusal to answer his question would signal their unwillingness to accept his implied answer to theirs' (France, p. 454). Jesus' question about John's baptism is a question about his entire ministry, which was focused on repentance, on the forgiveness of sins experienced in connection with immersion in the Jordan river (outside Jerusalem!) in preparation for the coming of the Lord, and on the announcement of the One more powerful who would initiate the fulfilment of the promise of the Holy Spirit (1:2–4, 7–8). If the Jewish leaders accept John's authority as sanctioned by God, they have to accept the authority of Jesus, who also claims authority to forgive sins (2:1–12) and who has done what John did not do: drive out demons, heal the sick and raise the dead.

31–33. Jesus' question provokes a discussion, not because they are unsure about their own opinion but because they are unsure about the consequences if they speak their mind. Mark's editorial comment *They feared the people, for everyone held that John really was a prophet* indicates that the Jewish leaders in Jerusalem did not share the opinion of the people who had walked to the Jordan river in great numbers to hear John preach and who had responded to his message by being baptized (1:5). Popular opinion held that John's baptism, which 'summarized' his entire ministry, was *from heaven*, that is, from God, which is why they believed in John and accepted his call to repentance and forgiveness of sins. If the Jerusalem officials answered in an attempt to demonstrate agreement with popular opinion, Jesus would ask them why they did not accept John's ministry as authentically prophetic, sanctioned by God's authority. It was evidently public knowledge that the officials in Jerusalem did not in fact regard John as a prophet. Since they were afraid to say that John's authority was *of human origin*, they replied, *We don't know*. The Jewish leaders prefer to lose face in claiming not to have an opinion about John the Baptist rather than risk public criticism.

Since they refuse to admit that they do not believe John was God's prophet, Jesus refuses to answer their question *by what authority* he has been disrupting commercial activity in the Outer Court. Jesus' answer effectively compares his own authority with the authority of John and thus invites two conclusions (France, p. 453). Just as John was authorized by God for his ministry of preaching repentance and forgiveness of sins in preparation for the coming of the Lord, so Jesus is authorized by God to act the way he acts and to teach what he teaches. Also, as John announced the coming of a messianic figure who would be more powerful, and as Jesus' ministry is clearly more powerful than John's, there is the strong possibility that he, Jesus, is the 'one more powerful' who fulfils God's promises for the last days. If the officials are not willing honestly to say what they think about John because they fear the people, there is no point in Jesus explaining the source of his own authority.

Theology
The Jewish authorities never accepted John as a prophet, and neither do they accept Jesus as prophet, let alone as Messiah with the authority to reform the temple. If his exorcisms, his argument why he cannot possibly be driving out demons by Satan's power (3:23–29) and his dramatic healings cannot convince the Jerusalem authorities that his authority is divine authority, nothing will convince them. Jesus refuses to answer their question about the source of his authority because he has long answered it in his words and actions. Jesus' authority has been implicit throughout Mark's Gospel: he forgives sins, commands the wind and the waves, and raises the dead – like God, who has affirmed Jesus' divine dignity and thus his authority twice (1:11; 9:7). In the following parable Jesus portrays himself as the Son sent by the Father, with the Father's authority, which leads to opposition, rejection and death. It is the rejection of

his authority by the Jewish leaders that leads to his death three days later (Strauss, p. 507) – which is not a tragedy but the divine purpose of his mission as the authoritative Son of Man who has come to give his life as a ransom for many (10:45).

d. *The parable of the tenants (12:1–12)*
Context

The parable of the tenants, also called the parable of the vineyard, is the second of six controversy episodes (11:27 – 12:37) subsequent to Jesus' prophetic action in the temple's Outer Court (11:12–25). The challenge to Jesus' authority by the Jewish officials in the previous incident (11:27–33) is symbolically portrayed in the figure of the vineyard tenants, who challenge the authority of the owner of the vineyard (God), of the owner's messengers (prophets) and of the owner's son (Jesus). The owner's judgment of the tenants symbolizes God's judgment of the temple and of Israel's leaders alluded to in Jesus' teaching that explained his disruption of commercial activities in the temple. The Jewish leaders who had decided after Jesus' demonstration in the temple that Jesus must be executed (11:18) conclude that the time has come to plan Jesus' arrest (12:12).

Comment

1. Having forced the Jerusalem authorities to admit, tacitly, that their question about the source of his authority was a ploy to trap him rather than an honest query (11:27–33), Jesus proceeds to comment on the authority that they have as Israel's leaders, an authority that they are going to lose. Jesus' pronouncement is given in a parable which the officials understand all too well (v. 12). The choice of a vineyard as the setting for the parable signals that Jesus is telling the story of God's dealings with Israel: the vine or vineyard is a well-known symbol for Israel (Judah) regarding the nation's relationship to Yahweh (Ps. 80:8–18; Isa. 1:8; 5:1–7; 27:2–6; Jer. 2:21; 12:10; Ezek. 19:10–14; Hos. 10:1). The wording of the parable echoes the introduction of Isaiah's 'Song of the Vineyard' (Isa. 5:1–2).

The *man* who *planted a vineyard* symbolizes God, who chose Israel as his people. Building a *wall* (*phragmos* denotes a partition such as a fence, hedge or wall) around the vineyard signals ownership, cultivation and protection; it corresponds to the clearing of stones in Isaiah 5:1, with the stones used to build the wall. A *hypolēnion* ('pit') is 'a trough placed beneath the wine-press to hold the wine'; a *pyrgos* ('watchtower') is 'a tall structure used as a lookout' (BDAG, pp. 1039, 899). There were several varieties of grapes and several types of wine. Most of the grapes were used for making wine, although they were also used to make syrup and vinegar, and raisins for raisin cakes (cf. *OEBA*, I, p. 16). While the vineyard clearly symbolizes Israel, the details of the wall, the winepress and the tower probably do not have allegorical significance.[6]

Compared with Isaiah 5, a new element is the leasing of the vineyard to tenant farmers and the departure of the owner. After the initial capital investment and the preparation of the vineyard, the owner *rented the vineyard to some farmers and moved to another place*. In first-century Palestine much of the land was owned by absentee owners and farmed by tenant farmers who leased individual plots. Many of the aristocratic priestly and non-priestly families owned estates farmed by local tenants. Since vineyards were often farmed commercially and since the high-handed behaviour of the tenants in the parable implies a high level of presumed authority, the *farmers* of the parable should be viewed as 'wealthy commercial farmers' (Evans, p. 233). The chief priests, scribes and elders (11:27) recognize that Jesus tells the parable 'against them' (v. 12): they understand that the tenant farmers in the parable represent the leaders of the people to whom God entrusted his 'vineyard'.

2. The language of the sentence is typical of lease agreements: *sent* (*apostellō*) means here 'send for payment'; *time* (*kairos*; NIV *harvest time*) means 'in due course', after the time prescribed in the lease agreement which here, in the case of a newly planted vineyard, would probably be three to five years; *collect* (*lambanō*) means collecting the agreed-upon payment. The owner sends a *doulos* (*slave*, NRSV). The slave is the owner's agent who has been given the task of collecting the payment which was stipulated in the lease agreement. The owner expects the payment of *some of the fruit of the vineyard*, which

---

6. Cf. Strauss, p. 514. Differently Brooke, *Scrolls*, pp. 78–79, 235–260, who points to 4Q500, which interprets the vineyard as Jerusalem, the tower as the temple and the winepress as the altar of burnt offering.

is an agreed-upon portion of the harvest paid in kind (perhaps grapes at the time of the harvest, later wine, transported in amphorae, and syrup, vinegar and raisins if such were produced), or money from the sale of grapes and wine.

3–5. The tenants' response to the owner's demand for payment is incomprehensibly irrational, a fact that challenges Jesus' listeners (and Mark's readers) to see the symbolic meaning of the story. The response to the owner's slave who has arrived to collect the payment is described with three verbs: they *seized him*, they *beat him* and they *sent him away empty-handed*. They not only refuse to pay the owner, but they mistreat his agent. There is no indication that the tenant farmers are destitute and cannot pay or that the demands of the landlord were excessive. In a papyrus letter preserved in the Zenon archive, Zenon's agents who wanted to recover money or seize securities were assaulted and driven out of the village (P. Cair. Zen. I 59018, dated 4 April 258 BC). In Jesus' parable, the tenants' behaviour suggests that they repudiate the legal claims of the owner with respect to the vineyard and its crops. They challenge the owner to enforce his demands, if he can. The owner sends *another slave* (NRSV) to collect the payment. He is treated even worse than the first slave: they *struck this man on the head*, presumably inflicting a wound, and *treated him shamefully*, perhaps spitting at him and ripping off his clothes. The owner is undeterred and sends *still another* slave, whom they *killed*. As the mistreatment of the owner's agents increases, the number of verbs used to describe the mistreatment decreases. As the owner of the vineyard is Yahweh and the vineyard represents the people of God, the emissaries of God are the prophets. In Amos 3:7 LXX the phrase 'slaves of the Lord, the prophets' makes this connection. The comment that *he sent many others* after these three agents, *some of whom they beat, others they killed*, seems incredible. As the Jewish leaders who were the intended target of the parable understood the symbolic meaning of the story, they would have recognized the Old Testament prophets behind the figure of the slaves: God sent many prophets to Israel, not just three, and many of them were rejected and mistreated, and some were killed (Jer. 26:20–23; 2 Chr. 24:20–22; and note the traditions of the martyrdoms of Isaiah, Jeremiah, Ezekiel, Micah and Amos in the Jewish text *Lives of the Prophets* written in the first century AD; cf. Matt. 5:12; 13:57; 23:34,

37; 1 Thess. 2:15; Heb. 11:36–38). The most recent prophet to be killed was John the Baptist (6:14–29). The inconceivable behaviour of the owner underlines God's seemingly endless patience with Israel, and the outrageous behaviour of the tenants emphasizes the guilt of Israel's leaders.

6. The phrase *he had one left to send* and the word *last of all* means that the sending of the son is not just one more attempt to collect, but God's last appeal to Israel. The word *one* (*hena*) emphasizes the finality of the owner's action as well as the uniqueness of the son over against the multitude of slaves. The verisimilitude of the story reaches its breaking point: in these circumstances no estate owner would risk *a son whom he loved*, an expression that could be the equivalent of 'his only son' (the LXX often renders Hebr. *yāḥîd*, 'only', with *agapētos*, 'beloved'). The owner of the vineyard expects that the tenant farmers will respect at least, and at last, his son. For Mark's readers, the expression 'beloved son' recalls the voice of heaven addressing Jesus as 'my beloved son' (1:11; 9:7). The chief priests, scribes and elders would not have known about the heavenly voice. However, since they had heard of Jesus' dramatic exorcisms and healings which went beyond anything any prophet had ever done, and since they had just challenged Jesus regarding the source of his authority (11:28), with his answer implying that his authority was 'from heaven' (11:30–31), they would have understood the single, climactic figure in the parable as pointing to Jesus, who implicitly refers to himself here as the one 'son of God'. In Jesus' trial two days later, the high priest will ask Jesus point blank: 'Are you the Messiah, the Son of the Blessed One?' (14:61).

7–8. The assumption of the tenant farmers that if they kill the heir, *the inheritance will be ours* has been explained in terms of the owner having died or being too far away to continue to insist on his ownership rights; or that being in possession of the property without paying rent for four years constituted a title of ownership, with the killing of the son giving the tenants the crucial fourth-year harvest (the legal basis of this explanation has been questioned). The tenant farmers' hope of owning the vineyard sets up their expulsion at the end of the story. They implement their plan: *they took* the owner's son, they *killed him* in the vineyard, then they *threw him out* without giving him a proper burial, demonstrating their contempt not only for the son but for his father as well. For leaving bodies without burial see Genesis 40:19; Joshua 8:29; 1 Samuel 31:10; 1 Kings 13:22–30.

9. Jesus' question *What then will the owner of the vineyard do?* challenges the chief priests, scribes and elders to provide the obvious answer which will constitute a pronouncement on their own fate. Jesus relates the decisive response of the owner with three verbs (compare the three verbs of the tenants' initial response in v. 3): the owner (*kyrios*) of the vineyard *will come*, personally; he *will destroy* (NRSV) the tenant farmers, exacting capital punishment for the killers of his slaves and his son; and he will *give the vineyard to others*. The action of the owner is not necessarily illegal vigilante justice: he would have worked through the proper authorities – the courts of Antipas in Tiberias if the story is pictured in Galilee, the court of the Roman prefect if the story is pictured in Judea. The use of the word 'destroy' (*apollymi*) rather than 'kill' (*apokteinō*; vv. 7–8) probably signals, ominously, not just the penalty for murder but 'the destruction of all that the old régime has stood for' (France, p. 461). In 3:6 and 11:18 the authorities want to 'destroy' (*apollymi*) Jesus. The Jewish leaders perceive that Jesus directs the parable at them (v. 12): Jesus announces the ruin of the Jewish leaders to whom God has entrusted his people Israel. When Jesus announces the destruction of the temple in 13:1–2, the Twelve (and Mark's readers) are prompted to connect the destruction of the tenant farmers in the parable with the destruction of the temple and Jerusalem. However, the destruction of the tenants does not mean the ruin of the vineyard (in Isa. 5:5–6 it is the vineyard that yielded only bad grapes that is destroyed). The owner will *give the vineyard to others*. In view of Jesus' actions and teaching in the temple (11:15–17), the subsequent inquest regarding Jesus' authority (11:28) and, more generally, the astounding power demonstrated in Jesus' exorcisms and miracles, the chief priests and elders would have connected the 'others' with Jesus and the Twelve.[7]

---

7. Evans, p. 237; Gundry, pp. 688–689; Strauss, p. 517. Others interpret the 'others' in terms of the early church (France, p. 462; Pesch, II, pp. 220–221; Stein, p. 537); if the latter interpretation is followed, one should note that the early church consisted of Jewish believers and Gentile believers, which makes references to 'supersessionism' (Marcus, pp. 808, 814) unwarranted.

10–11. Jesus interprets the parable with a quotation from Psalm 118:22–23 (LXX Ps. 117), one of the Hallel psalms recited at Passover; verses 25–26 of the psalm were cited by the pilgrims who celebrated Jesus when he approached Jerusalem (11:9). The introductory question *Have you not read this scripture?* (NRSV) is rhetorical and may mean, 'you have surely read, but obviously not understood' (Strauss, p. 517). Psalm 118:22–23 recalls the rejection and celebrates the deliverance of Israel, or of an individual, by God. This was understood in the Aramaic tradition as a reference to David: initially rejected by the establishment, he comes to be recognized and blessed from the house of the Lord by the priests (*Tg.* Ps. 118:19–27). It is in the light of this tradition that Jesus uses Psalm 118: he approached Jerusalem accompanied by shouts of pilgrims, who celebrated 'the coming kingdom of our father David' (11:10), following a quotation from Psalm 118 celebrating Jesus as the one 'who comes in the name of the LORD' (11:9); he was not greeted by the ruling priests when he first entered the temple (11:11); when he entered the temple for the second time, they rejected his actions and teaching and decided that he must be killed (11:18); when he came to the temple for a third time, they challenged his authority (11:27–33) – they 'do not realize who he is and what is happening' (Evans, p. 238). The *stone the builders rejected* is Jesus, whom the Jewish leaders (called 'builders' in CD IV, 19; VIII, 12, 18; cf. Acts 4:11) refuse to acknowledge as God's envoy who is building a new 'building'.

The *cornerstone* could be an elevated cornerstone (the capstone that completes an arch), the capital atop a column or the pinnacle of a building. Since *kephalē* can denote 'extremity, end, point' (BDAG, p. 542, meaning 2b) and thus not only vertical but also horizontal extension, the meaning 'cornerstone' seems more likely as the reversal referred to in verses 10–11 suggests more likely a reference to the beginning (foundation) of the new work of God rather than its completion; in the later passages 1 Corinthians 3:11, Ephesians 2:20–22, 1 Peter 2:6–8 the stone is foundational. Jesus, who has been proclaiming the coming of the kingdom of God (1:14–15), is the cornerstone of a new 'building': he determines the identity and purpose of Israel which now will include Gentiles as well, as the quotation of Isaiah 56:7 in 11:17 asserted. In verse 11 the new 'building' which will be shaped by 'the stone the builders rejected' is the work of *the Lord*, a work that *is marvellous in our eyes*. In the parable the son of the 'Lord' of the vineyard dies. The quotation of Psalm 118:22–23 pushes the meaning of the parable beyond the story to the figure of the son and its symbolic reference: the rejected son whom the tenant farmers kill is the messianic 'stone' of Psalm 118 that is also rejected but is subsequently vindicated and given supremacy by the work of God that amazes everybody.

12. The *chief priests, the teachers of the law and the elders* (cf. 11:18, 27) understood that the parable was spoken *against them*: they know that the tenant farmers who mistreat and kill the owner's agents and at the end kill the owner's son represent Jesus' view of their role as God's appointed leaders in Israel – leaders who ignore, mistreat and kill God's prophets. They want *to arrest* Jesus in preparation for a trial. The fact that they do not dare apprehend Jesus on the spot is explained by the comment that *they were afraid of the crowd*, which implies that the crowd in the Outer Court of the temple where the incident took place supported Jesus. While the parable was directed at the Jerusalem authorities, the crowd consisting of perhaps hundreds of festival pilgrims seems to have been listening. Since the authorities knew that the crowd regarded John the Baptist as a prophet authorized by God (11:32), a view which they rejected, they knew that the crowd would agree with Jesus' portrayal of Israel's leaders as killing prophets. They let Jesus go, for the time being. They will need to win the support of one of the disciples in order to carry out a secret arrest (14:1–2, 43–50).

Theology
The themes of rejection, vindication, supremacy, the initiative of God and amazement in the quotation of Psalm 118:22–23 characterize Jesus' entire ministry, celebrated by large crowds who are amazed at Jesus' teaching, exorcisms and miracles of healing, at the same time he is rejected by Pharisees, scribes, the Herodians, his own family and now by the Jerusalem authorities. In the next few days, Jesus' rejection will reach its climax in his crucifixion, while his vindication in his resurrection will be the most amazing 'work' of God. The parable confirms what Jesus had taught in his passion predictions (8:31): his death as son (12:8) will not be a tragedy but a death as a servant of God and thus a divine necessity, a 'work' of

the Lord that will be marvellous in the eyes (12:11) of Mark's Christian readers who will perceive that Jesus' vindication comes through his resurrection from the dead (Phil. 2:8–11). The 'rejected son' becomes, after his death, the supreme figure in the 'vineyard' that is restored to God's 'ownership': Jesus' death and resurrection are the foundation of the restored people of God.

The parable also speaks of a coming judgment involving the chief priests, scribes and elders – a judgment, however, that will also fall on the temple and on Jerusalem, as Jesus' quotation of Jeremiah 7:11 in the Outer Court intimated (11:17) and as his prediction in 13:1–2 (cf. 15:29) will clarify. While Jerusalem was rebuilt after the First Revolt (AD 66–70) which led to the deaths of over one million Jews (Josephus, *War* 6.9.3), the temple was never rebuilt, a fact that made the chief priests redundant. After the Second Revolt (AD 115–117) in which nearly six hundred thousand Jews perished, fifty fortified towns were destroyed and 985 villages razed to the ground (Cassius Dio 69.14), Jerusalem and Judea ceased to be the centre of the Jewish commonwealth. That Christians later interpreted the parable of the tenants in an anti-Jewish (anti-Semitic) fashion was misguided, ignoring the fact that Jesus engaged in 'prophetic criticism' in the same spirit as Israel's prophets, who criticized kings, priests and other leaders (Evans, p. 239). He did not prophesy the destruction of Judea or of the Jews: it is not the vineyard that is destroyed, but the tenant farmers. And the 'others' who are given the vincyard do not represent the Gentile church but Jesus, the vindicated Son, and the Twelve whom he has been training as those who will 'fish' people for the kingdom of God (1:17; 3:13–14; 6:7–12) and who will be the leaders of the congregation made up of the restored remnant of Israel and the Gentiles who respond to the proclamation of the good news.

e. Paying taxes to the emperor (12:13–17)
Context
The third controversy in the temple is initiated by the chief priests, scribes and elders, who send Pharisees and Herodians to entice Jesus to say something that they might be able to use in the criminal trial they are in the process of planning. The question about paying taxes raises political questions that are dangerous to answer: a pro-Roman

answer might make Jesus unpopular with pious Jews, and an anti-Roman answer would provide the authorities with a reason to denounce Jesus to the provincial authorities.

Comment

13. The *Pharisees* (cf. 2:16) and the *Herodians* (cf. 3:6) had collaborated in Galilee in opposition to Jesus, sharing ideas on 'how they might kill Jesus' (3:6). The Pharisees had been critics of Jesus in Galilee regarding matters of purity and the Sabbath (2:16, 24; 3:1–6; 7:1–5) and more generally regarding the question of his legitimacy (8:11). The Herodians might have been supporters of the Herodian dynasty in Galilee who accompanied Antipas on his Passover visit to Jerusalem (Luke 23:7). Alternatively, the Herodians mentioned here were representatives of Judean families who owed their influence and wealth to Herod and continued to support the Herodian dynasty. Since Herod and his sons and grandsons were supporters of Rome, the Herodians would have had a pro-Roman stance. They were *sent*, presumably by the chief priests, scribes and elders (12:12). These emissaries of the authorities want to *catch* Jesus off guard (*agreuō* means 'to take by hunting or fishing, catch', *LSJ*, p. 14) in what he might say in answer to their question about Roman taxation.

14–15a. Since the Pharisees and Herodians want to catch Jesus off guard, the address *Teacher* is insincere flattery. First, they claim that they *know* or acknowledge that he is *a man of integrity* (lit. 'that you are truthful, honest'), a person whose teaching is not guided by prejudice or special interests. Second, they claim to acknowledge that he is not *swayed by others* (lit. 'you don't care about no one'), that he is not beholden to the opinions of other people. Third, they claim to acknowledge that he pays *no attention to who they are* (lit. 'you don't look at the face of human beings'), that he shows no favouritism or partiality. Fourth, they claim to acknowledge that he teaches *the way of God in accordance with the truth* as God's unprejudiced spokesman. Coming from the Pharisees and Herodians who want to entice Jesus to say something that could be used against him in a trial, this is hypocritical flattery. Mark's readers who believe in Jesus would know that these four statements are true assessments of Jesus.

The question they finally ask concerns the Roman authorities, who control Judea: *Is it right to pay* (lit. 'give') *the poll-tax to Caesar or not?* The formulation translated *Is it right?* (*exestin*) asks whether it is permitted under God's law. The question concerns the possibility of a conflict between divine (Jewish) law and human (pagan) law. The term *kēnsos* ('imperial tax'; BDAG, p. 542: 'tax, poll-tax') is a Latin loanword (*census*) used in Greek, Aramaic and Hebrew. The *census* is the registration of names and assessment of property for the purpose of levying taxes. Roman taxation had been a reality in Judea since 63 BC (Josephus, *War* 1.154); it continued after 40 BC when Herod was named King of Judea, Galilee and Perea by the Senate of Rome. When Judea came under direct Roman control in AD 6, Judas of Galilee started a revolt, calling his countrymen 'cowards for consenting to pay tribute to the Romans and tolerating mortal masters, after they had God for their Lord' (Josephus, *War* 2.118; cf. *Ant.* 18.4–10). The revolt was quickly crushed. Josephus calls Judas, who was a religious teacher, the founder of the 'fourth philosophy' of the Jews, an early representative of the later insurgents called Zealots who started the First Revolt in AD 66. Whether the passions that Judas aroused in AD 6 were still felt in Judea in AD 30 seems unlikely. The outbreaks of violence that Josephus reports for the long tenure of Pontius Pilate as prefect of Judea (AD 19–36) were not triggered by questions related to taxation.

The authority to collect taxes was a responsibility retained by the imperial procurator of the province of Syria, to which Judea was attached (Eck, *Rom*, pp. 42–43). The people of Judea had to pay the *tributum soli* ('land tax', perhaps including a tax on annual produce and a flat tax on land) and the *tributum capitis* ('head tax', or poll-tax) on every male between the ages of fourteen and sixty-five. The tax might have been one denarius per person, as verse 15 suggests; or it could have been one denarius plus a percentage of movable property such as animals, wagons and slaves (Fiensy, *Origins*, p. 122). Since Jesus lived in Galilee, he did not have to pay the Roman poll-tax. The Pharisees and Herodians expected, perhaps, to entice Jesus to give an 'objective' answer to a politically charged question which was of no direct relevance to himself, an answer that would surely be pro-Jewish and anti-Roman, considering the fact that the conversation took place on the Temple Mount. Even though Jesus was not under the direct jurisdiction of the Roman governor, the latter might be persuaded to take action against an immensely popular Galilean who had revealed his opposition to Roman taxation and who would have to be regarded as a threat.

The word *Caesar* (Gr. *Kaisar*) was the cognomen of the family of Julius Caesar. Octavian, his adopted son who became the emperor Augustus, transmitted the cognomen Caesar to those whom he adopted and their direct descendants, including the emperors Tiberius and Caligula. Later emperors also called themselves 'Caesar' even though they did not descend from Julius Caesar. Eventually the name became synonymous with 'emperor' (the German *Kaiser* and the Russian *Tsar* are versions of the name). The current 'Caesar' in AD 30 was Tiberius, who called himself Tiberius Caesar Augustus (co-regent with Augustus since AD 11/12, emperor AD 14–37). The second question, *Shall we pay or shall we not pay?* (NASB), formulates the only two options that are available for Jews.

15b. Jesus perceives what the Pharisees and Herodians think (cf. 2:8). He is aware of their *hypocrisy*: he knows that their question is insincere. They do not want an answer to a question they are wrestling with: they are all paying the Roman poll-tax; otherwise they will be in serious trouble. They are *putting* Jesus *to the test* (NRSV; cf. 1:13; 8:11; 10:2); they want to entrap him by their enquiry. Jesus asks them to produce a *denarius* so that he can *look at it*. A denarius was a standard Roman silver coin; it had approximately the same value as the Greek drachma and represented a day's wages of a labourer (Matt. 20:2). It was the coin in which taxation was calculated and paid. In the Roman province of Syria, silver coins were minted in Tyre, Antioch and other subsidiary mints; the Roman imperial denarius minted at Lugdunum in Gaul (and perhaps Rome) circulated in Syria and in Judea. It should not be automatically assumed that the denarius in question was minted by Tiberius, the incumbent emperor: denarii minted by Augustus were still in circulation. Most of Augustus' coins showed the emperor's head on the obverse, sometimes with the legend 'Imp Caesar' (Imperator Caesar) or 'Augustus Divi F[ilius]' (Augustus, Divine Son'), while the reverse used to celebrate his achievements, his family and his honours (e.g. 'champion of the liberty of the Roman people'). The silver denarii minted by Tiberius in Lugdunum showed the head of Tiberius laureate on the obverse, with the legend

'Ti[berius] Caesar Divi Aug[usti] F[ilius] Augustus' (Tiberius Caesar, Son of the Divine Augustus, Augustus), and on the reverse a seated lady (perhaps Livia) as Pax (peace) and Tiberius' title 'Pontif[ex] Maxim[us]' (High Priest).[8] The depiction of a 'graven image', Augustus' title 'Divine (Son)' and Tiberius' title 'High Priest' were provocations for Jewish sensibilities, although Jews would have been used to seeing and using coins with imperial propaganda. Hippolytus relates that the Essenes would not touch a coin with an image (*Haer.* 9.26). When the Zealots rebelled against Rome in AD 66, one of their first actions was to mint new coins. At Jesus' time, offensive coins could be avoided by using the copper coins minted by Herod and by Antipas which bore no image.[9]

16. That Jesus asks for a denarius indicates that he did not have such a coin, nor presumably did the disciples. The fact that the Pharisees and Herodians did have a denarius in their possession suggests that they were not as patriotic or as religiously scrupulous as they seemed to pretend. Jesus looks at the coin to confirm what type of coin it is before he asks whose *image* (*eikōn*) and whose *inscription* (*epigraphē*) are on the coin. They identify both the image and the legend as being of *Caesar*, which was either Caesar Augustus or Tiberius Caesar Augustus.

17. The logic of Jesus' pronouncement is indicated by the command *Give back* (*apodote*). The Pharisees and Herodians had asked whether Jews should 'give' the poll-tax to Caesar (v. 14). Jesus says that since Caesar's image and inscription are on the denarius, the coin belongs to Caesar and therefore one should 'give back' what belongs to him. Since they have a denarius minted by Caesar, they implicitly acknowledge their indebtedness to Roman rule, and when they use the denarius to pay the poll-tax they explicitly acknowledge that indebtedness. What *is Caesar's*, what belongs to Caesar, is the obligation of the poll-tax. Jesus did not comment on the fact that the legend of the coin asserted the divinity of Augustus (if it was a denarius minted by Tiberius). Jesus limited his comment to the question that was asked, the payment of the poll-tax.

---

8. Seaby, *Roman Silver Coins* I, pp. 138–148.

9. Jensen, *Herod Antipas*, pp. 187–217.

The second element of Jesus' pronouncement is open-ended: *Give . . . to God what is God's*. As Jews believed that they were created in God's image (Gen. 1:26–27), the thought may be that since people bear God's image, they owe themselves to God. Jesus' response does not contain echoes of Genesis 1, and such a connection is not required to understand Jesus' answer. The Pharisees and Herodians had not asked Jesus about what to give to God, but this is what Jesus emphasizes (Dschulnigg, p. 316). Jesus challenges his listeners to establish what God's claims are. Jesus does not elaborate at what point or in which areas God's claims and the emperor's claims conflict. The formulation of the pronouncement seems to suggest that such conflicts are 'exceptional rather than normal' (France, p. 469, who rejects the suggestion that this is 'bourgeois' exegesis). The first part of Jesus' pronouncement asserts that they don't clash in the matter of paying the poll-tax.

The Pharisees and the Herodians, and presumably the disciples and the crowd in the Outer Court who were listening to the dialogue, *were amazed at him*. They had never heard a remotely similar answer to the question whether Jews should pay the poll-tax to the Roman authorities. Jesus advocated paying the taxes that the Roman authorities demanded. He did not support a tax rebellion against Rome. At the same time, Jesus did not simply make a pro-Roman statement: he challenges his questioners to take seriously the much more important truth that they need to give to God what belongs to God.

Theology

Jesus affirms that loyalty to God and loyalty to legitimate claims of Caesar are not in opposition to each other. The use of the denarius with Caesar's image and inscription to pay the required poll-tax is legitimate. More important than the political point is Jesus' theological assertion that God also has his rights – implying, in the context of his proclamation of the kingdom of God, that what God demands is repentance in view of the coming of God's kingdom and faith in him as God's envoy. Jesus' counsel of non-resistance to the Roman authorities corresponds to Jeremiah's counsel of submission to Babylon. The kingdom that Jesus proclaimed 'would indeed supersede the current world-empire, but the triumph of the kingdom of God would be inherited by the "little flock", not by the men of violence'.[10] Paul and Peter similarly argued that Christians can be loyal both to Roman authorities and to God (Rom. 13:1–7; 1 Peter 2:13–17). Jesus, Paul and Peter do not speak of conflicts between the claims of God and the claims of the Roman emperor. Such conflicts arise when the sovereignty of the one true God is questioned and when civic authorities demand absolute obedience or worship (cf. Dan. 3:16–18; Acts 4:19; 5:29). When later emperors demanded that Christians acknowledge their divinity in the imperial cult, Christians refused to give to 'Caesar' what he demanded because it did not belong to him. Divine dignity belongs only to the one true God and to Jesus, the Messiah and the only true Son of God. This is a truth that Christians have been willing to die for.

f. The question about the resurrection (12:18–27)
Context
In the fourth of six controversies in the Outer Court of the temple, the Sadducees ask Jesus a question concerning the resurrection of the dead. The question is not intended to clarify a theological matter but to discredit Jesus before the crowd and make him look a fool. The Sadducees, a term mentioned in the Gospel of Mark only here,[11] represent the chief priests (cf. 2:26; 8:31; 10:33; 11:18, 27). The first of three questions put to Jesus was raised by Pharisees and Herodians (12:13–17), the second question is raised here by the Sadducees and the third question will be raised by a teacher of the law (12:28–34).

Comment
18. The *Sadducees* represent a religious party of elite priests with significant influence in the priesthood and in the Sanhedrin. The name is probably derived from Zadok, a descendant of Aaron who flourished at the time of David (2 Sam. 8:17; 15:24; 1 Kgs 1:34; 1 Chr. 12:28) and whose descendants were regarded as the legitimate high-priestly line (Ezek. 40:46; 43:19). At least two high priests of the first century were Sadducees (Acts 5:17; Josephus,

---

10. F. F. Bruce, in Bammel and Moule, *Jesus*, p. 260.
11. Cf. Matt. 3:7; 16:1, 6, 11–12; 22:23, 34; Luke 20:27; Acts 4:1; 5:17; 23:6–8.

Ant. 20.197–199); as the high priest Ananus (Annas) II was a Sadducee in AD 62 (so Josephus), his father Ananus (Annas) I and the latter's four other sons and his son-in-law Caiaphas were probably Sadducees as well. If that is correct, the Sadducees supplied high priests for thirty-four of the sixty years of Roman rule in Judea, between AD 6 and 66.[40] They were conservative politically, pro-Roman, supporting the status quo while resisting assimilationist tendencies of some Jewish leaders. They rejected belief in the resurrection and final judgment as more recent innovations not part of the written law of Moses. Mark's comment that the Sadducees say *there is no resurrection* is confirmed by Josephus (*War* 2.165; *Ant.* 18.16). This characterization points to the 'tactical' nature of their question which is based on a belief which they themselves reject.

The idea of resurrection is found most clearly in the Prophets (Isa. 26:19; Ezek. 37:1–14) and Writings (Dan. 12:2, 13). Throughout much of the Old Testament, the dead are seen as having been gathered to their ancestors (Gen. 49:29; Judg. 2:10; 2 Kgs 22:20; 2 Chr. 34:28), experiencing a shadowy existence in the underworld ('Sheol', translated as *hadēs* in the LXX), from where they do not return (2 Sam. 12:23; Job 7:8–10), cut off from the land of the living (Ps. 88:10; Isa. 26:14); the living were prohibited from feeding (Deut. 26:14) or consulting with the dead (Lev. 20:27; Deut. 18:11; 1 Sam. 28:7; 2 Kgs 23:24; Isa. 8:19). The resurrection hope in the Prophets is associated with the conviction that Yahweh is the source of (new) creation and thus the Lord over life and death, that he is the covenant God of Israel who keeps his covenant promises, and that his kingdom will ultimately triumph and will include the final exaltation of God's covenant faithful.[41] Jesus' teaching presumes the reality of a future resurrection in 9:43–48; 10:17–25, 29–30 (Luke 14:14; 16:19–31; cf. 23:43); and Jesus predicted his own resurrection in 8:31; 9:9, 31; 10:34. The Sadducees' question assumes that Jesus shares the Pharisees' belief in the resurrection of the dead.

---

40. Meier, *Marginal Jew*, III, pp. 396–399; Marcus, p. 1121.
41. K. L. Anderson, *DJG*, p. 775; R. Martin-Achard: belief in resurrection from the dead was 'etched within the logic of OT concepts' (*ABD*, V, p. 683).

19. The Sadducees address Jesus as *Teacher* since they (ostensibly) seek an answer to a theological question connected with the Scriptures. They paraphrase the specific stipulation of the law of Moses later called 'levirate law' (Deut. 25:5–6; Latin *levir* means 'brother-in-law') which is based on the notion that the 'survival' of a man after death happens through the continuation of the family line. If a man dies and *leaves a wife but no children*, the man's brother is obligated to marry the widow (his sister-in-law) and *raise up offspring for his brother* (an exception to Lev. 18:16, which forbids having sexual relations with a brother's wife). The verb *raise up* (*exanastēsē*), which echoes Genesis 38:8 LXX, a classic example of the levirate law in practice (Onan; cf. Ruth 4:6–8), suggests that this is the only sort of 'resurrection' (*anastasis*) they anticipate.

20–23. The Sadducees present a scenario of *seven brothers*, the first of whom marries and dies without leaving any children. The second brother marries the widow and dies without leaving children, then the third, and so on, until all seven brothers have married the same woman who never had any children. When the woman dies, the question arises *At the resurrection* – if indeed there is a future resurrection – *whose wife will she be, since the seven were married to her?* The Sadducees present a *reductio ad absurdum* argument: since belief in resurrection leads to ridiculously complex marital situations in the afterlife, it must be absurd.

24. The tone of Jesus' reply is aggressive, matching the duplicitous purpose of the Sadducees' question meant to ridicule Jesus. Jesus charges the Sadducees that they are *in error* (lit. 'misled, deceived'), mistaken in judgment, in two areas. First, they *do not know the Scriptures* because, as Jesus will demonstrate in verses 26–27, even the Pentateuch teaches the continued existence of God's servants after their physical death. Second, they *do not know . . . the power of God*, who will create resurrection life which is much more than the mere continuation of earthly life, as verse 25 will show. For the aristocratic Sadducees, this twofold critique would have been insulting since they exercised authority in the Sanhedrin and since they regarded themselves as champions of the law of Moses.

25. Jesus explains his charge that the Sadducees do not know the power of God with a statement about resurrection life. *When the dead rise* asserts the bodily resurrection of the dead. The phrase *they* *will neither marry* refers to the husband's actions in acquiring a wife; the phrase *be given in marriage* refers to a father giving his daughter in marriage. Resurrection is different from earthly life: the latter is characterized by the social institution of marriage; the former is not. This is followed by the statement *they will be like the angels in heaven.* Jesus' argument does not require the implication that angels are genderless beings, but merely that angels do not need to reproduce, thus obviating the need to marry. Since earthly life is temporary, procreation is essential for further life, a fact that highlights the importance of marriage for the continuation of life. Heavenly life in the presence of God is eternal, not temporary, and thus procreation and marriage are no longer necessary. Jesus does not say that believers 'become' angels when they die. He asserts that they become 'like' angels, having an exalted existence and eternal life.

Jesus' argument would be irrelevant if the Sadducees did not believe in the existence of angels. Luke's comment to that effect in Acts 23:8–10 does not need to be interpreted in this sense: angels and spirits are frequently mentioned in the Pentateuch,[42] which the Sadducees accepted as authoritative. Since they denied the resurrection of the dead, they would have rejected an interim state between death and the day of resurrection during which the deceased were assumed to exist as angels or spirits. Alternatively, since angels were part of the apocalyptic worldview which they rejected, and since angels served as God's servants to administer his providence, a notion that the Sadducees rejected as well, the Sadducees might be described by Luke as objecting to angels carrying out the will of God 'in the fulfillment of a preordained eschatological program and to their interfering with the will of an autonomous human being' (Parker, 'Angel', p. 364).

26–27. Jesus turns from the specific question of the status of married people in a presumed future resurrection to the basic question of the belief in a resurrection of the dead. He challenges the Sadducees on the basis of the *Book of Moses* which they have cited as an authority for their test case in verse 19. Jesus identifies not only the *Book* (the Pentateuch) in which we read the story of Moses

---

42. Cf. Gen. 16:7–11; 19:1, 15; 21:17; 22:11, 15; 24:7; Exod. 3:2; 14:19; 23:20.

(specifically Exodus), but the section: *in the passage about the bush* (RSV; NIV 'in the account of the burning bush'). In the absence of numbered sections and paragraphs,[43] teachers referred to striking features of the text they wanted to expound – key words as in 11:17 ('den of robbers') or, as here, a well-known event. Jesus quotes what we call Exodus 3:6, prefaced by the statement *God said to him*, that is, to Moses, *I am the God of Abraham, the God of Isaac, and the God of Jacob*. Jesus' argument is not based on the present tense of the verb (*I am*) which is absent from Mark's Greek and the Hebrew text (the LXX has *eimi*, as does the parallel in Matt. 22:32). Jesus concludes from these words that God *is not the God of the dead, but of the living*. The logic of this conclusion depends on the conviction that God is a living God, that God established a covenant relationship with Abraham, Isaac and Jacob, that God's covenant with the patriarchs is eternal in nature, and that long after their deaths he still identifies himself as their God, demonstrating that 'they are alive and in fellowship with him' (Stein, p. 555). If not, the expression *God of the dead* would be an entirely inappropriate description of Yahweh as he had revealed himself (France, p. 475). Jesus ends his argument by accusing the Sadducees again, with even stronger words, of being *badly mistaken*: they are very much in error when it comes to the question of the resurrection of the dead. Mark does not relate a reply from the Sadducees.

Theology
Jesus demonstrates his wisdom and authority as a teacher, his knowledge of Scripture, his creative argumentation with Scripture, his consistent focus on God and his power, and his courage in accusing members of the priestly elite of not knowing Scripture the way they should and of committing a serious theological error. Jesus argues for the reality of the resurrection. Resurrection life is not a

---

43. The chapter numbering system was introduced by Stephen Langton, the Archbishop of Canterbury, in 1207–1228, and the verse numbering system was introduced by Robert Stephanus, aka Estienne, in his 1551 edition of the Greek New Testament printed with Erasmus' Latin translation.

continuation of earthly life but eternal life made possible by the power of God. Life after death is a new, glorified existence compared to that of the angels. Paul argues that just as God gives to each kind of seed, flesh, animal and celestial body its particular body, so he will give to believers a real, imperishable spiritual body in the resurrection (1 Cor 15:35–55).

g. The question about the commandments (12:28–34)
Context

The fifth of six controversy dialogues in the Outer Court of the temple (beginning in 11:27) relates the story of a teacher of the law asking which of the commandments is the most important. The introduction of the scribe does not portray him as hostile and the entire episode lacks the polemical tone of the previous dialogues, facts that prompt most scholars to view the episode not as a controversy dialogue but as a pronouncement story or a scholastic dialogue (Stein, p. 558). However, the final clause in verse 34 and the subsequent warning against the teachers of the law (12:38–40) gives one pause. The question about the greatest commandment offers the possibility for an undiplomatic answer (France, p. 476), or an answer that disputes the scribal consensus concerning the most important commandment. In view of Jesus' provocative actions in the temple and his prophetic announcement of its destruction, both implying the abrogation of the temple cult of atoning sacrifices (11:12–25), and given the unsuccessful attempts of the chief priests, scribes and elders to elicit an answer from Jesus about the source of his authority in the first controversy dialogue (11:27–33), the scribe of 12:28 may not be entirely sincere. The scribe might have hoped to draw Jesus into giving an answer about the source of his authority that would elevate his authority over the authority of God as revealed in the law.

Comment

28. The *teacher of the law* (cf. 1:22) agreed with the *good answer* that Jesus had given to the Sadducees (12:18–27), a fact that suggests that he belonged to the Pharisees (cf. 2:16). If the scribe was favourably disposed towards Jesus, his question would have to be interpreted in terms of the 'hope for an equally enlightening (not just clever) answer to his more fundamental question' (France, p. 479). If the scribe was hostile and wanted to try his own hand at a question that would help the plans of the Jewish authorities to eliminate Jesus (11:18; 12:12–13), he would have been hoping for an answer that differed from the consensus, perhaps in the sense that Jesus elevated his authority over the authority of the commandments of the law – explicitly abrogating the purity laws as human traditions (cf. 7:1–23) and claiming the power to forgive sins (2:3–12) in competition with the sacrifices offered in the temple, a claim that could have been derived from Jesus' actions in the temple (11:12–25).

The question *Of all the commandments, which is the most important?* (lit. 'the first') takes up a legal question debated in scribal circles. Later scribes distinguish between 'heavy' commandments – commandments that require the expenditure of a large amount of money, commandments that involve a threat to one's life or important commandments, for example, commandments that are connected with the death penalty, such as those concerning idolatry, adultery, murder, profaning the divine name, keeping the Sabbath holy – and 'light' commandments which make little claim on one's power or possessions or which are unimportant (Collins, pp. 571–572). The desire for a convenient summary of the commandments of the law in terms of a foundational principle from which the rest of the law could be derived (called *kelal* by the rabbis) is evident in later rabbinic passages (*b. Shab.* 31a; *b. Ber.* 63a; *b. Mak.* 24a). Whether such traditions go back to the time of Jesus is unclear. While the combination of Deuteronomy 6:5 and Leviticus 19:18 (vv. 29–31) is not found in any ancient Jewish text, several formulations come close. In *Jubilees* 20:2 it says, 'And he commanded them that they should guard the way of the Lord so that they might do righteousness and each one might love his neighbour, and that it should be thus among all men so that each one might proceed to act justly and rightly toward them upon the earth' (the enumeration continues to list circumcision, fornication and ritual pollution; see also *T. Dan* 5:3; Philo, *Spec. leg.* 2.63; *b. Shab.* 31a; *Sipre* 200 on Lev. 19:15–20). The gist of Jesus' response to the scribe's question would have caused no surprise, which suggests that the scribe expected Jesus to give a response that significantly modified, or contradicted, traditional formulations.

29–30. Jesus agrees to answer the scribe's question: there is a *most important* commandment, and he cites Deuteronomy 6:4–5. This text is the first part of the Shema ('Hear'), Israel's basic declaration of faith which, according to the Mishnah, was recited daily in the temple, together with the Decalogue (*m. Tam.* 5:1). Pious Jews recited the Shema every morning and every evening (*m. Ber.* 2:2). The 'first' commandment is Deuteronomy 6:5: *Love the Lord your God with all your heart and with all your soul and with all your mind and with all your strength*. The point of this commandment is to be totally, unreservedly committed to God with one's entire being. The Hebrew text has only three elements (heart, soul, strength). The terms *heart*, *soul* and *mind* are all roughly equivalent, describing the human mind and will from slightly different perspectives: the *heart* is the centre of human thinking and affections; the *soul* is the source of desires and feelings; the *mind* signals thinking and understanding. The term *strength* points to one's energy and power.

Jesus grounds this 'first' commandment in Deuteronomy 6:4, the basic confession of monotheism: *the Lord our God, the Lord is one*. This 'preface' to the citation of the most important commandment is surely deliberate. Jesus had refused to answer the question regarding the source of his authority. Here he establishes that he is committed to the Jewish belief in the exclusive existence of one God who is the Lord of creation and the Lord of Israel. In the very next passage (12:35–37), Jesus comes close to describing himself as 'David's Lord' who sits on the throne beside God, understanding the oneness of God to include a unity between God and himself. If Jesus can indeed forgive sins (2:7, 10), he is 'inseparable from the object of the Shema's devotion' (Marcus, p. 843, with regard to Mark). At the same time, Jesus demonstrated throughout his ministry what it means to love God with one's whole being, willing to 'serve, and to give his life as a ransom for many' (10:45).

31. Without having been asked, Jesus provides a *second* commandment which, together with the 'first' commandment, is *greater* than all other commandments. Jesus cites Leviticus 19:18: *Love your neighbour as yourself*. This commandment is linked with Deuteronomy 6:5 by the verb *love* and by the fact that Deuteronomy 6:5 is a summary of the first part of the Decalogue while Leviticus 19:18 summarizes the second part. While loving God and loving one's neighbour are the most important commandments, there is a clear priority: loving other people is authentically possible only on the basis of one's love for God. The phrase *as yourself* does not commend self-love but assumes that people love themselves: people have a basic self-interest which they should extend to their *neighbour*, to the people to whom they are close (in the family, in Israel). In Matthew 5:43–48/Luke 6:27–36 (cf. Luke 10:29–39) Jesus extends the understanding of 'neighbour' to one's enemies. These two commandments form a commandment that is *greater* than any other commandment. Jesus does not abrogate all other commandments of the law: the commandment to love God and to love one's neighbour is the foundation on which all the other commandments rest, the basic principle from which all the other commandments derive and on the basis of which they can be understood.

32–33. The fact that the scribe now addresses Jesus as *teacher* implies his acknowledgment of Jesus' expertise as teacher. The phrase *you are right (ep' alētheias)* echoes the phrase *You are truthful (alēthēs ei;* NASB) of verse 14, where it denoted flattery of Jesus in the context of an attempt to trip him up (Gundry, p. 711). The scribe continues with a paraphrase of Jesus' answer. The phrase *God is one* comes from Deuteronomy 6:4, while the phrase *there is no other but him* is a more explicitly monotheistic formulation that echoes Deuteronomy 4:35 (cf. Isa. 45:6, 21; 47:8, 10; Ps. 86:8) and links the statement with the Decalogue (Exod. 20:3). The scribe's quotation of Deuteronomy 6:5 in verse 33 omits 'with all your soul' and replaces 'mind' with *understanding*, which has a similar meaning. The comment following the quotation of Deuteronomy 6:4–5 and Leviticus 19:18 – *is more important than all burnt offerings and sacrifices* – seems to apply Jesus' pronouncement that 'There is no commandment greater than these' (v. 31) to the sacrificial commandments, in particular the burnt offerings (*holokautōmata*) and various kinds of other sacrifices (*thysiai*). Since the summaries of the law attributed to Hillel and Akiba do not mention sacrifices, the scribe's statement is not particularly striking. In Hosea 6:6, sacrifice and burnt offerings are subordinated to 'mercy' and 'acknowledgment of God', which emphasizes their merely relative importance.

34. Mark asserts that Jesus saw that the scribe *answered intelligently* (NASB), a comment which includes the scribe's assertion that the sacrifices are subordinate to the commandment to love God and to love one's neighbour. Jesus does not elaborate on the status of the sacrifices, but comments on the status of the scribe: *You are not far from the kingdom of God*. If the scribe seriously means what he has said, abandoning his initial antagonism – if indeed that was his attitude – he may be on the verge of appreciating not only Jesus' teaching about the law but the connection between Jesus and the kingdom of God. Jesus asserts that entering the kingdom of God requires that people acknowledge the primacy of the love of God, the primary importance of loving one's neighbour and the relative significance of the sacrifices, as the scribe has just done. The phrase *not far* implies that more is required: repenting and believing in the good news of the coming of the kingdom of God that Jesus has been preaching (1:14–15), and committing himself to Jesus (1:18, 20; 5:18) on the way of self-denial and the cross (8:34). The phrase *not far* means that the scribe is still an 'outsider' who needs God's revelation of the secret of the kingdom of God (4:11).

The episode ends with Mark's comment that *from then on no one dared ask him any more questions*. This ending is surprising only if one assumes that the scribe's question in verse 28 was friendly. Jesus has successfully fended off hostile questions from the chief priests, scribes and elders (11:27; 12:12), from the Pharisees and Herodians (12:13) and from the Sadducees (12:18), and now 'even one of his enemies' own experts – a scribe – has confessed the truth of his teaching' (Gundry, p. 712). In the next episode Jesus will take the initiative.

Theology
Jesus' emphasis on the monotheistic teaching of Deuteronomy 6:4–5, a passage that was part of the daily prayers of the Jews, reminds Mark's Gentile Christian readers of the crucial truth of the existence of one true God and the non-existence of the deities they worshipped before their conversion. The quotation of the love command Leviticus 19:18, whose importance is demonstrated by its frequent repetition in the New Testament (Matt. 5:43; 19:19; Rom. 13:8–10; Gal. 5:14; Jas 2:8), reminds both Jewish and Gentile Christians of their obligation to love their fellow believers *and* those who persecute them – an obligation that is a direct, inseparable result of

loving God unreservedly with heart, soul, mind and strength. The reference to the lesser importance of sacrifices would have been combined by Jesus' followers before AD 70 with Jesus' statement about his authority to forgive sins (2:1–12), his death as a ransom (10:45), the destruction of the temple (11:17; 13:1–2) and his blood as the blood of the (new) covenant (14:24). They would have understood that the sacrificial cult of the Jerusalem temple was not only of relative importance compared with the two love commandments but that it had been superseded by Jesus' atoning death on the cross. Jesus' comment about the scribe being not far from the kingdom of God would have reminded the early Christians that eventually thousands of priests, Pharisees and Jews zealous for the law had come to faith in Jesus as Israel's Messiah (Acts 6:9; 9:1–19; 21:20), challenging them not to give up on people who were 'not far from the kingdom of God'.

h. The question about David's Son (12:35–37)
Context
The last of the six controversy dialogues with Israel's religious leaders reports Jesus asking a question about the Son of David in the context of scribal views of the Messiah. The identification of the view that the Messiah is the Son of David as scribal teaching connects this passage with the previous and the following passages (12:28, 35, 38). Jesus goes on the offensive and demonstrates their inadequate views of the Messiah.

Comment
35. The episode takes place in the *temple* (*hieros*), in the Outer Court (cf. 11:11, 15). Since the last reference to the temple court (11:27) marked the beginning of a new day (Wednesday), it is plausible to assume that this episode takes place on the following day (Thursday morning). The reference to the temple is significant since Jewish tradition posited a connection between Jerusalem, the temple and the coming Davidic Messiah, who would purge Jerusalem of pagan defilement, restore the temple and teach the ways of the Lord (cf. *Pss Sol.* 17:21–46). Jesus' question *Why do the teachers of the law say that the Messiah is the son of David?* challenges the view that the identity of the Messiah is fully understood with the designation 'the Son of

David'. For the title *Messiah* (*ho Christos*; Hebr. *ha-māšîaḥ*) see on 8:29; for the title 'Son of David' see on 10:47. *Messiah* ('the Anointed One') had become a recognized title of Jewish hopes for the time when God would fulfil his promises for his people. While the figure of the coming deliverer was understood in various ways by different Jewish movements and authors, an influential view believed, on the basis of Nathan's prophecy in 2 Samuel 7:12–16, that God would raise up a new king from the line of David who would liberate and restore Israel (cf. Isa. 9:2–7; 11:1–9; Jer. 23:5–6; 33:14–18; Ezek. 34:23–24; 37:24; Hos. 3:5). Since kings were anointed, 'Son of David' was a convenient title that encapsulated these hopes of a coming Messiah (*Pss Sol.* 17:21; *b 'Erub.* 43a; *b. Meg.* 17b; *Gen. Rab.* 97 on Gen. 49:10).

The first premise of Jesus' argument is the identity of the Messiah as the Son of David. This was not controversial. The fact that Jesus formulates the statement as a question signals that there is more to the identity of the Messiah than the title 'Son of David' suggests: how, in what sense, on what basis, do the scribes say that the Messiah is the Son of David?

36. Jesus proceeds to quote Psalm 110:1 (the most-quoted OT passage in the NT), introducing it as a declaration of *David*. In the first century, nobody would have disputed that the formula *lĕ-Dāvîd mizmôr* ('Of David. A psalm'; RSV 'A Psalm of David') meant that the psalm was written by David. The second premise of Jesus' argument is the Davidic authorship of the psalm. The phrase *speaking by the Holy Spirit* describes David as a prophet (cf. Josephus, *Ant.* 6.166; Acts 2:30–31) inspired by the Spirit (cf. 2 Sam. 23:2; Acts 1:16; 11QPs[a] XXII, 2–4, 11); and it portrays the Holy Spirit as the medium of divine inspiration (cf. Acts 28:25; 2 Peter 1:21; cf. CD A IV, 13–14: 'as God spoke through the hand of Isaiah').

In Psalm 110:1 the phrase *the Lord said* refers to Yahweh. The referent of the phrase *to my Lord* is disputed. If the author of the psalm is not David (as modern scholars think), 'my Lord' is the ruling Davidic monarch 'who is symbolically exalted to co-regency with God on the day of his coronation' (Marcus, p. 846). However, as Jews accepted Davidic authorship of the psalm, this interpretation becomes impossible: this psalm and the other so-called enthronement psalms were interpreted as prophecies of the establishment of God's reign through a coming king, the Messiah. This means that 'my Lord' refers to the Messiah. This is the third premise of Jesus' argument: David refers to the Messiah when he speaks of 'my Lord'. The Hebrew text of Psalm 110 uses two different words for 'lord': *yhwh* ('Yahweh') and *'ădōnāy* ('lord'); in the LXX both words are translated *kyrios* ('lord'). If Jesus quoted the psalm in Aramaic, both Hebrew words would be translated *mārē'* ('lord'). In spoken Hebrew, *yhwh* ('Yahweh') would be pronounced as *'ădōnāy* ('lord'). The wordplay is preserved in any case. To be seated at the *right hand* is the position of highest honour beside the king (cf. 10:37). It indicates here that David's Lord (the Messiah) is God's co-regent, ruling at his side. Jesus will allude to Psalm 110:1 in the Jewish trial to assert that he himself will be seated at the right hand of God (14:61–62). The phrase *until I put your enemies under your feet* promises that God will defeat the enemies of his king and make them subservient to him.

37. Given the premises that David wrote the psalm and that David calls the Messiah 'my Lord', the question arises, *How then can he be his son?* – given the fact that fathers do not call their sons 'my Lord'. This means that the Messiah is David's Lord rather than David's son and that the traditional view of the Messiah as 'Son of David' is inadequate. Since Jesus did not object to Bartimaeus calling him 'Son of David' (10:47–48), brought into a sharper, messianic focus by the shouts of the crowds as Jesus approached Jerusalem (11:10), he did not find the title 'Son of David' unacceptable. Jesus' argument from Psalm 110:1 signals that the Messiah is neither exclusively nor primarily defined by his Davidic descent but by his relationship to God who makes him co-regent on the heavenly throne. In the parable of the tenants Jesus had implicitly identified himself as the Son of God, who would be killed by Israel's leaders (12:6–8). When Caiaphas asks Jesus whether he is 'the Messiah, the Son of the Blessed One', Jesus acknowledges that he is indeed the Messiah, the Son of God, describing his position as the Son of Man at the right hand of God (14:62). Since Jesus poses the question of the Messiah's true identity as an academic exegetical discussion, and since he does not identify himself here as the Messiah who is the Son of God, this incident is not used against him in his trial as a false messianic claim or a blasphemous statement.

Mark continues to report the approval of the people of Jerusalem (and of pilgrims) who listen to and enjoy Jesus' teaching (cf. 11:18, 32; 12:12, 17). It is because of the popularity of Jesus and his teaching that the chief priests and scribes are afraid to arrest him in public (11:18, 32; 12:12; 14:2). The phrase *listened to him with delight* is also used in 6:20 to describe Antipas gladly conversing with John the Baptist, which did not prevent him from executing John. The attitude of the crowd towards Jesus will change as well: only two days later they will choose Barabbas over Jesus (15:11).

Theology
Genealogical descent from David is an essential part of Jesus' credentials (Matt. 1:20; Luke 1:27, 32, 69; 2:4, 11; Rom. 1:3–4; 2 Tim. 2:8; Rev. 5:5; 22:16): Jesus is the Son of David, the promised deliverer-king, the Messiah. Jesus proves from Psalm 110:1 that it is insufficient to think of the Messiah/Son of David as a king who restores Israel's greatness: the Messiah is Lord, God's co-regent and thus Lord of all, even of David, indeed of the whole earth (Phil. 2:11; Rev. 19:16). He is the messianic Son of David and he is the Son of God (1:1, 11; 9:7; 14:62). For Mark's readers, to confess Jesus as the only true King and Son of God was potentially dangerous since the emperor had exclusive royal status in Rome and its provinces, claiming to be *divi filius*, the son of a god (i.e. of the previous emperor regarded as divine), the source of life, dominating the world. Followers of Jesus know that there is only one Son of the one true God: Jesus, whose sonship is the basis for their own adoption as God's children (Rom. 8:17).

i. Warning against the teachers of the law (12:38–40)
Context
The denunciation of the teachers of the law follows repeated clashes with the legal and religious experts and, in the previous episode, Jesus' challenge of the scribes' views of the Messiah being the Son of David. Jesus now censures the behaviour of the scribes as a class of people. The sweeping denunciation results from the fact that the scribes were Jesus' enemies from the early days of his Galilean ministry, and climactically so in Jerusalem where they are intent, together with the chief priests, on killing Jesus. The denunciation is

surprising only if the encounter with the scribe in 12:28–34 is regarded as friendly. In 8:15 Jesus gave a shorter but equally sweeping warning against the Pharisees and Herod, formulated after the Pharisees and Herodians had started to plot how to kill him (3:6). Jesus engages in polemics 'in the context of a highly charged and potentially fatal confrontation' and thus applies 'a suitably broad brush' (France, p. 489). His denunciation of the scribes' character as ostentatious, exploitative and hypocritical does not obviate the fact that he agrees with some of their positions (9:11–13; 12:28–35).

Comment

38–39. The phrase *watch out for* means to 'be ready to learn someth[ing] that is needed or is hazardous' (BDAG, p. 132, *blepō* meaning 5). The same verb is used in 8:15 for the Pharisees and Herod, who resisted Jesus. Jesus points out and warns of four objects of desire that are characteristic of the teachers of the law.

The statement that the teachers of the law *like to walk around in flowing robes* means that they take pleasure in impressing other people by their outward appearance. The most common outer garment for men was the *himation* (cf. 5:15). The *stola* (Lat. *toga*) was a long flowing robe that signified wealth. In the LXX the term is used for particularly impressive clothing such as priestly garments or royal attire (Gen. 41:42; Exod. 28:2; 29:21; 2 Chr. 18:9; 23:13; Esth. 6:8; 8:15). According to Sirach 38:4–11, the social status of experts of the law and of teachers was relatively high. The desire (which not all scribes would have been able to indulge in) to appear in public with such a robe indicates a desire to display one's high status. The reference to the long robes could suggest that the scribes in view here are scribes who are priests or who advise the priests as experts of the law. Scribes are mentioned together with the chief priests in 8:31; 10:33; 11:18, 27; 14:1, 43, 53; 15:1, 31.

The scribes like to *be greeted with respect in the marketplaces*, hoping that people will either recognize them or conclude from their attire that they are important people who deserve a deferential greeting. The desire to be greeted in the marketplace signals a yearning for honour. They like to *have the most important seats in the synagogues* (lit. 'first seats', 'seats of honour' or 'best seats'), the seats facing the congregation reserved for honoured persons (called 'cathedra of Moses'). As leadership in the synagogues was decentralized, in many congregations more than one person occupied the cathedra, depending on the particular activity taking place: the person leading prayers, preaching the sermon, teaching, the persons responsible for court proceedings, or special guests. The scribes like *the places of honour at banquets*. This reflects the ancient meal customs in which guests were placed according to their social status. The host would usually take the first position, his honoured guest being placed on his right. The honoured guests would receive not only the best places on the couches on which the dinner guests reclined but also the best food.

40. The reason for Jesus' harsh judgment of the scribes is connected with the way they treat widows. Their outward respectability is contradicted by their brutal behaviour: *they devour widows' houses*. Widows, together with orphans, resident aliens and the poor, are often mentioned in the Old Testament as people for whom God has a special concern since they do not enjoy the benefits of the usual social support system (Marcus, p. 855). The people of God are called upon to guarantee their well-being, with the warning that God is their defender and will avenge any exploitation of them (Exod. 22:22; Deut. 10:18; 24:17; 27:19). To defraud them is a heinous crime, as the prophets repeatedly assert (Isa. 10:1–4; Jer. 7:6–7; Ezek. 22:7; Zech. 7:10–14; Mal. 3:5). The house of a widow would often be her entire inheritance. The verb *devour* is a vivid description of the scribes' uncaring treatment of widows, appropriating their houses in an unethical manner. This could happen through charging excessive legal fees when they worked as probate lawyers, deliberate mismanagement of a widow's estate of which they had been made trustees, taking their houses as pledges for unpayable debts, prompting them to support the temple with resources they could not really afford, or exploiting their hospitality and trust. The phrase *for a show make lengthy prayers* indicates either the means by which the scribes manage to defraud widows of their possessions or the manner in which they cover up what they have done. Jesus does not criticize lengthy prayers as such but prayers that are said with ulterior motives: prayers addressed not to God but to others in order to impress them or to calm them.

Jesus' verdict corresponds to the prophets' condemnation of people who defraud widows: *These men will be punished most severely.* God will judge them. In Ezekiel 22:7, 15 and Zechariah 7:10–14 the threatened punishment for defrauding widows, orphans and the poor is the dispersion of Israel among the nations; in Jeremiah 22:3–6 it is the destruction of the king's palace; in Deuteronomy 27:19, the loss of fortune in this life.

Theology
The ostentatious, exploitative and hypocritical behaviour of the scribes that Jesus condemns is a lesson for Mark's readers, especially for the leaders in the churches. True disciples do not seek to gain this world but the next (8:36–37). Christian leaders must be authentically focused on the Word of God, which they study, preach and teach, not on their appearance or social status. They must be servants, not profiteers. They must love others at least as much as they love themselves (12:31); indeed they ought to be willing to be the 'last' (9:35–37; 10:31).

j. Commendation of the widow (12:41–44)
Context
The incident of the widow and her great gift to the temple is connected with the preceding episode by the term 'widow' and by its geographical location in one of the temple courts. The behaviour of the widow is implicitly contrasted with the behaviour of the scribes in the previous episode.

Comment
41. The *treasury* (*gazophylakion*, 'a place for the storing of valuables') refers in Josephus' description of the temple to the treasury chambers between the gatehouses at the northern and southern ends of the Inner Enclosure surrounding the Court of Israel, the Court of Priests and the temple proper (*War* 5.200; *Ant.* 19.294). The wealth stored in the temple was enormous; besides the half-shekel temple tax paid by each Jewish man twenty years or older, both wealthy and poor Jews contributed to the temple treasury. Here, the term refers to one of the thirteen receptacles for money offerings called 'shofar chests' in *m. Sheqalim* 6:5 due to their trumpet-shaped

construction which tapered at the top; seven of these receptacles were used for fixed duties, five for specific appropriations and one for voluntary contributions; they seem to have stood in the Court of Women (H. Balz, *EDNT*, I, p. 232). The Court of Women (*ezrat nashim*), which, despite its name, was intended for all members of the Jewish faith, was entered from the Outer Court via three gates. Jesus watched *the crowd putting money into the treasury*, and observed that *many rich people put in large sums* (NRSV). The latter would be discernible when they gave their generous contributions – silver and gold coins – to the priests for the necessary scrutiny. A denarius (silver coin) was a day's wage of a labourer (cf. 12:15); an aureus (gold coin) was valued at 25 silver denarii, representing nearly a month's wages.

42. A *poor widow* put in *two very small copper coins*. A leptos was worth 1/128 of a silver denarius. *Leptos* means 'small, thin, light'; the word is used here for *leptos nomisma*, 'small copper coin' (BDAG, p. 592; Hebr. *pĕrûṭâ*). The small copper coin was 0.43 inches (11 mm) in diameter and weighed 0.03 ounces (0.9 g; fixed under John Hyrcanus II and Herod I). In contemporary numismatic publications these tiny copper coins appear as 'half-*perutah*' or half-*pruta*. Mark informs his Roman readers that the two small copper coins were worth a *kodrantēs*, a term that transliterates the Latin word *quadrans*, the smallest Roman coin worth 1/4 of an as or 1/64 of a denarius. English translations which use terms like 'penny' (ESV, GNB, NRSV, RSV), 'a cent' (NASB) or 'a few pence' (NIV) are not quite accurate: since a quadrans is earned by a day labourer in about eight minutes of work (assuming an eight-hour work day to earn a denarius; cf. Matt. 20:2), at a low hourly wage of $7.50 (USD), a quadrans would be about $1 (USD). This is more than a 'penny' or a 'few cents', but still only 'small change', barely enough to purchase a meagre meal (Strauss, p. 559). Jesus and other observers would have learnt of the woman's contribution on account of the priests scrutinizing everybody who wanted to put an offering into the box. The later rabbinic text *Leviticus Rabbah* 107a describes how a poor woman had to endure public ridicule by the priests because of a small gift.

43–44. The fact that Jesus *called his disciples* (NRSV) and the phrase *Truly I tell you* (cf. 3:28) signal that the following pronouncement is important. Jesus asserts that *this poor woman has put in more* than anyone else because others *contributed out of their abundance*, that is, they gave from their surplus without pain, whereas *she out of her poverty has put in everything she had* (NRSV). She had two coins, and she gave both of them. The concluding phrase *all she had to live on* (lit. 'her entire life') may mean that after she had donated two *perutot*, she was without the ability to pay for her next meal. She is an example of what it means to fulfil the greatest commandment: loving God with one's entire self (12:29–32).

Theology
Jesus emphasizes yet again the 'upside-down' values of the kingdom of God compared with the traditional values of society: a wealthy person who contributed an aureus gave 1,600 times as much as the poor widow who gave 1/64 of a denarius. Jesus can say that the poor widow gave more than anyone else because he focuses not on the amount of money given but on the giver. While the wealthy may be pious, demonstrating their devotion to God by their generous giving, the poor widow is so totally devoted to God that she is willing to give everything that she has, without regard for the consequences, trusting that God will provide because he is 'a defender of widows' (Ps. 68:5).

ii. Jesus on the Mount of Olives (13:1–37)
As Jesus leaves the Temple Mount (13:1) in whose Outer Court he has been acting and teaching since 11:15, he abandons the controversy with the political and religious authorities and predicts the destruction of the temple. This prediction plays a central role in the trial (14:57–58), and it was remembered by those who mocked him on the cross (15:29–30) and by those who later put Stephen on trial (Acts 6:13–14). The prediction, which was uttered in public, may have been in large measure responsible for the loss of the popularity that Jesus had enjoyed among the crowds up to this point (France, p. 495).

The structure of the extended discourse in 13:5–37, the longest speech of Jesus in Mark's Gospel, has been much debated, particularly on account of the fact that Jesus addresses not only the destruction of the temple and Jerusalem but also the coming of the Son of Man and the end of the age. Most see a reference to both as distinct events – the destruction of Jerusalem and Jesus' return.

A simple outline of the discourse relates the first half (vv. 5–23) to the coming destruction of Jerusalem and the second half (vv. 24–37) to Jesus' parousia. This interpretation runs into problems in verses 10, 19, 29–30 (particularly the phrase 'this generation' in v. 30). Others suggest an A–B–A–B pattern, the most convincing of which relates verses 5–23 to the destruction of Jerusalem, verses 24–27 to the second coming of Jesus and the end of the age, verses 28–31 to the destruction of Jerusalem (lesson of the fig-tree) and verses 32–37 to the second coming of Jesus (Stein, pp. 593–597; Strauss, p. 566). This structure can be simplified: we relate verses 5–23 to the destruction of the temple, verses 24–27 to Jesus' second coming, and verses 28–37 to the consequences for the disciples both with regard to the destruction of Jerusalem which will take place very soon (vv. 28–31) and with regard to Jesus' parousia which will take place on an unknown date (vv. 32–37).

a. Prophecy of the destruction of the temple (13:1–2)
Context
Following his debates with the Jewish authorities in the Outer Court, his denunciation of the scribes and his commendation of a poor widow, Jesus leaves the Temple Mount to return to Bethany via the Mount of Olives. The admiration voiced by one of the disciples at the magnificence of the buildings on the Temple Mount prompts Jesus to prophesy the total destruction of the Mount.

Comment
1. As Jesus leaves the temple complex, an unnamed disciple draws Jesus' attention to the magnificence of the temple. He marvels at the massive *stones* (*lithoi*). If these had left the Temple Mount, he might be referring to the stones of which the retaining walls of the Temple Mount were built. These stones were generally about 3.3–3.9 feet (1–1.2 m) high and 6.5–13 feet (2–4 m) long; the largest stones were in the twenty-eighth course in the south-eastern corner (the 'master course'), twice as high as the other stones, with one stone more than 43 feet (13 m) long and 10 feet (3 m) high, its weight estimated at about 100 metric tons (Netzer, *Architecture*, pp. 161–164). Their outer faces were dressed with a margin 4–8 inches (10–20 cm) wide and a smoothed boss in the centre, creating an effect of light

and shade which emphasized 'the beauty and dramatic appearance of the massive walls' (H. Geva, *NEAEHL*, II, p. 738). The magnificent *buildings* (*oikodomiai*) could be a reference to the Royal Portico, a triple colonnade 787 feet (240 m) long and 108 feet (33 m) wide, its central hall 90–100 feet (30–33 m) high, with a total of 160 columns. The reference would surely include the temple building proper (*naos*), with dimensions of 164 by 164 by 164 feet (50 by 50 by 50 m), and described by Josephus as follows:

> The exterior of the building wanted nothing that could astound either mind or eye. For, being covered on all sides with massive plates of gold, the sun was no sooner up than it radiated so fiery a flash that persons straining to look at it were compelled to avert their eyes, as from the solar rays. To approaching strangers it appeared from a distance like a snow-clad mountain; for all that was not overlaid with gold was of the purest white. (*War* 5. 222–223)

In the light of *Jewish War* 5.208, it is not clear whether the whole façade was covered with gold, or only its central higher part, or the inside of the vestibule visible through the portal. If the disciple's comment was made in front of the Royal Portico, he would have seen only the upper 92 feet (28 m) of the *naos* which stood 492 feet (150 m) to the north, with the high wall of the Inner Enclosure obstructing from view nearly half of the building.

2. The disciple's pride in the grandeur and beauty of the walls and buildings of the temple complex was not misplaced but, as Jesus' response implies, doomed to be dissolved in the not-too-distant future. Jesus acknowledges *these great buildings* but predicts their demolition: *Not one stone here will be left on another; every one will be thrown down.* This is the first specific prediction of the destruction of the temple by Jesus, after he alluded to coming judgment in his symbolic action in the temple (11:15–17) and in the parable of the tenants (12:1–12). Jesus uttered the prediction in public, as he was leaving the Outer Court. In his trial Jesus will be accused of having threatened to destroy the temple and rebuild it in three days (14:58; cf. John 2:19). Mark treats this accusation as false testimony (14:57): Jesus did not say that he would destroy the temple himself.

Theology
Jesus' knowledge of future events points on the one hand to God's sovereign control of history and on the other hand to Jesus' inspiration as a prophet. If Mark wrote his Gospel before AD 70, his readers would not yet know that Jesus' prophecy had been fulfilled. Jesus seems to imply that the destruction of the temple is connected with his ministry and with who he is (11:15–25; 12:1–12; 14:58; 15:29). Mark 'wants his readers not to be disturbed by what is taking place in Jerusalem and Judea' (Stein, pp. 591–592). Some link Jesus' leaving the temple with Ezekiel's description of the departure of God's glory from the temple (Ezek. 10:18–19; 11:22–23), stopping 'above the mountain east of it' (Ezek. 11:23); that is, the Mount of Olives (cf. France, pp. 495, 507). This allusion may be too subtle to be noticed by Mark's readers, and may not be intended by Mark.

b. The destruction of the temple (13:3–23)
Context
Jesus' prophecy of the destruction of the temple buildings prompts the brothers among Jesus' disciples to enquire about the date when this prophecy will be fulfilled. The first part of Jesus' discourse describes the time between the present and the destruction of the temple, informing the disciples of a specific sign that will signal the imminent destruction of the temple, a sign that will allow them to leave the city and escape from Judea. The lack of detail and the lack of precise correspondence with the events in AD 70 confirm the historicity of Jesus' prediction: there is, for example, no reference to the great fire that engulfed the temple, graphically described and repeatedly emphasized by Josephus, culminating in the statement 'You would indeed have thought that the Temple Mount was boiling over from its base, being everywhere one mass of flame.'[44] Jesus' admonition to pray that the destruction might not happen in winter would be curious as a prophecy invented 'after the event': the city was captured and the temple burned in August and September AD 70.

---

44. Josephus, *War* 6.275; cf. 6.165–168, 177–185, 190–192, 228–235, 250–284, 316, 346, 353–355, 407, 434; cf. Evans, p. 295.

Comment

3. As Jesus and the disciples were sitting *on the Mount of Olives*, rising some 330 feet (100 m) above the city (cf. 11:1), they had a splendid view of Jerusalem and the Temple Mount. Their question is prompted by Jesus' prediction of the destruction of the temple (v. 2) and by their location *opposite the temple*, across the Kidron Valley. As in 4:10, 7:17, 10:10, Jesus gives a private explanation of a public pronouncement. The four disciples who were the first to be called by Jesus (1:16–20) – Peter and his brother Jacob (James), and John and his brother Andrew, all former fishermen – *asked him privately*. The verb *asked* is singular, presumably referring to Peter as their spokesman.

4. The disciples' question has two parts. They want to know, *when will this be* (NRSV), the demonstrative pronoun *this* (*tauta*, lit. 'these events') referring to the destruction of the temple that Jesus has just predicted (v. 2). They want to know the time or date when the temple will be demolished. And they want to know, *what will be the sign that all these things are about to be accomplished?* (NRSV). The plural *these things* (*tauta panta*) anticipates a series of events, and the verb 'accomplish' points to the completion of the historical process that will lead to the destruction of the temple. In Matthew 24:3 the disciples ask two questions referring to the destruction of the temple and the return of Jesus (parousia), and some understand the second part of the question here in verse 4 in the same way.[45] However, Mark's readers would have no way of knowing that *tauta panta* refers to a different event from *tauta*, and the verb *accomplished* does not change the subject matter either. It is better to understand the two-part question as referring to the same event: the destruction of the temple.

The word *sign* (*sēmeion*) refers here to 'a distinguishing mark whereby someth[ing] is known' (BDAG, p. 920), here specifically an event that signals that the process that will lead to the destruction of the temple is under way. In verses 5–13 Jesus mentions six developments leading up to the destruction of the temple (implied in vv. 19–20), with the sixth event being a 'sign' – the 'abomination' that desecrates the temple (v. 14), the one sign that one will clearly

---

45. Boring, p. 355; Collins, p. 602; Beasley-Murray, *Last Days*, p. 387.

be able to 'see' in order to conclude that now is the time to flee Judea. The first five developments are not 'signs' that allow the disciples to calculate the nearness of the end (cf. v. 7: 'but the end is still to come'). It is in the nature of the events described in verses 5–13, 20–23 that they do not unfold one after the other: they may take place simultaneously. Of decisive significance as 'sign' is the 'abomination that causes desolation' standing in the temple.

5. Jesus begins his description of the time between 'now' (April AD 30) and the prophesied destruction of the temple (September AD 70) with the imperative *Watch out* (*blepete*), an exhortation that is repeated in verses 9, 23, 33 (note the similar exhortations in vv. 33, 35, 37). Jesus' main concern is not the prediction of future events but the warning that the disciples must be prepared for anything that may happen and must understand that people and events may deceive them into arriving at erroneous conclusions.

6. The first development is the seduction of many people by messianic pretenders. The statement *many will come in my name* seems to suggest that there will be people who claim to represent Jesus. The claims of these people are expressed (in direct speech) in the sentence *I am he* (Gr. *egō eimi*). The verb *I am* needs to be supplied with a predicate, which most plausibly is 'the Messiah' in the context of 11:1–11, 12–25; 12:35–37. These people who will be active in the future will claim to 'be' what Jesus is: Israel's Messiah. They are in the same category as the 'false messiahs' and 'false prophets' of verse 22: Jewish would-be leaders who claim to have royal dignity and the ability to redeem Israel. In verse 6 they are messianic pretenders that appear before the war against Rome; in verse 22 they are messianic pretenders during the war (AD 66–70). Messianic pretenders did indeed appear in the years before the destruction of Jerusalem in AD 70: Josephus mentions a Samaritan, a certain Theudas, Judas of Galilee, and a Jew from Egypt, who all seemed to have had political or 'messianic' aspirations (*Ant.* 18.85–87; 20.97–99, 102, 169–172, 160–161, 167–168, 188; for Theudas, who had four hundred followers, cf. Acts 5:36; for the Egyptian Jew who had four thousand followers cf. Acts 21:38).

7–8. The second development refers to *wars and rumours of wars*. The word *rumour* refers to reports of wars in more distant provinces and regions. The expectation that *nation will rise against nation* and *kingdom against kingdom* corresponds to the wars mentioned in the previous statement, describing international conflicts and unrest. Although the period AD 30–66 was relatively peaceful in the territories controlled by the Roman Empire, there were armed conflicts and civil disturbances in the East: disturbances in Armenia caused by the Parthian king Artabanos (AD 33); war between Rome and Parthia (AD 36); war between Herod Antipas, the ruler of Galilee, and the Nabatean king Aretas IV (AD 36); large Jewish demonstrations in Ptolemais and Tiberias against the Roman legate in Syria, who had moved two Roman legions to Judea (AD 39/40); rebellion in Mauretania (AD 42); invasion of Britain under the emperor Claudius (AD 43); unrest in Jerusalem and Judea resulting from the provocative behaviour of Roman soldiers, with 20,000 Jewish citizens killed (AD 48); armed conflict between the Roman legate in Moesia and northern tribes resulting in the forced resettlement of 100,000 people (AD 57); conquest of Armenia by the Roman general Domitius Corbulo (AD 58); Parthians threatening Syria (AD 61); and the Roman general Caesennius Paetus arriving in Cappadocia with the task of annexing Armenia, forcing the Parthian king Vologaeses I to capitulate (AD 62).

Jesus warns the disciples, *do not be alarmed*, because *such things must happen*. Wars have always characterized history, both in Israel and in other regions and nations, which means that even though one may think that a particular war or an intense sequence of wars may signal the end, that is *not* the case: *the end is still to come*. Wars by themselves are not a 'sign' that the *end (telos)*, the end-point of the process leading to the destruction of the temple (cf. v. 4), is imminent. That such events *must happen* reminds Mark's readers of the depravity of humankind and points them to God's sovereignty in the events of history.

There were indeed *earthquakes* (*seismoi*) in *various places* (the third development). There was an earthquake in Philippi in AD 49 (Acts 16:26), a serious earthquake in Palestine some time before AD 60 (Josephus, *War* 3.286–287), and there were earthquakes in Asia Minor in AD 61 and in Rome in AD 67 (Pliny, *Nat.* 2.84). Earthquakes continue to be part of the human experience in many parts of the world, including the Middle East. It should be noted that Jesus did not predict that there was to be an increase in earthquakes, as 'end-time specialists' often claim.

The fourth development refers to *famines*. There was a famine in Rome in AD 41, a severe famine in Judea in AD 46 (Acts 11:28; Josephus, *Ant.* 3.320; 20.51–53, 101), and there were famines in various regions of the Roman empire in AD 51.

In the context of Old Testament passages in which wars, earthquakes and famines signal divine judgment[46] or the coming day of the Lord,[47] it is not surprising that Jesus links his prediction of the destruction of the temple with such events. Jesus explains that such events are *the beginning of the birth-pains*. The image of *birth-pains* describes both intense suffering and anxious longing for the joy of the birth of the child. The labour pains of women are used in both the Old Testament and the New Testament in a variety of contexts as a metaphor for suffering.[48] The term does not have the technical sense of the expression 'birth pang' (singular) which refers to the period of tribulation and distress before the coming of the Messiah and the messianic age that we find in later rabbinic literature.[49] When the disciples hear of wars, earthquakes and famines, they should not think that the destruction of the temple is imminent: history will continue until Jesus' prediction comes true. These events related to world affairs are false alarms.

9. The fifth development is persecution. The more general events described in verses 5–8 become personal. Jesus repeats the exhortation 'Watch out' (v. 5; NIV *You must be on your guard*). Jesus warns the disciples to be ready to face persecution and to bear it faithfully. Jesus does not specify who will 'hand them over'; that is, arrest them and take them to be tried before *local councils*, the Sanhedrin in Jerusalem and local Jewish courts of law in Judea and beyond, including Jewish diaspora communities; *synagogues* (cf. 1:21) which

---

46. Wars: 2 Chr. 15:6; Isa. 19:2; Jer. 4:16–20; Dan. 11:44; Joel 3:9–14; Zech. 14:2; earthquakes: Isa. 5:25; 13:13; 29:6; Jer. 4:24; Amos 1:1; Hag. 2:6, 21; famines and plagues: Isa. 14:30; Jer. 14:12; 21:6–7; Ezek. 14:21.
47. Isa. 2:19, 21; 13:13; 24:18; 29:5–6; Ezek. 38:19; Joel 2:10; Strauss, p. 573.
48. 2 Sam. 22:6; Ps.18:4; Isa. 26:17–18; Hos. 13:13; symbolizing the suffering of nations and cities in crisis: Isa. 13:8; Jer. 6:24; 22:23; Hos. 13:13; Mic. 4:9–10. Cf. John 16:21; Acts 2:24; Rom. 8:22; 1 Thess. 5:3; Gal. 4:19.
49. Cf. *b. Sanh.* 97a, 98a–b; *b. Shab.* 118a; *Gen. Rab.* 42:4.

had the authority to inflict corporal punishment such as flogging with forty lashes minus one (Deut. 25:1–3; 2 Cor. 11:24); *governors*, the administrators of Roman provinces who tried cases that the local courts were not able to decide as well as capital cases; *kings*, rulers such as the Jewish king Agrippa I (AD 41–42), the Nabatean king Aretas IV (9 BC – AD 40) and the emperor in Rome. Jesus prepares the disciples for official opposition in local Jewish courts and in Roman provincial and imperial courts.

Jesus explains both the reason for and the results of persecution. The disciples will suffer official opposition *on account of me*: because they follow Jesus, who is himself about to stand before the Jewish court of the Sanhedrin (14:53–72) and the Roman court of Pontius Pilate (15:1–20), and because they proclaim the good news about Jesus, which will get them into trouble. But they know that to lose one's life for Jesus and for the good news is gain (8:35). While flogging and worse is the result of persecution, the more important result is that they will stand before local, provincial and imperial courts *as witnesses*: they will be able to present the gospel before the members of the local, provincial and imperial elites. Not long after Jesus' arrest, torture and crucifixion, Peter, John and others of the Twelve were repeatedly arrested (Acts 4:3; 5:18; 12:3). Later Stephen, one of the Seven, and the apostle Jacob (James) were killed (Acts 7:58–60; 12:1–2). Luke relates in the book of Acts that Paul was repeatedly arrested and put in prison.

10. The assertion that *the gospel must first be preached to all nations* is related to the previous sentence in which the missionary witness of the disciples before their local and international opponents was described as a result of the persecution which they will face. The word *first* means that the worldwide proclamation of the good news of Jesus, Israel's Messiah and Saviour of sinners, has to happen before the destruction of the temple. The word *ta ethnē* (*the nations*) could refer in a basic sense to nations or peoples defined as a 'body of persons united by kinship, culture, and common traditions', ethnically homogeneous groups such as the Jewish people, the Lycians, the Achaian people, the nations of the Greeks besides the Macedonians, the Egyptian nations (cf. BDAG, p. 276); in inscriptions, the cities are sometimes contrasted with the 'people' (*ethnē*) living outside the cities (*I. Miletus* III 1052), and a governor of a province can be called 'the governor of the *ethnos*' (*P. Oxy.* VII 1020). The term *all* refers to nations, clans, tribes or provinces, not to every single person of a nation; it may not refer literally to every single nation without exception but hyperbolically to a multitude of nations. Jesus' announcement of the international proclamation of the gospel (according to Acts 1:8 a worldwide proclamation 'to the ends of the earth') was impressively fulfilled in the first century before AD 70: the gospel reached the ends of the earth in the south (Ethiopia; cf. Acts 8:26–40), west (Spain; cf. Rom. 15:24, 28), north (Scythia; cf. Col. 3:11) and east (India; cf. *Acts of Thomas*).[50] Paul writes in the AD 50s and early 60s that the gospel is being proclaimed 'throughout the whole world' (Col. 1:6), to 'every creature under heaven' (Col. 1:23) and to 'all the Gentiles' (Rom. 16:26).

11. The proclamation of the good news in the context of persecution in which the disciples may be *arrested and brought to trial* is a prospect which should give them confidence. Jesus assures them that they should *not worry beforehand about what to say* because the Holy Spirit will supply them with words to speak. Since none of the disciples were members of the elite, standing before councils, governors and kings would be a daunting prospect. The assurance of divine aid reminds later readers who know John's Gospel of the role of the Holy Spirit as *paraklētos* ('one who is called to someone's aid', advocate, helper, intercessor; John 14:26; 15:26–27; 16:8–11).

12–13. Followers of Jesus will face not only official persecution but fierce opposition even within their own families. The phrase *betray . . . to death* suggests that family members will inform on each other: brothers on their Christian siblings, fathers on their Christian children, and children on their Christian parents. The breakdown of family relationships echoes the description of the collapse of Judean society in Micah 7:6. There is little evidence for this level of persecution in the first century before AD 70, although we do not know what transpired in the persecution that followed Stephen's execution (Acts 8:1, 3; 9:1–2). In the Neronian persecution in AD 64 Christians were arrested, convicted and executed on the testimony of informers (Tacitus, *Ann.* 15.44). The phrase *everyone will hate you* is hyperbolic,

---

50. Cf. Schnabel, *Early Christian Mission*, pp. 373–376, 444–498, 880–895.

underlining the very widespread hatred that his followers will encounter. People will hate the disciples *because of me* (lit. 'because of my name'), because of their allegiance to Jesus and their proclamation of Jesus as Israel's Messiah and Saviour of sinners. Jesus assures his disciples that those who suffer for him will be saved. The singular phrase *the one who stands firm* points to the fact that endurance is an intensely personal matter: each and every disciple needs to stay committed to Jesus. The expression *to the end* does not refer to the destruction of Jerusalem as the end of the historical process described earlier, nor to the end of the world (which is not in view here); it is best taken as a general expression meaning 'for ever' in the sense of 'as long as it takes' (France, p. 519), or as referring to the end of one's life, given the context of martyrdom in verse 12. The word *saved* does not mean physical deliverance – martyrdom is a real possibility – but spiritual preservation in the faith in the midst of persecution, and eternal life if and when they are martyred.

14. The phrase *when you see* introduces the sixth development which is specific and readily identifiable, in contrast to the earlier events that have been and continue to be part of human history in a fallen world. The visible 'sign' (*sēmeion*) that signals the imminence of the destruction of the temple is the *abomination that causes desolation*. This 'sign' is Jesus' answer to the disciples' question in verse 4. The Greek phrase *bdelygma tēs erēmōseōs* (NRSV 'desolating sacrilege'; NASB 'abomination of desolation') is used in Daniel 11:31, 12:11 (cf. 9:27) to translate Hebrew *šiqqûṣ šōmēm*, which means 'a detested thing [normally used of idols] which desolates', or perhaps 'appals' (France, pp. 522–523), referring to the ritual desecration of the temple and the cessation of the regular burnt offering. In Matthew 24:15 Jesus explicitly mentions Daniel's prophecy. The phrase is not used anywhere else except in 1 Maccabees 1:54, where it describes the events of 167 BC when the Syrian king Antiochus Epiphanes IV ordered the abolition of the temple cult, resulting in the fact that 'they erected a desolating sacrifice on the altar of burnt offering'. Josephus relates that pigs were sacrificed (*Ant.* 12.253). The phrase *where it does not belong* describes the introduction of pagan objects of worship (such as a pagan statue of a deity) and/or pagan worship into the temple. As Daniel's prophecy was fulfilled in the profanation of the temple, which involved the cessation of regular sacrifices and the worship of pagan gods on a pagan altar, two hundred years before Jesus' prophecy, the disciples are being told that before the destruction of the temple an event will happen that is in some way recognizable as resembling both Daniel's prophecy and the events of 167 BC.

The phrase *let the reader understand* suggests that the reading of Daniel's prophecy and the recognition of a connection between a specific future event with Daniel's prophecy and the fulfilment of that prophecy in the events of 167 BC require careful interpretation and insight, since the precise nature of the *abomination* is not specified. This interpretation takes the phrase to be part of Jesus' discourse (France, p. 523). If the phrase is an aside by Mark, it is evidence for an early date of Mark's Gospel, who warns his readers 'to keep their eyes on Jerusalem' (Strauss, p. 580).

Jesus' prophecy refers to the temple that he and his disciples saw as they sat on the Mount of Olives (v. 3). This means that it is not plausible to link this 'sign' with events after AD 70, in the twenty-first century (or later centuries), somehow related to the appearance of a 'blasphemous Antichrist' before Jesus' second coming (Edward, p. 398; cf. Evans, pp. 319–320; such interpretations require for a literal fulfilment the construction of a third temple in Jerusalem which is then desecrated at some point). Such a reference would have had no meaning for the disciples, whose question was related to the destruction of the Second Temple.

Some connect the prophecy with the order of Emperor Gaius Caligula in AD 40 to set up a statue of himself in the temple in Jerusalem, an order that caused disturbances among the Jews; the plan was averted when Gaius was assassinated (Josephus, *Ant.* 18.261–272; Tacitus, *Hist.* 5.9). This crisis was real, but the 'abomination' was never brought into the temple. It is more plausible to connect Jesus' prophecy with events leading up to the destruction of the temple in AD 70. Some think of the events of August AD 70: after Roman troops broke through to the Temple Mount, the Roman commander (and later emperor) Titus entered the temple and viewed 'the holy place of the sanctuary and all that it contained'; subsequently Roman troops 'carried their standards into the Temple court and, setting them up opposite the eastern gate, there sacrificed to them, and with rousing acclamations hailed Titus as imperator'

(Josephus, *War* 6.260, 316). The main problem with this interpretation is the fact that Jesus advises his disciples to flee once they see the *abomination of desolation* standing in the temple: when Titus entered the temple and when the Roman standards were set up in the temple court, it was too late to leave the city; by that time the city had already been destroyed, having been surrounded by Roman troops for months.

A more plausible suggestion is the desecration of the temple not by pagans (which would be obvious) but by Jews, which would require readers to *understand* that Jesus prophesies not a repeat of the events of 167 BC but a different kind of abomination that desolates the temple. At the beginning of the war, in the winter of AD 67/68, Jewish militants (the Zealots) occupied the Temple Mount and usurped the high priesthood (Josephus, *War* 4.147–157). Ananus, the oldest of the chief priests, is reported as saying, 'How wonderful it would have been if I had died before seeing the house of God full of countless abominations and its unapproachable, sacred precincts crowded with those whose hands are red with blood!' (*War* 4.163; cf. 4.150, 182–183, 201, 377–379, 388; 6.95). Josephus states that 'the Zealots caused the prophecies against their country to be fulfilled' (*War* 4.387). In this interpretation, the *abomination of desolation*, linked with the masculine participle *hestēkota* ('standing'), refers to revolutionary leaders such as Eleazar son of Simon who occupied the Temple Mount and stained it with blood (*War* 4.225; 5.5), or to Phannias who was appointed high priest despite the fact that he was not of high-priestly descent (*War* 4.155–157).[51] The timing of these events would have allowed the Christians to flee Jerusalem and Judea.

After the reference to the *abomination* which desecrates the temple, Jesus issues several imperatives, formulated in the third person and directed at people in Judea rather than the disciples. The disciples may not be involved in these events personally, and if so, may be part of the general Judean population without having a special role to play. When people *who are in Judea* see the *abomination* that defiles the temple, they should *flee to the mountains*. Since Mark distinguishes

---

51. Marcus, p. 891; Stein, p. 604; Strauss, pp. 578–579; Breytenbach, *Nachfolge*, pp. 314–315; Balabanski, *Eschatology*, pp. 122–134.

Judea and Jerusalem (cf. 1:5; 3:7; 10:1), the admonition presupposes that Judea as a region, not only Jerusalem, is in danger. Since Judea is a mountainous region, *the mountains* seem to refer to a different mountain range, probably the mountains east of the Jordan Valley. Many link Jesus' command to flee with the tradition about the flight of Jerusalem Christians to Pella prompted by 'a certain oracle given by revelation to the approved people there' before or during the Jewish War (Eusebius, *Hist. eccl.* 3.5.3; cf. Epiphanius, *Mens.* 15).[52] Since one would expect people who lived in the unwalled towns and villages of Judea to flee into the city of Jerusalem in times of war, the exhortation to flee to the mountains implies that the city of Jerusalem is doomed. It is not only the temple that will be destroyed, but the entire city.

15–16. The imperatives in these verses reinforce the first exhortation and underline the urgency of the need to flee Jerusalem and Judea once the 'abomination' has desecrated the temple. The imperative*s Let no one on the housetop go down* and *[Let no one] enter the house* form a hendiadys, meaning 'Let no one come down for the purpose of entering the house': in order to flee, they will have to come down from the (flat) roof, but the situation is so urgent that they should not gather their belongings, which would take time and which would burden them and slow them down as they fled from the region. Similarly, if they work in a *field* outside Jerusalem, they should not return to the city in order to fetch essential gear such as a *cloak* (*himation*; cf. 5:15). When the Zealots took over the Temple Mount in the winter of AD 67/68, there was ample time to leave Jerusalem and Judea.

17–18. The phrase *in those days* refers to the time when the disciples see the 'abomination' desecrating the temple, prompting their flight from Jerusalem and from Judea. The hardship of being a refugee is particularly severe for *pregnant women* who cannot walk fast and for *nursing mothers* who need time to feed their babies. If the flight were to happen *in winter*, the colder temperatures and the wadis filled with

---

52. Accepted by Pesch, II, p. 293; Marcus, p. 891; defended by Balabanski, *Eschatology*, pp. 101–134; cf. Sowers, 'Pella Flight', pp. 305–320. Others remain sceptical: cf. Evans, p. 320; France, p. 526; Stein, p. 604.

water would make the plight of the refugees even more miserable, and there might be snow both in the Judean hills and in the hills they would be heading for. It is not clear what the command *Pray that this will not take place in winter* specifically means. Should they pray about the timing of the flight? If so, do their prayers concern others or should they expect that they will be among the refugees? Or is it the pregnant women and the nursing mothers who are called to pray? A general exhortation to prayer 'addressed to anyone whom it may concern' (France, p. 527) is plausible.

19. The phrase *those . . . days* refers to the events after the flight described in the previous verses; that is, to the war in Judea and the siege of Jerusalem. Jesus predicts that the *distress* (Gr. *thlipsis*; BDAG, p. 457: 'trouble that inflicts distress', 'oppression, affliction, tribulation') of these days will be *unequalled from the beginning, when God created the world, until now*. This comment refers to the destruction of the temple and Jerusalem, with the population suffering beyond imagination. Josephus describes the horrors of that time in lurid detail (*War* 5.242–438, 512–518, 567–572; 6.193–213). In order to 'encourage' the Jews in the city to surrender, the Romans crucified many Jews who had fled – as many as 500 a day – in front of the city walls that they ran out of wood for crosses (*War* 5.549–551). When a woman in the city had her food stolen, she was so desperate that she killed and cooked her own infant, offering half of it to defenders who had smelled cooking and demanded food (*War* 6.201–213). According to Josephus 1,100,000 Jews were killed during the siege and 97,000 were enslaved (*War* 6.420–421). Even if these figures are exaggerated, they illustrate the unspeakable intensity of suffering endured by the inhabitants of Jerusalem and the people who had sought refuge in the city. The statement that the distress of those days was *unequalled . . . until now* and *never to be equalled again* is hyperbolic language that is often used for great suffering (see Exod. 9:18; 10:14; 11:6; Deut. 4:32; Jer. 30:7; Dan 12:1; Joel 2:2 [cf. Rev. 16:18; 1 Macc. 9:27; 1QM I, 11–12; *Test. Mos.* 8:1]). The comment *never to be equalled again* points to the continuation of history: Jesus describes events connected with the destruction of the temple (cf. vv. 1–4), not the end of history.

20. People would not *survive* ('lit. 'be saved', here of physical survival) the intense suffering of the calamity that will fall on

Jerusalem *if the Lord had not cut short those days*. The idea of God 'shortening' days or 'hastening the time' is occasionally found in Jewish texts.[53] Some link the idea with Isaiah 60:21–22 and 65:8, where the threatened judgment is held back for the sake of the servants of God. The expression *the elect*, emphasized by the phrase *whom he has chosen*, refers in the Old Testament to Israel as God's covenant people,[54] and in the New Testament to the believers in Jesus as people saved by God's grace.[55] As Jesus describes events connected with the destruction of Jerusalem, *the elect* most likely refers to the Jewish Christians as the faithful 'remnant' among the people of Israel left in the city during the siege which lasted, as terrible as it was, only five months (France, p. 528; Stein, p. 607).

21–22. The description of the developments leading up to the destruction of the temple began and now ends with a warning against people who claim to be the *Messiah* (cf. v. 6). The *false messiahs* and *false prophets* are Jewish would-be leaders who will evidently appear during the war that will engulf Judea and Jerusalem and who will claim to have royal dignity and the ability to redeem Israel. In AD 66 Menahem, son of Judas of Galilee, entered Jerusalem 'as if he were really a king' and worshipped in the temple 'arrayed in royal robes' (Josephus, *War* 2.434, 444). In AD 69 Simon, son of Giora from Gerasa, gathered a strong force in the hills and became a terror to the towns; his army included serfs, brigands and 'citizen recruits, subservient to his command as to a king' (*War* 4.510). After the fall of Jerusalem, Simon was paraded in Titus' triumphal procession in Rome and subsequently executed, which suggests that the Romans saw him as a king of the Jews (*War* 7.154).

Jesus predicts that these false prophets will seek to deceive people with *signs and wonders*. Josephus relates that in the later stages of the siege of Jerusalem, prophets deluded the people by promising 'signs'

---

53. Sir. 36:10; *2 Bar.* 20:1; 54:1; 83:1; 4Q385 Frag. 3, 3–5; *Tg. Neof.* Gen. 28:10.
54. Cf. Deut. 7:6; 14:2; 1 Chr. 16:13; Pss 33:12; 105:6, 43; Isa. 41:8; 44:1; for the concept of the faithful 'remnant' cf. Isa. 42:1; 43:20; 65:9–11, 15.
55. Cf. Rom. 8:33; 16:13; Col. 3:12; 2 Tim. 2:10; Titus 1:1; 1 Peter 1:1; 2:4, 6, 9.

(*sēmeia*) of salvation, deceiving them by interpreting 'wonders' or portents (*terata*) as foretelling deliverance (*War* 6.285–300; for the terms *sēmeia* and *terata*, cf. ibid., 285, 288). If the *elect* whom they want to deceive are Jewish Christians, verse 22 could be a prophetic description of Christians who, during the siege of Jerusalem, might accept the claims of people who say that they are the returning Jesus, and who might believe false Christian prophets who predict an imminent date for Jesus' second coming (France, p. 529).

23. The command *be on your guard* ('watch out') reiterates the identical exhortations of verses 5 and 9. This is the main theme of Jesus' prediction of events leading to the destruction of the temple (vv. 1–4). The disciples must be aware of *everything* that Jesus has told them *in advance*, whether they personally will experience all or only some of the events described in verses 5–22, so that they are prepared to face the hardships that may come their way, hardships that will certainly include persecution on account of their allegiance to Jesus (vv. 9–13).

Theology

Jesus answers the disciples' question about the time of the destruction of the temple and the sign that will signal the imminence of this event with repeated warnings not to be deceived by claims of messianic pretenders and false prophets. The history of the church demonstrates that Christians have often not heeded this exhortation. The confusion about Jesus' 'eschatological discourse' in Mark 13 stems largely from the fact that so-called end-time 'specialists' do not interpret the text in its historical context but 'mine' these verses for predictions that are seen to be fulfilled in the most recent past, in the present and/or in the imminent future, often in an attempt to pinpoint the time of Jesus' second coming. The historical context forces responsible interpreters to explain Jesus' prophecy with regard to the Second Temple, whose destruction, predicted by Jesus in 13:2 (and implicitly in 11:17), is of concern to the disciples (13:4). In 13:4–23 Jesus prophesies events that will take place before the destruction of the temple, and that means events that took place during the forty years between AD 30 and 70. Jesus gives no reason for the destruction of the temple: he does not censure the Jewish leaders nor the Jewish people, and he does not link the destruction of the temple with a critique of the Jewish leaders in terms of either their corruption or their desire to kill him (11:18).[56]

c. The coming of the Son of Man (13:24–27)
Context
The second part of Jesus' discourse shifts the topic from the destruction of the temple to the new and, for Mark's readers unexpected, topic of Jesus' return. These four verses imply that after his death and resurrection predicted earlier (8:31; 9:31; 10:33–34), Jesus will leave the earth and come back at a later date. While Jesus provided signs that allowed the disciples to be prepared for the destruction of Jerusalem and the temple so as to be able to flee to safe regions (13:4–23), the timing of the return of the Son of Man will not be signalled by signs that will allow his followers to know its imminence.

Comment
24–25. The phrase *But in those days, following that distress* signals that Jesus now addresses a new subject matter, one different from the 'distress' (*thlipsis*; cf. v. 19) connected with the 'abomination' that desecrates the temple and the armed conflict in Judea and Jerusalem that the disciples are directed to avoid by fleeing into the hills (vv. 14–18). The phrase 'I have told you everything in advance' in verse 23 also signals that verse 24 begins a new section, as does the subject matter of verses 24–27, which are no longer focused on the temple, the city of Jerusalem and Judea (vv. 1–4, 14–16), local councils, synagogues, governors and kings (vv. 9–11) and whether it is winter or not (v. 18), but on the sun, the moon, the stars, the clouds, the ends of the earth and the ends of the heavens. Jesus does not indicate how much time will pass between the destruction of the temple and Jerusalem (13:1–23) and his coming at the end of the age. All that the formulation says is that 'the End is more distant in time than the events of 13:5–23' (Geddert, *Watchwords*, p. 310). The phrase *following that distress* indicates that the phrase *in those days*

---

56. The parable in 12:1–11 speaks of judgment of the tenants (Israel's leaders), not of judgment of the vineyard (Israel, or Jerusalem, if the wall around the vineyard is interpreted allegorically).

does not refer to 'those days' of verses 17, 19, the days connected with the siege of Jerusalem and the destruction of the temple, but to a time 'after' (*meta*) these events. The word *distress* or 'tribulation' is not a technical term for a 'great tribulation' immediately before Jesus' second coming, not even in Revelation 7:14 where that expression is used.

The following description parallels several Old Testament prophetic texts, especially Isaiah 13:10, 34:4 (cf. Joel 2:10, 30–31; 3:4, 15), which mention the same cosmic signs: the darkening of the *sun* and of the *moon*, the falling of the *stars* from the sky and the shaking of *the heavenly bodies*. Such language can be used of historical events: for example, the destruction of Babylon by the Medes (Isa. 13:1, 9–11, 17–19), the destruction of Jerusalem by the Babylonians (Jer. 4:11, 23–28; 15:5, 9), the destruction of Pharaoh's army (Ezek. 32:2, 7–8, 12, 18, 20) or the destruction of Samaria (Amos 8:9). Since Jesus speaks of his return in glory, the cosmic language in verses 24–25 does not describe metaphorically the destruction of Jerusalem in AD 70.

The question remains whether the description of the darkening of the sun and moon and the falling of the stars from the sky is meant to be understood in a metaphorical or a literal sense. Since the New Testament anticipates 'a new heaven and a new earth' (2 Peter 3:13; Rev. 21:1), in agreement with Isaiah 65:17, not in terms of a metaphor but in terms of new experiential reality, the cosmic terms could be meant to be understood literally – the darkening of the sun and moon returns the universe to the situation like that before the fourth day of creation (Gen. 1:14–19; Gundry, p. 782) or before the first day of creation (cf. Jer. 4:23: 'I looked at the earth, and it was formless and empty; and at the heavens, and their light was gone'; Gen. 1:2: 'Now the earth was formless and empty, darkness was over the surface of the deep'; cf. Marcus, p. 907). Alternatively, the language, while referring to a real historical event, could be metaphorical: the order of the space–time universe with seasons, days and years is dissolving, making way for the reality of the glory of the Son of Man. Jesus announces that the elements of creation that make life possible will react to his coming.

26–27. The phrase *at that time* refers to the time when the sun and moon have become dark and the stars fall from the sky. This is the time when *people will see the Son of Man coming in clouds with great power and glory*. 'Son of Man' has been Jesus' favourite self-designation (cf. 1:10–11; 8:31, 38), based on Daniel 7:13–14, where 'one like a son of man' (a human being) comes on the clouds of heaven, approaches God and receives from God 'authority, glory and sovereign power'. In 8:38 Jesus spoke of himself as the Son of Man who will come in the Father's glory with the holy angels, an allusion to the Daniel passage, as is his statement at the climax of his trial in 14:62. In Acts 1:9 Jesus, after his death and resurrection, returns to the Father in heaven (Luke 24:51) with a cloud hiding him from sight, and in Acts 1:11 angels tell the disciples that 'this same Jesus' will 'come back in the same way you have seen him go into heaven'.[57]

The details of the description of the coming of the Son of Man emphasize the awesomeness of Jesus in the future. First, *people will see* him coming – people in general (the verb *opsontai*, 'they will see', is an indefinite third person plural). Second, he will be *coming in clouds*, a divine mode of transport (9:7; 14:62; Dan. 7:13).[58] Third, he will come *with great power*, establishing the kingdom of God in power (9:1). Fourth, he will come with *glory*, sharing the glory of God himself (8:38; 10:37; cf. Ps. 8:5). Fifth, *he will send his angels*; that is, he will have authority over God's angels who will do his bidding. Sixth, he will *gather his elect from the four winds, from the ends of the earth to the ends of the heavens*, because they belong to him and because they are so numerous. When he returns, his followers will live east, west, south and north of Jerusalem and Judea, at the ends of the earth, where they have been reached with the good news (cf. Acts 1:8). Jesus' coming 'will need no heralding', in contrast to the false messiahs who need heralds to advertise their coming ('Look, here

---

57. Some scholars connect vv. 24–27 with Jesus' prophecy of the siege of Jerusalem and the destruction of the temple, and interpret vv. 26–27 in terms of the vindication of the Son of Man; cf. France, pp. 501, 530–531, 534–535; France, *Jesus and the Old Testament*, pp. 235–236; Wright, *Jesus and the Victory of God*, pp. 360–365. For a critique see Stein, pp. 613–614; Strauss, pp. 591–592.

58. Cf. Exod. 34:5; Lev. 16:2; Num. 11:25; Pss 18:12–13; 97:2; Isa. 19:1; Nah. 1:3; Rev. 1:7; 10:1; 14:14–16.

is the Messiah!', v. 21): 'It will herald itself in the heavens and across the expanse of the earth' (Gundry, p. 745). Jesus returns to gather God's people, his followers. The Old Testament theme of God gathering his people in the last days[59] is taken up in the description of Jesus gathering his followers upon his return. No details are given concerning what follows, such as the resurrection of the dead, the judgment of the wicked (8:38; Matt. 24:36–44, 45–51; 25:1–12, 31–46; Rev. 18 – 19; 20:11–15), the consummation of the kingdom or the heavenly banquet (Luke 14:15; Rev. 19:9).

Theology
One day, the order of the world with days, nights and seasons will come to an end – the day when Jesus, the heavenly Son of Man, returns with great power and glory. There are no 'signs' that allow Jesus' followers to establish the imminence of this event. Christians have been waiting for it since the first century. Even then they were mocked on account of their hope in Jesus' return and the inauguration of a new heaven and a new earth (2 Peter 3:3–4). Christians keep waiting, confident that the One who died for their sins and who rose from the dead will fulfil his promise and return bodily and visibly, delivering his people from suffering (cf. 2 Thess. 1:6–7; 1 Peter 4:13), wiping away every tear from their eyes (Rev. 7:17; 21:4), bringing back to life those who have died 'in Christ' (1 Cor. 15:22–23; 1 Thess. 4:16), giving his people imperishable bodies (1 Cor. 15:42–44, 51–54) and giving them the reward promised to those who persevere (Matt. 16:27; 2 Tim. 4:8; Heb. 9:28) – life everlasting in his presence and in the presence of God (John 14:2–3; 1 Thess. 4:17; 2 Thess. 2:1; Rev. 21:1–7, 22–23; 22:1–5; cf. Strauss, pp. 598–599). Jesus' followers can rest assured, even and especially in the midst of persecution and suffering, that their faithfulness will be rewarded. The passage also emphasizes Jesus' authority and foreknowledge as a prophet and his future glory as the glory of God: language that in the Old Testament describes theophanies, the appearances of God on earth, is used for Jesus who comes in divine glory and power.

---

59. Isa. 11:11–16; 27:12–13; 43:5–7; 49:12; 60:1–9; Pss 107:2–3; 147:2; Jer. 23:3; 31:10–12; Ezek. 11:16–17; 39:27; Neh. 1:9.

d. The consequences for disciples (13:28–37)
Context
Jesus' prophecy of the destruction of the temple (13:1–2) is followed by a discourse about the time between now (April AD 30) and the war that will lead to a fulfilment of his prophecy (13:3–23), answering the disciples' question as to the timing of the destruction of the temple and regarding a sign that will signal the imminence of this event. Then, changing the discourse from specific terms connected with Judea (13:14) to universal terms, Jesus, who earlier announced his death and resurrection several times (8:31; 9:31; 10:33–34), described his return at the end of the age (13:24–27). Jesus exhorted the disciples to 'watch out' (13:5, 9, 23) so as to be prepared for suffering and to avoid being deceived. Now, at the end of the discourse, Jesus revisits both predictions – the destruction of the temple and his return – urging the disciples to watch for the sign that will signal the imminence of the siege of Jerusalem and the destruction of the temple (the lesson of the fig-tree, 13:28–31) and to be ready for the day when Jesus returns (13:32–37).

Comment
28–29. The *fig-tree* is not the fig-tree of 11:12–14, 20–21. Jesus refers to a fig-tree in a *lesson* (*parabolē*; cf. 3:23) illustrating the significance of a sign that signals a coming event. The analogy of the fig-tree compares the visible changes in a fig-tree that sprouts new leaves in spring signalling the arrival of summer to the sign of the 'abomination' that desolates the temple (v. 14), signalling the destruction of the temple and Jerusalem (vv. 2, 19–20). In late March/April, the fig-tree's *twigs get tender and its leaves come out* (see on 11:12), signalling the coming *summer* when the mature figs become ready for harvest, which starts in August (the early harvest of the first-ripe figs in May/June is not in view). The appearance of the leaves announces that the summer will follow.

In a similar manner, when the disciples *see these things happening*, they will *know* that *it is near, right at the door*. The phrase *these things* (*tauta*) refers back to the phrase 'these things' (*tauta*) in verse 4 which refers to the destruction of the temple predicted by Jesus in verse 2. And the phrase 'all these things' (*tauta panta*) in verse 30 refers to 'all these things' (*tauta panta*) in verse 4. The sequence 'these things . . .

all these things' in verses 29–30 follows the order of 'these things ... all these things' in verse 4. The lesson of the fig-tree relates to the destruction of the temple and Jerusalem (rather than to Jesus' second coming). This is confirmed by the phrase *when you see* (Gr. *hotan idēte*) which reiterates the same expression in verse 14 that speaks of seeing the 'abomination' that desecrates the temple – the sign that the destruction of the temple that Jesus predicted is coming soon, signalling that the disciples should leave the city and indeed Judea. Just as the new leaves of a fig-tree signal that summer is near, so the 'abomination' that desecrates the temple is a sign that the destruction of the temple and Jerusalem is imminent and that it is time to leave Judea.

30. The authoritative significance of the following pronouncement is underlined by the expression *Truly I tell you* (cf. 3:28). In the context of the disciples' question 'When?' (v. 4), the word *generation* (*genea*) here has a temporal meaning (BDAG, p. 191, meaning 2: 'the sum total of those born at the same time, expanded to include all those living at a given time'). *This generation* means the people alive when Jesus is speaking (in AD 30), many of whom will still be alive in AD 67/68 when the Zealots establish themselves in the temple, desecrating both the temple and the high priesthood (cf. v. 14).[60] In 8:12, 38, the term 'generation' also refers to Jesus' contemporaries. The phrase *all these things*, following the phrase 'these things' in verse 29, picks up the phrases 'these things' and 'all these things' in verse 4 in the disciples' question about the destruction of the temple that Jesus predicted in verse 2. Jesus announces that the generation of his contemporaries will not die out before the 'abomination' that desecrates the temple has been seen and before the temple and the city are destroyed. People of the same age as Jesus would be about seventy years old in AD 67/68. Jesus' prediction in verse 30 turned out to be correct: the destruction of the temple and Jerusalem took place within a lifetime.

---

60. To reckon that a biblical generation is forty years and to point to the forty years between Jesus' prediction in AD 30 and the temple's destruction in AD 70 (mis)understands the phrase 'this generation' to refer to the *next* generation.

Jesus' pronouncement in verse 30 poses problems only if the expression *all these things* is related to Jesus' second coming predicted in verses 24–27. This interpretation is implausible, however: if verses 29–30 are connected with anything subsequent to the destruction of the temple, which happened in AD 70, Jesus' lesson would be useless as a response to the disciples' question concerning the destruction of the temple (v. 4; France, p. 538). If *all these things* is connected with the 'signs' of verses 5–13, and particularly with the visible 'sign' of the 'abomination' that desecrates the temple (v. 14) that signals the imminence of the fulfilment of Jesus' prophecy of the temple's destruction, the phrase *this generation* has its usual meaning (and does not need to be interpreted in the sense of 'race' – the Jewish race was not in any danger of extinction in the first century).

31. Jesus affirms the truthfulness of his pronouncement in verse 30 and thus the truthfulness of the discourse on the destruction of the temple and Jerusalem (vv. 5–23) with the statement *my words will never pass away*. The contrast with *heaven and earth* that will one day pass away to make room for a new heaven and a new earth (Isa. 65:17; 2 Peter 3:13; Rev. 21:1) is striking. The words of Jesus, the Messiah and Son of God (1:1), the heavenly Son of Man (13:26), are more enduring than creation itself, a statement that implies divine dignity. Like the word of God (Matt. 5:18; Luke 16:17), Jesus' words are eternal. Mark's readers would have understood Jesus' statement to apply beyond verse 30 and beyond the discourse in chapter 13, to the totality of Jesus' teaching.

32. The opening phrase *but about* signals a change of subject. The phrases *that day* and *that . . . hour* are introduced for the first time. The plural '(those) days' has been used in verses 17, 19, 20 to describe the siege of Jerusalem and in verse 24 the time after the destruction of Jerusalem, but no singular 'day' has been mentioned. The statement *no one knows* contrasts strongly with the certainty of Jesus' pronouncement in verse 30 regarding the time within which his prediction of the destruction of the temple and Jerusalem will occur. The *day* and *hour* that no one knows is the date of the coming of the Son of Man described in verse 24–27. The phrase *that day* refers to the day of judgment (cf. Matt. 7:22; Luke 10:12; 2 Tim. 1:12, 18; 4:8), as does the phrase 'the Day' in 1 Corinthians 3:13. In the Old Testament the phrase 'that day' is a standard reference to the 'day of the Lord' or judgment day.[61] In the context of the return of the Son of Man in verses 26–27 and the return of the owner of the house in verses 34–36, *that day* refers to the day of Jesus' return. While the time of the siege of Jerusalem is signalled by the 'abomination' that desecrates the temple (v. 14, illustrated in the lesson of the fig-tree in vv. 28–29), the time of Jesus' return is unknown.

The phrase *no one knows* is explained as including *even the angels in heaven*, who are in God's presence, and even *the Son*, Jesus himself. For Jesus referring to himself as 'the Son' without qualification see 12:6 and Matthew 11:27/Luke 10:22.[62] Jesus 'the Son' is 'closest to God and thus can represent him' (France, p. 543). Since God knows everything, including the future (Isa. 46:10; Zech. 14:7; cf. *2 Bar.* 21:8; *Pss Sol.* 17:21), *the Father* knows the date of the Son's return. The point of the statement that Jesus does not know the date of his return is, in context, not Jesus' humanity but his heavenly status: in the heavenly hierarchy the Son is higher than the angels, possibly implying Jesus' pre-existence. Yet he does not know the date of his return. Mark evidently did not regard this 'confession of ignorance' to be embarrassing; perhaps, if asked about the meaning of the statement, he would have answered that divine attributes such as omniscience should not be assumed for Jesus' human existence (thus later Christological arguments; France, p. 544). The point is that Jesus' followers must be ready at all times, which is emphasized in the following verses.

33. In verses 5, 23, the exhortation 'be on your guard' or 'watch out' (Gr. *blepete*) was an admonition not to be deceived by people who claim to be able to announce future events. In verse 9 the exhortation was a call to prepare to face suffering. Here the command is a summons to vigilance, an exhortation to 'keep your eyes open' (BDAG, p. 179 meaning 6), a call directing attention to the fact that nobody knows the date of Jesus' return. The second imperative, *Be alert!* (or 'don't fall asleep'), is a call 'to be vigilant in awareness of

---

61. Joel 3:18; Amos 8:3, 9, 13; 9:11; Obad. 8; Mic. 4:6; Zeph. 1:9–10; 3:11, 16; Zech. 9:16.
62. Cf. John 3:17, 35–36; 5:19–23, 26; 6:40; 8:35–36; 14:13; 17:1.

threatening peril' (BDAG, p. 16). The danger is to be caught unprepared in view of the fact that *you do not know when that time will come*. To be prepared for Jesus' second coming means for Jesus' followers to make sure that they are not deceived by false messiahs and false prophets (vv. 5, 21–23) and to follow Jesus on the way of the cross, 'losing' their lives for Jesus and for the gospel which guarantees their salvation (8:34–38).

34–36. The phrase *like a man* introduces a parable which reinforces the exhortation to watchfulness in verse 33, leading to a similar exhortation in verse 35. The parable describes a *man* who *leaves his house* as he is *going away* on a journey, which might be a short visit or an extended absence. He puts his *slaves* (*douloi*, NRSV; see on 12:2) *in charge*, giving them the 'authority' (*exousia*) to make decisions with respect to the *task* (*ergon*) assigned to each, telling the doorkeeper (*thyrōros*) to keep watch. It was the task of the doorkeeper to exclude unwanted visitors and to admit those who were welcome, including the master himself, letting them enter the house through the doors which were locked from the inside (cf. Luke 12:36). Dereliction of duty might have grave consequences for the people living in the house (cf. 2 Sam. 4:6–7; Esth. 2:21). The doorkeeper has to stay alert at all times since he does *not know when the owner of the house will come back*: he could return later in the *evening*, at *midnight*, *when the rooster crows* or at *dawn*. Mark mentions the four watches of the night of three hours each according to the Roman system. The names of the watches (*vigiliae*; details of Latin terminology vary) are 'late' or 'evening' (Gr. *opse*; Lat. *prima nox* or *intempesta nox*, 6–9 pm); 'midnight' (*mesonyktion*; Lat. *media nox*, 9 pm–midnight); that is, ending at midnight; 'cock-crow' (*alektorophōnia*; Lat. *gallicinium*, midnight–3 am), referring to the crowing of a cock at the end of the third watch, shortly before first light, 'which was used as an important indication of time during the hours of darkness, marking the time at which most people woke up and got up in preparation for beginning work as soon as there was sufficient light';[63] and 'early' or 'morning' (*prōi*; Lat. *conticinium*, *mane*, 3–6 am).

---

63. Cf. Bauckham, *Jewish World*, pp. 412–414; quotation p. 414.

Since the master might come *suddenly* (*exaiphnēs*), with very little time between his being seen on the road approaching the house and his standing in front of the door, the doorkeeper would have to stay awake at his post throughout all four watches. Since travelling at night was precarious, the master would be most plausibly expected to return in the evening, during the first watch, shortly after sundown when it was still possible to see the road; or after first light, during the fourth watch when sunlight made travel possible again. The imperative *keep watch* (*grēgoreite*), formulated in the second person plural even though in the story it concerns only the one doorkeeper, effectively draws Jesus' listeners (and Mark's readers) into the story, highlighting the focus of the application for the listeners.

The parable has several points of analogy: the master of the house who leaves is the risen Jesus after his death and resurrection (predicted in 8:31; 9:31; 10:33–34). The slaves are Jesus' followers, who are on duty between his going away and his coming back; in the context of verses 9–13 their main tasks are preaching the good news and enduring under persecution. The doorkeeper is one of the slaves. Since his task was to protect the property of the master, and considering the imperative in verse 35, his task may correspond to the warnings against false messiahs and false prophets (vv. 5–6, 21–23), and may point to the leaders of the community represented by the four disciples mentioned by name in verse 3 who must be alert to unmask the prophecies and pretensions of false prophets and thus prevent the deception of the community of Jesus' followers (Collins, p. 618). The return of the master is the coming of the Son of Man in the clouds (v. 26). The reference to all four watches, including the second and third watches when people avoided travel, underlines the fact that Jesus' return may happen when it is least expected, and emphasizes that Jesus' followers are always 'on duty': they must always, constantly, be alert, prepared for Jesus' sudden, unexpected return.

37. Jesus widens his final exhortation *Watch!* (*grēgoreite*) from being addressed to *you*, the four disciples mentioned in verse 3, to all disciples and to *everyone* or 'all' (*pantes*), each and every one of his followers (cf. Luke 12:41). The question of the timing of the destruction of the temple (v. 4) is directly relevant only to a limited audience, while the return of Jesus which will happen some time after the destruction of Jerusalem concerns all followers of Jesus wherever they live on the face of the earth (v. 27), including the Gentile believers (v. 10).

Theology

Jesus' disciples have been given a sign that allows them to anticipate the destruction of the temple and, by fleeing from Judea, escape the intense distress that will accompany this event. The appearance of the 'abomination' that desecrates the temple (v. 14) is like the twigs of a fig-tree that become green in the spring, signalling that summer is close. As regards Jesus' return, which will happen some time after the destruction of the temple, the disciples are given no clues. On the contrary, they are told in no uncertain terms that, with the exception of God himself, nobody knows the date and time of Jesus' second coming, not now and not ever (cf. Acts 1:6–7). Jesus tells his disciples to be vigilant (vv. 33–35, 37), an exhortation that is necessary because there are no signs that allow them to calculate the nearness of the end. Christians live in eager anticipation of Jesus' return (1 Thess. 4:13–18; 2 Tim. 4:8; Titus 2:11–14), praying *marana tha*, 'Lord, come' (1 Cor. 16:22; Rev. 22:10), and *your kingdom come* (Matt. 6:10), and carrying out the tasks that the Master has given to each believer in such a manner that the sudden return of the Master will not catch them unprepared.

C. The suffering and death of Jesus Messiah (14:1 – 15:47)

In the third section on Jesus' messianic suffering (8:22 – 15:47), Mark reports the events of the last two days of Jesus' earthly life in seven subsections: the preparations for Jesus' arrest (14:1–11); Jesus' last supper with his disciples (14:12–31); Jesus on the Mount of Olives in Gethsemane, where he is arrested (14:32–52); Jesus' trial before the Sanhedrin, with its climax of Jesus' declaration that he is the Messiah, the Son of God, the Son of Man enthroned at the right hand of God, which leads to the pronouncement of a death sentence (14:53–72); Jesus' trial before Pontius Pilate (15:1–20); Jesus' crucifixion (15:21–32); and Jesus' death and burial (15:33–47). Though Mark largely reports what other people do to Jesus, it is the sovereign purpose of God that holds the narrative together (cf. 14:18, 21,

22–24, 28, 36, 48–49, 61–62; 15:2, 39). The chronology of these days can be set out as follows, accepting AD 30 as the most plausible date for Jesus' crucifixion.[64]

arrest plot	14:1	Thursday (13 Nisan, 6 April)
preparations	14:1–11	Thursday early evening (13 Nisan)
Last Supper	14:12–25	Thursday evening (14 Nisan, 7 April)
Gethsemane	14:26–42	Thursday late evening (14 Nisan)
arrest	14:43–52	Thursday late evening (14 Nisan)
Jewish trial	14:53–72	Thursday night, Friday early morning (14 Nisan)
Roman trial	15:1–20	Friday morning (14 Nisan, 8 April)
crucifixion	15:21–39	Friday late morning, afternoon (14 Nisan)
burial	15:40–47	Friday before sundown (14 Nisan)

i. The preparations for Jesus' arrest (14:1–11)

Context

The preparations for Jesus' arrest involve three groups: the chief priests and the scribes who plot Jesus' arrest (14:1–2), a woman who anoints the feet of Jesus, interpreted as preparation for Jesus' burial (14:3–9), and Judas Iscariot, who betrays Jesus' (14:10–11). The devotion of the woman to Jesus stands in stark contrast to the plans of the religious leaders and the actions of one of Jesus' disciples.

Comment

a. The scheme to arrest Jesus (14:1–2)

This brief section sets the scene for the following events. Mark provides a date for when the events are set in motion leading to Jesus' arrest, trial and conviction. It is significant that this is the first reference in Mark to a specific time of year or a specific Jewish festival (the only other time reference earlier in Mark's account is in 9:2), and it is significant that this is Passover. Mark mentions the two groups responsible for Jesus' arrest: the chief priests and scribes.

1. The *Passover* (*to pascha*; Aramaic *pasha'*; Hebr. *pesaḥ*, rendered as *phasek* or *phasech* in the LXX) was the annual Israelite festival that commemorated Israel's rescue from slavery in Egypt, specifically the tenth plague in which the firstborn sons of the Egyptians were

---

64. On the date of Jesus' crucifixion cf. Riesner, *Chronology*, pp. 35–58.

killed, while the firstborn sons of the Hebrews were spared on account of the sacrifice of a lamb whose blood had been smeared on the doorposts and lintels of their houses (Exod. 11:1 – 13:22; Num. 9:2–14; Deut. 16:1–8). Passover was celebrated on the 14th/15th of the month of Nisan (April/May). The lambs for the Passover meal were slaughtered in the temple during the afternoon of 14 Nisan. After sunset, which according to the Jewish calendar marked the beginning of Nisan 15, the Passover meal was eaten in the homes. The *Festival of Unleavened Bread* (*ta azyma*; Hebr. *maṣôt*), originally a separate festival, followed directly after Passover and lasted seven days (Nisan 15–21), and commemorated Israel's exodus from Egypt when the Israelites ate unleavened bread during their deliverance (cf. Exod. 12:15; Num. 28:16–17). These holidays of eight days could be referred to as *to pascha* or as *ta azyma*; the use of the two terms together is more precise. The chronological reference *two days away* is most plausibly reckoned inclusively, indicating that the day in question was 13 Nisan (Wednesday 6 pm to Thursday 6 pm, 6/7 April AD 30).

On the *chief priests* see 8:31; on the *teachers of the law* see 1:22. They appeared together in two of Jesus' predictions of his arrest and execution (8:31; 10:33), and they are mentioned as the two groups plotting Jesus' death after his prophetic demonstration in the temple (11:18). The religious and political elite had already decided that Jesus must be killed (11:18 used the word *apollymi*, 'destroy'; in 14:1 the word *apokteinō*, 'kill', is used, as in 8:31; 9:31; 10:34; 12:7–8). Now they *were looking for a way* (NRSV; Gr. *zēteō* means here 'investigate, examine, consider, deliberate') to *arrest* Jesus. The imperfect tense of the verb suggests extended deliberations. The fact that they plan Jesus' arrest very carefully indicates that they envisage a trial which will lead to a conviction on a capital charge, guaranteeing Jesus' execution. They don't attempt to organize a lynch killing, nor do they plan a violent vigilante action. The Jewish elite seems to have acted out of a sense of judicial fairness: the law prohibited extrajudicial killings. Alternatively, they may have made the strategic calculation that a legal execution of Jesus would squash the movement he had set in motion.

Once they decided to arrest Jesus and put him on trial, they knew they had to proceed *by stealth* (NASB, NRSV; NIV 'secretly'; *dolos* means 'taking advantage through craft and underhanded methods' and can be translated as 'deceit, cunning, treachery'; BDAG, p. 256). The authorities apparently regard Jesus as a *mesît* and *maddiaḥ*, whose prosecution allows entrapment, which is otherwise prohibited (*m. Sanh.* 7:10); see Context for 14:53–72.

2. The reason why the Jewish leaders do not arrest Jesus in public is Jesus' popularity and a history of disturbances on the Temple Mount during Passover (cf. Josephus, *Ant.* 17.213–215; 20.105–112; *War* 2.224–227). The fact that Jesus, who enjoyed immense popularity in Galilee and beyond, was in Jerusalem meant that Passover week would have been regarded as more worrisome than usual by the Jerusalem authorities. The population of Jerusalem, estimated at around 60,000 to 70,000 (see on 1:5), swelled during the major festivals to perhaps 300,000 to 500,000 people,[65] which made it next to impossible to control the crowds. The report of Jesus' welcome when he approached the city (11:1–11) and the popular support among Galilean pilgrims and the crowds in Jerusalem before the festival (11:18, 32; 12:12, 37) made a *riot* (Gr. *thorybos*, *LSJ*, p. 803: 'the confused noise of a crowded assembly, uproar, clamour') a serious possibility if they arrested Jesus in public. When Judas Iscariot offered to give them information about Jesus' whereabouts (14:10–11), this was the 'stealth' they had been looking for.

b. The anointing at Bethany (14:3–9)

Mark's account of the deliberations of Jesus' enemies, who plan his arrest (14:1–2), continues with the betrayal of Judas, who offers to help the chief priests (14:10–11). Sandwiched between these two passages is the account of Jesus' anointing by a woman which Jesus interprets as preparation for his burial (14:8). Jesus thus confirms his earlier predictions of his arrest and death (8:31; 9:31; 10:32–34), and Mark's readers are told that the plan to arrest Jesus will succeed, leading to Jesus' execution and burial. If we accept that the woman's action was meant to signal Jesus' messianic status and mission, then this is the third event – after Jesus' triumphal approach to

---

65. Cf. Sanders, *Figure*, pp. 125–127. Josephus' figure of 3,000,000 pilgrims in Jerusalem at Passover in AD 64 (*War* 2.280) seems exaggerated.

Jerusalem and his prophetic action in the temple – that underlines that mission and that motivates the Jewish leaders to act. On the timing of the anointing, see p. 260.

3. Since Jesus and the disciples stayed in *Bethany*, located on the eastern slope of the Mount of Olives, the first night after his arrival in Jerusalem (11:11–12), it can be assumed that they spend all nights in Bethany during this week. The phrase *reclining at the table* signals dining in the context of a banquet (cf. 2:15). *Simon* may be the (deceased?) father of Lazarus, Martha and Mary (cf. John 12:1–3). He had the nickname *the Leper* (*ho lepros*; cf. 1:40) since, presumably, he had had a skin disease and was cured, presumably by Jesus. If he had been a leper at the time of Jesus' stay in Bethany, he could not have entertained people in his home. Since Simon was the most common Jewish name (see on 1:16), the description *the Leper* stuck with him as a useful nickname; or perhaps he never had leprosy but resembled a leper in some way. The *woman* who anoints Jesus is not named by Mark, despite Jesus' comment that what she did would be told 'in memory of her' wherever the gospel was preached (v. 9). Between AD 30 and 50 when the passion narrative took shape, or when Mark wrote his Gospel, 'the woman would have been in danger were she identified as having been complicit in Jesus' politically subversive claim to messianic kingship'.[1] When John writes, at a later date, he has the freedom to mention her name (John 12:3: Mary, the sister of Martha) since she no longer needed the anonymity.

An *alabaster jar* (Gr. *alabastros*; also a loanword in Latin) was 'a vase for holding perfume/ointment, often made of alabaster'. The stone referred to as *alabaster* is onyx-marble, known as Egyptian alabaster or Oriental alabaster, a limestone with swirling bands of cream and brown admired as a decorative stone. Mark describes the content of the alabaster jar with four terms. *Myron* refers to fragrant ointment or *perfume*. *Nardos* indicates that the perfume was made from the aromatic oil of the spikenard plant; nard was imported from India, but it was also produced in Italy, and Corinth specialized in the

---

[1]. Bauckham, *Eyewitnesses*, p. 190; on Simon, p. 81. For the concept of 'protective anonymity' see Theißen, *Gospels*, pp. 186–189.

production and export of fragrant oils.[2] Most ancient perfumes were based on oils derived from plants, unlike modern perfumes which are alcohol-based, and thus were thicker than modern perfumes. The word *pistikos* means 'genuine, unadulterated' (Pliny, *Nat.* 12.26.12: 'Pure nard is distinguished by its lightness, its reddish-brown colour, the sweetness of its fragrance, its pleasant flavour'). The term *polytelēs* means 'very expensive, costly'; in verse 5 the value of the perfume is specified.

The woman *broke the jar*, that is, the neck of the jar, rather than pouring the perfume, which was technically not necessary. It was a dramatic gesture which demonstrated the woman's unreserved devotion to Jesus, holding nothing back. Jesus' anointing would probably have been understood to have messianic significance,[3] and it is conceivable that the woman planned the anointing 'in association with others, who may have thought it best to take Jesus by surprise and so encourage him to undertake the messianic role about which he may have seemed to them very ambivalent'.[4] It would have been very surprising for a woman to anoint the messianic king; she may have been seen in the role of a prophet recognizing God's Anointed One (cf. 1 Sam. 16:1–13). Since anointing the head was not uncommon at banquets, recognizing the messianic significance of the action depended on the context – Bartimaeus' public designation of Jesus as 'Son of David', Jesus' triumphal approach to Jerusalem and his actions in the temple. The dinner guests who object to the waste do not recognize the messianic meaning. That Jesus interprets the woman's action in terms of his burial does not rule out messianic significance: since Jesus had linked Peter's messianic declaration with his death (8:29, 31), he would have recognized the messianic significance while emphasizing the nature of his messianic mission as involving suffering and death. Both the arrest plot of the Jewish

---

2. Cf. *Navigation of the Erythraean Sea* 49; Pliny, *Nat.* 13.18, 21, 135.
3. Evans, p. 360; Hooker, p. 328; Garland, p. 516; Bauckham, *Eyewitnesses*, pp. 190–192; cf. Collins, p. 642. For the anointment of kings cf. 1 Sam. 10:1; 16:1, 13; 1 Kgs 1:39; 19:15–16; 2 Kgs 9:3, 6; Ps. 89:20.
4. Bauckham, *Eyewitnesses*, p. 191; for the following points see ibid., pp. 191–192.

authorities (14:1–2) and the betrayal of Judas, who visits the chief priests (14:10–11) – the two actions before and after the account of Jesus' anointing – point to the messianic significance of Jesus' anointing. Jesus' reaffirmation of his messianic role as a mission that involved his death might have led to Judas' defection.

4–5. The woman's action provoked criticism. Mark speaks of *some*, referring to other dinner guests, while Matthew 26:8 identifies them collectively as 'the disciples' and John 12:4–6 speaks specifically of Judas Iscariot, noting that Judas' real concerns were not the poor but taking money from the money bag. The attitude of the critics is expressed with strong language: they spoke *in anger* (NRSV); they were indignant against what they thought was highly problematic behaviour. They characterize the woman's action as a *waste*, and they *rebuked her harshly*, expressing their anger and displeasure when they speak with the woman in a tirade of some length (*enebrimōnto* is imperfect tense). The critics seem to know which perfume ointment was used; at least, they claim to know that the alabaster jar with the nard could have been sold *for more than three hundred denarii* (NRSV), which is fifty weeks' or about a year's wages (cf. Matt. 20:2). In light of what Jesus had said to the rich man in 10:21, the critics are right: the alabaster jar and its contents could have been sold and *the money given to the poor*, particularly since it was a custom to give gifts to the poor on the evening of Passover (cf. John 13:29; *m. Pes.* 9:11–10:1).

6–7. Jesus defends the woman's actions. He commands her critics to *leave her alone*, to stop denouncing her for what she has done. He asks *why* they are *bothering her* in the first place, implying that they should have understood the woman's action. Then he states that *she has done a beautiful thing to me* (NRSV: 'she has performed a good service for me'; lit. 'she has worked a good work'). Jesus then comments on the suggestion that the perfume could have been sold and the proceeds given to the poor: they can *help* the poor *any time* they want because *the poor you will always have with you*. The opportunity to help the poor, which was mandated by the law (Deut. 15:1–11), will not go away. The woman's action is an exception, prompted by the fact that *you will not always have me*: his death, predicted in 8:31, 9:31, 10:32–34, is imminent. This is another, implicit, passion prediction. Jesus' statement is shocking only if the focus is on the poor rather than on Jesus. Jesus' imminent death, which is an integral part of his mission (cf. 10:45), is unique and significant and warrants the extravagant action of the woman which is not a waste of resources but an appropriate response to Jesus' messianic mission. Indeed, 'the poor can wait; something more vital is taking place, and the woman has proved more sensitive to it than even Jesus' closest companions' (France, p. 551).

8. Jesus declares that the woman *did what she could*. Since the woman had the perfume in her possession, to use it to anoint Jesus was the one unique action she was able to perform. The best thing she could do with the expensive perfume ointment was to anoint Jesus, which could be understood as an act of love from all her heart, soul, mind and strength (12:30; Stein, p. 635), but which is also, more plausibly, connected with the messianic mission of Jesus which the woman seems to have perceived (and which Mark's readers would certainly understand). Jesus interprets the anointing as preparation for his imminent death: *she poured perfume on my body beforehand to prepare for my burial*. The reference to *body* may imply that the woman anointed not only Jesus' head, but his feet as well (John 12:3). The reference to his *burial* (*entaphismos*) is another implicit passion prediction. If the woman anointed Jesus in order to highlight publicly his messianic mission, which seems likely, Jesus is asserting, as he did in 8:29, 31, that his mission as Israel's Messiah is integrally linked with his suffering and death and thus with his burial.

9. Jesus concludes with the authoritative pronouncement *Truly I tell you* (cf. 3:28) that the woman's action will be remembered *in memory of her*. Mary's action was honourable and uniquely significant, which is the reason why it is remembered in the tradition of the early church. It is telling that Jesus speaks of a memorial not for himself but for the woman who has anointed him, which implicitly points to the fact that 'the burial of Jesus will not be an end but a beginning. He will not require a memorial, because he will not remain dead, and the power that his resurrection will unleash in the cosmos will transform the deeds of those who serve him . . . in the worldwide triumph of the good news' (Marcus, p. 942). The *gospel* (*euangelion*, cf. 1:1) is here not the message preached *by* Jesus but the message *about* Jesus, here especially the message about his death and burial. Jesus declares that his death and burial is 'good news', part of God's redemptive purposes. Jesus affirms again – following the resurrection predictions in 8:31; 9:31; 10:32–34 – that the good news that his disciples will preach will not only explain the significance of his death: it will also proclaim his resurrection. The proclamation of the gospel that Jesus envisions is no longer limited to Galilee, or to Judea and Jerusalem, but extends to *the whole world* (NRSV *eis holon ton kosmon*), indeed to 'all nations' (*panta ta ethnē*, 13:10).

c. The betrayal by Judas Iscariot (14:10–11)

The account of the betrayal of Jesus by Judas, who contacts the chief priests, informing them of his willingness to inform on Jesus and his movements, forms an *inclusio* with the account of the arrest plot discussed by the chief priests and scribes (14:1–2). Mary's messianic action of anointing Jesus, interpreted by Jesus as pointing to his death and burial, seems to have prompted Judas to betray Jesus, setting in motion the events that will lead to Jesus' trial and execution.

10. Mark reminds his readers that *Judas Iscariot* had been mentioned with the rest of Jesus' disciples in the list of the *Twelve* (cf. 3:19). The group of the Twelve was selected by Jesus from a larger group of disciples (3:14, 16) and was trained, taught and sent out on a mission through Galilee by him (6:7; 9:35; 10:32; 11:11). Judas, who had spent the last three years with Jesus and the other eleven disciples, *went off* (NASB), an expression that at a historical level describes his departure from the group to seek out the chief priests; in terms of Judas' biography and in the context of theological considerations, it connotes apostasy. Judas goes over to Jesus' opponents, whose intentions he is clearly aware of – according to John 11:57 Jesus had been officially declared a 'wanted man' – in order *to betray Jesus*: to help with arrangements that would allow the *chief priests* (cf. 8:31) to take Jesus into custody. The verb *paradidōmi* means 'hand over, deliver' and is used here in the technical sense of 'hand over into the custody of' the police or the courts.

Some have suggested on the basis of the verb *paradidōmi* that Judas was an honest disciple who wanted to arrange a meeting between Jesus and the high priest in order to promote a constructive dialogue, allowing Jesus to rebuke the high priest directly, perhaps questioning Jesus about his faithfulness to his mission; others have suggested that Judas believed Jesus to be the messianic deliverer and he wanted to assist Jesus in offering himself as a ransom for many.[5] Some have suggested that Judas was a Zealot and hoped to force Jesus to act when he faced arrest, finally becoming the political messiah he, Judas, hoped for. Such views are contradicted by the strongly negative portrayal of Judas in all Gospel accounts, and in particular by Jesus' pronouncement in Mark 14:21. Mark does not mention a motive: he merely relates that Judas gave Jesus up to those who were determined to kill him (11:18; 14:1). Money is mentioned only after Judas went to the chief priests. Matthew specifically mentions greed as motivation (Matt. 26:14–15). Luke refers to Satan entering Judas (Luke 22:3). John refers to greed and satanic influence (John 13:2, 27). Some have suggested that Judas had become disillusioned: he had joined Jesus because he longed for the appearance of the kingdom of God, and now he realized that the ruling priests did not welcome Jesus but opposed him, while Jesus was talking of martyrdom (Evans, p. 366); he was finally swayed perhaps by the accusation that Jesus was a lawbreaker and blasphemer (Hurtado, p. 230).

11. The chief priests *were delighted* when they *heard* (NRSV). The verb *heard* has no object in the Greek sentence; Mark leaves it to his readers to supply the information from the context, which suggests two possibilities. The context of the arrest plot in verses 1–2 suggests that what Judas betrayed to the Jewish leaders was *how* Jesus could be arrested with stealth while he was separated from the festival crowds (Stein, p. 637). The messianic anointing of the woman suggests that Judas may also have provided the chief priests with material information: Jesus had not publicly asserted that he was the messianic king, but in private such language had been used more openly (8:29), and Judas would have been able 'to fill out a dossier of Jesus' words and actions which could be used against him at his trial, to prove that the incautious words of his followers (11:9–10) had not been unfounded' (France, p. 557; cf. Evans, p. 365). The

---

5. Cf. Klassen, *Judas*, pp. 62–76. The apocryphal *Gospel of Judas* (third/fourth century) portrays Judas as an agent in the divine plan acting on Jesus' orders.

chief priests promise Judas *money* once he provides the information on Jesus' whereabouts. According to Matthew 26:15, Judas received thirty pieces of silver, a month's wages. Mark mentions the money not as Judas' motivation but as sealing the agreement. Judas is a paid informer. He *began to look for an opportunity* (NRSV), for a 'convenient' (*eukairōs*) time and place when Jesus could be arrested. Once he knew that Jesus would spend the night after the Passover meal in Gethsemane on the Mount of Olives, he arranged for an arrest party (v. 43).

Theology
The three passages in 14:1–11 delineate the two main responses to Jesus in stark contrast: the chief priests want to arrest, try and execute Jesus, with one of the Twelve assisting them, while a woman disciple sacrifices a costly perfume to anoint Jesus as an act of total devotion, implicitly (or explicitly) acknowledging Jesus' messianic mission. The chief priests act out of calculations of political expediency, Judas perhaps out of disillusionment. The woman acts out of love and humility. Jesus' comment on the woman's action highlights the relative place of social action: helping the poor is important, and it is never merely optional, but it takes second place to devotion to Jesus and support for his mission.

ii. The Last Supper (14:12–31)
Context
The final phase of the Jerusalem visit begins with the last meal that Jesus and the disciples share together. As Passover is celebrated among families, Jesus celebrates a meal with his disciples, his new family (3:34–35), the first of whom he had called on the shores of the Lake of Galilee (1:16–20) and with whom he had travelled and lived for the last three years. The timing of the meal (v. 12), the detailed instructions for the preparation of the meal (vv. 12–16), Jesus' prediction of being betrayed (vv. 17–21) and his interpretation of the meal (vv. 22–25) signal that this is not a traditional Passover meal but an event that symbolizes the redemption of Jesus' followers as the effect of Jesus' death.

The nature of Jesus' last meal with the disciples has occasioned much discussion on account of the fact that John's chronology presupposes that the Passover meal had not yet been eaten in Jerusalem when Jesus was tried by Pontius Pilate (John 13:1; 18:28; 19:14). The Passover meal was traditionally eaten on the evening which began 15 Nisan, after Jesus' crucifixion which happened as the lambs were being slaughtered in the temple on 14 Nisan. Mark implies that Jesus ate a Passover meal a day earlier (Mark 14:12, 14, 16), on the evening which began 14 Nisan. Both rabbinic evidence (*b. Sanh.* 43a: Jesus died 'on the eve of Passover') and astronomical evidence confirm John's chronology (Friday is required by John's chronology, and in AD 30,[6] 15 Nisan fell on a Saturday, while Friday fell on 14 Nisan). Thus, the Last Supper took place on Thursday evening (14 Nisan, beginning at sunset), a day in advance of the official Passover festival. At the same time, the evidence is overwhelming that the meal that Jesus celebrated with the disciples was a Passover meal.[7] The fact that Jesus celebrated a Passover meal on 14 Nisan, one day in advance of the official Passover (15 Nisan), with the Passover lambs being slaughtered in the temple later, during the afternoon of 14 Nisan, has been explained by some in terms of calendar differences (the Essenes followed the solar calendar, in contrast to the traditional lunar calendar; they would have eaten the Passover meal on Tuesday evening; this is not very plausible).[8] Others point out that premature sacrifices of Passover lambs in the temple did take place in Jerusalem on 13 Nisan before AD 70 due to the overwhelming number of pilgrims in the city (*m. Zeb.* 1:1, 3),[9] which would allow Jesus to eat Passover on 14 Nissan. And it is worth noting that 14:12 does not necessarily give 15 Nisan as the date of Jesus' last supper: it plausibly refers to the preparation of the meal taking place on the day when the Passover lambs are sacrificed – after sunset on Thursday when 14 Nisan began, on the evening *before* the lambs were slaughtered on Friday afternoon, which concluded 14 Nisan (France, p. 561; Strauss, p. 619).

---

6. Also in AD 33, which some scholars prefer as the year of Jesus' crucifixion.

7. Jeremias, *Words*, pp. 51–62; Marshall, *Supper*, pp. 57–75.

8. Jaubert, *Date*; cf. Marshall, *Supper*, pp. 74–75.

9. Casey, *Sources*, p. 224; Instone-Brewer, 'Sources', p. 295.

Comment

a. Preparation for the Last Supper (14:12–16)

12. The chronological marker *on the first day of the Festival of Unleavened Bread*, in the context of the sentence *when it was customary to sacrifice the Passover lamb*, refers to 14 Nisan, the first day of the entire festival 'Passover-with-unleavened bread' (cf. Josephus, *War* 5.99). The second phrase explains the first phrase: the priests sacrificed the Passover lambs in the temple on the first day of the festival, on the afternoon which concluded 14 Nisan, after the events of verses 12–16. When the disciples ask, *Where will you have us go and prepare for you to eat the Passover?* (RSV), they probably think that they have an entire day to prepare the Passover meal, which will be eaten the next evening. Since the Passover meal had to be eaten within the city limits, Jesus and the Twelve had to move from Bethany (the last location indicated, v. 3) into the city, and so the disciples enquired as to what arrangements they should make.

13–16. Jesus' instructions remind the reader of 11:2–6. The detailed knowledge about what will happen could signal divine insight; more plausibly, in view of the large number of pilgrims in the city, it indicates a prearranged plan (cf. Matt. 26:18). Jesus seems to have already arranged with a contact in Jerusalem to have the use of a room, as verse 15 indicates (the room is *furnished* and *ready*). Jesus sent *two of his disciples*, as he had done earlier (6:7; 11:1). The *jar of water* is obviously a prearranged sign, even if the disciples' meeting with the man is providential timing foreseen by Jesus. The fact that the man with the water jar *will meet you* (rather than 'you will meet the man') signals, again, a prearranged plan, as does the title *the Teacher*, indicating that *the owner of the house* (*oikodespotēs*) knew Jesus. The man carrying the water jar would have been a slave or servant of Jesus' contact, who owned a two-storey house in the city. Jesus does not tell the disciples the name of the owner of the house or its location, probably because he knows that Judas will deliver him to the chief priests; since he is determined to celebrate with his disciples a last meal during which he will explain the meaning of his death, he does not want to reveal his whereabouts just yet. The prearranged plan of having a man with a water jar lead the two disciples to the house where Jesus wants to eat the Last Supper with the Twelve ensures that the two disciples will know the location only when they get to it. The word translated *guest room* (*katalyma*) denotes a 'lodging place' – in the context of a Passover meal, a 'dining room'. The room is a *room upstairs* (*anagaion*); it is *large* (*megas*), suggesting a relatively wealthy household, *furnished* (*estrōmenon*) with 'carpets or couches for the guests to recline on as they ate' (BDAG, p. 949) and *ready* for a communal meal. The imperative *Make preparations for us there* presumably refers to preparing the food. Jesus' contact in the city could have brought a lamb to the temple to have it slaughtered, which seems to have been possibly a day ahead of the regular slaughter of the Passover lambs (see Context above), and he might have bought other provisions with which the two disciples could prepare for the meal once they were in the guest room. The two disciples follow Jesus' instructions.

b. *Prediction of Judas Iscariot's betrayal (14:17–21)*

17. Jesus and the other ten disciples join the two disciples perhaps an hour later, two hours after sunset. The Passover meal is eaten not like regular dinners in late afternoon but at night (Exod. 12:8; cf. *m. Pes.* 10:1). The word *evening* (*opsios*) can refer to the time before sunset (see on 15:42) but also to the time after work was finished (1:32; Matt. 20:8) when it was already dark (in 6:47 for the time not long before dawn). The term *the Twelve* designates the group as a whole, whether or not all are present.

18–20. The comment that Jesus and the Twelve were *reclining at the table* indicates a formal dinner (cf. 6:26). Jesus had predicted that he would be 'handed over' to his enemies (9:31; 10:33), but he had not specified who would be responsible for the betrayal. Mark's readers know what to expect (cf. 14:10–11), but for the disciples it was disturbing news when Jesus said, *one of you will betray me – one who is eating with me*. The introduction *Truly I tell you* (cf. 3:28) underlines the certainty of the prediction. The expression *one who is eating with me* echoes Psalm 41:9 ('Even my close friend, someone I trusted, one who shared my bread, has turned against me'; quoted in John 13:18), a text that describes the painful experience of another righteous sufferer. Sharing a meal was an expression of trust and friendship. Being betrayed by a trusted friend is the worst kind of betrayal (Strauss, p. 621).

All disciples (except Judas, surely) were *saddened*, incredulous that one of their group would be involved in Jesus' arrest. The Greek wording of the question *Surely you don't mean me?* expects a negative answer. Yet the fact that they even ask the question *one by one* seems to express some self-doubt. In Mark's account, there is no specific focus on Judas Iscariot (unlike Matt. 26:25; John 13:23–30). Jesus' answer is not specific. He reiterates that it will be *one of the Twelve*, a disciple who is present at the table, *one who dips bread into the bowl with me*. Dipping food in sauces and relishes was a standard feature of Greco-Roman meals; it had become a fixed part of the Passover meal: 'On all the [other] nights we dip once, this night twice' (*m. Pes.* 10:4). Mark does not inform his readers whether Judas left at this point to go to the chief priests; the sentence 'they all drank from [the cup]' (v. 23) suggests that Judas stayed throughout the entire meal, leaving the group when they started to walk in the direction of Gethsemane.

21. Jesus states the consequences of the act of betrayal for himself and for his betrayer. Jesus had asserted in 9:12 that the suffering, rejection and death of the Son of Man were in accordance with the Scriptures (cf. the word 'must' in 8:31). The word *go* (*hypagō*) is here not a neutral term ('to go away'): it summarizes the fate Jesus predicted for himself in 8:31, 9:31, 10:33–34 in terms of his rejection, trial and death;[75] in the context of the following pronouncement it is functionally equivalent to 'betray'. If betrayal is in view, the phrase *it is written* could refer to Psalm 41:9 (see on v. 20), or to Zechariah 13:7; Isaiah 53:11; Daniel 7:13–14; 9:26. Jesus' death which results from the betrayal is not a tragedy that should never have taken place: it fulfils God's purposes.

The *woe* (Gr. *ouai*) formula introduces the severe condemnation that Jesus pronounces on the betrayer. It indicates disaster resulting from God's judgment.[76] Even though Jesus' betrayal, arrest, trial and death are the fulfilment of God's plan, Judas is responsible for his

---

75. For death as a journey cf. LXX 1 Kgs 2:2; Job 10:21; 16:22; Eccl. 9:10; 12:5; also *Jub.* 36:1; *4 Ezra* 8:5; *y. Ketub.* 12:3 [35a]; *Gen. Rab.* 100:2. See John 7:33; 8:21–22; 13:3, 33, 36; 2 Cor. 5:6, 8–9.

76. Num. 21:29; 1 Sam. 4:7; Job 10:15; Isa. 3:11; 5:8; Matt. 11:21; 23:12–29.

c. The bread and cup and Jesus' death (14:22–26)

22. The phrase *while they were eating* points to the Passover meal that Jesus deliberately celebrated with his disciples a day earlier (14 Nisan) rather than on the traditional date (15 Nisan). It is unclear how Passover was celebrated around AD 30. Later rabbinic sources[77] describe the Passover meal as structured around four cups of wine. After blessings over the bread and over the wine, the first cup was drunk; after vegetable appetizers were eaten, the second cup of wine was taken; then the youngest son asked the father, 'Why is this night different from other nights?', which resulted in the father recounting the exodus story, explaining the Passover (God passing over the houses of the Israelites), the unleavened bread (because God redeemed the fathers from Egypt) and the bitter herbs (the Egyptians had made the lives of the fathers bitter); this was followed by the singing of the first part of the Hallel (Pss 113 – 115); then the father pronounced a blessing over the bread, broke it and distributed it to the dinner guests; then the main meal was eaten, including the unleavened bread and the lamb; then the third cup of wine was drunk, followed by the singing of the second part of the Hallel (Pss 116 – 118); a fourth cup of wine then concluded the meal. Parallels to Jesus' last supper with the Twelve include the blessing (v. 22), the breaking and distribution of bread (v. 22), the description of the significance of the meal (v. 22), a cup of wine (v. 23) and the singing of a hymn (v. 26). Mark does not relate commands to 'eat' and 'drink' (as in Matt. 26:26–27), although they are implied in verses 22 ('Take it') and 23 ('they all drank'). Nor does Mark include the command 'do this in remembrance of me' (Luke 22:19; 1 Cor. 11:25), which would have been taken for granted by Mark's readers. Mark consistently focuses on the symbolism of Jesus' death (vv. 22, 24) and on the future messianic banquet in God's fully realized kingdom (v. 25).

The *bread* (*artos*) is the unleavened bread (*azymos*) of the Passover meal. The fact that *Jesus took bread* indicates that he was the host of

---

77. *m. Pes.* 10:1–9; *t. Ber.* 4:8; *t. Pes.* 10:1–14; *y. Ber.* 10d.

the meal. As in a traditional Jewish Passover meal, Jesus 'gave thanks': he pronounced a blessing. The traditional prayer of thanksgiving was: 'Blessed are you, O Lord our God, king of the universe, who brings forth bread from the earth' (*m. Ber.* 6:1; cf. Evans, p. 389). Then he *broke* the bread, *gave it* to his disciples and said, *Take it; this is my body*. Jesus explains the unleavened bread, not in terms of Israel's exodus story, which the Twelve would have expected in accordance with the Passover ceremony, but in terms of his body, the breaking of the bread symbolizing the fact of the death of his body (*sōma*). Jesus had predicted his death in 8:31; 9:31; 10:33–34. Now he symbolically enacts his prediction for the disciples, who should have no doubt at this point that he means what he has said. Luke and Paul add the phrase 'which is [given] for you', implying the redemptive significance of Jesus' death. Mark may allude to this with the imperative *take*: although distributing broken-off pieces of unleavened bread was part of the Passover ceremony, in the context of Jesus' statement *this is my body* the imperative *take* points to the redemptive significance of Jesus' death in which they participate. As a sacrificed lamb was the central feature both of the exodus story and of the Passover meal, eaten right after the explanation of the Passover, sacrificial imagery would have determined how the disciples understood Jesus' words. The explanatory words spoken over the bread speak symbolically of Jesus' inevitable death which will benefit the disciples.

23–24. The *cup* was a common cup from which Jesus and all the disciples drank wine. The later rabbinic accounts of the Passover meal mention individual cups. Either Jesus deliberately changed the usual practice to focus the symbolic meaning on the one cup that he shared with the disciples, or the later rabbinic practice was not yet observed in the first century. In the context of the Passover celebration, this cup seems to have been the third cup, taken after the main meal (see on v. 22; the second cup was taken before the breaking of the bread before the main meal). Jesus 'giving thanks' (Gr. *eucharisteō*, from which we get the word 'eucharist') means that he spoke the traditional blessing that was said over the cup (perhaps the blessing mentioned in *m. Ber.* 6:1: 'Blessed are you, O Lord our God, King of the universe, who creates the fruit of the vine'). Then Jesus passed the cup around, so that *all drank* from the one cup.

As Jesus symbolically identified the bread with his body, so he identifies the wine in the cup with his blood: *this is my blood of the covenant*. Like the pronouncement over the bread, the word over the cup asserts that Jesus' death is inevitable and that the disciples will benefit from it. In 10:38–39 the word 'cup' (*potērion*) was used to describe Jesus' coming death. The word *blood* (*haima*) indicates a violent death. The pronouncement over the cup is more explicit than that over the bread: the explanatory *of the covenant* and *which is poured out for many* significantly alludes to several Old Testament passages. The phrase *blood of the covenant* alludes to Exodus 24:1–8 and Moses' words at the covenant ceremony at Mount Sinai which followed the Passover and exodus events, consummating the process of the re-establishment of Israel after the rescue from Egypt. The blood of the sacrificial animal that was offered on this occasion was thrown over the people of Israel, with Moses shouting, 'Behold the blood of the covenant' (NASB, Exod. 24:8). The original covenant was sealed with the blood of an animal sacrifice; another covenant is sealed with the blood of Jesus' sacrifice on the cross. While Mark's text does not explicitly refer to a 'new covenant' (explicit in Luke 22:20; 1 Cor. 11:25), the symbolism implied by the allusion to Exodus 24:8 does not work unless a new covenant, as promised in Jeremiah 31:31–34, is in view here. An echo of Zechariah 9:11 LXX may be in view as well, a passage that alludes to Exodus 24:8: Israel's captives will be set free from exile, a new redemption grounded in Israel's redemption from Egypt. Here, the new beginning for the people of God is grounded not in the ritual slaughter of an animal, nor in the Sinai covenant sealed with the blood from an animal sacrifice, but in the death of Jesus. The phrase *which is poured out for many* alludes to Isaiah 53:11–12 LXX, a passage that connects the shedding of the blood of the Servant of the Lord with redemption through the vicarious death that he died instead of the 'many' and for the benefit of the 'many'. The verb *poured out* indicates violent death, as did the word *blood*. The explanation in 10:45 of Jesus' death in terms of a vicarious death is reinforced in the pronouncement over the cup with another allusion to Isaiah 53. On that night and in this context, whether or not the disciples understood (at the time) the allusions to Jeremiah 31 and Isaiah 53, they would have understood this much: Jesus was speaking of his death as the basis of redemption; and as

Jesus invited them to drink the wine which bore this symbolism, they would have realized that they belonged to the 'many' who benefited from Jesus' death.

25. Jesus concludes the meal with another solemn, authoritative pronouncement introduced with *Truly I tell you* (cf. v. 18; 3:28). Jesus asserts that his life on earth is now coming to an end: *I will not drink again from the fruit of the vine*. This is the last time that Jesus will share a celebratory dinner with the disciples. A new element is introduced in the next clause: *until that day when I drink it new in the kingdom of God*. The expression *kingdom of God* referred to the dominion of God becoming a reality through Jesus' earthly ministry (cf. 1:15 and the passages that spoke of entering or receiving the kingdom of God – 10:15, 23–25). The statement recalls Old Testament and Jewish language related to the 'messianic banquet' to be celebrated when God has made all things new (Isa. 25:6–9; 65:13; *1 En.* 60:7; 62:14; *2 Bar.* 29:5–8; 1QSa II, 11–22; in the NT see Matt. 8:11–12; Rev. 19:9). 'New wine' is often mentioned in the context of prosperity and well-being (Gen. 27:28; Deut. 33:28; Zech. 9:17). Jesus looks forward to the day when he will celebrate with the 'new wine' of the messianic banquet God's ultimate salvation with the 'many' who have benefited from the salvation effected by his death.

26. The *hymn* was the second part of the Hallel. Jesus concludes the Passover celebration by singing Psalms 115 – 118. Unlike on previous evenings, Jesus and the disciples did not return to Bethany. They went to the nearer slope of the *Mount of Olives* (cf. 11:1) which, during Passover, counted as being within the boundaries of the city. It was probably at this point, when Jesus announced their destination, that Judas left the group and went to the chief priests.

d. *Prediction of Peter's denial (14:27–31)*

27. Jesus' prediction of Peter's denial seems to have taken place when Jesus and the disciples left the city, perhaps by the Gate of the Essenes in the south-west section of the city, heading for the Kidron Valley and Gethsemane on the Mount of Olives (vv. 26, 32). The phrase *you will all fall away* (NIV, RSV; NRSV 'you will all become deserters'; for the verb *skandalizō* cf. 4:17; 6:3; 9:42–43, 45, 47) predicts that the disciples' loyalty will be tested, and that they will not pass the test. Jesus connects the 'fall' of his disciples with Zechariah 13:7. The same prophet who described the Messiah as a king riding into Jerusalem on a donkey (Zech. 9:9–10; cf. Mark 11:1–10) speaks of the suffering of the *shepherd*, God's associate, with the result that *the sheep will be scattered*. Zechariah prophesies that God will command that his appointed leader be struck down so that the people of Israel will be scattered, as judgment for their sin. In Mark's text, the imperative is reformulated as a first person verb: *I will strike*, underlining that God is the ultimate agent in the events that follow, including the dispersal of the disciples, who abandon Jesus: the coming events are the will and design of God. The 'falling away' of the disciples is part of God's initiative in the mission of the Shepherd-King. It is not clear whether Zechariah 13:7 is the source of Jesus' prediction or whether it served 'as supporting evidence to what he already knew' (Stein, p. 654). Some see an allusion to Isaiah 53:4, 6, 10.

28. As Jesus' predictions of his arrest and death were followed by a prediction of his resurrection (8:31; 9:31; 10:34), so here: *after I have risen* describes Jesus' vindication after his execution in his resurrection and signals the disciples' restoration as Jesus' followers. Jesus promises that he will *go ahead of you into Galilee*, a promise that is reaffirmed when the angel at the empty tomb announces Jesus' resurrection (16:7). The symmetry in verses 27 and 28 is significant: as the 'striking' of the shepherd results in the scattering of the sheep, so Jesus' resurrection will result in the gathering of the 'sheep' in Galilee. In both cases, the initiative lies not with the disciples: as their act of disloyalty is part of God's plan, so their restoration and their future mission as Jesus' followers rests on Jesus' power, the reality of which becomes visible in his resurrection. For Jesus' meeting with the disciples in Galilee after the resurrection see Matthew 28:16–20; John 21:1–23.

29–31. Peter acts again as a spokesman for the disciples, as verse 31 indicates. Peter concedes that *all [will] fall away*, with himself as the one exception: *I will not*. It appears that each of the eleven disciples (Judas seems to have left) considers it possible that his fellow disciples will be tripped up, confident that he is the exception. The self-confidence of all of the disciples that they will stay loyal to Jesus contrasts with the self-doubt earlier in verse 19. Two factors have changed: since Jesus' unsettling prediction that one of the Twelve will betray him, made earlier in the evening, they have had time to reflect on their own loyalty to Jesus, and they have evidently determined that they will stay with Jesus rather than abandon him. Also, since active betrayal is more serious than abandoning Jesus, they are convinced that they can avoid the lesser evil (cf. France, p. 578). Jesus addresses Peter's self-confidence with a solemn *amēn* saying (cf. 3:28; also 14:9, 18, 25), predicting that Peter will indeed *disown* him (*aparneomai* means 'to refuse to recognize or acknowledge, to deny'). The word is the opposite of 'to confess' (cf. Matt. 10:32–33; John 1:20). Jesus provides detailed information about Peter's refusal to acknowledge that he belongs to Jesus' followers: (1) it will happen *today*; that is, on the day which began when they left Bethany and returned to Jerusalem for the Passover meal; (2) it will happen *tonight*; that is, within the next six or seven hours; (3) it will happen *before the cock crows twice*; that is, before the cock-crow before first light, before the end of the third watch of the night (called 'cock-crow'; see on 13:35); (4) it will happen *three times*, which underlines the prediction of Peter's complete failure to acknowledge his loyalty to Jesus. These specifics signal that Jesus' arrest and death are imminent. Peter *emphatically* protests against Jesus' pronouncement that he will deny him. He asserts that he is willing *to die with* Jesus if he has to (*ean deē*; lit. 'if it may be necessary'), probably thinking that Jesus' arrest and execution will trigger the arrest and execution of Jesus' followers as well. Peter is certain that his courage will guarantee his loyalty to Jesus, so much so that he *will never disown* Jesus. He is wrong, as verses 66–72 will show. Peter's professed superiority over the other disciples was not necessarily 'shameful' (Stein, p. 655) if indeed he expressed only what they were thinking as well, as suggested by the phrase *and all the others said the same*. Peter and the other ten disciples have the right attitude, but they will lack the courage to act on it.

Theology
Mark emphasizes God's sovereign control of the events connected with Jesus' arrest and death. The earlier references to divine necessity (8:31; 9:31; 10:33–34, 45) are reinforced by Jesus' prediction of the betrayal of Judas and of the disciples' denial (14:17–21,

27–31), by Jesus' anticipation of the messianic banquet (v. 25) and by the prediction of his resurrection and his subsequent meeting with the disciples in Galilee (v. 28). Jesus and the Gospel writers (cf. Matt. 26:24; Luke 22:22) do not explain how the sovereignty of God, who directs history, including Judas' betrayal which fulfils Scripture, exists together with Judas' freedom to choose a different course of action, 'but they do not compromise one for the sake of the other' (Stein, p. 649).

During his last supper with the disciples, Jesus reiterates that his death has redemptive significance (cf. 10:45). In the context of Old Testament allusions and echoes, Jesus asserts that his death is a self-sacrifice which brings about the redemption of sinners and inaugurates the promised new covenant whose climax will be the future messianic banquet in the kingdom of God (14:22–25). My comments on Jesus' explanatory words over the bread and wine used the term 'symbolical' without attempting to provide a precise definition of the Greek verb *estin*, translated 'is': 'this *is* my body ... this *is* my blood'. Elaborate and, in the history of the Protestant Reformation, divisive attempts to determine the 'presence' of Jesus in the church's celebration of the Lord's Supper (Eucharist), arguing from the Greek verb *estin* (or, in the Vulgate, the Latin verb *est*), 'are built on a shaky foundation' (France, p. 569). It is generally agreed that in Aramaic, the language Jesus would have been using, Jesus' explanatory pronouncements would not have had an expressed verb. Jesus does not promise his presence when his followers eat bread and drink wine in remembrance of his death. Rather, he identifies the bread with his body and the wine with his blood – both literally present *apart* from the bread and the wine that were consumed on that fateful night. Jesus' symbolic identification of bread and wine focuses not on his presence but on his death.

iii. *On the Mount of Olives (14:32–52)*
Context

The third of seven scenes which depict Jesus' suffering and death follows the preparations for Jesus' arrest (14:1–11) and Jesus' last supper with the disciples (14:12–31). Mark relates Jesus' prayer in Gethsemane (14:32–42) and Jesus' betrayal and arrest (14:43–52).

Comment

a. Jesus' prayer in Gethsemane (14:32–42)

Before the violent action takes place that readers expect in view of Jesus' prediction of Judas Iscariot's betrayal (14:17–21), of his own violent death implied in the reference to his blood (v. 24) and of Peter's denial that same night (v. 30), there is a pause. Jesus and the disciples leave the city and walk to a garden on the slopes of the Mount of Olives, where Jesus prays, overwhelmed by the prospect of his imminent death, while the disciples sleep, unable to keep watch with Jesus. The time is probably an hour before midnight.

32. The *place* (*chōrion*, 'piece of land') called *Gethsemane* was, according to John 18:1, a 'garden' (*kēpos*) across the Kidron Valley from the city of Jerusalem. According to Luke 22:39 the place was on the Mount of Olives, which is implied in Mark 14:26. The Greek word *Gethsēmani* is a transliteration of the Hebrew/Aramaic expression *gat šemaney* ('oil press'), evidently the name of an olive orchard which had an oil press on the Mount of Olives. According to Luke 22:39, Jesus went regularly to Gethsemane, and John 18:2 says that Judas Iscariot knew that this was where Jesus would be. Gethsemane would have been inside the boundaries of 'greater Jerusalem' which were extended for the Passover festival. Since it was the night before the regular Passover celebration, Jesus' movements were not restricted: he could have returned to Bethany (the previous night, 6 April, was full moon, which means there would have been sufficient light in the night of 7 April to walk to Bethany). Perhaps Jesus observed the tradition of staying in Jerusalem on Passover night since he treated his last meal with the disciples as a Passover meal. Alternatively, he wanted to give the authorities the opportunity to arrest him in a quiet spot. When Mark earlier depicted Jesus praying (1:35; 6:46), he was praying alone. Now, again, he goes away from the disciples to pray.

33–34. Jesus leaves eight disciples behind, taking with him the 'inner circle' consisting of *Peter, Jacob [James] and John* (5:37; 9:2). It has been suggested that Jesus took these three disciples deeper into the garden with him because all three had expressed their willingness to suffer for him (10:38–39; 14:31). He brings them along as witnesses who see at least something of his agony before they fall asleep. And he brings them along for support, as the last sentence in verse 34 indicates: *Stay here and keep watch*. Jesus, the Son of God, but also the son of Mary (6:3), is distressed at the prospect of imminent death and asks his three closest companions for their support, informing them of his anguish.

Mark describes Jesus' emotional anguish with four terms: Jesus is *deeply distressed* (*ekthambeō*), overwhelmed and alarmed; he is *troubled* (*adēmoneō*), anxious, in anguish; *overwhelmed with sorrow* (*perilypos*), very sad, deeply grieved; and his distress is *to the point of death* (*heōs thanatou*), which means either sorrow so deep that it feels as if he is dying, or extreme distress in view of his imminent death. The sentence *My soul is overwhelmed with sorrow* recalls the repeated refrain of the righteous sufferer in Psalms 42:5–6, 11; 43:5 (LXX 41:6–7, 12; 42:5). Jesus perhaps uses these psalms of lament to express his distress and then regains confidence in God, in tune with the psalms where the mood of despair is eventually transformed into a calm trust in God. Jesus' command to the three disciples, *keep watch* (vv. 34, 37–38), means to stay awake and alert (rather than keeping watch for the betrayer).

35–36. Jesus left Peter, Jacob and John behind, *going a little farther*, the disciples remaining within earshot (according to Luke 22:41 a stone's throw away) and witnessing his prayer. Jesus *fell to the ground*, perhaps because of his sorrow, perhaps as a posture of reverent submission to the will of God (cf. Gen. 17:3; Num. 16:22, 44–45; 20:6). Mark first relates Jesus' prayer in indirect speech: he prayed that *if possible the hour might pass from him*. The *hour* is the appointed time of Jesus' arrest and death (cf. John 12:27). The expression *if possible* means 'if God wills'. The content of Jesus' prayer is given in direct speech. Jesus, praying in Aramaic, addresses God as *Abba*, which Mark translates *ho patēr* ('the father', here 'my father'). The Greek phrase *Abba ho patēr* also appears in Romans 8:15, Galatians 4:6 as an address to God: Jesus' use of *Abba* in prayer 'left a deep impression on early Christians' (Evans, p. 413), so much so that the word was repeated in the original Aramaic in the prayers of the Greek-speaking early church.

The word *Abba* is the emphatic (definite) form of *'ab* ('father'), which accounts for the Greek translation. The word *'abba* was not limited to the speech of small children: it was used by grown men (*m. Sanh.* 4:5), sometimes as a form of address for old men. While the Aramaic word *'abba* is not found as a direct address to God, the Hebrew equivalent *'ābî* ('my father'), used as an address in prayer, is found in the Old Testament (cf. Ps. 89:26) and in Qumran (cf. 4Q372 1 16); the Greek expression for 'my father' is used for God in Palestinian Judaism (cf. Sir. 51:10) and in Diaspora Judaism (cf. Wis. 14:3). Even though 'a fundamental difference from Jewish usage cannot be demonstrated' for Jesus' use of *'abba* (H.-W. Kuhn, *EDNT*, I, p. 1), the lack of attestation of an individual addressing God as *'abba* may indeed signify a distinctive of Jesus' prayer language (Evans, pp. 412–413; Marcus, p. 978).

Jesus acknowledges that for God, *everything is possible*: God is omnipotent; all things are possible for God (cf. 10:27). Jesus knows that God the Father can *take this cup from* him – the cup of God's wrath (cf. Isa. 51:17, 22; Ezek. 23:32–34; Lam. 4:21; Ps. 11:6), the 'cup of death' (cf. *t. Ab.* 1:3; 16:11; *Tg. Neof.* Gen. 40:23 for 'cup' symbolizing the death of an individual). See earlier on Mark 10:38–39; 14:23. The two aspects seem to be combined here: the cup as Jesus' death, and the cup that connects his death with the judgment that God renders on others, as in 14:23–24 where the cup symbolizes the 'blood of the covenant, which is poured out for many' (Marcus, p. 978). The notion of the cup of suffering, death and judgment being given to Jesus by his Father again emphasizes the conviction of Jesus (and of Mark, as indicated by his narrative) that Jesus' death is the will of God and that God controls the events that will lead to Jesus' execution by crucifixion. Jesus does not quail at the thought of physical death, which would be 'a poor example for his followers of how they should face death and martyrdom' (Stein, p. 662; contrast Heb. 11:32–38; Acts 7:54–60). He does not have inner doubts about the value of his death. Jesus' prayer to be spared death conveys the excruciating anguish that senses the terrible reality of suffering the judgment of God, dying as a ransom for the many (10:45), shedding his blood to seal the new covenant (14:24), dying as a sin offering (Rom. 8:3), becoming the place of God's atoning presence (Rom. 3:25), becoming a curse for us (Gal. 3:13).

The cry *Abba, Father* signals Jesus' filial obedience. His appeal to God is based on the knowledge that nothing is impossible for God, and on the acknowledgment that God's will 'is to be accepted rather than altered by prayer' (France, p. 585). Thus Jesus prays: *Yet not what I will, but what you will*. The conditions for effective prayer mentioned in 11:22–25 have been met. Jesus' deliverance from death *is* possible, if it is the will of God. However, if it *is* the will of God that he should die, Jesus does not want to change God's mind: Jesus wants his will to be aligned with the will of God.

37–38. When Jesus returned to the three disciples, he *found them sleeping*. This happened three times (v. 41). Mark does not explain the disciples' sleep by the late hour, the effects of the Passover meal or exhaustion after the tension of the last few days (relevant as such explanations might be). He wants his readers to see the contrast between the disciples' repeated sleep and Jesus' repeated prayers. Jesus rebukes Peter, probably because of his self-confident assertions earlier in the evening (vv. 29, 31). Peter has abandoned Jesus by falling *asleep* and by failing to *keep watch for one hour*. Soon, when Jesus is arrested, Peter will abandon him literally (v. 50), and then he will deny knowing him (vv. 66–72). The expression *mia hōra* ('one hour') is sometimes used for a short period of time (cf. *Test. Job* 7:12; Rev. 18:10, 17, 19).

The command *watch and pray* is formulated with the plural, addressed to all three disciples. The imperative *watch* calls on the disciples to stay alert, something they can do and should be doing. The imperative *pray* reminds the disciples of their dependence on God and the need to align themselves with the will of God, which happens through extended times of prayer in which they acknowledge God's omnipotence and their willingness to accept the will of God. The word *peirasmos* describes the *temptation* of the disciples to run away and to value their own safety more highly than their loyalty to God, to whom they pray, and to Jesus, the Son of God; the word also describes the 'test' of denying Jesus (v. 50), a *trial* (NRSV) in which they might fail. Perhaps the meaning is '[so that] when the test comes, you may not be tempted to disloyalty' (France, p. 587). The sentence *The spirit is willing, but the flesh is weak* is a statement on human nature. The *spirit* (*pneuma*) is the breath of human life, the inward person, the God-given capacity for right thinking, right decisions and right living. The *flesh* (*sarx*) is the general weakness of human beings, their vulnerability, their self-absorption, the human propensity to rebel against the will of God. The flesh is *weak* (*asthenēs*), which includes physical weakness (and thus refers to the disciples' sleep) but extends to all human limitations which render people incapable of consistently, joyfully and sacrificially doing the will of God. That the spirit is *willing* (*prothymos*, 'being eager to be of service') means that as far as the God-given spirit is concerned, people are eager to do the will of God. Jesus exhorts the disciples to be alert and to pray so that the weakness of the flesh does not control their actions; so that they can do the will of God, which in the context of Gethsemane means that they remain loyal to Jesus when the hour of testing comes and when the temptation to run to safety is overpowering.

39–40. Jesus left the three disciples and *prayed, saying the same words* (NRSV). Mark does not restate the prayer of verse 36. When he returned, *he again found them sleeping*. The explanation *because their eyes were heavy* now suggests exhaustion due to the time approaching midnight. They wanted to stay awake, but they could not keep their eyes open. This does not excuse their failure to stay awake. Evidently Jesus rebuked them again, but *they did not know what to say to him*. Their embarrassed silence recalls 9:34.

41–42. Jesus left the three disciples and prayed for a third time; Mark relates only that Jesus returned to the disciples *the third time*. Praying three times in distress is mentioned in Psalm 55:17 and 2 Corinthians 12:7–9. Jesus' praying three times is contrasted with the disciples' falling asleep three times, which foreshadows Peter's three denials. Jesus' words to the disciples can be interpreted as a command ('Go ahead and sleep. Have your rest', NLT), an ironic comment ('You can sleep on now and have your rest. It is all over', NJB) or an indignant question ('Are you still sleeping and resting? Enough!', NIV; cf. GNB, NASB, NRSV). The last two possibilities are plausible: Jesus has finished praying, the disciples have fallen asleep again, so Jesus wakes them up and rebukes them a third time. The next sentence consists of one Greek word (*apechei*), usually translated *Enough!* (NIV, NRSV) or *It is enough* (NASB, RSV). The meaning 'it is enough' is supported only in later Greek texts, but it makes sense as a colloquialism in a dramatic statement (BDAG, p. 102, *apechō* meaning 2). Jesus perhaps means to say, 'You have been sleeping enough', or 'I have tried enough to keep you awake' (Collins, p. 682). The word can also mean 'to be distant': Jesus might be asking, 'Is it far away?', a question that he answers in the following statement, 'The hour has come' (Evans, pp. 416–417; Marcus, p. 981). The statement *The hour has come* takes up the term 'hour' of verse 35: the time has arrived when Jesus' predictions of arrest, betrayal, trial and execution will be fulfilled. The first event in this sequence of events is Jesus' betrayal. The twofold *behold* (NASB; translated only in v. 41 in NIV; only in v. 42 in NRSV) functions here as 'a summons to a more careful consideration and observation' (G. Schneider, *EDNT*, II, p. 173). The expression *into the hands* can be understood literally – the arresting party 'laid hands on him' (NRSV, v. 46) – as well as figuratively, expressing the person(s) whose hands are mentioned as the source of activity: the time has come when others control Jesus and Jesus ceases to be a free agent. The *sinners* are, in the context of verses 42, 43–52, Judas who betrays his teacher and the Jewish authorities who have sent the arresting party as they have been plotting Jesus' death for some time. Repudiating the Son of Man is rebellion against God and thus constitutes sin (8:38). In Jewish tradition, sinners are delivered into the hands of the righteous for judgment (*1 En.* 91:12; 95:3, 7; 1QpHab IX, 9–12; 1Q171 IV, 7–10; Marcus, p. 989). Here, paradoxically, the one who forgives sins (2:5) is turned over to sinners. Even more paradoxically, it is *the Son of Man* – the one who is given dominion, glory and kingship according to Daniel 7:13–14 – who is turned over to sinners.

Judas' arrival spurs Jesus into action. The words *Rise! Let us go!* are a call to advance and meet Judas, who is coming and bringing with him people who will arrest Jesus. Jesus does not seek to escape. His prayers have led him to accept the will of God (v. 36). He is ready to go through the events that he has predicted.

b. Jesus' betrayal and arrest (14:43–52)
The first section of Mark's description of Jesus' suffering and death (14:1 – 15:47) ended with the betrayal by Judas Iscariot (14:10–11). In the second section Jesus predicted that he would be betrayed by one of the Twelve (14:17–21). The third section ends with Jesus' betrayal by Judas and his arrest (14:43–52). Jesus' arrest in Gethsemane sets in motion the sequence of events in which Jesus' trial before the Sanhedrin, his trial before Pontius Pilate and his crucifixion figure most prominently. This is the last text in which

Jesus and the disciples are together. After his arrest, Jesus is alone, his fate in the hands of the Jewish authorities and the Roman prefect – fulfilling the will of God, who ransoms sinners and initiates his new covenant.

43. The description of Judas as *one of the Twelve* emphasizes the depth and tragedy of his treachery. For Judas Iscariot see 3:19. Jesus' prediction that one of the Twelve would betray him (14:17–21) is now fulfilled. The phrase *just as he was speaking*, referring back to Jesus' words in verses 41–42, shows that Jesus is not taken by surprise. The *crowd* that arrives is not a mob, nor thugs working for the ruling priests, but people who are on an official mission, sent by *the chief priests, the teachers of the law, and the elders*. Since these three groups (cf. 8:31; 11:27; 14:43, 53; 15:1; cf. 14:55) made up the Sanhedrin in Jerusalem, the highest Jewish court, the people who arrested Jesus would have been their authorized representatives. Jesus' statement that he could easily have been arrested on the Temple Mount (v. 49) indicates that he recognized some of the people who arrested him, which suggests that the arresting party comprised mostly the temple guards, who were controlled by the chief priests. In the ancient world, municipal aristocracies were responsible for securing public order. In Jerusalem, the temple guards fit this pattern. Members of the elite used their retainers (freedmen, slaves) for self-protection, and they would have called on the same if they wanted to make an arrest. In Jerusalem, both the aristocratic priests (cf. v. 47) and the elders owned slaves whom they could employ to arrest people. Thus, Jesus was arrested by the temple guard and by retainers of the chief priests and the elders. The arresting party was armed with *swords and clubs* that would allow them to put down any resistance Jesus and his disciples might make.

44–46. A prearranged *signal* was an action or gesture previously agreed upon as a 'sign'. Since Jesus had taught publicly on the Temple Mount he would have been easily recognizable. However, since Judas had arranged an arrest during the night in Gethsemane, a sign that would point to Jesus might have been thought necessary, especially if other pilgrims had stayed overnight in Gethsemane: only Judas could get close enough to Jesus without arousing suspicion. Judas had made arrangements that he would greet Jesus with a *kiss*. A kiss was used as a greeting (2 Sam. 19:39; Acts 20:37); it was a sign of hospitality and friendship (2 Sam. 20:9; Luke 7:45), signalling family affection (Gen. 27:26; 33:4; 45:15; Luke 15:20; Rom. 16:16; 1 Cor. 16:20). Kisses given to a superior expressed honour and respect from the one who was inferior. The kiss of honour was usually given on the hand. The expression *under guard* (*asphalōs*, 'in a manner that ensures continuing detention'; BDAG, p. 147) suggests that Judas expected resistance, if not from Jesus himself then from his fellow disciples. After Judas identified Jesus with a kiss and the greeting *Rabbi!*, the arresting party *laid hands on him* (NRSV), grabbing him physically to prevent resistance. With verse 45, Judas disappears from the story. Mark is not interested in reporting his subsequent suicide (cf. Matt. 27:3–10; Acts 1:15–26). Judas' perfidious behaviour recalls Proverbs 27:6: 'Wounds from a friend can be trusted, but an enemy multiplies kisses.' In 2 Samuel 20:9–10 Joab greets Amasa with a kiss and then stabs him to death.

47. All four Gospels record the event of the high priest's slave having his ear cut off. Mark's account is the shortest. The reference to *the slave of the high priest* (NRSV) confirms that the members of the aristocracy in Jerusalem had sent their retainers to arrest Jesus (see on v. 43). Mark describes the person who attacked the arresting party with a sword as *one of those standing near*. John identifies him as Simon Peter, and he also provides the name of the slave as Malchus (John 18:10). Peter probably aimed at the neck of the man but managed only to hit the right ear. The name Malchus or Malichus is attested for Gentiles[78] and for Jews.[79] In all four Gospels, the man who lost his ear is called '*the* slave of the high priest'; since the high priest would have had more than one slave, the article may suggest that the person in question commanded the arresting party. The article may also suggest that the early church remembered this person 'because the injury to him remained, so to speak, an unsolved crime of which Peter was the as yet undetected perpetrator. Malchus was an influential person in the high priest's entourage with a personal grudge against the disciples of Jesus.'[80] It may not be a coincidence

---

78. Josephus, *Ant.* 13.132; 14.370–375; *War* 1.276; Eunapius, *Lives* 456.
79. Josephus, *Ant.* 14.84; *War* 1.162, 223–235.
80. Bauckham, *Eyewitnesses*, p. 195; the following point ibid.

that John mentions Malchus again in the account of Peter's third denial (John 18:26), which would explain Peter's fear: he is afraid of being identified not only as one of Jesus' disciples but as the one who assaulted the high priest's slave and cut off his ear. The anonymity both of Peter as the assailant and of Malchus as the victim can again be explained in terms of 'protective anonymity' (see on 14:3). Matthew, Luke and John report that Jesus called for a halt to the violent resistance, and Luke reports that Jesus healed the man's ear (Luke 22:51). Peter evidently still did not understand that Jesus' arrest, trial and death *had* to happen.

48–50. Jesus challenges the manner of his arrest. He argues that the group is armed with swords and clubs as if he were *a bandit* (NRSV), which he is not. The word *lēstēs* means 'robber' (ESV, NASB, RSV), 'highwayman, bandit' (cf. 11:17; Luke 10:30, 36; John 10:1, 8; 2 Cor. 11:26), but it can also mean 'revolutionary, insurrectionist, guerrilla' (cf. NIV 'Am I leading a rebellion?'). In John 18:40 Barabbas is called *lēstēs*, and in Mark 15:7 Barabbas is described as having committed murder in a *stasis*, which means 'riot' (GNB) or 'insurrection' (NASB, NRSV, NIV 'uprising'). Jesus will eventually be crucified between two *lēstai* (15:27). The term 'robber' or 'brigand' was often used as a code word for social-political revolutionaries who unsettled Palestine. Since Jesus was taken as a seditious messianic pretender to Pilate (cf. 15:2), who crucified him as 'king of the Jews' (15:26), it is possible that the Jewish authorities who had organized his arrest believed that Jesus was close to the movement started by Judas the Galilean (Josephus, *Ant.* 18.23; 20.102; *War* 2.118, 433; cf. Acts 5:37; cf. Hengel, *Zealots*, p. 340). If the Jewish authorities believe that Jesus is leading a rebellion, the arrest by armed men is neither cowardice nor duplicitous, but a necessary precaution. Jesus asserts that 'bandit' (or 'insurrectionist') is an inappropriate term for him: neither the goals nor the methods of his mission are those of brigands. As proof Jesus points to his activities since his arrival in Jerusalem (five days earlier): *Every day I was with you, teaching in the temple courts, and you did not arrest me*. Jesus implies that someone who regularly teaches in the temple is hardly an insurrectionist. Jesus concludes his statement with the assertion *But the Scriptures must be fulfilled*, implying that he is submitting to those who are arresting him because it is God's will and a fulfilment of prophecy. Mark does not indicate which text

Jesus had in mind. He may have alluded to Zechariah 13:7 ("'Awake, sword, against my shepherd, against the man who is close to me!' declares the LORD Almighty. "Strike the shepherd, and the sheep will be scattered"'), quoted in 14:27.

Jesus did not expect his words to have any effect on the arresting party. He knew that what was happening was God's will. But Jesus' words had an effect on the disciples. They realized that Jesus did not intend to resist his arrest, and so they *deserted him and fled*. The stark statement does not blame the disciples for abandoning Jesus. It is hard to see what other options they had, given that Jesus was not willing to sanction violent resistance, which would be futile even if all eleven disciples fought the arresting party.

51–52. The incident of the young man who is seized and then manages to flee naked is mysterious. He is described as a *young man* who was wearing a *linen sheet over his naked body* (NASB). The word *sindōn* describes 'fabric made from linen' and thus 'a light piece of clothing like a chemise, *shirt*' (BDAG, p. 924). Usually people wore two items of clothing, an undergarment (*chitōn*) and an outer garment (*himation*; cf. 5:15), but it was not indecent to wear only one item of clothing. The man is described as *following* (*synakoloutheō*) Jesus; he seems to have been a follower of Jesus who accompanied the other disciples to Gethsemane. When those who had arrested Jesus wanted to arrest the young man as well – perhaps he wanted to help Jesus after the eleven disciples had fled (v. 50) – a struggle ensued in which his clothing came off, with the result that he left it behind and *fled naked* (*gymnos*).

The young man is anonymous. It is a plausible assumption that we have another example of 'protective anonymity': the early church new the identity of the young man who could 'corroborate the story of his undignified escape through the olive groves'.[81] Victor of Antioch, who wrote the first commentary on Mark's Gospel (late fifth century), suggested that the young man was a resident of the house in which Jesus and the disciples had eaten the Last Supper; in the nineteenth century this suggestion was

---

81. France, p. 595; cf. Theißen, *Gospels*, pp. 185–186; Bauckham, *Eyewitnesses*, pp. 185, 197–201. Bauckham thinks that he might have been Lazarus.

specified in terms of John Mark, who lived in Jerusalem with his mother Mary (Acts 12:12). Ambrose (fourth century) identified the young man with John, the son of Zebedee (cf. John 18:15–16). Theophylact of Ohrid (eleventh century) suggested Jacob (James), Jesus' brother, who dressed in a linen garment all his life (according to Eusebius, *Hist. eccl.* 2.23.6).[82] The anonymity of the man cannot be penetrated. Mark included this story to underline the complete desertion of Jesus. The flight of the young man caps the account of Jesus' arrest, and 'the motif's vivid picture of abject terror and shameful nudity in cowardly flight admirably reinforces a scene in which the ruling emotion is the desperate impulse to save one's own skin, the mood of "Every man for himself!"' (Jackson, 'Youth', p. 286).

Theology
The theme of God's sovereign purposes is highlighted several times (14:27, 36, 49). Jesus' prayer to God demonstrates that God, not the Jewish authorities, is in charge of Jesus' fate. Jesus' agony in Gethsemane underlines his humanity and demonstrates the unfathomable seriousness of God's judgment that is about to fall on him, with its climax in God's abandonment of Jesus on the cross (15:34). Jesus' acceptance of the will of God, who will not take away the 'cup' of suffering and death, demonstrates that he is the Messiah, the Son of God and Son of Man who does God's will.

Both episodes teach about discipleship. One disciple betrays Jesus. The other eleven disciples are unable to watch and pray in Gethsemane, which leaves them unprepared for the following events. One disciple thinks that violent action is appropriate for defending Jesus. All disciples desert Jesus, abandoning him to the authorities. In contrast, Jesus' behaviour provides a model for Mark's readers: he submits to the will of God (14:36); he is alert and prays (14:35–39); he restores the disciples after their failure (14:28; 16:7); he submits to the arrest (14:43–49).

---

82. Cf. Brown, *Death*, I, pp. 294–302; Evans, pp. 427–429; Marcus, pp. 1124–1125; Strauss, p. 645, lists nine identifications and four symbolic interpretations.

iv. Jesus' trial before the Sanhedrin (14:53–72)
Context

The account of Jesus' trial before the Jewish authorities is the climax of Mark's Gospel. Since Caesarea Philippi, where Jesus first predicted his arrest, trial and death by the hands of the chief priests, the teachers of the law and the aristocratic elders (8:31), Jesus had repeatedly predicted that this would happen (9:31; 10:32–34; cf. 10:45; 14:8, 22–24). Now he finds himself in the house of the high priest, facing the chief priests, the elders and the teachers of the law (14:53) – the entire Sanhedrin (14:55). The climax of the trial is Jesus' declaration – which immediately leads to the death sentence – that he is the Messiah, the Son of God; indeed the Son of Man sitting at the right hand of God (14:62).

The Roman prefect of Judea had jurisdiction in capital cases, but the Roman administration allowed Jewish authorities to impose the death penalty in cases of the violation of the temple (Philo, *Legat.* 306–308; Josephus, *Ant.* 18.2; 20.199–203; *War* 2.117; 6.126).[83] The fact that the Sanhedrin first sought to indict Jesus on the charge of planning the destruction of the temple (Mark 14:57–59) fits the evidence of Jewish jurisdiction: if their trial strategy had been successful, the chief priests might have been legally able to order Jesus' execution. Lack of jurisdiction in capital cases not involving the defilement of the temple did not preclude the Sanhedrin from interrogating persons on relevant charges with the goal of taking the case to the Roman prefect (see on 15:1). It is a moot point whether the episode of Jesus before the Sanhedrin should be called an interrogation, an examination or an official judicial trial. The Jewish authorities certainly would have had the last view. That Mark describes a trial cannot really be in doubt: the court interrogates witnesses whose testimony is dismissed when it is established that it is contradictory; the high priest manages to elicit a statement from Jesus which is evaluated as constituting blasphemy (14:61–64). Since Jesus' statement involved the claim to be the Messiah, the religious blasphemy charge could be extended to the political charge

---

83. Chapman and Schnabel, *Trial and Crucifixion*, pp. 15–31. Cf. Blinzler, *Prozeß*, pp. 229–244; Brown, *Death*, I, pp. 363–373; Eck, *Rom*, p. 40.

of sedition: as Jesus claims to be the messianic king, the Roman authorities have jurisdiction. Jesus' trial before the Sanhedrin was not a kangaroo court (France, p. 604; Marcus, p. 1127), and the outcome was not a travesty of justice (Strauss, p. 652). Since the high priest did not accept Jesus' statement (14:62) as true, he did what he had to do and obtained a death sentence from the Sanhedrin. That a death sentence was the intention of the chief priests all along does not constitute evidence that they manipulated the trial.

The historicity of the details of Mark's account has been questioned on account of discrepancies with Jewish law,[84] particularly the stipulations for capital cases in *m. Sanhedrin* 4:1: Jesus was tried during the night (implied in Mark 15:1; cf. Matt. 26:34, 57; John 13:30; 18:2, 13, 24); he was tried on the day before Passover (John 18:28); he was convicted of a capital crime on the same day his trial had begun – there was no interval of at least a night between the judges' arguments and Jesus' conviction. Some argue that the legal stipulations of the Mishnah (written c. AD 200) reflect the more humane Pharisaic viewpoint: they were not in force before AD 70 when the Sadducean chief priests controlled the temple and the Sanhedrin.[85] Others argue that if the gathering of priests and elders at the home of Caiaphas during the night is regarded as 'an informal hearing designed to gain a consensus among Jewish authorities that Jesus should be handed over to the Romans with a capital recommendation', there is no violation of the rules of capital trials.[86] Most plausible is the analysis of A. Strobel, who argues: (1) in central legal questions there is no basic difference between Sadducean law, which the Sanhedrin would have followed before AD 70, and Mishnaic law; (2) the stipulations of the Mishnah (and Tosefta), particularly regarding capital cases, reflect the legal situation during the first century; (3) capital cases involving a seducer – a *mesît*, a (lay) person who proclaims heretical teachings, or a *maddiaḥ*, a demagogue who leads the masses astray – followed different rules from ordinary

---

84. Cf. Brown, *Death*, I, pp. 358–359; Juel, *Trial*, pp. 59–60.
85. Blinzler, *Prozeß*, pp. 216–229; Brown, *Death*, I, pp. 357–363.
86. Evans, p. 444. Cf. Marcus, p. 1127; Chilton and Bock, *Mark*, p. 487.

criminal cases.[87] Since Jesus was tried as a seducer of the people (cf. Luke 23:2, 5, 13–14), no legal rules were broken.[88]

The fact that the trial was held at night shows the Jewish authorities' fear of Jesus' popularity and confirms their decision to treat Jesus as a *mesît*, who seduced people to idolatrous worship. Jesus publicly claimed to have the authority to forgive sins, which provoked a blasphemy charge by teachers of the law (2:5–7). He healed provocatively on the Sabbath, which prompted Pharisees and Herodians to plot his death (3:1–6). Teachers of the law from Jerusalem concluded that Jesus acted with satanic authority (3:22). And when he arrived in Jerusalem, he claimed authority over temple procedures (11:15–18) and announced the destruction of the temple (11:17; 13:2). The fact that Jesus taught and acted in the way he did, and the fact that he was attracting permanent followers as well as large crowds of thousands of people, would, from the perspective of the Jewish authorities, warrant the charge of being a *mesît* and *maddiaḥ*. The permission to entrap the *mesît* in order to obtain the required number of witnesses (*m. Sanh.* 7:10) can be linked with Mark 14:1 as an explanation for the irregularities in Jesus' trial.

Comment
a. Peter follows Jesus (14:53–54)
After Jesus' arrest in Gethsemane, the disciples fled. However, Peter (and, according to John 18:15–16, also John, son of Zebedee) evidently follows Jesus from a distance, daring to enter the premises of the high priest's residence where the members of the Sanhedrin are gathering. His earlier confidence that he will stay loyal to Jesus (14:29, 31) proves true, so far.

53. The arresting party took Jesus to the residence of the *high priest* (*ho archiereus*). Mark does not name the incumbent high priest; the other Gospels identify him as Caiaphas (Matt. 26:57; Luke 3:2; John 11:49; cf. Acts 4:6). His name was Joseph; 'Caiaphas' (Hebrew Ha-Qayaf, Aramaic Qayafa) was a nickname or family name

---

87. *m. Sanh.* 7:10; *t. Sanh.* 10:11; 11:7; *y. Sanh.* 25c–d; cf. 11QTemple LVI, 8–11; cf. Chapman and Schnabel, *Trial and Crucifixion*, pp. 67–81.

88. Cf. Strobel, *Stunde*, pp. 46–92.

(Josephus, *Ant.* 18.35, 95). He was the third member of the family of Annas, whose son-in-law he was, to serve as high priest (see on 11:27). Caiaphas was high priest for eighteen years (AD 18–36). His exceptionally long tenure under two prefects (Valerius Gratus and Pontius Pilate), hardly rivalled by the long nine-year tenure of his father-in-law Annas, attests to his shrewd political talent. Mark relates that *all the chief priests, the elders and the teachers of the law came together* (cf. 8:31). The word *all* may signal full attendance of all members of the Sanhedrin, or underline the contrast between the assembled members of the Jewish court and the lone figure of Jesus without necessarily implying that all members without exception were present. According to later tradition, the Sanhedrin had seventy-one members: seventy council members plus the presiding high priest (*m. Sanh.* 1:6); but these figures cannot be confirmed for the first century. The reference in verses 53–55 to a courtyard suggests the high priest's residence as the venue for the night gathering, perhaps the home of Annas, the *éminence grise* of Jerusalem politics (note the preliminary hearing before Annas reported by John 18:13–24). The so-called Palatial Mansion in the Upper City (in Area P of the Herodian Quarter, c. 270 yds or 250 m south-west of the likely location of the Sanhedrin building and the western gate of the Temple Mount), a large and magnificent two-storey house with numerous ritual baths, was the residence of 'a particularly notable and wealthy family, and the exceptional number of miqvehs may indicate that they were a family of high priests' (N. Avigad, *NEAEHL*, II, p. 733); perhaps this was the residence of the family of Annas, including Caiaphas.

54. The comment regarding Peter following the arresting party *at a distance, right into the courtyard of the high priest* prepares for the report of his betrayal in verses 66–72. The word *aulē* can describe a dwelling complex (Luke 11:21) such as a royal palace (Mark 15:16; Matt. 26:3: the praetorium of the Roman prefect, which had been Herod's palace); here it describes a courtyard surrounded by buildings (BDAG, p. 150): Peter *sat with the guards and warmed himself at the fire.* The Palatial Mansion (v. 53) had a large courtyard (c. 26 by 26 ft or 8 by 8 m) paved with stone tiles around which the ground-floor rooms were grouped. The reception hall of the Palatial Mansion (36 by 21 ft or 11 by 6.4 m) in the west wing was large enough for a substantial gathering. The *guards* are the retainers of the elite families, who had arrested Jesus (see on v. 43).

b. Trial before the Sanhedrin and verdict (14:55–65)

After noting the arrival of the arresting party in the city and the gathering of the Jewish authorities in the residence of the high priest (v. 53), as well as the arrival of Peter in the courtyard of the high priest's residence (v. 54), Mark reports Jesus' trial by the 'whole Sanhedrin' (v. 55). The account consists of five parts: (1) review of evidence that would allow conviction of Jesus on a capital charge, dismissed because of contradictory testimony (vv. 55–56); (2) review of evidence that Jesus planned the destruction of the temple, dismissed because of contradictory testimony and because Jesus refuses to make a statement (vv. 57–61a); (3) direct interrogation of Jesus by the high priest regarding Jesus' messianic identity, which Jesus confirms (vv. 61b–62); (4) indictment of Jesus on the charge of blasphemy (vv. 63–64); (5) mistreatment of Jesus by the members of the Sanhedrin and their retainers (v. 65).

55. Jesus' trial before the Sanhedrin begins when the *chief priests and the whole Sanhedrin* are assembled. The chief priests are members of the Sanhedrin; they are singled out because the high priest chaired the proceedings of the Sanhedrin, and because of their leading role in seeking Jesus' conviction. The fact that they were examining *evidence* (*martyria*, 'testimony in court'; BDAG, p. 619 meaning 2) suggests that even though they had concluded three days earlier, after Jesus' symbolic action in the Outer Court of the temple (11:18), that Jesus needed to be eliminated, they did not have a master plan for Jesus' prosecution, nor had they arranged for witnesses who could prove that a particular teaching or action of Jesus' was criminal. If this had been a kangaroo court with a predetermined outcome, as is sometimes alleged, there would have been no need to examine or look for evidence that could be used in court – they would have arranged reliable witnesses beforehand. The chief priests were committed to getting a conviction, but they certainly did not 'railroad Jesus' (Myers, *Strong Man*, p. 371).

The verb translated *looking* (*zēteō*) in NIV means in judicial contexts 'inquire into, investigate, examine' (*LSJ*, p. 756, *zēteō* meaning I.4). The members of the Sanhedrin are 'investigating the evidence against Jesus'. The imperfect tense of the verb suggests that this examination was going on for some time. The goal of their examination of the testimony of witnesses is formulated with a purpose clause: *so that they could put him to death*. The Jewish authorities knew what verdict they wanted. But they did not know how to obtain that verdict: *they did not find any* – they were not able to discover testimony, confirmed by at least two witnesses in cross-examination, that could be used in the death-penalty case against Jesus.

56. The members of the Sanhedrin called witnesses and cross-examined them. According to *m. Sanhedrin* 5:1–5, the interrogation of witnesses had to cover seven questions in order to establish the date, time and place of the crime. The sentence *Many testified falsely against him* does not necessarily suggest that people invented fictitious stories which they advanced as accusations against Jesus. The verb *pseudomartyreō* ('to give false testimony') does not address the reason for the false testimony. A witness might maliciously invent a charge, or he might make an innocent mistake – about the identity of the accused, the place or time when something took place or the intended meaning of a particular statement made by the accused. See Context for 14:53–72 for material that opponents of Jesus could use as incriminating evidence.

The statement *and their testimony did not agree* (NRSV) signals that the witnesses who spoke out against Jesus were cross-examined. The view that the council wished 'to preserve at least the semblance of justice' (Collins, p. 701) is unwarranted: this would be the case if witnesses whose testimony contradicted something said by an earlier witness were kept on the witness stand as long as it took to harmonize the contradictory statements. The Jewish authorities followed the stipulations of the law not to accept false testimony (Exod. 20:16; Deut. 5:20) and that there must be at least two witnesses (Deut. 17:6; 19:15). No violation of the Jewish legal tradition is discernible. Passages such as Mark 2:6–7, 3:2, 22 could be interpreted in the sense that Jesus was warned that his actions and words violated the law, in agreement with the opinion of the legal experts of the Qumran community that required that an offender be warned of the consequences of a capital offence before being accused in court.[89]

---

89. CD IX, 2–8; 1QS VI, 1; cf. Schiffman, *Qumran and Jerusalem*, p. 105.

57–59. The phrase *some stood up* might signal that these particular plaintiffs were not witnesses brought before the court but members of the Sanhedrin themselves who sat (literally) as judges. Mark reports that some plaintiffs *gave false testimony* (v. 57) because *their testimony did not agree* (NRSV, v. 59). In other words, it was established in the cross-examination that their testimony differed – regarding the date, the time, the place of the crime or the intended meaning of a statement. The content of the teaching that Jesus is allegedly criminally guilty of is related in verse 58: *I will destroy this temple made with human hands and in three days will build another, not made with hands.* Mark has not recorded a pronouncement of Jesus in which he stated that he himself would destroy the temple, nor a pronouncement in which Jesus announced that he would build a new temple.

The first part of the charge – that Jesus said that he planned to destroy the temple – has its basis in Jesus' prediction in 13:2, which was made in public as Jesus and the disciples were leaving the Outer Court. Jesus did not assert that he personally would organize the temple's destruction, but the statement, particularly if connected to Jesus' symbolic action in the temple with its allusion to Jeremiah 7:11, provided the starting point for describing Jesus' prophetic objective as involving the destruction of the temple. Mark's wording of the charge is important: while up to this point he had referred to the temple with the term *hieron* (11:11, 15–16, 27; 12:35; 13:1, 3; 14:49), a term that refers to all the buildings and courts on the Temple Mount (cf. 11:11), he now uses for the first time the term *naos* which refers specifically to the building in which the Inner Sanctuary and the Holy of Holies were located (see on 11:15). Some witnesses may have asserted that Jesus planned to destroy the main temple building with the Holy of Holies, which could be construed as blasphemy and as a disturbance of public order; other witnesses may have testified that they had heard Jesus say that he would destroy the courts of the temple (for which the term *hieron* could be used), perhaps to make room in the Outer Court for the worship of God by the Gentiles (cf. 11:17).

The second part of the charge – that Jesus said that he planned to build another temple 'within three days' (*dia triōn hēmerōn*)[90] – might

---

90. Cf. BDAG, p. 224: *dia* meaning A.2b.

be connected with Jesus' prediction that he would be raised from the dead 'after three days' (*meta treis hēmeras*; 8:31; 9:31; 10:34). This connection would be particularly plausible if someone knew that Jesus had linked the destruction of the temple with the resurrection of his body, the latter constituting a new 'temple', a connection that John 2:19–22 reports for a public pronouncement Jesus made regarding his symbolic action in the temple. Some witnesses evidently knew that Jesus had stated that the temple *made with human hands* (*cheiropoiētos*) would be destroyed – the temple as a physical building, a human construction. In the Greek Old Testament and in Jewish literature, the term *cheiropoiētos* was consistently linked with idols manufactured by human beings.[91] If Jesus indeed described the temple as 'handmade' (this characterization of the temple could have been added by witnesses in an effort to describe Jesus' alleged contempt for the temple), witnesses could have construed this to portray Jesus as rejecting the worship of Yahweh in the temple as idolatrous. And some witnesses evidently knew that Jesus had stated that he would build *another* (*allon*) temple *not made with hands* (*acheiropoiēton*) – not a new temple replacing the temple presently standing in Jerusalem,[92] but a temple of a different kind, a non-physical reality connected with his resurrection. The point that God's presence is no longer located in the physical building of the temple in Jerusalem but in Jesus, who *is* the presence of God and thus a 'temple not made with human hands' (cf. 12:10–11; cf. Matt. 12:6: 'I tell you that something greater than the temple is here'), expresses the reality of a new relationship with God that becomes possible through Jesus' resurrection (France, p. 607). It is quite conceivable that members of the Sanhedrin learned of Jesus' predictions of his resurrection after three days from Judas Iscariot, 'and, not having heard Jesus speak them yet wanting to accuse him of a capital

---

91. LXX Lev. 26:1, 30; Isa. 2:18; Philo, *Mos.* 2.168; *Sib. Or.* 3.604–606.
92. For the idea of a new 'messianic' temple cf. Ezek. 40 – 48, expected to be built by God (11QTemple XXIX, 7–10), or, based on 2 Sam. 7:13 and Zech. 6:12, by the Messiah (*Tg. Isa.* 53:5; *Tg. Zech.* 6:12). In 4QFlor 1 I, 2–6 and *4 Ezra* 10:54 the building of a new temple is associated with the end of days, without the Messiah specifically mentioned as the builder.

offense, did give false testimony by mingle-mangling them' (Gundry, p. 906). The testimony of the second charge was false because the witnesses might have given different versions of Jesus' claim to build a different temple which is not made with human hands, or different versions of what Jesus meant; or they did not agree about the date, the time and the location when Jesus allegedly made the statement.

The testimony of the combined first and second charges – verse 59 implies one single charge – was a witness statement that accused Jesus of three crimes: he pejoratively called the most sacred of the buildings 'handmade'; he arrogated to himself the authority to destroy the temple; and he arrogated to himself the authority to build a superior new temple, implying the authority to do what only God or the Messiah could do. Jesus was not convicted on the charge that he planned to destroy the temple and wanted to build a new temple: the testimony of the witnesses who testified on this matter *did not agree*. However, the charge that Jesus planned the destruction of the temple was significant: it was the basis of Jesus' rejection by the wider population of Jerusalem, demonstrated by taunts uttered at his crucifixion (15:29), and it remained a central part of the authorities' rejection of Jesus, as the Stephen episode (Acts 6:13–14; 7:44–50) demonstrates.

60–61a. At this point the high priest, the presiding official of the Sanhedrin, intervened. He *stood up before them*, signalling his intention personally to interrogate Jesus. His intervention indicates that the trial had reached an impasse. The Sanhedrin did not have any evidence that could be legally used to convict Jesus. Caiaphas' only recourse was to attempt to obtain from Jesus, in direct cross-examination, a statement that could be used to obtain a legal conviction. Caiaphas begins his interrogation with the question *Are you not going to answer?* Mark's readers learn that Jesus had remained silent during the cross-examination of witnesses. Their case had collapsed without Jesus challenging details of their testimony.

Jesus' silence is striking.[93] When his followers ask about the meaning of parables and puzzling sayings (4:10; 7:17), their inability to cast out an evil spirit (9:28), acceptable grounds for divorce

---

93. Cf. Schnabel, 'Silence', pp. 203–257.

(10:10), procuring eternal life (10:17), eschatological questions (9:11; 13:3–4) or about who will betray him (14:19), Jesus always gives an answer. When evil spirits ask Jesus a question (1:24; 5:7), he responds. When opponents approach him with queries, he always replies – whether they are scribes and Pharisees (2:7, 16, 24; 7:5; 10:2), Sadducees (12:18) or chief priests (11:28). However, during his trial, Jesus has been silent, a fact that has no genuine analogies in Greek, Roman or later Christian trials. Jesus' silence has often been explained with reference to the silence of the Suffering Servant in Isaiah 53:7 (with whom Jesus is thus identified),[94] but Mark and the other Gospel writers do not alert their readers that such an allusion is intended; or with the silence of the righteous sufferer (Pss 38:14–16; 39:9); as fulfilment of Psalm 22:15 (MT v. 16); as a reflection of Jesus' portrayal as a sage or teacher of wisdom; as an expression of self-control and perhaps nobility; as Jesus proving that he is in command or showing his contempt for those who sit in judgment over him; or as showing that he is the eschatological judge before the final verdict. There may be some truth in some of these explanations. The most plausible explanation of Jesus' refusal to participate in the cross-examination of the witnesses reckons that he is willing to accept any sentence to which the legal proceedings might lead – which most likely would be a death sentence, given the circumstances of his arrest, the cross-examination during the night immediately before a major festival and the sensitive subject matter of temple destruction. Jesus' silence indicates his willingness to die, his acceptance of suffering and death as the will of God (cf. 8:31; 9:31; 10:32–34, 45; 14:36, 39; cf. Gundry, p. 886).

The high priest's question *What is this testimony that these men are bringing against you?* challenges Jesus to discuss his views on the temple. Jesus continues to remain silent because there is no need to answer contradictory accusations, and because an answer may 'reveal a reluctance to deny categorically the Temple charge' (Marcus, p. 1004). The grammatical form of the verb *apekrinato*, translated 'he gave [no] answer' (aorist middle), is used in the papyri as a technical legal term for 'response': the phrase describes 'Jesus' failure

---

94. Cf. France, p. 608; Pesch, II, p. 435; Moo, *Passion Narratives*, pp. 148–151.

to cooperate with the high priest' (Brown, *Death*, I, p. 464). The unique double mention of Jesus' refusal to answer (*Jesus remained silent and gave no answer*) highlights Jesus' determination not to defend himself regarding the temple charge. Jesus accepts suffering and impending death as the will of God.

61b. The high priest continues his attempt to elicit a statement from Jesus. His next question goes to the heart of Jesus' ministry because it is a question about his identity: *Are you the Messiah, the Son of the Blessed One?* Mark had not portrayed Jesus as publicly claiming to be the Messiah (cf. 1:1). However, Jesus' claim to have the authority to forgive sins which resulted in a charge of blasphemy (2:5–7), his provocative healings on the Sabbath showing a willingness to contravene the law in its traditional interpretation (3:1–6), his public demonstrations of unrestricted power over demons which led to the charge that he acted with satanic authority (3:22) – all this raised the question of what kind of authority Jesus claimed to have, since he never appealed to human authority and since he often explained his actions with reference to God's actions, particularly in his parables. Then, in the last few days, Jesus' actions and teaching raised the question of his messianic identity more explicitly: his triumphal approach to the city, his symbolic action in the temple, his words about the destruction of the temple (11:17; 13:2) and about the arrival of the time when Gentiles would worship in the temple (11:17), his claim to have the status of the Son of God (in the parable of the tenants, 12:1–12), and his pronouncement that the enthroned Son of Man will come with universal power (13:26–27, uttered in a discourse to four disciples, but a statement that 'evidently in some form leaked out to a wider public', France, p. 600).

The high priest's question is thus not a non sequitur. He attempts to provoke Jesus into stating his claim to have unique, messianic authority imbued with divine character, as he had implied in his exorcisms, in his teaching and most recently in his threat against the temple. Jesus had accepted the disciples' identification of him as Messiah, warning them not to speak about him in these terms in public (8:29–30). He had referred to himself as 'Messiah' only once (9:41), and otherwise used the phrase 'the Son of Man' to refer to himself and his mission (cf. 8:31; 9:9, 12, 31; 10:33, 45; 14:21, 41). As regards the expression *Son of the Blessed One*, a Jewish circumlocution for God (cf. Matt. 26:63), Jesus had been called 'Son of God' by God himself (1:11; 9:7) and by demons (3:11; 5:7); he had referred to himself as the Son of God in a parable which he had not explicitly interpreted.[95] The high priest wants to know whether Jesus claims to be the Messiah and to have a special, unique relationship to God with the authority to rule as God's Anointed.

62. Jesus breaks his silence – not in an attempt to defend himself but with a statement that asserts his messianic identity and divine authority, a statement that must lead to the death sentence given the hostile intentions of the chief priests, elders and scribes. Jesus answers Caiaphas' question in the affirmative: *I am*.[96] He affirms, without hesitation, that he is indeed the Messiah and the Son of God. Jesus expands his affirmation, explaining his status and mission: *'you will see the Son of Man seated at the right hand of the Power' and 'coming with the clouds of heaven'* (NRSV). Jesus speaks of himself as the Son of Man, now not in terms of his rejection and death (8:31) but in terms of his glory and power – albeit in a context of a legal trial that will lead to suffering and death. The phrase *you will see the Son of Man* comes from Daniel 7:13, the phrase *sitting at the right hand of the Mighty One* comes from Psalm 110:1, and the phrase *coming on the clouds of heaven* comes again from Daniel 7:13. The word *the Power* (NRSV *hē dynamis*) is a circumlocution for God. In Isaiah 9:6 the coming Davidic ruler is described as 'Wonderful Counsellor' and as 'Mighty God' (Hebr. *'ēl gibbôr*, 'God, the Powerful One'). Sitting 'at the right hand' was the position of greatest influence beside the king. Jesus had cited Psalm 110:1 in 12:36 to demonstrate that the Messiah must be more than a royal son of David since he is David's Lord. Now Jesus asserts that he is indeed the Davidic Messiah, but he is not a national

---

95. The Qumran text 4Q246, which connects the messianic Son of God with the Son of Man of Dan. 7, is evidence that 'the notion that the messiah was Son of God in a special sense was rooted in Judaism' (Collins, *Scepter*, p. 190).

96. The expression *egō eimi* ('I am') is a standard Greek idiom of affirmation. Jesus' words are not an echo of Isa. 43:10, 13 or Exod. 3:14; he does not pronounce the divine name or claim equality with God: uttering the divine name would not answer Caiaphas' question.

deliverer – his sovereign authority is exercised at the right hand of God. They will see him enthroned at the right hand of God, sharing God's sovereign authority, like the Son of Man of Daniel 7:13–14 who comes before God in the clouds of heaven and who is immediately given 'dominion and glory and kingship' (NRSV) which are universal and unending. In the context of the trial before the Sanhedrin whose members want to condemn him to death, a verdict which they are about to pronounce, Jesus' statement speaks of his vindication. Jesus' vindication takes place in his exaltation in his resurrection (cf. Rom. 1:4; Acts 2:32–33) and his ascension to the right hand of God (cf. Heb. 10:12–13) – 'seen' by the Jewish leaders in the courageous and powerful mission of Jesus' disciples who establish congregations of followers of Jesus in Jerusalem, Judea and Samaria and in many provinces of the Roman world, congregations in which Jews and Gentiles worship God and his Son, Jesus Messiah. As far as the members of the Sanhedrin are personally concerned, Jesus' ultimate vindication will take place when Jesus returns in the role of the Son of Man, who will judge those who are now sitting in judgment over him.

63–64. The high priest *tore his clothes*, not as a sign of grief[97] but as a formal judicial act indicating a guilty verdict. Since the high priest was forbidden to tear his priestly vestments (Lev. 21:10), he was either wearing regular clothes when he chaired Sanhedrin sessions or he tore the inner tunics (*chitōnes*) that he was wearing under his liturgical garments.[98] The question *Why do we need any more witnesses?* is not a rhetorical question: no witnesses are needed since the members of the Sanhedrin have heard Jesus' pronouncement concerning his identity.

The high priest classifies Jesus' pronouncement (v. 62) as constituting *blasphemy*. The general definition of the Greek term *blasphēmia* is 'speech that denigrates or defames' (BDAG, p. 178). In *m. Sanhedrin* 7:5, blasphemy is defined as 'clearly pronouncing the Name', referring to the tetragrammaton YHWH (usually transcribed as

---

97. Gen. 37:29; Num. 14:6; Josh. 7:6; 2 Sam. 1:11–12; Job 1:20; Isa. 36:22.
98. Stein, p. 685; Matt. 26:65 uses the word *himatia*. Josephus, *Ant.* 17.136 mentions that some people wore two inner tunics.

Yahweh). Some argue that Jesus did in fact pronounce the name of God when he used Psalm 110:1 in his answer to Caiaphas' question (Gundry, pp. 915–918); the fact that Mark reports Jesus referring to the circumlocution 'the Power' (NRSV) is explained in terms of later tradition that substituted other terms for the name of God in order to avoid offence. This explanation is neither plausible nor necessary since the Mishnah's definition of blasphemy is narrower than general usage. Besides pronouncing the divine name,[99] other actions and other speech were regarded as blasphemy: claiming divine prerogatives,[100] despising the law and profaning holy things,[101] threatening the temple[102] and attacking the divinely appointed leadership.[103] The charge of blasphemy against Jesus is most plausibly connected with the fact that Jesus identified himself with the authority of the enthroned royal figure of Psalm 110:1 and with the authoritative figure of the One like a Son of Man of Daniel 7:13, with his claims of sitting next to God in heaven[104] and being instrumental in the final judgement, and with his attack on Israel's leadership with his threat that he would sit in judgment over them. In the wider context, the charge of blasphemy could also be linked with Jesus' statements concerning the temple which evidently were interpreted as a threat, and with his statements that could be interpreted as despising the law and profaning holy things, although any such charges made by witnesses had not been proven (vv. 55–59).

With the question *What do you think?* the high priest asks the members of the Sanhedrin to render a verdict. Mark notes that *all*

---

99. Philo, *Mos.* 2.203–208; Josephus, *Ant.* 4.198, 202; *m. Sanh.* 6:4; 7:5.
100. Philo, *Somn.* 2.129–132; *Decal.* 61–63l; *y. Ta'anit* 65b; *b. Sanh.* 38b.
101. *Sifre Bamidbar* §112 on Num. 15:30–31.
102. Josephus, *Ant.* 12.406; *War* 6.300–309.
103. Josephus, *Ant.* 13.293–296. Cf. Bock, *Blasphemy*, pp. 30–112; Chapman and Schnabel, *Trial and Crucifixion*, pp. 98–130.
104. While Jewish tradition knows of figures such as Adam, Abel, Abraham, Job, Moses and David being exalted to heaven, and David and Moses sitting on a throne in the heavenly throne room, it is 'a very different thing from confronting a living human being who predicts that he himself will be so enthroned' (Collins, 'Charge', p. 399).

condemned him as worthy of death. Death (*thanatos*) is the punishment that the Jewish authorities impose on Jesus. The penalty for blasphemy was death by stoning (Lev. 24:10–16; *m. Sanh.* 7:4–5). Since the Sanhedrin could not execute criminals, with the exception of offences that involved the sanctity of the temple, they had to transfer the case to Pontius Pilate, the Roman prefect, which is what they do (cf. 15:1–2).

65. Some of the members of the Sanhedrin *began to spit at him.* Spitting at a person shamed and demeaned (cf. Num. 12:14; Deut. 25:9; Job 30:10). The Servant of the Lord in Isaiah 50:6 is spat upon as well. Some *blindfolded* Jesus, *struck him with their fists, and said, 'Prophesy!'* They want Jesus to say who is hitting him. Jesus' reputation as a prophet (6:15; 8:28) and his prophecies in 14:58, 62 explain this cruel game which is meant to mock Jesus. Mark's readers would have noted the irony that Jesus had predicted precisely this kind of treatment (10:33–34). When they were done mocking and insulting Jesus, they handed him over to the *guards* (cf. v. 54), who *took him and beat him,* continuing the physical abuse of the prisoner who has just been condemned to death. Josephus confirms the practice, if not legality, of 'distinguished citizens' of Jerusalem physically abusing prisoners who stood before a Jewish court of law (*War* 6.302).

c. The denial of Peter (14:66–72)
Before Mark reports the transfer of Jesus to the Roman authorities and the trial before Pontius Pilate, he picks up the story of Peter, who had followed Jesus and the arresting party into the courtyard of the high priest's residence (14:53–54). Peter's earlier denial that he would ever disown Jesus, even if it meant death (14:31), is now put to the test, a test that he fails, thus fulfilling Jesus' prediction (14:30). The event described here occurred during Jesus' trial before the Sanhedrin.

66–67. Peter was last mentioned in verse 54 sitting with the authorities' retainers at a fire in the courtyard of the high priest's residence. The *servant girl* is a female slave who belonged to the high priest's family. She is thus a 'colleague' of Malchus, whom Peter had assaulted in Gethsemane (cf. v. 47), a fact that made her approach to Peter doubly dangerous. She seems to have been in the courtyard on her duties; according to John 18:16–17 she was 'the slave who kept the door' (BDAG, p. 749). The progression from *she saw* to *she looked closely at him* indicates that she recognized Peter, probably because she had seen him with Jesus and the other disciples on the Temple Mount, alerted to them when the popular prophet from Galilee, deemed dangerous by the chief priests, was discussed in the household of the high priest. There is nothing threatening about her assertion *You also were with Jesus, the man from Nazareth* (NRSV). People were regularly identified with reference to the city in which they were born or in which they lived (cf. Acts 21:39: 'I am a Jew, from Tarsus in Cilicia'); there is no hint in the text that the description of Jesus as 'inhabitant of Nazareth' (or 'the man from Nazareth', NRSV; 'the Nazarene', NASB, RSV) is derogatory or signalling contempt (as assumed by commentators, reflected in NIV 'that Nazarene'). There is no reason to assume that Nathanael's prejudice against Nazareth (John 1:46) was shared by the slave girl or the authorities' retainers in the courtyard (not all of whom may have been Judeans; in John 7:41, 52 people express the opinion that neither the Messiah nor a prophet can come from Galilee, which is not the same as contempt for Galilee).

68. Since Peter always seems to be more than willing to speak, he *denied* having been with Jesus. The verb *arneomai* means 'to refuse consent', 'to state that something is not true'; here, 'to disclaim association with a person or event' (BDAG, p. 132). Peter repudiates his association with Jesus. He disowns Jesus, who had called him as his first disciple (1:16–18) and who had selected him to be one of the Twelve (3:13–19). Mark relates the denial in direct speech: *I do not know or understand what you are talking about* (NRSV). He not only denies that he has been in Jesus' company; he also categorically denies knowing him. He claims that he has no idea what she is talking about, suggesting that she should drop the matter. Mark's readers would remember that Jesus had predicted Peter's denial (v. 30), and they might have remembered Jesus' word about his being ashamed of anyone who is ashamed of him (8:38).

Peter left the courtyard (*aulos*) and went to the *proaulion*, a word that denotes the place in front of a house; it can be translated 'forecourt' or 'gateway'. He left the courtyard, perhaps because he remembered Jesus' prediction of three denials and wanted to move to a location that would not be lit by the fire. But he decided to stay close, which should be understood as a sign of courage. Some manuscripts include the sentence *Then the cock crowed* (NRSV; cf. ESV, GNB, KJV), while other (earlier) manuscripts omit the phrase (NASB, NIV, RSV). Either a later copyist introduced the first cock-crow to prepare for the reference to a second crock-crow in verse 72, or early copyists adapted to the text of the other three Gospels which narrate three denials of Peter but only one cock-crow. The standard edition of the Greek text includes the phrase within square brackets.

69–70a. Peter's categorical denial of knowing anything about Jesus was not plausible: there was no reason for anybody to be in the courtyard of the high priest's residence around 2 or 3 am, with a Sanhedrin session held inside the house, unless his presence was in some way connected to Jesus. So the same female slave, when she saw Peter in the gateway, said *to those standing round them* that *This man is one of them* (NRSV; NIV 'this fellow' is derogatory, which is not indicated in the text). She appeals to bystanders – presumably slaves and assistants of the members of the Sanhedrin who had accompanied their masters as they walked after nightfall to the high priest's residence – to corroborate her assertion that Peter is *one of them*, a phrase that indicates that Jesus' disciples were perceived and known as a coherent group. Peter again *denied* that he belonged to Jesus and his disciples. The imperfect tense of the verb (*ērneito*) could suggest that Peter denied Jesus repeatedly, perhaps being challenged by several of the bystanders; or it may indicate that he 'tried' to deny it (conative imperfect). Mark does not relate the words that Peter spoke at the second denial; they may have differed little from those of the first denial. While Peter's first denial probably also took place in front of an audience (implied in vv. 54, 66), his second denial explicitly takes place in front of a crowd.

70b–71. It took only *a little while* (or 'after a short while') for *those standing near* to address Peter again. This time Mark relates their words in direct speech: *Surely you are one of them, for you are a Galilean.* They recognize Peter's Aramaic Galilean accent (explicitly stated in Matt. 26:73). According to *b. Berakot* 32a, Galileans are said to pronounce *'aleph* as *'ayin* and *'ayin* as *'aleph*: that is, their *'aleph* is too guttural and their *'ayin* is not guttural enough (Evans, p. 466). The fact that some of the authorities' retainers identify Peter as belonging to the group of people who have attached themselves to Jesus is dangerous: they may force Peter to be a witness in the trial; and Peter may be afraid to be recognized as the person who attacked and cut off the ear of Malchus, a retainer in the high priest's entourage (cf. v. 47).

Peter's third denial is again reported in direct speech: *I do not know this man you are talking about* (NRSV). This is more explicitly a repudiation of Jesus than the first denial (v. 68). The expression *this man* is dismissive, a striking formulation for Jesus' premier disciple who had identified him as Messiah (8:29). Mark prefaces Peter's declaration with the comment that *he began to curse, and he swore an oath* (NRSV). The term 'swear an oath' (*omnyō*) means 'to affirm the veracity of one's statement by invoking a transcendent entity, freq[uently] with the implied invitation of punishment if one is untruthful' (BDAG, p. 705). This means that Peter emphasized his statement by swearing that it was true, using a formula such as 'May God do . . . to me if . . .' The word 'to curse' (*anathematizō*) means 'to invoke consequences if what one says is not true'. If the word is understood in a transitive sense and taken as synonymous with the term 'to swear' (Mark often uses two roughly synonymous expressions to emphasize a point; cf. 1:40; 11:31; 13:19; 14:61), Peter invokes a curse on himself (RSV, ESV 'he began to invoke a curse on himself'; NLT 'a curse on me if I'm lying'). In this interpretation, Peter puts himself under a curse if what he says is not true.[105] However, since the verb is not linked with a reflexive pronoun (as in Acts 23:12, 14, 21), it can be taken in the intransitive sense 'to put someone under a curse'. Many commentators think that Peter is cursing Jesus.[106] This seems unlikely.[107] Jesus predicted that Peter would 'deny' him, not that he would 'curse' him, and, significantly, Matthew, who often presents Peter in a more positive light, uses the equally strong verb *katathematizō*, which suggests 'that he does *not* view Mark's language as particularly

---

105. BDAG, *anathematizō* b; Bayer, p. 545; Collins, p. 708; Pesch, II, p. 450.
106. France, p. 622; Gundry, p. 890; Marcus, pp. 1019–1020; Brown, *Death*, I, pp. 604–605; H. Merkel, 'Peter's Curse', in Bammel, *Trial*, pp. 66–71.
107. Note Pliny, the governor of Bithynia, who states in a letter to Trajan that 'real Christians' cannot be compelled to curse Jesus (Pliny, *Ep.* 10.96.5).

offensive' (Strauss, p. 665). It seems preferable to think that Peter called down curses on the bystanders who identify him as one of Jesus' companions, essentially saying, 'Go to hell for making such accusations against me! I swear to you I do not know the man' (J. Behm, *TDNT*, I, p. 355).

72. When *the cock crowed the second time*, at the very moment when Peter spoke the words reported in verse 71, Jesus' prediction that Peter would deny him three times (v. 30) was fulfilled. Matthew, Luke and John follow the usual practice of calling this simply *the* cock-crow, the cock-crow usually referred to in ancient literature that people would have heard when they woke up at the end of the third watch (called 'cock-crow'; see on vv. 27–30). Mark 'follows the apparently rare practice of calling it second cock-crow. Perhaps, since Peter spends the third watch of the night with people who, like him, stayed awake all night, it seemed appropriate to Mark to refer to cock-crow as those on watch through the night might do'.[108]

Mark describes Peter's response to the cock-crow with three terms. He *remembered* the word of Jesus' prophecy (quoted in direct speech). He *wept*: he shed tears. The reference to the shedding of tears is modified by a participle which many translations render *he broke down* (ESV, GNB, NIV, NLT, NRSV, RSV); the basic meaning of the verb *epiballō* is 'to throw upon', which fits the present context only if the participle (which here has no object) is understood reflexively, in the sense that Peter began attacking himself, beating his breast. Since the verb often denotes putting on clothing, some suggest that Peter covered his head, expressing shame. A rare meaning is 'to begin': Mark would then be saying that Peter 'began to weep' (NASB). Another possibility is the meaning 'to throw [into one's mind]'; that is, 'to think about, consider': Peter thought about Jesus' prediction (KJV). In line with the geographical progression implied both in the verb and in the context – Peter had moved from the courtyard to the gateway – is the suggestion that the verb means 'to rush outside': he 'runs out of the house altogether', which explains 'how Peter manages to avoid arrest if his tears clearly identify him as a follower of Jesus' (Marcus, p. 1021).

---

108. Bauckham, *Jewish World*, pp. 417–418.

Theology
Jesus is the Messiah, the Son of God, the Son of Man who shares God's divine dignity. The declaration that the high priest elicits from Jesus is the climax of Mark's Gospel in terms of his portrayal of Jesus, and it is the heart of Mark's paradoxical presentation of Jesus. In 'narrative reality', Jesus' opponents who have plotted for some time to kill him have arrested him, put him on trial and managed to get an incrimination statement that they can use for a death sentence, but in 'theological reality' Jesus is the Messiah, the unique Son of God, the heavenly Son of Man (France, p. 599). The significance of Jesus' silence throughout the trial becomes understandable when he finally speaks, challenged directly by the high priest to state who he thinks he is: he declares his messianic identity and his status as the unique Son of God and Son of Man enthroned at the right hand of God, a declaration that he knows will lead to a death sentence since the Jewish authorities will not accept it as truth.

v. Jesus' trial before Pontius Pilate (15:1–20)
Context
The report about Jesus' trial before Pontius Pilate follows immediately after the report about Jesus' trial before the Sanhedrin chaired by the high priest. Mark's account of the trial conducted by Pilate is very concise. Pilate focuses on the central question of whether Jesus claims to be king (15:2), mentioned before the reference to the charges against Jesus brought by the chief priests (15:3), and on Jesus' refusal to answer their charges (15:4–5). Mark does not report Jesus' transfer to Herod Antipas or the punishment of flogging executed by Pilate. Mark reports Pilate's attempt to free Jesus by means of a Passover amnesty (15:6–11) and by means of popular acclamation (*acclamatio populi*) (15:12), and that the crowd wants Jesus to be crucified (15:13–14). Pilate's verdict of punishment by flogging and crucifixion is implied rather than reported (15:15). Roman governors had exclusive jurisdiction in capital cases, without any limitations on their *coercitio* (power to correct and enforce), especially when law and order needed to be maintained against troublemakers. Penal *coercitio* measures included imposition of fines, seizing of property, corporal punishment and capital punishment. In the case of provincials who did not have Roman citizenship, the governors

had the authority to impose penal *coercitio* measures at their discretion.

Comment
a. Pilate's interrogation of Jesus (15:1–5)
Mark relates an early-morning session of the Sanhedrin in which the chief priests, the elders and the scribes finalized the outcome of the trial during the previous night, planning the transfer of the death-penalty case involving Jesus to the Roman prefect. Jesus is taken to Pontius Pilate, who tries Jesus on capital charges.

1. The expression *very early in the morning* (Gr. *prōi*) refers here to the time after the cock-crow that ended the third watch of the night (cf. 14:30). The morning session took place between 4 and 6 am. The location of the session was most probably the venue of Sanhedrin meetings (cf. 14:53), not far from the residence of the high priest. The sentence *the chief priests held a consultation with the elders and scribes and the whole council* (NRSV) can be understood in different ways: (1) the participial clause summarizes the trial that was held during the night ('having held their council'); (2) it indicates that the chief priests (re)convened a session of the full Sanhedrin; (3) it refers to the Sanhedrin's decision to take Jesus to Pilate (NIV 'made their plans'; NLT 'met to discuss their next step'). While the first explanation is possible,[109] the second and third options, which can be combined, are more plausible: the time indicator (*very early in the morning*) signals a new event. A full session of the Sanhedrin formally ratified the result of the trial held during the previous hours. According to Josephus, the *boule* ('Council') met in a venue which was located where the first city wall coming from the Xystus met the west wall of the temple (*War* 5.144), in or above the Tyropoeon Valley immediately west of the Temple Mount, a location perhaps to be identified with the magnificent hall (the so-called Hasmonean Hall) excavated near Wilson's Arch (cf. H. Geva, *NEAEHL*, II, p. 742).

The people responsible for Jesus' death sentence in the Sanhedrin and for his transfer to the Roman authorities are the same three

---

109. Evans, p. 475; France, p. 626; Stein, p. 697; Brown, *Death*, I, pp. 629–632.

groups mentioned in 8:31; 11:27; 14:43, 53. The formulation in verse 1 underscores the leading role of the chief priests; after verse 3 it is always the chief priests who are named as Jesus' accusers. The authorities *bound Jesus* and *led him away*. This is the first reference to Jesus being bound, in all likelihood with chains, signalling to Pilate that Jesus is publicly confined and that he is a dangerous criminal.[1] Chaining usually involved an iron collar and iron manacles on one hand; the chains often weighed over 10 pounds (4.5 kg).

The sentence *they . . . handed him over to Pilate* signals the transfer of Jesus' case to the Roman prefect. The expression *handed over* describes historically the transfer to Pilate, but theologically the fact that behind all this was divine necessity (8:31; 14:21) in which God 'handed over' his Son as a ransom for many (10:45; 14:27, 36). Literary and documentary sources illustrate the complex relationship between Roman provincial administrations and the local courts. The papyrus *P. Oxy.* II 237 refers to the 'law of the Egyptians' that was adhered to in early Roman Egypt when the Roman governor would take cases that lower courts could not decide, which indicates that it was legally appropriate for the Jewish leaders to affirm in Jesus' trial before Pilate that 'We have a law, and according to that law he must die, because he claimed to be the Son of God' (John 19:7).[111] When the prophet Jesus ben Ananias, active in Jerusalem in AD 62–64, predicted that a disaster would fall on Jerusalem, the temple and the people, the Jewish authorities were not able to silence him: they took him to Albinus, the Roman prefect (Josephus, *War* 6.303–305). This incident indicates that the Jewish authorities were responsible for preventing riots and maintaining law and order in case of disturbances, and for arresting and imprisoning criminals and transferring them to the Roman authorities, assisting the Roman prefects in matters of criminal justice. It has been suggested that due to the messianic implications of the *seditio* charge, the Roman prefect temporarily yielded the preliminary investigation to the Sanhedrin, a procedure that neither robbed the sentence and

---

1. Cf. Rapske, *Paul*, pp. 25–28; on chains, pp. 206–209.
111. Cf. Chapman and Schnabel, *Trial and Crucifixion*, pp. 147–149. For the following example see ibid., pp. 123–127, 149–151.

execution imposed on Jesus of the character of a Roman trial, nor called into question the monopoly of Roman capital punishment.[112]

Pilate, whose full Latin name was Pontius Pilatus,[113] may have belonged to the old Samnite family of the Pontii. He was a Roman knight (*eques*) who was appointed *praefectus Iudaeae* by the emperor Tiberius, perhaps as early as AD 19 (the traditional date is AD 26), administering Judea until AD 36. Pilate was not an independent provincial governor but a prefect (*praefectus*; Gr. *eparchos*), subordinate to the consular legate of the province of Syria (Eck, *Rom*, pp. 1–51). The competencies of Pilate included the responsibility to maintain law and order, especially as far as Roman citizens were concerned; he monitored the Jewish authorities; he alone had the authority to try capital cases (*ius gladii*) in the region he administered; he had auxiliary troops at his disposal (cf. v. 16). Pilate's long tenure indicates that he was successful in maintaining a balance between his loyalty to Rome and his authority in Judea. Josephus and Philo report disturbances under Pilatus. The Roman authorities seem to have treated these and similar incidents as insignificant. In contrast to (largely earlier) scholars who assumed that Pilate hated the Jews on account of his close relationship with Lucius Aelius Sejanus, who was an enemy of the Jews, scholars today generally no longer describe Pilate as being hostile to the Jews. Some emphasize the difficulty of Pilate's task as prefect of Judea and explain his clashes with the Jewish people and his behaviour during Jesus' trial by a mixture of obstinacy and weakness of character. Some explain the clashes between Pilate and the Jewish population by Pilate's character on the one hand and his understanding of the role of a prefect in a Roman province on the other hand: he expected acceptance of his role as Roman prefect by the population of the province, and he sought to honour the emperor by bringing Judea into line with the Roman provinces, despite Jewish sensibilities.[114]

Since the working day began at daybreak and since Roman officials, like other people, began work as early as possible, 'there is

---

112. Wieacker, *Rechtsgeschichte*, II, p. 366.
113. Cf. *CIIP* II 1277; Josephus, *Ant.* 18.35; Luke 3:1; Acts 4:27; 1 Tim. 6:13.
114. Strobel, *Stunde*, pp. 99–131; Lémonon, *Ponce Pilate*, pp. 221–277.

no difficulty in supposing that the evangelists represent the Jewish authorities as taking Jesus to Pilate a considerable time' before sunrise.[115] According to Seneca, Roman trials began at daybreak (*De ira* 2.7.3). The discussion of Jesus' case may have started as early as 5 am. The trial took place at the official judgment seat (*bēma*) which had been placed in a spot outside the Praetorium, the governor's official residence (Mark 15:16; cf. Matt. 27:27). There is general agreement that the Roman prefects of Judea, when they were in Jerusalem, took up residence in Herod's palace situated against the western wall of the city south of the three Herodian towers. In John 19:13 the place outside the Praetorium where Jesus' trial took place is called Lithostrotos (Hebr. Gabbatha). The Lithostrotos is most likely to have been located in the courtyard inside a gateway into the city about 330 feet (100 m) south of Herod's palace (near today's Jaffa Gate),[116] a place where the Roman prefect would be able to hold court without bringing people into the palace proper. (The Lithostrotos was not in the Antonia Fortress on the north-west corner of the Temple Mount where a stone pavement under the Convent of the Sisters of Zion with the lines of a 'king game' played by Roman solders is shown to tourists as the place of Jesus' trial; this pavement belongs to the later Roman city of Aelia Capitolina.)[117]

2. Pilate's question, *Are you the king of the Jews?*, implies that charges have been filed by the Jewish authorities, reported by Mark in verse 3; see verse 12, where Pilate refers to the fact that Jesus was called 'the king of the Jews' by Jews. The title *the king of the Jews* (*ho basileus tōn Ioudaiōn*) has not been used by Mark until this point. The phrase *of the Jews* indicates that the title was more likely used by people who were not Jews themselves. In verse 32 the Jewish leaders use the

---

115. Bauckham, *Jewish World*, p. 418 (who writes 'before sunset' but means 'before sunrise'). Sherwin-White, *Roman Society*, p. 45: Pliny had completed his whole working day by 10 am when he was prefect of the fleet (*Ep.* 3.5.9–11; 6.16.4–5). Cf. Brown, *Death*, I, p. 629.

116. Cf. M. Broshi and S. Gibson, in Geva, *Ancient Jerusalem Revealed*, pp. 147–155; Gibson, *Final Days*, pp. 96–106 (takes this gate to be the Essene Gate).

117. Cf. U. C. van Wahlde, in Charlesworth, *Jesus and Archaeology*, pp. 572–575.

expression 'king of Israel'. The title is an appropriate 'translation' of the title 'Messiah' (*Christos*) into language which the Roman prefect would understand and which he would recognize as potentially treasonous. Jewish leaders of insurrections regularly called themselves *basileus* (Josephus, *Ant.* 17.285). According to *Jewish Antiquities* 16.311, Herod I, who was confirmed by the Roman Senate as king, had the title 'the king of the Jews'.

Since the emperor had not appointed Jesus to be king in Judea or Galilee, the charge that Jesus claimed to be king could be construed as falling within Cicero's definition of the crime of *maiestas* (Cicero, *Inv.* 2.53: the person who has *maiestas*, that is, unquestionably superior power and dignity, is owed respect, deference and obedience). Merely making impious comments (*inreligiose dicta*) about the deified emperor could be construed as constituting *crimen maiestatis*, the crime of *lèse-majesté* (Tacitus, *An.* 2.50). Some regard a conviction of Jesus for *maiestas* difficult: since Jesus was a provincial non-citizen belonging to the lower classes, a 'foreigner' (*peregrinus*), a conviction on the charge of sedition (*seditio*) or troublemaking seems more likely.[118] Others argue that in the imperial period *seditio* could be understood as *crimen maiestatis* (or *crimen laesae maiestatis*).[119] See further on verse 15.

Since Jesus had proclaimed 'the kingdom of God' (*hē basileia tou theou*),[120] the title 'the king of the Jews' had a positive meaning for Mark, also indicated by the fact that it is used six times in the passion account (15:2, 9, 12, 18, 26, 32). The claim that Jesus is king is the reason for the soldiers' mocking of Jesus (15:16–20) and for the official written notice attached to the cross summarizing the charges (15:26). Mark expects his readers to recognize that 'Jesus does enter into his true kingship, paradoxically, enthroned on the cross' (France, p. 628).

Jesus' response, *You have said so*, is most plausibly taken in the sense that 'what has been phrased as a question is true; yet the one who phrased it must take responsibility for it – in this case, must

---

118. Cook, 'Crucifixion', pp. 199–203.
119. Heusler, *Kapitalprozesse*, pp. 202–203, 239–266.
120. Cf. 1:15; 4:11, 26, 30; 9:1, 47; 10:14–15, 23–25; 11:10; 12:34; 14:25.

take responsibility for any political interpretation that would have Jesus overthrowing the Roman administration of Judea' (Brown, *Death*, I, p. 733). Mark's readers would know that Jesus did not make political, nationalistic, anti-Roman claims, even as he is a king. Neither Jesus' understanding of his mission nor Mark's description of Jesus' ministry indicates the political connotations that Pilate would be assuming. Jesus affirms that he is 'the king of the Jews' – he is the Messiah, as he affirmed in the Jewish trial (14:62) – even though he is reluctant to use the language of 'king' connected with the ethnikon 'the Jews'. The continuation of Mark's report of Jesus' trial indicates that Jesus' brief reply was not sufficient to convince Pilate that Jesus' answer conveyed royal claims.

3–5. Mark now reports that *the chief priests accused him of many things*. As in the trial before the Sanhedrin (14:56), Mark does not specify the charges, although verse 12 implies the charge that Jesus claims to be king. We should note that the charge that Jesus threatened to destroy the temple, which played a central albeit unsuccessful role in the Sanhedrin trial (14:58), is not mentioned, perhaps because this charge had been so thoroughly discredited due to the conflicting witness testimony that the chief priests did not dare hurt their case by using this tainted charge. According to Luke 23:2, they brought the following charges: 'We have found this man subverting our nation. He opposes payment of taxes to Caesar and claims to be Messiah, a king.' The charge of 'misleading' the Jewish people corresponds to Jesus' treatment as a *mesît* and *maddiaḥ* by the Sanhedrin (see Context for 14:53–72). The question of taxes had been the subject of one of the discussions on the Temple Mount a few days earlier (12:13–17). In the trial before the Sanhedrin, Jesus had affirmed that he was 'Messiah, a king' (14:62). Pilate's question in verse 1 indicates that this is the charge he focuses on.

Jesus remained silent, as in the trial before the Sanhedrin. On Jesus' silence see on 14:60–61. When Jesus was directly challenged by the high priest, he gave an (incriminating) answer. Jesus answers affirmatively Pilate's question whether he is the king of the Jews, but then remains silent. The fact that he does not defend himself suggests, again, that he is willing to accept any sentence to which the legal proceedings may lead – which will be a death sentence, given the charge that Jesus claims royal status. Since Pilate is suspicious of the chief priests' motives (v. 10), Jesus may be able to impress upon him his innocence regarding the political charges. His silence indicates that he does not want to avoid the 'cup' that he accepted in Gethsemane as the Father's will. Pilate *was amazed* that Jesus did not answer the chief priests' charges or respond to his suggestion to defend himself against their charges. Pilate's subsequent attempts to release Jesus suggest that he was impressed by Jesus' unintimidated silence, perhaps admiring his stoic silence in the face of suffering.[121]

Jesus' affirmation that he is the king of the Jews, which would be taken as a confession of guilt of this particular charge, together with his refusal to defend himself, warranted Pilate's eventual judgment of guilt. The Roman prefect was bound to condemn him since in the Roman legal system a formal verdict and a regular *quaestio* became unnecessary if the accused admitted his guilt or if he abandoned defending himself (*defensionem relinquere*). Relinquishing the demand that the plaintiff prove his guilt signalled the renunciation of claims to be innocent. An accused person who confesses guilt brings the trial to an end: *confessus pro iudicato est* (he who has confessed is as if convicted).[122]

b. Unsuccessful attempts to release Jesus (15:6–15)
Pilate's admiration for Jesus' consistent silence leads to attempts to release Jesus. Alternatively, he wanted to free Jesus in order to demonstrate to the Jewish authorities that he could not be pressured into making whatever decisions they wanted him to make. Pilate evidently did not take Jesus' assertion that he was indeed the king of the Jews as indicative of subversive political activities that deserved to be punished.

6. The Passover amnesty, referred to as *privilegium paschale*, is specifically mentioned in John 18:39, more generally here and in Matthew 27:15 with reference to *the festival*. The translation *it was the*

---

121. Evans, p. 479; cf. Plutarch, *Mor.* 498D–E; Plato, *Resp.* 2.5.361e. Marcus, p. 1035, sees an echo of Isa. 52:15.

122. Kunkel, *Schriften*, pp. 19–20. Garnsey, 'Lex Iulia', p. 173: 'The *confessus*, the *non respondens*, and the *indefensus*, were all *iudicati*, or *iure lege damnati*.'

custom (NIV) introduces the term *synētheia* ('custom') from John 18:39 into the Markan text (*he used to release* [NRSV]; Matthew uses the word *eiōtha*, 'to maintain a custom'). The available sources do not confirm that Roman prefects in Judea regularly released a prisoner on the occasion of the Passover festival, which celebrated Israel's liberation from Egypt. However, several texts demonstrate that provincial governors had the authority to grant amnesties.[123] The term *venia* was used to refer to the pardon of people who had been convicted of a crime, either as an act of clemency in view of extenuating circumstances or as an act of grace irrespective of the question of guilt (usually) before the verdict was pronounced. There is no good reason to doubt that a particular amnesty tradition could have been established under local circumstances, such as granting one prisoner *venia* at the Passover festival.[124]

7. The name *Barabbas* (Aramaic *bar 'abba'*, 'son of Abba') is a patronymic used as a personal name (like Bartimaeus). Both 'Abba' and 'Barabbas' are attested as personal names. In Matthew 27:16–17 he is called 'Jesus Barabbas' (in later manuscripts, but 'Jesus' is accepted as the original reading by many scholars). Mark describes Barabbas as being *in prison* (lit. 'bound'), waiting to be tried in court, perhaps on this very day when the Roman prefect was in the city. He was connected *with the insurrectionists* (NASB); the word *stasiastēs* describes a person 'who stirs up sedition' (*LSJ*, p. 1633), 'a factious pers[on] who causes public discord', a 'rebel, revolutionary' (BDAG, p. 940). These rebels *had committed murder in the uprising*; the word *stasis* can be translated as 'uprising, riot, revolt, rebellion'. Several people, Barabbas among them, had started a riot which some interpreted as an insurrection. According to Luke 23:19, the riot had taken place in Jerusalem; Luke says that Barabbas had been thrown into prison because of the riot and for murder. In John 18:40 Barabbas is called a 'brigand' (*lēstēs*). Jesus was crucified together with two *lēstai* (Mark 15:27; Matt. 27:38, 44): they probably belonged to the same group

---

123. Livy 8.35.4–10; *P. Flor.* I 61; Josephus, *Ant.* 20.215; Pliny, *Ep.* 10.31–32. According to *m. Pes.* 8:6, Jews expected Jewish prisoners to be released at Passover. Cf. Chapman and Schnabel, *Trial and Crucifixion*, pp. 255–269.
124. Cf. Waldstein, *Begnadigungsrecht*, pp. 41–44.

as Barabbas (see on v. 27). Since Barabbas was, provocatively, singled out for a pardon, he was probably the leading insurrectionist. According to Josephus, *Jewish War*, 2.253, 'brigands' were often understood to be revolutionaries. It is not clear that Barabbas was a 'popular hero' (France, p. 631): the crowd asks for Barabbas because it is incited by the chief priests to do so (v. 11). When war came in AD 66, 'most of southern Syria and most Judaeans in the province wanted no part of a showdown with the legions, no matter how intense the grievances . . . As a result, there was little fighting, even of a guerrilla kind' (Mason, *Jewish War*, p. 588). This was a dangerous time to be charged with *seditio*, more so if one claimed to be a king, as several insurrectionists were tried by Pilate and executed on this Friday, 8 April AD 30.

8. The *crowd* of Jews *came up*; that is, arrived at the Praetorium in Herod's former palace (cf. v. 1). Since Mark does not comment on the composition of the crowd, it is plausible to assume that they were inhabitants of Jerusalem and festival pilgrims getting ready for Passover. They came to Pilate and asked him *to do for them what he usually did*, knowing that the prefect would release a prisoner if they asked for a pardon.

9–10. Pilate seeks to release Jesus by means of the Passover amnesty. He considers Jesus to be innocent of *seditio* charges. He *realized that it was out of jealousy* (NRSV) that the chief priests had asked him to put Jesus on trial on a criminal charge. The word *phthonos* describes 'ill-will' or 'malice', especially 'envy or jealousy of the good fortune of others' (*LSJ*, p. 1930; NIV 'self-interest' neutralizes the negative meaning of the word). The authorities were envious of Jesus' popularity with the crowds (11:18; 12:12, 37), indicated by the fact that they did not dare arrest Jesus in public (12:12; 14:1–2). Mark has repeatedly emphasized Jesus' popularity.[125]

Pilate surmised, perhaps, that since the chief priests were more concerned with their own authority than with Jesus' guilt, releasing the popular Jesus would be a gesture that would enhance his own goodwill among the Jewish people. His attempt to *release* Jesus – the

---

125. 1:33–34, 37; 2:2, 4, 13; 3:7–9, 20; 4:1, 36; 5:21, 24, 30–32; 6:14–15, 31–34; 7:24; 8:1–3; 9:14–15, 30; 10:1, 13.

Greek verb *apolyō*, used as a legal term, means 'to grant acquittal, set free, release, pardon' (used in vv. 6, 9, 11, 15) – is related by Mark with three questions (vv. 12, 14), given in direct speech, which underlines their importance. Pilate first asks the Jewish crowd whether they want him *to release to you the king of the Jews*. The expression *to you* corresponds to the statement of C. Septimius Vegetus, the prefect of Egypt, reported in the minutes of a trial in which he presided: 'You deserve to be flogged for keeping in your custody a decent man and his wife. But I give you to the people, and I will treat you with utmost kindness' (*P. Flor.* I 61, lines 59–62).[126] The use of the title *the king of the Jews* is taken from the authorities' charges, as verse 12 indicates.

11. The crowd ask Pilate to *release Barabbas instead*: they want Jesus to be executed, not Barabbas. Mark reports that it was *the chief priests* who *stirred up the crowd* who suggested Barabbas as the candidate for the Passover amnesty. In ancient sources crowds are often portrayed as 'fickle, malleable, and readily manipulated' (Gruen, *Heritage*, p. 174). Some suggest that while Jesus was popular among his fellow pilgrims from Galilee, he was rejected by the inhabitants of Jerusalem, many of whom were dependent on the temple for their livelihood and who had been provoked by Jesus' attitude to the temple (see on 14:58). The Jewish aristocracy would have hated Barabbas, whose activities threatened their authority, but they feared Jesus because he was a greater threat on account of his popularity among the people.

12–13. When the attempt to release Jesus by means of the Passover amnesty failed, Pilate tried to achieve a favourable verdict for Jesus by means of popular acclamation (*acclamatio populi*), a measure that is documented in Roman sources (cf. Livy 8.35.4–7; on *venia* see on v. 6). His question, addressed to the crowd, is again given in direct speech: *What shall I do, then, with the one you call the king of the Jews?* If they call Jesus king, why would they want him to be executed? Pilate seems to probe beneath the meaning of the Jewish charge with which he confronted Jesus (v. 2), as indicated in verse 10 (Brown, *Death*, I, p. 824).

---

126. Cf. Chapman and Schnabel, *Trial and Crucifixion*, pp. 258–262; Strobel, *Stunde*, p. 124; Waldstein, *Begnadigungsrecht*, pp. 42–43.

The shouted reply is shockingly brutal: *Crucify him!* (*staurōson auton*). The verb is used by Mark here and in verses 15, 20, 24–25, 27; 16:6. Earlier references to Jesus' death used the verbs 'destroy' (NASB, 3:6; 11:18), 'kill' (8:31; 9:31; 10:34; 14:1), 'condemn to death' (10:33; 14:64), 'put to death' (14:55). The crowd could have demanded moderate punishments such as having to work as a slave in a mine or deportation to an island, or lesser penalties such as banishment, exile, public work and chains; instead they demand the severest of the 'extreme punishments' (*summa supplicia*): crucifixion, listed in a later text before burning and beheading (*Pauli Sententiae* 5.17.2). Crucifixion, bodily suspension on a wooden post, was used in the Roman Empire for the public execution of slaves, brigands and rebels, and occasionally for conquered enemy generals; Roman citizens were exempt from crucifixion except in cases of high treason. The Romans 'typically reserved the cross for the crimes they feared most undermined Roman rule and society'.[127] The crowd's demand – which Mark does not connect with the chief priests – that Pilate crucify Jesus is consistent with the accusation that Jesus claimed to be 'king'. Crucifixion was the form of execution deserved by rebels who were guilty of *seditio* and even by Roman citizens if they were guilty of high treason (*perduellio*). Judea was surrounded by, and often under the control of, civilizations that practised human bodily suspension in various forms (Egyptians, Philistines, Persians, later the Greeks, Ptolemies, Seleucids, Romans). In the Hellenistic period we find Jewish authors approving of crucifixion[128] and Jewish leaders practising it: the Jewish king Alexander Jannaeus massacred 800 opponents in Jerusalem in 90 BC by having them crucified (Josephus, *War* 1.96–97; *Ant.* 13.380–381).

14. Pilate's third question, again reported in direct speech, enquires as to the justification for the demand that Jesus be crucified: *Why? What crime has he committed?* The imperfect of the verb *asked* suggests that Pilate persisted in asking for evidence that would warrant a death sentence – evidence that would prove that Jesus, who, according

---

127. Chapman, in Chapman and Schnabel, *Trial and Crucifixion*, p. 533; on victims of crucifixion see ibid., pp. 533–638.
128. Cf. 11QTemple LXIV, 6–13; Philo, *Flacc.* 72, 83–84; *Prov.* 2.24.

to his Jewish adversaries, claimed to be the king of the Jews, was indeed an insurrectionist. The formulation of Pilate's question suggests that he believed Jesus to be innocent. His questions as to the crimes Jesus committed would have been directed at the chief priests. The subject of the sentence *they shouted all the louder* is surely the crowd. They demand, again reported in direct speech, *Crucify him!* For the Jewish authorities and the crowd outside the Praetorium, Jesus' guilt has been proven – in the trial before the Sanhedrin and when Jesus affirmed during his interrogation by Pilate that he was indeed the king of the Jews.

15. Pilate's verdict has two parts. The first part relates to the Passover amnesty: he *released Barabbas to them* – he gave the convicted brigand to the people. The second part of the verdict sentenced Jesus to flogging and to execution by crucifixion: he ordered *Jesus* to be *flogged* and then *handed him over to be crucified*. As is common in crucifixion accounts, the cross is preceded by flogging and a variety of other forms of torture.[129] The verb *phragelloō* refers to the Roman *flagellum*, the scourge consisting of a wooden handle to which were attached leather thongs, often weighted with pieces of metal or bone to inflict maximum damage. One could die as a result of this punishment (which was not Pilate's intention), or one could end up being crippled for life. Mark does not specify how many lashes Jesus received. As verse 16 implies, the flogging took place in public.

Pilate sensed that the reason for the charges the Jewish authorities advanced against Jesus was a pretence in the context of a contest about popularity and local authority, rather than the result of a concern for the inviolate safety of Roman imperial authority (see v. 10). At the same time his hands were bound by the fact that Jesus had waived a defence and asserted that he indeed was the king of the Jews. Pilate had to take Jesus' behaviour as a confession that he was guilty as charged.[130] Seen in this context, Pilate's verdict was not a miscarriage of justice. Both the literary sources and his long tenure as prefect in Judea indicate that he was an essentially capable and

---

129. Josephus, *War* 2.306–308; *Ant.* 12.255–256; Seneca, *Ep.* 101.14; Dionysius of Halicarnassus, *Ant. rom.* 7.69.1–2; 12.6.6.

130. Cf. Kirner, *Strafgewalt*, pp. 269, 284–285; Kunkel, *Schriften*, pp. 17–21.

prudent governor, who would not take any nonsense from the people but who was able to show flexibility and a willingness to stand down in the interests of preserving the peace.[131] This is why he did not resist the wishes of the chief priests and the Jewish crowd, which he had the authority to do. Pilate was not manipulated into following the wishes of the priestly aristocracy and the Jewish crowds, who wanted Jesus to be executed. He demonstrated his cooperation with the Jewish authorities, who were responsible for public order, which was presently disturbed by the clamour of the crowd for Jesus' execution. Whether Jesus, a *peregrinus* belonging to the lower classes, was guilty or not was a minor concern for him. While Pilate seems to have believed that Jesus' confession (v. 2) implied a non-political meaning of the title 'the king of the Jews', a meaning that did not require the death sentence, and while his attempts to release Jesus suggest that he did not think that Jesus was a *confessus* in terms of the charges brought by the Jewish authorities, Jesus' refusal to make a statement during the interrogation would have to be interpreted as recalcitrance (*contumacia*) not only against the prefect but also against the emperor whom the prefect represented.[132] From a Roman legal standpoint, Pilate's decision to grant the wishes of the Jewish authorities and order Jesus' crucifixion was legal. A Roman prefect examining the alleged crime of a 'foreigner' did not need to identify a specific criminal law for conviction,[133] especially if his legal ruling agreed with the wishes of the local aristocracy.

c. *The soldiers' mocking of Jesus (15:16–20)*

Before Mark reports Jesus' crucifixion (15:21–32), he describes Jesus' mistreatment and mocking by Pilate's soldiers which takes place not in public but in the Praetorium.

16. After the public flogging (v. 15), *the soldiers led Jesus away into the palace*. The soldiers (*stratiōtai*) belonged to auxiliary troops which Pilate had at his disposal as *praefectus* of Judea (Roman legions were stationed in the province of Syria, not in Judea, before AD 70). When

---

131. Cf. Bond, *Pontius Pilate*, pp. 203–204.
132. Cf. Schuol, *Augustus und die Juden*, p. 193.
133. Kirner, *Strafgewalt*, p. 285.

Judea came under Roman control in AD 6, the Roman prefect inherited the army of King Herod, which consisted of one cavalry unit and five infantry cohorts; their names (*Kaisareis* and *Sebastenoi*) indicate that the soldiers were locally recruited among the non-Jewish population of Caesarea and Sebaste (Josephus, *Ant.* 19.365); a sixth infantry unit was the 'Italian cohort' mentioned in Acts 10:1. Since a cohort (Lat. *cohors*; Gr. *speira*) had nominally 480–500 men,[134] Pilate would have had a total of about 3,000 men at his disposal. The term *aulē* refers either to the *courtyard of the palace* (NRSV) or to the *palace* (NASB, NIV, RSV). The explanatory comment *that is, the Praetorium* makes the latter more likely, although the courtyard is easier to picture as the place of the following scene. When they were in Jerusalem, the Roman prefects of Judea took up residence in King Herod's palace, which thus became the *praetorium* (Lat.; Gr. *praitōrion*), the official residence of the Roman official in charge of Judea (cf. v. 1; cf. Matt. 27:27; John 18:28, 33; 19:9). The soldiers who had executed the flogging took Jesus into the Praetorium, where they assembled *the whole cohort* (NRSV; France, p. 637: 'all' refers to 'all the soldiers there on duty'). Since before the Passover festival Pilate might have brought another cohort from Caesarea to Jerusalem, in addition to the cohort that was permanently stationed in Jerusalem in the Antonia Fortress (Acts 21:31–32), the scene in the courtyard of the Praetorium involving 500 men is not necessarily implausible: there would have been sufficient troops available keeping an eye on the crowds on the Temple Mount. The following scene fulfils two further parts of Jesus' prediction saying that they would mock him and spit on him (10:34).

17–19. The soldiers stage a mock coronation, for which there are parallels (Philo, *Flacc.* 36–40; *P. Louvre* 68). Jesus had just been flogged and must have been barely able to stand or walk, his back soaked in blood. The soldiers' mock play makes sense only in the context of Jesus' indictment and condemnation as the king of the Jews (vv. 2, 9, 12, 26, 32). The soldiers put *a purple robe* (*porphyra*) on Jesus. Since there were different grades of purple dye, and since the

---

134. J. C. Campbell, *BNP*, VII, col. 358: a legion consisted of 'around 5,000 men together with 120 cavalry serving as body-guards and messengers'.

wearing of purple was not restricted by law to royalty, purple robes were more commonly available than one might think and could indeed be used by soldiers taunting Jesus with a mock 'royal robe'. According to Matthew 27:28 the soldiers used a scarlet cloak, the normal garment of a Roman soldier. They *twisted together a crown of thorns* and put it on Jesus' head. The term *stephanos* (*crown*) generally describes 'a wreath made of foliage or designed to resemble foliage and worn by one of high status or held in high regard' (BDAG, p. 943). It has been suggested that the *thorns* in question were what was later called the Syrian Christ thorn (Lat. *Ziziphus spina-christi* or *Rhamnus nabeca*), with smooth white branches, leaf blades between 1.57 and 2.36 inches (4 and 6 cm) long and petioles averaging longer than 0.11 inches (3 mm). The white branches would resemble a golden or silver diadem, while the thorns perhaps simulated the light rays emanating from the heads of rulers on Ptolemaic, Seleucid and Roman coins (Marcus, p. 1048). The question whether the crown of thorns was just for scorn or also to cause pain poses false alternatives. After the mock robing and the mock crowning, the soldiers continue with a mock royal acclamation, reported by Mark in direct speech: *Hail, king of the Jews!* The scene is a burlesque of the 'Ave Caesar' acclamation of the emperor. The verb *they began to call out to him* suggests that the soldiers persisted in this mockery for some time, playing with Jesus, shaming him, ignoring his pain.

The mockery involved physical abuse. The imperfect tense of the verbs *they struck him* and *they spat on him* indicates that this happened *again and again*. The soldiers brutally abused Jesus and treated him with contempt. The *staff* with which the soldiers struck Jesus on the head had previously been put in his hand as a mock sceptre (Matt. 27:29). Then the soldiers fell on their knees and *paid homage to him*, a fake expression of reverence considering that the verb *proskyneō* means 'to express in attitude or gesture one's complete dependence on or submission to a high authority figure' (BDAG, p. 882). Mark's description echoes the violence, insult and spitting endured by the Servant of the Lord in Isaiah 50:6: 'I offered my back to those who beat me, my cheeks to those who pulled out my beard; I did not hide my face from mocking and spitting.'

20. After the soldiers *had mocked* Jesus, they replaced the purple robe with Jesus' *own clothes*. The return of his clothes for the walk to

Golgotha may have been a concession to Jewish sensibilities which regarded public nudity as offensive (*Jub.* 3:30–31; 7:20; *m. Sanh.* 6:3). According to verse 24, Jesus' clothes were removed at the cross. That Mark mentions the removal of the purple robe but not the removal of the mock crown suggests that the thorns stayed on Jesus' head. Then the soldiers *led him out*, from the courtyard of the Praetorium into the streets of Jerusalem, in order to walk to the place of execution where they had been ordered to *crucify him*. According to John 19:23, the execution squad consisted of four soldiers (Lat. *quaternion*; cf. Acts 12:4). Jesus was probably taken through the narrow alleys of the western part of the city: from the gateway south of Herod's palace in a northerly direction along the eastern side of the Praetorium, then a short distance west towards the Temple Mount, then north again through the Gennath Gate to the quarry east of the city wall, a distance of about 765 yards (700 m).

Theology
In the Sanhedrin trial, Jesus acknowledged that he was the Messiah, the Son of God. In the Roman trial, he acknowledges that he is the king of the Jews. In the Sanhedrin trial, Jesus clarified the title 'Messiah' by stating that he was the enthroned royal figure of Psalm 110:1 and the authoritative figure of the One like a Son of Man of Daniel 7:13, the judge who sits next to God in heaven. He was not a nationalist political leader but a royal figure in the presence of God. In the Roman trial, Jesus' affirmative answer to Pilate's query indicates that he will not describe himself as 'the king of the Jews', even though the title applies, implying that he does not claim the political authority that the Jewish authorities connect with it. John makes this explicit: Jesus tells Pilate that his kingdom is 'not of this world' but 'from another place' and focused not on political kingship but on truth (John 18:33–37). Jesus is the king of the Jews, but in a sense that is integrally connected with his rejection, death and resurrection, as he predicted (Mark 8:31; 9:31; 10:32–34). His trial by a Gentile judge, his scourging and his condemnation to death fulfil his earlier prediction (10:33–34). That the insurrectionist Barabbas goes free and Jesus is condemned to death shows not so much Roman indifference to justice for provincials but the hand of God, who is behind these events (8:31; 14:21; Stein, p. 703). Jesus

has not committed any crime (cf. 15:14), but he refuses to defend himself (15:3-5). He accepts death as his God-given mission, which is to give his life as a sacrifice for many (10:45; 14:24).

vi. Jesus' crucifixion (15:21-32)
Context
Mark reports the events of Jesus' crucifixion in four parts: the conscription of Simon of Cyrene to carry the cross (15:21-22), the soldiers' offer of wine mixed with myrrh (15:23), the crucifixion between two bandits (15:24-27) and the mocking of Jesus at the cross (15:29-32). The act of being affixed to the cross is only implied (15:25). Jesus' crucifixion took place on Friday, 14 Nisan (8 April) in the year AD 30, at nine in the morning (15:25).

Comment
a. Conscription of Simon of Cyrene to carry the cross (15:21-22)
21. *Simon* was the most popular male Jewish name (see on 1:16), and so this Simon is identified by his place of origin: he was 'Simon the Cyrenian'; that is, Simon of Cyrene, the capital city of a region in north Africa (mod. Libya) which formed, together with Crete, a senatorial province governed by a proconsul. Luke mentions a synagogue in Jerusalem in which Jews from Cyrene and Alexandria worshipped (Acts 6:9); a Lucius of Cyrene belonged to the leaders of the church in Antioch in Syria (Acts 13:1). Mark mentions Simon and also his sons *Alexander and Rufus* evidently because he is 'appealing to Simon's eyewitness testimony, known in the early Christian movement not from his own firsthand account but through his sons. Perhaps Simon himself did not, like his sons, join the movement, or perhaps he died in the early years, while his sons remained well-known figures, telling their father's story of the crucifixion of Jesus.'[135] Rufus may be identical with the Rufus of Romans 16:13, who must have moved to Rome from the East where Paul had known him well. Simon seems to have been a resident of Jerusalem who was coming *from the country* or 'from his farm' (BDAG, p. 15, *agros*) into the city, getting ready for Passover.

---

135. Bauckham, *Eyewitnesses*, p. 52; the following point ibid., n. 49.

The soldiers who led Jesus from the Praetorium to the place of execution (v. 20) forced Simon *to carry the cross*. The word for cross is *stauros*, which originally referred to upright posts; at some point, the word became associated with a T-shaped crucifixion device.[136] Here the word refers to the horizontal crossbeam (Lat. *patibulum*) to which the outstretched arms of the convicted criminal were attached with nails or ropes before the body was hoisted upright on a pole that stood at the usual place of execution so that the crucified criminal could be exposed to the public until he died. The flogging and beating (15:15, 19) had weakened Jesus to the point where he was no longer able to carry the heavy crossbeam on his bloody shoulders. Since there was not a standardized method of crucifixion (see on v. 24), one cannot say that 'normally' the condemned man carried the crossbeam. The soldiers who took Jesus to Golgotha *forced* Simon. The word *angareuō* means 'requisition', 'press into service, and so force, compel' (BDAG, p. 7); it is a Latin loanword (*angaria*) which describes compulsory public service imposed on the local population (cf. Matt. 5:41).

22. The execution squad took Jesus *to the place called Golgotha*, with Simon carrying the crossbeam. The Greek word *Golgotha* reproduces Aramaic *gulgultha'* and Hebrew *gulgōlet* ('skull'). Mark translates the term for his readers as *the place of the skull* (Gr. *Kraniou Topos*). According to John 19:20, the site was 'near the city'; that is, outside the city walls; there was a garden in the place (John 19:41) as well as at least one new (unused) tomb nearby (John 19:41). The traditional localization of Golgotha (and the tomb) underneath the Church of the Holy Sepulchre[137] is very probably correct. Excavations have shown that the place was once a quarry, extending south of the Church, an area of about 500 by 650 feet (150 by 200 m), as indicated by chisel marks and partly hewn blocks of limestone still attached to the bedrock; tombs had been cut into the rock of the quarry,

---

136. Cf. Chapman and Schnabel, *Trial and Crucifixion*, pp. 674–675; on the crossbeam (*patibulum*) see pp. 282–292.

137. The first church on the site was built by Helena, the mother of Constantine, in the fourth century. Cf. Murphy-O'Connor, *Holy Land*, pp. 49–62.

some tombs dating to the first century AD.[138] There is evidence that the quarry pit had been filled in and overlaid with reddish-brown soil, which could be the garden mentioned in John 19:41 (cf. 20:15). The quarry and the fill are adjacent to the Gennath Gate (Garden Gate) mentioned by Josephus as the spot where the second wall (extending north) of the city began (*War* 5.146). The identification of the place as looking like a skull 'reflects knowledge that the area where the crucifixion took place was a protruding, bare, and rocky area, probably a hillock not quarried because of the poor quality of the stone there'.[139]

b. Offer of wine mixed with myrrh (15:23)

23. The subject of the verb *they offered* is the soldiers who were about to affix Jesus to the crossbeam. They offered Jesus *wine mixed with myrrh*. The wine (*oinos*) would have been red wine; the verb *smyrnizō* means 'to treat with myrrh'. The noun *smyrna* refers to the resinous gum of the bush *Balsamodendron myrrha* (BDAG, p. 933). The substance is used for perfume (Matt. 2:11), as an embalming ointment (John 19:39), as a salve, for burning as incense and for flavouring. Some suggest a narcotic effect[140] and point to *b. Sanhedrin* 43a, which refers to women of Jerusalem giving wine containing frankincense as an act of mercy to numb the pain of those led out to execution, guided by Proverbs 31:6. Since the wine was more likely offered by soldiers who would not have been interested in dulling the pain of a *cruxificus*, and since wine mixed with myrrh was regarded as a delicacy (Pliny, *Nat.* 14.92), the offer seems to have been part of their mockery of Jesus: the soldiers were offering the finest wine to the 'king of the Jews' (Evans, p. 501). Jesus' refusal to take the wine indicates that he refuses to play the soldiers' game, 'facing his death with dignity and courage' (Strauss, p. 690). Jesus

---

138. Cf. Corbo, *Il Santo Sepolcro di Gerusalemme*; V. C. Corbo, 'Golgotha', *ABD*, II, p. 1072; Gibson and Taylor, *Golgotha*; R. Riesner, *DJG*, p. 55.
139. U. C. von Wahlde, in Charlesworth, *Jesus and Archaeology*, p. 578.
140. With reference to Dioscorides 1.64.3, an army physician in the first century AD.

had accepted in Gethsemane that God wanted him to drink the 'cup' of suffering (14:35–42). As he is about to be nailed to the cross, he refuses the soldiers' offer and focuses on the task that the will of God has entrusted to him.

c. Crucifixion between two bandits (15:24–27)

24. Jesus' crucifixion is reported in three terse words: *kai staurousin auton – and they crucified him.* Seneca, writing in the middle of the first century AD, describes three forms of crosses: 'I see there crosses, not merely of one kind, but fashioned differently by different people: a certain one suspends [a person] with his head up-side down towards the ground, others impale a stake through the sexual organs, others extend the victim's arms by a yoke' (Seneca, *Marc.* 20.3; the word translated 'yoke' is *patibulum*). Many texts suggest that people usually assumed the third type of cross, a crucifixion involving arms outstretched and attached to the cross(beam). The traditional view that Jesus was crucified on a T-shaped cross rests on early evidence: several early Christian authors equate the cross with the letter *tau* (T)[141] and in some of the earliest New Testament manuscripts the copyists combined the letters *tau* (T) and *rho* (R) of the Greek word *stauros* ('cross') to form a staurogram that looks like the head of a person atop the *tau*, implying a man crucified with outstretched arms.[142] While both nails and ropes were employed in crucifixions, Luke 24:39 ('Look at my hands and my feet') and John 20:20 ('he showed them his hands and side') indicate that in Jesus' crucifixion nails were used (cf. Col. 2:14). The nails would have been inserted not through the hands (which would not be able to hold the weight of the body) but between the two bones of the forearm near the wrists. Sometimes a *sedile* was provided, a small seat attached to the vertical pole, intended to prolong the time it took for the criminal to die; we do not know whether Jesus died on a cross with such a device.

Death on a cross was slow and agonizing. Seneca provides the most memorable description:

---

141. *Barn.* 9:8 (c. AD 130); Justin, *1 Apol.* 55:1–8; Irenaeus, *Haer.* 2.24.4.
142. Cf. Hurtado, *Artifacts*, pp. 135–154.

Can anyone be found who would want to waste away amid
punishments and to perish limb by limb and to emit his soul
(as so often occurs) by dripping bodily fluids, rather than to expire
at once? Can he be found who – having been driven to that cursed
tree, already weak, already deformed and in an abominable way
thrusting out swellings from his shoulders and chest, for whom
many causes of death would have been even nearer than a cross –
would want to drag out a soul that has been dealt so many torments?
(Seneca, *Ep.* 101.14)

Cicero called crucifixion 'this cruelest and vilest penalty' (*Verr.* 2.5.165). Death was due to asphyxiation (the weight of the body pulling on the outstretched arms made breathing increasingly difficult) and/or hypovolemic shock leading to cardiac and respiratory arrest.[143] Mark is not interested in portraying Jesus' suffering on the cross so much as the fact and the circumstances of his crucifixion and the text of the official written notice that here died 'the king of the Jews' (v. 26).

Mark notes that the soldiers were *dividing up his clothes* and that they *cast lots to see what each would get*. Jesus was stripped before he was affixed to the cross. The executioner's squad had the right to take the minor possessions of the victim. Clothing was one of the more important possessions of the poor, thus there was a good reason for the soldiers to want his clothing. John comments that Jesus' tunic was a special seamless one (John 19:23–24). It is unclear if any undergarment was removed from Jesus. John, who describes the scene in more detail than the other Gospel authors, 'is so specific about every item of clothing that one would have the impression that nothing was left' (Brown, *Death*, II, p. 953) – that is, that Jesus was crucified naked (thus in the late second century Melito of Sardis, *Pasch.* 97). The apocryphal *Acts of Pilate* 10:1 have Jesus girded with a loincloth (Lat. *subligaculum*), which may be supported with reference to Mark 15:20. It is impossible to know with certainty whether or not Jesus was completely exposed. The casting of lots might have been a game of dice, or a version of the Roman game of *morra* which

---

143. Cook, *Crucifixion*, pp. 430–435.

involved guessing the number of fingers held behind one's back (Brown, *Death*, II, p. 953).

Mark's description of the dividing of Jesus' clothing echoes Psalm 22:18 ('They divide my clothes among them and cast lots for my garment'); John 19:24 explicitly cites the passage. Other statements of Psalm 22 are echoed in verse 29 (Ps. 22:7) and in verse 34 (Ps. 22:1). Following Jesus' use of the opening words of Psalm 22 on the cross (v. 34), his followers very early on recognized the psalm as a prefiguring of Jesus' passion on the cross. What is happening as Jesus dies on the cross happens, even in detail, 'according to the Scriptures', as Jesus had predicted.

25–26. Having noted Golgotha as the place of Jesus' crucifixion (v. 22), Mark reports the time of the crucifixion: *the third hour* (NASB), 9 am.[144] And he reports that the reason for the execution was published in a *written notice of the charge* (Gr. *epigraphē tēs aitias*). It was Roman practice to record, painted on a *tabula albata*, the reason for the punishment of a condemned person.[145] John provides more details: Pilate had the reason for Jesus' death sentence written on a *titulus* in three languages – in Hebrew (Aramaic), in Latin and in Greek (John 19:19–20). Matthew says that the notice was placed 'above his head' (Matt. 27:37). This was an 'unparalleled case of a quasi-official (but ironical) use by the Romans of a vernacular language (an act of offensive accommodation . . . meant to annoy the Jews)' (Adams, *Bilingualism*, p. 268). Mark relates the Greek version as *ho basileus tōn Ioudaiōn* ('the king of the Jews'); Matthew and John provide slightly expanded versions: *houtos estin Iēsous ho basileus tōn Ioudaiōn* ('This is Jesus, the king of the Jews', Matt. 27:27);

---

144. Stein, p. 713, explains the discrepancy with John 19:14 (Pilate rendered his verdict 'about the sixth hour') by pointing out that we need to 'recognize the general preference of the third or sixth hour to designate a period between 9 a.m. and noon and the lack of precision in telling time in the first century'.

145. Cf. W. Eck, in *CIIP* I/1, p. 62, who discusses the *titulus* on Jesus' cross as inscription No. 15: 'There is no reason to doubt the tradition that a titulus with the reason for his condemnation by Pilatus was affixed on Jesus' cross.'

Iēsous ho Nazōraios ho basileus tōn Ioudaiōn ('Jesus the Nazarean, the king of the Jews', John 19:19). The Vulgate provides the Latin translation *Rex Iudaeorum* (Mark 15:26), and *Iesus Nazarenus rex Iudaeorum* (John 19:19).[146] The Hebrew version would be *melek ha-yĕhûdîm* and *yešua' ha-nozry melek ha-yĕhûdîm*. The *titulus* was probably carried by Jesus himself when the execution squad walked the three condemned men from the Praetorium to Golgotha. A relief discovered in Miletus depicts three prisoners, led by an armed guard, shackled together around the neck, the first of whom carries a placard which presumably identifies the miscreants and their crime. Jesus was convicted of claiming to be king in a region controlled by Rome, without having been appointed king by Rome, which amounted to insurrection (*seditio*) and challenging the power and dignity of the emperor (*crimen maiestatis*). The publication of the title 'the king of the Jews' above Jesus' head as he died in agony and disgrace was meant as a joke and a blunt deterrent to would-be royal pretenders.

27. The execution squad erected three crosses on Golgotha, two being occupied by *two rebels* (NIV; NRSV 'bandits'; ESV, NASB, RSV 'robbers'; NET 'outlaws'; NLT 'revolutionaries'). The word *lēstai* can mean 'robber, highwayman, bandit' or 'revolutionary, insurrectionist, guerrilla' (see on 14:48). Even though Mark does not link these two men with Barabbas, whom Pilate thought to be a more logical candidate for execution than Jesus (vv. 7–11), it is probably not a coincidence that Pilate had recently presided in death-penalty cases of three *lēstai* as well as Jesus, convicting Jesus on a charge involving treason. The two men were most likely insurrectionists (who would have been regarded as 'freedom fighters' by some Jews). Jesus was placed in the middle because he was the more prominent victim.[147]

d. *Mocking of Jesus at the cross (15:29–32)*

29–30. After Pilate's mockery of Jesus, indicated in the *titulus* (v. 26), three groups of people who are present at the crucifixion mock him. The first group is *those who passed by*, confirming that

---

146. Abbreviated INRI, often seen in later depictions of Jesus' crucifixion.
147. Some late manuscripts insert a verse 28 citing Isa. 53:12 with a fulfilment formula; this is a later gloss reflecting Luke 22:37 in a different context.

Golgotha, the place used for executions just outside the walls of Jerusalem, was at a public thoroughfare. These onlookers could be inhabitants of Jerusalem who came out to witness the execution of the famous Galilean preacher and two insurrectionists, besides festival pilgrims who walked between the city and their lodgings in neighbouring villages. They *hurled insults* (on the verb *blasphēmeō* see on 2:7) at Jesus, verbally humiliating him, perhaps using the text of the *titulus* to taunt Jesus just as the soldiers had taunted him as a pathetic royal pretender. For Mark, these insults would constitute 'blasphemy' since Jesus, indeed Jesus at the cross, is the Messiah and the Son of God (cf. 1:1). They were *shaking their heads* as a sign of scorn and derision (BDAG, p. 545, *kineō* meaning 2a; cf. Lam. 2:15). According to Psalm 22:7, the enemies of the righteous sufferer 'hurl insults, shaking their heads'. Mark relates the mockery of Jesus' immobility on the cross in direct speech. In the context of their taunts, the interjection *Aha!* (NRSV) conveys 'vindictive sarcasm' (France, p. 647). The charge that Jesus wanted to *destroy the temple and build it in three days*, which in the trial before the Sanhedrin could not be proven, was public knowledge. The onlookers combine Jesus' alleged claim to be the destroyer and rebuilder of the temple with his ability to save himself: if he has the power to do the former, he surely has the power to do the latter. Thus they challenge Jesus, *save yourself, and come down from the cross!* NRSV). They find Jesus' helpless position on the cross – his outstretched arms nailed to the crossbeam and his feet nailed to the vertical pole – ironically funny. The suggestion that Jesus should 'save' himself recalls Jesus' healings in which he 'saved' life (for the verb *sōzō* cf. 3:4). As Jesus had demonstrated his authority over nature (4:35–41), over death (5:35–43) and over natural resources (6:30–44), he did have the ability to come down from the cross. Apart from the fact that even had he done so the authorities and the onlookers would have found some rationalizing or demonological explanation (cf. 3:22), Jesus did not *want* to come down from the cross. He had accepted the will of God involving the 'cup' of his death (8:31; 9:31; 10:32–34) effecting a ransom for the sins of many (10:45) in Gethsemane (14:32–42).

31–32. The second group of people mocking Jesus at the cross are the *chief priests and the teachers of the law*, the two groups who represent the Jewish authorities in Jerusalem (cf. 11:18; 14:1; 15:1).

The chief priests and scribes seem to have accompanied the soldiers of the execution squad who took Jesus from the Praetorium to Golgotha. They want to witness Jesus' death. They join the mocking of the soldiers (vv. 16–20) and of the onlookers (vv. 29–30). The fact that they ridicule Jesus *among themselves* indicates that they congratulate themselves for having achieved their aim of killing Jesus by stealth (11:18; 14:1). They make fun of his claim to be the *Messiah*, the *king of Israel*, by stating that *he saved others but he can't save himself* and by challenging him to *come down now from the cross, that we may see and believe*. The titles *Messiah* and *king of Israel* confirm that Jesus was condemned to death on the charge of sedition and challenging the power and dignity of the emperor. The word 'save' (*sōzō*) had been used by Mark mostly in the sense of physical healing and restoration (3:4; 5:23, 28, 34; 6:56; 10:52), a meaning which could be in view here as well (see v. 30). In the context of the title *Messiah* it is equally possible, and more plausible, to understand *sōzō* in the broader sense of messianic salvation (cf. 8:35; 10:26; 13:13). If Jesus cannot save himself, he can hardly be the Messiah; and, conversely, since Jesus is not the Messiah (in their view), his immobility as he is affixed to the cross proves that he cannot save either himself or others. If he cannot save himself, he cannot be the Son of Man sitting at the right hand of God (cf. 14:62). The suggestion that they would *believe* if they could *see* him dismounting the cross is not an honest promise: the Jerusalem scribes who had assessed Jesus' ministry in Galilee did *see* him exorcizing demons but then believed that he was possessed by Satan (3:22). They would have arrived at the same 'conclusion' had Jesus extracted the nails and climbed down from the cross. They do not understand that Jesus' messianic mission was indeed to bring salvation – not in terms of national restoration and not just in terms of physical preservation and restoration of life in healings and exorcisms, but in terms of ultimate salvation connected with the coming of the kingdom of God and the forgiveness of sins through his death (2:1–12; 10:45; 14:22–25). They cannot grasp the irony that it is by staying on the cross that Jesus is Israel's Messiah and the Saviour of many, including people among all nations (13:10).

The third group of people who mock Jesus are the two brigands: they *also heaped insults on him*. This is the final indignity: the two people who share Jesus' terrible fate of being crucified on Golgotha join the onlookers and the Jewish authorities in mocking him. The imperfect of the verbs suggests that the mockery of the three groups went on for some time. Jesus is truly alone.

Theology
Jesus' crucifixion at Golgotha is the fulfilment of Jesus' repeated predictions (8:31; 9:31; 10:34). Jesus, the Messiah, Israel's King and Son of God (1:1; 14:61–62; 15:2), is executed with the most fearful, painful and shameful punishment that is inflicted on human beings. Mark also points to the fulfilment of the Scriptures, as indicated by the allusions to Psalm 22 (15:24, 29, 30–31). The description of the mockery is full of paradoxical irony. Israel's leaders mock Jesus for claiming that he would replace the temple, that he is the Messiah and brings salvation, and that he is Israel's king, not realizing the fact (that Mark's readers know to be true) that Jesus is fulfilling this mission 'by being where he is' (France, p. 649). In the context of the allusions to Psalm 22 where the mockers call on *God* to save the innocent sufferer, Mark's description of the mockers who call on *Jesus* to save himself is significant: 'the mockers do not realize that Jesus and God are so intertwined that Jesus' salvific power *is* the power of God . . . and that Jesus' kingship, far from being a joke, participates in that of God'; the description of the onlookers' taunts as blaspheming suggests to Mark's readers that 'those who oppose Jesus are guilty of the "blasphemy" of separating Jesus from God and of seeing his present powerlessness as an indication of permanent divine abandon' (Marcus, p. 1051). The power of the kingdom of God that Jesus has been proclaiming, manifest in exorcisms, healings and nature miracles, reaches its saving climax in Jesus' death on the cross.

vii. Jesus' death and burial (15:33–47)
Context
The description of Jesus' death and burial marks the conclusion of Mark's passion narrative. Mark relates in quick succession the darkness that descended on the region, Jesus' last words, further mocking, Jesus' death, the splitting of the veil in the temple, the declaration of the centurion who witnessed Jesus' death, the presence of women supporters and Jesus' burial in the tomb of Joseph of

Arimathea. In the previous section, Jesus was passive; now he speaks – out of the darkness, or as the darkness lifts. Jesus' death is as extraordinary as his life (France, p. 650), its implications underlined by the tearing of the veil in the temple and by the declaration by a pagan soldier that Jesus is indeed the Son of God.

Comment
a. Darkness and Jesus' last shout (15:33–34)

33. Jesus was crucified at the third hour (9 am; v. 25). *Darkness fell over the whole land* at the *sixth hour* (noon) *until the ninth hour* (3 pm; NASB). The pace of events that had happened so far during 14 Nisan, which started seventeen hours earlier, had been hectic: preparations for the Passover meal (14:12–17), the Last Supper (14:18–25), prayer in Gethsemane (14:23–42), arrest (14:43–52), trial before the Sanhedrin (14:53–72), trial before Pontius Pilate with the death sentence and flogging (15:1–15), mocking by the soldiers (15:16–20) and crucifixion at Golgotha (15:21–32).

When darkness descends on the land (*gē*, here probably a reference to Judea), no events are recorded for three hours. Darkness is sometimes a symbol of God's displeasure and judgment (Deut. 28:29; Isa. 13:9–13; Jer. 4:28; 13:16; Ezek. 32:7–8); the ninth plague in Egypt, before the death of the Egyptians' firstborn and the first Passover, was darkness (Exod. 10:21–23). In Greek and Roman tradition, darkness is reported with reference to the deaths of Alexander the Great and Caesar (Ps.-Callisthenes 3.33.26; Virgil, *Georg.* 1.463–468). The symbolism of the darkness does not mean that there was no physical darkness. Luke says that 'the sun stopped shining' (Luke 23:45), which cannot refer to a solar eclipse since the time of Passover is the period of the full moon when solar eclipses cannot happen (they happen when the moon is new; Marcus, p. 1054). Some have suggested a desert sand storm (the famous sirocco or khamsin); others think of heavy dark clouds; others, of a supernatural darkening of the sun. The darkness signals that Jesus' death is an extraordinary death.

34. Mark reports Jesus' last words to have been spoken *at the ninth hour* (NASB), when the darkness still persisted (the word 'until' in verse 33 includes its terminus; Marcus, p. 1054) or when the darkness lifted (the word 'until' excludes the terminus; Gundry, p. 964: the darkness 'veils and thus counteracts the shame of crucifixion'). The ninth hour is the hour of Jewish prayer (cf. Acts 3:1), which Mark's Gentile readers would not know since they require explanation of Jewish customs, which Mark does not provide here. Jesus has been on the cross for six hours, which, as far as crucifixions go, is not very long (cf. v. 44) but, for the person on the cross, a drawn-out time of inconceivable agony. Jesus will die shortly (v. 37). Since his declaration before Pilate that he is indeed the king of the Jews, Jesus has not spoken (but see Luke 23:28–31). Now, suddenly and dramatically, *Jesus cried out in a loud voice*. Mark's description is doubly emphatic: Jesus *cried out*, 'shouted', and he did so with a *loud voice*. This description indicates Jesus' intense emotion, his intense physical suffering or his strength as the Son of God.

Mark relates Jesus' words first in Aramaic and then provides a translation: *Eloi, Eloi, lema sabachthani?*, in Greek, *ho theos mou, ho theos mou, eis ti engkatelipes me?*, which means, in English, *My God, my God, why have you forsaken me?* Jesus uses the words of Psalm 22:1, although not in Hebrew but in Aramaic, the language in which he used to expound Scripture.[148] In Gethsemane, Jesus had addressed God as *Abba*, Father. Now he addresses him as *Eloi*, 'my God', which expresses a continuing, personal relationship with God. The fact that Psalm 22 ends with hope, confidence, praise and the proclamation of God's dominion to the ends of the earth (Ps. 22:22–31) 'must not be allowed to override its distressed beginning in exegesis of Jesus' cry of dereliction' (Marcus, p. 1063). Jesus quotes not the ending of Psalm 22 but its beginning with its sense of the terrifying agony of real abandonment by God. After being on the cross for six hours, and after three hours of darkness, Jesus shouts out his sense of having been forsaken by God who is *his* God, the God whose Messiah and Son he is, the God whose throne is next to his own throne as the heavenly Son of Man. Jesus' shout is not merely an expression of emotion. In view of Jesus' previous emphasis on the necessity of his death (8:31; 9:31; 10:34; 14:21), on God's purpose for his mission that he become a ransom for many (10:45), on his

---

148. Cf. Casey, *Sources*, p. 88; Moo, *Passion Narratives*, pp. 264–268; Brown, *Death*, II, pp. 1051–1053. For quotations in Aramaic see on 5:41; 14:36.

sacrificial pouring out of his blood which inaugurates the new covenant (14:24) and on knowing that his death means God striking the Son according to the Scriptures (14:27), Jesus' shout is the acknowledgment that his abandonment by God is real. God has placed the sin of the world upon him, the one who has completely identified himself with sinners. Jesus experiences the stark reality of the 'cup' of God's judgment (14:36). Mark's readers, particularly if they lived in Rome and knew Paul and his theology, would have understood this in the light of passages such as Romans 3:24–25; 2 Corinthians 5:21; Galatians 3:13. God abandoned Jesus because God cannot be where sin is. Mark does not explain Jesus' death. He wants his readers to see the agony of Jesus' commitment to God, who has abandoned him.

b. *Mocking of Jesus (15:35–36)*

35. The Aramaic word *Eloi* ('my God'; Matt. 27:46 has the Hebrew word *Eli*) sounds similar to the Hebrew name *'Eliya* ('Elijah') so that onlookers think that Jesus is calling out to the prophet Elijah to rescue him. The people who understood Aramaic would have included the soldiers who belonged to Pilate's auxiliary troops recruited in the region. The mistake – unless it was a malicious mockery – alludes to the expectation that Elijah would precede the Messiah (cf. 6:15; 8:28; 9:11–13; cf. 2 Kgs 2:11; Mal. 3:1; 4:5), which prompted the hope that Elijah might appear from heaven to help in times of need (thus later rabbinic texts; cf. *b. 'Abod. Zar.* 17b: a certain Rabbi Eleazar was rescued from a Roman trial by Elijah, who, disguised as a Roman official, intercepted a messenger sent to bring evidence and hurled him a considerable distance so that he did not return; cf. J. Jeremias, *TDNT*, II, p. 930; France, p. 654).

36. The *someone* who *ran* was probably a Jewish spectator: the soldiers would not have been in a hurry to run and get a sponge, and they would not have understood a reference to Elijah. The *sponge* (Gr. *spongos*; Lat. *spongia*) is the bath sponge (*Euspongia officinalis*) which grows in the Mediterranean, with black and white subspecies. The *wine vinegar* (Gr. *oxos*) was sour, cheap wine which 'relieved thirst more effectively than water and, being cheaper than regular wine, it was a favorite beverage of the lower ranks of society and of those in moderate circumstances' (BDAG, p. 715). The *staff* could be a 'reed' or a 'stalk'; the term does not allow us to estimate the height of the cross. The offer of something to drink can be understood as an act of kindness since, according to John 19:28, 30, Jesus said that he was thirsty and accepted the offer; or as cruel mockery, prolonging his life and suggesting that they are willing to wait and see whether *Elijah comes to take him down*.

c. Jesus' death (15:37)

37. Mark does not indicate whether Jesus' *loud cry* was an inarticulate cry, expressing again desolate dereliction, or a loud verbal utterance expressing trust (Luke 23:46: Jesus called out with a loud voice, 'Father, into your hands I commit my spirit') and triumph (John 19:30: Jesus died with the words, 'It is finished'). The declaration of the centurion who 'sees' how Jesus died (v. 39) suggests that Jesus' last words indeed expressed confidence in God and the triumph of having accomplished his mission. The expression *breathed his last* (most English versions; GNB: 'Jesus died') translates the verb *ekpneuō*, which means 'breathe out' (*LSJ*, p. 517) and is used here (and in Luke 23:46) in the sense of 'breathe out one's life/soul, expire' as a euphemism for 'to die' (BDAG, p. 308). Jesus seems to have died soon after the ninth hour (v. 34); that is, around 3 pm, on 8 April (14 Nisan) AD 30. On the cause of death, which did not interest the evangelists, see on verse 24.

d. Splitting of the curtain in the temple (15:38)

38. The second supernatural event associated with Jesus' crucifixion, after the three-hour-long darkness, happened on the Temple Mount. It is not clear which *curtain* (*katapetasma*) of the temple is meant. The LXX uses the term *katapetasma* for the curtain through which one entered from the courtyard into the Inner Sanctuary where incense was offered (Exod. 26:37), and for the curtain separating the Holy of Holies from the Inner Sanctuary (Exod. 26:31). Josephus describes two curtains (*katapetasmata*) in the same two positions (*War* 5.212, 219; *Ant.* 8.75). He describes the outer curtain which was visible to the public, placed every morning in front of the sanctuary doors (55 cubits or 90 feet [27.5 m] high), as a work of art ('of Babylonian tapestry, with embroidery of blue and fine linen, of scarlet also and purple, wrought with marvelous skill . . . it typified the universe . . . On this tapestry was portrayed a panorama of the heavens, the signs of the Zodiac excepted'; *War* 5.211–213). The inner curtain was visible only to the priests who served in the Inner Sanctuary, consisting of two curtains (*traksin*), one behind the other, evidently 60 cubits (98 feet [30 m]) high. Both curtains were very long, which means that the tear that split the curtain *in two from top to bottom* could not have been caused by human hands. The tearing of the outer curtain would be a more public event. The tearing of the inner curtain, tearing open the Holy of Holies, would be theologically more telling; this is the understanding of the writer of Hebrews who speaks of the 'second curtain' (Heb. 9:3; cf. 6:19; 10:19–20). Some argue that the tearing of the more visible and magnificent outer curtain picks up more naturally the theme of the references to Jesus claiming to destroy and replace the temple (France, p. 657). It would indicate that the fulfilment of Jesus' prediction in 14:58 and 15:29 had already begun, to be physically 'completed' in AD 70 when Roman troops destroyed the temple. In this interpretation, the splitting of the curtain signals God's judgment on the temple. Others argue that the verb *schizō* ('to split, divide, separate, tear apart') points to 1:10, the only other place where Mark uses the verb: as the heavens are split at Jesus' baptism, revealing the unique, direct access that Jesus has to the Father as his Son, so now Jesus' followers have direct access to the Father on account of Jesus' death (Hooker, p. 378; Hurtado, p. 268). It is possible that Mark intends both the 'judgmental' and the 'revelatory' interpretation.

e. Declaration of the centurion (15:39)

39. The *centurion* (Gr. *kenturiōn*; Lat. *centurio*; cf. v. 44; otherwise *hekatontarchēs*; cf. Matt. 8:13; Luke 7:6; 23:47; Acts 10:1, 22; 21:32, etc.) was a Roman officer commanding about a hundred men (a *curia* or 'century'; in the first century BC a *centuria* consisted of eighty men). A centurion was responsible for the administration and discipline of his *centuria*; as they were experienced soldiers, senior officers would seek their advice. They could take command of a limited number of troops for special duties, as was the case here: the centurion commanded the squad that executed two insurrectionists and Jesus, the royal pretender.

The centurion stood *in front of* Jesus (NRSV 'facing him') and *saw how he died*. This could refer to the preternatural darkness, to Jesus' final words, to Jesus dying' with a loud shout rather than with his life slowly ebbing away, or to Jesus' quick death. The centurion's declaration, *Truly this man was the Son of God!* (NASB), has been variously understood. Since the expression 'Son of God' has no article in the Greek text, some have suggested that the pagan centurion exclaimed that Jesus is *'a* son of God' (REB, JB; cf. note in ESV, NRSV). The Greek construction suggests that the expression should be understood as definite, which is supported by the consideration that the title 'Son of God' is used with the article throughout Mark's Gospel and should be so understood here as well. Some have suggested that the centurion's declaration is sarcastic: Jesus' humiliating death demonstrates that he cannot possibly be the Son of God. This is not convincing since the centurion is linked not with the chief priests and the onlookers who mock Jesus (vv. 29–32) but with the women (vv. 40–41) who are Jesus' supporters. Also, the centurion's declaration is one of three 'architectonic acclamations of Jesus as Son of God, which are similar in form' – 1:11; 9:7; and here in 15:39 – appearing significantly at the beginning, middle and end of the Gospel (Marcus, p. 1059).

Jesus' divine, messianic sonship was announced in the title of the Gospel (1:1) and affirmed by God at Jesus' baptism (1:11) and transfiguration (9:7); it was recognized by demons (3:11; 5:7), implicitly affirmed by Jesus in a parable (12:6) and in the discussion about the Son of David and the Messiah (12:37), and explicitly affirmed by Jesus in the trial before the Sanhedrin (14:61–62). Now, at the cross on which Jesus has just died, a pagan centurion is the first human witness to describe Jesus as the Son of God. While the Jewish authorities declared as blasphemy Jesus' assertion that he was indeed the Messiah, the Son of the Most High, the Gentile army officer, who has no connections with Jesus, perceives that Jesus' manner of death proves the truth of Jesus' claims. His insight is extraordinary: *this man*, whom he sees in front of him still nailed to the cross, is dead, his body mistreated and bloodied, but yet he is the Son of God. How much the centurion understood cannot be ascertained. What Mark's Christian readers understood is easier to highlight: Jesus' divine sonship and his messianic identity are confirmed 'not through conquest, but through suffering' (Strauss, p. 706). In the light of 1:1, 14–15, 13:10, the Gentile readers of the Gospel see that the salvation accomplished by Jesus is 'good news' for Israel *and* for the whole world.

f. Presence of women supporters (15:40–41)

40. The male disciples had all deserted Jesus when he was arrested (14:50), and Peter, who had followed the arresting party into the courtyard of the high priest's residence, had, before breaking down, denied knowing Jesus (14:66–72). But three women disciples had followed the execution squad. They had been *watching from a distance*, observing Jesus' crucifixion and witnessing his death. This is the first time that Mark explicitly mentions female disciples. Jesus' statement in 3:34–35 that his disciples are his new family consisting of brothers, sisters and mothers implicitly referred to female followers. Mark states that *there were also women* (NRSV) at the cross (cf. v. 41: 'many other women ... were also there'; cf. Matt. 27:55–56: 'many women were there', with three mentioned; cf. Luke 23:49), and then names three of them.

Mary Magdalene is distinguished from other Marys by the addition of her place of origin: she is from Magdala/Tarichaeae, a town on the western shore of the Sea of Galilee, south of Capernaum (see on 1:16, 19–20; 6:53). She is present at Jesus' burial (15:47) and she is among the women who visit the empty tomb (16:1).

The second *Mary* is described as *the mother of Jacob [James] the little and of Joseph*. Since Jacob (James) was a very popular Jewish name, he is distinguished from other Jacobs by the addition of his nickname 'the little' (*tou mikrou*, usually translated *the younger*, but the reference is probably not to age but to stature; cf. BDAG, p. 651). Mark mentions this Mary, with more concise descriptions, in 15:47 ('Mary the mother of Joseph') and in 16:1 ('Mary the mother of Jacob/James'). Like Mary from Magdala, she is also present at Jesus' burial and at the empty tomb. The fact that she is identified by reference to her sons (see also Matt. 27:56, 61; 28:1; Luke 24:10) rather than to her husband suggests that her sons were well known in the early Christian community.

Salome was also present at the empty tomb (16:1) but is not mentioned as being present at Jesus' burial (15:47). Many combine the reference to Salome in verse 40 with its parallel Matthew 27:56, where Mary Magdalene, Mary the mother of Jacob and Joseph, and 'the mother of Zebedee's sons' are mentioned, concluding that Salome was the wife of Zebedee and the mother of Jacob/James and John,[149] but this is not likely.[150]

These three women, especially the two Marys, have a crucial role as eyewitnesses: they saw Jesus die (v. 40), they saw Jesus' body laid in the tomb (v. 47, the two Marys) and they found the tomb empty (16:1). The fact that Mary Magdalene and Mary the mother of Jacob/James and Joseph were present at all three events 'means that they can testify that Jesus was dead when laid in the tomb and that it was the tomb in which he was buried that they subsequently found empty'.[151]

41. Mark notes that these three women played an important role not only as eyewitnesses of Jesus' crucifixion, burial and resurrection, but already during Jesus' Galilean ministry. The sentence *In Galilee these women had followed him* uses the same verb (*akoloutheō*) that Mark used to describe Peter and Andrew receiving and accepting Jesus' call when they left their nets and 'followed' him (1:18; cf. 2:14; 10:28). The three women had *cared for his needs*: they were at Jesus' service. Luke relates that many women, including Mary Magdalene, Joanna the wife of Chuza, who was an official at the court of Herod Antipas, and Susanna 'provided' for Jesus and the Twelve 'out of their own means' (Luke 8:2–3). Mark notes that *many other women* who had accompanied Jesus from Galilee to Jerusalem were also at the cross.

---

149. BDAG, p. 912; cf. Evans, p. 511; France, p. 664; Strauss, p. 707.
150. Bauckham, *Eyewitnesses*, p. 50 n. 45: the fact that Matthew does not put the mother of the sons of Zebedee in the group who find the empty tomb is 'conclusive evidence' that she is not the same person as Mark's Salome; cf. Bauckham, *Gospel Women*, pp. 235–236; for later traditions, pp. 237–247.
151. Bauckham, *Eyewitnesses*, p. 48, who emphasizes that all three Synoptic Gospels repeatedly make the women the subjects of verbs of seeing (Matt. 27:55; 28:1, 6; Mark 15:40, 47; 16:5–6; Luke 23:49, 55).

g. Jesus' burial (15:42–47)

42. The expression *Preparation Day* (*paraskeuē*) refers to the day of preparation for a festival. The characterization *the day before the Sabbath* (*prosabbaton*) indicates that the day in question was the day that had begun on Thursday evening and that would end on Friday evening at sundown (the Sabbath began at sundown Friday evening). The same time frame is given in Matthew 27:62 and John 19:31 (John links 'the day of Preparation' with the next day that is to be a 'special Sabbath'; i.e. it is the day of Preparation both for the Sabbath and for the Passover; cf. John 19:14). The phrase *as evening approached* refers to the time between Jesus' death shortly after 3 pm and sundown around 7.20 pm. According to Deuteronomy 21:23, an executed criminal had to be buried before nightfall in order to avoid defilement of the land, and the Sabbath regulations would not allow the work involved in burying a person after sunset.

43. All four Gospels report that *Joseph of Arimathea* took the initiative to organize Jesus' burial (cf. Matt. 27:57; Luke 23:51; in John 19:38–39 he is accompanied by Nicodemus). Joseph came from Arimathea, a town in the Shephelah hills about 20 miles (32 km) north-west of Jerusalem. Joseph was a *member of the Council* (Gr. *bouleutēs*), a member of the Sanhedrin in Jerusalem (see on 8:31; 14:55). Mark describes him as *prominent* (as was Nicodemus; cf. John 7:50). He evidently belonged to the non-priestly aristocracy, owned estates near Arimathea but mostly lived in Jerusalem, where he was called 'Joseph of Arimathea'. Mark describes Joseph as *himself waiting for the kingdom of God* (cf. 1:15). The word *himself* is best related to the women mentioned in verses 40–41 who followed Jesus in Galilee and came with him to Jerusalem. Given the context of Mark's Gospel, the reference to the kingdom of God signals that Joseph was sympathetic to Jesus' teaching and thus was on Jesus' side. Matthew and John call him 'a disciple of Jesus' (Matt. 27:57; John 19:38), and Luke says that he had not agreed to the 'plan and action' of the other members of the Sanhedrin (NRSV Luke 23:51). Some suggest that he may not have been present during that particular Sanhedrin meeting (Pesch, II, pp. 512–513), others that the 'all' in 14:64 is not to be taken literally and that there were dissenters when the Sanhedrin condemned Jesus. Another suggestion is that Joseph was 'more a sympathetic fellow traveller than an openly committed member' of Jesus' followers (France, p. 667; cf. Marcus, pp. 1075–1076: 'incipient allegiance to Jesus'). We do not know whether Joseph was present at the cross and saw Jesus die, or whether he was informed of Jesus' death by one of the women (v. 41).

The fact that Joseph was a prominent member of the Council explains why he had access to the Roman prefect. The verb *[he] went boldly* (or 'he summoned up courage', BDAG, p. 1010) indicates that it was a risky undertaking when he *asked for Jesus' body*. The term used for Jesus' body is *sōma* (which can also mean 'dead body, corpse', as *ptōma* in v. 45). If a pious Jew wanted to bury an executed criminal in accordance with Deuteronomy 21:23, no courage would have been required, especially if the one asking for the body were a member of the Sanhedrin who had been involved in convicting the criminal. However, showing interest in the body of a man who had been crucified as an enemy of the state 'might identify the benefactor as a member of a subversive group' (Marcus, p. 1076). A passage in Josephus suggests that the authorities did give crucified bodies back for burial (*War* 4.317; cf. Philo, *Flacc.* 83).

44–45. Pilate was *surprised* to hear that Jesus had already died. Dying on a cross could take a long time (see on v. 24). Before Pilate could release Jesus' body, he had to ascertain whether the royal pretender whom he had sentenced to be executed by crucifixion had actually expired, and so he summoned the *centurion* – presumably the leader of the execution squad who had been at Golgotha – who confirmed *that it was so*. The sentence *he gave the body to Joseph* means that he gave him permission to take Jesus' body down from the cross and bury him, as verse 46 confirms. The word *body* (*ptōma*; lit. 'that which has fallen') is always used for a dead body, of animals or humans, and can be translated 'corpse' (many manuscripts read the less drastic word *sōma*, but *ptōma* is better attested and to be preferred).

46. Mark reports five actions of Joseph. He *bought some linen cloth*. The word *sindōn* refers to 'fine cloth', usually 'linen' (*LSJ*, p. 1600). The fact that linen cloth was light, cool and dirt- and even louse-resistant made it an ideal material for the production of textiles; the quality of linen varied from coarse to extremely fine (Pliny, *Nat.* 19.7–11). Before Joseph walked to Golgotha, he bought new linen cloth. After arriving at Golgotha, he *took Him down* (NASB). This would have involved extracting the nails and taking Jesus' body down from the *patibulum* and the vertical pole, an operation that would have required several men to accomplish (see 16:6 the plural 'the place where *they* laid him'). Joseph would have had slaves and servants at his disposal to handle Jesus' body, which addresses the problem that a member of the Sanhedrin would not want to become unclean for seven days by contact with a dead body (Num. 19:11). It is perhaps significant that Mark uses here (and with the next two verbs) the masculine personal pronoun *him* (NIV and NRSV translate 'the body'): while Joseph and Pilate consider that Jesus has been reduced to a corpse, Mark views the deceased Jesus as still an animate person, perhaps foreshadowing Jesus' resurrection (Marcus, p. 1077).

Presumably Jesus' body was washed. Washing the body of a deceased person was an important part of Jewish burial ritual; it was even permitted on the Sabbath (*m. Shab.* 23:5). John relates that Nicodemus brought a mixture of myrrh (*smyrna*) and aloes (*aloē*), evidently prepared as dry spices (*arōma*) which were wrapped in the linen around Jesus' body (John 19:39–40). John and the other evangelists do not relate that Jesus was anointed with oil between death and burial (Brown, *Death*, II, pp. 1261–1264), which the three women intended to do on Sunday morning (Mark 16:1). Mark merely reports that Joseph *wrapped Him in the linen cloth* (NASB).

Then Joseph *laid Him in a tomb which had been hewn out in the rock* (NASB). A typical Jewish tomb (*mnēmeion*) in Roman Palestine consisted of a short entranceway leading into one or more burial chambers. Tombs cut into the rock had two forms: *kokhim* (Lat. *loculi*), long narrow niches cut back into the rock into which the wrapped body was slid; or *arcosolia*, shallow, transverse, bench-shaped tombs cut into the rock with an arch extending over the resting place which allowed the entire body to be visible. The description of John bending down, looking into the tomb and seeing the linen lying there, with the headpiece lying separately (John 20:5–8), indicates that the niche within the tomb was an *arcosolium*.[152] In the quarry that archaeologists have found underneath the Church of the Holy Sepulchre (see on v. 22), tombs have been found, cut into the rock

---

152. U. C. von Wahlde, in Charlesworth, *Jesus and Archaeology*, p. 581.
Cf. H. Geva and N. Avigad, *NEAEHL*, II, pp. 747–757.

of the quarry, dating to the first century, including one tomb of an *archosolium* type carved into the eastern scarp of the quarry; this may very well be the tomb of Joseph of Arimathea in which Jesus was placed.[153] If correct, the tomb would have been only about 50 m or 55 yards from the traditional site of Golgotha. If the site of the crucifixion is placed further south, close to the intersection of the roads leading into the Gennath Gate, the distance from Golgotha to the traditional site of the tomb would be 250 m or 273 yards (Taylor, 'Golgotha', pp. 183–203). The fact that the women are shown the spot where Jesus had been laid (16:6) may suggest that the tomb had been cut for multiple occupancy. Since tombs sealed with circular stones seem to have belonged to prominent people, and since Joseph had ready access to a rock-cut tomb close to the city, Mark's account points to Joseph, the prominent member of the Sanhedrin, as the owner of the tomb.

Finally, Joseph *rolled a stone against the entrance of the tomb*. Circular stones that were set upright in transverse channels facilitating their being rolled into place with the aid of levers weighed some 1,500–3,000 pounds (680–1,361 kg). Mark notes in 16:4 that the stone was 'very large'. Joseph seems to have had help in taking Jesus down from the cross, preparing him for burial and moving the rolling stone in front of the grave entrance.

47. Two of the women mentioned as witnesses of Jesus' crucifixion (v. 40) are present when Jesus is buried by Joseph: *Mary Magdalene* and *Mary the mother of Joseph*. They knew where to go on Sunday morning. The comment that they *saw where he was laid* suggests that they went into the tomb and saw the bench on which Jesus' wrapped body was placed. The word translated *saw* (*theōreō*) means 'to observe someth[ing] with sustained attention' (BDAG, p. 454) and suggests to Mark's readers that his account is based on eyewitness testimony.

---

153. Wahlde, in Charlesworth, *Jesus and Archaeology*, p. 5. Cf. Gibson, *Final Days*, pp. 149–157, who suggests that the tomb had a square inner chamber measuring 6.5 by 6.5 feet (2 by 2 m) and at least one bench measuring 6.5 by 1.6 feet (2 by 0.5 m), with the door leading into the tomb measuring 1.3 by 1.9 feet (0.4 by 0.6 m).

Theology
Jesus' death is as extraordinary as his life – preceded by three hours of unnatural darkness, accompanied by his shout that asserts God's absence while clinging to his commitment to 'his' God, followed by the splitting of the curtain in the temple and by the declaration of a Roman officer who acknowledges Jesus to be the Son of God. In Mark's report of Jesus' death there is no call for forgiveness (Luke 23:34), no concern for his mother (who is not reported to be present, unlike in John 19:26–27), no offer of salvation to the repentant brigand (Luke 23:43), no final words of assurance that he is about to enter into God's presence (Luke 23:46) and no triumphant shout that his mission is 'finished' (John 19:30). 'Mark's entire focus is on the gloomy darkness of the scene, the agonizing suffering and aloneness of the Son of God' (Strauss, p. 702). And yet, even though God has abandoned Jesus as he dies on the cross over the course of six hours, Jesus does not let go of God. The confidence that God is 'his' God affirms, implicitly, his prediction that he will be raised on the third day (8:31; 9:31; 10:34). And the centurion's declaration, reported as a reaction to the manner of Jesus' death, confirms for Mark's readers that Jesus' humiliating, shameful death is intimately connected with Jesus' mission as the Messiah who is the Son of God and with the good news of the coming of the kingdom of God (1:1, 14–15). The Son of God (15:39) is abandoned by God (15:34) because Jesus is giving his life as a ransom for many (10:45; 14:24), a reality that now, after his crucifixion, extends the good news of the kingdom of God to Gentiles as well.

Mark leaves no doubt that Jesus died. His dead body is explicitly mentioned twice (15:43, 45). His death is mentioned twice in Pilate's presence (15:44). The centurion confirms Jesus' death (15:45). Jesus' resurrection was not a resuscitation of a person who was merely comatose. The women did not go to the wrong tomb: the women who were present at the cross were present at Jesus' burial and *saw* where Jesus' body had been placed inside the rock-cut tomb. Mark's account of Jesus' death and burial, which fulfilled Jesus' predictions (8:31; 9:31; 10:34), prepares his readers for the fulfilment of the rest of Jesus' prophecy – that he will rise from the dead after three days.

4. JESUS' RESURRECTION ANNOUNCED (16:1–8)

Context

In the two main sections of his Gospel, Mark described Jesus' messianic authority (1:14 – 8:21) and Jesus' messianic suffering (8:22 – 15:47). The last section (16:1–8), which relates Jesus' resurrection, is even briefer than the first section, which related the beginning of the gospel (1:1–13). In his account of events connected with Jesus' resurrection, Mark reports no appearances of the risen Jesus to the women or to the disciples, no explicit words of Jesus and no missionary commission, in contrast to Matthew, Luke and John. The Gospel ends with the message of Jesus' resurrection entrusted to three women who are afraid to say anything about it (for 16:8 as the end of the Gospel see Introduction 3e). The abrupt ending leaves the women – and the disciples whom they have been asked to inform about what has transpired at the tomb – in the same position as Mark's readers: with the announcement of Jesus' resurrection from the dead and a call to faith and renewed discipleship.

Comment

A. The women at Jesus' tomb (16:1–5)

1. Jesus' burial happened shortly before the start of the Sabbath which began with sunset on Friday evening. Now *the Sabbath was over* – it was past sunset on Saturday – this allowed the women to buy *spices (arōmata)*. The three women – *Mary Magdalene, Mary the mother of Jacob [James]* (and Joseph) and *Salome* – had been present at the crucifixion and saw Jesus die (15:40). The two Marys had been present when Joseph of Arimathea had buried Jesus' body (15:47). The women had bought spices *so that they might go to anoint Jesus' body*, finishing the burial procedures which had been interrupted by the Sabbath. Since they had come to Jerusalem with Jesus from Galilee (15:41), they would have been aware of Jesus' predictions of his death and resurrection (8:31; 9:31; 10:32–34). Evidently they did not take seriously Jesus' prophecy that he would rise from the dead after three days. The reference to anointing (*aleiphō*) indicates that the spices were not dry powders and small pieces of myrrh and aloe (used on the occasion of the burial, according to John 19:39) but an ointment based on olive oil rendered fragrant by spices. In a customary honourable burial, the body was washed, anointed with aromatic oil, wrapped in cloth with aromatic spices placed within the wrappings, and clothed (Brown, *Death*, II, pp. 1243, 1261). The aromatic spices and ointment were a sign of respect, they compensated for the odour of decomposition and they kept the corpse fresh for some period of time. Having bought the spices on Saturday evening, the women were ready to walk to the tomb the next morning (Sunday) after first light.

2. Mark provides three temporal references for the time when the women came to the tomb. The phrase *very early* suggests a time soon after first light, perhaps as early as 4 or 5 am. According to John 20:1, the women went to the tomb 'early ... while it was still dark'. The phrase *on the first day of the week* indicates that it was the day after the Sabbath. Since it was just before sunrise on that day, the time in question was Sunday morning. Given that the Sabbath is the last day of the week and Jesus' resurrection happened on the first day of the week, Jesus' prediction that he would rise from the dead 'after three days' (8:31; cf. 9:31; 10:34) seems problematic. However, since Jewish custom treats any part of a day as a full day, the phrase 'after three days' is the same as 'on the third day': Jesus was buried late on Friday (14 Nisan), he was in the grave on the Sabbath (15 Nisan) and he was raised from the dead on the first day of the new week (16 Nisan). Even though the time between Jesus' burial and Jesus' resurrection was at the most not much more than thirty-six hours, Jesus was in the grave during (parts of) three days.

The phrase *just after sunrise* (NRSV 'when the sun had risen'), which would be around 6.20 am in April, seems to indicate a later time than the first temporal reference. If we view the (genitive absolute) participle not as expressing antecedent time, but coincidental action (cf. 2 Peter 1:17; Acts 28:3), Mark might be saying that the women left shortly after first light, while the sun was rising.[1] The women *went to the tomb* (NRSV): they knew where to find the tomb in which Jesus was buried since they had accompanied Joseph of Arimathea from Golgotha to the site of the tomb (15:47).

3–4. The women had made their preparations without considering *Who will roll the stone away from the entrance of the tomb?* Given Mark's report of the disciples' abandonment of Jesus and Peter's denial (14:50–52, 66–72), the reference to the women's question, given in direct speech, seems less a comment on their unpreparedness than on the disciples' unwillingness to take the risk and visit Jesus' tomb, given the probability that the women would have been in contact with the disciples.

When they arrived at the site of the tomb and *looked up* to the entrance, they *saw* that the stone *had been rolled away*. The comment that the stone *was very large* underlines the women's knowledge that they would not be able to move the stone by themselves: several men would be required to roll the stone away from the entrance (cf. 15:46). The passive verb (*had been rolled away*) leaves the agency open. There is no indication here, nor in the other Gospels, that Jesus'

---

1. Robertson, *Word Pictures I*, p. 406, suggests that the women started out from Bethany while it was dark and arrived at the tomb when the sun had risen.

resurrection required the removal of the stone from the entrance of the tomb. In Matthew 28:2 it is 'an angel of the Lord' who rolled back the stone, but the tomb was apparently already empty when the stone was rolled away. Mark does not explain the removal of the stone, which creates 'a sense of superhuman agency in the narrative' (France, p. 678).

5. The women *entered the tomb* because they wanted to anoint Jesus' body with aromatic spices. The entrance tunnels leading into the inner burial chambers were often very low and required crawling on all fours. On the type of tomb in which Jesus had been laid to rest see on 15:46. Finding the stone rolled away, they might have anticipated seeing Joseph of Arimathea and his servants completing the burial rites. Instead, they see *a young man dressed in a white robe sitting on the right side*. Since he points out the place where Jesus' body was laid (v. 6), he sits on a bench opposite the bench-shaped resting place. The man is not an observer who happened to pass by but an 'interested party' who had gone through the narrow entrance into the tomb. Although Mark does not explicitly say that the man was in reality an angel, his description leaves little doubt that this is his understanding. A *white robe* (*stolē leukē*) connotes, in other contexts, festivity or formal occasions. In a tomb, a man in a white robe conveys a supernatural impression, particularly if the whiteness of the robe is something out of the ordinary, like Jesus' clothes on the mountain which were 'dazzling white' (*himatia leuka lian*; 9:3); Luke 24:4 speaks of 'clothes that gleamed like lightning' (*esthēs astraptousē*) when he describes two 'men' at Jesus' tomb. White, shining clothes are marks of a heavenly visitation (Matt. 28:3; John 20:12; Acts 1:10; 10:30; cf. Dan. 7:9; *1 En.* 62:15–16; 87:2). Angels are sometimes described as 'young men' (2 Macc. 3:26, 33; 5:2; Josephus, *Ant.* 5.522). A man with an extraordinarily white robe *sitting* suggests authority. The words that he speaks (vv. 6–7) could hardly come from an anonymous passer-by. And the women *were alarmed*: shock and fear are the responses to an encounter with heavenly envoys (Judg. 6:22–23; 13:6, 22; Dan. 8:16–18; Tob. 12:16; Luke 1:12–13; 2:9). In verse 8 Mark further describes the women's reaction: they were 'trembling and bewildered' and 'fled from the tomb'. They knew that they had met an angel.

B. The announcement of Jesus' resurrection (16:6–7)

6. The first part of the message of the 'young man' is expressed in five short 'staccato'-style sentences. *Don't be alarmed* is a word of reassurance (which was not successful; see v. 8), a common feature in connection with the appearance of angels (Gen. 21:17; Judg. 6:23; Dan. 10:12, 19; Matt. 28:5; Luke 1:13, 30; 2:10; Acts 27:24). The young man 'speaks from a position of authority and of privileged knowledge, not as an equal' (France, p. 680).

Next comes a statement of fact: *you are looking for Jesus of Nazareth, who was crucified* (NRSV). The 'young man' knows why the women have come to the tomb and, indirectly, he affirms that the tomb in which they are standing is indeed the tomb in which Jesus was buried (Collins, p. 796). Jesus is identified with reference to Nazareth, the village in which he lived for most of his life (cf. 1:24; 10:47; 14:67). The Jesus of history who preached and healed in Galilee and the Jesus of the resurrection are one and the same 'Messiah, the Son of God' (1:1). The description of Jesus as *who was crucified (estaurōmenon)* records the reality of what happened the previous Friday and it indicates the reason why the women came to the tomb. They had watched Jesus being affixed to the cross and hanging on the cross for over six hours. They had watched when Joseph of Arimathea removed Jesus' body from the cross. Now they have come to the tomb in order to anoint Jesus' battered, dead body that bears the marks of flogging and crucifixion. The perfect of the participle *estaurōmenon* indicates, in the context of the following statement of Jesus' resurrection, that the fact of Jesus' crucifixion continues to be the defining reality of Jesus' identity and existence. Jesus has not left the crucifixion behind: as the Risen One he is still the Crucified One who died as a ransom for many (10:45) and inaugurated God's new covenant (14:24). Jesus' death on the cross has continued significance for his followers, who will soon preach the good news of Jesus' life, death and resurrection to all nations (13:10).

The next sentence consists of one single word: *ēgerthē* ('He has been raised', NRSV). The passive voice signals that it was the power of God that brought Jesus back from the dead and out of the tomb – the divine power that had been present in 'Jesus of Nazareth' when he ministered in Galilee. Since the absence of Jesus' body could be explained in different ways, the 'young man' interprets what has happened: Jesus' body has not been removed – God has raised him from the dead.

In the next two sentences the 'young man' states that Jesus' body is gone: *He is not here*, a fact that can be ascertained once the women *look* at *the place they laid him* (NRSV). The tomb is empty. There is no body on the bench-shaped *place* (*topos*) where Jesus was laid on Friday evening, a fact that the two Marys personally witnessed (15:47). These two statements signal that what happened with Jesus' body was a physical event: Jesus' crucified, dead body has gone, not in the sense of a removal of the body but in the sense of a new physical existence which allows him to travel to Galilee (v. 7). Mark describes Jesus' bodily resurrection as leading to continuing life and activity on earth (France, p. 680).

7. The announcement of Jesus' resurrection is the basis for action, both for the women and for Peter and the other disciples. The 'young man' commands the three women to *go*, to leave the tomb and to contact the *disciples and Peter* (who may have stayed in the city since the events on Friday, or who may have returned to Bethany where they had stayed earlier in the week). Peter is singled out on account of his leadership role (3:16; 5:37; 8:29; 9:2; 10:28; 14:29, 33, 37, 54) and, especially, because of his denial of Jesus (14:66–72). Perhaps Peter has not rejoined the other surviving disciples (Gundry, p. 1003) and needs a personal message. The disciples' desertion of Jesus and Peter's denial of him does not lead to the dissolution of the group of disciples who were Jesus' close companions during his Galilean ministry. The message that the women are to convey to the eleven remaining disciples signals the assurance of forgiveness and restoration, 'the more impressive for being left unsaid' (France, p. 681).

The disciples are assured that Jesus *is going ahead of you into Galilee*, a statement that repeats the promise of 14:28, as referred to in the phrase *just as he told you*. The verb *going ahead* indicates here not a literal journey from Jerusalem to Galilee but a meeting in Galilee. The only post-resurrection appearance of Jesus is not to the women (as in the other Gospels) but to the disciples and to Peter, although this is not narrated but indicated as an event that will happen soon. Matthew and John report a meeting of the risen Jesus with the disciples (Matt. 28:16–20; John 21:1–23). Jesus called the disciples in Galilee (1:16–20; 3:13–19) and trained them to fish for people (1:17). The commission to continue Jesus' mission 'to all nations' (13:10), now that Jesus has completed his mission to give his life as a ransom for many (10:45), will be reaffirmed in Galilee. The announcement *there you will see him* does not imply that there will be no meeting before Galilee (reported by the other evangelists for Jerusalem later that Sunday); it merely states that Jesus will fulfil his earlier promise and meet them in Galilee. The sentence *you will see him*, understood in the context of verse 6, promises not a visionary experience but a physical encounter with the risen Jesus, whom they will see face to face.

C. The reaction of the women (16:8)

8. Mark describes the women's reaction to their encounter with the 'young man' with six phrases. They *went out* of the burial chamber and went through the narrow entrance of the tomb. They *fled from the tomb*, leaving the area of the rock-cut tombs outside the city walls and seeking safety by returning to the city and/or Bethany. They were *trembling*, quivering with fear. They were *bewildered* (NIV; cf. NLT), in a state of consternation due to the profound and entirely unexpected emotional experience of being inside the tomb where Jesus' body had been, meeting an angel and being told of Jesus' resurrection to bodily life. It is no surprise that they were 'amazed' and 'astonished' (cf. NASB, NRSV, RSV) about what they had just seen and heard. They *said nothing to anyone* (Gr. *oudeni ouden*); they were silent; they did not recount the experience they had just had. Mark leaves his readers with the impression that the angel's message was not delivered to the disciples. And *they were afraid*, fear being a common reaction to the presence of the supernatural (cf. 4:41; 5:15, 33; 6:50; 9:6).

We learn from the other Gospels that the women's silence was temporary. Matthew states that the women hurried away from the tomb 'afraid yet filled with joy, and ran to tell his disciples' (Matt. 28:8). Luke writes that the women were frightened but returned from the tomb to the city, where 'they told all these things to the Eleven and to all the others' (Luke 24:5, 9). John reports that Mary Magdalene 'ran and went to Simon Peter and the other disciple, the one whom Jesus loved', and told them that the tomb was empty (NRSV John 20:2). We can explain the silence of the women in Mark's Gospel in the sense that 'they may have said "nothing to anyone" only until, passing soldiers changing the guard and merchants opening their stalls and shoppers heading for the market, they reached the disciples'.[2] Mark, of course, does not say that. The puzzling ending at verse 8 is interpreted by many as showing that Mark did not in fact end his Gospel at this point but continued his account of Jesus' resurrection along the lines of Matthew 28:9–10, 16–20 and Luke 24:9–12: the women told the disciples about the empty tomb and Jesus met with the disciples in Galilee, a meeting during which Jesus commissioned them to go to all nations. The later manuscript tradition has provided endings for Mark's Gospel. See the Introduction (section 3e) for a discussion of Mark's ending at 16:8 as the most plausible explanation of the evidence.

Considering verses 7 and 8 together, Mark's ending can be understood as a typically Markan 'paradigm for the interplay between divine promise and human failure in Christian experience' (Lincoln, 'Promise', p. 34). Alternatively, Mark provokes his readers to think out for themselves the challenge of the Gospel: 'it is like one of Jesus' own parables: the hearer is forced to go on thinking' (Best, *Story*, p. 132). The ending with 16:1–8 fits Jesus' three predictions of his death and resurrection in 8:31, 9:31, 10:32–34, each of which is followed by corrective teaching on the nature of discipleship in the light of Jesus' death and resurrection. The announcement of the angel ('He has risen'), who speaks the words that the women will speak to the disciples, stands for the event of the resurrection and makes Jesus present in the minds of Mark's readers. The ending is therefore satisfactory. The suspense it creates causes the reader to act and to choose among the various options that Mark's account of Jesus' life, suffering, death and resurrection presents to its readers – from inappropriate action to inaction, from indiscriminate communication to no communication, from rejection to obedient following (Magness, *Ending*, pp. 111, 123). Mark ends his Gospel

---

2. Magness, *Ending*, p. 100; cf. Dwyer, *Wonder*, pp. 191–192.

with a note of fearful wonder about the resurrection of Jesus, who was, is and remains the Messiah and the Son of God.

Theology

The most important character in the last eight verses of Mark's Gospel is Jesus, not the 'young man' or the women. Mark had announced that his book is about 'the good news about Jesus the Messiah, the Son of God' (1:1). He ends his book with the extraordinary news that the body of Jesus, who has just been crucified, is no longer in the tomb: Jesus' body has been raised from the dead and will be seen by the disciples in Galilee. Just as 4:35–41 was not about the fear of the disciples during the storm on the Sea of Galilee which Jesus commanded to subside but about 'Who is this?', so 16:1–8 is not about the fear of the women who came to the tomb but about Jesus who has been raised from the dead (Stein, p. 737). The focus of Mark's ending is the angel's message in verses 6–7: the crucified Jesus of Nazareth has been raised from the dead, Jesus' body is no longer in the tomb, the place on the rock-cut bench is empty and the disciples will see Jesus in Galilee. Jesus' absence in the tomb signals divine action, and Jesus' presence in Galilee signals divine identity: death could not hold Jesus' crucified body – Jesus is alive as only God is alive. Yet Jesus the Risen One remains the Crucified One since it is his death that effects a ransom for sinners (10:45) and inaugurates the new covenant (14:24). The angel's message calls the women, and through the women the disciples, to faith in the crucified Messiah Jesus, who is the risen Jesus, to perseverance in restored discipleship, and to an obedient participation in Jesus' mission which now extends to all the nations.